KANT'S CONCEPTION

OF MORAL CHARACTER

Kant's Conception of Moral Character

THE "CRITICAL" LINK OF
MORALITY, ANTHROPOLOGY, AND
REFLECTIVE JUDGMENT

G. Felicitas Munzel

THE UNIVERSITY OF CHICAGO PRESS
CHICAGO AND LONDON

G. Felicitas Munzel is assistant professor in the College of Arts and Letters at the University of Notre Dame.

The University of Chicago Press, Chicago 60637
The University of Chicago Press, Ltd., London
© 1999 by The University of Chicago
All rights reserved. Published 1999
08 07 06 05 04 03 02 01 00 99   5 4 3 2 1

ISBN (cloth): 0-226-55133-4
ISBN (paper): 0-226-55134-2

Library of Congress Cataloging-in-Publication Data

Munzel, G. Felicitas.
    Kant's conception of moral character : the "critical"
link of morality, anthropology, and reflective judgment /
G. Felicitas Munzel.
        p.   cm.
    Includes bibliographical references (p.   ) and index.
    ISBN 0-226-55133-4. — ISBN 0-226-55134-2 (pbk.)
    1. Kant, Immanuel, 1724–1804.   2. Ethics.   3. Character.
I. Title.
B2799.E8 M849 1999
170'.92—dc21   98-47957
                                                         CIP

⊖ The paper used in this publication meets the minimum requirements of the American National Standard for Information Sciences—Permanence of Paper for Printed Library Materials, ANSI Z39.48-1992.

TO MY MOTHER AND IN MEMORY OF MY FATHER

Üb' immer Treu und Redlichkeit,
Bis an dein kühles Grab;
Und weiche keinen Fingerbreit
Von Gottes Wegen ab.
Ludwig Christoph Heinrich Hölty, 1748–1776

Sapere aude; incipe!
qui recte vivendi prorogat horam,
rusticus exspectat dum defluat amnis;
at ille labitur et labetur in omne volubilis aevum.
Horace, 65–8 B.C.

Contents

PREFACE

The ideas developed in this book represent the culmination of a number of stages of inquiry that began with my exploring the parallels between Kant's concept of conduct of thought (*Denkungsart*) and elements of the Greek quest for *phrōnēsis*. This book develops the conclusions resulting from my initial research: that at the heart of Kant's moral thought is a fundamental concern with the possibility, nature, and formation of moral character. These ideas have matured in tandem with considerable shifts over the past decade in Kant scholarship, in particular the increasing appreciation of the systematic significance of his aesthetics and anthropology for his critical and moral philosophy. Of the many who, over the course of this time, have supported my efforts, my special thanks go first and foremost to those individuals who took my ideas seriously at their early, incomplete stages, at a time when, from the standpoint of the received view, the conjunction of Kantian ethics and moral character could only be deemed an oxymoron.

For his steadfast encouragement and concrete support throughout this project, for his patient and close reading of multiple drafts, and for his ongoing sympathetic and constructive criticism, I am deeply grateful to Rudolf Makkreel.

For his insightful critique of the earlier phase of my work, my thanks are due to Alasdair MacIntyre. Others who have made helpful comments on various drafts and who graciously gave of their time to discuss my ideas include Karl Ameriks, Volker Gerhardt, Ann Hartle, Alven Neiman, Ludwig Siep, Phillip Sloan, and Richard Velkley. I also wish to thank Werner Stark for his willingness to share some of his own work in progress on Kant's lectures on anthropology.

For various forms of substantive communications in regard to my work and from which I have benefited at particular stages, I owe my thanks to

Lewis White Beck, Manfred Frank, Otfried Höffe, Pauline Kleingeld, Paul Kristeller, Manfred Kuehn, Christian Laursen, Walter Nicgorski, Clark Power, Birgit Recki, Mark Roche, Peter Rohs, Philip Rossi, S.J., Thomas Seebohm, David Solomon, Manfred Sommer, Katherine Tillman, Frederick Van De Pitte, Michael Waldstein, Robert Wokler, Allen Wood, and John Zammito.

My sincere thanks are due also to David Brent of the University of Chicago Press, both for his encouraging support and for his vision, which, over the past decade, has led to the publication of important developments in the Kant scholarship—developments that point toward the reevaluation of Kant's philosophy entailed by the analysis of his conception of character. I wish further to acknowledge the assistance of Patrice Horan and the efforts of Irmgard Stein in supporting my work.

Finally, for her help and support in all things without which this project could not have been completed, my deepest debt is to my mother, Marianne Munzel.

Research support was provided by the Institute in the Liberal Arts, University of Notre Dame. Earlier stages of the project were supported by grants from the American Association of University Women Educational Foundation, the Robert H. Horwitz Memorial Trust, the German Ministry for Wissenschaft und Forschung of Nordrhein-Westfalen, and the Lewis White Beck Fellowship, Emory University.

Earlier essays that anticipate some of the interpretation developed in this book are "Reason's Practical Idea of Perpetual Peace, Human Character, and the Pedagogical Function of the Republican Constitution," *Idealistic Studies* 26 (1996): 101–34; "'The Beautiful Is the Symbol of the Morally-Good': Kant's Philosophical Basis of Proof for the Idea of the Morally-Good," *Journal of the History of Philosophy* 33 (1995): 301–30. My thanks to the journal editors for permission to republish parts of these essays.

*   *   *

The epigraphs are taken from the following works of literature. The first one consists in the opening lines of one of the poems written by Hölty in his last year. The poem presents an address of an "alten Landmann an seinen Sohn" [an old farmer to his son]. "Act always faithfully and honestly, / Until death claims you; / And do not stray even in the slightest / From the ways of God." As played by the carillon of the Garnisonkirche (built under Frederick the Great) in Potsdam, these opening lines of the poem were set to music from Mozart's *The Magic Flute* (one of Papageno's pieces).

The second is an excerpt from Horace's *Epistles*, I.ii. This poem is addressed to a young man who is studying rhetoric in Rome. It is an exhortation to "dare to be wise; begin! He who puts off the hour of right living is like the bumpkin waiting for the river to run out: yet on it glides, and on it will glide, rolling its flood forever" (Loeb Classical Library).

A Note on Translation

In current scholarship, attention is being given to problems with a number of received translations of Kant's terminology. However, two terms central to Kant's strict sense of moral character, in its mature formulation, still require reexamination. The more familiar is *Gesinnung.* The other, *Denkungsart,* has received little recognition as a technical term in Kant's writings. The translations for these terms vary considerably, and if there is a point of agreement that consultation with different scholars brings to light, it is the difficulty of finding a satisfactory way to render these concepts in English. While one can certainly concede the value of retaining conventional translations, these are themselves also problematic.

With no simple solution readily available, the following approach has been taken in this book. To preserve the nuances of the German—particularly since Kant's mature sense of these terms and their connection with moral character is not fully evident in each usage—when the reference is Kant's own voice (in either direct quotation or paraphrase), the forms *Denkungsart* and *Gesinnung* are retained. To capture as nearly as possible the technical sense of these terms as they define moral character, in discussion and interpretation they are rendered as "conduct of thought" and "comportment of mind," respectively.

The reasons for these choices of translation are as follows. First, *Denkungsart* as "conduct of thought": in the available English translations it has been rendered variously as "disposition of mind," "cast of mind," "mental attitude," and "mode of thought." Even within a single text the translation shifts, as in the *Critique of Pure Reason,* in which Norman Kemp Smith uses "thought," "way of thinking," "manner of thinking," and "modes of thought," while rendering the phrase "revolution of *Denkungsart*" as "intellectual revolution," "revolution in point of view," and "changed point of view." Pluhar uses "way of thinking." From an ordinary-language perspective, none of these translations is incorrect, but collectively they lose the fact that we have a *single* term in the German, one that comes to be consistently identified by Kant with the concept of character. In my own earlier research, I used "mode of thinking" or "mode of thought" to render *Denkungsart*. "Mode" is not so informal or loose a term as "way," but even so, *Denkungsart* is not a mere mode of thinking—not a mode, for example, such as empirical, mathematical, logical, or illogical thinking. "Conduct of thought" retains the ordinary meaning of *art* as "way" or "mode," but it conveys the distinction of a specialized "way" that is at stake in the activity of thought constituting the absolute sense of character. It also expresses the issue (namely, how we conduct ourselves in thought) that Kant connects with character and with the conduct of human life. "Art of thinking" would have had the merit of being consistent with standard English translations of the French *l'art de penser* (a parallel notion in the literature of the period). It would also have implied the connection with the sense of *art* that is applicable to the formation of character. In the *Critique of Judgment,* Kant notes that "by rights, only a production [literally a bringing forth] through freedom, that is, through a power of choice that grounds its acts on reason, ought to be called art" (*Ak* 5:303). As is shown in the course of the investigation here, cultivating moral character is precisely such a "bringing forth" on the ground of freedom. However, one would first have to make the case that the German *art* has been given such a specialized sense (differing from its ordinary usage) before employing the translation "art of thinking."

At stake in Kant's concept of *Denkungsart* is an *activity* of thought informed by certain principles (moral law plus principles of reflective judgment). The translation "conduct of thought" attempts to capture this essential aspect of activity; that is, the term "conduct" conveys the general sense of activity consciously informed by guiding principles. Normative dimensions depend upon what these principles turn out to be. There is further a direct link with conducting ourselves in thought in accordance with definitive principles and having a corresponding *Gesinnung*.

Gesinnung is one of the most difficult words to render in English. Again variations may be found in the extant translations. "Disposition" is the term most frequently used, while in his recent translations of the first and third *Critiques*, Pluhar has rendered it as "attitude." One of the volumes in the Cambridge complete works uses "sentiment." This last is a translation with which I am particularly hard pressed to agree, but all of these conventional choices are problematic. On the face of it, "attitude" seems to be the most promising alternative, but it bears psychological connotations (of mood and/or emotion) that would literally falsify the meaning of *Gesinnung* in Kant's strict sense. A compromise might be "mental attitude," but as noted, *Denkungsart* has sometimes been translated this way, and one would still need some explanatory apparatus to ensure that the sense conveyed is that of "attitude as informed by principles."

The most frequently used translation, "disposition," brings a number of difficulties. Here again, other terms have been translated by the same English word, namely *Anlage* and, in one of the recent Cambridge volumes, even *Fügung*. Moreover, in both his *Anthropology* and his *Groundwork*, Kant explicitly rejects the Latin cognate *dispositio*. On his view, dispositions have for their basis circumstantial causes, not the natural aptitudes found in the nature of every human being; that is, dispositions have cultural, empirical origins (as Kant explicitly makes the point in his published anthropology lectures, *Ak* 7:286). When discussing *Gesinnungen* as maxims of the will in the *Groundwork*, Kant notes that they do not require the recommendation of either a "subjective disposition or taste" (*Ak* 4:435). "Disposition," in other words, has too close a connection with the sense of habit (*Gewohnheit*) that Kant explicitly rejects—that is, something mechanically produced through repeated actions. *Gesinnung* is closely connected with *Denkungsart* in the sense of referring to the enduring quality of mind made manifest in consistent acts of thought given expression in words and actions, but it is produced anew with each exercise of *Denkungsart*.

The Latin equivalent for *Gesinnung* provided by Kant is *animus* (*Ak* 6: 477). Even here a subtle, but important, distinction is involved. In contrast to *anima* (which means soul as the principle of life), *animus* refers to soul as principle of intellection and sensation. Its range of meaning includes intellect, understanding, mind, thought, reason, and spirit. Kant holds to this distinction; for example in the *Critique of Pure Reason*, he identifies "soul" (*anima*) as the "principle of life in matter" (A345/B403).

The ordinary-language sense of *Gesinnung* is *sittliche Haltung* (the *Haltung* may be either morally good or evil); this sense is consonant with Kant's discussion in the *Anthropology* and elsewhere. In *Ethik und Politik. Grundmodelle und Probleme der praktischen Philosophie*, Otfried Höffe affirms this fundamental sense, especially as the term is used by Kant. A literal rendering (suggested to me by several German scholars) that conveys the connotations of rigorous principles this sense of *Gesinnung* bears for, and since, Kant is "moral-mindedness," or "morally principled–mindedness." The less awkward translation "comportment of mind" seeks to capture both the notion of *Haltung* and the latter's achievement by rigorously maintained principles, while also conveying the Latin reference to mind that is included in *animus*. *Haltung* also suggests the nuance of attitude, and "comportment" is intended to convey the specific sense thereof as one's mental bearing, informed by principles one consistently adopts in setting and pursuing one's purposes and in guiding one's choice making.

The foreign ring of "conduct of thought" and "comportment of mind" underscores the absence of exact English equivalents for Kant's terms. This absence further signals that Kant's sense of character differs from the more familiar, Aristotelian-based sense of acting in accord with the habituated disposition of our inclinations. The support for this claim, of course, requires the full argument presented in the course of this book.

Abbreviations

Ak   *Kants gesammelte Schriften.* Ed. Preussischen Akademie der Wissenschaften. Berlin: Walter de Gruyter, 1902–.

A   "Beantwortung der Frage: Was ist Aufklärung?" ("An Answer to the Question: What Is Enlightenment?"). 1784. In *Ak,* vol. 8.

ApH   *Anthropologie in pragmatischer Hinsicht (Anthropology from a Pragmatic Point of View).* 1798. In *Ak,* vol. 7.

B   *Beobachtungen über das Gefühl des Schönen und Erhabenen (Observations on the Feeling of the Beautiful and the Sublime).* 1764. In *Ak,* vol. 2.

BB   *Bemerkungen in den "Beobachtungen über das Gefühl des Schönen und Erhabenen" (Remarks on "Observations on the Feeling of the Beautiful and the Sublime").* 1764–65. Gerhard Lehmann edition in *Ak,* vol. 20. Cited in this book is the annotated edition by Marie Rischmüller in *Kant-Forschungen.* Vol. 3. Ed. Reinhard Brandt and Werner Stark. Hamburg: Felix Meiner Verlag, 1991.

BG   *Der einzig mögliche Beweisgrund zu einer Demonstration des Daseins Gottes (The Only Possible Argument in Support of a Demonstration of the Existence of God).* 1763. In *Ak,* vol. 2.

BM   "Bestimmung des Begriffs einer Menschenrace" ("Determination of the Concept of a Human Race"). 1785. In *Ak,* vol. 8.

DO   "Was heißt: Sich im Denken orientiren?" ("What Is Orientation in Thinking?"). 1786. In *Ak*, vol. 8.

ED   "Das Ende aller Dinge" ("The End of All Things"). 1794. In *Ak*, vol. 8.

F   *Zum ewigen Frieden: Ein philosophischer Entwurf (Toward Perpetual Peace: A Philosophical Sketch).* 1795. In *Ak*, vol. 8.

G   *Grundlegung zur Metaphysik der Sitten (Groundwork of the Metaphysics of Morals).* 1785. In *Ak*, vol. 4.

GTP   "Über den Gebrauch teleologischer Principien in der Philosophie" ("On the Use of Teleological Principles in Philosophy"). 1788. In *Ak*, vol. 8.

IG   "Idee zu einer allgemeinen Geschichte in weltbürgerlicher Absicht" ("Idea for a Universal History with a Cosmopolitan Intent") 1784. In *Ak*, vol. 8.

KpV   *Kritik der praktischen Vernunft (Critique of Practical Reason).* 1788. In *Ak*, vol. 5.

KrV   *Kritik der reinen Vernunft (Critique of Pure Reason).* 1781/1787. In *Ak*, vol. 3–4. Cited in accord with standard practice of distinguishing the 1781/1787 editions as A/B.

KU   *Kritik der Urteilskraft (Critique of Judgment).* 1790. In *Ak*, vol. 5.

LJ   *Immanuel Kant's Logik: Ein Handbuch zu Vorlesungen (Logic).* Ed. G. B. Jäsche, 1800. In *Ak*, vol. 9.

M   "Mutmaßlicher Anfang der Menschengeschichte" ("Conjectural Beginning of Human History"). 1786. In *Ak*, vol. 8.

MSI   *De mundi sensibilis atque intelligibilis forma et principiis ([Inaugural Dissertation:] On the Form and Principles of the Sensible and Intelligible World).* 1770. In *Ak*, vol. 2.

MSR   *Die Metaphysik der Sitten. Metaphysische Anfangsgründe der Rechts-*

lehre (Metaphysics of Morals: Metaphysical Principles of Justice). 1797. In *Ak*, vol. 6.

MST   *Die Metaphysik der Sitten. Metaphysische Anfangsgründe der Tugendlehre (Metaphysics of Morals: Metaphysical Principles of Virtue).* 1797. In *Ak*, vol. 6.

N   "Nachricht von der Einrichtung seiner Vorlesungen in dem Winterhalbenjahre von 1765–1766" ("Announcement of [Kant's] Lectures for the Winter Semester of 1765–66"). In *Ak*, vol. 2.

NG   *Versuch den Begriff der negativen Größen in die Weltweisheit einzuführen (Attempt to Introduce the Concept of Negative Magnitudes into the Philosophy of Nature).* 1763. In *Ak*, vol. 2.

NH   *Allgemeine Naturgeschichte und Theorie des Himmels (Universal Natural History and Theory of the Heavens).* 1755. In *Ak*, vol. 1.

P   *Über Pädagogik (On Pedagogy).* Ed. F. T. Rink. 1803. In *Ak*, vol. 9.

PG   "Entwurf und Ankündigung eines Collegii der Physischen Geographie" ("Outline and Announcement of Lectures in Physical Geography"). 1757. In *Ak*, vol. 2.

Ph   "Aufsätze, das Philanthropin betreffend" ("Essays concerning the Philanthropin"). 1776–77. In *Ak*, vol. 2.

Pro   *Prolegomena zu einer jeden künftigen Metaphysik, die als Wissenschaft wird auftreten können (Prolegomena to Any Future Metaphysics).* 1783. In *Ak*, vol. 4.

RA   *Reflexionen zur Anthropologie, Handschriftlicher Nachlaß (Reflections on Anthropology).* In *Ak*, vol. 15.

RL   "Über ein vermeintes Recht aus Menschenliebe zu lügen" ("On the Supposed Right to Lie for the Sake of the Love of Humanity"). 1797. In *Ak*, vol. 8.

RM   *Reflexionen zur Metaphysik, Handschriftlicher Nachlaß (Reflections on Metaphysics).* In *Ak*, vols. 17 and 18.

RV   *Die Religion innerhalb der Grenzen der bloßen Vernunft (Religion within the Limits of Reason Alone).* 1793. In *Ak*, vol. 6.

SF   *Der Streit der Facultäten (The Conflict of the Faculties).* 1798. In *Ak*, vol. 7.

T   "Von einem neuerdings erhobenen vornehmen Ton in der Philosophie" ("On the Recently Adopted Refined Tone in Philosophy"). 1796. In *Ak*, vol. 8.

TG   *Träume eines Geistersehers, erläutert durch Träume der Metaphysik (Dreams of a Spirit-Seer Elucidated by Dreams of Metaphysics).* 1766. In *Ak*, vol. 2.

TP   "Über den Gemeinspruch: Das mag in der Theorie richtig sein, taugt aber nicht für die Praxis" ("On the Old Saw: That May Be Right in Theory, but It Won't Work in Practice"). 1793. In *Ak*, vol. 8.

VR   "Von den verschiedenen Racen der Menschen" ("On the Different Human Races"). 1775. In *Ak*, vol. 2.

VT   "Über das Mißlingen aller philosophischen Versuche in der Theodicee" ("On the Failure of All Attempted Philosophical Theodicies"). 1791. In *Ak*, vol. 8.

INTRODUCTION

Moral philosophy today expresses a general lack of confidence in our culture's Enlightenment roots. We are told that we have lost our moral bearings, that the Enlightenment project has failed, that reason itself has failed us, and that we must move on to a postmodern ethics, or turn back to some version of Aristotelian virtue. Within this context, moral philosophers have charged Kant's ethics with exemplifying all that is wrong with the Enlightenment and, above all, with failing to provide an account of character and its formation in moral and political life. The very fact that until now no systematic study has been made of Kant's conception of moral character seems to confirm the charge. This book, the first such study, challenges the conventional reading of Kant's thought, claiming not only that he has a very rich notion of moral character, but also that it is a conception of systematic importance for his thought, linking the formal moral with the critical, aesthetic, anthropological, and biological aspects of his philosophy.

Scholarly interest in the notion of moral character and in character development has only recently enjoyed a renewal in the fields of psychology, philosophy of education, and moral philosophy. A review of the Anglo-American philosophical literature shows scant reference to these topics in the sixties and seventies. More attention is evident in the eighties, but a general admission of the concept of moral character to contemporary discourse is established only in the nineties. In this current literature, however, Kant's ethics for the most part either fares poorly among critics of its perceived pure formalism or is defended as a virtue ethics. This defense tends to begin with a traditional conception of virtue ethics and attempts to show how Kant fits *its* terms.[1] By contrast, the present study seeks to

---

1. In the current literature on moral psychology, the central theme of the criticism of Kant has to do with the status of the emotions. "Unfortunately," write John Sabini and Maury Silver, "the tradition that has found the most sensible location for choice, responsibility, and objectivity,

illuminate his account of moral character on Kant's own terms, with the additional aim of gleaning new insights into how we think about character at all.

For Kant, character is a moral task definitive of our vocation as members of humanity. Morally speaking, character is the steadfast commitment to virtue that is realized through a resolute conduct of thought (*Denkungs-art*)[2] that is morally good in its form and that, in its exercise, entails both causal and reflective elements. Anthropologically speaking, it is the formative task of the specific rational being we are, that is, of the rational human being in relation to living nature. Aesthetically speaking, it is the task of producing, on the ground of freedom, the work of art proper to us qua humanity. Ontologically speaking, it is the achievement of the unity of the natural and moral orders in the individual, a unity that results in the concrete actualization of the moral law in the world. Only when all these dimensions are taken into consideration does one begin to have a complete account of Kant's conception of moral character.

A number of recent developments in Kant scholarship point in the general direction of conclusions reached in the analysis here.[3] The deontologi-

---

the Kantian, precludes an honorable place for these unchosen feelings. We argue that this difficulty can be repaired once we see that Kant's exclusion of emotion relies on a faulty psychological model of the emotions working with an overly narrow conception of character" ("Emotions, Responsibility, and Character," in *Responsibility, Character, and the Emotions: New Essays in Moral Psychology*, ed. Ferdinand Schoeman [New York: Cambridge University Press, 1987], 165). Lawrence Thomas concludes that "for Kantians, the mere fact that the emotions are part of the nature of human beings makes it impossible that living morally could receive its fullest expression in the lives of human beings, since their existence make it impossible for us to be certain that we act for (and only for) the sake of the moral law" ("Trust, Affirmation, and Moral Character: A Critique of Kantian Morality," in *Identity, Character, and Morality: Essays in Moral Psychology*, ed. Owen Flanagan and Amélie Oksenberg Rorty [Cambridge: MIT Press, 1990], 235). Nancy Sherman's work is a recent example of a direct response to such criticisms. A central argument in the Kant portion of her book on Aristotelian and Kantian virtue is that in Kant's account "we are to develop our talents and emotional capacities as part of virtue (and so conceive of virtue along the ancient model of an empirical project of character habituation)"; that, further, "responsiveness to morality, as rooted in the rational nature of persons, flourishes best in someone who has cultivated emotional capacities" (*Making a Necessity of Virtue: Aristotle and Kant on Virtue* [New York: Cambridge University Press, 1997], 143, 144). While Sherman balances the view of Kant operative in the psychological criticisms, the implication that Kant's account fits that of "an empirical project of character habituation" will be challenged in the present study. It will also be shown that aesthetic capacities of feeling are of the essence, not emotions and inclinations.

2. For the translation of *Denkungsart* as "conduct of thought," see the "Note on Translation."

3. Authors of such monographs appearing in just the Anglo-American Kant literature since 1989 include Barbara Herman, Rudolf Makkreel, Onora O'Neill, Susan Meld Shell, Richard Velkley, and John H. Zammito. These advances are represented too (among other German scholars) in the work of Dieter Henrich and Otfried Höffe, translations of some of whose writings have also appeared during this time.

cal reading of his ethics has been seriously challenged, and Kantian ethics distinguished from Kant's own ethics. The primacy of practical reason has been generally acknowledged and it has been examined in relation to both Rousseau's influence and the question of the justification of reason. It has been argued that practical rationality and the practice of moral judgment, not duty, are central. A debate comparing Kant's "virtue ethics" and Aristotle's has ensued. The *Critique of Judgment* has gained acceptance as an integral part of the critical philosophy. Continuities between the precritical and critical writings have been explored, while the later writings (broadly viewed as Kant's philosophy of history) have been reexamined in relation to the critical philosophy, especially with respect to nature and freedom. The philosophical import of connections between Kant's life and thought has been recognized. Finally, the historical research recently completed by Reinhard Brandt and Werner Stark (compiled in volume 25 of the Academy edition) will undoubtedly lead to a serious reconsideration of the relation of Kant's *Lectures on Anthropology* to the critical ideas and principles. As Stark has documented, each of Kant's lectures on morality was given in conjunction with lectures on anthropology in the same semester; hence, for his immediate audience, there was "no morality without anthropology."[4]

This study of moral character fills a lacuna remaining in these welcome developments. Central to its argument is the view that character (or more precisely, a singular character) is the notion in terms of which Kant himself poses the question of the unity of forms of thought and life, that character is the primary instance of the way in which freedom and nature are related for him. In the wider philosophical discourse of the eighteenth century, the issue was posed in terms of the possible relation of reason and sensibility; Kant's account of character may be seen as his particular way of taking up this question. While the focus on the conception of character allows an approach hitherto not taken to issues such as the relation of nature and freedom in Kant's writings, it is compatible with the new directions in scholarly interpretations of his epistemological and moral positions: especially with Rudolf Makkreel's analysis of the role of reflective judgment in responding to and interpreting our world, and of the link between reflective judgment and the notion of orientation; Richard Velkley's examination of the justification of reason as inseparable from the issue of reason's telos; and Brandt and Stark's research. Character, seen as the system-

---

4. Werner Stark, "Kant's *Lectures on Anthropology*" (paper presented at the Central Division meeting of the American Philosophical Association, Pittsburgh, April 1997), 7.

atic link between the moral, aesthetic, and anthropological elements of Kant's works, provides an interpretation of the philosophical import of the historical links documented by Stark.[5] The attention given here to the *Critique of Judgment* includes important dimensions generally neglected in current studies of practical rationality and the comparisons with Aristotle. Of greatest significance are (1) the role of specific principles of reflective judgment (for the concrete exercise of moral character in the world and for securing its orientation to humanity's final purpose, the highest good) and (2) the role of aesthetic feeling for moral spiritedness.

At this point, the question naturally arises: why, if the conception of character is so central to Kant's thought, has it not received due attention before now? At least three explanations may be given in response: (1) Kant's own manner of presenting his examination of character, (2) the foci in the scholarly treatments of his thought, and (3) the meaning of *character* itself, particularly as it is associated in virtue ethics with a habitual inclination to act in certain ways. Aristotle is very explicit that practical wisdom belongs to intellectual virtue, while the moral virtue that he describes as of the essence for moral character—being gentle or temperate[6]—is, in Kant's account, a matter of temperament and sensibility. Hence, in light of its classical sense, the very notion of character seems

5. Stark only goes so far as to propose that the theme of Kant's anthropology lectures, "namely to investigate human character," is "no mere construct derived from the [student] transcriptions" thereof, but is extant elsewhere, noting a passage from Kant's *Reflections on Anthropology* and the first *Critique* passage that first identifies conduct of thought (*Denkungsart*) and sensibility (*Sinnesart*) with intelligible and empirical character ("Kant's *Lectures on Anthropology*," 12). The present study, essentially completed before Stark made his findings public, confirms what he suggests and, on the basis of a systematic account based on a philosophical analysis of relevant terms and principles (first as found in Kant's published writings and further as evident in lectures and reflections), independently reaches a similar conclusion to that of Stark's historical investigation in regard to the centrality of character in Kant's thought. Because volume 25 of the Academy edition appeared when the manuscript for this book was nearing completion, few selections from the transcriptions of the lectures have been cited here. A preliminary review indicates that one may expect to find further corroborating citations in these lecture transcriptions for points made in the present interpretation. The fact that the latter is primarily based on Kant's published writings strengthens the case for the thesis that Stark is now also proposing.

6. Aristotle, *Nicomachean Ethics*, trans. Martin Ostwald (New York: Macmillan, 1962), 1103a4–10: "Virtue, too, is differentiated in line with this division of the soul. We call some virtues 'intellectual' and others 'moral': theoretical wisdom, understanding, and practical wisdom are intellectual virtues, generosity and self-control moral virtues. In speaking of a man's character, we do not describe him as wise or understanding, but as gentle or self-controlled [a phrase also translated as "good-tempered or temperate"]; but we praise the wise man, too, for his characteristic [also translated "disposition" or "state"], and praiseworthy characteristics [or dispositions] are what we call virtues." Compare the Loeb Classical Library edition and the revised Oxford translation edited by Jonathan Barnes.

at odds with Kant's formalism and rationalism. Thus too, virtue ethicists, in their recent efforts to locate a conception of character in Kant, have turned primarily to his discussion of the "matter" of duty found in the *Metaphysical Principles of Virtue*.[7] Kant's conception of character is, however, unique in the history of philosophy just because it is not based on inclination. Moreover, Kant's position on radical evil, perhaps more than any other factor, dictates that the habituation of desire to take pleasure in the good can never be an adequate foundation for character. While light shed on parallels between his position and Aristotle's is quite helpful, it is precisely the differences that give us another way to think about character.

Second, in the scholarly treatment of Kant's thought the emphasis that continues to be found in analytical moral philosophy on the formal principle of the moral law from an *objective* point of view, one that is informed by a Hegelian type of critique, has a long history. The concerns of Kant's successors, logically and metaphysically to ground the moral law, the thing in itself, and the categories—their efforts, in other words, to "make Kant more rational" (as Fichte, for example, saw his own work)—continue to exert a strong influence on scholarly approaches to Kant. One sees this tendency even in the work of someone like Dieter Henrich, who has argued for the origins of Kant's moral thought in his precritical work, for the importance of Rousseau, and for intrinsic connections with Kant's aesthetics. Henrich still treats these elements primarily as sources for elucidating the origin, deduction, and ontology of moral insight as expressed by the "fact of reason" and the categorical imperative, precisely, that is, in regard to an objective grounding for the latter.[8]

Third, in regard to its meaning, the most familiar reference to the no-

---

7. In line with this, Barbara Herman takes it to be the case that moral development and character can be understood in a Kantian sense, but must be "added" to the account Kant has given us; we must first "develop a Kantian idea of character," by drawing on textual resources dealing with the "relation between motive and desire" ("Making Room for Character," in *Aristotle, Kant, and the Stoics: Rethinking Happiness and Duty*, ed. Stephen Engstrom and Jennifer Whiting [New York: Cambridge University Press, 1996], 37, 40, 44).

8. Henrich himself notes that "Kant scholarship was so determined by Hegel" that (for example) in the case of Heidegger's interpretation of the transcendental deduction, "it let pass as unproblematic the attempt to interpret" the deduction "in complete analogy to Hegel" ("On the Unity of Subjectivity," trans. Guenter Zoeller, in *The Unity of Reason*, ed. Richard Velkley [Cambridge: Harvard University Press, 1994], 46). Nonetheless, Henrich's concern, in seeking to recover the depth, complexity, and continued urgency of the "problematic character of reason" (as Richard Velkley characterizes his project in the introduction to this volume of essays), is the foundation of the Kantian fact of reason and its autonomy—the necessity of this question being carried forward by Kant's successors.

tion of character, which occurs in the opening passages of the *Groundwork*, seems simply to identify character with will. Readings that take the *Groundwork* as their point of departure understandably see little that the notion of character adds to the familiar issues of the will.[9] In addition, the works in which the terminology central to Kant's investigation of character is explained and related to the other human capacities (his *Lectures* and *Reflections on Anthropology*) have, with some exceptions, been widely regarded as peripheral at best to Kant's main critical effort.[10] Hence, when Kant uses the terminology relevant to character without further explanation, as he does in other writings, it goes largely unnoticed by readers today. With that omission, one also loses the philosophical dimension the terminology gives to the passages and texts in which it appears. Finally, because character is a pervasive issue with which Kant is grappling throughout his works, no one text spells out what one might call his complete doctrine. Its components, their own development in Kant's writings, and their relation to other terms and distinctions must be gleaned from the corpus as a whole. To do just that has constituted the fundamental research and interpretative effort of this book.

This effort aims to contribute to a richer understanding of Kant's moral thought, especially within the context of new directions in Kant scholarship. It is not, of course, intended to be the last word on the subject. Examination could be extended to the scientific discourse of the eighteenth century, to its employment of terminology such as the aptitudes and rudiments of human nature, terminology central also to Kant's account of character.[11] The systematic importance of the notion of aptitudes for Kant's own thought is generally underappreciated in the Anglo-American literature, and an understanding of its role in the biological discourse of

9. As Werner Stark has recently noted, even in the case of German-speaking readers of Kant, a kind of unquestioned assumed identification of the notions of "having a character" and "acting morally" has resulted in their not finding anything "of note or special" in regard to the use of the word *character* in Kant's critical writings ("Anthropologie und Charakter. Beobachtungen und Überlegungen zur Entstehung von Kants Lehre vom intelligiblen Charakter" [paper presented at the conference "L'Antropologia di Kant" at the Institute for Philosophy, University of Padua, Italy, March 1998]).

10. These exceptions include Frederick P. Van De Pitte and Volker Gerhardt, among others. In his "Kants kopernikanische Wende," Gerhardt makes the explicit claim that the "critical philosophy is at its core an 'anthropo-logy'" (*Kant-Studien* 78 [1987]: 148). Van De Pitte's study appeared earlier: *Kant as Philosophical Anthropologist* (The Hague: Martinus Nijhoff, 1971). Most recently, Werner Stark (in papers cited elsewhere in the present study) too advocates a close connection between the *Anthropology* and the critical philosophy.

11. The work of Johann Friedrich Blumenbach, with which Kant was familiar, is particularly important in this regard.

the age would further elucidate its meaning in Kant. Another area of investigation would be current issues in moral education and moral psychology.[12] Given the range of Kant's writings, the scope and variety of interpretations of his thought,[13] and the implications of the present analysis for understanding the critical philosophy itself,[14] this study does not exhaust

12. The complexity of garnering and analyzing the components of Kant's account of character precludes engagement of contemporary moral educational theory here. Especially in its analytical, rule-driven reading, Kant's ethics have generally not been well received by contemporary feminists in psychology, moral education, and moral philosophy. Differences will likely remain, but a more complete picture of Kant's moral thought can more fruitfully advance the contemporary discussions of these issues. Authors and works to be considered in reevaluating the relation of Kant to today's discourse include Carol Gilligan, *In a Different Voice: Psychological Theory and Women's Development* (Cambridge: Harvard University Press, 1982); and Nel Noddings, *Caring, a Feminine Approach to Ethics and Moral Education* (Berkeley and Los Angeles: University of California Press, 1984). For a collection of essays in which the contributors seek to "bridge the worlds of both Kantian scholarship and contemporary feminist debate," with many explicitly engaging the "ethics of care" debates, see Robin May Schott, ed., *Feminist Interpretations of Immanuel Kant* (University Park: Pennsylvania State University Press, 1997). Kohlberg scholars, on the other hand, working toward a conception of character (developed through empirical investigation) that is focused on achieving high levels of moral judgment, may welcome a philosophically worked-out account of Kant's conception of character. Since the latter in its full sense involves both the rational moral and natural human aptitudes, a new basis for dialogue with the "ethics of care" position may be possible. Comparisons and contrasts between the Kantian and Kohlberg accounts would likely begin with Lawrence Kohlberg, *The Philosophy of Moral Development: Moral Stages and the Idea of Justice* (San Francisco: Harper and Row, 1981); and F. Clark Power, Ann Higgins, and Lawrence Kohlberg, *Lawrence Kohlberg's Approach to Moral Education* (New York: Columbia University Press, 1989).

13. On the "colossal proportions" of Kant scholarship over the past twenty-five years, "effectively defying summary assessment and manageable presentation," see Guenter Zoeller, "Main Developments in Recent Scholarship on the *Critique of Pure Reason*," *Philosophy and Phenomenological Research* 53 (1993): 445–66; cited are Zoeller's opening lines. For another attempt to categorize the different approaches that have been taken in the Kant scholarship to his philosophy, identified in terms of the work of Strawson, Popper, Heisenberg, Vollmer, Apel, and Henrich, see Manfred Zahn, "Contemporary Trends in the Interpretation of Kant's Critical Philosophy," *South African Journal of Philosophy* 8 (1989): 129–47.

14. Distinguishing his position from that held by Reinhard Brandt, Werner Stark supports the interpretation that "there is a positive relation between Kant's lectures on anthropology and his moral philosophy," and that further, "the *Anthropology* constitutes an integral part also of Kant's critical philosophy and is not to be relegated to [the status] of a mere appendix to its system" ("Kant's *Lectures on Anthropology*," 5). In their introduction to volume 25 of the Academy edition, Brandt and Stark trace the changing conceptions of anthropology as a discipline, from an initial speculative treatment by Baumgarten to an empirical psychology, to its pragmatic conception in Kant (i.e., as a popular, philosophically practical discipline), culminating in "pragmatic anthropology as knowledge of the world (*Weltkenntnis*)," instruction in which was to serve the apprentice in making the transition to life in the world, in being "introduced to the stage of his destiny" (Reinhard Brandt and Werner Stark, introduction to *Kant's Vorlesungen über Anthropologie*, vol. 25, bk. 2.1 of *Kant's gesammelte Schriften* [Berlin: Walter de Gruyter, 1997], vii–xx). The conclusion reached in this introduction is that "in none of its phases of development is the pragmatic anthropology identical with that anthropology" which Kant after 1770 intends as a "comple-

the notion of character and its attendant issues within Kant research, but rather invites further development.

In her most recent work, Onora O'Neill argues for a comprehension of universal principles as leading "neither to dangerous rigourism nor to vacuous formalism."[15] "Ethical thinking," she goes on, "can move beyond the groundless rejection of abstraction and universality that has preoccupied so much writing on virtue and community not by rejecting principles, but by establishing and defending specific claims about action-guiding principles."[16] That character should be conceived in terms that are both formal and rigorous is perhaps even more difficult to admit than are such universal principles. The challenge confronted in the present interpretation is to articulate the substantive sense of formalism that makes up Kant's conception of character. The conclusions to which this effort leads may be summarized as follows. Kant's mature conception of moral character is essentially a critical concept; that is, while nascent versions of the *issues* involved are discernible in the early works, its ultimate *formulation* is made possible by the critical turn. In the works published by Kant, the first explicit connection of the notion of character with its divisions (as these are given in the *Anthropology*) appears in the discussion of intelligible and empirical character in the *Critique of Pure Reason.* Kant immediately parallels this way of discussing character with the notions of "conduct of thought" (*Denkungsart*) and conduct of "sensibility" (*Sinnesart*). In the *Critique of Practical Reason,* in the context of that text's discussion of how the soul is to be morally cultivated, one finds a statement of Kant's mature definition of character: "practical resolute *Denkungsart* in accordance with invariable maxims" (*KpV* 152).[17] It comes a few passages after the identification of what one may call the primary issue for the establishment and exercise of moral character: how can objective practical reason also be made *subjectively* practical (*KpV* 151)?

In one sense, this book is an articulation of the full entailment of this critically technical and tersely expressed statement. Central to it is the problem especially well articulated for our purposes here in the introduc-

---

ment to his moral teaching" (xlvi). However, the admission is made that it becomes "obligatory to take the moral teaching [or doctrine] into account wherever character as conduct of thought (*Denkungsart*) is discussed" (xlviii). The strong stance taken in the present study, identifying character as a critical link, is thus not obvious to all and will undoubtedly be controversial for some.

15. Onora O'Neill, *Towards Justice and Virtue: A Constructive Account of Practical Reasoning* (New York: Cambridge University Press, 1996), 90.

16. O'Neill, *Towards Justice and Virtue,* 90.

17. Detailed discussion is given in chapter 1 for the translation of "consequente Denkungsart" as "resolute conduct of thought"; see also "Note on Translation."

tion to the *Critique of Judgment:* "that the lawfulness of nature's form will harmonize with at least the possibility of effecting in her these purposes according to the laws of freedom" (*KU* 176). Upon its solution depends the possibility of realizing character (as it is described in the *Anthropology*) as the formative activity peculiar to human, rational beings in relation to living nature (*ApH* 321). It is an activity that concretely actualizes moral law in the world, imparting its form to sensibility and effecting literally a counterimage of the objective law under the conditions of the latter. In realizing this counterimage, character makes its appearance in the world and achieves the elevation of nature called for in the *Critique of Practical Reason* (*KpV* 43).

Character, as Kant conceives of it, is both formal and rigorous, but not in the usual abstract sense of these terms. It is formal in a structuring, ordering sense, as that which unifies the human capacities in relation to one another, to the world as human community and nature, and to the transcendent. So too, Kant (in his *Anthropology*) identifies the "establishment of a character" with the "absolute unity of the inner principle of the conduct of life (*Lebenswandels*)" (*ApH* 295). The formal definition of character in the *Critique of Pure Reason* as the law of causality of an efficient cause is directly relevant. Thus considered, character is the actual, operative law governing the interrelation and form of activity of the human capacities involved in choosing, moral judging, and acting. In other words, it governs the relations that make up its structure. It is also rigorous, in that it is a matter of resolute and steadfastly held principles, of an unwavering commitment to virtue. It entails self-control as an essential attribute of conduct of thought, not control of the inclinations as in an Aristotelian account. It requires spiritedness, again not derived from the inclinations, but as achieved through the aesthetic capacity for taking pleasure in purposive form. As the work specific to human beings, character formation is the effect (*Wirkung*) we produce, that which we are obligated to bring about in the world, in relation to nature, as a result of our own act (*Handlung*). As such, character formation turns out to meet Kant's general definition of what may be properly called a work of art. For it is the ultimate "production through freedom, that is, through a power of choice that bases its acts on reason" (*KU* 303).

The account of character, then, constitutes the subjective (and one might add, neglected) side of Kant's moral philosophy. The subjective conditions of the possibility of the concrete instantiation of the moral universal and its exercise in human life are discussed by Kant, broadly speaking, under two main headings: (1) his anthropological doctrine of the natural human aptitudes (*Naturanlagen*), developed primarily in his *Religion within the Limits of Reason Alone* and *Anthropology,* and (2) the exercise of character in the particular situations of human life, the exercise, that is, of moral judgment that is reflective in its form. All the relations and factors involved, first in establishing and maintaining moral character and, second in exercising it as one's conduct of life in a way that the latter itself constitutes the good in appearance, comprise its two moments: causal and reflective. In the first moment, reason's relation to the understanding and to human volition, respectively, constitutes a synthetic unity of causality whereby reason's empirical character is realized as a rule in appearances. Thus, morally good form is enacted in human life. The second moment involves the outcome realized in human life on the basis of such morally good character. Properly guided by specific, subjective principles of judgment or maxims, human orientation toward its own proper destiny (as defined by the idea of the highest good) is secured.

The book is divided into two parts. Textual exegesis is more heavily concentrated in the first part, interpretation in the second. In part 1 (consisting of three chapters), the inquiry into Kant's notion of conduct of thought (*Denkungsart*), into how and why it is definitive of character, locates his conception of moral character in his writings: that is, in relation to his precritical concerns, to central ideas and principles of his critical philosophy (of all three *Critiques*), and to his anthropological, biological, and aesthetic concepts. The second part (consisting of two chapters) examines the structure of character, the principles formative of its actual exercise in the world. On that basis, the question that naturally arises, the pedagogy whereby moral character may be achieved, is addressed. Finally, an epilogue draws upon and gives an extended interpretation of a metaphor, the horticultural art of grafting (used by Kant), in order to depict his account of character as securing the unity of thought and the life of sensibility, of *Denkungsart* and *Sinnesart.* Turning first to the epilogue may be helpful for the reader not completely familiar with the Kantian critical terminology.

Chapter 1 begins with a brief historical sketch showing that the term central to Kant's mature definition of character has a significant background in eighteenth-century discourse beyond Kant's contribution to it. We learn that "conduct of thought" gives expression to a concern raised by other major figures of the day; namely, the quest for wisdom understood (in Goethe's words, for example) as requiring a relation of thinking and acting that is as interconnected as are exhaling and inhaling in a singular act of breathing. With the historical context defined, Kant's own development of the meaning of "conduct of thought" is traced from his precritical to his critical philosophy. The chapter introduces three main issues, leaving complete discussion to the second and third chapters: (1) the relation of Kant's account of character to the primacy of practical reason and its moral law; (2) his focus on thought—not, as in traditional accounts, on the inclinations—as constitutive of character; (3) his conception of the moral agent as "efficacious cause." Also introduced and examined is the notion of "comportment of mind" (*Gesinnung*), which refers to the qualitative dimension of character, the state and spirit of our moral consciousness, and is the companion notion to "conduct of thought" (which defines the essential activity of character).[18] The analysis of Kant's account of character as a whole reveals a richer sense of familiar notions of his moral philosophy than is generally appreciated. Here we broach (and complete in the fourth chapter) the discussion of the first of these notions: the much-debated concept of maxims. In their function as principles for orienting or guiding the activity of thinking and thereby informing the entire comportment of mind (and not now as rules for direct application to matters at hand), a number of specific maxims are shown to be principles formative of morally good character and its exercise in the world.

The second chapter comprises the most technical discussion of the book. It explores the relation of character to the intelligible/empirical distinction and to the natural human aptitudes, especially volition and aesthetic feeling, in light of the problem of achieving the unity of the activity of the human agent as efficacious cause in the world. What is required is a positive account of how the two orders of moral and natural causality can and do work together, and to what end they do so. In this regard, the following questions are addressed: How is it, when empirical character is determined by temporal conditions, that we can be responsible for our character as a whole, or even consider our character to be a whole? How can this whole be more than a mere conjunction, a cooperative relation, at best, of dual orders of causality? How can these different orders form an integrated whole, a synthetic unity?

The analysis focuses on how empirical causality may itself be an effect of intelligible causality. The solution includes the relation of reason to the understanding, a relation not usually attended to as being of central importance for morality. The conclusion drawn is that intelligible character is the a priori moral form that requires the schema of empirical character for its concrete actualization. To express the point less technically,

---

18. For the translation of *Gesinnung* as "comportment of mind," see "Note on Translation."

reason as higher and directing cause avails itself of the form of the causal order of the understanding in order to bring its rule to bear in the world. The point identifies, in turn, one major component of the way in which reason becomes subjectively practical. Another central element thereof is for the human power of choice to become a *free* power of choice, through the exercise of which reason "acts in the place of a natural cause in the world."

The discussion of choice turns the focus of the chapter to how reason's more familiar objective, moral determination of human volition fits together with the account of its relation to the understanding. Realizing a synthetic unity of causality, now taken up in regard to volition, turns out to depend on the modality of that volition. What is called for is that volition (which, being human, cannot escape the natural necessity of its temporal relations) nonetheless concretely manifest practical (moral) necessity as characteristic of its nature. In other words, volition does not simply agree with what is objectively required, but what it *wants* includes in itself wishing to be in such agreement. Here the conclusion is drawn that, where these relations both to the understanding and to volition obtain, the result is the realization of character as the counterimage of the supersensible within sensible nature.

With this notion of the counterimage, we have also addressed what is entailed in character as the formative activity peculiar to the rational being in relation to living nature. The full account includes tracing the transition of Kant's concept of natural aptitudes from his biological writings, specifically in regard to the character of a natural being, to his use of this terminology in reference to moral character. We learn that this notion of natural aptitudes allows for a positive account of the responsiveness of human subjective capacities to practical necessity and of their resulting active role in the realization of moral universals in particular, concrete form. The transition from the notion of the character of the human race to that of the species morally conceived retains basic assumptions of the former, but now considers these assumptions in regard to a different set of *relations* involved in the response and development of the original aptitudes of human nature. As introduced in this chapter and developed throughout the remainder of the book, these relations include those to reason, to others in community, to political forms of organization, and to the transcendent.

One of the main conclusions that emerges from the discussion in chapter 2 is that the inner unity of the human conduct of life is ultimately achieved, not in terms of a kind of defeat, or passive subordination of

human nature to reason's causal exercise, but rather by a genuine, cooperative responsiveness of the human subjective capacities that allows for a
single, united effort in concretely actualizing moral form. In this regard,
the aesthetic capacities of feeling are seen literally as a partner in reason's
efforts to bring about the requisite enlargement of sensibility for the sake
of producing within it the counterimage of the moral law. The examination begun here is completed in the inquiry into pedagogy (in chapter 5).
The second chapter concludes with Kant's portrayal of the individual in
whom the unity of conduct of thought (character in its absolute sense)
and of sensibility (the subjective conditions of its concrete realization)
reigns: the magnanimous soul.

The account of the natural aptitudes would appear to lend itself to a
developmental interpretation of Kant's conception of moral character, but
in fact character is a *moral task* explicitly to be adopted and executed, one
that coincides with the moral task of establishing peace within the individual (that is, between human moral and natural capacities) and without (in
human social and political relations). This task is the focus of discussion
in the third chapter. At issue is the inherent problem of radical evil, identified by Kant as the ultimate source of all human conflict. The chapter
begins from a reconsideration of the status of this notion in Kant's writings, challenging the theological terms in which it has been read since
Goethe's initial reaction, terms that still today lead to its being called a
"fallen freedom." As essentially a problem of moral character, the notion
of radical evil is pivotal for addressing the apparent gap between the human moral possibilities promised by Kant's formal, moral philosophy and
the evident historical record of what human beings are actually able and
willing to do. Neither the anthropological portrayal of human nature
(what it *can* do) taken by itself, nor the account of the formal, moral principles (what it *ought* to do) taken by itself, ultimately deals with employment
(what *is* actually done).[19] By addressing this question of employment

19. An explanatory note is in order for thus delineating this distinction as a threefold one
(rather than the usual twofold "is" and "ought," *sein und sollen*). Development of the distinction
is given in the third chapter, but a few words of clarification may be helpful here. The twofold
version stems from an early description of the relation between anthropology and morality in
which Kant is less clear on the distinction between "can" and "is" (as I have characterized it here).
As found in the lectures first published by Paul Menzer in 1924, Kant is reported to have called
"practical philosophy the science of the rule whereby human beings ought to conduct themselves,"
while "anthropology" is said to be the "science of the rule of their actual conduct." However, in
the lines immediately following, in his assertion that these "two sciences are closely connected
and that morality cannot subsist without anthropology," Kant is reported to have gone on to say
that "we must first know the subject, whether the latter is *capable* of achieving what is demanded
that he ought to do" (emphasis added). This second way of expressing the matter points to the

(which is central to the exercise of character in the world), radical evil fulfills a systematically necessary role in Kant's thought and, thus too, may be philosophically interpreted. As is argued in the chapter, properly speaking there is no "fall" here from which to recover, neither in the strong theological sense of a fall from grace and a loss of immediate relationship with God, nor in the sense of a loss of a previously possessed human perfection. To attain such perfection is just the task first to be undertaken, and, to do so is to effect a state of peace, that is, to effect the subjective conditions under which laws have force.

The intrinsic connection thus entailed between character and human social and political contexts is discussed in the chapter in terms of the following questions: Exactly how does Kant understand this essential connection between the inner root of moral evil in human nature and external conflict among whole peoples? How does one reconcile the pedagogical with the moral order? (The discussion of this issue is completed in the fifth chapter.) The chapter reviews Kant's conception of the inclinations and passions, and of the relation between character and virtue. The meaning of virtue under examination is virtue in its formal sense as a singular commitment and as synonymous with the "embattled moral *Gesinnung* (comportment of mind)," or with the "strength of resolve" that is the hallmark of moral character. The conclusion reached is that virtue does in fact consist in self-control, not of the inclinations, but of the human processes of thinking; specifically, of choice making, or the subjectively practical use of reason in human moral life. The realization of greatest overall significance that emerges from the discussion in the third chapter is that there is an intrinsic interdependence of the cultivation of the subjective employment of freedom (and hence of character) with human civic relations. This points to the next step: carrying out the subjectively practical in relation to human life and nature. Again, translated into less technical language, what must now be explored is the employment of moral judgment in such a way that it realizes and preserves the resolute conduct of thought in a lifetime of the daily vicissitudes of the human condition. What is at issue and what is required to accomplish this is the subject matter of the fourth chapter of the book.

---

further distinction between "can" (what human beings can do based on their natural aptitudes) and what the historical record shows them actually doing. By 1793, Kant has developed his account of radical evil to address this question. By 1795 (in *Perpetual Peace*), the required pragmatic anthropology, the science needed by the moral politician, is further delineated as the knowledge of what can be made out of the human being. For the early description, see Kant, *Lectures on Ethics*, trans. Louis Infield (1930; reprint, Indianapolis: Hackett, 1963), 2.

Both chapters 4 and 5 (part 2 of the book) deal with the more inter-pretative issues surrounding the structure and formation of character. Chapter 4 arrives at the conclusion that Kant's account of reflective judg-ment proves to be indispensable for completing his account of human morality. It begins with an examination of the notion of orientation, spe-cifically Kant's engagement of this issue in response to Mendelssohn's discussion in his *Morgenstunden*. Mendelssohn's allegorical dream of the dispute between speculation and common sense depicts an issue latent in Kant's own writings up to this point (1786), one that must be addressed for the sake of the exercise of character in human life. Where character is established, the morally good order of maxim adoption characterizes free choice, while firm resolve characterizes comportment of mind. Poten-tial hindrances to morally good choice and conduct arising from inclina-tions, passions, and the propensity for evil have all been successfully con-fronted. The oscillation between incitement and command has been overcome. However, within the operations of thought and judgment, a further divide appears, namely, between theoretical doubts and practical commands. At stake now is the preservation of resolute conduct of thought, and it is to this end that practical reason avails itself of subjective principles or maxims of orientation whereby human life may be directed in a way befitting its moral vocation or destiny. The maxims required are very specific and fall under three headings.

First are the maxims directly related to the fulfillment of the human vocation and the assessment of our efforts in this regard: rational faith and conscience. In short, the argument developed is that rational faith is essentially a subjective principle of reflective judgment addressing two is-sues: the intelligibility of human final purpose and the maintenance of conviction, of a single-mindedness or wholeheartedness of effort on the part of the human agent called upon, in the face of the perceived human inadequacy to fulfill the task, to be proactive concerning the idea of the highest good in relation to human life in the world. Thus Kant's notions of rational faith and the highest good can be appreciated in a new light. Conscience is equally interpreted as a "subjective reflective principle," that is, as an ongoing self-assessment by reason to ensure that its guiding activ-ity, the bringing of all contemplated and executed actions before it for moral judgment, is not allowed to lapse.

Second is the set of the three maxims of sound understanding that prove, in the final analysis, to be principles for securing (both negatively and positively) the orientation of individuals to the other (both to the self as other and to the community) in such a way that the unanimity of particular and universal in the resolute conduct of thought is assured. Each of these maxims—thinking for oneself, thinking from the standpoint of others, and thinking with unanimity—is separately analyzed in the chapter.

Finally, there are those maxims identified by Kant as specifically "relating to character," principles that bear a remarkable affinity to the initial preliminary articles of the just constitution. This final set of five principles provides governance or guidance for human discourse, for the human means whereby acts of judgment are expressed and character is made manifest; they concern the cultivation and preservation of character in these human relations. The first principle, truthfulness, is fundamental to the remaining four principles, and the discussion concentrates on it. The interpretation developed offers a unique insight into the prohibition against lying that most of Kant's critics have found so troublesome. Once it is understood that truthfulness is the formal condition for having character at all and, hence, that the act of lying violates this condition, Kant's absolute stance in this regard becomes more comprehensible. "Having made truthfulness one's highest maxim both in one's inner admissions to oneself and in one's bearing toward everyone else," writes Kant in the *Anthropology*, "is the only evidence in one's consciousness that one has character" at all (*ApH* 295). At issue is the integrity of moral judgment itself as it is expressed in human discourse before ourselves and others. The conclusion drawn is that truthfulness is the formal subjective condition providing surety against the instrumentation (actual or potential) of the moral universal itself by the human subject. Its opposite, falsity, by contrast leads human travelers on life's journey away from the true guides, the subjective principles of orientation, indispensable for maintaining their course toward the realization of human purpose.

The fourth chapter concludes with the observation that the relational unity achieved through reflective principles for guiding thought or judgment, and hence life, fulfills Kant's general definition of the work of art; that is, this unity may be understood to fulfill human vocation or final purpose precisely by being the work of art, the work of beauty, specific to humanity. The question that naturally arises, then, is how such a work is to be produced. Consequently, the formation (*Bildung*) of character and what Kant offers in the way of a pedagogy are the focus of the fifth and final chapter.

Chapter 5 is divided into two parts: an initial general discussion of issues, aims, and nature of pedagogy (particularly as discussed in the eighteenth century), followed by three sections that respectively examine Kant's conception of (1) propaedeutic functions in relation to character development, (2) moral education proper, and (3) the roles and limits of communal and individual responsibility. The chapter both completes discussions begun in earlier sections of the book and offers further insights into Kant's thought. In the first place, what emerges from the analysis is that pedagogy is not simply another topic about which Kant writes, but that the critical philosopher is at once the educator, for whom the "formation (*Bildung*) of human beings" is "the only thing necessary" (*Ak* 10, no. 125, 221). His pedagogical position is gleaned from a wide range of texts, including both the *Anthropology* and the *Critique of Judgment,* as well as *Religion within the Limits of Reason Alone,* the *Critique of Practical Reason,* and *Metaphysical Principles of Virtue.* In addition to elucidating Kant's position by recognizing the intrinsic connection of pedagogy with the critical philosophy, the discussion also appeals to the historical background of the debate over educational reforms (including the influence of Locke and later of Rousseau) that was well in progress by the time of Kant's birth. His direct interaction with this debate came in the form of his support for the educational movement known as *Philanthropinismus.* The background, both of the main principles of this movement and of the widespread conception of the purpose of pedagogy as consisting in the production of a moral and civic-minded citizenry, helps complete the picture of Kant's views on the subject.

Overall, the fifth chapter affords a reply to those critics who maintain that Kant's formal moral philosophy has no place for moral education. In general, the approach taken here is to show that the pedagogical efforts, whether on the part of nature or community, relate to the fostering of those conditions under which the ultimate individual moral responsibility is most likely to be brought to a successful conclusion, that is, conditions under which the formation of character is best realized. In connection with this, the examination completes the account of the reconcilability of the pedagogical and moral orders. The question addressed in particular is how and why Kant deems the republican constitution an indispensable vehicle of moral cultivation.

The entire discussion of the chapter is structured in terms of the three-fold stages in pedagogical praxis: discipline, cultivation, and formation. The chapter shows how and why these (rather than the fourfold division commonly appealed to) are the main distinctions. The terms are individually analyzed, and the conclusions reached are drawn upon to address the central question at stake; namely, how these pedagogical stages and principles relate to the task of character formation. Discussion of the first two, discipline and cultivation, as the negative and positive propaedeutic functions, respectively, examines the role of the example and of aesthetic education in relation to moral education. In regard to the latter, Schiller's relation to Kant is briefly reconsidered. The use of the example, with its inherent connection with aesthetic pleasure in response to purposive form (such as character itself consists in), is related both to the place for moral spiritedness in Kant's moral thought and to the role of religion (in particular, the maxim of rational faith). The claim (already introduced in the third chapter) that aesthetic responsiveness serves as reason's partner in the realization of the moral task of procuring character is here defended further.

The phrase "cultivation of morality," often (understandably) seen as an oxymoron in the context of Kant's philosophy, is given particular attention in the discussion. Entailing the cultivation of the use of reason, its exercise being subject to its own law, it includes an aesthetic dimension that has an even more direct role in moral education proper, in (that is) the cultivation of moral judgment. For it is not only the feelings of the sublime and of pleasure in the beautiful that play a role (primarily in relation to spiritedness), but it is aesthetic judgment as a power of discernment that is important. The explanation of this point draws on the observation made by Kant himself in regard to the etymological connection between taste (*sapor*) and wisdom (*sapientiae*). The conclusion reached is that the development of the aesthetic quality of the comportment of mind (developing what one might call a "taste for the law") necessarily goes hand in hand with the cultivation of the powers of moral discernment and judgment. In regard to judgment, the discussion returns to the topic of human discourse (introduced in the fourth chapter), to its natural display of human aptitudes that moral education, in turn, cultivates by means of the Socratic method into a *habit* of moral judging. An explication of the Kantian sense of "habit" concludes this part of the inquiry.

The chapter ends with the identification of the limits of responsibility for moral formation on the part of all agencies (especially the republican constitution) involved in the stages of discipline and cultivation. The connection between these two stages and formation is drawn upon to elucidate how the individual act of responsibility for establishing character stands in relation to these other agencies. The epilogue further explains how these dimensions may be reconciled. The metaphorical appeal to the horticultural praxis of grafting both illuminates the possibility of achieving the unity of the natural and moral orders and clarifies the limits and relation of cultivation to the attainment of this unity. On the basis of understanding this unity and its realization, the ontological achievement, the successful formation of character, may be comprehended as inextricably associated with human community and political praxis and, at the same time, as a supreme act of individual autonomy.

PART ONE

Development of the Conception of Character and
Its Relation to Other Terms and Distinctions
of the Critical Philosophy

Character Conceived as an Issue of the Conduct of Thought (*Denkungsart*)

THEMATIC OVERVIEW

If any sense of Kant's notion of character is generally familiar among Kantians and other scholars alike, it is the statement found in opening of the *Groundwork* that "the peculiar property of the will is therefore called character," since the will "is to make use of [our] natural gifts," our "talents of mind," and our "qualities of temperament" (*G* 393). Allan Gibbard, for example, remarks quite matter-of-factly that Kant "insists that morally good character is the place to start. He starts out by arguing that the only thing good in itself, without qualification, is a good will— a morally good will."[1] The passage has occasioned a number of different interpretations of the will, its identification with character being seen as only one possible meaning.[2] The greater interest of Kant's statement may

1. Allan Gibbard, *Wise Choices, Apt Feelings: A Theory of Normative Judgment* (Cambridge: Harvard University Press, 1990), 310n.
2. Scattered, brief, and undeveloped allusions to Kant's concern with moral character are found in the literature. For example, Lewis White Beck, in "Kant's *Weltanschauung*," in *Early German Philosophy: Kant and His Predecessors* (Cambridge: Harvard University Press, 1969), simply states that for Kant, "progress in history and improvement in man are not measured by happiness and well being, but by the development of moral character and freedom" (427–28). Robert Pippin notes, almost in passing, in his discussion of perfect and imperfect duties in Kant, that "I need to be concerned about my own character, about not just doing my duty in this or that instance, but about adopting as my end the development of a character committed over a long stretch of time, a lifetime, to a moral sensitivity and a kind of moral disposition" ("Hegel, Ethical Reasons, Kantian Rejoinders," *Philosophical Topics* 19 [1991]: 117). Allen W. Wood, responding to the Hegelian charge of the emptiness of the will, refers briefly to Kant's contrast between qualities of temperament and "the worth of character, or moral worth," concluding that "Kant's conception of the good will and moral worth is simply the most courageous, candid admission in the history of philosophy of what we are committed to if we hold consistently to the moral conviction that the real worth of people and their actions cannot depend on nature or luck, but must lie entirely in what is up to the agent" ("The Emptiness of the Moral Will," *Monist* 72 [1989]: 475–76).
Karl Ameriks analyzes "three major interpretations of the term [will]: (1) the 'particular inten-

very well lie in the indicated relation to our natural, human capacities; moreover, the connection between the notions of character and will turns out, on a comprehensive reading of the corpus, to be one that Kant explicitly draws relatively infrequently.[3] This is not to say that the connection

---

tion' view, (2) the 'general capacity' view, and (3) the 'whole character' view." Referring also to Kant's *Reflections* (*Ak* 19, no. 7314, 310–11), Ameriks (rightly, I think) takes Kant to mean that "commitment to such principles" of a good will is "the essence of a proper Kantian character" and that the "whole character" is entailed because "it is not a matter of being good in one particular intention, or even through a series of events; it is a matter of being good in the free and overriding principle behind the more particular maxims which are behind all our even more particular and numerous actions" ("Kant on the Good Will," in *Grundlegung zur Metaphysik der Sitten. Ein kooperativer Kommentar*, ed. Otfried Höffe [Frankfurt am Main: Vittorio Klostermann, 1989], 45, 54–55). Not only does the notion of commitment itself bear development, but what is here being called "whole character" will (in the present study of Kant's conception of character) be shown to be the strict sense of character, with the "whole" involving the full range of the human aptitudes (*Anlagen* and *Keime*). This latter point is important because, among other reasons, the centrality of the notion of will has in the past led to Kant's ethics being labeled as a kind of subjectivist voluntarism.

As Otfried Höffe argues, Kant in fact is not a *Gesinnungsethiker*, at least "not in the sense that his moral principle, the good will, designates an externally inactive inwardness (*Welt tatloser Innerlichkeit*) without any manifestation in political, social, and private life" (*Ethik und Politik. Grundmodelle und Probleme der praktischen Philosophie* [Frankfurt am Main: Suhrkamp Verlag, 1979], 88).

The interpretation that Friedrich Kaulbach gives to the notion of the "good will" in his commentary on the opening passage of the *Groundwork* accords with central aspects of character as they are developed in the present study. As the inner source of the subject's activity, to designate the will as good, writes Kaulbach, is to say the subject's "character" is "trustworthy" and "steadfast" (*Immanuel Kants "Grundlegung zur Metaphysik der Sitten"* [Darmstadt: Wissenschaftliche Buchgesellschaft, 1988], 199–200).

For Barbara Herman, the opening passage of the *Groundwork* has served to support her version of the current argument against the deontological reading of Kant: "It seems to me now incontrovertible that the chief source of misunderstanding of Kantian ethics is the almost universal commitment to treating it as a moral theory without a notion of value as its fundamental theoretical concept. . . . Were we able to set aside the canon that sorts all moral theories as deontological or teleological—with Kant the defining exemplar of the former—we might recognize in this opening sentence a variant on the familiar first move of classical ethics. . . . the point of insisting that the two texts [i.e. the *Groundwork* and the *Nicomachean Ethics*] can be compared is to make it easier to see the *Groundwork* embarking on a familiar path of inquiry into the nature of the good" (*The Practice of Moral Judgment* [Cambridge: Harvard University Press, 1993], 208–9).

Most recently, Stephen Engstrom has interpreted the notion of the "good will" as identified with wisdom: "Kant has very good reason—deep and important ones—for thinking that the idea of the good will lies at the bottom of the ancient idea of wisdom" ("Kant's Conception of Practical Wisdom," *Kant-Studien* 88 [1997]: 17). Such emerging richer readings of Kant's notion of *Wille* are complementary to a thoroughgoing analysis of his conception of character.

3. Another example of these relatively infrequent (as compared with the express link with *Denkungsart*) direct associations of will and character is made by Kant in his *Reflections on Anthropology*, paragraph 1113 (whose range of possible dates is reported by Adickes as being anywhere from 1769 to 1776–78). Except for the transposition of the notions of character and will in

of these terms is insignificant, but it does indicate, as Karl Ameriks has pointed out, that "one must be careful not to assume that the notion of the good will by itself is an unambiguous and unquestionable starting place."[4]

In the *Critique of Practical Reason*, it is character that is named as the "highest good in a human being" (*KpV* 157), and its identification here (as in other texts) is made with the notions of power of choice (*Willkür*), conduct of thought (*Denkungsart*),[5] and comportment of mind (*Gesinnung*).[6] Further examination of Kant's writings reveals the notion of character to be multifaceted, complex, and intimately linked with a number of terms and distinctions central to both the critical philosophy and the *Anthropology*. The most general and also the most formal sense of character is given in the *Critique of Pure Reason:* "Every efficient cause must have a character, that is, a law of its causality, without which it could not be a cause" (*KrV* A539/B567).[7] The continued discussion in these sections of the first *Critique* ("The Possibility of Causality through Freedom," and "Explication of the Cosmological Idea of Freedom," A538–58/B566–86) is also replete with terminology from the *Anthropology*, in particular the paired set of terms "conduct of thought" (*Denkungsart*) and "conduct of the sensibilities" (*Sinnesart*).[8] As the following listing of citations from various

---

regard to which follows from the other, Kant's statement here is virtually identical to that of the *Groundwork.* "Character is the general governing principle in human beings of the use of their talents and attributes. Therefore it [consists in] the constitution of their will and [is either] good or evil" (*RA* 496). A very similar statement appears in the Mrongovius lecture notes (from the winter semester of 1784/85); see *Ak* 25.2.2, 1385. The passages here continue in a vein similar to that of the opening discussion of the published anthropology lectures (*ApH* 285). In further passages that Werner Stark alludes to in his papers (in which he discusses the import of the now published lecture notes found in volume 25 of the Academy edition), it is evident that the identification of character and will is one that Kant gave expression to in his classroom (at least as late as the mid 1770s).

4. Ameriks, "Kant on Good Will," 45.

5. For the translation of *Denkungsart* as "conduct of thought, see "Note on Translation."

6. For the translation of *Gesinnung* as "comportment of mind," see "Note on Translation." Kant's terms, *Gesinnung, Gesinnungen*, and *sittliche Ordnung der Gesinnung* are among some of the most difficult to translate. A detailed discussion of these notions is given at the end of this chapter.

7. In order to retain the distinction in the English, I will be rendering *Ursache* simply as "cause," or also as "causal agency" or "causal agent," while *Kausalität* (literally the connection or relation between a cause and its effect) appears as "causality." As a philosophical term, *wirkende Ursache* means "efficient cause," but where it is important to underscore its meaning of "having the power to and producing the intended effect," I will also translate *wirkend* as "efficacious."

8. *Sinnesart* refers to mental and emotional attributes, inclinations, states as these are empirically evident in physical and linguistic forms of expression. In Kant's account these belong to human sensible (as contrasted with intelligible) nature and the literal "conduct of the sensibilities" parallels its counterpart, "conduct of thought." In most cases, the less awkward translation "sensibilities" will be given.

texts shows, whatever other associations are made, it is "conduct of thought" that appears as a common denominator in their references to character.⁹

In the *Anthropology*'s discussion "The Character of the Person," character is (*a*) a concept embracing the tripartite levels of aptitudes inherent to human nature (physical, psychological and practical);¹⁰ (*b*) it is that which is "characteristic" of our "capacity of desire" (*Begehrungsvermögen*) considered in terms of this tripartite division (also expressed as our natural aptitudes, temperament or sensibilities, and conduct of thought); while, (*c*) in its "absolute sense," character is said to refer to *Denkungsart* (*ApH* 285ff.). This latter identification is consistent with the texts in Kant's *Reflexionen* assembled by Adickes under the title "Of Character as *Denkungsart*" (*RA* nos. 1155–1232, 511–42, spanning the period 1772–88), and with *Reflexion* number 1518, "Character or *Denkungsart*" (subtitled as "that which defines [*fixirt*] freedom") (*RA* 867, from the early 1780s). In the *Critique of Pure Reason*, Kant develops his discussion of character in terms of his critical empirical/intelligible distinction, which, in turn, he explicitly identifies with the paired set "sensibilities" and "conduct of thought"; that is, "empirical character (sensibilities)" is said to be "determined by intelligible character (*Denkungsart*)" (*KrV* A551/B579). In relation to the law of causality, this intelligible/empirical (sensible) distinction is further described in terms of the two aspects of any causal action, namely the "act" (*Handlung*)¹¹ and its "effect" (*Wirkung*), with thought explicitly

9. Peter D. Fenves has recognized that *Denkungsart* is a term with considerable depth (*A Peculiar Fate: Metaphysics and World-History in Kant* [Ithaca: Cornell University Press, 1991], 251ff.). As he sums it up, "by virtue of its cosmic context, the word *Denkungsart* can thereafter comprise those fundamental ways in which one takes the Idea of freedom itself into consideration; morality thus belongs to modes of thinking as well. . . . It is not surprising that modes of human existence in their entirety are often presented primarily in terms of *Denkungsarten* throughout Kant's later writings" (252).

10. In *Religion within the Limits of Reason Alone* (*RV* 26–28), Kant identifies the three levels of aptitudes (of animality, i.e. of the human as a living being; of humankind, i.e. as a living, rational being; and of personality, i.e. as a rational and at once morally accountable being) as "original aptitudes for good in human nature." The notion of personality is given in the *Critique of Practical Reason* (87) as the conception of the person as a being belonging to the sensible world, but as subject to one's true personality as belonging to the intelligible world. In the *Anthropology* (*ApH* 285) the analogous tripartite division of human aptitudes is given as a basis for the discussion of character. Later in the same text, still within the context of a discussion of "character" that "we procure for ourselves," Kant draws the distinction in terms of resulting kinds of abilities we possess: technical/mechanical, pragmatic/prudential, and moral (*ApH* 321–23). In the second chapter, an extended discussion is given of Kant's use of the term aptitude (*Anlage*), often written as *Naturanlage*, and its significance for his conception of character.

11. For the sake of clarity as to whether the intelligible activity (*Handlung* as *Tat* equals *factum noumenon*), or its *Erfolg* or *Wirkung*, its consequent manifestation, in the concrete (*Handlung* as *Tat* equals *factum phaenomenon*) is being referred to, I am rendering the distinctions by using the

identified as the causal source of effects in the world (*KrV* A538–39/ B566–67, A546/B574, A551/B579). Turning to the *Critique of Practical Reason*, one finds character defined as "practical resolute *Denkungsart* in accordance with invariable maxims" (*KpV* 152), a definition developed further by the *Anthropology*'s account detailing those fundamental maxims proper to the one who can be said to have character (*ApH* 294–95) and reiterated by a statement in the essay *On Pedagogy* that "character consists in proficiency in acting in accordance with maxims" (*P* 481).[12] The discussion in the *Critique of Judgment* (sec. 42) of what counts as an indication of morally good character is also developed in terms of the notion of conduct of thought; previously in the text, *Denkungsart* (rather than nature) has been identified as that to which the sublime (properly speaking) refers (*KU* 246, 274, 280). *Religion within the Limits of Reason Alone* continues the parallel of conduct of thought/intelligible character and sensibilities/ empirical character; a new dimension is added, the problem of overcoming the human propensity for evil, in relation to which a "conversion of *Denkungsart*" is essential for the "establishment of character" (*RV* 47–48).[13] Virtue (itself multifaceted in its usage and meaning in the Kantian texts) is here associated with empirical character (*RV* 47), while in a later essay one reads that the "true valor" of virtue consists in "squarely facing and vanquishing the maliciousness of the evil principle in ourselves" (*F* 380).[14]

---

translations "activity" (for *innere Handlung*, for example, the activity in general of reason), "act" (for either *Handlung* or *Tat* as *factum noumenon* as the inner moral acts or judgments upon which external moral action depends), and "action" (for *Handlung* when it refers to concrete actions in space and time).

12. The discussion in section 40 of the *Critique of Judgment* is directly relevant here also, since the culminating principle of these maxims of an ordinary human understanding is expressed in terms of Kant's central notion for his definition of character—the resolute conduct of thought (*Denkungsart*).

13. The *Anthropology* discussion parallels this discussion of character as *Denkungsart* and its establishment consisting in a conversion (*Umwandlung*) or rebirth (*Wiedergeburt*) (*ApH* 294–95).

14. The relation of the notion of virtue to the meaning of *character* will be a separate topic of discussion. In the *Critique of Pure Reason*, virtue is identified with the application of moral principles under the subjective conditions of feelings, inclinations, and passions (A54–55/B79). Kant also uses this term (*a*) as another name for the "morally good comportment of mind" (*sittlich gute Gesinnung*, which is in turn closely connected with resolute conduct of thought, or *consequente Denkungsart*, *G* 435; see also *KpV* 160), (*b*) as the highest possible level of human morality (*MST* 383), (*c*) as signifying spirit (*Mut*) and courage, while also presupposing an enemy (namely, the propensity for moral evil) (*RV* 57), (*d*) as derived from a root word meaning "fit for" or "adequate for" (*taugen*) (*MST* 390), while the "fitness" (*Tauglichkeit*) or "adequacy" (*Zulänglichkeit*) of something for various purposes is, in turn, given explicitly as the "practical meaning" of the "concept of perfection" (*KpV* 41). Human "inner perfection," however, consists in "having control over the use of all our capacities, in order to subordinate them to our free power of choice" (*ApH* 144). This state of perfection is synonymous with a virtuous state.

In addition to these aspects of character, all involving conduct of thought, or *Denkungsart* (as well as other aspects familiar to Kant's readers), character is explicitly related to "conduct of life" (*Lebenswandel*)— to its unity, purpose and vocation. "Establishment of a character," Kant writes, "is the absolute unity of the inner principle of the conduct of life" (*ApH* 295). The "character of a living being" first allows us to recognize "its vocation" (*Bestimmung*), its "purpose," which in the case of human character as conduct of thought is "not given by nature, but must always be secured by one's own efforts"; our natural endowments or aptitudes "indicate what can be made" of us, while character in its absolute sense as *Denkungsart* indicates "what one is prepared to make of oneself" (*ApH* 329, 294, 285; see also *KpV* 98–99). Here the most general thing to be said is that character formation is the work specific to the human being, the effect (*Wirkung*) we produce, indeed are obligated to bring about, in the world as a result of our own act (*Handlung*)—a way of considering the matter that indicates its intrinsic relation to the passages cited previously.[15] As Kant notes at one point, "The leading (*erste*) character of the human genus is our capacity as rational beings, for [the sake of] our own person as well as for the society in which nature has placed us, to procure a character at all; and that we do so presupposes there is already a favorable natural aptitude and a propensity for good" inherent in the individual (*ApH* 329). "To set a purpose for oneself at all is the capacity characteristic of humanity (in contrast to animality)" (*MST* 392). Such "superiority over nature is the basis of a self-preservation entirely different in kind" from the one that can be threatened by the forces of nature outside of us, and hence, too, we are able to feel our "own sublimity of our vocation" (*KU* 261–62). That cultivation of our final purpose is what Kant has in mind when he thinks of pedagogy is also evident: "Many rudimentary things (*Keime*) lie within human nature, and now it is our affair proportionally to develop these natural aptitudes and to unfold our humanity out of its rudiments, and to see to it that human beings achieve their vocation" (*P* 445). From his review of the student transcriptions of Kant's lectures,

---

15. Kant consistently distinguishes between what is simply given, the innate attributes of our nature (what is *natürlich, angeborn*) and what is acquired by our own efforts, our own work (*erworben*). It is our "duty" to make the "perfection proper to our human nature" our "purpose," and such duty refers to that which "can be an effect (*Wirkung*) of our action (*Tat*), and not something that is merely a gift for which we must thank nature" (as he puts it in the *Metaphysical Principles of Virtue*, for example, *MST* 386–87). This distinction is made explicitly in the discussion of character in the *Anthropology* (*ApH* 285).

Stark concludes that the "decisive point" evident in them as well is that "character, defined as the highest power of availing ourselves of our capacities and abilities, is the source of human actions"; "character is an achievement, a morally estimable activity of the subject."[16]

While connecting threads are discernible in these varying references to character found in the Kantian corpus, nonetheless tensions are also evident. Further, the wide array of terms and distinctions involved might, prima facie, give the impression of an ubiquitous term (or set of terms, character and conduct of thought) that defy any effort to locate a single, definitive meaning. Questions such as the following readily come to mind. How, in light of standard interpretations of Aristotle's account, as well as contemporary moral, psychological discourse, in both of which moral virtue and character have to do first and foremost with the human inclinations, are we to understand character described in terms of the notion of conduct of thought? What exactly does the latter mean? What is its connection to the classical moral issue of the conduct of life? What precisely is the relation between character and nature (or our natural human capacities), given that the concept of character embraces *all* the human aptitudes in one sense, while in an apparently narrower sense referring to both the act and result of human rational effort? Just what does this effort consist in? How is character so construed to be cultivated? Do the varying elements—intelligible, empirical, and aesthetic dimensions, virtue, radical evil, and so forth—ultimately form a unified whole (as implied in the identification of character with the unity of an inner principle of the conduct of life), or does the account simply consist in an aggregate of interesting connections? How does one distinguish and/or relate the character of the individual and that of the human species? How do all the other dimensions mentioned fit with the general definition of character in terms of law from the first *Critique*? Is there a systematic, or at least cohesive, account of character to be gleaned from all this? These are challenging issues, but well worth the effort to address them. We begin with an overview of the historical context in which the association between the forms of thought and life, between conduct of thought and character, is made— both in selected elements of eighteenth-century discourse and in Kant's own writings.

16. Stark, "Kant's *Lectures on Anthropology*," 10. "The task of anthropology," Stark goes on, "at least through the middle of the 1770's, is to investigate what use human beings make of their capacities" (11).

HISTORICAL CONTEXT

The literature from the seventeenth and eighteenth centuries reveals that the notion of an immediate connection between conduct of thought and conduct of life is not new with Kant. A work as early as Antoine Arnauld's *La Logique ou l'art de penser* (1662) begins with the assertion: "Other qualities of mind are of limited use, but precision of thought is essential to *every aspect and walk of life*. To distinguish truth from error is difficult not only in the sciences but also in the *everyday affairs* that men engage in and discuss" (emphasis added).[17] While not widely read today, this was a text, Charles Hendel points out, whose "wide dissemination . . . from the time of its first appearance and the constant demand for it that produced edition and edition over the subsequent centuries . . . suggest an importance of the work in the education of many another thinker and man of letters." It was widely "familiar to the learned and the philosophers of the seventeenth, eighteenth, and nineteenth centuries," a book "over which some of them certainly pored with profit if not even with some measure of inspiration."[18] Arnauld's contemporary, Blaise Pascal, also raises conduct of thought as an issue of utmost significance for human life: "Man is obviously made for thinking. Therein lies all his dignity and his merit; and *his whole duty is to think as he ought*. Now the order of thought is to begin with ourselves, and with our author and our end. Now what does the world think about? Never about that, but about dancing, playing the lute, singing, writing verse, tilting at the ring, etc., and fighting, becoming king, without *thinking what it means* to be a king or *to be a man*" (emphasis added).[19] The discussion of *l'art de penser* of greatest interest, perhaps, in relation to Kant is Rousseau's *Emile; or, On Education.*

17. Antoine Arnauld, *The Art of Thinking: Port-Royal Logic,* trans. James Dickoff and Patricia James (Indianapolis: Library of Liberal Arts, 1964), 7. I am indebted to Christian Laursen for a very helpful conversation on Arnauld's text.

18. Charles W. Hendel, foreword to Arnauld, *The Art of Thinking,* xxiii, xxiv–xxv. Hendel remarks that "it would be interesting to explore its relevance . . . to Kant's view of judgment," and notes further that "it was indeed *au fait* with contemporary science and philosophy as well as moving in the newer spirit of religion drawing upon Augustinian theology. It bespoke a lively concern too about the moral and even political problems of the modern world. It was something new and fresh" (xxiii, xxiv–xxv). I agree with Hendel's intuition, but rather surprisingly (given the wealth of authors named in Kant's corpus), Kant makes no explicit reference either to Arnauld or to his work (at least none that the Personindex, a CD-ROM search, or extensive reading of Kant's works has turned up).

19. Blaise Pascal, *Pensées,* trans. A. J. Krailsheimer (New York: Penguin Books, 1966), 235, no. 620.

On the opening page of its preface, one is told that this work, concerned with the "first of all useful things, the *art* of forming men," grew out of a "collection of reflections and observations . . . begun to gratify a good mother who knows how *to think*" (emphasis added).[20] Throughout the text, Jean-Jacques repeats that learning to think, acquiring judgment (as a prerequisite both to entering society and to the acquisition of any science) is a central aspect of Emile's education.[21] In book 5, he underscores the point by asserting that "by nature man hardly thinks. To think is an *art* he learns like all the others and with even more difficulty" (emphasis added).[22] Emile, he claims, is able to benefit from travel, is able to inform himself (in this case about the most appropriate form of government for a human community) precisely because he, unlike his peers, possesses the "art of thinking."[23]

The classic exemplar of the bildungsroman in German literature also raises the issue of thinking, specifically its requisite unified and interdependent relation with the active life. Although the completion of this work postdates Kant's lifetime, its clear expression of the question as an ongoing one of the age makes it worth noting. In Goethe's *Wilhelm Meister's Travels,* the answer to Wilhelm's question, on what does everything depend? reads as follows: "*Thinking and acting* [or doing, *Tun*], *acting and thinking, that is the sum of all wisdom,* appreciated and drilled into us from time immemorial, but not realized by a single person. Like exhaling and inhaling, each must be forever exercised in life in a continuous back-and-forth manner; like question and answer, the one should not take place without the other. Whoever makes into a law for himself what the genius of the ordinary human understanding secretly whispers into every newborn's ear, namely to test acting against thinking, thinking against acting, cannot go wrong, and if he should err, he will soon find his way back to the right path" (emphasis added).[24]

While one thus finds the notion of conduct of thought as an issue of immediate concern for human life in the discourse leading up to the eighteenth century and beyond, these examples provide no clear evidence of Kant's *sources* for his own use of the concept and his identification of it

20. Jean-Jacques Rousseau, *Emile; or, On Education,* trans. Allan Bloom (New York: Basic Books, 1979), 33.
21. For example, see *Emile,* 125, 192, 205, 241, 316.
22. *Emile,* 408.
23. *Emile,* 452.
24. Johann Wolfgang von Goethe, *Wilhelm Meisters Wanderjahre,* in *Goethes Werke,* ed. Erich Trunz, 14 vols. (Munich: C. H. Beck, 1981), 8:263.

with character. Kant implies that the term is generally used and indeed expresses an issue of the day, in his comment on his contemporaries' complaints about the insipid *Denkungsart* of the times (*KrV* Axi). However, he does not cite Arnauld at any point, his references to Pascal regard other topics, his uses of the term *Denkungsart* never mention any other author, and his own first employment of the notion predates his reading of Rousseau's *Emile* by no less than seven years, although his subsequent development of the meaning of conduct of thought may well owe some inspiration to the central importance Rousseau gives it in cultivating Emile's character.[25] Notably, Kant's own explicitly stated pedagogical principle (in his 1765 Announcement of his lectures, that students were "to learn not thoughts, but how to think" (*N* 306), a principle that biographical accounts attest actually characterized his manner of instruction, echoes Emile's tutor, Jean-Jacques.[26] The same emphasis on the activity of thinking, rather than the mere learning of propositions, is repeated a number of times in Kant's lectures on logic (specifically in regard to what it means to philosophize, *LJ* 22–26).

It is fair to surmise that Kant himself was at least a contributor to the use and meaning of the term, through his published writings and, in particular, his lectures on anthropology.[27] Relying primarily on Goethe, Kant,

25. Analyzing in his *Anthropology* Rousseau's intentions in his "three writings" dealing with the "injury" sustained by humankind in its transition from a state of nature to civilization, Kant explicitly notes that Rousseau's account includes the problem of "malformation of *Denkungsart*" (*ApH* 326).

26. The most current archival research on Kant's lectures, in particular his lectures on anthropology, completed by Werner Stark and Reinhard Brandt for volume 25 of the Academy edition, confirms earlier testimonies to Kant's pedagogical style (Brandt and Stark, introduction, lxvii).

27. The term *Denkungsart* (with its plural and the shorter version, *Denkart*) appears in each of the first nine volumes of the Academy edition, a total of 163 times, with over half (93) of these usages concentrated in five texts. These are, in descending order of number of occurrences, *Critique of Judgment, Critique of Pure Reason, Religion within the Limits of Reason Alone, Critique of Practical Reason*, and *Anthropology from a Pragmatic Point of View*. *Character* appears a total of 261 times in these nine volumes, with three-quarters (195) found in these same texts plus the essay *On Pedagogy*, again listed in descending order of number of occurrences: *Anthropology* (98 occurrences), *Critique of Pure Reason, On Pedagogy, Religion within the Limits of Reason Alone, Critique of Practical Reason*, and *Critique of Judgment*. A comparison that gives some perspective on these statistics is, for example, the famous Kantian notion of the "noumenon." In all its variations (including the Latin versions) the term appears a total of 145 times in the first eight volumes (with no instances in the ninth volume), half (74) concentrated in a single text, the *Critique of Pure Reason*, with 90 percent of those instances found in the third chapter of the first division of the "Analytic" (the section on the distinction of noumena and phenomena and its appendix, A236–92/B295–347, thirty-nine pages of text in the Kemp Smith translation). Whatever criteria decide what makes a term a "technical term" of the critical philosophy, pervasiveness and frequency cannot count against *Denkungsart*. It proves to be an ongoing concern throughout Kant's writings, one that increases in importance as one moves through their critical period. In light of these

and Herder, Grimm reports that the term *Denkungsart* (along with its less used synonyms, *Denkart, Denkungsweise, Denkweise*) appears for the first time in German in the latter half of the eighteenth century.[28] We know of Kant's relation with his student, Herder, and we also know that, while Goethe was reading Kant (especially the third *Critique*, the text with the single greatest number of occurrences of the term), there was no such reciprocal engagement with Goethe's work on Kant's part.[29] Among the meanings of conduct of thought (*Denkungsart*) in the period, Grimm includes viewpoint or direction of mind or spirit (*Ansicht, Richtung des Geistes*), comportment of mind (*Gesinnung*), character, and mode of thinking (*modus cogitandi*)—concepts found in the passages quoted earlier referring to Kant's account of character. In addition, Grimm cites passages, many from Goethe, that express three further dimensions of the notion of conduct of thought that are consistent with Kant's usage. First is the call for a logically appropriate conduct of thought for a given problem, on which the logical validity of our conclusions depends, for our judgments naturally follow from the conduct of thought (its direction, orientation, point of departure) brought to bear on a situation. This is just the sense of the term as Kant first uses it in *Universal Natural History* (*NH* 235). Second, conduct of thought is described as having two basic modes: active—thinking for oneself, a mode intrinsically connected with the notions of maturity, of thinking as an adult, of being responsible for one's thoughts and actions—and passive—the mere appeal to the opinions of others, to books, to custom, a mode that displays immaturity, thinking as a child, that takes flight from one's inherent self-responsibility. The parallel to Kant's discussion of the meaning and issue of Enlightenment

---

statistics, too, one might suspect that the recognition given to particular concepts is a function (at least in part) of the interests of Kant's readers and critics.

28. *Deutsches Wörterbuch*, ed. Jacob and Wilhelm Grimm, 16 vols. (Leipzig: S. Hirzel, 1860), 2:926–97, 943. Referring to the same source, but in regard to the term *character*, Werner Stark (in his paper "Anthropologie und Charakter") arrives at a similar conclusion, that "Kant's critical writings" effected a "redefinition of 'character' in German" usage, one that also differed from its usual connotations in English and French literature up to that point. Stark observes that already in the first Collins lecture notes, an "entirely different definition of 'character'" is found, one connected with the "concept of purpose." In the Parow lecture notes, not the drives and desires themselves, but the principle in accordance with which use is made of all human talents and attributes, is said to be determinative of character. Such statements of course resonate with the opening passage of the *Groundwork* (discussed earlier). Stark further observes that, based on the lecture notes, in Kant's own thinking, the "doctrine of human character underwent dramatic changes in the years of the 1770's."

29. Kant's inattention to Goethe did not, of course, escape the latter's notice. Goethe's accolade and complaint are both well known: the "old Königsberger" was "beyond any doubt the superlative philosopher of the day," but "never took any notice of him [Goethe] at all."

is self-evident.[30] Moreover, the transition from the passive to the active mode, as presented in the quotes from Goethe, involves a "genuine transformation of heart and thought" that again bears resemblance to Kant's call (in his account of radical evil) for a conversion in one's conduct of thought. The suggestion is not that Goethe is influenced by Kant and the reverse can certainly be held to be unlikely. Rather than deciding any question of influence, Grimm's assessment of the usage of this term indicates a genuine issue of the age, capturing the attention of its major thinkers and expressed through the notion of conduct of thought (*Denkungsart* or *art de penser*).

Finally, Grimm's selected passages connect the concepts of revolution and conduct of thought. Kant's reference to the shift from the Ptolemaic to the Copernican worldview as a fortunate "revolution in the *Denkungsart*" of the age is perhaps his best-known use of the concept of *Denkungsart*. The expression is not unconnected with the other aspects already noted, for not only was scientific inquiry thereby reoriented to begin from completely different premises, but the comprehended relationship of humanity to the world (individually and collectively) likewise received a wholly new orientation. It stands to reason that implications for morality and other dimensions of human life would be drawn. By 1793, Kant refers to the requisite conversion in conduct of thought (in order to overcome radical evil) as just such a "revolution of *Denkungsart*." In a wider sense, revolution was, of course, characteristic of the age; the changes (political, social, cultural, religious, as well as scientific) were recognized and welcomed by its major figures. One scholar has remarked that "long before Kant, the concept of revolution became a shibboleth for all the changes that humanity could henceforth, in light of the newly discovered knowledge, expect from itself."[31] And those changes included a call for revolu-

---

30. For a discussion of the dialectic and relation of enlightenment and counterenlightenment, see Vittorio Hösle, "Moralische Reflexion und Institutionenzerfall. Zur Dialektik von Aufklärung und Gegenaufklärung," in *Praktische Philosophie in der modernen Welt* (Munich: Verlag C. H. Beck, 1992), 46–58. The attempt to establish ultimate criteria not on the basis of tradition, but as derived from reason, is seen by Hösle as having been undertaken the first time by Plato and again most recently by the German Idealists (58).

31. Gerhardt, "Kants kopernikanische Wende," 136. Gerhardt provides a very instructive discussion of the transformation from a negative to a positive sense of "revolution" in the eighteenth century and of its intrinsic connection with the issue of conduct of thought. It is also noteworthy that one finds Enlightenment scholars employing the conception of conduct of thought in their descriptions and assessments of the thinking and events of the century. Hermann Timm, for example, calls the period one of a "revolution in the theological *Denkungsart*," a characterization that is the basis for his entire study, *Gott und die Freiheit. Studien zur Religionsphilosophie der Goethezeit*, vol. 1, *Die Spinozarenaissance* (Frankfurt am Main: Vittorio Klostermann, 1974). Peter

tion in the thinking of the people: "Even a skeptical realist such as Frederick the Great held a 'revolution in the conduct of thought (*Denkweise*) of the people' to be a possibility."[32]

What sort of possibility Kant ultimately had in mind, as indicated by our introductory overview, was character in its absolute sense as *Denkungsart*, a conception in which responsibility for self inhered, for it entailed "what one was prepared to make of oneself." Kant's most sustained discussion of this concept appears in his *Reflexionen* and the lectures published as *Anthropology from a Pragmatic Point of View*, but his contemporaries did not have to wait for the publication of the latter in 1798. As reported in earlier biographies and confirmed by the archival research on student transcriptions appearing in volume 25 of the Academy edition, starting in the academic year of 1772–73 and continuing regularly each winter semester for the next twenty-four years, Kant gave his very popular lectures on anthropology.[33] Kant himself describes them (in a footnote to the preface of their published version) as "initially freely undertaken," but later as part of the assignments of his position he delivered "two branches of *Weltkenntniß*" (literally, knowledge of the world) in the form of the "popular lectures" on anthropology and physical geography (*ApH* 122).[34] The knowledge of human beings considered "pragmatically" refers just to the investigation of "what individuals as freely acting beings make of

---

Gay in *The Enlightenment: A Comprehensive Anthology* (New York: Simon and Schuster, 1973) entitles one whole section, "Changing the General Way of Thinking" (283–415).

32. Frederick's hope is expressed in a letter he writes to Voltaire in August 1766. Gerhardt cites the passage ("Kants kopernikanische Wende," 137) from W. Mönch's *Voltaire and Friedrich der Große. Das Drama einer denkwürdigen Freundschaft. Eine Studie zur Literatur, Politik und Philosophie des XVIII. Jahrhunderts* (Stuttgart and Berlin: W. Kohlhammer, 1943), 383.

33. Brandt and Stark, introduction, 25.2.1, c; see also J. H. W. Stuckenberg, *The Life of Immanuel Kant* (1882; reprint, Bristol: Thoemmes Antiquarian Books, 1990), 70–80. The following data on student transcriptions and their dissemination is taken from Stark's conclusions, which are based on his archival research. The existence of these transcriptions, as Stark notes, was known previously to others, for example, Adickes, Menzer, and Krauss. Not all the biographies pay equal attention to the anthropology lectures. For example, Friedrich Paulsen gives them little more than a mention. Ernst Cassirer mentions them only once, but his brief statement in their regard is worth noting: "Thus it is in general an ideal of comprehensive practical human wisdom at which Kant aims in his own growth as well as in his teaching. Like the lectures on physical geography in the beginning, the later lectures on anthropology pursued this goal." In his description of Kant's earlier years, Cassirer observes, "Nowhere does Kant stand closer to the ruling eighteenth-century ideal of 'philosophy,' to the ideal of 'popular philosophy,' than at this point" (*Kant's Life and Thought*, trans. James Haden [New Haven: Yale University Press, 1981], 52–53).

34. As Brandt and Stark also report, from the mid-1770s on, Kant treated his lectures on physical geography as a "discipline complementary to that of pragmatic anthropology"; as such, the intent of the instruction was to "prepare" the students for "practical reason" (Brandt and Stark, introduction, xix, xxiii).

themselves, or what they can and should" make of themselves, and it considers "human beings as cosmopolitan citizens (*Weltbürger*)"; a "physiological" investigation, by contrast, explores "what nature makes out of human beings" (*ApH* 119, 120). As Brandt and Stark further report, due in large measure to a kind of cottage industry of producing and disseminating copies of student transcriptions of these lectures (a throwback to the ages before the invention of printing), the "history of their influence" entails "dimensions going far beyond what the normal publicity through the student forum could provide"; the demand for the copies came from a wide audience beyond the students.[35] Kant was aware of the dissemination of these copies and to some extent participated in it himself, as early as 1778, for example, seeing to it that his former student Marcus Herz received copies in Berlin. Again in the preface to the published edition, he refers to the "benefit for the reading public" that such a "systematic" and yet "popular" anthropology from a pragmatic point of view provides (*ApH* 121). The lectures themselves (including those on physical geography) attracted persons other than students, among them "officers, professional men, and merchants."[36] Brandt and Stark confirm Moses Mendelssohn's personal visit in the summer of 1777 and Von Zedlitz's interest expressed in a 1778 communication to Kant.[37] In addition, they note a further, more indirect route whereby Kant's teachings circulated, namely, as passages from the student manuscripts incorporated into Theodor Gottlieb von Hippel's writings. In particular, the first part of the latter's four-volume novel (appearing in Berlin between 1778 and 1781) included text from Kant's lectures on anthropology.[38]

35. Brandt and Stark, introduction, lxvi. In Protestant universities, this practice was continued during the Reformation for pedagogical reasons that valued this way of handling the materials of instruction (lxvii).

36. Stuckenberg, *Life of Immanuel Kant,* 71, 75.

37. Brandt and Stark, introduction, lv. Zedlitz was head of the ministry overseeing the affairs of church and education.

38. Brandt and Stark, introduction, lvi ff. By the mid-1760s, Hippel was one of the circle of friends that met frequently for the main meal of the day at Kant's house. The relationship began while Hippel was still a law student at the university, during which time he attended Kant's seminar on physical geography, among others. Eventually Hippel became mayor of Königsberg and during the course of his career published his writings anonymously. See Karl Vorländer, *Immanuel Kant. Der Mann und das Werk* (Hamburg: Felix Meiner, 1977), 3:34ff. Also see Joseph Kohnen, *Theodor Gottlieb von Hippel. Eine zentrale Persönlichkeit der Königsberger Geistesgeschichte. Biographie und Bibliographie* (Lüneburg: Verlag Nordostdeutsches Kulturwerk, 1987). A reference is given in the *Allgemeine Deutsche Biographie* (Leipzig: Duncker & Humblot, 1875), 12:463–66. A comparison of texts showing just where Hippel borrowed from Kant has been prepared by Hamilton Beck in "Kant and the Novel: A Study of the Examination Scene in Hippel's 'Lebensläufe nach aufsteigender Linie,'" *Kant-Studien* 74 (1983): 271–301.

Copying of the student manuscripts continued even after Kant's 1798 publication, indicating how Kant was received by his contemporaries and what attracted their attention, but of even greater importance from a philosophical standpoint is the way Kant's lectures were scheduled: each of his fourteen lectures on morality was given in conjunction with his lectures on anthropology in the same semester. As Stark has observed, in presentation there was "no morality without anthropology" and, in the decade of the seventies, it was equally the case that there was "no anthropology without morality."[39] The student manuscripts indicate that Kant necessarily had to count on students taking both lectures in the same semester and had to take care that the respective lectures did not contradict one another. For such students, then, unlike many modern readers, the experience and comprehension of Kant's moral teachings were always holistic, including both the objective and subjective dimensions that Kant tells us (in each of his major published writings on moral philosophy) belong to the complete subject. In the Mrongovius transcripts of his lectures on morality, Kant is reported to have asserted that the two sciences of practical philosophy and anthropology "cannot subsist as one without the other," for "one must know human beings in order to know whether they are capable of performing all that is demanded of them. The consideration of a rule is useless, if one cannot make people prepared to fulfill it" (*Ak* 27.2.2, 1398). Kant notes too in the *Groundwork* that "morality requires anthropology for its application to human beings" (*G* 412), or as he puts it ten years later in *Perpetual Peace,* the true political leader, the moral politician

---

39. Stark, "Kant's *Lectures on Anthropology*," 7. Basing his conclusion also on Kant's letter to Marcus Herz at the end of 1773 (depending on the edition, *Ak* 10, no. 71, 136–39, or no. 79, 144ff.), Stark claims that Kant here is already explicit about the fact that "a change in his lectures on morality is connected with the establishment of his lectures on anthropology"; that it is clear both that "morality and anthropology must be separated" and that "at the same time neither can be considered independent of the other" (6–8). Elsewhere, Stark points to the Parow lecture notes as explicit evidence for the relation between morality and anthropology expressed in the identification of the question of someone's morality with that of the moral quality of the individual's character (the supporting passages are found in *Ak* 25.2.1, 438). In his most recent paper, "Anthropologie und Charakter," Stark continues to develop and defend his thesis that for Kant "there was a close, inner relation" between the two disciplines of morality and anthropology.

Very recently, research in the Anglo-American Kant scholarship has begun to turn its attention to the relation of anthropology and morality in Kant's thought. Allen W. Wood prefaces his article on the subject by articulating the assumption that has stood in the way of taking this connection seriously until now: Kant's ethical theory has been thought to be "an exception, even an intended counterexample" to the notion that "basic to any practical science is a knowledge of its materials," that the "intellectual power of an ethical theory is mainly a function of its anthropological insights" ("Unsociable Sociability: The Anthropological Basis of Kantian Ethics," *Philosophical Topics* 19 [1991]: 325–51).

(whose task it is to educate people morally), possesses that "higher stand-point of anthropological observations" (rather than the political moralist's empirical ones) and so "knows what can be made of human beings" (*F* 374). For the reader cognizant of Kant's account of character, of the discussion in the *Anthropology*, the reference and significance of such a phrase and others like it scattered through all the texts (including all three *Critiques*) carry an import otherwise easily overlooked. In Kant's own day, as the historical findings imply, explanations of the anthropological or "character" terminology when used in other contexts were unnecessary—and indeed Kant uses it without such explication. In our contemporary readings, much of the terminology has gone largely unnoticed and with it the philosophical dimension it gives to the passages and texts in which it appears: namely, the allusions to moral character and its relation to those aspects of the critical philosophy in which the references are made.

Some time ago, Hans Seigfried wrote, "More is needed than a linguistically accurate translation in order to make Kant's writings fully accessible to Anglo-American philosophers who come from a different tradition than the one in which Kant wrote; the tradition in which and against which Kant was writing has to be made accessible as well. Like the more general need to read Kant's writings *entwicklungsgeschichtlich*, so this more particular need, too, has been recognized relatively late."[40] The scholarship has since then been developing along just such lines,[41] but of course work remains to be done. The foregoing discussion is a mere historical sketch,

40. Hans Seigfried, "Kant's 'Spanish Bank Account': *Realität* and *Wirklichkeit*," in *Interpreting Kant*, ed. Moltke S. Gram (Iowa City: University of Iowa Press, 1982), 115.

41. Recent changes of direction in Anglo-American scholarship, especially in regard to Kant's ethics, include the following: Kant's moral philosophy is now generally recognized to be more than a deontological ethics, the *Critique of Judgment* has won scholarly respect, current work promises to do the same for the *Anthropology*, and the Cambridge edition is making more and more works available in translation and correcting older versions. Many authors have and are participating in these new directions. Examples of recent titles that relate Kant's writings to various areas of eighteenth-century discourse include Michael Friedman's *Kant and the Exact Sciences* (Cambridge: Harvard University Press, 1992), Richard L. Velkley's *Freedom and the End of Reason: On the Moral Foundation of Kant's Critical Philosophy* (Chicago: University of Chicago Press, 1989), and John H. Zammito's *The Genesis of Kant's Critique of Judgment* (Chicago: University of Chicago Press, 1992). The English translations of essays by Dieter Henrich make available some of the efforts in the German scholarship to read Kant *entwicklungsgeschichtlich*; see Richard L. Velkley, ed., *The Unity of Reason: Essays on Kant's Philosophy*, (Cambridge: Harvard University Press, 1994). Older works of note include Beck, *Early German Philosophy*; Josef Schmucker, *Die Ursprünge der Ethik Kants in seinen vorkritischen Schriften und Reflektionen* (Meisenheim am Glan: Anton Hain, 1961); Paul A. Schilpp, *Kant's Pre-Critical Ethics*, 2d ed. (Evanston: Northwestern University Press, 1960); Keith Ward, *The Development of Kant's View of Ethics* (Oxford: Basil Blackwell, 1972); and Max Wundt, *Kant als Metaphysiker. Ein Beitrag zur Geschichte der deutschen Philosophie im 18. Jahrhundert* (1924; Hildesheim: G. Olms, 1984).

but it introduces us to the term central to Kant's mature definition of character, as having its own history in eighteenth-century discourse and as expressing a concern of the day. The next step is to trace Kant's own use and development of its meaning in his writings.

From Precritical to Critical Philosophy: The Path to Character as an Issue of Thought

The anthropology lectures span the time period from eight years prior to the appearance of the first edition of the first *Critique*, through ten years after the publication of the B edition, and if we had all of the lectures in Kant's own hand, we might begin our examination there. We will, however, begin the following examination with his writings published from 1755 through to the critical turn. Strictly speaking, the path within the precritical period to Kant's mature definition of character is short (at least within the works he published), with only ten occurrences of the term conduct of thought (*Denkungsart*), and with an explicit discussion of character in its moral sense found in only one essay, *Observations on the Feeling of the Beautiful and the Sublime,* from 1764. The connections in these writings between conduct of thought and character are tenuous; the 1764 essay, for example, never employs the former term, although it refers to "comportment of mind" (*Gesinnung*) relatively frequently, particularly in connection with the notion of virtue.

In these limited early references, however, nascent versions of the *issues* involved in Kant's mature definition are discernible. His very first use of *Denkungsart* appears in *Universal Natural History and Theory of the Heavens* (1755) in relation to rightly conducting one's thinking in those cases where geometrical accuracy and mathematical certainty cannot be expected (such as theories about the actual mechanics of the creation of the universe) (*NH* 235). A similar sense characterizes Kant's use of the notion in *The Only Possible Argument in Support of a Demonstration of the Existence of God* (1763), in which he discusses rules for methodology in physico-theology, asking (for example) in accordance with what premises we can or should think about the advantages accruing to us from a given phenomenon of nature, what the consequences are for our thinking when we begin from an assumption of divinely ordained purpose (*BG* 126–27). Implicit in these first discussions is an issue explicitly articulated in 1786, in the essay "What Is Orientation in Thinking?" Namely, what are the appropriate principles to guide judgment in reflections involving questions that go beyond possible experience?

The road to connecting these issues with moral character is a long one, but we can learn something about Kant's point of departure, what in these first writings already gives rise to the question of rightly conducting oneself in one's thinking. To understand *why* Kant focuses on thought rather than inclinations as the fundamental constitution of, and problem for, character, it is instructive to begin with his initial and abiding concern with the attributes of "thinking natures" (among whom human beings are the ones we know best). An implicit moral concern—specifically, how perfection of their natures as thinking beings may be attained—is present in Kant's very first considerations in the *Universal Natural History;* how, he asks, does their placement in the universe in relation to distance from the sun affect their possibility of realizing a "perfection of the capacity of thought," even if such occurs only in the form of a kind of "perpetual progress" ("Fortschreitung . . . ins unendliche wachsenden Graden") (*NH* 331, 351–52, 355)? That coming to an understanding of human nature requires studying human *Denkungsart,* as well as inclinations and prejudices, is explicitly stated in Kant's 1757 announcement of his lectures on physical geography (*PG* 9), while in "On the Different Human Races" (1775) a consideration of the influence of the earth's climatic zones is discussed in terms of "character" resulting from the development of "a particular germ (*Keim*) or natural aptitude (*Anlage*)" (*VR* 432, 435, 442)— the earliest instance of the conjunction of this terminology of *Anlagen* with that of character. Development of the connection, however, is found only in the *Anthropology* and in other writings published after the 1781 edition of the first *Critique.* The essay *Observations on the Feeling of the Beautiful and the Sublime* (which predates the advent of Kant's annual anthropology lectures by nine years) discusses "character" in terms of temperament divided along the same lines as the medieval humors (*B* 218ff.), a division found also in the *Anthropology,* where, however, Kant goes on to identify this second level of the human aptitudes explicitly as the sensibilities (*Sinnesart*). Otherwise, within the precritical period, the term *character* is used only in its ordinary sense, referring simply to the nature of the thing under discussion; for example, the "fluid character of forces," or the "character of the permanence of creation," or even the "character of the beautiful."

Beyond the explicit use of the terms *Denkungsart* and *character,* a number of other points are worth noting.[42] Already in 1755, Kant describes

---

42. The remaining instances of the use of *Denkungsart* that have not been discussed are as follows: (1) the essay on the four syllogistic figures (1762) in which Kant critiques this logical division of the figures as giving expression to an "oddity of *Denkungsart*" (*Ak* 2:56); (2) the essay

thinking as an "inner activity," a "power of thought" (*Denkungskraft*) that, when exercised as the "light of judgment" (*Urteilskraft*), as the "activity of deliberating," struggles to overcome the "sluggishness" resulting from the corporeal association in which human reason finds itself (*NH* 355–58). These early reflections are pessimistic, but again implicitly moral, tied as they are to concerns about human existence. Among all the earth's creatures, human beings are held least likely to attain the "purpose of their existence," for our capacity of connecting concepts and ruling over our propensity to passions by a "free use of insights" develops late, if at all (*NH* 356). The 1763 essay on negative magnitudes too speaks of the "power of thought" whose "inner activity" is not necessarily ascertainable from external actions, for the opposed forces of (for example) a desire for money and the capacity to act in accordance with basic principles of obligation may net each other out. Hence, Kant already here draws a conclusion familiar to his readers of the critical moral philosophy: on the basis of their actions, it is "impossible for human beings to infer the degree of the virtuous *Gesinnung*" (*NG* 199–200). In addition, the *Observations* (1764) discusses "true virtue" (as distinguished from "good-naturedness, an attribute of the sensibilities) as being "sublime" and as necessarily grounded on principles (*B* 214–17). The positive side of the melancholic character is described in terms that coincide with attributes elsewhere characterizing morally good conduct of thought: such a character is motivated by principles, is steadfast and truthful, has a deep sense of the dignity of human nature, is free and judges and thinks for himself (*B* 221). In this essay too, Kant implicitly alludes to what comes to be called the "enlarged *Denkungsart*";[43] in a discussion which recalls later descriptions of nature's role in civilizing human beings (especially for readers familiar with the essays usually referred to as his philosophy of history), Kant here notes how, on the stage of the world, human beings are brought to a juncture in their thinking such that they take a point of view lying beyond themselves (*B* 227).

Finally, on the other side of the "great light" of 1769, Kant in his *Inaugural Dissertation* of 1770 spells out a number of crucial distinctions in-

---

on principles of natural theology and morality (1764) in which Kant reflects that Crusius's new point of departure in metaphysics is not as far removed from the "*Denkungsart* of philosophy" as it might first appear (*Ak* 2:294); (3) *Dreams of a Spirit-Seer* (1766), in which Kant refers to *Denkungsart*—his own and that of those who put credence in the seer's tales—as being of discernible, different kinds, having (in effect) very different characteristics (*TG* 347, 351, 356, 357).

43. This maxim has recently become more familiar as increased attention is given to the *Critique of Judgment*, but in fact the set of three maxims (of which it is the second one) is found repeated at five different points in the corpus and will be discussed later.

cluding: (1) the intellect's "real" use (giving rise to "concepts of objects or relations" independently of the senses) to which moral concepts belong, versus its "logical use" (ordering given concepts and sensitive cognitions), which is "common to all the sciences"; (2) two kinds of "perfectio noumenon"—theoretical (belonging to God) and practical or moral; (3) sensibility and intelligence as two capacities of the subject distinct in kind and role—as "receptivity" and as a spontaneity that corresponds to the intellect's real use (*MSI* 392–96).[44] Before Kant's mature conception of character is completed, these and other distinctions are explicitly brought to bear on it. The earliest indication appearing in the published writings that Kant (in the course of his "silent decade") proceeded to do so, comes in 1781 in his explicit connection of character with *Denkungsart* and with the sensible/intelligible distinction defined in 1770. In a first *Critique* passage, Kant asserts that the "empirical character" of an action in its appearance, that is, the empirical character "of sensibility" (*Sinnesart*) is itself determined in "intelligible character (of *Denkungsart*)"; insofar as *Denkungsart* is the "cause" of the action, the latter is not the result of the operation of empirical laws (*KrV* A551/B579). In the second *Critique*, the moral sense of *Denkungsart* identified with character is unequivocally expressed, notably in the context of that text's discussion of how the soul is to be morally cultivated (an issue which is, of course, related to the concerns of the *Anthropology*): "Character (practical resolute *Denkungsart* in accordance with invariable maxims)" can only be "established" through "the pure moral ground of motivation" (*KpV* 152).

The essays of the intervening years between the first edition of the first *Critique* and the second *Critique* are peppered with similar references, all without definitive explanations of the meaning of the terminology, but through its very usage alluding to the on-going discussions of the lectures

44. The relevant discussion is concentrated in the second part of the *Inaugural Dissertation*, secs. 3–9. English translations consulted are *Kant's Latin Writings: Translations, Commentaries, and Notes*, ed. and trans. Lewis White Beck et al. (New York: Peter Lang, 1986) and the more recent volume of *The Cambridge Edition of the Works of Immanuel Kant: Theoretical Philosophy, 1755–1770*, trans. David Walford and Ralf Meerbote (New York: Cambridge University Press, 1992). Manfred Kuehn has argued for the importance of Kant's *Inaugural Dissertation* for his moral philosophy, as both representing a break with his ethical positions prior to 1769 and establishing the all-important "new conception of the intellect as a spontaneous faculty, radically different and independent from, sensation," as well as "at least two of the fundamental features of his mature ethical position": Kant's "insistence that the principles of judgment in morals are not in any way based on sensibility, and [that] morality is fundamentally the point of view of freedom" ("The Moral Dimension of Kant's *Inaugural Dissertation:* A New Perspective on the 'Great Light of 1769'?" in *Proceedings of the Eighth International Kant Congress*, ed. Hoke Robinson [Milwaukee: Marquette University Press, 1995], vol. 1, pt. 2, 374, 376, 378.

in anthropology. In his 1784 "Idea for a Universal History," Kant calls for the cultivation of human nature out of its natural state of brutishness to one of "inner perfection of *Denkungsart*," a cultivation requisite too for ultimate human happiness, but one which is continually obstructed by the political leaders and institutions of the states (*IG* 20–21, 26). The essay "What Is Enlightenment?" also speaks of a "true reform of *Denkungsart*" that is not achievable by mere political revolutions (*A* 36). In the *Groundwork*, the sort of *Denkungsart* one is dealing with in a given case—base or virtuous—is identified as being a function of the maxims which have been adopted (*G* 423, 426, 435). The "Conjectural Beginning of Human History" of 1786 implies the importance of the notion of orientation for conduct of thought: "A small beginning, . . . in that it gives to *Denkungsart* a wholly new direction, is more important than the entire unforeseeable series of expansions in culture which follow from it" (*M* 113).

Pinpointing the origin(s), then, of Kant's conception of conduct of thought as a moral issue, indeed its identification with moral character in its strict sense, is not a simple matter. The extant accounts of the development of Kant's moral philosophy focus on the question of the origin and development of the *objective principles* of Kant's ethics. In themselves, these scholarly readings constitute a very interesting debate involving at least the following three issues: (1) When did Kant establish the basic principle of his formal ethics? (2) What is the relationship between the development of Kant's theoretical and moral philosophy? Does the moral precede, or do theoretical insights inform the moral ones, or do the essential developments of both stem from the same origins? (3) What role did either inspiration by, or reaction against, his contemporaries play?[45] Relying on Kant's remarks in his interleaved copy of his *Observations on the Feeling of the Beautiful and the Sublime*, Dieter Henrich argues that "[t]he development of Kantian ethics had its beginnings in the context of the presuppositions formulated by Wolff, Crusius, and Hutcheson. This context led Kant to the discovery of the formula of the categorical imperative as early as 1765."[46] The conclusions of the older studies of Kant's pre-

---

45. These questions have each been addressed by Lewis White Beck in the following articles: "The Fact of Reason: An Essay on Justification in Ethics: Internal and External Questions," in *Studies in the Philosophy of Kant*, ed. Lewis White Beck (Indianapolis: Bobbs-Merrill, 1965), 200–214; "Kant and His Predecessors," in *Critique of Practical Reason and Other Writings in Moral Philosophy* (Chicago: University of Chicago Press, 1949); "Kant's Theoretical and Practical Philosophy," *Studies in Kant*, 3–53.

46. Dieter Henrich, "The Concept of Moral Insight and Kant's Doctrine of the Fact of Reason," trans. Manfred Kuehn, in Velkley, *The Unity of Reason*, 72. The translation is of the essay "Der Begriff der sittlichen Einsicht und Kants Lehre vom Faktum der Vernunft," which appears

critical writings are familiar to most. Paul Arthur Schilpp sees a "straight line of development," a "remarkable steadfastness of insight and belief" in Kant's "labors of the sixties" through to their "temporary culmination and most deliberate expression in the Dissertation of 1770," but rejects the view that Kant was ever a "disciple either of Rousseau or of the British moralists."[47] Josef Schmucker (who challenges various points of Schilpp's reading) concludes that the "fundamental principles" of Kant's "critical ethics" were established in the "first half of the sixties" and that, under Rousseau's influence, the development of Kant's ethical principles were transformed.[48] More recently, Manfred Kuehn argues that the 1770 Dissertation represents a break with previous positions both in Kant's theoretical and moral philosophy.[49] While Henrich too emphasizes the importance of the 1770 changed "concept of reason," on his analysis it takes Kant until after the 1785 *Groundwork* to shift from an effort of "deducing moral insight from theoretical reason" to conceiving of "moral insight as the fact of reason."[50] Kuehn, by contrast, views "Kant's new theory . . . of the intellect as a spontaneous faculty" forged in 1770 as decisive: "The origins of Kant's theoretical thinking are also the origins of his practical philosophy" and it is "wrong to assume that his critical ethics originated much earlier than 1769."[51]

On Richard Velkley's interpretation, "Kant is a critical philosopher in the theory of practical reason before becoming a critical philosopher in the account of theoretical reason some time after 1770."[52] Velkley takes the assessment of Rousseau's influence further than either Henrich[53] or

---

in *Die Gegenwart der Griechen im neueren Denken,* ed. Dieter Henrich et al. (Tübingen: J. C. B. Mohr, 1960). See also two other essays by Henrich: "Über Kants früheste Ethik. Versuch einer Rekonstruktion," *Kant-Studien* (1963): 404–31; and "Über Kants Entwicklungsgeschichte," *Philosophische Rundschau* 13, no. 3 (1966): 252–63.

47. Schilpp, *Kant's Pre-Critical Ethics,* 105, 170. Schilpp notes that Kant was "grateful" to Rousseau and the British moralists for "noting and emphasizing previously neglected aspects of human conduct," but that "nonetheless, there is no evidence that Kant ever accepted their doctrines without important reservations."

48. Schmucker, *Ursprünge der Ethik Kants,* 24, 143ff. Schmucker's discussion of the importance of Rousseau for Kant's moral thought spans pages 143–252.

49. Kuehn, "Moral Dimension," 374.

50. Henrich, "Concept of Moral Insight," 72.

51. Kuehn, "Moral Dimension," 374, 375.

52. Richard L. Velkley, "Freedom, Teleology, and Justification of Reason: On the Philosophical Importance of Kant's Rousseauian Turn," in *Rousseau in Deutschland. Neue Beiträge zur Erforschung seiner Rezeption,* ed. Herbert Jaumann (Berlin: Walter de Gruyter, 1995), 182. This essay develops the interpretation presented in *Freedom and the End of Reason.*

53. In *Aesthetic Judgment and the Moral Image of the World,* Henrich (as he also does elsewhere) interprets Kant with a view especially to the Platonic tradition. However, here Henrich notes

Schmucker: "Rousseau's importance for Kant after 1764 goes beyond providing the self-legislative model for practical, and more derivatively, theoretical rationality. And [it] also goes beyond providing a certain moral
impetus, or a new enthusiasm for a moral conception of humanity, to
motivate the activity of theoretical science. More fundamentally, Rousseau
proposes to Kant a way of thinking about the *justification* (*Rechtfertigung*)
of reason as a whole. This issue of justification is inseparable from the
issue of the end, *Zweck,* or telos of reason."[54] As Velkley develops his
point elsewhere, "the true destiny of instrumentalist Enlightenment is, as
Rousseau shows Kant, a paradoxical decay of the rational advance of mas-
tery over nature and society, into a progressive enslavement of man to his
own creations. . . . Among thinkers influencing Kant, Rousseau has most
responsibility for the Kantian effort of saving modern rational emancipa-
tion from its self-undermining tendencies, in a project of redefining Enlightenment and the forms of reason upon which Enlightenment must
rest."[55] In agreement with Velkley at least in this regard, Frederick Beiser

---

that there is "another philosopher to whom [Kant] constantly refers but whom he never quotes
when he tries to understand and justify the moral image of the world. Here Kant finds himself
in almost complete accord with him, and one can describe Kant's entire philosophy as the result of
an attempt to transform this philosopher's thoughts into a scientifically respectable and universally
applicable theory. The philosopher is Jean Jacques Rousseau" (*Aesthetic Judgment and the Moral
Image of the World,* Stanford Series in Philosophy, Studies in Kant and German Idealism [Stan-
ford: Stanford University Press, 1992], 10).

54. Velkley, "Freedom, Teleology, and Justification," 183.

55. Richard L. Velkley, "The Crisis of the End of Reason in Kant's Philosophy and the Remarks of 1764–1765," in *Kant and Political Philosophy: The Contemporary Legacy,* ed. Ronald
Beiner and William James Booth (New Haven: Yale University Press, 1993), 78. Velkley provides
an analysis of the project of modern philosophy, dividing it into three eras, with Rousseau and
Kant falling in the second era, the "response to 'alienation by Nature and Reason.'" Specifically,
Kant's response is twofold: a recognition of the crisis at hand, as well as of its intrinsic opportunity,
if rightly directed, for a new, comprehensive ordering of reason: "The weakness that Kant discovers
in the modern foundations leads him to believe that his age is one of unprecedented dangers to
rationality and humanity. The possibility arises of loss of all faith and confidence in the capacity
of reason to guide human affairs. But statements about the 'current crisis in learning' in Kant's
letters of the 1760s are accompanied by declarations that the present age is one of unprecedented
opportunities for philosophy to assert its leadership in human affairs and to 'establish the lasting
welfare of mankind.' Thus Kant supposes that Enlightenment in his time is undergoing a critical
test from which it should be able to emerge stronger and victorious" (82). As Velkley notes, the
main points of Rousseau's analysis are so familiar that "one might fail to appreciate how a reader
of Kant's age might be shocked by them. What is more, one might fail to grasp how this analysis
might compel a thinker of Kant's stature to reshape his whole conception of reason" (84). "At
this moment in history, which is like an 'absolute moment,' reason's dialectical fate has been
exposed, and now its inner structure and law can be discovered. The threat of chaos and collapse
is veiling the grandeur of the possible providential justification of reason, now emerging. Shortly
after he finds the 'hidden law' in Rousseau, Kant begins to develop the science of reason's self-
knowledge; philosophy is above all the science determining the end, powers, and limits of reason,

too argues for a "very marked and radical change" in Kant's views "sometime in late 1764 or early 1765," due to the "influence of Rousseau" which caused Kant "drastically to redefine the role of reason and his entire conception of metaphysics."[56]

The operative hypothesis of the current investigation is that the account of character, as the concrete manifestation of reason in the world, is the fulfillment of the reconception and justification of reason as a whole. Thus it takes the point regarding the role of reason one step farther. There are, moreover, at least two basic differences between the preceding varying interpretations and the present effort of elucidating Kant's conception of moral character. These differences relate to the question being asked and the source texts to which the answers are traced. Most of the authors cited share in common the effort to locate the roots of Kant's *objective* principles of morality. Further, those who decide on a point in the time period prior to 1769 tend to rely on Kant's 1764–65 *Remarks on "Observations on the Feeling of the Beautiful and the Sublime"* for their assessment. In our inquiry here, not the objective principles considered in themselves, but the nature of the relation of Kant's conception of character to his formal, moral principles is the question to be addressed, as part of the examination of what character means. Second, to this end, the lectures on anthropology, not the *Remarks*, provide the important archival data.

That is not to say that relevant notions are not raised in Kant's *Remarks*; especially when read from the vantage point of hindsight, as is also the case for the other precritical writings, many interesting statements stand out. Besides the reflections in Latin emphasized by Henrich, important distinctions and concepts are identified throughout. For example: Kant points to the differences between (1) being "good-natured" and "well-mannered" or civilized, (2) being a "good person" (*Mensch*) and a "good

---

for the sake of its own soundness and well-being. The language of the 'critique of reason' arises in 1765–66, out of the reflection on 'crisis' " (86).

56. Frederick C. Beiser, "Kant's Intellectual Development," in *The Cambridge Companion to Kant*, ed. Paul Guyer (New York: Cambridge University Press, 1992), 42, 43. Attaining a more complete picture of Kant's conception of reason is particularly important in the context of contemporary ethical discussion. As Onora O'Neill too, has pointed out, at the heart of (for example) MacIntyre's criticism of Kant is his view that Kant makes a "misguided attempt to base ethics on an impoverished conception of human reason"; O'Neill's own response to this charge is found in *Constructions of Reason: Explorations of Kant's Practical Philosophy* (New York: Cambridge University Press, 1989), 148–62. Another recent study tracing Kant's conception of willing to his precritical writings and, in particular, Rousseau's influence is Giovanni B. Sala's two-part essay "Das Gesetz oder das Gute?" *Gregorianum* 71 (1990): 67–95, 315–52.

rational being" (*vernünftiges Wesen*), (3) moral taste and virtue, (4) life in an aristocracy and one in a republic (already at this early date rejecting both the arcadian and courtly forms of life as "vapid and unnatural") (*BB* 21, 24, 43, 46).[57] Virtue is associated with strength, freedom is seen as the highest principle both of virtue and of happiness, and our absolute duty that our actions be (morally) good is expressly asserted (*BB* 75, 29, 24). However, like the *Observations*, the *Remarks* refer to character only in terms of the sanguine, melancholic, and choleric humors (for example, *BB* 57). Not only do they not employ the notion of *Denkungsart*, but—unlike the *Observations*—they also rarely mention *Gesinnung* (comportment of mind).

Nonetheless the issues, in terms of which the debate among Kant's commentators is carried out, are highly relevant for analyzing his account of character, especially in its strict sense. Following is an assessment of what may be gleaned in light of these issues from the passages cited previously from Kant's early works. From the very outset in 1755, we saw Kant concerned with the question of conducting oneself rightly in one's thinking and, indeed, in a sense going beyond strictly the requirements of formal logic; the discussion in the *Universal Natural History* refers to the use of analogy and rules of plausibility (*NH* 235). Arguably, in view of Kant's well-known self-description—a "researcher by inclination" who was "set right by Rousseau" and taught that the quest for knowledge did not constitute the "dignity of humanity" (*BB* 38)—the articulated concern in 1755 and again in 1763 is still primarily theoretical in nature. Yet even the first mention is raised in connection with the issue of the perfection of our nature, given the place in which we find ourselves in the universe. According to the variation of this concern in the *Remarks*, humanity's most urgent business is "to know how to fulfill its place in creation properly and to understand rightly what it is to be a human being" (*BB* 36). By the time of the *Inaugural Dissertation*, perfection has been explicitly distinguished between the theoretical form proper to God and the moral or practical form. The use of the *Kraft* language, again as early as 1755 and explicitly in relation to exercise of the power of thought over other human capacities and propensities such that the purpose of human existence might be fulfilled, is at least a nascent version of the intelligible causality all-important to the moral life and to character as the unity of its inner principle. It would seem that a case could plausibly be made for a "line

57. All references to the *Remarks* are to the Rischmüller annotated edition.

of development" taken back even prior to the sixties, to Kant's first published work.

Certainly too, the *Remarks* in particular clearly manifest a serious engagement of Rousseau's writings. That it is a reproving engagement is important: Kant underscores his different starting point, namely the civilized and not the "natural man"; he remonstrates against Rousseau's style of expression and criticizes his portrayal of the tutor as an "unnatural" model (*BB* 16, 27, 28). Further, given that in this text Kant makes relatively frequent explicit mention of Rousseau, it is all the more striking that he passes over in silence just the issue of conduct of thought as it is raised in *Emile*. The affirmation of the primacy of the practical over the theoretical is, of course, crucial, but as the cited passages from 1755 and 1763 show, at the very least in its implicit form, the concern with the practical characterizes Kant's reflections from the beginning. In short, if one applies Kant's own statement in the *Remarks* to himself, "I can never persuade someone else except through his own ideas" (literally, "thoughts" [*Gedanken*], *BB* 30), then one may see his relation to Rousseau as classically Socratic: the teacher not as the source of the ideas, but the midwife aiding their birth and stimulating what proves to be their long journey of clarification in Kant's own thinking.

Whether one wishes to press for an account of development that reaches back into the sixties and even the fifties in Kant's writings, depends on the weight one accords to the presence therein of identifiable elements of his later positions. In regard to the specific question of the "establishment" of Kant's conception of character as conduct of thought, it is decisive, I think, that while one finds both discussions about character and explicit inquiry about rightly conducting oneself in one's thinking, juxtaposed in turn with other elements important to these notions in later writings, *no systematic connection* is made by Kant (in the writings examined) between these concerns about character and conduct of thought as related to the fulfillment of human purpose. The portrayal of character in these texts is left in terms of what the *Anthropology* describes as the level of the sensibilities. The first and second *Critique* passages cited provide the first stated connection in the works published by Kant; beyond these, one must turn to the student transcriptions of the anthropology lectures and to Kant's anthropology *Reflexionen* in order to locate an earlier date when it is evident that he has begun to see these two concerns as essentially related. In this regard, the recently compiled data by Werner Stark shows that by the 1777–78 academic year, documentation appears for the first time for Kant's use of the terms conduct of thought and of the sensibilities (*Den-*

kungsart and *Sinnesart*) as a paired set.[58] Given that this is how Kant also begins the discussion of the "Character of the Person" in his published lectures, we have here a good indication that by four years before the appearance of the first edition of the *Critique of Pure Reason* (but over a decade after the *Remarks*), he has already begun to formulate his mature conception of character. This time frame is also consonant with what one may glean from earlier student transcriptions and from Kant's *Reflections on Anthropology*. While juxtaposed usages of *Denkungsart* and *character* appear in the student notes from the start (in the winter semester of 1772–73),[59] and while possibly as early as 1769, but more certainly by 1772–75, Kant discusses character in his *Reflections* in such terms as firm resolve in one's maxims, explicit statements defining character in terms of *Denkungsart* are identified by Adickes (without a question mark) beginning with the period of 1776–78 (for example, *RA* no. 1230, 541). In any event, *all* these references, implicit and explicit, are subsequent to the "great light of 1769"; subsequent, that is, to the period designated by Kant himself as one in which he achieved new clarity of insight.

For character to come to be defined in terms of conduct of thought, another connection had to be forged, one that goes against the grain of the philosophic position that would view the activity of thinking as independent, even necessarily isolable, from the *vita activa*. The divide (perceived or real) between thinking and acting, between the life of thought and the active life, must be overcome. To this end also the model of rationality, the sense of thinking that is called for, must be given careful consideration. In our own century, these are just the issues Hannah Arendt takes up in her inquiry into an inherent connection between the activity of thinking and moral good and evil in human life.[60] It is also the topic

58. This again corresponds with what is found in Kant's *Reflections on Anthropology*. Among those passages not accompanied by Adickes with a question mark, the explicit distinction of the "natural" and of character as *Denkungsart* appears in a time period between 1773–75 and 1776–78 (for example, *RA* no. 1125, 502).

59. For example, in the Collins transcriptions one reads that Kant stated that a person's character could pretty well be inferred from the company they were keeping, their habitual choice in dress, and their favorite amusements. Further, for one who had a preference for strong color tones, one could surmise many corresponding attributes in their character, but one could not presume a balance in the contrast with their *Denkungsart* (*Ak* 25.2.1, 231–32; Collins 197:13–198:5).

60. Specifically, Arendt poses the question whether "the activity of thinking as such . . . could . . . be among the conditions that make men abstain from evil-doing or even actually 'condition' them against it" (*The Life of the Mind* [New York: Harcourt Brace Jovanovich 1978], 5). Arendt's reading of Kant has (justifiably, I think) drawn criticism, but she does deserve credit for attending to the importance of the issue of thinking in Kant. *The Life of the Mind* identifies as Kant's "greatest discovery" his distinction between "knowledge which *uses* thinking as a *means to an end*, and thinking itself as it arises out of 'the very nature of our reason' " (64, emphasis added; see

broached by Goethe in the passage cited from *Wilhelm Meister:* just as
breathing requires both inhaling and exhaling, so thinking and acting are

also 14, 123–24, 170). For Arendt, this distinction is related to instrumental reason's having been
adopted even within the political realm. The scientific model of rationality, with its mathematical,
logical processes and its experimental methodology, has become accepted as *the* way we come to
know anything and, in turn, is assumed to be synonymous with thinking. This model, in effect,
realizes a problem latent already in the ancient conception of the thinking activity. As Arendt
describes it, in the ancient sense, contemplation and fabrication share an inner affinity, in that
in the latter what one beheld by the mind both guided the making of, and served as a standard
to judge, its product (*The Human Condition* [Chicago: University of Chicago Press, 1958], 301–
4). Yet, even here the mentality of the maker qua craftsman is one of instrumentality; he works
with things as means to an end. The orientation of thought governing the building of the world,
if it were generalized to the world and relations of men, would lead to limitless devaluation, the
loss of intrinsic worth, and growing meaninglessness (*Human Condition,* 157–58). For Arendt, this
explains the contempt in which the philosophers held the craftsmen; they were of *banausic* mentality
(unable to think and judge a thing apart from its function or utility) and as such posed a threat to
the political realm (*Human Condition,* 156–57; *Between Past and Future* [New York: Penguin Books,
1977], 215–16). When the questions changed from "what a thing is and what kind of thing is to be
produced, to the question of how and through which means and processes it had come into being
and could be reproduced," when the true was itself held to be the made, not given, when process,
not the idea, guided the activity, Arendt sees just such a generalization occurring as was feared by
the Greek philosopher: in the modern political realm it is taken "for granted that action, even more
than fabrication, is determined by the category of means and ends" (*Human Condition,* 228–29,
296–97, 299–300, 304, 307; *Between Past and Future* 217, 228–29). See also Hannah Arendt,
"Thinking and Moral Considerations: A Lecture," *Social Research* 38 (1971): 417–46.

It is beyond the scope of the present project to take up Arendt's reflections and their relation
to Kant in any detail. Writings that deal with her inquiry into the relation between acting and
thinking include Seyla Benhabib, "Judgment and the Moral Foundations of Politics in Arendt's
Thought," *Political Theory* 16 (1988): 29–51; Leah Bradshaw, *The Political Thought of Hannah
Arendt* (Toronto: University of Toronto Press, 1989); Michael Denneny, "The Privilege of Our-
selves: Hannah Arendt on Judgment," in *Hannah Arendt: The Recovery of the Public World,* ed.
Melvyn A. Hill (New York: St. Martin's Press, 1979), 245–74; Robert J. Dostal, "Judging Human
Action: Arendt's Appropriation of Kant," *Review of Metaphysics* 148 (1984): 725–55; Bernard
Flynn, "Arendt's Appropriation of Kant's Theory of Judgment," *Journal of the British Society for
Phenomenology* 19 (1988): 128–40; Volker Gerhardt, "Vernunft und Urteilskraft: Politische Philo-
sophie und Anthropologie im Anschluss an Immanuel Kant und Hannah Arendt," in *John Locke
und Immanuel Kant. Historische Rezeption und gegenwärtige Relevanz,* ed. Martyn P. Thompson
(Berlin: Duncker & Humblot, 1991), 316–33; Michael W. Jackson, "The Responsibility of Judge-
ment and the Judgement of Responsibility," in *Hannah Arendt: Thinking, Judging, Freedom,* ed.
Gisela T. Kaplan and Clive S. Kessler (Sydney: Allen and Unwin, 1989), 42–55; Hans Jonas,
"Acting, Knowing, Thinking: Gleanings from Hannah Arendt's Philosophical Work," *Social Re-
search* 44 (1977): 25–43; James T. Knauer, "Hannah Arendt on Judgment, Philosophy, and
Praxis," *International Studies in Philosophy* 21 (1989): 71–83; Jerome Kohn, "Thinking/Acting,"
Social Research 57 (1990): 105–34; Elizabeth K. Minnich, "To Judge in Freedom: Hannah Arendt
on the Relation of Thinking and Morality," in Kaplan and Kessler, *Hannah Arendt* 133–43; and
William J. Richardson, "Contemplation in Action," in *The Public Realm: Essays on Discursive
Types in Political Philosophy,* ed. Reiner Schürmann (Albany: State University of New York Press,
1989), 206–24. For a recent study responding to criticisms of Arendt's thought see Margaret
Canovan, *Hannah Arendt: A Reinterpretation of Her Political Thought* (New York: Cambridge
University Press, 1992).

likewise to be understood as a whole in which the one does not take place without the other. The point at issue here is not one of procedure or methodology in ethical decision making: that is, the question is not one of applying theoretical principles, first ascertained by various forms of scientific and philosophical inquiry (by a thinking activity carried out independently of actual agency in the world), to subsequent practical and pragmatic concerns. Rather, it is the conception of the moral agent that presents the difficulty. For if thinking is to be the activity constitutive both of character in its absolute sense and of the highest term of character conceived as the unity of the human intelligible and sensible capacities, then the agent must be identified with this activity—and not simply as an active individual in the world who happens to make use of powers of rationality.[61] Nor can such an agent be construed as a purely rational being. Hence it is significant to find Kant's continued attention not only to *Denkungsart*, whereby we may be a "subject responsive to the good," but also to what it takes to be a "good human being" (or good person, *guter Mensch*); the latter is achieved only "in continual acting and becoming" (literally, "bringing about effects" or "being efficacious" in the world and "developing oneself," *wirken und werden*) (*RV* 48; recall the distinction noted in the *Remarks* previously, *BB* 24). Character as conduct of thought that is at once the character of the active agent in the world and, indeed, as we have seen, the "unity of the inner principle of the conduct of life" requires an account of the unity of thinking and acting.

The point may be restated in Kant's own terms as these appear already in the few passages cited thus far, showing both its translation into the technical, critical terminology and the relation of the development of the conception of character to the critical formulations and insights. The most general definition of character given in the *Critique of Pure Reason*, "every efficient cause (*wirkende Ursache*) must have a character, that is, a law of its causality, without which it could not be a cause" (*KrV* A539/B567), referring (as it does) simply to the law of a given thing's efficacious causality in the world, is applicable even to Kant's earliest uses of the notion, such as the "fluid character of forces." Here the physical laws of nature

---

61. Lewis White Beck observes that the fact "that thought and action are intimately related in Kant's philosophy is evident from the very title of the book." He stops short of making a connection with character, developing his point in terms of the different points of view, the different concerns of the spectator and the actor ("Thought, Action, and Practical Reason," in *A Commentary on Kant's "Critique of Practical Reason"* [Chicago: University of Chicago Press, 1960], 29ff.). Beck later developed a book-length study of the relation of acting and thinking human beings and how they understand one another and themselves: *The Actor and the Spectator* (New Haven: Yale University Press, 1975).

that determine how such forces move within and in relation to the world are also definitive of the character of these forces. However, to be an efficacious cause as a *moral* being is to bring a different order of causality to bear on and in this physical world. How the relation of these orders of causality is to be conceived, if one is to have a single unified action brought about by an agent in whom these orders of causality themselves work together in a unified whole, is stated by Kant a few passages later in his first use of the paired terms (conduct of thought and sensibilities) in the first *Critique:* the "empirical character" of an action in its appearance, that is, the empirical character "of sensibility" (*Sinnesart*) is itself determined in "intelligible character (of *Denkungsart*)" (*KrV* A551/B579). Such agency is not to be construed merely negatively, as being independent of empirical conditions, but positively; namely as a "power" that "initiates of its own accord a series of events (*Begebenheiten*)" in the world (*KrV* A553–54/B581–82). Or, as Kant puts it in the introduction to the *Critique of Judgment*, where he again explicitly raises the issue of the connection of the theoretical and practical, discussed in terms of the determination of the sensible by the "supersensible in the subject," the "word *cause*," when "used in regard to the supersensible, means only the ground (*Grund*) that determines the causality of natural things to bring about an effect (*Wirkung*) in accordance with their own laws of nature, but at the same time also in *unanimity* (*einhellig*) with the formal principles of the laws of reason" (*KU* 195, emphasis added). That such a possibility is not inherently contradictory, continues Kant, has been shown elsewhere (referring obviously to the third antinomy).

The 1755 and 1763 *Kraft* language, the exercise of the power of thought whereby even then Kant had held that human beings attain the "purpose of their existence," has in these and other like passages received its critical translation. In the third *Critique* Kant goes on to put it this way: "The effect in accordance with the concept of freedom is the final purpose, which itself (or its appearance in the sensible world) ought to exist, and for which the condition of its possibility in nature is presupposed; that is, in the nature of the subject as a sensible being, namely as a human being" (*KU* 195–96). The unanimity, that is, the working together of the two orders of causality toward a single end (final purpose), the unity of reason and sensibility, of *Denkungsart* and *Sinnesart* in moral character concretely exercised in the world, requires attending not only to what the objective principles are (the work of the second *Critique*), but also to the conditions of the possibility of the realization of these principles in and through sensible nature. Having defined the objective principles in the second *Critique,* Kant's subsequent writings turn their focus to these subjective conditions. Among these later texts, *Religion within the Limits of Reason Alone* deals at length with the stumbling block to the unanimity required for character: the human propensity for evil inherent to the subjective conditions.

The unity to be achieved can only be a synthetic (not an analytic) unity. It is not deductive; one term is not derived from the other. A synthetic unity, as Kant, still in the introduction to the *Critique of Judgment,* spells it out, "arises from the union of the conditioned with its condition" (*KU* 197n). It is in these terms that the account of character as the unity of the thinking and acting, efficacious moral agent in the world must be considered. That Kant thus grapples with the issue of the connection of thinking and acting is recognized; yet it is just in this regard that his work draws criticism from one of the commentators who defends an early date for the establishment of Kant's ethical principles. Responding to statements in the *Reflections,* Dieter Henrich remarks: "While writing this text Kant obviously still believed that the phenomenon of demand and obligation can be shown to exist in both the theoretical and the moral realm, and that it signifies the necessity of both thinking and acting. Yet we must make a distinction between the two realms that Kant did not consistently observe even after his publication of the *Critique of Practical Reason.*"[62] There is a distinction, certainly, but if the conception of character as de-

---

62. Henrich, "Concept of Moral Insight," 81. Henrich's objection here is that the characteristics constitutive of moral insight, specifically "approval" as "the answer to the demand with which the good confronts the self," are not to be attributed to theoretical reason: "Thinking and its laws do not require the approval of the self in order to be evident truth. . . . I know that a pure thought is true and that the self can verify it at any time, but because this possibility itself is selfless, it cannot provide the foundation for our consciousness of the freedom of the self" (81). The claim that truth does not require the approval of the self is a rather different one from Henrich's final statement in this paragraph: "The truth of thinking, though achieved within me, does not arise as a demand on me" (81). Not only is this latter claim much less obvious, even debatable, but the thrust of Henrich's objections here is very different from our present project. Henrich is tracing out what he concludes are Kant's failed attempts at providing either a direct or indirect deduction of morality (more precisely, moral insight) from theoretical reason. Thus too, his criticism is based on the equation of "thinking" with "consciousness of self" (83). Our question is the relation of a priori moral insight to the self as moral agent in the world (a specific version of the question of the relation of reason and sensibility). For a discussion of moral insight as affirmation of the good and as promoted by reflective judgment, see chapter 4. Although Henrich observes both that the "method of critical philosophy, which establishes relations between its different disciplines, can best be seen in Kant's introduction to the *Critique of Judgment*" and that "Kant's theory of moral insight exhibits to a great extent the same structure that determines the critical system in its entirety," he does not take up Kant's account of reflective judgment in his analysis of moral insight (85–86).

fined is to be successful, then the account of the unity is all-important. And the notion in terms of which Kant so frequently gives expression to these questions is precisely the one whose elucidation (as he tells us in the preface to the second *Critique*) can be provided only by "an exhaustive critique of practical reason"; itself "constituting the greatest merit" of this work, the same term later in the *Critique of Practical Reason* is given as the definition for character: the consistent or resolute *Denkungsart* (*KpV* 6–7, 152).

To complete tracing out the path through the Kantian corpus from the precritical writings to the critical formulation of character as conduct of thought, a few words are in order concerning the meaning of this latter notion and the modifiers employed in connection with it. Just as the term *Achtung* is used by Kant in the full range of its nuances, from simply being attentive to something, to showing a deep respect that borders on reverence, so *consequente Denkungsart* expresses a range of meaning from basic consistency to resoluteness. For example, Kant's initial use of the term in the preface to the second *Critique* refers to *Denkungsart* as it is employed in the first two *Critiques* themselves, specifically in regard to the question of ascertaining the reality of supersensible objects. While it is certainly the case that a basic sense of Kant's statements here refers to maintaining consistency in the inquiry, even in relation to such cognitive activity (whether as theoretical or practical cognition), *more* than simple, logical consistency is conveyed by the term *consequent*. For the inquiry was steadfastly pursued, undaunted by the apparent contradictions (such as denying objective reality to the supersensible use of the categories by speculative reason, but affirming it in its use by practical reason). Directed toward a purpose, in this case showing how and when the concepts of supersensible objects are not empty for us, perseverance in the inquiry resulted in the "satisfying confirmation" of just that purpose.[63] To articulate the complete sense of Kant's statements in this way is consonant with the whole description he gives of his enterprise in these passages and with the meaning of the term in ordinary language: consistent (*folgerichtig*), persevering, unwavering (*beharrlich*), constant, steadfast (*beständig*), true to fundamental

63. In "Determination of the Concept of a Human Race," Kant uses the notion of resolute *Denkungsart* as characterizing his use of reason in pursuing this inquiry in the natural sciences. In this context he speaks of following his maxim without allowing himself to be distracted by other alleged facts (*Ak* 8:96). In other words, here, too, more than mere logical consistency is at stake; this investigation is to be pursued with a firm adherence to the appropriate principle of the use of reason in this case.

principles (*grundsatztreu*), goal-directed or (literally) conscious of one's goal (*zielbewußt*).[64]

In Kant's discussions of conduct of thought in relation to character, he makes explicit use of such adjectives. Beginning with the second *Critique*'s definition of character, the qualifying description reads "in accordance with *invariable* maxims" (*KpV* 152, emphasis added). In the *Anthropology*, in the discussion of the establishment of character, Kant speaks of the requisite firmness (*Festigkeit*) and perseverance (*Beharrlichkeit*) in holding one's principles (*ApH* 294). The essay *On Pedagogy* describes character as "consisting in the firm resolve to will to do something and then also in the actual carrying out of the same"; to quote from Horace, it means to be a "man of firm resolve" (*vir propositi tenax*) (*P* 487). Kant's *Reflections on Anthropology* ("On Character as *Denkungsart*") repeats the point: the "cultivation of character" requires "firm resolve in the adoption of certain maxims" (no. 1162; see also nos. 1179, 1230, 1232, 1517). As indicated in the *Critique of Judgment* (and elsewhere), belief (which itself means "to trust in the attainment of a goal that we are duty bound to advance, but for which we lack insight into the possibility of its realization") also enters into the discussion precisely in relation to its role in securing the "firm perseverance" of the "moral *Denkungsart*" (*KU* 472). In short, *consequent* includes a qualitative dimension over and above simple consistency; to convey the complete sense of the term, the translation "resolute" will here be used.

The examination of Kant's path to the conception of character in these terms has led to the following conclusions. While, from the very beginning, Kant inquires into the activity of thinking in a way that implicitly and explicitly involves moral aspects, strictly speaking it is only in conjunction with insights into essential distinctions of the critical philosophy that he definitively articulates the formulation of character as resolute conduct of thought.[65] To make sense of this notion as definitive of the moral char-

---

64. Reference works consulted are *Wahrig. Deutsches Wörterbuch,* ed. Gerhard Wahrig et al. (Munich: Mosaik Verlag, 1987); and *Der Duden. Das Standardwerk zur deutschen Sprache,* ed. Wissenschaftlichen Rat der Dudenredaktion (Mannheim: Bibliographisches Institut & F. A. Brockhaus, 1986).

65. Stark makes a similar statement. The "presentation [or conception, *Darstellung*] of the difference between *Sinnesart* and *Denkungsart,* that is between empirical and intelligible character enables the critical philosophy to presume human freedom. Kant could only have worked out this decisively important position in the course of the years of the 1770's. In the mid 1770's, Kant still did not have this concept, this conceptualizing at his disposal, as the transcriptions of the anthropology and ethics [lectures] show" ("Kant's *Lectures on Anthropology,*" 12).

acter of an agent in the world raises the issue of just how the relation of thinking and acting, of conduct of thought and the sensibilities, is to be understood. Just as the notion itself (as *art de penser* and as *Denkungsart*) is found in the wider discourse of the eighteenth century, so in Kant's use of it in relation to character we find that, in effect, Kant's development of the latter is a particular rendition of the "broader problem" of the "relation of reason and sensibility in general" preoccupying philosophical discourse in the latter half of the century.[66] As conceived by Kant, thinking, especially as resolute conduct of thought, is understood as something more and something other than a calculative, logical, or mathematical function. While consistency certainly is called for, it is steadfastness in its exercise on which the emphasis is placed.

Moreover, beyond this essential qualitative dimension, as the passages cited previously further indicate, maxim adoption is definitive of the conduct of thought itself. Reflection 1518 puts it most succinctly: "To make maxims for oneself: *Denkungsart*. Otherwise, *Sinnesart*.[67] Not to permit oneself to be deterred [from one's principles]. To be resolute" (*Ak* 15: 870).[68] At issue here is not only *what* these principles are (and Kant in the *Anthropology* does explicitly identify those essential to character). Maxims are usually considered in the context of Kant's universalizability criterion; that is, as rules of actions to be tested for their agreement with the moral law before being applied in a given case. In a more general sense, they are "subjective principles" whose source lies in the "interest of reason" (*KrV* A666/B694); as such "regulative principles" they allow, for example, inferences regarding the reality of supersensible objects. Rightly formulated, they result, in other words, in an orientation of thinking that avoids the pitfalls of relegating ideas intrinsic to morality to the status of mere

66. Kuehn's relevant historical observations here include: "Mendelssohn's contribution was important. He set for himself and others a most important task, namely that of explaining how the rational principles are related to what appear to be the completely different moral sentiments. It was precisely this task that defined one of the central concerns of German moral philosophers during the second half of the eighteenth century. . . . These Germans thought that the two accounts [Wolffian and Hutchesonian ethics] could be combined. . . . 'moral sense' . . . was one important part of the broader problem concerning the relation of sensibility and reason in general. Indeed, this broader problem became the most important concern of German philosophers between 1750 and 1780" ("Moral Dimension," 380).

67. (Conduct of the) sensibilities.

68. In aesthetic and pedagogical contexts, for example in the third *Critique*, Kant likewise links conduct of thought and maxims: "Thus the sublime must always have reference to *Denkungsart*, i.e., to maxims [which direct us in our thinking] to secure the supremacy of the intellectual and the ideas of reason over sensibility (*Sinnlichkeit*)" (*KU* 274). One of the definitions of character in *On Pedagogy* reads: "Character consists in the accomplished ability to act in accordance with maxims" (and character has here too been explicitly discussed in terms of *Denkungsart*) (*P* 481).

ideals (*DO* 139). Here we have, in effect, a thematic continuation from Kant's earliest use of conduct of thought, the question of rightly conducting our thinking precisely in those cases where empirical verification is precluded. We saw Kant attesting (in the preface to the second *Critique*) to the indispensable role played by the resolute conduct of thought in the satisfactory conclusion to this problem in its critical formulation. Our next step is to ask what the translation of the meaning and function of these notions in their practical employment entails. How are maxims in relation to conduct of thought definitive of character to be understood? Thus posed, we have yet another way of considering the issue of the unity of thinking and acting as an efficacious moral agent in the world.

Maxim Adoption and the Moral Comportment of Mind (*Gesinnung*)

The first point to be made is that "resolute *Denkungsart*" is itself a *maxim*—namely (as Kant spells it out in the third *Critique*) a maxim of reason and the third and final maxim of the three making up the "ordinary human understanding"; it is the one most difficult to achieve and attainable only as the union of the maxims of (1) thinking for oneself (maxim of the understanding) and (2) thinking from a universal standpoint (maxim of judgment), when repeated adherence to the latter two has developed into an accomplished observance (*Fertigkeit*) thereof. As meaning further to think in one voice (*mit sich selbst einstimmig*), this description of the third maxim calls to mind its identification in the *Anthropology* with the unity of the inner principle of the conduct of life (*KU* 294–95, *ApH* 295).

With the recent increased scholarly attention to the *Critique of Judgment*, these maxims (found in the context of the comparison Kant draws to elucidate the *sensus communis, KU* sec. 40) have become more familiar, and, of course, they are also central (the second one in particular) to Hannah Arendt's political reading of the third *Critique*. However, this set of three maxims appears at least five times in the corpus, including twice in the *Anthropology*, in both cases as the avenue to attaining wisdom, but notably once in a practical (*ApH* 200) and once in a theoretical (*ApH* 228) context. Their presentation in the lectures on logic appears in the context of a discussion of the source and nature of error, which Kant concludes with a call to "orient oneself in thinking, or in the speculative use of reason, by the ordinary human understanding"; the latter is identified as a "touchstone for discovering error" and is presented as another name for *sensus communis* (*LJ* 57). The maxims are here said to be the "universal rules and conditions for the avoidance of error in general," and the third, resolute *Denkungsart,* is given as being synonymous with "bündige Denkart" (binding, valid, conclusive, to the point) (*LJ* 57). Reflection 1508 (from the first half of the 1780s and so at least five years before the publication of the third *Critique*) begins with the definitions of each of the three maxims and ends by naming them as the "maxims of a mature (*reifen*) reason" (*Ak* 15:820–22). In this "Reflection" Kant alludes to a number of important relations. Academic learning is said to require "memory and understanding," but its "application in life" requires "judgment," a statement followed by a repeated listing of the three maxims. Reason (which, rightly used, allows us to go beyond what we have learned) may be sophistical, or legislative, or administrative (or governing). Its legislative function relates to "*Denkungsart,* not [the] thoughts" themselves, or as Kant also puts it in a similar point in the *Logik,* it has to do with the "use of reason" and not the actual "propositions"; in both texts, this exercise of reason constitutes what is, properly speaking, philosophy (*RA* 820, 821; *LJ* 26). By contrast, "all the other sciences consist only in the administration of our affairs through [the use of] reason" (*RA* 821); its governing function here, in other words, relates to theoretical knowledge.

From this summary, we see that a single set of principles or maxims pertains to sound reasoning, whether in its practical (legislative), or theoretical (governing) employment. These are not principles directly applicable as procedures for decision making or problem solving (as, for example, a series of steps to be followed to arrive at prudent choices in life's daily affairs, or a formula to solve a question in physics or mathematics). In Kant's essay devoted to the maxim of thinking for oneself, he explicitly repudiates the appeal to "rules and formulas, those mechanical instruments of a rational use, better said, *misuse* of our natural gifts" as the "shackles of chronic immaturity" (*A* 36, emphasis added).[69] One way to understand his point here is that such mechanical procedures in fact entail a passive use of one's rational powers, a mere following of learned steps, while the cultivation of the capacity for thinking itself goes unheeded. In the *Anthropology* Kant explains that "instruction consists in the communication of

69. In *Reflections on Anthropology* paragraph 1164 (from the period between 1772 and 1773–75), Kant explicitly states that rules ought to be subordinate to maxims: "Character requires in the first place that one makes maxims for oneself and then rules. But rules that are not limited by maxims are pedantic when they restrict oneself and stubborn, unsociable, when they restrict others. They are the strings leading (*Gangelwagen*) the immature along" (*RA* 514–15).

rules," and by means of such instruction, the human understanding may be furnished with many concepts and rules, but the ability to judge (whether as technical, aesthetic, or practical judgment) if a given case is an instance of the rule or not, cannot be taught; only years of practice can yield maturity and understanding in this sense (*ApH* 199). Reason, which has the power of representing the particular in accordance with universal principles, may thus be viewed as the capacity to judge and to act (with respect to the practical) in accordance with principles; but especially in morality, in matters involving acting and refraining from acting (*Tun und Lassen*), people are inclined to forgo the use of their reason and passively and obediently observe given statutes (*ApH* 199, 200). The opposite, "wisdom," the idea of perfection in the practical use of reason, a use in accordance with law, cannot in the least degree be infused by another; each must give rise to it from within, and the road to its attainment, for Kant, lies just in the adoption and exercise of these three maxims culminating in the resolute conduct of thought (*ApH* 200). Later in the text, referring back to these maxims as having already been identified as leading to wisdom, Kant recommends them as "invariable commands" too for thinkers engaged in the pursuit of knowledge; a pursuit in which the questions are (1) what is to be held to be true? (asked by the understanding), (2) on what does it depend? (asked by judgment), (3) what comes from it? (asked by reason) (*ApH* 227–28).

A number of important points are brought to light by these passages of what, in some respects, is familiar ground to Kant's readers. The thinking at issue, whether theoretical or practical, involves the use of all three capacities of reason, judgment, and understanding. The maxims are not rules for direct application to matters at hand; rather they are principles for orienting or guiding the activity of thinking itself as it is carried out in an interdependent relationship among the three capacities. Maturity consists in maturity of thought, that is, in the latter having attained, after long practice, a state of perfection in the exercise and realization of these maxims as formative for it, implicitly also entailing a state of unanimity or agreement among these human capacities. At maturity, they speak with one voice. The perfection of human nature as a thinking nature, expressed by Kant as a basic concern in 1755, is here given a much more detailed articulation.

The question that must be confronted is self-evident and has already been alluded to. By thus conceiving of character, the moral self (in effect) is identified as a thinking self; not only must its relation to the moral self as an acting self be elucidated, but the nature of the analogy drawn between achieving wisdom in moral and epistemological senses must be analyzed.[70] For Dieter Henrich (as already indicated) the essential question is the source of the objective principles of Kant's moral philosophy. In this regard, Henrich concludes that "a deductive justification of ethics [from the theoretical] must necessarily turn out to be unsatisfactory and contradictory" and that Kant "overstat[es] the analogy between the epistemological self and the moral self."[71] The focus of the present discussion is on the subject, more explicitly on the subject's activity of thinking; from this perspective, it is the principles or maxims for orienting that activity in general that have turned out to be the same. How is the analogy to be understood from the subjective (rather than objective) point of view?

The subjective side, as an indispensable part of the complete account of morality, has long been overshadowed by Kant's famous "ought, therefore can," the formulation responding to Hume's objections that "ought" cannot be derived from "is." Kant has not, however, simply inverted the relationship of the factual and the normative. "Can" is not equivalent to "is." "Can" asserts that our endowment of the human capacities must be such that it is possible for these to be responsive to reason's imperative, for them to instantiate the intelligible moral form under the conditions of space and time and in and through human choosing and inclinations. It is an assertion about the normative viewed in relation to human nature, from the transcendental, critical standpoint, which is to ask the question, how is morality (*Moralität*) as objective principles possible as a lived morality (*Sittlichkeit*) by the human subject?[72] The objective account of the

70. The issue at stake here has been variously cast and answered in contemporary philosophy, both independently and in explicit relationship to Kant. Foucault's analysis reads, "Before Descartes, one could not be impure, immoral, and know the truth. . . . After Descartes, we have a nonascetic subject of knowledge . . . which poses for Kant the problem of knowing the relationship between the subject of ethics and that of knowledge. There was much debate in the Enlightenment as to whether these two subjects were completely different or not. Kant's solution was to find a universal subject, which, to the extent that it was universal, could be the subject of knowledge, but which demanded, nonetheless, an ethical attitude—precisely the relationship to the self which Kant proposes in the *Critique of Practical Reason*" (Michel Foucault, *The Foucault Reader*, ed. Paul Rabinow [New York: Pantheon Books, 1984], 372).

71. Henrich, "Concept of Moral Insight," 81. See also his "Das Problem der Grundlegung der Ethik bei Kant und im spekulativen Idealismus," in *Sein und Ethos. Untersuchungen zur Grundlegung der Ethik,* ed. Paulus Engelhardt (Mainz: Matthias-Grünewald Verlag, 1963), 350–86.

72. The overshadowing of the subjective by the objective has included the practice in the English translations of not retaining the distinction between *Moralität* and *Sittlichkeit* (in spite of the fact that with Hegel the latter is rendered as "ethical life"). For a discussion of Kant's use of the three levels of *Sitten, Sittlichkeit, Moralität*, see my article " 'The Beautiful Is the Symbol of the Morally-Good': Kant's Philosophical Basis of Proof for the Idea of the Morally-Good,"

effect of the law as the immediate ground of determination of the will, the essence of *Moralität* (*KpV* 72), does not yet tell us what it is that the human agent actually does; that is, it gives us no basis for expectations or predictions as to what such an agent will actually do amid life's circumstances. Here it is no longer simply a question of the "representation of duty" but of the "observance of duty"; for the latter we have to ask, "not about the objective [ground of the action], what [human beings] ought to do," but rather about the "subjective ground of the action, on the basis of which, when one may presume its [presence], one may first anticipate what human beings will do" (*ED* 337). For what *is* likely to be the case, we must ask about the presence or absence of character, about the subjective, human conditions of the adoption and concrete realization of maxims; we must ask about the essential affair of "conduct of thought," about its own firmness or lack of resolve, as well as about the maxims in accordance with which its own activity is directed.[73] Only on the basis of "resolute *Denkungsart* in accordance with invariable maxims" can we expect of ourselves, and may others expect of us, that we actually will choose and act on the basis of the moral law, no matter what the surrounding difficulties of choice might be.[74]

Hence, too, the "first effort in moral education is to establish a character," and by "character" we mean the "accomplished ability to act in accordance with maxims" (*P* 481). We require, in short, practical or moral anthropology, that part of ethics containing such doctrines and prescriptions based on experience as (1) the subjective conditions that both hinder and promote the execution of the laws of (rational morality) in human nature, and (2) the engendering, propagation, and strengthening of moral principles (in upbringing, in school, and in popular instruction) (*G* 388, *MSR* 217). While this is the "empirical" part of ethics, it does not refer to the kind of historical, empirical familiarity with human behavior possessed, for example, by Kant's political moralist (in his 1795 essay on perpetual or eternal peace), but rather entails knowledge of what can be made of the human being (a phrase by now familiar to us as referring to character

---

Journal of the History of Philosophy 33 (1995): 315–17. For a detailed analysis of the notion of *Sittlichkeit*, see Otfried Höffe, "Grundbegriff Sittlichkeit," in *Ethik und Politik*, 281–310.

73. Kant's *Reflections on Anthropology* give some of his most explicit and concise statements about these terms. For example, one reads that "character consists in *Denkungsart*, namely acting from principles" (*RA* no. 1230, 541) (and *handeln* here most likely refers both to the reasoning activity as well as action in the world).

74. Kant makes this point explicitly. For example, *Reflections on Anthropology* number 1158 states: "A definite [or determined, *bestimmter*] character: of whom one can judge in advance everything which may be determined (by it) in accordance with rules" (*RA* no. 1158, 512).

in its absolute sense); for this, writes Kant, the "higher standpoint of anthropological observation is required" (*F* 374).

It is just in terms of the relation between these two parts comprising the whole of ethics that Kant himself in the *Critique of Pure Reason* draws the analogy between what one could broadly refer to as epistemology and morality. "What I call applied logic . . . is a representation of the understanding and the rules of its necessary use under the concrete, namely contingent, conditions of the subject, which may either hinder or advance its use, . . . and universal, pure logic relates to it as pure morality, which only contains the necessary moral law of a free will, relates to the true doctrine of virtue, which takes these laws into consideration under the hindrances of the feelings, inclinations, and passions to which human beings are more or less subject" (*KrV* A54–55/B79). The point of the comparison here does not lie between the objective principles respectively of logic and morality, nor is there any notion of a derivation of one from the other. Rather, the comparison lies in the relation of the effect to the objective principles causally brought to bear on it; it is this *relation* between universal and particular, objective and subjective, causality and its effect, ground and consequence, that is claimed to be analogous in the case of logic and morality. Kant's presentation here is in fact in agreement with the form of analogy as he develops its legitimate use within the critical limits. In its critical sense, analogy is the "identity of the relationship between ground and consequence (cause and effect), insofar as it takes place irrespective of the specific differences of the things, or their properties themselves that contain the basis of the similar consequences" (*KU* 464n; see also *Pro* secs. 57 and 58, *KrV* A179–80/B222–23).[75] It provides an avenue for comprehending the connection of supersensible and sensible, not by giving us cognition of the supersensible cause, but by means of concepts that "express its relation to the sensible world" and thus allow us "to think" such a "connection" itself (*Pro* 355).

The importance—and difficulty—of this relation is what makes the account of the subjective side of morality so crucial. The "idea of freedom" itself, writes Kant, "occurs only in the relation of the intellectual as cause to the appearance as effect" (*Pro* 344n). It is not enough either to stop with the articulation of the moral law and the objective account of its

75. A virtually identical statement appears in Kant's "Lectures on Metaphysics and Rational Theology," *Ak* 28.2.2, 1023. The ultimate goal of the analogy is to articulate a way of making comprehensible to us those supersensible objects of the ideas of reason for which we have no capacity of intuition. A discussion of this analogy is included in my article " 'The Beautiful Is the Symbol of the Morally-Good,' " 302–9.

effect as a determination of the will, nor simply (on the subjective side) to investigate the human conditions. The latter must be comprehended in terms of what can be made of them, how they may constitute the effect (*Wirkung*), the concrete realization of what is in itself objective, universal, intelligible. Thus they must be considered both in regard to their fitness (*Tauglichkeit*) for realizing such principles and the nature of their relation to them. Just these considerations constitute the inquiry into the concept of character. Moral concepts, in turn, "if they are to become subjectively practical," as Kant notes in the *Critique of Practical Reason*, "must not be left [at the level of] the objective laws of the moral life (*Sittlichkeit*), to be admired and highly esteemed in relation to humanity [as such]; rather we must consider their representation in relation to human beings and to them as individuals" (*KpV* 157).

It is, of course, the critical task for all such ideas of the supersensible to make them "fit for use in experience" (*DO* 136),[76] a task that includes (1) being able to regard their reality as true (for which, as we saw, Kant credits the employment of resolute conduct of thought in inquiry), (2) making the ideas comprehensible, attaining practical cognition of them (by means of the critical sense of analogy), and (3) giving them their critical, moral formulation. An idea for which, at best, only partial and fleeting empirical examples might be found to correspond to its object, an idea that brings with it a tradition of varying meanings, an idea that in its theoretical sense is deeply problematic, is recast as a moral task, specifically as a maxim that it is our duty to adopt. As a result, the validity of the idea for our actions is rendered independent of any particular instantiation present, past, or even in the future. The moral, philosophical emphasis shifts the meaning of the idea from either its historical fulfillment (which, of course, we are still to work toward, for that is just the dictate of the maxim), or the metaphysical efforts to define it, to its conception as a formal principle for our conduct of thought—to its immediate connection with our character. In short, the *actuality* of moral ideas within the world (for example, of the highest good, or eternal peace) depends upon their adoption and execution as maxims for human choice-making and actions.

Hence character as the resolute conduct of thought that recognizes the truth of such ideas and firmly and consistently resolves to choose and act

76. It is of course the well-known solution of the critical philosophy to define ideas of reason practically in order to make them comprehensible in and for human experience. In "What Is Orientation in Thinking?" Kant gives a step by step summary of how we must treat such ideas of reason for which it is necessary that we make judgments (*DO* 136–37).

in ways that will result in their concrete realization is all important.[77] The critical philosophy, in particular the third antinomy, on Kant's own assessment has completely allayed the suspicion or even fear of the impossibility and hopelessness of such an enterprise (engendered by Humean skeptical suspension of judgment or outright Voltairean rejection): "The problem that we had to resolve, . . . whether freedom contradicts the necessity of nature in one and the same action, . . . has been adequately answered" (*KrV* A557/B585). The analysis of the form of analogy legitimate within the critical limits has provided an avenue for intelligible speech about and comprehensibility of the supersensible objects of reason's ideas. With the negative, critical task thus having removed the impediments, having (as Kant's well-known statement puts it) "level[ed] the ground beneath the majestic moral edifices and made it capable of supporting them" (*KrV* A319/B376), the positive account of *the* moral edifice, human moral character, may be confidently undertaken. To do so is to give an account of the effect (*Wirkung*) of the idea of freedom, not simply as providing the rule for particular actions, but as formative of human moral nature. That its causality extends even to being the presupposition for the behavior of our inclinations is expressly discussed by Kant in the *Anthropology* (*ApH* 268–69).[78]

Nonetheless, even if moral concepts "must not be left [at the level of] the objective laws of the moral life," most will be left wondering at this point just how and where freedom's supreme law of causality fits in.[79] More detailed attention will be given to this question in the examinations of the relations of the notion of character (1) to the capacity of desire (in particular to the will) and (2) to the problem of moral evil, but an introduc-

---

77. The suggestion is *not* being made here that engagement of the critical philosophy is in any way requisite to the establishment of such character. The moral ideas are, for Kant, an inherent vague metaphysics of the soul and not called into question by the ordinary human understanding. It is the philosophers to whom Kant is recommending the explicit adoption of the fundamental maxims of this ordinary understanding (as we saw in the passages cited from the *Anthropology* and the lectures on logic) for pursuit also of their theoretical enterprises. Indeed, as Kant states in the *Anthropology*, "To be a person of principles (to have a definite character), must be possible for the most common understanding (*gemeinsten Menschenvernunft*) and thereby [must be] in regard to its dignity, superior to the greatest of talents" (*ApH* 295).

78. Kant's discussion is found in the section "The Inclination of Freedom as Passion." The passage referred to in the text reads verbatim as follows: "Thus the concept of freedom under moral laws not only awakens an affect that is called enthusiasm, but the mere sensible representation of outer freedom gives rise to the inclination to persevere therein or to enlarge [this outer freedom], by analogy with the concept of justice, to the point of a fierce passion" (*ApH* 269).

79. Otfried Höffe discusses the categorical imperative as the "criterion for lived morality (*das Sittliche*)" in which he includes a summary of the usual interpretations and objections raised in the scholarship in regard to it ("Kants kategorischer Imperativ als Kriterium des Sittlichen, in *Ethik und Politik* 84ff.).

tion is in order here. In Kant's own discussions of character, overt mention of the categorical imperative is conspicuously absent. Instead he uses the term given elsewhere in his explanations of the notion of the maxim: *principle*, or more literally, "fundamental principle[s]" (*Grundsatz*) (for example see *KpV* 20, or the earlier citation from the first *Critique*). To be a person of character is to be a person of firm principles; indeed, to lack such firm principles is to be without character altogether (and not simply to have an imperfect or weak one) (*MST* 420; *ApH* 285, 295; *RA* no. 1156, 512). Even Kant's itemization of "principles relevant for character" does not name reason's practical law (*ApH* 294). While this might initially strike one as puzzling, full consideration of the matter leads us to appreciate the import of Kant's distinction between objective law and subjective principle (or maxim), of his repeated insistence that "the law applies only to the maxims, not to particular actions" (*MST* 393), and of the priority he gives to the "form and principle from which [the action] itself follows" (*G* 416).

For evidence that reason has causality at all, Kant appeals even in the *Critique of Pure Reason* to "those imperatives . . . whereby [in the form of] rules we direct our performative powers in all practical matters" (*KrV* A547/B575). Such causality is always indirect in relation to the world. As we saw in the case of the resolute conduct of thought itself, formative, orienting, guiding principles were defined for conducting the activity of thinking, in relation to which reason was presented in an interdependent partnership with the capacities of judgment and understanding. For human reason to be efficacious, for it to relate its law, principles and ideas to the concrete world, the faculties more directly concerned with the latter must themselves be directed in accordance with maxims that result in their cooperative and able response to reason's direction. Or, as Kant has discussed the relation of reason to the other capacities of mind under the rubric of the "primacy of practical reason" in the second *Critique*, "reason as the capacity of principles determines the interest of all the other powers of mind (*Gemüthskräfte*), but its own for itself" (*KpV* 119–20; compare *KrV* A666/B694). The familiar account of its exercise of its practical interest is that of its determination of our capacity of desire, or capacity for setting ends (which insofar as it is thus objectively determined by reason is Kant's famous notion of *Wille*).[80] In this account of reason bringing its

---

80. I agree with Meerbote's assessment that "will" is inadequate as a translation of *Wille* and that in Kant's mature philosophical definition of the latter, it is practical reason itself considered in its function of determining (more or less successfully) the power of choice (*Willkür*). See Ralf Meerbote, "*Wille* and *Willkür* in Kant's Theory of Action," in Gram, *Interpreting Kant*, 69–84.

imperative to bear on human agency, the moral law is generally considered in relation to the contemplated or executed action; hence, too, its well-known role is that of a rule for deciding the moral worth of that action, by testing the maxim of the action for its formal conformity with the imperative.

There is, however, another dimension to practical reason's relation to other human capacities in the exercise of its practical interest. Kant spells out its central issue in the second part of the *Critique of Practical Reason* (in the "Doctrine of Method," whose relative shortness of length belies its proportionate significance, for here Kant explicitly takes up the question of the cultivation of moral character): "How is one to secure the admission of the laws of pure practical reason into the human mind (*Gemüt*), to introduce their influence on the maxims of the latter; that is, how can objective practical reason also be made *subjectively practical*" (*KpV* 151, emphasis added). As we have already seen, to be able to speak of the presence of character at all means that firmly adopted principles (maxims) are attributes of such a mind; the activity constituting character (in its strict sense) is the resolute conduct of thought. In turn, character has also been defined (in the first *Critique*) as the *law* of an efficient causality, or alternatively (in the *Anthropology*) with the unity of the inner principle of the conduct of a human life. Thus considered, it is the actual, operative law governing the interrelation and form of activity of the human capacities involved in human choosing and acting. As such a law considered in its instantiated form (embodied, so to speak), character may also, therefore, be seen as formally constitutive of the concrete relation itself of the intelligible as cause and the sensible as its effect in the individual human being. In the Kantian universe, however, there are only two kinds of laws: laws of nature and laws of freedom. Moral character, what human beings make of themselves, as a law can only be a form of law of freedom. In short, where moral character is good, it is the particular, subjective counterpart of practical, universal reason in the human individual; or to put it in the preceding terms, it is just what it means for reason to be subjectively practical. Where in the conduct of thought, judging, choosing, the moral law has itself been consistently and resolutely adopted as the supreme maxim governing all other maxim adoption, moral insight, the *factum der Vernunft*, has received *its* concrete realization.[81] As Kant observes at a much

---

81. Dieter Henrich's essay "The Concept of Moral Insight" is directly relevant here. For his discussion of moral insight versus evil and their relation to character, see 65–66. It is also worth noting that the term *factum* (which is usually translated as "fact") means "deed" or "act"; it is the Latin, in other words, for *Tat* or *Handlung* and is thus explicitly translated by Kant (see, for

earlier point in the second *Critique,* "The law is given graphic form (*anschaulich gemacht*) through the example" of an individual of "upright character" (*KpV* 77).[82]

Such a morally upright individual has achieved moral insight as an accomplished state (*Fertigkeit*) of the capacities involved when choosing and acting in the world. Kant's explication of how the moral law thus gains entry into these subjective conditions entails a further concept that must be brought into the discussion, the notion of *Gesinnung* ("comportment of mind").[83] As Grimm already noted—and it is also true in Kant's writings—there is a certain identification being made in the eighteenth-century usage of the notions of conduct of thought, character, and com-

example, *MSR* 227). This consciousness of the moral law is a fact of reason, but it is a fact that is itself an act; see *KpV* 5, 31, 43, 103–6, 147. Again, see Henrich's discussion of Kant's notion of the *factum der Vernunft* ("Begriff der sittlichen Einsicht," 93, 113; translated as "Concept of Moral Insight"; see 82–87).

Oswald Schwemmer underscores the point that when Kant speaks of the *Faktum der Vernunft,* he is not using the term in the sense of a factual given to be found (by investigation, for example) but gives an active sense to the term, using it even explicitly synonymously with *Tathandlung* (i.e., as an identifiable act of the activity that is reason) (*Philosophie der Praxis. Versuch zur Grundlegung einer Lehre vom moralischen Argumentieren* [Frankfurt am Main: Suhrkamp Verlag, 1971], 198). See also his discussion "Das 'Faktum der Vernunft' und die Realität des Handelns. Kritische Bemerkungen zur transzendentalphilosophischen Normbegründung und ihrer handlungstheoretischen Begriffsgrundlage im Blick auf Kant," in *Handlungstheorie und Transzendentalphilosophie,* ed. Gerold Prauss (Frankfurt am Main: Vittorio Klosterman, 1986), 271–302.

Wilhelm Teichner is in agreement with Schwemmer's point, noting that in the "moral self-consciousness, in the *factum* of practical reason, I recognize myself as the activity of reason (*Vernunfthandlung*), or as pure practical desire (*Wille*), that is, as *Tat-sache* (as acting thing)" (*Die Intelligible Welt. Ein Problem der theoretischen und praktischen Philosophie I. Kants* [Meisenheim am Glan: Verlag Anton Hain, 1967], 115–16).

That the law is intrinsic to the nature of reason and not the product of subtle reasonings is underscored again in *Religion within the Limits of Reason Alone* (*RV* 26) and accords with Kant's frequent remark about the law written on the human heart. In his *Metaphysical Principles of Justice,* Kant explicitly clarifies the distinction between being an author, a cause of obligation in accordance with the moral law and being the author of the law (*MSR* 227). A legislator (which is Kant's common name for reason, i.e., *Gesetzgeber*) is the author or cause of the obligation, not of the law. See also Klaus Konhardt, "Faktum der Vernunft? Zu Kants Frage nach dem 'eigentlichen Selbst' des Menschen," in *Handlungstheorie und Transzendentalphilosophie,* 160–84; Manfred Riedel, "Imputation der Handlung und Applikation des Sittengesetzes. Über den Zusammenhang von Hermeneutik und praktischer Urteilskraft in Kants Lehre vom 'Faktum der Vernunft,'" in *Urteilskraft und Vernunft* (Frankfurt am Main: Suhrkamp, 1989), 98–124. Philip J. Rossi's earliest research focused on Kant's "Doctrine of the 'Fact of Pure Reason,'" which Rossi connected in turn with character; i.e., his operative hypothesis in the text was that "Kant's notion of the fact of pure reason" is a "concrete representing of our responsibility for our character" (*Kant's Doctrine of the "Fact of Pure Reason": The Foundation for Moral Rationality* [Ann Arbor: UMI, 1975], 20).

82. In his translation, Lewis White Beck drops the word *character* altogether, rendering "Rechtschaffenheit des Charakters" simply as "righteousness."

83. For the translation of *Gesinnung* as "comportment of mind," see "Note on Translation."

portment of mind. Yet, there are (albeit subtle) distinctions that address various dimensions involved in Kant's conception of character. In the first place, "responsiveness to a pure moral interest" is an "attribute of our mind (*Gemüt*)" (*KpV* 152).[84] The three main ways in which Kant uses the notion of *Gesinnung* describe (at least in part) how such responsiveness takes place. One way he speaks of it is as "the first subjective basis of the adoption of maxims"; as such it is (and consistently so by 1793) identified specifically as a "property of the faculty of our power of choice," and, moreover, when the latter has taken respect for the moral law up in its maxims (is characterized by such a *Gesinnung*), "constitution of such a power of choice" is "good character" (*RV* 25, 27, 51). This is consonant both with Kant's references to the power of choice in his discussion of intelligible character (examined in the next chapter) and his point that the subjective ground of an action is the basis on which we may expect what someone will actually do.

For understanding the connection that Kant draws here to character, it is important to bear in mind that we have seen maxims as orienting, directing principles for the use of the various faculties of mind, not simply as principles of actions in the world. Thus when Kant further calls *Gesinnung* the "inner principle of maxims" (*RV* 23n, 37), goes on to identify it with the "spirit of the [moral] law" (*KpV* 85),[85] and holds that practical causality is realized "in concreto in *Gesinnungen* or maxims" (*KpV* 56), the role of maxims as in fact constituting principles formative of character, as being (literally speaking) "character-building devices," begins to come into view.[86] In and through the "embodiment" of the spirit of the law in

84. I am following Rudolf Makkreel here in rendering *Empfänglichkeit* as "responsiveness" rather than receptivity, because of the passive connotation of the latter term (for example, see Makkreel, *Imagination and Interpretation in Kant: The Hermeneutical Import of the Critique of Judgment* [Chicago: University of Chicago Press, 1990], 94). *Gemüt* is not merely receptive to reason's imperative; it acts on it.

85. See also *KpV* 33, 72n., 79, 82, 86, 99, 152, 160–61; *MST* 390–91, 446; *G* 412, 416.

86. The question of what exactly maxims are in Kant's moral philosophy has given rise to a number of interpretations. Otfried Höffe sees them essentially as rules for one's conduct of life (*Lebensregeln*): "Resolutions" (*Vorsätze*) or "rules of action one posits for oneself," they differ "quantitatively" from "ordinary intentions" (*gewöhnliche Vorsätze*) in that they are the "primary, fundamental determinations of volition" that "give expression to what kind of individual one wants to be. . . . Maxims comprise the manner in which we conduct life as a whole" (*Ethik und Politik*, 90). "The maxim designates a general comportment of volition (*Willenshaltung*), which imparts a common sense of direction to a multiplicity and diversity of intentions and actions." Maxims are the standard (literally the "provision of the measure," *maß-gebende*) or "formative principle in accordance with which we ultimately respond to a given kind of situation" (*Ethik und Politik*, 92). See also Oswald Schwemmer's discussion in "Vernunft und Moral. Versuch einer kritischen

the maxims adopted as principles for guiding the activities of judging and choosing, in such maxims further being held firmly, resolutely, steadfastly in and by the activity of the conduct of thought, the moral law acquires its subjective, concrete actualization as the fundamental formative principle of the human moral agent and of such agency's basic motivation (*Triebfeder*).[87] Thus it is that "the moral law is for itself the motivation in

Rekonstruktion des kategorischen Imperativs bei Kant," in *Kant. Zur Deutung seiner Theorie von Erkennen und Handeln*, ed. Gerold Prauss (Cologne: Kiepenheuer & Witsch, 1973), 255–73.

Harald Köhl argues that maxims are ultimately attributes of character, but critiques this conception of Kant's as being unwieldy and unnecessary; i.e., on the one hand it is enough to know the intention underlying an action in order to assess it morally and, on the other, given the difficulty in ascertaining the operative maxims, it makes forming a judgment on someone's character needlessly difficult (*Kants Gesinnungsethik* [Berlin: Walter de Gruyter, 1990], 45–61; see especially 60–61). As we will see (particularly in our fourth chapter), the connection of maxims with character runs deeper than ascertaining consistent intentions. Kant identifies very specific maxims that must be in place for the formation and exercise of morally good character in the world. Köhl's main texts are telling for his interpretation: the *Groundwork*, first and second *Critiques, Metaphysics of Morals*, and the *Religion;* notably absent from his own list are the *Critique of Judgment* and the *Anthropology.* Manfred Kuehn (in conference presentations) has used the phraseology of "character-building devices" to characterize Kant's fundamental sense of the maxim. Thomas Nenon, who regards character as one of three elements making up Kant's conception of the person, also connects character (in its strictest sense) with the "form of maxims chosen"—which essentially agrees with the interpretation developed in the present study ("Freedom, Responsibility, Character: Some Reflections on Kant's Notion of the Person," *Jahrbuch für Recht und Ethik/Annual Review of Law and Ethics* 1 [1993]: 167). Further evidence that, even when maxims are connected with character, there remain differences in how the maxim and the connection are understood, is given by Michael Albrecht. For Albrecht character comes into play if and when there is agreement among the maxims (as rules for conduct) held by the agent ("Kants Maximenethik und ihre Begründung," *Kant-Studien* 85 [1994]: 129–46; especially 132–33). On Nelson Potter's interpretation, maxims are "products of our inner, deepest moral character," and their own nature and function is to "(i) formulate a rule of action and (ii) express the agent's resolve to act by that rule" ("Maxims in Kant's Moral Philosophy," *Philosophia* 23 (1994): 59–90; see especially 62, 82). Another example of the shift in interpretation of maxims from simply rules of action to "agent-centered standards of consistency" is Hugh J. McCann's "Practical Rationality: Some Kantian Reflections," *Journal of Philosophical Research* 15 (1990): 57–77.

Particularly in the final essay of *The Practice of Moral Judgment*, Barbara Herman critiques the conception of maxims as either conscious intentions or underlying rules, arguing instead for "packing everything into the maxim" (224), i.e., all aspects of actions and ends that make them choiceworthy for an agent. For Nancy Sherman, maxims seen in terms of the "notion of acting on principles responsive to the salient features of complex situations" provide yet another avenue for mitigating the traditional stark contrast between ancient and modern ethics ("Wise Maxims/Wise Judging," *Monist* 76 [1993]: 41–65).

87. The sense of *Gesinnung* as Kant uses it thus has an affinity with the meaning of the roots of the term in Old and Middle High German (ninth through fifteenth centuries). As reported by Wahrig, the now obsolete verb *gesinnen* means to think of something, or even to desire, or to demand. The verb *sinnen* (which is still in use) means to deliberate or ponder and takes its origins from *sinnan*, meaning "to direct one's thoughts toward something," while the fundamental meaning of *sin* is "way, path, journey," i.e., "to take a direction."

reason's judgment and those who make it their maxim are morally good" (*RV* 24). Moreover, Kant identifies very specific maxims needed for the concrete exercise of character in the world. It is only in the context of this discussion (which we take up in the fourth chapter and which will connect maxims with subjective principles of reflective judgment for orienting the human subject to the good) that we will see the full sense of what it is for a maxim to be "character building."

In light of what we have seen thus far, the objective and the subjective, morality and anthropology, moral law and character, may be understood as two sides of one whole, with the second dependent on the first for its supreme principle, but with the first also dependent on the second for its actuality (*Wirklichkeit,* in contrast to its reality, which is, of course, independent). While character is defined by Kant in terms of its essential activity, the resolute conduct of thought (*consequente Denkungsart*), the latter term is frequently used in conjunction with the notion of comportment of mind (*Gesinnung*)—with what one might call the qualitative dimension of character. Awareness of our moral state is bound up with just this dimension, in regard to which Kant often speaks of our consciousness of its moral condition (for example, *KpV* 157). In a morally good character, comportment of mind consists in conformity to the spirit of the law characterizing the maxims, activities, and capacities of mind; such a "moral *Gesinnung*" is held by Kant to be "necessarily connected" with "consciousness of the determination of the capacity of desire," specifically of the "determination of will" (*KpV* 116).

With the account of character thus located in relation to the primacy of practical reason and its law, the elucidation of character as the operative law of causality of the human agent and with the unity of the inner principle of the conduct of life is itself, however, far from complete. For, to be in one's *Denkungsart* a "subject responsive to the good" is not yet to be a "good human being," and it is just this latter that we are to become (*RV* 48, 51). The relation of conduct of thought (*Denkungsart*) and the sensibilities (*Sinnesart*), of intelligible and empirical, and the connection with virtue (the doctrine of virtue having been said to deal with just this relation) remain to be explained. Doing so entails further relating the notion of character to the tripartite division of the human aptitudes and investigating the nature and role of its aesthetic dimension. It is to these efforts that we turn our attention next.

Character and the "Unity of the Inner Principle of the Conduct of Life"

CHARACTER, EFFICACIOUS CAUSE, AND THE INTELLIGIBLE/EMPIRICAL DISTINCTION

Perhaps even more immediately than the question of the exercise of moral judgment, "conduct of life" (*Lebenswandel*) evokes the conception of the moral self as an active agency, as well as a desiring and feeling being. We will explore, then, what it means for the establishment of character to constitute the unity of the inner principle of the conduct of life, by examining its relation to Kant's understanding of the human capacities of causality, desire, and feeling.

Particularly decisive for his conception of character is Kant's point of departure: the notion of efficacious cause (*wirkende Ursache*). More familiar, traditional conceptions of character and moral virtue, informed by Aristotle's way of proceeding, begin from and center on the notion of a habituated disposition of the human inclinations.[1] To be sure, for a sense of character that would serve to give unity to our lives, the inclinations must be taken into account. It is just Kant's focus, however, on the "operations" (to render *Wirkungen* in its strongest sense) of "thinking and acting by the pure understanding"[2] as these are "met with in appearances" (*KrV* A546/B574) that affords him a unique approach to the issue of unity within the context of his own position (involving two operative modes of

1. As already noted in the introduction, Aristotle explicitly categorizes practical wisdom as an intellectual virtue, while specifying that the moral virtues include generosity and self-control. "In speaking of a man's character," he writes, "we do not describe him as wise or understanding, but as gentle or self-controlled; but we praise the wise man, too, for his characteristic, and praiseworthy characteristics are what we call virtues" (*Nicomachean Ethics,* 1103a6–10).

2. *Verstand,* as both German and Anglo-American commentators have noted, is relatively frequently used by Kant in the wider sense of rational comprehension (i.e., reason), rather than in its strictly technical, critical sense of the theoretical power of determinant judgment. The context here of empirical and intelligible character points to the wider sense of the term, as is supported also by the parallel discussion found in Kant's *Reflections on Metaphysics* (RM 252–59). Hannah Arendt has the following to say in regard to rendering *Verstand* in English: "Crucial for our

causality), as well as within the wider eighteenth-century discourse (specifically in regard to the problem of reconciling sensibility and reason).[3] Reason, he tells us, is "not merely a comprehending, but rather an efficacious and propelling principle" that "acts in the place of a natural cause" in the world (*RM* no. 5612, 253).[4] Reason's causality in its objective, determinant function in relation to the will is, of course, a well-known Kantian conception, but just how is its causality to be understood in relation to other human capacities and the conduct of life? The concepts of causality and freedom, too, are long-standing topics of scholarly discussion,[5] but the relevant question here concerns the role of the notions of intelligible and empirical causality in the critical, propaedeutic function of leveling the ground for the moral edifices, in particular the edifice of character.

On close examination, the phrase "efficacious cause" turns out to be highly significant, expressing both the essence of Kant's vision of human nature and the crucial issue it entails. *Caussalitatis* is the "law of cause *and effect*" (*RM* no. 5616, 256; emphasis added); to speak of causality is always to speak of such an inherently interdependent set of terms, of the law of the causal relation between them, a law whose concrete manifestation is

---

enterprise is Kant's distinction between *Vernunft* and *Verstand*, 'reason' and 'intellect' (not 'understanding,' which I think is a mistranslation; Kant used the German *Verstand* to translate the Latin *intellectus*, and *Verstand*, though it is the noun of *verstehen*, hence 'understanding' in current translations, has none of the connotations that are inherent in the German *das Verstehen*)" (*Life of the Mind*, 13–14).

3. Henrich focuses (in "Concept of Moral Insight" and other writings) on the question of derivation with the attendant failure of all attempts to derive the theoretical and practical from one another, while also recognizing that for Kant they do not simply stand independently side by side. He further analyses how the subsequent Idealist philosophers dealt with the issue. This focus and analysis leave out of consideration the different approach to the question of unity being investigated here, namely, that of unity as a task to be undertaken. Hence, too, in his essay "Ethics of Autonomy" (in Velkley, *The Unity of Reason*, trans. Louis Hunt), we read that "the demand that one must be able to comprehend the unity of reason in both functions [theoretical and practical], and as well the unity of reason and sensibility, can only be derived from the Kantian ethics if one misunderstands the theoretical grounds which oppose such a derivation" (92). In both essays, Henrich is completely silent on Kant's notion of the establishment character as the unity of the inner principle of the conduct of life.

4. The German reads "[wie die Vernunft] die Stelle einer Naturursache vertrete." Heinz Heimsoeth's "Freiheit und Charakter. Nach den Kant-Reflexionen Nr. 5611 bis 5620," in *Kant: Zur Deutung seiner Theorie von Erkennen und Handeln*, 292–309, gives a good discussion of these reflections as effectively constituting the preliminary work to the account of freedom and character found in the *Critique of Pure Reason*.

5. For a discussion of issues that have been raised in the scholarship and for his response based on his interpretation of transcendental idealism, see Henry E. Allison, *Kant's Theory of Freedom* (New York: Cambridge University Press, 1990), 29–46.

for human cognition met with only in experience, in the effect (*Wirkung*).[6] As themselves "appearance in the world of sense," human beings are "one of the causes of nature whose causality must fall under empirical laws. As such, like all other natural things, they must accordingly also have an empirical character" (*KrV* A546/B574). Such laws of nature are, of course, laws of the understanding (in its strict, critical sense), but it would not "in the least detract from" the operations of the latter if one were to "assume that among the causes of nature, there are some which have an intelligible capacity," such that while the actions determined thereby are not empirically conditioned, yet in their appearance the actions are in complete accord with the laws of empirical causality (*KrV* A542/B570, A545/B573). That we hold ourselves to be just such a kind of natural cause, one endowed with such intelligible powers, is for Kant "clear from the imperatives, whereby [in the form of] rules, we direct [our] performative powers in all practical matters" (*KrV* A547/B575). That it is further possible to think of ourselves as such a single agency operating in terms of two orders of causal relations, depends also on removing the concern of a necessary contradiction between them; this is the work, of course, of the third antinomy, to show "that nature at least does not contradict the causality of freedom" (*KrV* A558/B586).

Kant's discussion here in the first *Critique* (A538/B566ff.) is purely hypothetical in its modality. It is an investigation of what *would* be the case if there were such a being among the natural causes that possesses such an intelligible ground. The emphasis on "*natural* cause," when the subject matter is *intelligible* efficaciousness, is worthy of note: intelligible cause is "cause" just *in relation to nature*. In the *Critique of Judgment*, Kant

6. For an analysis of Kant's conception of action as the relation of cause and effect, see Volker Gerhardt, "Handlung als Verhältnis von Ursache und Wirkung. Zur Entwicklung des Handlungsbegriff bei Kant," in Prauss, *Handlungstheorie und Transzendentalphilosophie*, 98–131. Gerhardt traces the conception of action (*Handlung*)—both merely physical action and moral action (whose distinction from the former lies in its cause)—as it arises in Kant's early works and is carried into the *Critique of Pure Reason* with its meaning essentially unchanged. As the title indicates, Gerhardt's basic point is that the fundamental sense of *Handlung* (for which Kant gives the Latin, *actio*) is the relation of cause and its effect. Used by Kant initially as a term for the actions of natural, mechanical processes, it transfers to human action, to human acting and refraining from acting (*Tun und Lassen*), precisely because the latter shares this basic characteristic of producing a concrete effect on the basis of an ascertainable cause. Hence, acting on the basis of freedom, on the basis of the causality of reason, is only a special case of action per se (Gerhardt, "Handlung als Verhältnis," 118–19). In Kant's *Religion within the Limits of Reason Alone* (for example), the distinction of cause and effect is expressed as two senses of *Handlung*, since the effect can itself be a *Handlung* (deed or action) rather than a product such as an artifact (*RV* 31).

defines *cause*, when used in reference to the "supersensible," as "meaning only the ground (*Grund*) that determines the causality of *natural things* [to bring about] an effect (*Wirkung*) in accordance with their own laws of nature, but at the same time also in *unanimity* (*einhellig*) with the formal principles of the laws of reason" (*KU* 195, emphasis added). The effect in question is further identified as follows: "The effect in accordance with the concept of freedom is the final purpose, which [itself] (or its appearance in the sensible world) ought to exist, and for which the condition of its possibility in nature is presupposed; that is, in the nature of the subject as a sensible being, namely as a human being" (*KU* 195–96).

If there is to be a successful account of character as a source of unity for our conduct of life, then the earlier, hypothetical examination of whether and how one can think of these two orders of causality working together must be developed into a positive account of how they can and do work together and to what end they do so—issues that, as the preceding quote shows, continue to be central to the account of reflective judgment. Or, as Kant puts it in the *Religion within the Limits of Reason Alone*, the real problem of predeterminism is reconciling how our "chosen actions as events [in the world] have their determining ground in preceding [events in] time" and yet are genuinely chosen; that is, how determination in time "can be in agreement with freedom" (*RV* 49–50n). Or again, to cast the issue in the terminology of the *Anthropology*, if character in its strict sense is to be "what we are prepared to make of ourselves," then it is just this relation between empirical and intelligible character (with character understood in its most formal sense as the law of causality) that must be explained. How is it, when the first (empirical character) is determined by temporal conditions, that we can be responsible for our character as a whole, or that we can even consider our character to be such a whole? If there is such a whole, how can it be more than merely a conjunction, a cooperative relation at best of dual orders of causality? How can they form an integrated whole, a synthetic unity?[7]

7. Heimsoeth expresses the point as follows: "Human doings and becoming active (*Tun und Tätigwerden*) (*in* the world!) stand under a dual 'law,' and are already entirely generally of a dual 'character'—can fundamentally, therefore, neither be explained nor comprehended and assessed in one and the same way" ("Freiheit und Charakter," 293–94). The issue at stake here is, in fact, a very old one. For Aristotle, for whom it is axiomatic that "characteristics develop from corresponding activities" (*Nicomachean Ethics*, 1103b20) and who therefore agrees with Plato that "men must be brought up from childhood to feel pleasure and pain at the proper things; for this is correct education" (1104b11–13), matters take an interesting turn when the discussion moves to the question of responsible agency and voluntary action. There we read that we "share in some way the responsibility for our own characteristics" (1114b23). The point is developed in terms

Kant begins his discussion of the human being as "efficacious cause" with the "subject of the world of sense" considered initially apart from the question of reason's activity in its regard. As such a subject, human beings have an "empirical character" and in accordance therewith, as appearance, are determined by empirical laws of causal connections; likewise "all their actions are explicable by laws of nature" (*KrV* A539–40/B567–68). They are, ipso facto, subject to the law of all determination in time, of all that is mutable: namely, the law "that everything *that comes about* (*was geschieht*) finds its cause in the appearances (of the foregoing state [of affairs])" (*KrV* A540/B568). In the case of a chosen action, then, one can trace the source of its empirical character to an individual's upbringing, the company he or she has kept, to the tendencies one has by nature (what Kant here and in the *Anthropology* calls one's *Naturell*) (*KrV* A554/B582). In regard to "this empirical character," therefore, "there is no freedom," and our account of the "motivating causes" is a "physiological" one (*KrV* A550/B578).

In short, our explanations would be no different than for any animal behavior: "The determining causality of sensibility (*Sinnlichkeit*)" is "animality" (*RM* no. 5619, 258). If all "were determined by sensibility, nothing would be either good or evil; nothing would be practical at all" (*RM* no. 5611, 252). one could not speak of human beings as actors (*tätige Wesen*) in Kant's sense of that notion, that is, as beings actively initiating events in the world and accountable for such in accordance with standards of right or justice, independently of empirical conditions. The demand that human conduct in a given case could have and should have been otherwise is itself, however, a commonplace of human society and history (*KrV*

---

of a metaphor. "Let us assume the case of a man who becomes ill voluntarily through living a dissolute life and disobeying doctors' orders. In the beginning, before he let his health slip away, he could have avoided becoming ill: but once you have thrown a stone and let it go, you can no longer recall it, even though the power to throw it was yours, for the initiative was within you. Similarly, since an unjust or a self-indulgent man initially had the possibility not to become unjust or self-indulgent, he has acquired these traits voluntarily; but once he has acquired them it is no longer possible for him not to be what he is" (1114a14–22). In conclusion Aristotle writes that "our actions and our characteristics are not voluntary in the same sense: we are in control of our actions from beginning to end, insofar as we know the particular circumstances surrounding them. But we control only the beginning of our characteristics: the particular steps in their development are imperceptible, just as they are in the spread of a disease; yet since the power to behave or not to behave in a given way was ours in the first place, our characteristics are voluntary" (1114b30–1115a3). The point to be made is that in this ancient text too, the assignment of moral responsibility to the individual agent turns on being able to assign the responsibility for moral character itself to that agent. In this general sense, Kant and Aristotle stand in agreement. The question for the present study is how Kant's critical formulation addresses this issue. What difference does the critical formulation make? How successful is it?

A555/B583; see also *RM* no. 5612, 253). The moral, philosophical justification of this actual human practice requires an account of the human actor as an agent responsible for both the particular action and the agency (the character) from whence it flows.[8] In Kant's sense of it, the very expression *act* (or *deed* [*Tat*]) refers to the "use of freedom" construed either as the act of adopting "a highest maxim (which may be either in accordance with or contrary to the law) in one's power of choice," or as the "action itself in accordance with which such a maxim is carried out" (*RV* 31). The account of such an act and such agency is further necessary for ascertaining a "sufficient" and "complete reason" (*zureichenden* and *vollständigen Grund*) for a given action; appearances yield only a conditioned necessity (*RM* no. 5613, 254; no. 5619, 258). The causal series under temporal conditions leads to infinite regress and not to a first principle that would serve as complete and sufficient reason.

It is, then, just for the sake of accounting for the very possibility of human beings as *actors in the world* that Kant makes the prima facie paradoxical move of turning to intelligible or supersensible causality, to an "intelligible ground" that "does not bother at all with the empirical questions, but rather concerns only *thinking* in pure understanding" (*KrV* A545/B573, emphasis added). Most narrowly defined, intelligible causality means determination of choice and action independently of foregoing empirical conditions (*KrV* A545/B573). What has occurred in a natural course of events and what, in accordance with the latter's empirical grounds, unavoidably thus took place, when considered further in relation to reason, when compared with practical purpose, may very well be found deficient or reprehensible; through such comparisons we discover an "entirely different rule and order from the natural order" of things (*KrV* A550/B578). Only thought or judgment that does not begin from the empirical questions, but takes instead as its point of departure, its orientation for thinking, a universal, rational principle or idea, is capable of calling an entire series of otherwise naturally necessitated events into question, of pronouncing the assessment that it "ought not have happened at all."

Those who hold that reason is itself essentially historical would say that such principles too have empirical origins, but here a very interesting statement Kant makes in the *Critique of Pure Reason* is relevant: "Whether reason itself, in these acts whereby it prescribes laws, is not in turn deter-

8. As is evident from the passages cited from the *Nicomachean Ethics* (in the previous note), to this extent Kant and Aristotle share common ground at least in the purpose of their philosophical efforts.

mined by further influences, and whether what is called freedom in relation to the motives of sense might not in turn, in consideration of higher
and more remote efficacious causes, be nature once again, does not concern us in the practical realm, since above all we are asking reason for the
rule of conduct (*Verhaltens*)" (KrV A803/B831). For the question of what
is "to be done or left undone" (*Tun und Lassen*), Kant sets aside the question of reason's own potential origins or cause (indeed, declaring it a "speculative question") and focuses only on the issue of the exercise of its causality vis-à-vis actions in the world. Even a minimalist reading of what
reason's "independence . . . from all determining causes of the sensible
world" (*KrV* A803/B831) finally thus means, leaves intact the crucial issue
of practical causality considered in relation to character. That we are able
in and through thought to "step outside" (so to speak) a series of events
in the world, including and especially a series of our own actions as these
are determined by our desires and external influences, that we are able to
judge them morally, to direct them differently in the future as a result of
bringing that judgment to bear on them, that we are able in fact to initiate
a whole series of events in the world on the basis of rational judgment,
Kant takes to be noncontroversially the case. In taking this position, he
shares a long and venerable company. The difference in Kant's account
is that it is only in and through such causality that the moral first receives
its concrete actuality in appearance—both as actions and as character. To
give an account in his critical terms, of efficacious thought and judgment
exercising this moral role, is just to explain the relation of intelligible and
empirical causality in human character.

These various considerations, then, all point to this relation as a central
issue. Reason's causality in the world is mediated by the other human
capacities. As Kant also refers to it, practical causality, objectively speaking, consists in reason's determination of the will.[9] In the section of the
Critique of Pure Reason that deals explicitly with causality and character,
however, another avenue of mediation is the focus of his considerations.
Kant raises the question whether "empirical causality *itself* might not, after

9. See the complete text of the passages previously cited from the first *Critique*. The relevance
of practical causality objectively considered to this issue is discussed later in this chapter. The
inherent connections between what willing (capacity of desire determined by reason) means and
the mediation required for reason's efficaciousness in the world are very well put by Heimsoeth:
"Aber die Wirksamkeit solchen Wollens bedeutet doch eben wirkliche (empirisch-reale) Ein-
Wirkung auf den Lauf der Dinge! Und eben dazu bedarf es der *Vermittlungen*" [But the
efficaciousness/activity of such willing means just actual (empirically real) effect/acting upon the
course of things in the world. And just for this *mediation* is required] ("Freiheit und Charakter,"
296).

all, be an effect of nonempirical, intelligible causality" (without the former's connection with the causes of nature being in any way undermined) (*KrV* A544/B572, emphasis added). The answer is given in the affirmative, namely as the relation between the respective capacities of understanding and reason. The latter, which deliberates about its objects only in terms of ideas, "accordingly determines the understanding" (*KrV* A547/B575). Here then we have not two causal orders side by side, but a single efficacious cause in which the effect is realized through the determination, the ordering or directing of the level of causality in immediate connection with the world. This conception of "cause" accords with its definition in its supersensible meaning given in the *Critique of Judgment*. Thus we have a way of construing these causal orders as a synthetic unity: drawing on the formulation from the third *Critique,* character "arises from the union of the conditioned" (the empirical) "with its condition" (the intelligible).

The essential mediating role of the understanding for the realization of reason's causality in the world is developed too in the *Critique of Practical Reason.* In the "Typik of Pure Practical Judgment," Kant writes that "therefore the moral law has no other mediating cognitive capacity for its application to the objects of nature than the understanding," which, in lieu of a "sensible schema" and for the purpose of moral judgment, provides the "idea of reason" with the "form" of a "law of nature" (*KpV* 69). To put it another way, reason as higher and directing cause avails itself of the form of the causal order of the understanding in order to bring its rule to bear in the world.[10] Translating the point into Kant's paired set of terms constitutive of his conception of character, we can say that the law of intelligible causality definitive of character as conduct of thought (*Denkungsart*) is exercised in the world by means of this thinking, judging activity availing itself of the law of empirical causality definitive of character in its appearance in the conduct of the sensibilities (*Sinnesart*).

From here it is a relatively easy step to Kant's still further development of the intelligible/empirical relation in terms of the notion of schema and,

---

10. For a discussion of the relation of reason and understanding in the theoretical realm of constituting an "order of nature" and hence for completing Kant's theory of science, see Gerd Buchdahl, "The Relation between 'Understanding' and 'Reason' in the Architectonic of Kant's Philosophy," in *Kant's Critique of Judgment,* vol. 4 of *Immanuel Kant: Critical Assessments,* ed. Ruth F. Chadwick and Clive Cazeaux (New York: Routledge, 1992), 39–53. Buchdahl argues that since Kant "wants to avoid arbitrariness," the "activity of reason may borrow from the constitutive foundation of the understanding," but that Kant then "must insert 'relations' closing the gap between understanding and reason: relations loose enough not to endanger the necessary autonomy of reason" (41).

finally, of reason's *own empirical character.* Kant's qualification—"if this word is appropriate here"—in regard to the notion of a "schema" in the "Typik" of the second *Critique* indicates that he is using it in an analogous sense (*KpV* 68). In the first *Critique*, "schema" is said to be, "properly speaking, only the phenomenon, or sensible concept of an object, in agreement with the category" (*KrV* A146/B186). Reading, then, his further characterization of empirical character as the "sensible schema" of "intelligible character" (*KrV* A553/B581)[11] as an analogous statement, one can express the relation of these two senses of character as follows: empirical character is the phenomenon, or sensible concept of intelligible character in accordance with an idea of reason. Furthermore, since the "schemata of sensibility first realize the categories" (*KrV* A146/B186), so empirical character first realizes (or actualizes) intelligible character or freedom. Such a reading is consonant with and helpful for grasping the full import of Kant's statement regarding reason's empirical character. Under the assumption "that reason has actual causality in regard to appearances, it must nonetheless, notwithstanding that it is reason, manifest its empirical character. For every cause presupposes a rule in accordance with which certain appearances follow as its effects, and every rule requires uniformity in the effects that establishes the concept of cause (as a capacity [or power]). To the extent that [the cause] must be made evident through mere appearances, these may be called its empirical character; [this character] endures, while the effects, in accordance with the differences of the attendant and in part limiting conditions, appear in variable shapes" (*KrV* A549/B577).

The uniformity, then, which is not attributable to the laws of nature, but found in the divers effects or operations making up human life, is just the manifestation of reason's rule under the conditions of time and space. As phenomenon, it is actually reason's empirical character that reason shows of itself (*von sich zeigt*) in and through its causal relation to the understanding. So seen, this causal relation is fundamental to the constitution of the synthetic unity of character. In his *Reflections on Metaphysics,* Kant expresses these points as follows: "Actions here in the world are only schemata of the intelligible; and yet, these appearances (this word already means schema) hang together according to empirical laws, if one takes reason itself to be a phenomenon (of character) in accordance with their manifestations" (*RM* no. 5612, 253). "This connection of the actions in

11. Kant makes this point more than once. For example, at *KrV* A546/B574, he notes that the "transcendental cause" of empirical character, namely "intelligible character," is itself not cognizable, but is shown through the "empirical as its sensible sign."

accordance with the laws of appearance, without being determined by the same, is a necessary prerequisite for reason's practical rules, which [in turn] are in themselves the cause of regularity in the appearances" (*RM* no. 5619, 257).

In short, reason's empirical character is intelligible (practical) causality in its empirical dress (so to speak). So seen, empirical causality is not a separate, independent causality but is the very form in which intelligible causality is exercised in the world; thus these two senses of causality form a single unity. It is *through its empirical character* that *reason is subjectively practical,* that it and hence human beings as moral beings are genuinely "efficacious causes" in the world. Thus it is, too, that character in its absolute sense (conduct of thought) determines character as conduct of the sensibilities, and, in turn, to the extent we can have cognition of the former, we must rely on its indication given through the appearances, through empirical character (*KrV* A551/B579). Considered in itself, intelligible causality is the "sensibly unconditioned condition of appearances" (*KrV* A557/B585). To put the matter in general, critical terms: just as our cognition necessarily begins from, but does not arise out of, experience (*KrV* B1), so it is in the latter that we may recognize moral character, without therefore deriving it from experience. To repeat (in a slightly different way) the point made earlier, just as the categories are a priori, but empty forms of experience requiring the schemata for their application, so intelligible character may be seen as the a priori moral form requiring the schema of empirical character for its concrete actualization in the world.

This subjectively practical exercise of reason's causality is, moreover, just what it means (for Kant) to have power of choice (*Willkür*), indeed free power of choice: "Thus every individual's power of choice has an empirical character, which is nothing else but a certain causality of one's reason, insofar as the latter displays a rule in its effects in appearance; accordingly, we may gather, in respect to their kind and degree, what reason's grounds and the acts thereof are, and may assess the subjective principles of [the individual's] power of choice" (*KrV* A549/B577). The "empirical character" of "one's power of choice" is further asserted to be the "empirical cause of all of one's actions" in the world (*KrV* A552/B580), but itself, of course, "has a free causality as its basis" (*KpV* 100). Hence, as in the case of reason, Kant speaks of power of choice in terms of both the empirical and the intellectual. In the following passage from his *Reflections on Metaphysics,* power of choice is used literally in place of what is elsewhere given as the essence of the meaning of intelligible cause. Citing an example of what happens in the case of a sensual temptation, Kant notes that "it is nevertheless possible for intellectual power of choice, which is exempted from the law of dependency on the senses, to involve itself; this [intellectual power of choice] then determines a different course of [affairs at the level of] sensibility" (*RM* no. 5616, 255). It is, then, as just such a power of choice that one may understand Kant's designation of reason as a capacity that "acts in the place of a natural cause" in the world.[12]

The use and importance of the notion of power of choice continues to increase in Kant's writings subsequent to the *Critique of Pure Reason*. By *Religion within the Limits of Reason Alone* (1793), it is at the center of his discussion of radical evil (examined in the next chapter). For discussion here, we will only draw the lines of connection with the notions of comportment of mind (*Gesinnung*) and conduct of thought (*Denkungsart*). In his 1793 work, Kant describes what it means to speak of "freedom" in one's "power of choice." This "freedom" is that "highly peculiar property" of the power of choice such that one cannot, in its exercise, be "determined by any other motivating impulse [to perform] an action, except to the extent one has taken [such an impulse] up in one's maxim"; to have done so means "to have made it a general rule for oneself, in accordance with which one wishes to conduct oneself (*sich verhalten*)" (*RV* 23–24). The "rule that the power of choice makes for itself for its use of freedom" is just what it means to adopt a maxim; this "subjective ground of the use of our freedom," is itself an "act (*Actus*)[13] of freedom" and synonymous with what Kant means by "human nature" in the context of these passages

12. The issue involved here is also found in contemporary discussions of self, self-consciousness, and persons. For example, Dieter Sturma defends a dualism of self and reason in which these "irreducible concepts" signify "integrated components of the lives of persons in the world of events. . . . reason is the perspective of a person's specific potential for action, not a relationless noumenal realm." "The self as the subject of self-consciousness is the center of the experiential perspective of an individual who exists in space and time and whose essential properties include acting from reason. . . . It is a necessary condition of the life of persons as subjects of reflective and practical attitudes to be able to alter the world of events. On the basis of this property one must grant persons a special status in the world of events, for persons are not necessarily objects of change but are capable of altering the world of events in a reasonable way. To this extent the complete ontology of a person already involves a transition from self to reason. And this fact is the ontological cornerstone of the dual aspect theory that is defended here" ("Self and Reason: A Nonreductionist Approach to the Reflective and Practical Transitions of Self-Consciousness," in *The Modern Subject: Conceptions of the Self in Classical German Philosophy*, ed. Karl Ameriks and Dieter Sturma [Albany: State University of New York Press, 1995], 207).

13. The use here of *Actus* (and not *Handlung*) connotes the additional dimension of office or vocation.

(*RV* 21). Or, as he puts it later, the "human moral constitution" is just the "ground of the use of freedom" (*RV* 40; see also *ApH* 324). This subjective ground we have seen, however, as definitive of comportment of mind (*Gesinnung*); further, the activity of such maxim adoption and choosing in accordance with it is also just what it means to conduct oneself in thought (*Denkungsart*). In short, it is in terms of the notion of power of choice that Kant brings together the critical, causal account of character and its description in the *Anthropology*.

Before relating character (now understood as efficacious cause consisting in the synthetic unity of intelligible and empirical causality and exercised as power of choice) to its further aspects in Kant's account, his much-criticized insistence on the timelessness of intelligible character must be addressed. "Reason" is said to be the "persisting condition" of all actions resulting from the exercise of power of choice; the effects of "intelligible character" as actions do appear under the conditions of time, but these conditions are held to be nonapplicable to intelligible character itself (*KrV* A553/B581). Insofar as intelligible character is one with human moral agency this, of course, leads to the seemingly absurd proposition that we, as moral agents, are timeless creatures; that our character, which according to Kant's own account must be morally cultivated, nonetheless has an essentially timeless quality. As part of the investigation of what the conception of character means, we must reconsider, then, what is to a certain extent familiar ground in the scholarship.

As efficacious cause, intelligible character stands by definition in relation to empirical character, but the claim Kant is defending is that such a connection with appearances does *not* consist in a "connection with appearances *as causes*" (*KrV* A541/B569, emphasis added). To be outside all determination of time is to be untouched by the law of all that is mutable; that is, the causal, determining act of intelligible character does not, in turn, have a cause in a prior state of affairs among appearances (*KrV* A540/B568; see also A541/B569). The "rule of causal connections," whereby the realm of appearance forms a coherent and cohesive whole of its particular and individual events, does not apply to the intelligible world (*RM* no. 5612, 254).

Already in his 1755 *New Exposition of the First Principles of Metaphysical Knowledge* Kant had identified the issue still at stake in these assertions. In less technical and more familiar terms, he recounts a "well-known controversy" presented in a dialogue between Caius, a "defender of the freedom of indifference," and Titius, a "supporter of reasons of determination." Caius finds himself consoled by the doctrine that "since I have been bound by a nexus of reasons determining one another even from the beginning of the world, whatever I have done I could not fail to do, and whoever now reproaches me with my faults and fruitlessly urges that I should have entered upon another course of life proceeds as absurdly as he would were he to demand that I ought to have stayed the flow of time." Titius, by contrast, vehemently defends a notion of "spontaneity" as an "activity proceeding from an internal principle. What is determined in conformity with the representation of the good we call freedom. The more certainly anyone complies with this law, and therefore the more he is determined by all the posited motives for willing, the freer he is."[14] So presented, the issue is cast as the kind of interminable either/or that characterizes the later-articulated antinomies of reason. For character construed as efficacious cause, for the possibility of moral accountability both for character itself and the actions following from it, for the sake of the account of human beings as moral beings *in* the world who first bring the moral order of causality to that world and are in *this* respect (as source of moral necessity, of the way a thing must be if it is to be good) not determined by the world: for these purposes, the critical resolution of the third antinomy is indispensable.

In his early work, Kant identified the essential question to be that of the "*source* of the thing's necessity."[15] Now, law (in a very general sense) is a "formula giving expression to the necessity of an action,"[16] and the claim being made for intelligible character in the first *Critique* is that the necessity, whereby a given action appears in relation to foregoing conditions in time (laws of nature), does not impinge upon the reason why its existence as practically necessitated has been initiated at all. As Kant puts it in 1793, in his ongoing discussion of the determining grounds of the power of choice, the question of "source" (*Ursprung*) is that of the first cause of an effect, namely "of that cause which is not again the effect of another cause of the same kind" (*RV* 39). Consideration of an effect in light of reason as its source is only in regard to the fact that it exists (*Dasein der Wirkung*), while in relation to time, it is regarded as an event (*Begebenheit*) and hence causally connected to the series of temporal relations in which it is found (*RV* 39). Unlike such events, the condition or ground of determination lying in reason does not itself *begin*. "Reason is present and one and the same in all human actions under all circumstances of time"; it is "determining, but not determinable" in this regard, and,

<hr />

14. *Kant's Latin Writings*, 81, 82 (trans. John A. Reuscher).
15. *Kant's Latin Writings*, 78.
16. Mrongovius lectures on moral philosophy, *Ak* 27.2.2, 1421.

furthermore, such exercise of the causal capacity that it itself is does *not* place reason "in some new state in which it was not before" (*KrV* A556/ B584). Its effects (not its causality) have a beginning in the "series of appearances," but (and this qualification is also important) such effects "can never constitute an absolutely first beginning" in this series (*KrV* A554/B582). An analogy may be drawn with the understanding as a capacity or power of mind that remains ever present and one and the same under all circumstances: namely, as a determinative power invariably prepared to forge given, sensible intuitions into objects of cognition.[17] It is determining, but not itself determinable in regard to these intuitions, and its exercise of determinant judgment in relation to them does not bring about a changed state of the understanding.

To put the point in the foregoing terms of synthetic unity of intelligible and empirical causality, *as effects of reason's causal determination,* such effects are nothing more (but also nothing less) than the introduction of a practical/moral form or direction made manifest as a uniformity not attributable to the laws of nature, but characterizing both empirical character and events constituted by temporal relations. Temporal differences are fundamental for *appearances* in their relation to one another, but "cannot make a difference to the relation in which an action stands to reason" (*KrV* A556/B584). This relation, where intelligible character is morally good, is ultimately a relation to reason's objective practical law (which itself is, of course, one, universal, invariable, neither derived from nor affected by conditions of time). Where it has been resolutely adopted as the highest subjective principle (maxim) governing all other maxim adoption, subjectively practical reason is efficacious as a moral causality in human life. By 1793 Kant states the point even more strongly: "To think of oneself as a freely acting being and yet as absolved from such a proper law (the moral) would be as much as to think of an efficacious cause without any law at all . . . which contradicts itself" (*RV* 35). In the *Metaphysical Principles of Virtue,* the point is stated as follows. The vices opposed to the duty toward oneself as a moral being (to act in accordance with principles and not rob oneself of one's own inner freedom) have as their principle just to have "no principle and hence also no character" (*MST* 420). Another parallel expression of this point is found in the *Anthropology.* Here,

17. Heimsoeth raises just this point in "Freiheit und Charakter." He notes that the criticism of Kant's timeless intelligible character rests on its immediate distortion by Schelling and Schopenhauer as a single, pretemporal act from which the entire temporal state of a human life follows (298–99).

for Kant, being "changeable as the weather, moody, and (without malice) unreliable" is again tantamount to "having no character" at all (*ApH* 249).

In short, for Kant it is a contradiction in terms to speak of a "variable character." Principles resolutely adopted and guiding conduct of thought (*Denkungsart*) are either present or absent; where they are absent, one cannot speak of character, of the law whereby an efficacious cause first is such a cause. So, too, Kant designates moral character as being "singular" (*ein einziger*); one either has such a character, or one has "none at all" (*ApH* 285). Where the requisite principles are present, one speaks too of *Gesinnung* as "something supersensible and therefore not variable in time," as something that "abides and is constantly the same" (*ED* 334). Especially given the overall parameters of character defined in terms of law, perhaps an analogy with Kant's explanation (from *Metaphysical Principles of Justice*) of the meaning of eternal (*ewig*), when used as descriptive of a philanthropic foundation, would be most relevant and helpful. Here he notes that one may call such a foundation eternal (or perpetual) if and when the ordinance that both establishes and maintains it is a part of the constitution of the state (which is here itself considered as existing into perpetuity) (*MSR* 367). In other words, if provided for in the laws of the state, the foundation derives its own permanent status from that of the state. Similarly, intelligible character, conduct of thought, comportment of mind, as established and maintained by reason's law, share in the latter's unconditioned permanence and invariability.

As a corollary thereto, precisely to the extent that what is unconditioned and intelligible is in itself not available for human cognition, so we can have no certain insight into the moral state of our intelligible character, of reason's subjectively practical exercise. "In the assessment of free actions, in regard to their causality, we may get as far as intelligible cause but cannot [stand in judgment] over the same" (*KrV* A557/B585; see also A540/B568). As Kant often notes, that privilege is left to the "Searcher of Hearts." When such an action fails to accord with the moral law, the question is not "why did reason not determine itself otherwise, but rather, why did reason not determine the appearances differently through its causality. To this question, however, no answer is possible for us. For a different intelligible character would have yielded a different empirical one" (*KrV* A556/B584; see also *KpV* 99–100). How much of our empirical character is the "pure operation [or effect] of freedom, how much is to be ascribed to mere nature and to either the [morally] nonculpable fault of temperament, or the latter's fortunate constitution (*merito fortunae*), no one can penetrate and therefore also no one can pass completely just judgment upon it" (*KrV* A551/B579n; see also *ED* 329–30). We can and must judge empirical character *as it appears* and so indeed hold ourselves accountable, but it is only with regard to the "legality" of an action that we can be "completely certain," that it is "indubitable" whether or not it conforms to the law (*MST* 392–93). In Kant's *Reflections on Anthropology*, he puts it as follows (and it is noteworthy how pervasive in the corpus, as shown by the foregoing merely exemplary citations, the entire issue with all its related aspects is): "In order to know whether someone has a character, many observations are needed; but to know that a certain character is not present," meaning that a good character is lacking, "only a single observation is required. For, since character consists in *Denkungsart*, namely acting from principles, so a single exception is sufficient proof that the basis of the action was not a universal maxim" (*RA* no. 1230, 541; see also no. 1191, 526 and *RV* 20).

One of the questions we are left with at this juncture is how we are finally to understand the notion of empirical character. We began our discussion with empirical character accounted for in terms of the foregoing state of temporal affairs constitutive of it and human life, but we have also seen it referring (indeed, primarily so) to reason's empirical character, to the uniformity of its rule that reason brings to bear on and in these affairs through its determination of the understanding. Are there then two distinct senses of empirical character? Even in explicit reference to the "effects" of "thinking and acting" of pure human understanding (here taken in its broad sense), Kant asserts that these effects or operations in the realm of appearance "must be *wholly explicable* in terms of their cause in appearance in accordance with the laws of nature" (*KrV* A546/B574, emphasis added). How does one reconcile such an assertion with the foregoing account of intelligible cause in relation to such appearance? Or again, how are we to relate a statement such as the following to the account just presented of reason's empirical character? "Since this empirical character as effect must itself be drawn from the appearances and their rule made available by experience, so all human actions in appearance are determined by empirical character and the other cooperative (*mitwirkenden*) causes in accordance with the order of nature" (*KrV* A549/B577).

An avenue to seeing how it is that Kant is finally speaking of only one and the same empirical character lies in taking into account the essential meaning of his notions of actor (*tätiges Wesen*) and act or action (*Handlung* as *Tat*). Returning to a passage from the *Religion within the Limits of Reason Alone* already cited, further scrutiny proves Kant's parenthetical remark here to be significant. He explains that it follows from trying to think of oneself both as "a freely acting being" and "as absolved from the moral law," that one is therefore trying to think the inherently contradictory notion of "an efficacious cause without any law at all," because "the determination in accordance with the laws of nature would also be canceled (*wegfallen*) on account of freedom (*der Freiheit halber*)" (*RV* 35). Why would this be the case? Why would lack of determination by the law of freedom entail nullification of determination by laws of nature? Clearly, laws of nature remain operative where laws of freedom are absent; that is just the state of the entire natural universe considered apart from the inclusion therein of genuine actors (*tätige Wesen*).

Such actors, as we have already seen in the foregoing passages from the first *Critique*, are beings actively initiating events in the world and accountable for such in accordance with standards of right or justice, independently of empirical conditions (*KrV* A541/B569; see also A555/B583). Kant's explicit definitions of the notion of act or deed (*Tat*) reinforce this point. In a relevant passage in *Principles of Justice*, he further provides the Latin: "Accountability (*imputatio*) in its moral meaning is that judgment whereby someone is seen as the author [or agent] (*Urheber, causa libera*) of an action (*Handlung*), which is thereupon called an act (*Tat, factum*)[18] and stands under laws" (*MSR* 227). Other examples of Kant's specific use of *act* to refer to one's "use of freedom" have been cited earlier (*RV* 21, 31).[19] A state of a lack or absence of activity (*Tatlosigkeit*) includes, for Kant, just such a state of affairs in which a complete equilibrium of good and bad actions would effectively "neutralize" the principles of good and evil, neither being ultimately actualized by the empirical— a truly "Sisyphean" state of futility that is in reality to be at an utter "standstill" (*SF* 82). There would be perpetual movement, in other words, but no activity (in the proper sense of that term).

In short, it falls outside the very definition of what it means to be an

---

18. This is the same Latin term that Kant uses in his well-known notion of *factum der Vernunft* and that is usually translated as "fact" of reason; Kant's use of the Latin indicates the meaning of deed or act.

19. This meaning is further intrinsically bound up with the notion of efficacious cause (*wirkende Ursache*), for being active (*tätig sein*) is synonymous with the verb "to effect or bring something about" (*wirken*). That, for Kant, it is further inherently bound up with the issue of good or evil being brought about is clear from the contexts in which he uses these terms. To construe character as "that which we make of ourselves" is to conceive of it as an "effect of our act" [Wirkung unserer Tat]. In speaking of our duty to make the attainment of the perfection proper to us as human beings a purpose for ourselves, Kant notes that therefore such perfection must be posited as "an effect of one's act" [Wirkung von seiner Tat] (*MST* 386).

actor, an active being, to construe of such a being's actions solely in terms of the laws of nature. To act is to make use of one's freedom, and to do so in the world, as we have seen, entails the synthetic unity of causality whereby reason (through its direction of the activity of the understanding) realizes its principles and ideas in concrete, empirical form. To construe a being absolved from the moral law is to exclude the very notion of activity understood as the united effort under the essential direction or orientation of the law of freedom given to empirical causality to guide the latter's activity toward the realization of moral purpose. In Kant's words, "The determination in accordance with the laws of nature would also be canceled (*wegfallen*) on account of freedom." One could not, therefore, speak of action, activity, or acts. One could still see movement, including that driven by instinct, sensual impulses, and the like, but such would fall under laws of nature, such as those governing physical attraction and repulsion. Thus to consider these as wholly divorced from their standing in further relation to reason's causal capacity is, by definition, no longer to be speaking of what it is to be a human being.[20] In sum, to speak about the empirical character of a human being, of a *being essentially endowed with freedom*, is to be talking about the law of causality of this specific efficacious cause in terms of the synthetic unity of causality.

In this synthetic unity, reason's causality is not to be understood as standing in "competition" with inclinations and impulses deriving from our natural aptitudes, or foregoing states of affairs in life; reason is viewed as "complete in itself (*vollständig*)" (*KrV* A555/B583). Its effects (as effects in appearance) are actualized by its availing itself of the "cooperative causes in accordance with the laws of nature," but the latter are *not conditions of its own act of determination*. Where empirical character does not manifest this introduction of reason's rule, where an action contrary to the moral law has been perpetrated, one speaks not of sensual inclinations and the like "winning out," but rather of reason's "default" (*Unterlassung* rendered in its juridical sense) (*KrV* A555/B583).[21] One still speaks of an action,

20. In "Conjectural Beginning of Human History," Kant criticizes those who yearn for some so-called golden age, a time of instinct and natural impulses, a time before the realization of free choice in one's conduct of life, but also therefore a time of the pure pleasure of a carefree existence. "Reason," writes Kant, will "remind" those catering to such a wish "to give life worth through actions" (*M* 122).

21. Given Kant's pervasive use of judicial metaphors, the juridical sense is arguably the better translation for this term. Heimsoeth's discussion of the meaning of "default" or "omission" on the part of reason, as well as how reason both makes use of the mechanism of nature while still free from the latter's determination in relation to its own act of determination, is very clear and helpful ("Freiheit und Charakter," 295, 296–97).

because the agent in question, even if reason's causality has been omitted in the particular case, remains bound to its law. One has here a case of intelligible character failing to yield a "different empirical one" (*KrV* A556/B584). The why and wherefore of such default would require cognition of the intelligible cause and hence lies beyond human capacity to know. The condition of the possibility of default, the propensity for evil innate to the capacity of choice, does have ramifications for the account of character and will be discussed separately.

Here one can begin to appreciate the depth and import of the inherent moral uncertainty central to Kant's understanding of the matter. No account, however complete, of the determination of an action in terms of its causes in the nexus of appearances can ever answer the question of why intelligible character defaulted. To return to the analogy with the causal function of the understanding: suppose such instances that we designate (not insignificantly) as *absent-mindedness*. An object is before one, one is looking straight at it, and yet one truly does not "see" it. The operation of the understanding, to constitute an object of cognition out of the sensible intuitions, has not produced such an object of which one is conscious. We can and do give "reasons" for what has occurred in such an instance. Our attention is distracted by a background noise, our mind is preoccupied with another matter, our emotional state is blinding us to the world around us, and so forth. All of these are perfectly valid accounts of the empirical state of affairs and, from *that* standpoint, a complete account of how these phenomenal factors are linked together can be given. From this same standpoint, however (and it is of course the only one cognitively available to us as human beings), all that can be said in regard to the act of determinant judgment of the understanding is that its effect (*Wirkung*) has not been realized and so there is a failure, a default, on the part of its operation (*Wirken*). What has happened from *its* standpoint as *active causal capacity* (and not simply passive recipient of the sensible intuitions), we cannot judge. Its determinative activity of uniting the sensible intuitions under a concept has produced no such determination of which we are conscious. That is as far as we can go in our assessment. Likewise, in regard to reason's operation, "we may get as far as intelligible cause but cannot [stand in judgment] over the same" (*KrV* A557/B585). The further import for "moral self-knowledge," held by Kant to be the "beginning of all human wisdom" (*MST* 441), will be examined in the discussion of his account of conscience (in chapter 4).

Clearly, the underlying assumption operative here is Kant's conception of practical reason as *factum der Vernunft*. What follows from it for his conception of moral character is the focus of our discussion (and not the issue of the assumption itself, in regard to which the debate in the scholarship has a long history).[22] Thus far, we have seen that to speak of empirical character in the case of the human being as actor is, by definition, to entail the relation to intelligible character even if, in a given instance, our account (1) is limited to the discussion of the empirical causes in the nexus of appearances, or (2) it involves a case of default on the part of intelligible causality. Conversely, to speak of the intelligible causality of a human being is ipso facto to speak of the relation of such causality to the empirical; only so is intelligible causality an *efficacious* cause. As Kant very explicitly puts it in the second *Critique:* "In the moral law I have a pure intellectual ground of determination of my causality (*in the world of sense*) (*Sinnenwelt*)" (*KpV* 115, emphasis added).

Kant draws a still further, very direct connection in his references to the cultivation of empirical by intelligible character. In the *Critique of Practical Reason,* when he returns to the issues thus far discussed here primarily in terms of passages from the first *Critique,* he reiterates the point that, even in the case of an action contrary to the law, both the action and all those past events that determined it "belong to a *single phenomenon of one's character,* which one *procures* for oneself, and in accordance with which, as a cause independent of all sensibility, one holds oneself responsible for the causality of these appearances" (*KpV* 98, emphasis added). This notion of character's being what we acquire for ourselves echoes the fundamental assertion of the *Anthropology,* that character is just "what we are prepared to make of ourselves." The discussion of both texts indicates that he means thereby to incorporate the whole of our appearance in the world. Kant had begun the discussion in the *Critique of Pure Reason* with the question whether empirical causality might not itself be the effect of intelligible causality (*KrV* A544/B572), and we have seen that his answer is "yes," both for conduct in conformity with *and contrary to* the moral law. The preceding inquiry into the notion of reason's being in default in the latter case helps explain his conclusion. For, such default

22. Included in this debate are the two senses of freedom (practical and transcendental) identified by Kant in the canon of the *Critique of Pure Reason* (A803/B831). For a discussion thereof see Henry E. Allison, *Kant's Transcendental Idealism: An Interpretation and Defense* (New Haven: Yale University Press, 1983), 315–29. Allison argues that "in Kantian terms, the Idea of transcendental freedom has a regulative function with respect to the conception of practical freedom" (319). His discussion is continued in "Kant on Freedom: A Reply to My Critics," in *Idealism and Freedom: Essays on Kant's Theoretical and Practical Philosophy* (New York: Cambridge University Press, 1996), 109–28. See also Bernard Carnois, *The Coherence of Kant's Doctrine of Freedom,* trans. David Booth (Chicago: University of Chicago Press, 1987).

remains, in effect, an act of free choice, and hence in this case too, the resulting empirical character (inclusive of the natural necessity of the connections of appearances) remains one's own responsibility.

More positively expressed, intelligible character is portrayed as actively formative of empirical character. To be a good human being (and not simply a subject responsive to the good) requires a "revolution of *Denkungsart*" and a consequent "gradual reform of sensibility" (*RV* 47). "Reason gradually draws sensibility into a state of proficiency (*habitus*),[23] arouses motive impulses, and thereby cultivates a character that is itself, however, to be ascribed to freedom and is not completely based in appearances" (*RM* no. 5611, 252). Heinz Heimsoeth's conclusion in this regard is especially well articulated: "Intelligible character is thus not something that stands and endures in the sense of the permanence of a substance, upon whose surface (as it were) conditions and attributes change; rather, [intelligible character constitutes] a self-possession amid activity (*Selbststand im Tun*): it cultivates [or forms, *bildet*] empirical character."[24] Further development of how Kant understands this cultivation will be taken up in the examination of his pedagogy.

As has become evident by our discussion, character is also a specific way in which Kant addresses the wider issue of the relation of nature and freedom.[25] Character as the law of an efficacious cause (of the synthetic unity of intelligible and empirical causality) fulfills the explicit goal identified in the "Typik" of the second *Critique*: to impart the form of the moral and intelligible to the natural and sensible.[26] When one bears in mind that

23. In *Principles of Virtue*, Kant identifies the Latin *habitus* with *Fertigkeit*, an accomplished ability to "act with facility" or proficiently—a "subjective perfection of the capacity of choice" (*MST* 407). The accomplished ability of the will, in turn, lies in the ability of determining oneself to act on the basis of the representation of the law. In either case, Kant rejects the conception of such ability or facility as a habituated one (*Angewohnheit*). A few passages later he repeats the point. "Moral maxims, unlike technical ones, cannot be based on habit (*Gewohnheit*) (for the latter belongs to the physical constitution of the determination of one's willing); rather, even if their exercise were to become a matter of habit, the subject would thereby forfeit freedom in the adoption of maxims, just in what the character of an action from duty consists" (*MST* 409). The Latin term, *habitus*, itself has a wide range of meaning, including "condition (of the body)." This sense fits quite well with Kant's portrayal of reason's relation to sensibility as literally a cultivation of the condition of the latter, its fitness (*Tauglichkeit*) for realizing/actualizing moral form.

24. Heimsoeth, "Freiheit und Charakter," 301.

25. In regard to this relation of nature and freedom, perhaps the deepest tension in Kant's account occurs precisely in its pedagogical aspects, and thus the issue of this tension is addressed in a separate discussion.

26. Many elements of the issue of reconciling nature and freedom have received scholarly scrutiny independently of their role in Kant's conception of character. Among these, the "Typik" has perhaps received the least attention, and, in this case, it is just the relation of intelligible and

nature means the lawful connection of appearances effected by the synthesis of the understanding, it is not surprising to find that the relation of reason and the understanding is fundamental to Kant's conception of character, at least as it has thus far been identified with subjectively practical reason in the world. How reason's more familiar objective, moral determination fits into this account is addressed as part of the following examination of the relation of character and human desiring.

CHARACTER AND THE CAPACITY OF DESIRE

Kant's discussion of the "Character of a Person" in the *Anthropology* begins with what are perhaps his most inclusive and, hence, most complicated statements about what all is entailed by this concept. Parts of the passage have already been referred to, but it is useful to quote it here more extensively. Noting that "character" has a twofold meaning (physical and moral) in universal semiotics (*Zeichenlehre, semiotica universalis*), Kant here remarks that moral character can only be "singular" (*ein einziger*). He goes on to make the association between it and holding principles with a firm resolve: "The man of principles, in regard to whom one may safely rest one's expectations not on his instincts, but on his will, has a character."[27]

---

empirical causality in connection with character that underscores its importance; i.e. that reason have available to it a kind of schema (analogous to what the schematism does for the categories) in and through the form of the laws of nature. Thus it is possible to have efficacious "practical judgment, whereby that which is given general expression, is abstractly presented (*allgemein gesagt, in abstracto*) in the rule, is applied to an action *in concreto*" (*KpV* 67). The third antinomy is essential for establishing that such unity is not impossible. Another very familiar notion giving expression to a synthetic unity of nature and freedom (specifically as happiness and virtue) is, of course, the *summum bonum*, described in the second *Critique* as the "necessary object of a will determinable by the moral law" (*KpV* 122), as the "subjective effect of this law" (*KpV* 143). The postulates, in turn (in particular the existence of God as the "ground of the agreement not only with the law of the will of rational beings, but of the representation of this law with nature," *KpV* 125), address the issue of the wider metaphysical basis of agreement making possible the realization of such a highest good. In order that we as human beings might be able to think about nature in such unity with "what is practically contained in the concept of freedom," the notion of purposiveness as a principle of reflective judgment provides an avenue making "possible the transition from *Denkungsart* in accordance with [practical] principles to that in accordance with [theoretical] principles" (*KU* 176). There is also the further question of the relation of the judgment of taste with reason's intellectual interests that will be touched on in the discussion of the connection between character and the aesthetic capacities of feeling. The role on the side of nature in forging the unity of nature and freedom, discussed by Kant in his later essays, will be taken up in the examination of his pedagogy. Here too, the role that is played by the public, specifically the political constitution, speech, and culture, is addressed. Again, all of these notions and principles involve issues of their own that have received scholarly attention. The present study is limited to their role in Kant's conception of character.

27. Here we thus also have one of Kant's express associations of the notion of will with character.

In his further conclusions, Kant also incorporates the notions of capacity of desire, characteristic (which, in relation to semiotics and elsewhere, bears for him the special meaning of counterimage, *Gegenbild*), and his tripartite division of the human aptitudes: "Therefore, in the [portrayal of] character (*Charakteristik*), without [falling into] tautology, one may divide the characteristic [features] (*das Charakteristische*), of what belongs to one's capacity of desire (what is practical), into the following: (*a*) nature (*Naturell*) or natural aptitude, (*b*) temperament or sensibilities (*Sinnesart*), and (*c*) character per se (in an absolute sense, *schlechthin*) or *Denkungs-art*.—The first two aptitudes indicate what may be made out of the individual; the other (moral), what one is prepared to make of oneself" (*ApH* 285). We have seen the sensibilities and conduct of thought associated in the first *Critique* with forms of causality, with empirical and intelligible character. Here they are presented as divisions of what is characteristic of the human capacity of desire, which is further connected both with "what is practical" and with the complete spectrum of all the human faculties. To try and establish how all these apparently diverse elements are to relate to one another, and to ask what connection, in turn, there is between these and character in its strictly formal sense, or in its sense of serving a unifying function in regard to the conduct of life, we will begin by reviewing the meanings of the notions of capacity of desire, will, and power of choice.

Unity of Two Orders of Necessity

Given the degree of exegetical analysis that follows, an overview of what it shows may be helpful at the outset. Examination of what Kant has to say about these terms reveals that *Wille* and *Willkür* are each literally a specification of the capacity of desire insofar as the latter is determined by reason. The same issue of causality that we saw in the discussion of intelligible and empirical character is ultimately at stake; that is, the concern is the concrete realization, the actuality, of moral ideas and principles in the world. As Kant had put it in the *Critique of Practical Reason*, if moral concepts are to be "subjectively practical," then we must "consider their representation in relation to human beings and to them as individuals" (*KpV* 157). We find once again the significance of the notion of efficacious cause, with an emphasis on giving equal weight to both terms (cause and effect) and especially to the relations for which these terms serve as the definitive arche and telos. The relation between reason and the understanding, which turned out to be central to the first *Critique* reflections on intelligible and empirical character, may be seen as the account of the "how" on the side of efficaciousness; that is, it describes how what begins as supersensible can be realized in sensible form. In this regard, the question of results or success, which Kant again in the second *Critique* links to the role of the understanding, becomes important. More immediately we turn to the question of "how" on the side of causality. How reason can be construed to be such a causal capacity at all is addressed in Kant's account of the capacity of desire and its determination.

In the preface to the *Critique of Practical Reason,* one finds that Kant's basic conception of life already links the issue of its conduct with the determination of desire: "To live" (*Leben*) is the "capacity of a being to act in accordance with laws of the capacity of desire" (*KpV* 9n). The latter, in turn, is defined as follows: "The capacity of desire is the capacity of [living beings] to be, by means of their conceptions (*Vorstellungen*), the cause of the actuality of the objects of these conceptions" (*KpV* 9n).[28] A similar statement opens the discussion of the capacity of desire in Kant's *Anthropology:* "Desire [or appetite, *Begierde, appetitio*] consists in the self-determination of a subject's power[s] (*Kraft*) [to produce] an effect as a result of conceiving of something prospective" (*ApH* 251).[29] In the next line, Kant defines "inclination" as being a "habitual, sensible desire," but as we see in the remaining passages cited here, inclinations are not yet the pressing question. In the *Critique of Judgment,* we continue to see the same point, now expressed in terms of the notion of purpose and related to will. "The capacity of desire, insofar as it can be determined to act solely [on the basis of] concepts, that is, commensurate with the presentation [or conception] of a purpose, would be the will" (*KU* 220). Later Kant simply identifies "will" with the "capacity [of setting] purposes" or "acting in accordance with purposes" (*KU* 280, 370).

Ultimately, the setting of purposes for oneself is held to be definitive of what it is to be human: "The capacity to assume any purpose for oneself at all is characteristic of humanity (in contrast to animality)" (*MST* 392). Translating this point in regard to moral ideas, one recognizes here the critical solution to treating such ideas of the supersensible, which are theoretically incognizable for us. These are recast as a moral task, as a purpose;

---

28. While "representations" has long been the standard translation for *Vorstellungen,* other variations are found in recent translations. Werner Pluhar uses "presentations" in the *Critique of Judgment,* and Lewis White Beck has opted for "conceptions" in his revised translation of the *Critique of Practical Reason.* I do find that this latter best fits the context here.

29. Later in the *Anthropology,* Kant describes the "formal" part of "volition (*Wollen*) in general" as "acting in accordance with firm principles" (*ApH* 292).

specifically, it is our duty to adopt them as maxims for our actions. This we have further seen to be the essence of what is meant by reason's causality, but in the quotes just given from Kant's texts, it is the capacity of desire that is identified as a causal capacity whose role in the living being is just to effect the concrete actualization of what, in the case of human beings (at least), are first objects of thought. Continued perusal of the texts shows that the functions assigned to the will (setting purposes and, as we saw in the *Groundwork*, making use of our natural talents) are equally identified with reason itself. "Pure practical reason" is a "capacity of purposes in general; to be indifferent in regard to it, that is, to take no interest therein, is thus a contradiction" (*MST* 395). "Reason in a living being is a capacity for enlarging the rules and intentions of the use of all [of this being's] powers far beyond natural instinct" (*IG* 18).[30]

This all becomes less puzzling when one further explores the relation between reason and will, as well as the meaning of practical reason itself. "Practical reason is concerned, not with the cognition of objects (*Gegenstände*), but with its own capacity for making such objects (in accordance with its cognition of them) actual; that is, it is concerned with a will, which is a causality insofar as reason contains its determining ground" (*KpV* 89).[31] The conclusion that becomes apparent is that to speak of *Wille* is to speak of the capacity of desire as determined by reason and that, to this extent, practical reason and *Wille* are not merely identified by the same functions; rather, *Wille* is precisely nothing more than an expression for practical reason's exercise of causality in relation to the capacity of desire. It is reason in its causal capacity, which is the same as to say reason

30. In *Reflections on Anthropology* Kant even accords this role to the power of choice: "Character is the particular attribute of one's power of choice to avail oneself of all one's talents and to direct one's nature or temperament" (*RA* no. 1122, 501).

31. Other passages in which *Wille* is defined as just such a causal capacity for bringing about objects corresponding to representations are as follows. In its "practical use," reason "concerns itself with the grounds of determination of the will, which is a capacity that either brings about objects corresponding to conceptions, or that determines itself, that is, its causality, to effect such objects (whether the physical capacities to do so are adequate or not)" (*KpV* 15). The concepts of "good and evil always entail a relation to will, insofar as the latter is determined by reason's law to make something its object; . . . it is a capacity for rendering a rule of reason into the motivating cause of an action (whereby an object can be actualized)" (*KpV* 60). "Will is a capacity to choose only what reason, independently of inclination, recognizes as practically necessary, that is, as good" (*G* 412). "Will is thought to be a capacity that determines itself to act in accordance with the conception (or presentation) of certain laws" (*G* 427). The will is subject to the law in such a manner that it "must be seen as self-legislating" and may "regard itself as author" of the law (*G* 431). "Proficiency" in "determining itself in action in accordance with the conception of a law" is an "attribute not of the power of choice, but of the will, which is (together with the rule that it adopts) a universally legislative capacity of desire" (*MST* 407).

is practical. "Will is a kind of causality of living beings, insofar as they are rational" (*G* 446). The difference between laws of a system of nature to which will is subject and a system of nature subject to will is that, in the latter case, will is "the cause of the objects, so that the determining ground of their causality lies solely in the pure capacity of reason, which therefore can also be called pure practical reason" (*KpV* 44).

Some time ago, Ralf Meerbote pointed out the inadequacy of rendering *Wille* by its English cognate, *will*, defending instead the translation "practical reason." As Meerbote notes, eighteenth-century sources (in particular Grimm) adduce Kant as the authority for conceiving of volition (*Wollen*, a term that means both "to want" and "to will") as a power of acting, in contrast both to passivity and human natural drives. Kant's ultimate philosophical definition of *Wille*, Meerbote writes, is "practical reason determining the power of choice (*Willkür*)."[32] There is, in fact, much textual support in Kant's writings for Meerbote's conclusions. One of the best passages that delineates just how Kant sees all these terms in connection with one another is found in *Principles of Justice*.[33] "Insofar as the ground determining it to act is found in itself, and not in an object, the capacity of desire in accordance with concepts is called a capacity of doing or forbearing as one likes (*nach Belieben zu Tun oder zu Lassen*)." When "combined with the consciousness of the capacity of its activity to produce an object," the capacity of desire is known as the "power of choice" (*Willkür*). Without such consciousness, its act is called a "wish." Will is the "capacity of desire" insofar as its "inner ground of determination and, hence, even its likings (*Belieben*) are found in the subject's reason. Will is thus the capacity of desire considered, not in relation to the action (as is the power of choice), but rather [in regard to] the ground determining choice to an

---

32. Meerbote, "*Wille* and *Willkür*." This essay dates back to 1982; particularly relevant pages are 78–81.

33. There are numerous instances of Kant's own explicit identification of *Wille* with practical reason. Following are a few examples. For reason to hold a maxim up to the pure will is to hold it up "to itself, insofar as it regards itself as a priori practical" (*KpV* 32). The moral determination of an action must abstract from all objects so that these have no influence on the will, "in order that practical reason (will) does not merely administer interests external to it, but rather demonstrates its own commanding authority as the supreme legislation" (*G* 441). "As author of its principles, reason must regard itself as independent of external influences; thus, as practical reason or as the will of a rational being, it must regard itself as free" (*G* 448). "Since reason is required for the derivation of actions from laws, will is nothing else but practical reason" (*G* 412). "Laws proceed from will; maxims from the power of choice." Will is directly concerned, not with actions, but rather with the "legislation for the maxims of actions (and hence [is] practical reason itself); therefore, too, it is absolutely necessary and is itself incapable of being constrained" (*MSR* 226).

action and, in reality, has no [further] determining ground before it; instead, insofar as [reason] can determine the power of choice, [will] is *practical reason itself*" (*MSR* 213, emphasis added). In the next statement, Kant repeats the point: "Power of choice and also mere wish are included under [the concept of] will, insofar as reason can determine the capacity of desire at all" (*MSR* 213). He goes on: "Free choice is choice determined by pure reason. Choice determinable only by inclination (sensible impulse) is animality (*arbitrium brutum*). Human power of choice, by contrast, is one that is affected, but not determined, by impulses and . . . can be determined to action by pure will. The negative concept of freedom of choice is its independence from determination by sensible impulses. The positive concept is that of the capacity of pure reason to be practical in and of itself" (*MSR* 213–14). In light of all the citations thus presented and in accordance with Meerbote's observations, perhaps the best translation for *Wille* would be "practical desire." This rendering expresses both the essential components of practical reason and the capacity of desire, while still retaining a term distinct from practical reason itself (which is virtually the only objection one might have to rendering *Wille* as "practical reason"). All future references here to *Wille* will be made as "practical desire." Where Kant uses *Wollen* (or even *Wille/Willen*, as indicated by its context) in reference to the wider sense of the capacity of desire, which also includes possible determination by sensual impulses, the translation "volition" will be given.

The parallels between the descriptions involving desire and Kant's remarks in the first and second *Critiques* about intelligible and empirical character are self-evident. For purposes of recall and comparison, let us repeat a short passage here: "Every individual has an empirical character of his or her power of choice, which is nothing else but a certain causality of one's reason" (*KrV* A549/B577). The "empirical character" of "one's power of choice" is the "empirical cause of all of one's actions" in the world (*KrV* A552/B580) but itself, of course, "has a free causality as its basis" (*KpV* 100).[34] If, finally, we are talking about essentially *one* causal agency, namely reason, then how do all these distinctions cash out? If we have one main concern, efficacious cause bringing about the concrete actualization of supersensible moral ideas and principles in the world, why

---

34. In first chapter we saw the further identification of character and power of choice: when the latter has taken respect for the moral law up in its maxims (is characterized by such a comportment), Kant describes the "constitution of such a power of choice" as "good character" (*RV* 25, 27, 51).

is the discussion at one point made in terms of distinctions of character (distinguished further in terms of two kinds of causality) and, at another, in terms of specifications of desire?

Summarized in its simplest terms, all the textual passages considered in the present chapter prove to be an accounting of details of two fundamental relations of reason to other human capacities—namely, to understanding and to desire—whereby reason's causality can be brought to bear on the world. Through these relations, character (as law of causality) is realized as a rule manifest in appearances; in effect, moral form is thus imparted to the sensible world of which both the physical and volitional are a part. Character "consists in the firm resolve to want (*wollen*) to do something and then also in the actual carrying out of the same" (*P* 487). The question of character thus in fact encompasses all three levels (identified in the opening quote from the *Anthropology*): formal determination of maxim adoption and formal ground of determination of volition (*Denkungsart*), determination of volition in regard to purposes (*Sinnesart*), and the question of successful outcome (which involves, among other things, natural skills, abilities, and talents). The absence of the question of outcome in Kant's account of pure, objective principles of morality has, of course, occasioned much of the criticism brought against it.[35] It is through his conception of character that we come to see how Kant understands and treats the relation of this issue to morality objectively considered. Let us, then, turn again to the relevant texts themselves.

The importance of the relation to the understanding for the question of outcome has already been noted. We have seen its essential role, analogous to what the schematism does for the categories, in the application of the supersensible to the sensible. The form of the laws of nature provides the requisite test case for assessing the maxim of an action in regard to its moral possibility (*KpV* 69–70). Further, the very concept of efficacious cause entails the relation to the existent world, which exists as it does for us precisely as a result of the operations of the understanding. As Kant observes in the second *Critique*, "without something it can use in actual experience as an example," common sense (*gemeinste Verstand*) "could not make use of the law of pure practical reason in applying it" in the world (*KpV* 70). That the question of the execution of moral actions

---

35. Kant's well-known delineation of what concerns pure morality and what does not is exemplified in the following: Even in the case where the physical capacities are not adequate to bringing forth the object corresponding to one's conceptions, reason remains able to determine practical desire; to the extent that it is only a question of volition (*Wollen*), "reason always has objective reality" (*KpV* 15).

is related to theoretical cognition is alluded to again later in the text. Reviewing the difference in the way the analytic of theoretical reason proceeds, Kant notes that "practical reason is not required to provide an object of intuition"; instead, "since the concept of causality always entails the relation to a law that determines the existence of the many (*Mannigfaltigen*, manifold) in relation to one another" (the law provided by the understanding), "practical reason is only required to provide a law" to give moral direction to "such objects of intuition" (*KpV* 89). As he also stated earlier, "Whether the causality of practical desire (*Willens*) is adequate [to bring about] the actuality of the objects or not" is a question "left to the theoretical principles of reason for judgment"; these examine the "possibility of the object of volition (*Wollens*)" and concern themselves with the issue of "results," with the possibility of "success" (to put it more strongly, since Kant's term, *Erfolg*, connotes both) (*KpV* 45).

The possibility of success involves two levels of consideration. First, it must be the case that, in general, the action to be given moral direction is possible within the parameters of the natural conditions (*KrV* A548/B576). It is the understanding that provides us with the requisite cognition of the latter, with "what is, was, and will be the case" (*KrV* A547/B575), and so is essential to the link between causality objectively considered (as determination of practical desire) and subjectively considered (as efficacious cause in the world—with the emphasis on "efficacious"). Secondly, in the particular case and for human nature as such, one must ask whether the requisite capacities and resources are available. This is just the question of the indispensable study of anthropology, that is, whether human beings "are capable of performing all that is demanded of them." Strictly speaking, to say that pure reason is practical is to say that it is "directly determinant of volition" [unmittelbar willenbestimmend] (*KpV* 46), but as Kant himself noted in his lectures, "Consideration of a rule is useless, if one cannot make people prepared to fulfill it." Such fulfillment, being subjectively practical in the world, *includes* the manifestation of reason's character as empirical; that is, here too, the relation between reason and understanding is of central importance.

The determination of volition or desire (as we have seen from a number of different angles) ultimately concerns causality in regard to actualizing the objects of one's conceptions or prospective aims; or, as expressed in the third *Critique*, it is the human capacity for purposes. In this text, in his discussion of the "character of things" considered as "natural purposes," Kant notes yet again that for a thing to be "possible only as a purpose" means that the source of its causality cannot lie in the mechanism of nature, but in a cause whose capacity to be efficacious is determined by concepts." "Such a causality" must be regarded as "possible only through reason" and is therefore the "capacity to act in accordance with purposes (practical desire)" (*KU* 369–70).[36] By its objective determination of the capacity of desire, "reason as the capacity of principles determines the interest of all the other powers of mind (*Gemüthskräfte*)" (*KpV* 119–20), but as is well known, human volition (in particular, among these powers) is subject to being otherwise affected. Character as effecting the unity of the inner principle of the conduct of life in this regard, then, must essentially involve the question of achieving a *unity of human desire or volition*.

As Kant puts the matter in 1793, if either the motive impulses of our sensibilities or the motivation arising from the determination of practical desire in accordance with the moral law were considered in isolation from one another, we would find each, in and of itself, adequate for the determination of volition (*Willensbestimmung*) and of the power of choice (*RV* 36). Moreover, if in the determination of choice and action, reason were to make use of the "unity of maxims" (which is "peculiar [*eigen*] to the moral law") solely to forge a "unity of maxims, in the name of happiness, among the motive impulses of the inclinations" (for whom such a unity is otherwise not the norm), then in fact no true unity would be attained. In such a case, Kant writes, one may find "empirical character good, but [intelligible character] would still be morally evil" (*RV* 36–37). Instead, "legislative reason" must "constitute itself as a force (*Gewalt*) to execute the law," if practical desire is to be morally strong or virtuous (*MST* 405)—if human volition (*Wollen*) is to be directed (*gerichtet*) according to what reason discerns ought to be the case (*Sollen*). Thus, while by the end of the *Critique of Practical Reason*, Kant has turned his attention to the issue of how "objective practical reason can also be made subjectively practical" (*KpV* 151), it remains the case that objective determination must be prior. This priority, among other things, entails an ordering and unity in regard to the *modality* of our desiring or volition.

To speak of the issue of the modality of our desiring and willing is to underscore the point that to forge a unity in regard to this human capacity does not entail introducing something foreign to what we ordinarily, naturally, and humanly want. Not only is "responsiveness to a pure moral inter-

36. The complete discussion here parallels the first *Critique* distinction between accounting only for the very existence of a thing and the laws of the "how" of its existence (in appearance). Earlier in the *Critique of Judgment* we are told that the "judgments about the sublime in nature" contain "a purposive relation of the powers of cognition, which must be laid a priori at the basis of the capacity of purposes (practical desire) and therefore is itself a priori purposive" *KU* 280).

est" an "attribute of the [human] mind (*Gemüt*)" (*KpV* 152), but we may (and do) equally want and take pleasure in either the pleasant or the good (the objects respectively of sensibility and reason) even just on empirical grounds (*KrV* A548/B576).[37] The empirical and the practical acquire their characteristics, of course, precisely from the laws that first make them what they are. A law as such, in turn, is defined by Kant as a "formula giving expression to the necessity of an action" (*Ak* 27.2.2, 1421). Hence, two different modes of necessity are operative in the respective realms of the empirical and intelligible, and the fundamental issue is not the object desired, but the modality characteristic of the desire on the basis of which it is sought.

The necessity of the empirical realm is the necessity of "the way temporal relations in fact are," of what has, is, and will in fact take place, and for which cognition is provided by the understanding (*KrV* A547/B575). Thus desire, insofar as it is formed (or habituated) by the actual temporal relations constitutive of upbringing, interaction with others, culture, and so forth, will of necessity be predictably attracted and repulsed by certain things. Here indeed we would properly speak of our "dispositions" (*Disposition*), which refer to our feelings insofar as "circumstantial causes underlie them" and are to be distinguished from the capacity of desire and even temperament considered as natural aptitudes (*ApH* 286). From the standpoint of reason, such empirical grounds can only produce "conditioned volition (*Wollen*)" (*KrV* A548/B576), a familiar Kantian statement that may be understood in a fresh light when considered in terms of the notion of necessity. That is, what is necessary when considered in its natural relations is, morally speaking, contingent in its modality;[38] it is contingent on just its empirical circumstances. Even if what is desired and chosen on these grounds is good, in the sense that in its appearance it is legally conformable to the law, the modality of the volition motivating the action remains contingent from a moral point of view (or, as Kant also calls it, it is pathologically conditioned or necessitated).

---

37. The beautiful and the sublime will be the subject of a separate discussion.

38. Contingent is another possible translation for *bedingt*. The point here is that no theoretical account (however extensive it might be) of the cause and effect relations that have resulted in a state of affairs or object being what they are (and from this standpoint, given the existence of the cause or causes, they could not otherwise be), such causal necessitation can never be translated into "the kind of necessity" that is expressed by the "ought" (*KrV* A547–48/B575–76). It is true, of course, that in his earlier discussion "Synthetic Principles," Kant has identified contingency as such (*Zufälligkeit*) as something we recognize from the fact that "something can only exist as the effect of a cause"; thus once I have "assumed something to be contingent (*zufällig*), then to say that it has a cause is an analytical statement" (*KrV* B291).

To speak of practical necessity, by contrast, is to refer to the way an action or thing would have to be if it were to be good (whether or not it ever actually was, is, or will be) (*Ak* 27.2.2, 1398; *KrV* A547–48/B575–76). Where human volition is in fact operative on the basis of this mode of necessity, one looks to the concept that is its basis (not circumstances) in order to assess what one might expect in the choices and actions motivated by volition.[39] To put it in the terms of the *Anthropology*, desire in a particular case will necessarily follow from character (law of causality): "The man of principles, in regard to whom one may safely rest one's expectations not on his instincts, but on his practical desire (*Wille*), has a character" (*ApH* 285). For such an individual, as efficacious cause in the world, choices follow from practical necessity, from the overriding consideration, "how this must be if it is to be good." Hence, too, as Kant asserts in his now famous opening line of the *Groundwork*, "Nothing in the world . . . can be called good without qualification [or limitation, *Einschränkung*] except for a good practical desire (*Wille*) (*G* 393).

From the standpoint of the intelligible, such practical desire is simply again a "necessary volition (*Wollen*)," acquiring its further mode of compulsion as an imperative, as "ought" (*Sollen*) only in relation to our sensibilities (*G* 455). What naturally, of necessity, follows for us as beings of the empirical realm is confronted with what, of necessity, must be the case from the standpoint of our participation in the intelligible. What we naturally and actually want in the conduct of our sensibilities and what we morally and actually want in our conduct of thought (considered for the moment apart from the further problem of the innate propensity for evil) is connected, objectively considered, by the constraint (*Nötigung*) exercised by reason's causality in relation to the human volition. Hence too, to think of ourselves as bound or obligated is, by definition, to "consider ourselves as belonging both to the world of sense and at the same time to that of reason (*Verstandeswelt*)" (*G* 453), and to hold an action to be a "duty" is to understand that it is "practically [and] unconditionally necessary" (*G* 425).[40] It is to understand the action not as contingent on the particular, but as necessary in light of what is required for it to be a good one.

Does such a connection construed as constraint, or even coercion, satisfy, however, the notion of character as effecting the unity of the inner

39. As Kant puts it in the *Critique of Pure Reason;* "This ought (*Sollen*) gives expression to a possible action whose basis is nothing but a bare (*bloßer*) concept" (*KrV* A547/B575).

40. For a recent reevaluation and defense of what it is to act from duty, see Marcia W. Baron, *Kantian Ethics Almost without Apology* (Ithaca: Cornell University Press, 1995).

principle of the conduct of life?[41] To live, we recall, is just to act in accordance with laws of the capacity of desire in order that we might be an efficacious cause whereby our conceptions are concretely realized. Does the portrayal of a capacity of desire, in particular in its specification as power of choice, affected on the one hand by sensuous impulses and, on the other, subject to reason's self-constitution as authoritative power, provide anything more than an uneasy, even forced, union? To be sure, for many a reader, admittedly for good reason, just such a portrayal has seemed to capture Kant's ethical individual. Not only in the familiar passages of the *Groundwork*,[42] but elsewhere, Kant does employ the rigorous language of command (*Gebot*), prohibition (*Verbot*), and imperative. The issue broached hereby is in fact quite complex, and a complete response involves (1) the account of the true enemy of virtue, the inherent propensity for evil, (2) the pedagogical account of the cultivation of character (which includes, among other things, nature's providential role in regard to the moral purpose of humanity and the delimitation of constraint as appropriate to the child, meant literally and figuratively), and (3) in conjunction with the account of cultivation, the question of the form of (political) constitution most conducive to it. The question to be immediately

41. Dieter Henrich poses the problem in terms of the question of the comprehensibility of the "unity of both acts" of respect—the negative check of the inclinations and the positive elevation of subjectivity. His conclusion is that "Kant's theory becomes problematic because he has to assign the two acts which constitute 'respect' to two different 'faculties' of the human soul. The limitation of the inclinations occurs in 'sensibility,'" but "it is not possible to see on the basis of Kantian presuppositions how sensibility can acquire a positive connection to reason solely because its claims were rebuffed. For this reason Kant understands this elevation merely as a relation of practical *reason to itself*" ("Ethics of Autonomy," 109, 110). The force of our interpretation here is to show that Kant indeed has an avenue for securing the elevation of sensibility, that the task of moral character in its fullest sense requires it.

42. The most popularly known passages in this regard are found in the *Groundwork* in the course of Kant's discussion that, in the case of human beings, volition does not completely conform to reason but is also subject to sensual motives (G 412–13). Given the identification of *Wille* and practical reason, *Wille* (in this and other similar statements) must be understood in the broader sense of capacity of desire; i.e., capacity of desire, insofar as it can be determined to act solely (on the basis of) concepts (which is its specification as practical desire), is also subject to motives arising from our the inclinations. "The determination of such volition commensurate with objective laws is constraint (*Nötigung*)," meaning that it is envisioned as a determination by principles of reason to which volition is not necessarily submissive by virtue of its own nature (G 413). Hence, the causal relation of reason to the human capacity of desire is in the form of necessity expressed by the "ought," and "the conception of an objective principle, insofar as it constrains volition, is called a command of reason, and its formula is an imperative. All imperatives are expressed by an ought (*Sollen*) and thereby indicate the relation of an objective law of reason to volition that, in its subjective constitution, is not necessarily determined thereby (constraint)" (G 413).

addressed here is propaedeutic to these wider considerations. Does Kant offer another dimension beyond constraint (or perhaps as a supplement to "bare" constraint) as a vehicle for unifying these two modes of necessity operative in human volition?

Since necessity as a function of the actuality of temporal relations and necessity grounded on a concept are not derivable from one another, the unity we are seeking must again be a synthetic one, a union of the conditioned with its condition. Arguably, the preceding description in terms of constraint does fit these parameters; that is, volition contingent on empirical circumstance is constrained in its pursuits to those purposes that also satisfy practical necessity. So conceived, we have the familiar negative criterion of objective morality restated in terms of the modes of necessity involved. From the standpoint of the question of character, however, a positive account is called for. What is wanted is not simply a higher-ranking necessitation winning the day. Rather, analogous to the earlier account of reason's empirical character as a rule manifest in appearance, what is called for is that volition (which, being human, cannot escape the necessity of its temporal relations) nonetheless concretely manifest practical necessity as characteristic of its nature.[43]

The focus in this regard falls on the power of choice. In the mature and virtuous comportment of mind, choice (that is, volition in direct relation to action) is so constituted that it follows, not merely contingently in accord with, but necessarily from the consideration that a possible action be good. The synthetic unity thereby realized is of the specifications of volition itself: power of choice (the conditioned) and practical desire (as its condition). While philosophical analysis divides the matter into the two sciences of practical philosophy or morality and anthropology, dealing with the objective and subjective "laws of free choice" respectively (*Ak* 27.2.2, 1398), the *exercise* of volition as a genuinely unified whole must be such that practical necessity is inherent to what is actually wanted and

43. In the *Critique of Pure Reason,* in direct connection with its discussion of the two modes of necessity, one reads that "the ought expressed by reason confronts contingent [or conditioned] volition with a [standard of] moderation, even prohibition and superiority" (*KrV* A548/B576). Kant's phrase, "Maß und Ziel, ja Verbot und Ansehen," when rendered literally, means "measure and goal, indeed prohibition and high standing (or prestige, reputation)." However, *Maß und Ziel* is an idiomatic expression for "moderation." A call to do things with *Maß und Ziel* is a call to do everything with moderation. Given the wider context of Kant's writings, it is tempting to render the phrase (as Kemp Smith has done) along the lines of "limit and end," but doing so emphasizes, of course, the rigorous reading of what Kant is saying here. Read in terms of the first translation, this short passage incorporates both the negative, objective, legislative relation of reason to volition (notably as the second part) and a positive expression of a standard to be adopted by, subjectively realized on the part of, volition itself.

chosen. In other words, volition does not simply agree with what is objectively required, but *what it wants* includes *in itself wishing to be in such agreement.* As Kant puts it in 1793, the "moral *Denkungsart*" consists in that "*Gesinnung* which wants" something "only on the condition" that the objective condition, whereby all our maxims agree with the moral law, be met; that is, it desires that happiness be wished for only on the condition that one first be worthy of happiness (*RV* 46n). Or, to put it in the words of the *Groundwork,* it means that what is "recognized" as being "objectively necessary is also subjectively necessary" (*G* 412). To express the same point in still another way, it means that human volition is now in and of itself characterized by one overarching orientation or direction that encompasses and orders *all* its wanting and choosing. Volition and the actions to which it gives rise are directed or oriented toward the ought (*auf das Sollen gerichtet*) (*KrV* A548/B576).

For practical necessity thus to inhere in human volition means that it is an acquired characteristic, and, where it has so been acquired, one finds character both in the absolute sense of conduct of thought and in regard to the conduct of the sensibilities. One may safely rest one's expectations in regard to such individuals on their practical desire, for their capacity of choice has adopted the former's mode of necessity as its own. In our day-to-day colloquial expressions, on Kant's view, it is to just the capacity of choice that we are in fact referring when we speak of the "heart": the "capability or inability of the power of choice to adopt or not the moral law in its maxims" is called the "good or evil heart" (*RV* 29).[44] It is this heart or choice that makes itself actually manifest in the world, and, so too, by 1793 Kant is identifying it virtually exclusively with empirical character. Given further his identification of practical desire with practical reason, it turns out that the account of volition (as presented here) is not simply analogous to that of reason's empirical character understood in terms of the relation of reason and the understanding. In and through the capacity of choice characterized by practical necessity, reason is constituted as a subjectively practical, efficacious cause *in the world,* and not only as an objective, legislative capacity standing in relation *to* the world. In and through the actions resulting from such choice, practical necessity is further concretely realized as a factor within, now actually belonging to, temporal relations. What follows of necessity from relations so informed will

44. In *Reflections on Anthropology,* Kant provides a small table under the heading "Nature and Freedom." On the side of freedom, he lists mind (*Gemüth*), heart, and character as *Denkungsart.* On the side of nature, he lists the dispositions one has by nature (*Naturel*), talents, and temperament (*RA* no. 1135, 504).

subsequently, in virtue of what these relations are, entail also what follows from practical necessity.

What has been achieved by the adoption of practical necessity in and by human volition is thus precisely an elevation of nature as called for in the *Critique of Practical Reason:* the law shall give the form of supersensible nature to sensible nature; the result is to be the existence of a "counterimage" (*Gegenbild*) of the former within the latter, without thereby disrupting the operation of the laws of the sensible world (*KpV* 43). The notion of counterimage appears in Kant's writings in regard to the work of the imagination, but it is also explicitly identified with the notion of the "characteristic": "Characteristic is the counterimage of the other. Counterimage is a means of producing (literally, bringing forth) the image of the other thing" (*Ak* 28.1, 237).[45] Kant's discussion in the *Anthropology* begins from a reference to semiotics (cited previously) and speaks of the notion of characteristic in relation to the capacity of desire. As we also saw in the first *Critique*'s discussion of intelligible and empirical character, Kant refers to the empirical as the "sensible sign" of the former (*KrV* A546/B574). In short, the very notion of character as such connotes a counterimage found in the sensible world that inherently points to its supersensible "original" and makes the latter available for human intuition. The constitution of the counterimage is the positive account we were inquiring about in regard to practical reason's causality vis-à-vis the world. Its production is what it means for reason "to make for itself, with complete spontaneity, its own order in accordance with ideas, into which it fits the empirical conditions" (*KrV* A548/B576), or for reason to have its own "sphere, namely the order of purposes, which is at the same time an order of nature" (*KrV* B425). It is what it means to think of the subjection of our maxims to the law as tantamount to giving rise to an order of nature: "Through our reason, we are conscious of a law to which all our maxims are subject; [it is] as if, at the same time, an order of nature is bound to arise through our practical desire" (*KpV* 44).

The conception of character realized in the power of choice as the counterimage of legislative practical reason (through the determination of choice by practical desire) does not yet, however, answer whether some-

---

45. Rudolf Makkreel discusses *Gegenbild* as one of the modes of formation (*Bildung*) that are products of the imagination; *Gegenbild* here is a "counterimage that serves as a linguistic analogue." Makkreel remarks on the further identification with "characteristic" that appears in the Pölitz lectures on metaphysics (Makkreel, *Imagination and Interpretation*, 13–15, 19). In its second *Critique* sense, the counterimage is the world of sensibility to which the form of moral, intelligible causality has been imparted.

thing else beyond constraint is or can be operative in bringing about such unity in human volition. Nor does it by itself account for the wider association Kant makes (in the opening citation from the *Anthropology*) between our capacity of desire and our natural aptitudes—our endowments, talents, and temperament—said to be characteristic features of that desire. Kant's own attention and priority given to reason's objective determination involved first locating the source and supplying the causal moral direction or orientation, as the indispensable condition for introducing an "entirely different rule and order from the natural order" of things (*KrV* A550/B578). The subjective conditions of the realizability of such a rule, however, include just those natural aptitudes of which causality (whether it is said to be of reason, practical desire, or choice) makes use. In the wider context of Kant's employment of the notion of aptitudes (*Anlagen*) in his philosophy, it turns out that these too are construed as being purposive powers of human nature. Thus they offer yet another avenue to address the issue of how unity of the inner principle of the conduct of life might be achieved. In this regard then, as well as the question of their relation to desire, it is time to turn to Kant's tripartite division of the human aptitudes and to explore their relation to his conception of character.

Unity of the Human Aptitudes

The general definition of character as a law of causality, central to our discussion thus far, is obviously a very abstract and formal one. Without the additional account of what it is for the human being to be efficacious cause or actor (*tätiges Wesen*), or of the meaning of act or action (*Handlung* as *Tat*), the definition would hardly connote the human, either as person or species; nor would its moral implications be easily seen. In this regard, Kant's earliest description of character as defined by the governing species of feeling in human nature, distinguished in terms of the four medieval humors (sanguine, melancholic, choleric, phlegmatic) seems much more obvious (*B* 218ff.). In his *Anthropology* lectures, Kant applies his early description to our characteristic sensibilities; these, he states, are indeed what we ordinarily refer to when we speak of someone's character (*ApH* 286–91). As a basis for understanding how the natural human aptitudes now fit in, it is helpful to turn to what Kant has to say about the possibility of giving a definition of the character of the human genus (*Gattung*); that is, it helps us to see what basic conception of human nature is operative in his thought and how it relates to the critical account of character.

The very "vocation" or "destiny" (*Bestimmung*) of a "living being," writes

Kant, is ascertainable from its character (*ApH* 329). If one begins, however, with the "concept of the genus" as a "terrestrial rational being," one is precluded from giving any theoretical definition of it and from identifying its character; for, we cannot have the requisite knowledge of a "rational, nonterrestrial being" as the basis for comparison, so as to define its distinguishing property (*ApH* 321). Kant excludes from consideration altogether a definition of the human species *derived from* mundane, animal nature and, to this extent, retains his earliest point of departure (expressed in his *Universal Natural History*): his concern with thinking natures and the possible perfection of their capacity of thought.[46] However, with the genus of rational beings as such beyond our grasp (and so too the definition of its earthly member in its terms), if we are yet to "assign to human beings their species (*Classe*) *in the system of living nature* and thus to characterize them, we are left with no other option [but to say] that [human beings] have a character that they procure for themselves, in that they are able to perfect themselves in accordance with purposes that they adopt for themselves" (*ApH* 321, emphasis added). We are left, in other words, with a practical definition, one notably in relation *to* nature (cognition of which is possible for us), but not *from* nature. The "perfection proper" to "humanity" is not to be construed as a "gift for which we must thank nature"; it must be the "effect of our deed (*Tat*)" (*MST* 386; see also *ApH* 294).

Ultimately, of course, such perfection, vocation, or destiny is defined by the concept of good, and the most immediate vehicle of its possible actualization in the world (or system of living nature) is the exercise of the human power of free choice. In the *Anthropology* and elsewhere (as we have seen time and again), it is this capacity that is pivotal to. the discussion. "Human inner perfection consists in having the use of all one's capacities in one's power," so that their employment is "subordinate to a free power of choice" (*ApH* 144). While it is a "basic principle of nature's

46. Stanley Cavell's characterization of Kant's basic presuppositions about human nature is to my mind correct: Kant "regards the human being as a species of the genus of rational beings, to wit, the species that has the distinction of being animal." This conception of the human being as one species of rational being is significant, for it "reverses the Aristotelian field and thus redirects the problem of connection. . . . The direction to the human is not animation, but incarnation" (*The Claim of Reason* [Oxford: Clarendon Press, 1979], 399). From the perspective of this reversal, one now gives an account of the human, not in terms of the lower half of the "great chain of being" (which itself is redefined by Kant as a "ladder of [rational] being" in which the human occupies the middle rung, "between the two extremes of perfection," *NH* 359), but in terms of the measure provided by its extreme points. It is not a question of how far we are above the animals, the question naturally following from the ancient definition, but of how nearly we realize the genus to which we belong within the limits of our specific (i.e. human) form.

purposes" that "all living beings attain their destiny," in the case of the "human genus" we are able to see therein "only a tendency" on the part of "nature toward this purpose: namely, the development of good through their own activity" (*ApH* 329). Where the discussion is just of the development of this "rudiment of good" found within us (*Keim des Guten,* as Kant calls it in the *Religion within the Limits of Reason Alone* and *Perpetual Peace*), we are to understand by "human nature only the subjective ground of the employment of our freedom as such," which is the "first basis of the adoption" of maxims, a basis found in our capacity of choice (*RV* 21); our resulting moral state is an "effect (*Wirkung*) of a free power of choice" (*RV* 44).

These are, by now, very familiar notions: (1) the "subjective ground of the use of our freedom" (related to choice), (2) "making use" of the innate attributes and capacities of our nature (of what is *natürlich, angeborn*) by all three capacities (practical reason, practical desire, and free choice), and (3) what is acquired or procured (*erworben, verschafft*) by our own efforts (related primarily to the attainment of character). It is important to underscore the additional point we have just seen; namely, that the effort to procure character is defined in relation to living nature. It is in comparison with living beings (*Geschöpfe*) that we recognize that the essential property of the human being—the character of the human species—lies in this distinctive activity that human beings carry out in relation to the given.[47]

47. It is in this regard that Kant's so-called humanism is expressed most strongly. It is quite interesting to compare Kant's claims and conceptions here with the famous speech of God to Adam from Pico's *Oration on the Dignity of Man:* "We have given you, Oh Adam, no visage proper to yourself, nor any endowment properly your own, in order that whatever place, whatever form, whatever gifts you may, with premeditation, select, these same you may have and possess through your own judgment and decision. The nature of all other creatures is defined and restricted within laws which We have laid down; you, by contrast, impeded by no such restrictions, may, by your own free will, to whose custody We have assigned you, trace for yourself the lineaments of your own nature. I have placed you at the very center of the world, so that from that vantage point you may with greater ease glance round about you on all that the world contains. We have made you a creature neither of heaven nor of earth, neither mortal nor immortal, in order that you may, as the free and proud shaper of your own being, fashion yourself in the form you may prefer. It will be in your power to descend to the lower, brutish forms of life; you will be able, through your own decision, to rise again to the superior orders whose life is divine" (Giovanni Pico della Mirandola, trans. A. Robert Caponigri [Chicago: Regnery Gateway, 1956], 7–8). For Kant, of course, the "form" is mandated by practical reason and, arousing and sustaining preference for it, is just the issue of bringing human volition into accord with reason.

A recent reconsideration of Kant's humanism by John Luik argues that the notion of radical evil severely undermines the humanist enterprise that Kant might otherwise be seen to have: "An Old Question Raised Yet Again: Is Kant an Enlightenment Humanist?" in *The Question of Humanism,* ed. David Goicoechea and John Luik (New York: Prometheus Books, 1991), 117–37.

In this light, character is the *formative activity* peculiar to the rational being in relation to nature; it is not creative, for it can only give form, direction, orientation to what is already given.

To express it this way delineates more specifically our general definition of character in terms of the relation of cause to its effect. From the moral point of view, this relation is an expression of "ought" in that it expresses what reason wants. From the anthropological point of view, it entails the presupposition that it is characteristic of the given to be inherently amenable to the exercise of this causal activity in relation to it. Moreover, the benefit of this activity accrues to us as living, political beings: "So one may say that the leading (*erste*) character of the human genus is our capacity as rational beings, *for [the sake of] our own person as well as for the society in which nature has placed us,* to procure a character at all; and that we do so *presupposes* there is *already a favorable natural aptitude and a propensity for good"* inherent in the individual (*ApH* 329, emphasis added). To put the matter, then, again in our previous terms, character as effecting the unity of the inner principle of life expresses the relation of nature and freedom such that the latter is the basis employed as the source of the activity that, in turn, uses what is given effectively as its material. As Kant continues to maintain in 1798, innate to human nature is an "aptitude and capacity for the better" that "alone unites nature and freedom in accordance with internal principles of justice in the human race" (*SF* 88).

Articulated in terms of the specification of human desire as choice (the locus of effecting this unity), the relation consists in just what was so succinctly stated in the *Critique of Pure Reason:* volition and the actions to which it gives rise are directed or oriented toward the ought (*auf das Sollen gerichtet*) (*KrV* A548/B576), and this is possible also because natural volition (*Wollen*), indeed all the human natural aptitudes, are already "original aptitudes for good" (*RV* 26). To say they are "original" is to claim that they "necessarily belong" to the very "possibility of human nature"; that is, they are not "contingent," for without them what our "being" or nature (*Wesen*) as human beings is would not be "in itself possible" (*RV* 28). They are "aptitudes for good" both in the negative sense that they do not inherently conflict with the moral law and in the positive sense that they can serve to promote the observance of the law (*RV* 28). Again, the "basis both of insight and heartfelt participation (*Herzensanteils*) in the true and the good lies in each person's natural aptitude (*Naturanlage jedes Menschen*)" (*RV* 122). The cultivation of these capacities or aptitudes, of all of our "natural powers (*Kräfte*) (of mind, body, and soul) as means for all possible purposes, is a duty" (an action that is practically necessary) that "human beings owe to themselves"; for reason can employ these natural aptitudes and capacities that should not, therefore, be left unused and, as it were, to rust (*MST* 444; see also 445, 386–87).

The notion, then, of natural aptitudes (*Naturanlagen*) too is of central importance for the understanding of Kant's conception of moral character. It is a term whose meaning is grounded in Kant's biological reflections on the nature and generation of organized, living beings, but is also pervasive in Kant's other writings. In the *Groundwork,* when Kant emphasizes that the "reality" of the "highest moral principle" is "not to be derived from an attribute unique (*besonderen Eigenschaft*) to human nature," he goes on to identify what belongs to the "particular natural aptitudes of humanity"; namely, "certain feelings and propensities, even . . . a particular direction (*besonderen Richtung*) peculiar [or proper, *eigen*] to human reason" and, of course, our "inclinations" (*G* 425). In the *Anthropology,* we have seen the term related to the kinds of characteristic features into which one may divide what belongs to one's capacity of desire. In the *Religion within the Limits of Reason Alone,* a text in which almost one-third of Kant's uses of *Anlage(n)* (in works published in his lifetime) are concentrated,[48] Kant too qualifies its reference in this way: "We are here speaking only of those aptitudes that are directly related to the capacity of desire and the employment of choice" (*RV* 28). In turn, these aptitudes are repeatedly presented by Kant in a three-part hierarchy, whose levels are variously expressed as follows. In his 1793 work, the hierarchy is explicitly said to be drawn along the lines of the purpose of the aptitudes as "elements of [our] human vocation"; that is, our aptitudes as (1) living, animal beings, (2) living, rational beings, and (3) rational, morally accountable beings (*RV* 26). In the *Anthropology,* Kant also names these levels as our (1) "technical" aptitude, or our conscious, mechanical abilities to work with things, (2) "pragmatic" aptitude, or skill in dealing with others in regard to attaining our goals, and (3) "moral" aptitude, or ability to "act toward oneself and others according to the principle of freedom under laws" (*ApH* 322). Thus to set purposes for ourselves is identified in *Principles of Virtue* as precisely that which is "characteristic of humanity in contrast to animality," and, in this context, cultivation of our aptitudes is further held to be a duty, a matter of practical necessity (*MST* 392). From the standpoint of practical desire, in other words, it is not merely to be left as a matter

48. A search of the computerized Kant index shows that of the 225 occurrences of *Anlage(n),* 73 are found in this 1793 text. It is here too that Kant uses the related term, *Keim,* in direct relation to the notion of good—*Keim des Guten.* Other occurrences of the latter phrase are found in *Perpetual Peace* and *On Pedagogy.*

of contingency, of dependence on circumstances, that such cultivation take place; rather, it is an overarching purpose to "acquire or promote" our "capacity for carrying out all kinds of purposes" (*MST* 392). Pedagogically speaking, then, the cultivation of these aptitudes consists in developing "skillfulness" (*Geschicklichkeit*) in relation to our talents, "prudence" (*Weltklugheit*) or skillfulness in relations with others (which involves our temperament), and, third, attaining moral character in its absolute sense as *Denkungsart* (*P* 486).

While practical desire thus adds the dimension of practical necessity and moral orientation, the important word here is "adds." The impetus for pursuing purposes or goals, for cultivating and developing our natural aptitudes, lies already within the latter themselves. Hence, attending to the meaning and role of this neglected notion in Kant's writings concerning natural history and biology is helpful for elucidating Kant's conception of character. In his analysis of the term *aptitudes* from the standpoint of the philosophy and history of the life sciences, Phillip R. Sloan observes that Kant was developing his own thought "exactly in the period of a fertile and complex debate over the generation of organisms that within the life sciences served to define the parameters of important reflections on the nature of life, permanence of species, the origins of organic form, and the relation of nature to divine causation."[49] Sloan argues that much illumination can be gained by considering Kant's employment of these terms in relation to the "surrounding biological context of discussion."[50]

---

49. Cited from an unpublished manuscript by Phillip R. Sloan, "Preforming the Categories: Kant and 18th C. Generation Theory," University of Notre Dame, 6. My colleague Phillip Sloan and I have profited from mutual consultation on these terms from the standpoint of our respective interests in the sciences and moral philosophy. The translation of *Anlagen* poses particular difficulties. In its ordinary-language sense it has a wide range of possible meanings and applications. Thus far, it has here been rendered as "aptitude," but as Phillip Sloan also underscores, "nothing in English quite captures the full meaning" of Kant's usage, which Sloan finds to be "more equivalent to a 'structuring ability' in many contexts." The translation "disposition" is unsatisfactory both in light of its passive connotation, which fails to convey Kant's more active sense of the term (as expressed by "structuring ability," for example), and for the meaning (noted earlier in the text) that Kant associates with "disposition," namely, that dispositions have for their basis circumstantial causes—cultural, empirical origins—not the natural aptitudes found in the nature of every human being (*ApH* 286) that are the very basis for the organism's response to circumstances. Further, "disposition" too closely connotes the sense of habit (*Gewohnheit*) that Kant also explicitly rejects—i.e. something mechanically produced through repeated actions.

50. Sloan's immediate interest is in illuminating Kant's point in the first *Critique*, where he traces the pure concepts to their "first *Keimen* and *Anlagen* in human understanding" (*KrV* A66/ B91) ("Preforming the Categories," 1–6). In light of the citations given thus far of Kant's use of these terms in relation to character, its constitution and development, the relevance of their meaning for this issue is even more apparent.

To the extent that Kant is himself (in opposition to positions taken by such figures as Buffon and Maupertuis) formulating a "novel solution to the generation problem in terms of an endowment of organic beings with an inherent capacity that enables them to generate their offspring by genuine causal powers,"[51] and given his explicit reflections on the formation and perpetuation of human character (as a character of the species) in terms of just these notions, it becomes apparent that this dimension of Kant's thought impacts the sense of "character" that is at issue in his anthropological and moral reflections (in which, as we have seen, the association with *Anlagen* and *Keime* continues regularly).

In the earliest writings (from 1755 to 1775), the discussion of aptitudes and germs[52] inherent to the nature of organic beings is in regard to the latter's inherent ability to adapt to varying environmental conditions. The language used is that of development (*Entwickelung*), unfolding (*Entfaltung*), or uncovering (*Auswickelung*)[53] of what nature has provided for in the organism, enabling it to respond to the circumstances in which it finds itself in a given geographical location and, therefore, enabling it to maintain and preserve itself (*sich erhalten*). Such provision consists in an "advantageous aptitude of its structure" (*NH* 358). The wider context of this passage (from 1755) is Kant's concern with the possibility of the perfection of thinking natures, considered there in regard to the question of how such might be affected by their proximity to the sun (*NH* 351ff.). By 1763 Kant conceives of "aptitude" in terms of a single "dynamic principle that organizes the whole structure (*Bau*)" as well as "adapts" the organism "advantageously to many conditions" (*BG* 126).[54] Again, the language here

51. Sloan, "Preforming the Categories," 13.

52. The translation "germ" for *Keim* (other possible choices being seed, bud, sprout) is intended to convey the active connotation of germination (which a seed does not necessarily do) and the wider sense of origin, first principle, and rudiment, beyond that from which something can develop and grow.

53. The term *Auswickeln* means literally to unwrap, or in biological terms, to take off an outer shell, husk, or hull. Kant explicitly carries this notion of removing a hard outer husk into his discussion in his essay "What Is Enlightenment?" The following are the closing lines to the essay and are noteworthy for the many motifs of his thought that Kant brings together within such a short passage: "Wenn denn die Natur unter dieser harten Hülle den Keim, für den sie am zärtlichsten sorgt, nämlich den Hang und Beruf zum freien Denken, ausgewickelt hat: so wirkt dieser allmählig zurück auf die Sinnesart des Volks (wodurch dieses der Freiheit zu handeln nach und nach fähiger wird) und endlich auch sogar auf die Grundsätze der Regierung, die es ihr selbst zuträglich findet, den Menschen, der nun mehr als Maschine ist, seiner Würde gemäß zu behandeln" (*A* 41–42).

54. Sloan, "Preforming the Categories," 14; the important point here from a biological standpoint is that this conception "does away with the need to assume special separate adaptations or powers in each part that would adapt them to circumstances."

is striking; Kant speaks of a "single aptitude" entailing a "fruitful fitness for many propitious consequences" (or effects, *fruchtbare Tauglichkeit zu viel vortheilhaften Folgen, BG* 126), terminology that later appears in discussions of virtue and the moral cultivation of humanity. By 1797, what over thirty years earlier had been conceived as a natural process of the organic body provided for in its structuring principle is now explicitly formulated as a maxim for action that we (as moral beings) are obligated to adopt: "Cultivate (*anbauen*, build, add on to, structure) the powers of your mind and body such that they are adequate for fulfilling [literally, are in a condition of fitness for, *Tauglichkeit*] all purposes that you may have to face (*die Dir aufstoßen können*), uncertain [as you may be] as to which one of such purposes may become your own" (*MST* 392). In the essay *On Pedagogy*, such "development of our natural aptitudes" and the "unfolding of our humanity out of its rudiments (*Keime*)" is also identified as an explicit task we must undertake if "human beings are to achieve their vocation" (*P* 445).

By 1775, in his essay "On the Different Human Races," Kant makes his first explicit association of all three notions: character, natural aptitude, and rudiments (or germs). The "mere ability, even where nothing purposive shows itself, to propagate one's particular, acquired (*angenommenen*) character" is said to be sufficient evidence "that a particular germ or natural aptitude for such may be found in the organic living being" (*VR* 435). As before, character itself is acquired by the organism's adaptation to climatic conditions; the result is a "permanent development of the germs and aptitudes" that results in the establishment of a particular race (*VR* 436; see also 442). Moreover, Kant explicitly rejects the notion that either "chance or universal mechanical laws" could bring about such remarkable developments on the part of the organism consonant with its conditions (*VR* 435). The distinction and relation of germs and aptitudes in this essay are drawn along the lines of part and whole. Both are "grounds of a determinate unfolding lying in the nature of an organic body"; the notion of "germs" refers to such grounds when only "particular parts are affected," while "aptitudes" refer to them when either the "size or relation of the parts to one another are affected" (*VR* 434).

Admittedly, character here refers to the character of a particular race, not of the human genus as such; nor has any moral association (relation to capacity of desire or to choice) been made. Some crucial elements of the general conception of character have, however, been laid down. Even basic physical adaptations (such as birds developing an extra layer of feathers in cold climates) have been explicitly excluded as possible effects of mechanical laws. Instead, a dynamic principle within the living being, having the potential for actively responding in a fitting way to new conditions (that is, in a way serving its self-preservation amid new circumstances), for producing characteristics that become permanent attributes (and hence are hereditary, thereby serving the self-preservation of the race) has been formulated as a basic assumption to be made about the nature of a living being. The language of purposiveness has been introduced. By ten years later (in Kant's essay of 1785, "Determination of the Concept of a Human Race"), the purposiveness found in a given organization (of a living being, or of an entire race) is itself held to be the "general basis" upon which we "infer" that the "provision for this end was originally placed in the nature of a living being and, if such a purpose is to be achieved only at a later point," then we infer the presence of the requisite germs (*BM* 102–3). The 1788 essay "On the Use of Teleological Principles in Philosophy" uses *purposive* as a descriptive modifier for the aptitudes and germs themselves, as well as for "efficacious nature" (*GTP* 169, 170, 173), a use continued in the *Critique of Judgment,* where we find the phraseology of "inner purposive aptitudes" (*KU* 423). In the 1785 essay, the language of cause and effect too is explicitly used; both germs and aptitudes are identified as causes, with their effects including a character capable of being inherited (*BM* 97, 98).

The shift from such a character of a human race[55] to the character of the species morally conceived (of which the character of the individual is a particular instantiation) requires not so much a departure from the preceding basic assumptions underlying the notion, but the consideration of a different set of relations informing the response and development of the original aptitudes of human nature. The crucial environment is now not "air and sun," but the proximity of others in society, the political forms of organization, more precisely, the civil constitution, and arguably, above all, the awakening of reason—its active assumption of its role as initiator or first principle of these further changes in the human condition. The changes from the instinctual world once "reason awakened" are presented by Kant in "Conjectural Beginning of Human History" (1786) (with the following summary taken from pages 111 to 115 of that text). The description of reason here may still be seen as falling under the "particular natural aptitudes of humanity" that we saw (in the account of the *Groundwork*) included "a particular direction (*besonderen Richtung*) peculiar (or proper,

---

55. Race is defined by Kant simply as a "lineage that has an enduring hereditary set of properties grounded in the original *Keimen* and *Anlagen*" (Sloan, "Preforming the Categories," 22; see also *BM* 98–99).

eigen) to human reason" itself (*G* 425). The "development" of the other aptitudes, of the "innate abilities" of human nature, now takes place under the influence of the "driving force of reason," which they are "unable to resist." These developing skills are not acquired in the manner of the foregoing characteristics; their acquisition (*Anschaffung*) does not become a hereditary factor but must be acquired by each one themselves (*selbst erwerben*, which is the terminology used in both the second *Critique* and the *Anthropology* for the procurement of character). Foremost among these skills is the "organization (*Veranstaltung*) best suited for sociability," here held to be the "highest purpose of [our] human vocation [or determination, *Bestimmung*]."

The fundamental sense of reason presented in this 1786 essay is that of provoking the enlarged employment of our capacities beyond the "limits of instinct," a sense that agrees with "Idea for a Universal History with a Cosmopolitan Intent" (1784), in which "reason in a living being" is explicitly defined as a "capacity for enlarging the rules and intentions of the use of all its powers far beyond natural instinct" (*IG* 18). Another point to be underscored here (in addition to the fact that the development of the natural aptitude of human reason itself also is at issue) is that, without reason's influence, the other natural aptitudes are literally held back in the development of their own inherent potentialities. The path is not a smooth one. As Kant notes in 1786, in the exercise of reason's initial comparative powers in regard to the objects of sense, its own "attribute" soon comes to light, namely, "with help of the imagination," to give rise to "desires" (or appetites, *Begierden*) that not only lack a corresponding "natural drive," but that even stand "in opposition" to such natural drives. However, turning back to the 1784 piece, one reads Kant's well-known affirmation of "antagonism" and "opposition" (here cast as occurring between the inclination for societal organization promoted by reason and the inclination for individualism that seeks to order all in accordance with self) as just that which is conducive to (1) "awaken all human powers," (2) gradually "cultivate all talents" otherwise "forever hidden in their germs," and (3) ultimately lead to both the "inner perfection of *Denkungsart*" and the constitution of society as a "moral whole" (*IG* 19–21). Such opposition is a provision of nature itself without which "all the excellent natural aptitudes would lie forever asleep in humanity" (*IG* 21). In light of the foregoing model of natural adaptation (as the vehicle for producing the character of a race), this portrayal of how the character of the species develops toward its realization as a moral species is not, after all, surprising.

Returning to the relevant passages of the "Conjectural History," once again the capacity of choice turns out to be of central importance, specifically the discovery in ourselves of a "capacity to choose one's way of life (*Lebensweise*) for oneself." A second important step is the attainment of "consciousness of some measure of power on the part of reason over impulses," realized in conjunction with the step from "merely felt to idealized [objects of] attraction"; the latter is a result of covering the sensual, removing it from the physical senses. Reason's "third step" is "deliberated anticipation of the future," whereby too we realize the human ability to "prepare ourselves for purposes [that lie] far in the future," an ability "commensurate with our destiny" described several passages later as consisting in "progress toward perfection." The fourth step achieved by the use of reason is to conceive of ourselves as "the purpose of nature," a notion that receives its elaboration in the second part of the *Critique of Judgment.* This notion is the basis not only for equality among human beings as equal participants in nature's gifts, but for a status of equality with all rational beings.

The ultimate environment conducive to the complete development of all our natural aptitudes is itself a product of human effort, namely, the "completely just civil constitution" under whose governance "all the germs [lying in human nature] can be developed" and human "destiny" (or vocation, *Bestimmung*) "here on earth may be fulfilled" (*IG* 22, 25, 30). This is a claim repeated in many of Kant's writings, including *Critique of Judgment, Religion within the Limits of Reason Alone, Metaphysical Principles of Justice,* "Idea for a Universal History," *Toward Perpetual Peace, Conflict of the Faculties,* and the *Anthropology.* By 1795 Kant goes so far as to assert that the "good moral formation (*Bildung*) of a people is to be expected in the first place" as a product of "a good political constitution" (*F* 366). It is, of course, just in this connection that the persistent questions about the reconcilability of Kant's moral philosophy and the essays broadly referred to as his philosophy of history are raised, particularly in regard to the role accorded to nature in the latter. The texts provide grounds for this concern, and we will return to it as part of the inquiry into the pedagogical issues of character building. A number of immediately relevant points, however, come to light on the basis of Kant's account of the natural aptitudes.

In the first place, reason qua *human* reason is itself just such an aptitude. We saw the distinction made in the *Groundwork* passage between reason so considered and as practical (in a strict sense, that is, as law-giving and author of the moral imperative). The capacity of thinking for oneself is a germ innate to human nature and one whose development naturally has consequences for the human sensibilities and ultimately even for the forms of political organization. As Kant puts it in his essay on enlightenment: "When nature has uncovered under this hard husk the germ for which she cares most tenderly, namely, the propensity and calling to free thinking, this germ gradually in turn impacts (*wirkt zurück*) the *Sinnesart* (sensibilities) of the people (whereby they become more and more capable of acting [in accordance with freedom]). And, finally, it even [impacts] the principles of government, which itself finds it beneficial to treat human beings, who are now more than machines, commensurate with their dignity" (*A* 41–42). In the passages cited from the "Conjectural History," while the path depicted is that of development from the simply instinctual in the direction of the ethical, nonetheless these first stirrings (*Regungen*) of the rational capacity described there are of that capacity as belonging to the developing rational animal. To be such a rational animal is *not yet*, as Kant underscores more than once, to be the morally accountable, rational being. The distinction is spelled out, for example, as part of the hierarchy of our aptitudes for good presented in *Religion within the Limits of Reason Alone.* The second tier is that of the rational animal, and, as Kant makes explicit in his note, "it does not at all follow [from the fact that] a being [is endowed with] reason, that such contains a capacity unconditionally to determine the power of choice through the mere conception of the qualification of its maxims for universal legislation. . . . The most rational worldly being could after all require certain motivations stemming from objects of inclination in order to determine its choice, [and] apply thereto the most rational deliberations . . . without having any inkling . . . of even the possibility of something like a moral, absolutely commanding law" (*RV* 26n). The "aptitude for personality," the third and final tier, consists in the "responsiveness of respect for the moral law"; that is, it is the "subjective ground" of the adoption of "respect as motivation in our maxims" that "deserves the name of an aptitude for this purpose" (*RV* 27, 28).[56] It is this third aptitude that has reason as "unconditionally lawgiving for its root" (*RV* 28). The law itself is of course the fundamental assumption of Kant's moral philosophy (objectively speaking) and, as such, warrants the extent of the scholarship devoted to it. It is a given, nonderivable through rational inferences from human nature: "If this law were not

56. In the *Critique of Practical Reason,* the notion of "personality" is described as the conception of the person as a being "belonging to the sensible world, but as subject to one's true personality as belonging to the intelligible world (*KpV* 87).

given in us, we would not arrive at such through any subtle reasonings (*durch keine Vernunft herausklügeln*), nor foist it on the power of choice" (*RV* 26n).

In regard to the notion of character as the counterimage, then, the crucial point of unity that emerges from the preceding discussion is precisely between *reason as objective* (the fundamental assumption of the *factum der Vernunft*) and *reason as subjective* (as an aptitude of the rational animal, as which it already stands in relation with the remaining aptitudes and capacities of that being). We have come full circle to the essential question identified by Kant in the *Critique of Practical Reason* (*KpV* 151): how reason can become subjectively *practical*. For, it is in this further achievement (which, as we have seen, is synonymous with attaining a *free* power of choice) that objective and subjective are united as one. In the individual in whom this realization is met, the universal *is* the concretely realized, particular inner principle of the conduct of life. In a society governed by the completely just republican constitution (whose first principle is explicitly identified as the formal, moral principle, the categorical imperative, *F* 377), the universal is again realized as the supreme, particular principle uniting all others below it.

The force of necessity that is thereby brought to bear on the subjective capacities and conditions may be seen in a different light as a result of the account of the human aptitudes in general. The words of command and prohibition generally convey the image of an onerous taskmaster bearing down on the merely human. From the foregoing synopsis of the development of natural aptitudes as Kant understands the matter, it becomes clear that the force of necessity as such, opposition and resistance, are already inherent to the natural processes. Even, for example, in consideration of the more rudimentary (preconscious) levels of existence, these forces are unavoidable. The extra layer of feathers that ultimately becomes characteristic of a species of bird that now finds itself in a colder climate is a response to the necessity of the situation. When and where in life the adequate or appropriate response is not made, the organic being in an ultimate sense risks nothing less than self-preservation; that the response is made is a matter of an inherent aptitude. We have seen the explicit connection of this notion with character as the organization, or organized structure, of the organic being. The point is repeated in the *Critique of Judgment:* the hereditary character of organized species here too is said to indicate an "original, extant, purposive aptitude for self-preservation (*Selbsterhaltung*) of their kind" (*KU* 420).

Kant carries this motif of self-preservation over into both his moral thought and anthropological reflections.[57] In the *Metaphysical Principles of Virtue* he distinguishes between the "self-preservation of one's nature in its perfection," associated with the fulfillment of one's material duties to oneself, and "moral self-preservation," which is connected with formal principles of duty to oneself (*MST* 419). The latter is a matter of the "moral health (*ad esse,* for the being) of human beings, both as object of their inner and outer sense, so that their nature in its perfection (as receptivity) may be preserved" (*MST* 419). "Self-preservation of one's nature in its perfection" is a matter of "moral wealth (*ad melius esse,* for the better being; *opulentia moralis*); it consists in the possession of a capacity adequate for [realizing] all purposes . . . and belongs to the cultivation of the individual (as an active perfection)" (*MST* 419). In the *Anthropology,* Kant explains what is meant by procuring character (doing so, we recall, being characteristic of human beings in the "system of living nature") as follows: to have a character one has acquired for oneself is "to be capable of perfecting oneself in accordance with the purposes one has adopted for oneself." This in turn means that (1) one "maintains [or preserves] oneself and one's kind," (2) "practices, instructs, and disciplines" one's capabilities "for domestic social life," and (3) "manages (*regiert,* literally "rules") these as a systematic whole (ordered according to rational principles) appropriate for society" (*ApH* 321–22).

Character, then, not only of the physical order, but as the moral form of organization or structure of the human "system of powers (*Kräfte*)" as these are employed by reason, practical desire, and choice, likewise "indicates an original, extant, purposive aptitude for self-preservation (*Selbsterhaltung*) of their kind"; namely, the "germ of good" [Keim des Guten] whose uncovering and development in the nature of things takes place through the duress of both natural and practical necessity. All the human aptitudes, moreover, are classified by Kant as "original aptitudes for good." By implication, the potential for actively responding in general in a fitting way to new conditions includes the potential for responding in a fitting way to moral legislation. In short, seen in the light of the account of the human aptitudes, reason's causal, legislative activity presents human

57. Manfred Sommer, who reads Kant as having shown in exemplary fashion how the normative governance of our actions and the affirmation of contingency are systematically connected and how we can succeed in living with the contingent, interprets self-preservation as a fundamental principle of reason itself (*Identität im Übergang: Kant* [Frankfurt am Main: Suhrkamp Verlag, 1988]; see especially the chapters "Selbsterhaltung als rationales Prinzip" and "Mit dem Zufall leben").

choice specifically, and the other human capacities generally, with what is in its overall form a most familiar and indispensable situation: necessity, but now specified in a mode not otherwise found in nature.[58] Effectively, then, reason's authoritative exercise functions as the enabler of the realization of the potential already present. Under reason's initial awakening, human beings were enabled to choose their way of living (as we saw in the "Conjectural History"). Under the force of practical necessity, such choice is exercised in accordance with the overriding consideration that it be a good one. Thus the inherent capacity of the aptitudes for "directing" or "orienting" themselves (*sich richten, GTP* 173) is provided with a new direction or orientation that entails "a self-preservation of a completely different kind" (*KU* 261), namely, that of the individual and the species as moral being. We have, then, also finally gained a positive account of the constraint under which the unity of the inner principle of the conduct of life is forged.

Kant offers a portrayal of the individual in whom such unity reigns. On the side of conduct of thought, the steadfast commitment to certain practical principles constitutes "strength of mind" (*Seelenstärke*, literally "strength of soul").[59] When the sensibilities are good, these are characterized by "good-naturedness" or "friendliness" (*Gutartigkeit*). The union of such "kindheartedness" (*Seelengüte*, literally "goodness of soul") with "strength of mind" may be called "magnanimity" (*Seelengröße*, literally "greatness of soul"), albeit we are now referring to something that is "more ideal than real," just as good character in its strict sense is rarely found (*ApH* 291–93). Such "magnanimity" is identified too in the second *Critique* as that for which we see ourselves destined (*bestimmt*) (*KpV* 152). Moreover, such greatness of soul is said to constitute "abundant compensation" for the sacrifices that its independence from inclinations entails (*KpV* 152).

Thus far we have been referring to the "sensibilities" primarily in terms of just that general rubric. To continue to delve deeper into their relation to character, an identification of their components is needed. The human

---

58. It is interesting to note that one of the very first lessons that Jean-Jacques ensures that his student Emile learns is forbearance in the face of necessity. For example: "Let his haughty head at an early date feel the harsh yoke which nature imposes on man, the heavy yoke of necessity under which every finite being must bend" (*Emile,* 91). There are many important differences, of course, between Rousseau's and Kant's respective conceptions of this notion of necessity, but the attentiveness of both to this as a central issue is at least noteworthy.

59. In the *Metaphysical Principles of Virtue,* Kant employs this notion of strength of soul or mind (a strength of resolve) as a way of describing virtue. In the following chapter, we return to this point.

capacities on the side of the sensibilities given most discussion by Kant are feelings (in particular, of pleasure or displeasure), the inclinations (which are all said to "rest on feeling," *KpV* 74), passions, and the feelings referred to as the "aesthetic preconceptions of the responsiveness of the mind (*Gemüt*) for the concept of duty as such" (which include love of humanity, moral feeling, conscience, and respect for self, *MST* 399–403). In the *Anthropology*, Kant relates both the levels of nature (*Naturell*) and temperament (explicitly identified with *Sinnesart*) to the notion of a "good heart" and the feeling of pleasure or displeasure. The first (nature) is said to refer to how we are characteristically affected *by* others, the second (temperament) to how *we* affect others; it is related not only to inner feeling, but to the capacity of desire and manifests itself externally as activity (*Tätigkeit*) (*ApH* 286–87). The relation of character to the aesthetic capacities is quite involved and will be returned to a number of times in this study, with the first such discussion concluding this chapter. The inclinations too receive separate treatment as part of the explication of character and radical evil, but a few words are in order here to identify the main issue in regard to them.

The satisfaction of all the inclinations taken as a whole is called achieving happiness, and Kant's restriction of this endeavor of self-seeking to "rational self-love" is one of the more readily recognized concepts of his moral philosophy (*KpV* 73). Less clear is his affirmation of the inclinations as belonging to our natural aptitudes and thereby serving a role that is not to be ignored, or worse, thwarted altogether. We develop this point in our later chapters; here, the following third *Critique* passage is relevant for introducing Kant's conception of the requisite cultivation of the human aptitudes to make them fit for the fulfillment of our human purposes. While the cultivation of "skillfulness (*Geschicklichkeit*) is easily the foremost subjective condition of our fitness (*Tauglichkeit*) to further purposes in general," it is "not adequate for advancing the purposes determined by practical desire." The "condition" for "fitness for purposes" in the latter case may be called "cultivation by discipline" [Cultur der Zucht (Disciplin)]; it "is negative and consists in freeing volition from the despotism of the inclinations, due to which we, fixed upon certain natural things, are rendered unable to choose for ourselves, because we allow the instincts, given by nature only as guides so that we might *not neglect or even injure our animal nature (Bestimmung der Tierheit)*, to become our fetters"; when in fact we are free enough to adopt them or not, to extend or restrict them, in accordance with what best serves "reason's purposes" (*KU* 431–

32, emphasis added). Reason's purposes include, of course, the overall satisfaction of its demands, which, in both its speculative and practical functions, is "the absolute totality of conditions for a given conditioned thing" (*KpV* 107). Such an unconditioned totality for the "practically conditioned (which rests on the inclinations and natural needs [of human beings])" is the "object of pure practical reason, under the name of the highest good" (*KpV* 108), the synthetic unity of perfect virtue and complete happiness. Thus, what in earlier treatises appears as a provision in its structuring principle for the preservation of the organic body is later explicitly formulated as a maxim for action that we (as moral beings) are obligated to adopt, notably including the general maxim of cultivating all the powers of mind and body such that they are adequate for fulfilling *all* the purposes and situations that the living being might have to face (*MST* 392). Or, as another example, what on the one hand are natural provisions for guiding humanity to an organized whole under a republican constitution are again formulated as the explicit "duty to enter into such [a constitution]" (*SF* 91). For the moral being that finds itself necessitated to act under and through the conditions of the natural, organic being, the care of the latter is ipso facto its concern. Hence, for its free choice (which is "free" precisely in the sense that it is not determined by the inclinations and instincts), what is provided for in the direction inherent to the natural aptitudes, must now be recast as a consciously and freely adopted maxim.

As indicated by the foregoing passage from the *Critique of Judgment*, it is just the question of "determination" that is the crux of the issue. The independence from the inclinations that belongs to the magnanimous or great soul is *not* a flight from the sensible to the intelligible—such as explicitly called for by Socrates,[60] or as is characteristic of much of Stoicism's teachings; for example, Boethius's ascent to the citadel. The movement in Kant's thought is in the opposite direction, *from* the intelligible to the sensible, with a view to the relations that must obtain for the former's counterimage to be realized in and through the latter. The objective is the concrete actualization, the embodiment, of the intelligible. As Kant had already put it in 1766, the "higher ideas of reason" are to put on a "corporeal dress" (*TG* 339), and the result is at one and the same time an elevation of the sensible. Precisely therefore it is of the essence that voli-

---

60. For example, Socrates' exhortation in the *Theaetetus*: "evils . . . haunt mortal nature and this region here; it's for this reason that one ought to try to flee from here to there [among gods] as soon as possible. Flight is assimilation to a god as far as possible" (*Plato's Theaetetus*, trans. Seth Benardete [Chicago: University of Chicago Press, 1986], 176A–B).

tion not be *determined* (even if it necessarily remains affected) by the inclinations (*KpV* 117), which do not have inherent to them the practical necessity that is the hallmark of intelligible, moral form. An echo of this point appears as early as the 1755 *Universal Natural History,* in which he observes how difficult it is for most to gain "control, by free employment of [their] insights, over the propensity of the passions," and, yet, to fail to do so is also to fail to attain "the purpose of one's existence" (*NH* 356). In the *Anthropology,* Kant defines inclination (*Neigung, inclinatio*) as that desire [or appetite, *Begierde*] of our sensible nature which serves the subject as a rule or habit, while passion (*Leidenschaft, passio animi*) is an inclination that hinders reason in its function of making a choice from among the totality of all inclinations; or as he also puts it in *Religion within the Limits of Reason Alone,* inclination as passion "refuses to admit [any] control over itself" (*ApH* 265, *RV* 29n). This is the despotism referred to in the third *Critique,* and, in light of all that has been said, the problem with it is apparent. Where the "principle of independence" from such and, even more generally, "from all else besides the [moral] law" defines one's conduct of thought, "liberality (*liberalitas moralis*) of *Denkungsart*" has been achieved (*MST* 434). It is an attainment of a genuine freedom that, negatively construed, is a freedom from a "wild" state of freedom or "lawlessness"; the first step is to bring the inclinations under the governance of public law (*F* 357).

What is called for is the good-natured or friendly state of the inclinations that, formulated as a maxim of duty for human beings toward one another, is the "maxim of benevolence (*Wohlwollens*)" or "practical love for humanity" (*MST* 450ff.).[61] However, unlike his 1764 considerations, in his mature conception Kant does not accord the designation "good character," or even "character," to kindheartedness taken by itself (as simply characteristic of our inclinations). In the *Anthropology,* he goes so far as to say that in a choice between the alternatives of depravity of our sensibilities (or temperament) and their kindliness associated with a lack of character (understood in its strict sense and hence meaning a lack of firm principles or resolve), it is the *former* that is less grievous; for, without such principles (for example, the free and resolute adoption of the maxim of benevolence in one's conduct of thought), the requisite source of sovereignty over the sensibilities (to step in at any point that they are not so

---

61. Kant further specifies this overarching duty into the following threefold distinctions: beneficence (or acting on the behalf of others' well-being, *Wohltätigkeit*), gratitude, and sympathy (as it is usually translated, but which more literally means "participation," *Teilnehmung*).

inclined) too is lacking (*ApH* 293; see also *KpV* 155n).[62] It is the commitment by itself, the steadfastness and resoluteness of conduct of thought, the purely "formal [attribute] of volition" [Formelle des Wollens] that is decisive for character (*ApH* 292). It is the resoluteness that ensures that choice no longer wavers between hearkening to reason's command (imparted to it by practical desire) and the inclinations' demands. Where resoluteness characterizes the adoption of the moral law as the highest maxim, it is further characteristic of the capacity of choice consistently to choose from and in accordance with the moral law. This includes the resolute adoption of maxims that give formal expression to what the good moral state of the inclinations is and ought to be. The magnanimous soul thus entails the two general duties of respect for law and love of humanity, which are proper to morally good conduct of thought and the sensibilities respectively.[63] The conduct of thought in which these maxims are fundamental principles, which effects the "union of living well with virtue in human relations (*Umgange*)," and does so with these respective maxims rightly ordered, is called the *Denkungsart* of "humanity" (*ApH* 277).

The attainment of this union (rare as it is, as Kant notes several times) entails realizing the enlargement or expansion of human sensible nature beyond the instincts and inclinations—realizing the fulfillment, in other words, of the role we saw earlier being accorded to "reason in a living being" (*IG* 18). The aesthetic capacities, in particular the feeling of the

---

62. Kant repeats this point a number of times in his *Reflections on Anthropology* and very explicitly: "Morality in no way consists in the kindliness of the heart, but rather in a good character [that morality] is to cultivate" (*RA* no. 1179, 521; see also no. 1113, 496; no. 1156, 512; no. 1162, 514; no. 1165, 515; no. 1168, 516; no. 1218, 533; no. 1219, 534; no. 1232, 542). It is also for this reason that in the *Groundwork*, Kant gives subordinate importance to such "attributes of temperament" as "courageous spirit (*Mut*), determination (*Entschlossenheit*, also resolution), perseverance in one's resolve"; designated here as "natural gifts" (*Naturgaben*), the point is just that if practical desire were not good, then the use that it would make of these gifts would also not be good (*G* 393). Kant's later discussion of moral evil makes distinctions not captured in this 1785 passage; for a practical desire that would count as evil cannot (by his 1793 discussion) be found in anything other than a diabolical being. By more clearly delineating the problem in relation to that specification of volition termed the power of choice and by raising the issue of the latter's inherent propensity not to accord top priority to practical desire's command, that there be such resolve at all too becomes the central issue in conduct of thought. Kant does go on in the *Groundwork* just a few passages later to underscore that such "practical desire [that] is good in itself" is "*not* the only nor the complete [good], but it must be the highest good and the condition for all else, even all yearning for happiness" (*G* 396, emphasis added). This statement is in accord with the conception of character articulated in the present study; the aim here is to show what it is for this objective condition to be subjectively actualized.

63. These duties are again identified in *Toward Perpetual Peace* as the two with which politics (rightly understood and grounded on morality) must concern itself (*P* 385ff.).

beautiful and of the sublime, turn out to have a central role in relation to this enlargement and, hence, an important role in forging the unity of the inner principle of our conduct of life. Their relation to the conception of character is not limited to this, but to conclude our investigation of character and this unity, we now turn to this dimension of the role of aesthetic feeling.

CHARACTER AND THE AESTHETIC CAPACITIES OF FEELING

Kant's claims in regard to reflective judgment and the feeling of pleasure as middle terms between the sensible and supersensible (and the human capacities related to each respectively) are explicitly made in the introduction to the *Critique of Judgment*. The "power of judgment" (*Urteilskraft*) serves as a "middle term between the understanding and reason," with all three making up the "family of the higher cognitive capacities" (*KU* 177). Further, bearing in mind that the fundamental "capacities of soul" are threefold (the "capacity of cognition, feeling of pleasure and displeasure, and the capacity of desire"), we see that the "feeling of pleasure" found "between the capacities of cognition and desire" parallels the mediating role of judgment (*KU* 178). In general, what is at stake is the possibility of making the "transition from *Denkungsart* in accordance with the principles [of freedom] to that in accordance with the principles [of nature]"; since the "concept of freedom is to actualize in the world of sense the purpose enjoined by its law, we must therefore be able to think of nature as being such that the lawfulness of its form will harmonize with at least the possibility of effecting in her these purposes according to the laws of freedom" (*KU* 176). This statement, perhaps more directly than any other in Kant's writings, expresses what must be possible if character as the counterimage of the moral law is to be brought about in and through human, sensible nature. It articulates the problem to be solved in this regard, as it has become manifest in the presentation of the conception of character up to this point. In light of the attention in the *Critique of Judgment* to this problem, we may see this text as fulfilling a seminal role in Kant's moral thought; specifically, in relation to the task of reason becoming subjectively practical. Let us continue here, then, with a consideration of the role of aesthetic feeling as middle term, or literally reason's partner, in actualizing freedom's purposes and principles in human, sensible nature.

Previously, we have seen that to speak of the human, natural aptitudes is to refer to capacities inherently responsive in ways serving the living being's self-preservation and flourishing (if you will) in the face of changed external influences. This biological model, carried into Kant's moral thought in regard to character, through the continued use in the latter of the model's terminology, suggested a way of understanding human nature in terms of the anthropological question of its possibility of realizing moral universals in particular, concrete form, namely, by recognizing therein an inherent provision for responsiveness to the practical necessity that practical reason brings to bear. The human aesthetic capacities are even more explicitly described in terms of such responsiveness to moral determination. In this connection, the value of ascertaining a basis legitimate within the critical limits for ascribing purposiveness to nature is clear; the use of the biological language, particularly in regard to teleological judgment, too remains significant.

The most frequent, direct association made in the third *Critique* with character (that is, with character in its absolute sense as conduct of thought), however, is the feeling of the sublime. This relation is not new to the 1790 text. Already in his *Observations* (1764), Kant speaks of "true virtue," which "can only be grafted on principles that are the more sublime and noble, the more universal they are" (B 217ff.). In the *Critique of Practical Reason,* Kant observes that the moral law in its subjectively practical form as the "true motivation" that has its source in pure practical reason "allows us to perceive (*spüren*, literally "sense," "feel," or "get a taste of") the sublimity of our own supersensible existence" and "effects" (*wirkt*) within us, subjectively speaking, "respect for our higher vocation" (*KpV* 88). The repeated assertion in the *Critique of Judgment* is that the reference to the "sublime in nature" is misplaced. Truly speaking, the "sublime must always have reference to our *Denkungsart;* that is, to maxims that secure supremacy over sensibility for the intellectual and for the ideas of reason" (*KU* 274; see also 245, 246, 264, 265).[64] Or, in words that virtually echo the second *Critique,* "the feeling of the sublime in nature" is actually "respect for our own vocation" (*KU* 257).

Of importance in relation to the earlier discussion of practical necessity and the human response to its duress is that it is precisely the feeling of the sublime that manifests the double movement beginning from the negative feeling of displeasure on the side of sensibility and then, in a second step, culminating in a feeling of pleasure. Granted, strictly speaking, the "displeasure arises from the inadequacy of the imagination in its

---

64. Ronald Beiner explores this association of the sublime with our inherent moral nature in terms of the consequences for the human stance vis-à-vis nature ("Kant, the Sublime, and Nature," in Beiner and Booth, *Kant and Political Philosophy,* 276–88).

aesthetic estimation of magnitude" in comparison with such an "estimation by reason" (*KU* 257), but Kant himself draws the parallel with reason's subjection of sensibility to its moral determination. Human "lived morality" (*Sittlichkeit*) is, of course, the familiar case in which "reason must exert its dominance (*Gewalt antun*) over sensibility"; the difference from aesthetic judgment is that "in the judgment about the sublime, this dominance is presented as being exercised by the imagination itself," here construed as "reason's instrument" (*KU* 269). In general, "it is for us a law of reason and belongs to our vocation to estimate as small, in comparison with reason's ideas, everything found in nature that, as an object of sense, is large for us; and whatever arouses the feeling of this supersensible vocation in us agrees with that law" (*KU* 257). Indeed, the "feeling of the sublime in nature *is* respect for our own vocation," and the "substitution of respect for an object" for the respect for the "idea of humanity in ourselves" simply "makes intuitable as it were, the superiority of reason's determination . . . over the greatest capacity of sensibility" (*KU* 257, emphasis added; see also 262). That even the "greatest capacity of sensibility" is thus found "inadequate" is in "agreement with reason's ideas"; from this agreement with reason's laws and ideas ensues our feeling of pleasure (*KU* 257). To repeat, the "feeling of the sublime" is neither the product of culture nor a matter of convention; it "has its foundation in human nature . . . namely in the *aptitude* for a feeling for (practical) ideas, that is, for moral" feeling (*KU* 265, emphasis added).

Kant again restates the point in terms of the more general notion of being pleased (*Wohlgefallen*). The latter's object, intellectually speaking, is the "moral law in its might," a might that "reveals itself aesthetically only through sacrifice" (albeit one that "serves inner freedom"), and, hence, our sense of being pleased is "negative in relation to sensibility," but "positive considered from the intellectual side" (*KU* 271). This way of expressing the matter calls to mind the passage quoted previously from the second *Critique*, in which Kant asserts that greatness of soul or magnanimity provides "abundant compensation" for the sacrifices that its independence from inclinations entails (*KpV* 152). In fact, respect or moral feeling, as described in the *Critique of Practical Reason*, is just such a double movement. Displeasure is here a result of the humbling experience of falling short of the moral law considered either directly, or as manifest in the example of a just moral character; we naturally resist that to which we find we do not measure up. This resistance too is followed, once self-conceit is set aside, however, by a satisfaction (of which we cannot get enough) in the contemplation of the splendor of this law (*KpV* 77). In both texts, the negative is itself further accorded a positive function. The negative exhibition (*Darstellung*) of lived morality is said, in the third *Critique*, to serve to "avoid fanaticism"; that is, the "delusion of wanting to *see* something beyond all bounds of sensibility" (*KU* 275). As an "exhibition of the infinite" it can only be negative, but it remains "uplifting for the soul" (*KU* 274). In the second *Critique*, too, it is Kant's final position that the negative exhibition, that of the "law of duty that commands," is the "sole exhibition that cultivates the soul morally" (*KpV* 85). In short, the double movement of the feeling of displeasure and pleasure reinforces the point that moral determination is not simply felt as an onerous experience (as which it would entail an inner unity based on restraint and even coercion). Rather, in the feeling of the sublime, with its "attunement of mind (*Gemüt*)" that is "similar to that for moral" feeling (*KU* 268), we have an explicit manifestation of the capacity within human nature for responding positively to what, in relation to sensibility as such, is incommensurable and opposed to its interests.

Kant develops the point further. In the feeling of the sublime we find that which "repels sensibility" to be something that "at once attracts" us, because reason here "exercises its dominance solely in order to enlarge" the domain of sensibility "commensurate with its own practical domain" (*KU* 265). Hence, the exercise of causality that results in the production of character (in its wide sense in relation to our natural aptitudes) is ultimately attractive for us as human beings, due to the nature of the aesthetic response. Therefore, too, one can see the aesthetic capacity as literally a partner in reason's efforts to bring about this enlargement of sensibility, for the sake of producing within the latter the counterimage of the moral law. Moreover, in the recognition of a capacity within us that is superior to nature's might, we "discover at the same time a capacity" that is the basis of "a self-preservation of an entirely different kind than the one threatened by nature outside of us" (*KU* 261). It is different, in other words, from the one confronted by the vicissitudes of natural necessity. In and through aesthetic reflection we are "returned" so to speak from looking without, to reflection upon ourselves within; in just this turn we come to *feel* an appreciation for who and what we are, to feel the very dignity of our essential nature. The move is a characteristic one in Kant's philosophy. Only in and through the course of actual human experience can the grounds within us, which are the very basis of the possibility of that experience in its characteristic form, become perceptible for us. In the aesthetic contemplation of the starry heavens above us, with its felt sense of being overwhelmed by the forces of natural necessity that they represent, we are turned to an appreciative awareness of having within ourselves the source of a necessity different in kind, and, so too, an entirely different domain of existence comes into view for us.

Or, to put it in still another way, pleasure plays the role of middle term between reason and the capacity of desire just in relation to what is finally also the fundamental interest of the inclinations; namely, self-preservation and a desire for well-being. While reason determines volition through practical desire, the apparent rebuff to the inclinations' interests is translated into a newfound pleasure in service to an interest in a higher order of self-preservation. Nor is the aesthetic role in this regard limited to the feeling of the sublime, which, in the *Anthropology,* is described as the "counterbalance, but not the counteraction to the beautiful" (*ApH* 243). As early as the *Observations* (1764), Kant exhorts us to "consider the sensations of the sublime and the beautiful, above all insofar as they are moral" (*B* 220). The feeling of the beautiful is there said to be the basis of being generally well inclined to be friendly and kind (*allgemeinen Wohlgewogenheit*), while that of the sublime is the basis of "universal respect" (*B* 217). In 1790, Kant expresses a similar distinction: "The beautiful prepares us to love something, even nature, without interest; the sublime to esteem it even against our interest (of sense)" (*KU* 267). In the *Critique of Practical Reason,* Kant speaks of an "employment of judgment" that is "not yet an interest in actions and their morality"; it does, however, "give to virtue or *Denkungsart* in accordance with moral laws a form of beauty" that gives rise to "admiration," without yet therefore inspiring an effort "to seek it" (*KpV* 160). Here a two-step movement in the reverse order (from that which we saw in the feeling of the sublime) is called for; namely to get beyond a general sense of being pleased in which we remain indifferent to the existence of the object, to a felt realization of the positive worth of observing the law (*KpV* 160–61).

As Kant describes it in the *Critique of Judgment,* such pleasure arising from the judgment of taste in relation to conduct of thought (or character) nonetheless genuinely serves the latter as well. "Pleasure (*Lust*) in the beauty of nature," for example, "presupposes and cultivates a certain liberality of [our] *Denkungsart,* that is, independence of the sense of being pleased from mere sensual enjoyments (*Sinnengenusse*)" (*KU* 268). We have already seen the reasons for just such a need of freedom from the "despotism of the inclinations." Even more, through "the agreement of taste with reason, that is of the beautiful with the good, the former may be used as an instrument" on behalf of our "aims in regard to the good"; such use is achieved through the attunement of mind (*Gemüt*), which preserves itself and is subjectively universally valid, providing support for (literally, being laid under) that *Denkungsart* which can only be preserved (or sustained) through arduous resolve, but which is objectively universally valid (*KU* 230–31). Again, as Kant puts it in section 59, in his discussion of beauty as the symbol of the good, such a supportive attunement of mind is a consciousness "of a certain ennoblement and an elevation above the mere receptivity of pleasure from the impressions of the senses" (*KU* 353). The supportive relation is reciprocal: the "true propaedeutic to establishing taste is the development of moral ideas and the cultivation of moral feeling" (*KU* 356).

Of central importance for the elucidation of the relation of character and the human aesthetic capacities of feeling is just this: inner unity for our conduct of life is ultimately achieved, not in terms of a kind of defeat, or passive subordination of human nature to reason's causal exercise, but rather by a genuine, cooperative responsiveness that allows for a single, united effort in realizing moral form in its subjective, concrete actualization. In *Religion within the Limits of Reason Alone,* Kant takes the point one step further. "Frequently to arouse the feeling of the sublimity of one's moral (*moralischen*) vocation is to be recommended above all as a means for awakening the moral (*sittlicher*) *Gesinnungen;* for it acts (*wirkt*) just in opposition to the innate propensity for reversing the motive impulses in the maxims of our power of choice." Thus, it effectively acts "to reestablish, in the unconditioned respect for the law as the highest condition for adopting all maxims, morally [good] order among the motive impulses and, thereby [also to restore] the aptitude for good in its purity in the human heart" (*RV* 50).

Apart from this problem of radical evil (the perverse order of maxims and motive impulses), one might almost be tempted to begin to see the combined moral, anthropological, aesthetic, and biological dimensions involved in Kant's conception of character as lending themselves to an overall developmental account of a cooperative participation of the human aptitudes in the singular, moral purpose of human existence. On the preceding interpretation, even the duress of practical necessity has proven not to be a stumbling block in such a genuine, unified effort initiated by reason's legislation, but supported by inherent capacities of the human aptitudes. However, as the passage from Kant's 1793 text indicates, the complete story still remains to be told. The quote suggests the continued importance of the role of the aesthetic capacities. Yet in the identification of the real source and nature of the conflict (which must be dealt with if character as the subjective counterimage of objective morality is to be successfully realized), it becomes clear that the establishment of character is in fact a moral task to be explicitly adopted. It is, in the final analysis, itself the moral task of establishing peace in the inner principles of the conduct of life and, only thereby, ultimately forging their unity. It is to the conception of character as this task that we turn next.

❦ *3* ❦
Character and Radical Evil

STATUS OF MORAL EVIL IN KANT'S THOUGHT

Kant's notion of radical evil has been widely understood as a restatement of the Christian doctrine of the Fall, an interpretation evident in Goethe's negative reaction and persisting in the contemporary characterization of the notion as a "fallen freedom." Predictably, it has been criticized as an "incongruous result" in a moral philosophy whose central tenet is human autonomy.[1]

1. See Gordon E. Michalson's *Fallen Freedom: Kant on Radical Evil and Moral Regeneration* (Cambridge: Cambridge University Press, 1990). More recently, John E. Hare continues to interpret Kant's notions of "an original predisposition to the good, overlaid with an innate but imputable propensity to evil, which can be overcome only by a revolution of the will" as "replicating the structure of creation, fall, and redemption." Arguing further that Kant "translates these doctrines within the limits of the pure religion of reason," Hare concludes that Kant "is not able to make the translated doctrines do the work in his theory which he needs them to do" (*The Moral Gap: Kantian Ethics, Human Limits, and God's Assistance* [Oxford: Clarendon Press, 1996], 35). Rita Koppers treats the question of evil in terms of an issue of theodicy (*Zum Begriff des Bösens bei Kant* [Pfaffenweiler: Centaurs Verlagsgesellschaft, 1986]).
Interestingly enough, despite his criticisms of Kant elsewhere, Alasdair MacIntyre ("Can Ethics Dispense with a Theological Perspective on Human Nature?" in *The Roots of Ethics*, ed. Daniel Callahan [New York: Plenum Press, 1976], 122–28) finds Kant to be superior to Aristotle precisely in this point: the absolute and unconditional moral order in which "evil is the concept of that which is absolutely prohibited. No reason of any kind can justify or excuse the doing of evil. . . . An evil person is not just someone who has not yet approached the good closely enough; he or she is someone engaged in an attempt to disrupt the whole moral order by setting him- or herself and others to move in the opposite direction. . . . Kant's conception of moral progress is inseparable from his conception of the radical evil in human nature. . . . depravity lies in [persons] deliberately preferring other maxims to those of morality. . . . Within the framework of law and civility the individual progresses toward moral perfection. . . . Kant's moral philosophy thus has kinship to a whole family of narrative portrayals of human life. . . . Only if I place my own physical survival lower on the scale of values than other goods, can my self be perfected. Teleology has thus been restored, but in a form very alien to either Aristotle's thought or Mill's. It is no wonder that Kant finds in Greek ethics no adequate conceptual scheme for the representation of morality, but views Christianity as providing just such a scheme."

Kant's language, the references to "innate sin" or "guilt," provides good reason for beginning with such assumptions.[2] Moreover, in the relevant passages Kant himself draws parallels between his philosophy and biblical teachings. Less attended to, however, is the fact that he equally makes such comparisons with respect to his formal, moral philosophy (and not simply in regard to the postulates). In the second *Critique* he notes that the possibility of being commanded as we are by the law of the New Testament harmonizes with the conception of ourselves as subjects in a realm of morals, in which our relation to the moral law is characterized by duty and indebtedness (*KpV* 82–83). Further, this command of the Gospels is held by Kant to "exhibit the moral *Gesinnung* in its complete perfection" (*KpV* 83).

The use of the theological language and the parallels drawn in 1793 do not, then, necessarily signal a belated turn to admit orthodox, theological conceptions of human nature, nor is the significance of these allusions self-evident. The question to be asked is whether any internal connections may be seen between Kant's foregoing moral and anthropological reflections and the extended discussion of moral evil presented in his 1793 work. What emerges from the discussion in this chapter is that, if one approaches this topic from the standpoint of Kant's account of character, one finds a number of other important elements playing a significant role in the conception and introduction of the problem of evil in his writings. That is, aspects arising from within Kant's thought, rather than a theological doctrine imported from outside it, come into view. The topic is not

---

2. The most obvious examples, of course, are found in *Religion within the Limits of Reason Alone: peccatum originarium, angeborne Schuld (reatus), culpa, dolus, dolus malus,* the "foul spot of our genus" (31, 38). Moreover, Kant writes that in "moral instruction" we cannot take "natural innocence" as our point of departure; rather, we must begin from the assumption of the "viciousness of the power of choice in the adoption of its maxims" (*RV* 51). However, similar references are found both before and after the 1793 text. In the *Critique of Practical Reason,* Kant explores the notion of a "born villain" whom he deems equally responsible for, guilty of, his transgressions as any other human being; for all human beings, the free causality that is the ground of such actions is said to manifest "its character in the appearances of the actions from early youth on" (99–100). A discussion similar in spirit is found in the *Critique of Pure Reason,* where Kant distinguishes our fundamental responsibility based on our intelligible nature from what can be traced to empirical influences (*KrV* A555/B583). The "Conjectural History" (1786) reads as a philosophical interpretation of Genesis; the "moral of the story" is expressed in the statement that "human beings must wholly ascribe to themselves the blame for all ills arising from the misuse of their reason" (123). In 1798 Kant still speaks of "sin," of the "viciousness of human nature," which has made "penal law necessary," while on the other hand "Grace"—through the medium of "faith," the "original aptitude for good in us," and the "hope animated in the example of humanity pleasing to God in the Son of God"—is to prevail when we "allow the *Gesinnungen* of a conduct of life (*Lebenswandels*) comparable to this holy example to become active" in us (*SF* 43).

restricted to Kant's *Religion* of 1793. A discussion of the nature of evil is found in his writings as much as thirty years earlier, and observations made in 1763 are repeated as late as 1797 in *Metaphysical Principles of Virtue*. Distinct Rousseauian motifs characterize his position, which may further be seen in terms of an explicit response to certain aspects of the philosophical conversation of the time. Among the elements of Kant's account of character we have seen thus far, of particular importance to its connection with the problem of moral evil are the distinction between subjective and objective reason, the centrality of the power of choice, the notion of what it is to be a genuine actor in the world, and the biological concepts informing Kant's understanding of human nature.

We will begin, then, with an overview of this wider context, in order to convey a sense of the complexities involved in Kant's concept of moral evil and to suggest ways it is intrinsically connected with these dimensions of his philosophy. The subsequent, more detailed examination is divided into three parts. The first reviews Kant's account of all forms of human conflict as the manifestation of the root of evil in human character. Second, Kant's sense of virtue (as identified with the embattled comportment of mind) is reconsidered in this light, with particular emphasis on the meaning of virtue as progress or advance. Finally, the relation between the moral task of establishing character and that of establishing both inner and outer peace in human life is examined.

Establishing character, as we have learned, entails reason becoming subjectively practical, which is in turn synonymous with attaining a free power of choice. This task is of the essence if morality is to be concretely realized in the world, but we must first ask how its attainment is possible; these are the essential issues identified by Kant in the *Critique of Practical Reason*. As such a task, as something first to be achieved by human effort, the problem is not one of a "fallen" freedom, but of the possible and necessary translation of objective freedom into its subjective counterpart. It must be underscored that the integrity of objective, legislative reason, the ground of human freedom, remains intact. The achievement on the subjective side too is not a matter of recovering a lost status, but of something to be first realized as a result of human effort. This effort is understood in terms of a long line of development from childhood to maturity (speaking here both figuratively and literally). As Kant articulates it in the *Religion*: the "root (*Grund*) of this evil" can lie neither in "human sensibility" (*Sinnlichkeit*) and its "inclinations," nor in "a corruption of morally legislative reason" (*RV* 32–34). To attribute it to the former would be "too little," for the level of sensibility is only that of our aptitudes for animality, while a reason that releases itself from the moral law is too much; it would make of the subject a "diabolical being" (*RV* 34). Thus neither our inclinations, nor our moral capacity objectively considered, as author of the moral imperative and our power of practical desire determined by reason, is at issue. Rather, this propensity is "rooted in" and "interwoven with" our "*subjective highest basis*" of the adoption of "all maxims," our power of choice (*RV* 32, emphasis added). With this statement, Kant has squarely identified moral evil as a problem of moral character—as a problem for the realization of the subjective counterimage of morality in the world.

For it to arise as such a problem, however, presupposes also a capacity with which it stands at odds. In his essay on the relation of theory and praxis published in the same year as his *Religion within the Limits of Reason Alone*, Kant explicitly raises the question of the good that one may or may not expect of and love in a human being. The answer, he writes, involves addressing another question: "Are there aptitudes [found] in human nature that allow us to conclude that the race [as a whole] will always progress toward the better and that the evil of present and past times will disappear in the good of the future?" (*TP* 307).[3] This notion of an *aptitude* for good, a germ or rudiment of good inherent to human nature, is by now familiar to us as an essential aspect of Kant's conception of human nature expressed in terms of his biological model. It shares the stage of the discussion (in the *Religion*) of the equally inherent propensity for evil

---

3. It is perhaps on this point regarding human goodness, or at least its possibility, that Hannah Arendt most definitively parts company with Kant (despite the fact that she develops her own account of the intrinsic connection between moral good and evil and the human activity of thinking). Not only is Arendt highly uncomfortable with the *Critique of Practical Reason* and its legislative conception of practical reason (including, of course, the categorical imperative itself), but while Kant sees it as the highest human duty to perform the work necessary to make good human beings out of ourselves, Arendt interprets goodness (including good works) as having an essentially otherworldly quality. Hence on her reading it is a fundamental "insight that no man can be good" and that "[g]oodness, therefore, as a consistent way of life, is not only impossible within the confines of the public realm, it is even destructive of it" (*Human Condition*, 75, 77). Certainly, for Arendt, wrongdoing is directly destructive of the fabric of human relations, but her "moral category" (if one might call it that) is forgiveness. In this same work she identifies the faculties of forgiving and of promise making as redemptions (for action's predicaments of irreversibility and unpredictability) indispensable for the continuity and durability of human relations qua human (*Human Condition*, 236–37). Arendt writes of the "darkness of each man's lonely heart, . . . a darkness which only the light shed over the public realm through the presence of others, who confirm the identity between the one who promises and the one who fulfills, can dispel" (*Human Condition*, 237). While Kant (in a virtual echo of the early lines of Rousseau's *Emile*) asserts that in the case of human works one must begin with the presupposition of evil (that what begins with the hands of man is evil, while what begins from God is good), the presupposition of a "germ of good" (*Keim des Guten*) inherent to human nature, which it is our duty to nurture into the realization of the mature, good human being, carries equal weight.

(for example, *RV* 38), but as an aptitude it is more fundamental than a mere propensity. The latter is the "subjective ground of the possibility of an inclination" or "habitual desire"; or speaking more generally, it is "only the predisposition to desire something pleasurable," and once experienced, it further produces an "inclination" for such an object (*RV* 28–29, 28n). The aptitude for good, by contrast, refers to an original endowment of our human nature, a capacity of responsiveness for good in the given circumstances of life. While in general, as we have seen, all human aptitudes count as aptitudes for good, Kant also specifies the latter more precisely in his *Religion* as the ability of even the most limited individuals or of children for (1) ever greater respect for a lawful action, the more they distinguish in thought its motivations from those based on the maxim of self-love and (2) discerning what motivations inform a given action (*RV* 48). Or, to define it more narrowly, the germ of good is our aptitude for personality, our aptitude for responsiveness as respect for the moral law. As Kant also puts it later, it is a "natural aptitude" that, as it were, is "entrusted" to us, and thus it is incumbent upon us to cultivate and employ it (*RV* 161).

In his references to this cultivation occur the most striking parallels between Kant's and Rousseau's portrayals of good and evil in human life and nature. For example, in "Conjectural Beginning of Human History" we read that the "history of nature begins from the good, for it is the work of God, the history of freedom from evil, for it is the work of humanity" (*M* 115). The opening lines of book 1 of *Emile* proclaim, "Everything is good as it leaves the hands of the Author of things; everything degenerates in the hands of man. . . . He wants nothing as nature made it, not even man; for him, . . . man must be fashioned . . . like a tree in his garden. Were he not to do this, however, everything would go even worse, and our species does not admit of being formed halfway."[4] This latter qualification is the one to be attended to: human development is inextricably linked with, even held to be dependent upon, the evils that are part

---

4. *Emile*, 37. Rousseauian echoes in Kant's position go beyond this example. Consider the following passage from the *First Discourse*: "It is a grand and beautiful sight to see man emerge from obscurity somehow by his own efforts; dissipate, by the light of his reason, the darkness in which nature had enveloped him; rise above himself; soar intellectually into celestial regions; traverse with giant steps, like the sun, the vastness of the universe; and—what is even grander and more difficult—come back to himself to study man and know his nature, his duties, and his end. All of these marvels have been revived in recent generations" (Jean-Jacques Rousseau, *The First and Second Discourses*, ed. Roger D. Masters, trans. Roger D. Masters and Judith Masters [New York: St. Martin's Press, 1964], 35). In his "Conjectural History," Kant makes explicit references both to Rousseau's *Emile* and his *Second Discourse* (*M* 116).

of its history. Parallel expressions are found in Kant's *Critique of Judgment*, as well as in his essays regarded as his philosophy of history; namely, that the conflicts (including war) resulting from the propensity for evil are themselves to be construed as means employed by nature precisely on behalf of the realization of human moral purpose, of the attainment of highest good. That this history of the human race serves the outright "perfectibility" of human nature, in particular the aim "to perfect human reason," is an interpretation shared by Kant and Rousseau.[5] In "Conjectural Beginning of Human History," Kant goes so far as to criticize those who yearn for some so-called golden age, for a time of instinct and natural impulses viewed as the pure pleasure of a carefree existence. Such an age, for Kant, predates the all-important realization of the human as actor; it is a time before the realization of free choice in one's conduct of life. "Reason," he writes, will "remind" those catering to such a wish "to give life worth through actions" (*M* 122). Just what one is to make, then, of this notion of evil is complicated further by the apparent outright contradiction both with Kant's own statements and with the Rousseauian viewpoint when Kant (for example) also chides Rousseau and others for their "heroical view" of the world as unceasingly moving from a worse to a better state (*RV* 19–20). Whatever may thus be meant too by the notion of "advance" or "progress," it cannot be perpetual in the sense of persisting uninterruptedly in the events of time; historical facts speak otherwise. Kant explicitly acknowledges that regress is part of world events, that a given revolution or reform could very well be followed by a return to a former status quo (for example, see *SF* 88).

Yet Kant also expressly rejects Mendelssohn's position, describing the latter's argument with Lessing against the perfectibility thesis as a concession to the "stone of Sisyphus" (*TP* 307). Thus to conceive of humanity oscillating continually back and forth between fixed bounds, only to remain ultimately at the same "level of lived morality" and, more, to hold that the facts of history serve as evidence that such a state of affairs must have been condoned as part of the providential plan for the world (as Mendelssohn claims), flies in the face of Kant's understanding of what it is to be a genuine actor (*tätiges Wesen*) in the world (*TP* 308). He writes simply, "I am of a different opinion," noting that even if mere stage actors (fools) were to put on such a display, of every advance in virtue perpetually followed by an equal or even further regress into vice and misery, the

---

5. Rousseau's *Discourse on the Origin of Inequality* is very explicit on this point; see Jean-Jacques Rousseau, *Basic Political Writings*, trans. Donald A. Cress (Indianapolis: Hackett, 1987), 59.

audience (well-thinking, ordinary individuals) would soon cease to find the portrayal instructive and respond with ennui to such eternal monotony (*TP* 308). Such a state of oscillation, we recall, is effectively to be at a standstill, that is, not to be engaged in what counts for Kant as the activity proper to the human species. As noted previously, not even an initial state of innocent oneness with nature (as described in the "Conjectural History" and as would typify the arcadian form of life already rejected by Kant in 1764) could qualify as desirable, precisely because it is not yet to be an actor; the latter requires the awakening of reason.

At stake, then, is just this notion of the human actor, but upholding it turns out to be problematic. From our previous conclusions, we know that the notion is bound up with the self-preservation of the human as a moral species, conceived as a formation of moral character in a manner analogous to the development of the character of a human race on the biological model. To defend the notion (so conceived) philosophically requires an account of some form of genuine progress (in contrast to the perpetual seesaw between vice and virtue with which human history prima facie confronts us), but it also entails taking into account humanity's empirical history. As late as 1798, Kant candidly concedes (as he had already done in the *Groundwork*) that he "blames no one, in the face of the ills" perpetrated by the nation-states, "for beginning to despair of the well-being of the human race and of its progress toward a better" condition (*SF* 93; compare *G* 407). He makes his own appeal for not likewise despairing in terms of his biological model. From its standpoint, responsiveness to necessity (in this case the practical necessity presented by reason) is either successful and hence represents a real advance in the development of the organizational structure of the organism, or its failure ushers in the demise of the individual and the species (in this case as moral being). In his reflections on the French Revolution, Kant appeals (as he had also done in 1793) to the manifestation of the aptitude for good in human nature, in effect declaring that the requisite organizational structure has indeed irrevocably thus shown itself: an "aptitude and capacity in human nature for the better has been uncovered" that "unites nature and freedom in accordance with inner principles of justice in the human species," and so one can expect, when future circumstances are again fortuitous, that repeated efforts will be made to institute a just constitution (*SF* 85–88).[6] The uncovering of the inherent aptitude of the human spe-

---

6. For a discussion of Kant's response to the French Revolution in terms of "the art of interpreting historical events," see Rudolf Makkreel, *Imagination and Interpretation*, 149–51.

cies and its appearance as a concrete historical fact provide Kant with a basis for what he calls his "philosophical prophecy," namely, that the advance here made will not be wholly undercut and lost, that an elevated, permanent level has been achieved in the unfolding of humanity's capacities for the better (*SF* 88–89).

If he thus finds reason not to despair, Kant must nonetheless address the fact that unlike a purely biological aptitude, whose appearance heralds a steady and *hereditary* manifestation in present and future surviving members of the species, the history of the manifestation of the aptitude for good is in fact a very turbulent one. Why do the *appearances* of human history not present a straight line of development, given that both the objective (legislative reason) and subjective (aptitude for good) conditions are in place? How does moral transgression, apparent regress in human moral affairs, continue to be possible? The Rousseauian route of locating the source of the problem externally in society would be to deny individual human freedom for good. In light of both Kant's position on moral autonomy (freedom of self-legislation) and his account of character, his identification and placement of the source of the problem is ultimately not surprising.

The account of human moral character has all along indicated that the question of subjectively practical reason, that is, of the human subjective use of freedom, is just what is at issue. As we have seen, the positive account of the unity of objective and subjective and, hence, of the latter's concrete actualization of the former entails the unity of the modality of human desire, namely, that what human volition itself *wants* is first and foremost to be in agreement with the law. The "true enemy" of the good, what can truly said to be evil, is just a *Gesinnung* so oriented that when an "inclination entices one to the commission of a transgression" against the law, one "does *not want* to resist" the inclination (*RV* 58n). As essentially the spirit characterizing the "subjective highest basis" of the adoption of "all maxims," as the moral quality of our power of choice, the notion of comportment of mind expresses the subjective state or condition of this capacity as distinguished from the activity of maxim adoption identified with conduct of thought. Commentators have found Kant's distinctions here to be puzzling at best and useless at worst, and, indeed, the line being drawn is a fine one.[7] Is it overly subtle, tantamount to what Kant himself often enough criticizes as mere hairsplitting, or can it be seen to perform

---

7. For a discussion of the questions raised, see Allison, *Kant's Theory of Freedom*, 138ff.

some actual work when considered from the standpoint of his conception of character?

This much can at least be said thus far. While Kant makes proportionately more use of the notion of comportment of mind in his reflections on the problem of moral evil than in other texts, it is nonetheless not a new term either in his writing, or in the ordinary use of the language. With his appeal to this notion, Kant stays focused on the problematic of the "subjective basis of the use of our freedom" (*RV* 21) and seeks to avoid the two undesirable alternatives of (1) giving up freedom subjectively speaking, which would be the result of construing choice as determined by the object of one's inclination, or (2) giving up the very possibility of freedom to choose for the good, which would be the result of construing the problem as the adoption of the maxim to make evil (the perverse order of maxims) itself the motivating ground of the adoption of our maxims; such an order of perversity is no longer human, but diabolical (*RV* 21, 37).[8] Both of these alternatives would point to real regress, to an undoing of human capacities for the good. Kant's conclusion as to what the root of evil must then consist in, put into the terms of his conception of character, might read as follows.

The comportment of mind named as the "true enemy" is a, qualitatively speaking, moral perversity, literally a perversity of the spirit of mind we bring to choosing, and (as is generally known) it consists in and manifests itself as an inverted order (morally speaking) of the maxims in accordance with which choice is executed. The power of choice itself is a specification of our capacity of volition, and such an inherent propensity for evil attaching to it thus constitutes a predisposition of our volition to direct its responsiveness to the inciting inclination, instead of being of one voice (*einstimmig*) with the determination of practical desire. Where choosing is done in such a spirit, it constitutes in fact a failure in the subjectively practical employment of reason to make use of and foster our inherent aptitude for good (narrowly defined, as we have seen). Thus, and this has received little attention by Kant's readers, it is a failure that not only leaves the objective principle of morality concretely unrealized, but also leaves the potential of the natural human aptitude(s) for good unrealized. It is, of course, a failure, too, that manifests the absence of morally good charac-

---

8. Kant repeats this point in the *Anthropology* where he puts it as follows: one cannot say that "someone's malevolence is a property of their character, for then it would be diabolical; human beings never sanction evil in themselves and so there is actually no such thing as malevolence based on principles; rather [it can only be based] on a forsaking of principles" (*ApH* 293–94).

ter (in its absolute sense); where the spirit of the law is not embodied by the actual maxims adopted, there has also been no firm resolve on the part of the conduct of thought to make the law itself the condition of all maxim adoption. Put in terms of Kant's three maxims of the sound human understanding, where such unanimity of thought is lacking, the third maxim, reason's maxim of the resolute conduct of thought, also is lacking. In the language of the *Critique of Pure Reason,* what can be said in retrospect is simply that "a different intelligible character would have yielded a different empirical one."

In his *Religion,* Kant speaks of this problem as the "battle of the good principle with evil" and identifies this so-called battle as that of an "intelligible moral relation" whose historical and pictorial representation has been given in the images of heaven and hell (*RV* 78). What exactly is this relation as Kant understands it? Between what parties does it obtain? The duality of the laws of freedom and of nature prima facie would have made it easy for Kant simply to follow the model of outright opposition of reason and passion that characterizes in one form or another so many ethical theories. The conclusion to the third antinomy, however, namely that these laws are *not* contraries of one another, in effect already heralds the direction Kant takes (or one can even say, "must take" for the sake of consistency) in locating and articulating moral evil. The Pauline model (for example)—"I see in my members another law at war with the law of my mind"[9]—stands at odds with the entire account of the synthetic unity of causality, in which the direction or orientation of the law of freedom is given to empirical causality to guide the latter's activity toward the realization of moral purpose. In this unity, as we have seen, reason's causality is not to be understood as standing in competition with inclinations and impulses deriving from our natural aptitudes, or foregoing states of affairs in life; reason is viewed as "complete in itself." In short, Kant's doctrine of freedom, of the *factum der Vernunft,* not only remains fundamental to his account; it is the very basis on which moral good and evil as Kant construes them are first possible. The challenge in articulating what is meant by this assertion lies in restating what is largely familiar Kantian doctrine in a way that sheds some new light on it. We will start by reviewing our interpretation of the meaning of subjectively practical reason.

To call reason "practical" is to say that it is directly determinant of volition and that, as practical desire, it determines choice. To call reason "subjectively practical" is to say that it has procured for itself an empirical

9. Romans 7:23.

character, that is, a regularity manifesting the law of freedom in appearances that, in their relations to one another, are determined by the laws of nature. This empirical character is just what we call the free power of choice; it is the actualized synthetic unity of causality. As nothing but a "certain causality of reason," to speak of free choice is to say that reason now "acts in the place of a natural cause" in the world, that reason has procured for itself efficacious causality *in* the world (and not simply a legislative relation *to* the world). As a specification of volition, choice qua volition determined by reason has *acquired the latter's characteristic freedom; that is, the power of self-legislation (*autonomia*). Just so we find Kant describing the power of choice: as "making a rule for itself for the use of its freedom" (*RV* 21). Thus to have acquired this capacity of rule making means that the power of choice cannot be dictated to, determined by the inclinations. What does, however, attach to this power of self-legislation subjectively actualized as choice is the permanent possibility of its freely adopting, as its own highest maxim guiding choice, a motivating impulse whose source is the inclinations.

The moral relation at issue, then, is that of the exercise of this acquired power of making a rule for itself—how it actually relates itself to available maxims it may adopt to guide or orient choice making. Or as Kant so often puts it, it is the issue of the subjective use of our freedom. Through the actual acts of choice making, the power of choice itself acquires the moral comportment (*Gesinnung, sittliche Haltung*) of the spirit of the maxims it has adopted in its acts of choosing. For maxims are not only principles of actions, but constitutive principles formative of character. Thus, where the subjective power of self-legislation is used in accord with the propensity to direct its response to an inciting inclination, the result is a comportment of mind that does not *want* to offer resistance to an inciting inclination, rather than the morally requisite "subjective perfection of the capacity of choice," of its proficiency (*habitus*) in moral choice making (*MST* 407). Such a comportment of mind is the freely self-acquired "true enemy" of the morally good subjective employment of freedom, a perversity that attaches to the internal moral relation at the very heart of character as the subjective counterimage of objective morality.

That such a perversity constitutes a "real opposition" and not merely a deficiency, lack, or weakness relates to Kant's conception of the human as actor. As he repeats the point in the *Religion*, human beings cannot "through any cause in the world cease to be beings" capable of "acting freely" (*RV* 41). By definition, in such a being endowed with the ground of freedom, with an inner moral law, the failure to act in conformity with that law is ipso facto an act against the law. Kant had already given explicit expression to this claim in *Attempt to Introduce the Concept of Negative Magnitudes into the Philosophy of Nature*, from 1763. In the course of his critique of Maupertuis's attempt to calculate the sum of human happiness, he writes that the "error" that has spelled the "ruin of many a philosopher" is the failure to make the distinction between the notions of negation, or lack, and deprivation, or the positive ground of real opposition (*NG* 182). On this basis Kant here distinguishes two kinds of evil: the evil of the lack or absence of a good (*mala defectus*) and the evil of deprivation, of taking away an extant good (*mala privationis*). The latter is the "far greater evil," for it is the concept of a "real opposition." Vice (*Untugend, demeritum*) falls under this latter category; it is not a mere lack or absence of good because it can "only occur insofar as there exists in a being an inner law," a "positive ground of good action," against which that being's actual conduct stands in direct opposition. An animal lacking reason acts neither virtuously nor viciously, for in its nature there exists no inner (moral) law in conformity with, or in opposition to which, an action is carried out (*NG* 182–83). In *Metaphysical Principles of Virtue*, from 1797, Kant again refers to virtue and vice in these terms, describing vice as a "contrary" or "real opposition" (*MST* 384).[10] Thus we can see that Kant's conception of moral evil begins with his early conclusions of 1763 that "the concept of real opposition has its useful application in practical wisdom" and that the "state" of mind or spirit (*Geistes*), unlike matter, "can be altered by internal causes" (*NG* 182, 192). By 1793 an internal cause has become *the* issue: not only is it the central problem for moral character, but Kant further comprehends all human conflict as a manifestation of this inner root of opposition to moral good. Thus the establishment of good moral character is also ultimately of central importance to the solution of conflict in all its forms in human life.

HUMAN CONFLICT: ITS FORMS AND THEIR ROOT IN CHARACTER

Kant goes so far as to assert that the very "multitude of flagrant examples" found in human experience of this "corrupt propensity rooted in human nature" allows one to dispense with a "formal proof" (*RV* 32–33). He concludes his list of these examples with the observation that the civilized

---

10. In his "Reflections on Moral Philosophy" Kant makes a similar point: "Moral failures are actions [literally "works," *Tätigkeiten*] that [stand] in real opposition to impulses to certain actions" (*Ak* 19, no. 6647, 124).

nations continue to relate to one another at the level of the brutish state of nature (a state of continual war) (*RV* 34). He repeats the point about this most obvious example, of war among the nation-states and its moral, philosophical significance, in essays about the relation of theory and practice (1793) and about the concept of perpetual peace (1795). "Human nature nowhere appears less lovable than in the relation of entire peoples with one another" (*TP* 312). This "depravity of human nature" is openly visible in the free relations of people (outside of the constraints of a civil constitution), that is, in the "state of nature," which is a "state of war" with its, at the very least, "perpetual threat of hostilities," even when such "have not openly broken out" (*F* 355, 348–49). "If one were still to doubt that a certain depravity rooted in human nature" is to be met with "in those living together within a state, and if, instead, one were tempted to point to the shortcomings of an insufficiently advanced culture (brutishness) as the cause of the appearances of unlawfulness in their *Denkungsart*," one would certainly have to acknowledge this depravity "in the foreign relations of states toward one another," for there it "is apparent in a completely unconcealed and incontrovertible way" (*F* 375n). In this later essay, Kant also again finds a basis for asserting evidence of the human aptitude or germ of good.[11] The "tribute that each state (at least verbally) pays to the concept of justice surely proves that a still greater (albeit presently dormant) moral aptitude is to be found in the human being," an aptitude for "finally mastering the evil principle within" (a principle this being "cannot disavow") and "for hoping that others too" will master it (*F* 355).

To see how Kant understands this asserted link between external conflict among whole peoples and the inner root of moral evil in human nature, or even how internal conflict is to be understood, we will examine each of the manifestations of conflict he identifies in order to address three questions. How does Kant's conception of practical reason, objectively and subjectively speaking, inform his understanding of how inclinations and passions function in the human being? How do the inclinations, which play a central role particularly in external human conflicts, remain exonerated from moral culpability (strictly speaking)? How is it that the internal, intelligible moral relation is fundamental to all others? The inquiry leads us to see that this dimension of Kant's examination of human moral character, its inherent problem of evil, constitutes a major part of his own

---

11. As noted previously, it is in his 1793 and 1795 writings on religion and perpetual peace that Kant expressly combines the notions of germ and good in the phrase *Keim des Guten*.

systematic, philosophical connection between his formal moral philosophy and its further account as a "lived morality" in actual human social and political contexts.

In the first place, it must be remembered that choice making as such is a rational exercise and that simply to be a rational animal is not yet, as we have seen, to be the morally accountable rational animal. "The most rational worldly being could after all require certain motivations stemming from objects of inclination in order to determine its choice" and "apply thereto the most rational deliberations . . . without having any inkling . . . of even the possibility of something like a moral, absolutely commanding law" (*RV* 26n). Kant's note here underscores the point raised previously in regard to the human as a genuine actor; without the prior assumption of the moral law, the discussion of moral evil as Kant construes it could not take place at all. Hence, too, one cannot speak of the propensity for evil in connection with the capacity of choice insofar as the latter pertains to the human being as a natural being (*RV* 31). Only when the question is that of human moral character conceived as the subjective counterimage of objective practical reason realized in and through the capacity of choice is there even a context for the issue of a ground of formal opposition to the morally good.

In this light too, Kant's three gradations of the "ability or inability of the power of choice to adopt the moral law in its maxims" may be understood as follows (*RV* 29–30). The first two levels (of sheer weakness or frailty and of impurity of the moral condition of the power of choice) both admit the appropriate maxim but lack precisely the quality of resoluteness essential to character in its absolute sense. Hence, either the morally appropriate execution of choice does not occur, or it does so only when bolstered by compatible motive impulses drawn from the objects of choice. At the third level, the propensity for evil has been actualized as a formal condition of depravity of the power of choice. What makes the difference whether someone is "good or evil does not lie in a difference in the motive springs taken up in one's maxims . . . but in their order of subordination (in their form)" (*RV* 36). This morally corrupt order (as we already know from the second *Critique*) is to make the "motive spring of self-love" the "condition for the observance of the moral law" (*RV* 36, 45). Even if, under such conditions, an action were to result which externally (legally) conformed to the law, the "*Denkungsart* is thereby corrupted in its root (in what pertains to the moral *Gesinnung*), and the person is therefore designated as evil" (*RV* 30, 36; see also 21, 51).

Just as reason's formal determination has a material consequence in the world, where that determination is in default (as we have seen Kant elsewhere characterize the act of moral transgression), a material effect results. The intelligible act itself, as "that use of freedom . . . whereby the highest maxim (commensurate with or contrary to the law) is taken up in the power of choice" (*RV* 31), when considered in relation to the law lies outside the conditions of time. For as we saw in the case of "timelessness" in reference to character as conduct of thought, temporal differences are irrelevant for considerations of the nature of the "relation in which an action stands to reason" (*KrV* A556/B584). The perverse use of freedom as an "original act (*peccatum originarium*)" thus defined in relation to reason is, in turn, the "formal ground of the second sense of all actions contrary to the law . . . known as vices (*peccatum derivativum*)"; the latter are "sensible, empirical, given in time (*factum phaenomenon*)" and represent the conflict with the moral law "materially considered" (*RV* 31). At one level, Kant's conclusion here seems straightforward enough—within the context, that is, of his intelligible/empirical distinction. In a deeper sense, however, the statement glosses his entire conception of the relation of the moral and natural aptitudes, as well as the question of how the inclinations and passions fit into his account. Inquiry into these notions will help us clarify how and why Kant takes the inner, formal basis of moral corruption to be also the basis of external conflict in human relations.

For human character to effect the unity of the principle of our conduct of life requires that *all* of our aptitudes be cultivated. Yet Kant agrees with Rousseau that there exists another difficult problem to be resolved: namely, how such cultivation is to proceed so that "the aptitudes of humanity as a moral species are developed as is proper to its vocation," but also in such a way that "these no longer conflict" with its aptitudes as a "natural species";[12] the conflict between these two species of aptitudes, he

12. While Kant here and elsewhere agrees with Rousseau's recognition of the problem in human life, he parts company with him in regard to the source of that problem. In his *Anthropology* (*ApH* 326–27), referring explicitly to the social contract, Savoyard Vicar, and Emile, Kant offers the following interpretation of Rousseau's intentions. "His three works" in which he "conceived of the state of nature as a state of innocence" were only intended to provide "his social contract, Emile, and Savoyard Vicar with a guide to find [their way] out of the maze of ills with which our species has surrounded itself through its own fault." Rousseau's "three writings" described the "injury" sustained by "1. leaving nature for the cultivation (*Cultur*) of our species by means of weakening its strengths (*Kraft*), 2. civilizing by means of inequality and mutual oppression, 3. supposed moralizing through an education [that is] contrary to nature and [that produces] the malformation of [our] *Denkungsart*." Rousseau's source of the problem, however, the external "threat of being infected and corrupted by evil or incompetent leaders and examples," leaves out

writes, gives rise to all the "ills" and "vices" that "oppress" and "dishonor human life" (*M* 116).[13] In a note here, and again in the *Anthropology,* Kant also comments on the disproportion in the typical age of the possible attainment of physical and either moral or civil maturity (*M* 116–18n; *ApH* 325). The attentiveness in these passages to the need for alleviating conflict between human natural and moral aptitudes is not readily seen in the language of "force" (from both the second and third *Critiques*) most familiar to Kant's readers. In the context of his discussions of the proper order of subordination of our maxims in moral choice, Kant invariably describes pure, practical reason as literally "breaking off," calling a halt to our natural or pathological desires for well-being, as these are aroused in us even prior to the moral law; for such desires are to be restricted to the condition that they agree with reason's law and, to this extent, all the demands of self-love to the contrary be refused (*KpV* 73–74, 76). Again, in the *Critique of Judgment,* we read that "human nature does not of itself agree with the good" and can only be brought into such agreement "by the force reason brings to bear on sensibility" (*KU* 271).

The question that presents itself, then, is similar to the one we have asked before in regard to these notions of constraint and coercion defining the relation of human moral and natural capacities. The passages cited from his "Conjectural History" and *Anthropology* imply Kant's own awareness of this issue. Our previous conclusion, that the constitution of the counterimage was the positive account we were seeking in regard to practical reason's causality vis-à-vis the world, drew on the inherent capacity of the human aptitudes for directing or orienting themselves in response to the necessity with which they were confronted in their environment. Does the preceding assertion of human nature's lack of inherent agree-

---

of account the "innate evil propensity" and so leaves "unresolved" the "problem of the moral education of our species."

13. Tzvetan Todorov's interpretation of humanism and of Rousseau as adhering to this position speaks to just this issue. On Todorov's reading, humanism is the "refusal to choose between naturalism and conventionalism," the "refusal to choose between the two options that human beings are good or evil." Thus, this version of eighteenth-century humanism views the basic Enlightenment postulate that humanity can be cured of evil, specifically by the extension of the benefits of civilization, as illusory. Instead, it recognizes in civilization a source of human misery (arising from the conflicts that come with the necessity of living together), but equally recognizes the capacity of choice, the opening up of a "space beyond the genetic program," the ability to "choose to acquiesce or resist." So seen, human nature is characterized by both "determinism and potentiality" (Tzvetan Todorov, "Rousseau and Humanism" [paper presented at the twenty-ninth annual meeting of the American Society for Eighteenth-Century Studies, Notre Dame, Indiana, April 1998]).

ment with the good simply contradict that, or does Kant's conception of radical evil, while now opening an inner wound, so to speak, offer a more complex response? For understanding Kant's conception of how sensibility functions within its human environment, we will now turn to his account of the inclinations and passions. Thereby we will also come to see wider implications of the presence of reason (beyond its authorship of practical necessity) that are important for the whole relation of the natural and moral.

Unlike Rousseau's point of departure (in *Emile*) from the inclinations and passions as related to human gender and his effort to draw moral implications for civil life based on the gender distinctions, Kant leaves the sexual instincts related to the preservation of the human species as animal species (*ApH* 325). For the preservation of humanity as a moral species, he focuses his concern on those passions that he sees first arising on the basis of simple human associations: those that are "acquired" and only "emerge from" human civilization (*ApH* 267–68). It is in the relations between neighbors (whether the latter take the form of individuals or corporate, political bodies) that Kant sees those natural desires making themselves manifest that erupt into war and that must, from practical reason's point of view, be constrained (however useful conflict and war might also be in the initial stages of development of the human natural capacities). For this external form of conflict to make its appearance, Kant observes, "it is enough that others" are merely "present"; one need not assume moral evil on their part, nor view them as examples that lead one astray. Human nature (at its psychological level) is such that, whenever and wherever people come together, our sensibilities[14]—in themselves an "easily satisfied nature"—are "soon assailed" by "envy, thirst for power, greed, and all the hostile inclinations bound up with [them]" (*RV* 93–94).[15] Thus, instead of "love for humanity," one of those ends that are duties in themselves (as identified in the *Metaphysical Principles of Virtue*), or adherence to the obligation to "promote the happiness of others" (as Kant speaks of it already in the second *Critique*, 34–35), the felt response of humankind

14. Kant here is using the term that refers to the middle level of human character, as it is defined in the *Anthropology: Sinnesart* or *Temperament*, which, "psychologically considered" refers to our powers or capacities for feelings and desires (*Gefühls- und Begehrungsvermögen*) (*ApH* 285, 286).

15. In his *Reflections on Anthropology* Kant repeats his observation that it is a "peculiar property of human nature" that we cannot live as neighbors without discipline, constraint, and external rule (*RA* no. 1227, 540).

for its neighbor is characterized by the "vices of misanthropy" (*MST* 458).[16]

Perhaps most surprising is that Kant traces this stated peculiarity of the human sensibilities, when they find themselves in even the smallest social context, to an aspect of their environment that is equally peculiar to the human being; namely, to the concept of freedom. "Considered in themselves, the natural inclinations are good; no condemnation" is due them, and "it would not only be in vain, but harmful" and a matter of "reproach to wish to eradicate them" (*RV* 58). They do require discipline,[17] but more important here is Kant's further assertion that the "natural inclinations" have "no direct relation to evil"; rather, they "provide the opportunity for virtue" (*RV* 34–35). And, of course, the "satisfaction" of "all the inclinations together" constitutes just our natural purpose, "happiness," which belongs (albeit in a subordinate position) to our highest good (*KpV* 73). What then is the source of the above-claimed negative, felt response of humankind for its neighbor?

Kant's discussion of the inclinations and passions in his *Anthropology* (particularly *ApH* 265–70) offers some insight. Here he widens the discussion beyond that of the subjective use of freedom through the power of choice, to the difference it makes to human sensible nature (specifically the inclinations) for the conception of freedom (which is necessarily a rational concept) to be inherent in the environment in which the inclinations function.[18] The concept of freedom is identified as the very presupposition for the arousal of certain inclinations and even for the possibility of the notion of a passion (which in its nature stands essentially in conflict with the concept of freedom). Passions too can hence be properly spoken of only in relation to human beings, not to animals lacking the endowment of reason. To put it more explicitly, Kant conceives of this exposure (if one will) of sensibility to the rational concept of freedom as yielding a "sensible conception of external freedom" that, in turn, gives rise to "the inclination to persevere therein or even to enlarge it" (*ApH* 269). In addition, closely allied with our "technically practical reason, that is, the maxim of prudence," is our further inclination to seek to influence others in order

16. Kant continues here to describe these as that "abominable family" of vices consisting in "jealousy, ingratitude, and malicious delight in another's misfortunes" (*MST* 458). See also *MST* 394, 401–2, 450, 452.

17. This point is taken up in detail in the fifth chapter in the course of the inquiry into the pedagogy requisite for producing moral character.

18. In the *Groundwork* Kant defines "inclination" as meaning the "dependence of the capacity of desire on sensations" (*G* 413n). So one might restate the question here as what difference it makes to bring the concept of freedom to bear on such a dependent capacity of desire.

to procure their cooperation in promoting our own intentions (*ApH* 271). A more extreme version is spelled out by Kant in *Metaphysical Principles of Justice*. Here he claims we need only look within ourselves to acknowledge this "inclination of human beings in general to play the master over others," that is, "not to respect the rights of others when they feel themselves to be superior in power or cunning" (*MSR* 307). In this regard it is easy to see the relevance of the point made in the *Critique of Judgment* under the discussion of the "discipline of the inclinations"; as natural aptitudes in respect to our determination as an animal species these are said to be altogether purposive but are also held greatly to impede our development as humanity (*KU* 433). How do inclinations, in themselves blameless, become such impediments?

The connection lies in the awakened "enthusiasm" for freedom (which is particularly strong in the state of nature prior to cultivation of the natural aptitudes by discipline and outside of any assurance in the form of laws that one's own rights will be protected against potential encroachment by others) (*ApH* 269).[19] Heightened to the point of a "fierce passion," that is, to an inclination overriding the demands of all other inclinations, it is bound up with the further inclination to exert influence over others in order to use them for achieving one's own ends. This latter inclination, now as a passion, takes the form of those misanthropic vices Kant so frequently lists: greed (*Habsucht*), vainglory (*Ehrsucht*), and a craving for dominance (*Herrschsucht*) (*ApH* 271). One of Kant's passages summarizing the consequences in human history is found in the *Critique of Judgment:* in the absence of a "constitution in the relations of peoples with one another, whereby the infringement on freedom resulting from their mutually conflicting freedom is countered by a lawful authority in a whole called a civil society," and given, as a result of the "vainglory, craving for domination, and greed especially on the part of those who are in power, the hindrance to the very possibility" of forming a "cosmopolitan whole, a system of all states, war . . . is unavoidable" (*KU* 432–43). Kant's description here is of what he calls in *Perpetual Peace* the "wild" or "lawless freedom" engaged in by both individuals and entire peoples that reason opposes with its moral law (*F* 356–57).

---

19. Kant's discussion is found in the section entitled "The Inclination of Freedom as Passion." The passage, already referred to previously, reads verbatim as follows: "Thus the concept of freedom under moral laws not only awakens an affect that is called enthusiasm, but the mere sensible representation of outer freedom gives rise to the inclination to persevere therein or to enlarge [this outer freedom], by analogy with the concept of justice, to the point of a fierce passion" (*ApH* 269).

So the inclinations in question are directed outward, toward others in our human relations. Informed by the "sensible conception of *external* freedom," they are directed to achieving ends in the world; or more precisely, they seek to procure as enlarged a sphere of freedom within which to satisfy one's inclinations as one's means and power allow. Absent from this portrayal of the employment of the concept of freedom is just the latter's law, practical necessity. As natural aptitudes, the inclinations have here indeed responded to the presence of something only attributable to reason in the context within which they function, but the response is not yet informed by the moral law. Kant's point seems to be that absent such a *concept* of freedom, the striving of animal inclinations would simply cease with each immediate satisfaction; where hunger is satiated (for example) there is no need from the standpoint of the desire for food to persist in the pursuit and acquisition of new territory. So conceived, the inclination serves well the purpose of the self-preservation of the individual and species, physically speaking. However, even (or perhaps especially) a well-fed animal, if its priority in its inclinations is the satisfaction of an overriding demand to acquire the freedom always to be able to satiate its needs and desires, will soon expand its sphere of attempted domination to the point of inevitable conflict with the like effort of its equally minded neighbor. Such action and conflict is explicable only through an unmitigated desire, indeed passion, for external freedom. Hence, what is initially purposive for the preservation of human beings as a natural species proves at first (paradoxically under the introduction of a rational concept) to be detrimental to their development as a moral species and even harmful to their well-being as a natural species. The pursuit of these inclinations on the part of such rational animals (as they must be to have a conception of such freedom) further entails the exercise of the capacity of choice and "always *presupposes a maxim*" adopted by the "subject to act on the basis of a purpose (*Zweck*) that has been prescribed by the inclination" (*ApH* 266, emphasis added). Here, in the operation of choice as belonging to the rational animal, lies what from the standpoint of practical reason (but not from that of the human as a natural species) counts as an inherent propensity for evil—as a potential basis for opposition to objective reason's command.

Reason's role, then, proves to be far wider in this scenario than its familiar function as pure practical reason. It is "natural" (for example) to "take up" the desire for "well-being" in one's "maxims," and "reason" in this respect "only acts on the behalf of the natural inclination" (*RV* 45n). Such a statement brings to mind reason's role, which Hume took to be central, but which for Kant falls within the purview of technically practical and pragmatic/prudential reason. Such a maxim becomes a moral issue only if and when it is "made into an unconditioned principle of our power of choice" (*RV* 45n). In its "sensible-practical" employment, reason stands in relation to the inclinations as follows. Exercising its own nature (to seek in all its operations the maxim of unity), it moves "from the universal to the particular in accordance with the basic principle" of not allowing the satisfaction of one inclination at the expense of all others; rather, it sees to it that a given inclination is compatible with the totality of all the inclinations. A particular inclination has become a passion when it has become the rule or habit to be asserted without any such consideration of its agreement or lack thereof with the rest of the inclinations; it hinders reason in its function of making a choice from among the totality of all inclinations, and, hence, it contradicts reason in its formal principle (*ApH* 265–66).[20]

Two things are worthy of note. The reason/passion conflict, as portrayed in this ordering of the inclinations in accordance with the maxim of unity, involves a description of reason as we saw it in Kant's "Conjectural History" and "Universal History with a Cosmopolitan Intent," namely, reason as falling under the "particular natural aptitudes of humanity" and provoking the enlarged employment of the human capacities beyond the "limits of instinct." The further connection with pure practical reason has yet to be drawn. Second, as Richard Velkley has put it, "just through this hindering of reason, passion reveals its own rational character, for it makes a claim upon totality; it dictates a maxim or way of acting under all circum-

---

20. As Kant also outlines the distinctions in his *Religion:* propensity is a "predisposition for desiring," instinct is a felt need that is preconceptual, inclination is an habitual desire, and passion is an inclination that refuses to admit control over itself (*RV* 28–29n). Other points worthy of note from Kant's discussion in his *Anthropology* are (1) however violent the passions may be as sensible motive impulses, nonetheless from the point of view of what reason prescribes, they are "weaknesses"; (2) they constitute a servile or slavish mentality; (3) detailed in terms of Kant's three main passions of concern, one can gain influence over others through their own opinion where the weakness of vainglory holds sway, through fear in the case of the craving for domination, and through their own interests where greed is the master (*ApH* 271). The praise of justification of the passions voiced among humankind, namely that nothing great in the world can be achieved without them, is attributable to moral evil having first taken hold in their principles. Such a claim may be made, grants Kant, for various inclinations indispensable for humankind's living nature (*ApH* 267). In *On Pedagogy*, Kant divides the desires between formal (pertaining to freedom) and material (directed to an object); vainglory, craving for domination, and greed belong to the formal category, while pleasures related to sexuality, things, and company belong to the material category (*P* 492).

stances."[21] Kant himself writes that the passions "bear a semblance to reason" just to the extent that they "emulate the idea of a capacity connected with freedom, through which alone purposes in general may be attained" (*ApH* 270).

In this overview of the inclinations and passions, then, we see that in Kant's account of human nature we do not have a strict rational/nonrational divide. Human sensibility, by definition, functions within a rational environment, namely that of the human rational being, and, furthermore, shows rational characteristics of its own. The crucial distinction obtains between lawless and lawful employment of freedom (any employment of which presupposes rationality broadly speaking). To attain its moral form, external freedom must both be patterned after and based on what inner, *free* power of choice, strictly speaking, means for Kant. Enforcing a just civil constitution may effect the pattern externally among the inclinations; nature too is seen by Kant as lending its helping hand at this level.[22] Thus changes may be effected through the utilization of natural necessity (through the medium of force employing the laws of nature, whether psychologically or physically). While such external or legal conformity as may be attained might relieve the symptoms, it leaves the root of the illness (metaphorically speaking) untouched. For it is not the passions and certainly not the inclinations that raise the barrier to the *determination* of the power of choice as a *free* power of choice; this barrier lies within, in its own inherent propensity for the morally corrupt order in maxim adoption. That is, in the face of practical desire and the communication of practical necessity, the power of choice nonetheless exercises its natural propensity to act on the basis of a purpose prescribed by an inclination and even goes so far as to make the "motive spring of self-love" the "condition for the observance of the moral law." Or, as we have seen Kant put it, the "true enemy" is that comportment of mind which does not *want* to offer resistance to an inciting inclination. Where this enemy holds sway, the lawless employment of freedom at the level of the inclinations (which as natural aptitudes indeed lack an inherent moral order) is not confronted with practical necessity at all, for the power of choice has (so to speak) closed the door on this vehicle for the elevation of nature to the moral order. That such closure is not irrevocable is addressed by Kant in at least the three different ways already mentioned: nature's providential assistance,

21. Richard Velkley, *Kant as Philosopher of Theodicy* (Ann Arbor: UMI, 1978), 372; pages 368–75 give a clear, succinct outline of Kant's notion of passion and its relation to nature and freedom.

22. Elaboration of both points is given in the discussion of Kant's account of pedagogy.

the political avenue of the just constitution, and above all, the establishment of morally good character.[23]

As a more indirect consequence of the root of moral evil in human life, Kant notes that the thinking person who reflects upon all these ills of humanity is vulnerable to suffering yet one more kind of conflict; namely a dissatisfaction (*Unzufriedenheit*) with the entire, providential course of the world, a kind of sorrow Kant calls "inimical to morality," for it undermines the very courage and spirit required to face the need for "self improvement" and thereby to take on "the in all likelihood sole cause of all these ills" (*M* 120–21). The Stoical model, at least on Kant's description of it, missed the point altogether by failing to take into account the human natural purpose of happiness and well-being and by placing the motive impulse and actual ground of determination of practical desire in the elevation of *Denkungsart* over and above the lowly sensible impulses; thus virtue for the Stoic was a kind of "heroism" on the part of the "wise man who elevated himself above animal nature," instead of elevating the natural to the moral order (*KpV* 127n). In response to one of the naysayers of possible human moral improvement of his own day, Kant sees Mendelssohn's actions nonetheless belying the kind of resignation that he preached: for not even Mendelssohn could work, as he did, for the welfare of his nation without maintaining the hope that others would follow in his footsteps (*TP* 309). In fact, the more strenuous judgments of one's moral state, asserts Kant, come precisely at higher attained levels from where one can better see how far one has yet to go (*TP* 310). For his part, Kant affirms that where one can still find a live respect for justice and duty, he himself neither can nor wants to hold human nature as so far submerged in evil that morally practical reason could not ultimately emerge as victor over that evil (*TP* 313).

Of systematic significance is the fact that Kant's account of radical evil (at least in part) is a response to challenges raised by his contemporaries on the basis of the purported empirical evidence of human history, challenges that represent disagreement with human moral possibilities promised by Kant's formal moral philosophy.[24] Further, Kant's response is given

23. The discussion of the respective roles and connections of these three ways with one another is completed in the fifth chapter.

24. Günter Patzig's objection is also relevant here. He argues that it is the question of actually being moved to act on the basis of our assent (*Billigung*) to the moral good that Kant does not satisfactorily address ("Principium diiudicationis und Principium executionis: Über transzendentalpragmatische Begründungssätze für Verhaltensnormen," in *Handlungstheorie und Transzendentalphilosophie*, 204–18).

Kant, as Patzig points out, very clearly distinguishes moral judgment from moral execution in

in terms of moral character, of just the conception within his philosophy that has all along constituted the intrinsic link between the moral and the natural, between objective and subjective. To speak of character at all (as we recall) is to speak of the human moral capacity in relation to living nature. In these relations in their historical social and political forms, the issue of moral evil most clearly presents itself. To turn to the essential inner moral relation constitutive of character (which in general is the account of the subjective use of freedom) as also the locus of the externally manifest problem is, from this point of view, a natural sequitur in Kant's thought.

In contrast to Rousseau who cultivates his Emile outside of society and then enters him morally fait accompli for civic functions, in Kant's understanding of the matter it is just the engagement in civic relations that promotes the uncovering and development of the human aptitudes (on his biological model); civic relations bring the problems to light but also serve as the indispensable means or context for working toward their resolution. Kant writes: "Human beings are determined by reason to be in society with others and therein to cultivate, civilize, and moralize themselves through art and science" (*ApH* 324). The objective is precisely to become "active" beings and not leave their relation to nature at a "passive" stage in which they simply "give themselves over" to the stimuli for living well that they call "happiness" (*ApH* 325). "The dominion of the good principle, insofar as human beings are able to bring it about, is thus, insofar as we are able to see, attainable in no other way than through the founding and propagation of a society," both "in accordance with laws of virtue and for their sake" (*RV* 93).[25] The subjective employment of freedom is not,

---

his lectures: "When it is a question of what is morally good or not, this entails a principle of decision (*principium der dijudication*) in accordance with which the moral soundness or depravity of an action is judged. When, however, the question is, what moves me to live in a way that is commensurate with these moral laws, this is a question of the principle of the motive power of the action. The assent to or approval of the [morally good] action is its objective ground, but not yet its subjective [ground]. That which impels me to do what reason bids me do, is the subjective moving cause (*Motiva subjectiva moventia*). The highest principle of all moral judging lies in reason, and the highest principle of all moral impetus lies in the heart" (*Ak* 27.2.2, 1422–23).

25. In the *Religion* Kant keeps a sharper distinction between his ethical civil society and his just civil society than one finds in later essays such as *Perpetual Peace*. In either case, however, the important point here is the call to societal relations. Sharon Anderson-Gold has interpreted it as follows: "the moral law, which is a relation within the individual, simultaneously directs the individual to a common ground of personal relationships. It appears to be Kant's mature view that this 'command' which issues in 'reverence' must be a personal force, an activity directed to the wills of beings standing in moral relation to their fellows. The 'existential' import of this form of moral-religious experience does not lead to Kierkegaard's religious mysticism, but to Buber's

cannot, then, be cultivated outside of human relations. Indeed, "egoism" must be "opposed by pluralism," that is, with such *Denkungsart* whereby individuals do not hold themselves as "encompassing the entire world in their own selves, but rather regard and conduct themselves as mere world citizens" (*ApH* 130). Among other things, this entails not succumbing to "misanthropy" or that *Denkungsart* in which contempt rather than respect for humanity reigns; instead, the idea of "friendship," an "ideal of the participation in and imparting of mutual well-being" is to inform one's *Gesinnung* (*MST* 466, 469; see also 472–73).

The foundation of fundamental respect for humanity is of course pure practical reason's law, which, as a formal principle, must be prior in the order of maxim adoption to any material principle, that is, to any object of our power of choice, even when such objects constitute moral tasks that it is our duty to work toward (such as the highest good or perpetual peace). Hence too, Kant finds empiricism a greater threat to the morally good comportment of mind than even mysticism; for it is just in terms of empirical interests (which by definition are tied to objects) that the inclinations in general naturally relate to one another (*KpV* 71). The formal basis of the lawful employment of freedom, as a matter of the conduct of life individually and collectively (and not simply as a matter of determining a particular action), requires the "revolution of *Denkungsart*" definitive of establishing moral character and the consequent "gradual reform of the sensibilities" (*RV* 47). It requires making a commitment realized as resoluteness, as the adoption not merely of the moral law as the highest maxim guiding choice making, but first and foremost as the adoption of a firm resolve that it be such a highest maxim. Like the account of radical evil itself, this proposed solution gives rise to a number of questions.

First of all, as in the case of Kant's earliest use of it, one must ask just what is meant by the notion of revolution. In its first *Critique* sense, it entails a changed relation of the human subject in regard to nature, and, here too, from the foregoing discussion we can see that such a changed relation is implied. The passive relation to nature natural to the inclinations must be superseded by the active relation in which the subject as actor is henceforth the source of the law of causality governing all actions. A "revolution" or "transformation" (*Umwandlung*) in conduct of thought

---

ethical communalism. We know God only through his command to create ethical community as the abode of relationships between moral persons" ("God and Community: An Inquiry into the Religious Implications of the Highest Good," in *Kant's Philosophy of Religion Reconsidered*, ed. Philip J. Rossi and Michael Wren [Bloomington: Indiana University Press, 1991], 129–30).

is required in the first place to convert the power of choice as a capacity of the natural being, to a capacity operating on behalf of the moral being (which then also adopts maxims appropriate to the preservation of the natural and physical aspects of the whole human being). That is, even apart from the consideration of a realized propensity for evil (not wanting to resist an inciting inclination), the natural order of the capacity of choice making to adopt a maxim to act on the basis of a purpose prescribed by an inclination must undergo a "revolution." The transformation or revolution is, moreover, the act upon which the elevation of nature to the moral order depends. To put it once again in the terms of our earlier discussion, pure practical reason thereby succeeds in becoming subjectively practical; having procured an empirical character for itself in and through the capacity of choice, it imparts its rule as a regularity manifest in choice making and in the phenomenal appearances that result. As the act constituting the establishment of "character or *Denkungsart*," as Kant puts it in his *Reflections on Anthropology*, it "defines (*fixirt*) freedom" (*RA* no. 1518, 867); that is, it gives freedom its lawful form, a form that is henceforth resolutely and consistently maintained.[26]

Yet, this act of transformation itself (in the order of maxim adoption in the human capacity of choice) gives rise to a further issue that has been noted in the scholarship.[27] Kant's account prima facie involves a circularity that threatens to undermine the very possibility of such a revolution at all. *Gesinnung* is said to be the "first subjective ground of the adoption of maxims," and, further, it is a "characteristic (*Beschaffenheit*) of the capacity of choice that belongs to it . . . by nature" (*RV* 25). That is to say, our very ability mentally to assume a moral posture (*sittliche Haltung*) that we maintain or hold and consistently bring to bear on the circumstances of life is, subjectively speaking, a function of the nature of the human capacity of choice. Whether such a moral posture is good or evil depends on the further question of its relation to the moral law. In this regard, put into the terms used earlier, to be able to assume such a moral comportment is a condition of responsiveness inherent to the capacity of choice whereby the spirit of the moral law may receive its subjective actualization. If the

26. As is evident from the student transcriptions prepared by Brandt and Stark, Kant clearly and explicitly stated the point in his lectures that we have been arguing for here. As Stark quotes from the Parow notes in his paper, "The determination of human character does not depend on drives and desires, but solely on the way in which the individual modifies these. Our question therefore only concerns how human beings use their powers and capacities, for the sake of what final purpose they apply them" (Stark, "Kant's *Lectures on Anthropology*," 10; see the Parow transcriptions [306–7] in *Ak* 25.2.1, 438).

27. See, for example, Allison's discussion in *Kant's Theory of Freedom*, 139ff.

further problem of the propensity for evil were not present, the account of objective determination of the power of choice by practical desire, the introduction of practical necessity, would suffice to effect this transformation to a free power of choice. The question that arises is how a revolution in the order of maxim adoption is possible if and when this comportment of mind inherently tends toward a morally perverse order of maxim adoption.

A number of things may be said in response. The requisite "subjective ground," as referring simply to the ability itself of adopting a moral posture by means of maxim adoption, remains available as such an ability at either level of its (morally speaking) deficient exercise: the initial natural turn to maxims based on inclinations, or the morally corrupt order of subordination of the moral law to the maxim of self-love. In either case, Kant's conception of human nature and his articulation of the problem of evil also leaves intact the all-important objective ground of moral legislation, pure practical reason and practical desire, as well as the aptitude for good (the capacities of respect for the law and ability rightly to discern one's maxims) on the subjective side.[28] Kant explicitly asserts that we "cannot lose the motive impulse for the good, and if such were possible, we would also never reacquire it" (*RV* 46). The power of choice, just by virtue of being one of the human capacities, functions (or at the very least stands) at all times in relation to these objective and subjective grounds, as well as to the human inclinations. Without the act of resolve, that is, prior to its own actualization as a free power of choice, it is subject to influence from *both* the objective and subjective sides. Thus, even if choice as a specification of volition is in such a state that it does not want to resist an inciting inclination, nonetheless *no steadfast* comportment is in principle realizable prior to the establishment of character as the resolute conduct of thought. Both practical reason exercised through the determining power of practical desire and, on the subjective side, also conscience[29] (as one of the aesthetic preconceptions of responsiveness to concepts of duty, *MST* 399, 400–401) are ineliminable voices of opposition to moral transgression. The mechanisms of habit might be in place, but in its essential

---

28. Hence, too, as Kant explicitly notes, a morally corrupted comportment of mind ("perversity of the heart") may coexist with good practical desire ("kann mit einem im Allgemeinen guten Willen zusammen bestehen") (*RV* 37). Not only does the objective/subjective distinction allow for such a situation, but its possibility is necessary if a change from the corrupted to the morally good state is in turn to be possible by human effort.

29. Kant's conception of conscience and the role it plays in his account of character is discussed in conjunction with his pedagogy.

characteristic, choice making remains irresolute, both subject to being in-cited and opposed. The point in fact parallels the view Kant had Titius express thirty-eight years earlier in the dialogue with Caius (recounted in the 1755 *New Exposition*), that "sin is committed by mortals by a voluntary and innermost state of mind; the *chain of antecedent reasons does not urge and constrain them unwillingly, but induces them.* . . . since the origin of these evils lies in an inner principle of self-determination, it is entirely clear that the evil must be laid to the charge of the offenders themselves" (emphasis added).[30] Further, Kant rejects as inconceivable just that state or condition of the power of choice which would indeed present a virtually insurmountable obstacle to the required transformation: "Malevolence based on principles" is diabolical and not attributable to human beings (*ApH* 293–94; see also *RV* 21, 37).

The act of resolve is an act on the part of *Denkungsart* and is described by Kant, in both the *Religion* and the *Anthropology*, as a "kind of rebirth," a "transformation" whose moment of occurrence marks a "new epoch" in the life of the individual (*RV* 47; *ApH* 294). The language he uses here also recalls the point made in "Conjectural History" that even "a small beginning" that gives "a completely new direction to *Denkungsart*" initiates an "epoch" (*M* 113). In the *Religion*, reference is further made to a "new heart" that is now "constant" (*unveränderlich*) (*RV* 51). The theological overtones of Kant's language are reinforced by his explicit identification of the "Incarnate Word" as the "archetype of the moral *Gesinnung* in its complete purity" (*RV* 60–61) and by his claim in the *Anthropology* that it pertains to the "character of our species" that, while it "strives for a civil constitution," it "also requires discipline through religion" (*ApH* 332n). In short, by implication, a kind of conversion experience serves as Kant's model for this notion of a revolution in conduct of thought. The objection that presents itself in this regard, of course, is that while human history is replete with testimony to the possibility and reality of such conversions that result in a permanent, changed course of one's life, traditionally such conversions include an appeal to some form of divine aid. Faith (conceived as rational faith) does in fact play an important role in Kant's conception of character (and is examined in our next chapter as part of the principles of orientation making up the relational structure of character). Yet, in Kant's account of the establishment of character, the conversion not only is, but must be, made by individual human effort.

It is not, however, difficult to recall, or conceive of, life-changing mo-

---

30. *Kant's Latin Writings*, 87.

ments of resolve within the context of secular life; consider for example the firm resolve to reorder one's priorities in life, one that frequently entails career changes and the like. It entails precisely, in other words, going against long-ingrained habits and patterns of choice making, but that fact alone does not ordinarily cause us to reject it as being in principle impossible. Moreover, if infinite regress is to be avoided, it must be possible for the virtuous state to follow upon its contrary, the morally corrupt one. As Kant points out in his *Metaphysical Principles of Virtue*, one cannot understand the attainment of virtue in such a way that would require assuming a further preexistent virtue in order to bring it about (*MST* 406). Hence too, he observes, one must "regard virtue in its complete perfection" as if it "possesses the human being" and not as something possessed by the individual (*MST* 406). The likely age identified by Kant for the epoch-making moment of character establishment (few try it before thirty and even fewer succeed before forty)[31] makes the matter even more suggestive, as well as implying the role of life's vicissitudes—nature's helping hand and the social and political relations of the human community incorporated into Kant's account. Here we can at least conclude that, while room for disagreement is likely to remain in regard to the expected degree of probability that individuals with a morally corrupt order in their maxims will undergo the requisite revolution in their conduct of thought, within the parameters and assumptions of Kant's complete view of human nature, it is at least not impossible. Kant is, after all, also the first to admit that to be able to accord character (in its absolute sense) to someone is a rare thing indeed (*ApH* 291–92).[32] Moreover, given that human beings are

31. *ApH* 294. Earlier in the text, Kant is even less optimistic and identifies the ages marking the stages in the development toward the "complete employment of reason" as follows: skillfulness may be achieved in one's twenties, prudence by one's forties, but wisdom as the "idea of a practical employment of reason that is perfectly in accord with the law" may only be expected in one's sixties and even then, it is essentially negative, consisting primarily in recognition of the follies of the first two stages (*ApH* 200–201).

32. The echoing phrases in Aristotle's text read: "That is why it is a hard task to be good. . . . It is for this reason that good conduct is rare, praiseworthy, and noble" (*Nicomachean Ethics*, 1109a24, 29).

As indicated by these occasional comparative citations from Aristotle's text, I am very sympathetic with the efforts in the current scholarship to make the comparisons. A systematic comparison of Aristotle's and Kant's conceptions of character lies beyond the scope of the present project, for it rather presumes the latter's completion. However, I do want to remark on some reservations. As welcome as is the recent scholarly recognition of parallels between Kant and the ancients (Aristotle and the Stoics in particular), on my view there do remain differences that "make all the difference" and need to be kept in the forefront. Dieter Henrich (who is highly attentive to the comparisons and contrasts of Kant's thought to the ancients) notes that "the methodology of Kant's foundation of ethics is therefore neither the Aristotelian dualism of theoretical and

unable to penetrate the "depth of the heart," the "subjective primary ground of one's maxims," no one can be self-assured of having in fact achieved the establishment of character; however, "one must be able to

practical reason nor the Idealistic derivation of the one from the other. Kant is different from Aristotle because the fact, or the object, of moral insight is a fact of reason" ("Concept of Moral Insight," 85). Analogously, Martha Nussbaum cautions against giving a Kantian reading to Aristotle (see especially chapter 11 in *The Fragility of Goodness: Luck and Ethics in Greek Tragedy and Philosophy* [New York: Cambridge University Press, 1986]). As our analysis here points to the differences, they include the following. The "partnership" of reason and sensibility involves not so much the inclinations, but rather the aesthetic capacities, the power of reflective judgment that in turn gives rise to the aesthetic feelings of the sublime and pleasure in the beautiful, in purposive form (a point worked out in chapter 5). Moreover, because of the problem of the innate propensity for evil, the relationship must necessarily be hierarchical and not a cooperative conjunction (such as Aristotle's right reason and right desire). Further, this propensity, attaching as it does to the capacity of choice, entails that it is the subjective use of reason, the use of the human powers of judging, that is thus susceptible to corruption; hence, virtue as self-control is an attribute of conduct of thought and not the inclinations. In addition, the reason at issue is a *finite* human reason, an initial factor in denying to it the power of intuition of the supersensible. We have seen Kant's objections to a Stoical asceticism, and, whether or not he is being altogether fair (for surely the Stoic did see virtue as giving rise to its own proper pleasure), a more fruitful comparison is perhaps made with Socratic thought, not only because of Kant's explicit appeals to its methodology in cultivating reason (again developed in the fifth chapter), but precisely because (unlike Aristotle, who objects to the appeal to the Idea of the Good in moral affairs) the idea of perfection informs both Kant's objective and subjective morality, as well as his pedagogy. As Richard Velkley has observed, Kant's "central motivation for taking up the question of the 'foundations' of practical reason . . . is also different from Aristotle's aim of fully articulating common opinions and experiences relating to the human good, ordering and unifying them, tracing them back to first principles when possible, and in the process, correcting them" ("Crisis of End," 81). Allen Wood made one of the earliest cases in Anglo-American thought for Kant's connection with the Socratic tradition: "The critical philosophy, true to the Socratic tradition, is a philosophy of human self-knowledge" (*Kant's Moral Religion* [Ithaca: Cornell University Press, 1970], 2). Central to what also distinguishes Kant from the Platonic project, however, is his treatment of reason's ideas: that the Idea must be practically interpreted as a task to be performed, not contemplated and theoretically expounded. To say this is, of course, to gloss what quickly becomes a more complicated question of the relation of Kant to Plato; see, for example, David A. White, "Kant on Plato and the Metaphysics of Purpose," *History of Philosophy Quarterly* 10 (1993): 67–82. The fact of evil in Kant's conception of human nature also entails that duty and not an inclination to the good (the latter being a Thomistic/Aristotelian formulation) remains paramount (in contrast to Barbara Herman's recent line of argumentation). These differences are fundamental and, connected as they are with Kant's conception of character, entail that the latter too will ultimately be distinct from an Aristotelian or other ancient account. Important in the recent scholarly efforts is the realization that Kant is in fact engaged in a quest for wisdom (as opposed to the deontological reading of his ethics) and to this extent the parallels with the ancients are significant.

Two of the more recent publications on this subject are the collection of papers (representing a good selection of arguments for and against drawing parallels between Kant's position and the tradition) compiled under the title *Aristotle, Kant, and the Stoics*, ed. Engstrom and Whiting; and Nancy Sherman's *Making a Necessity of Virtue*. While Sherman notes that "Kant's anthropology is a part of his *full* moral theory in ways that are often not acknowledged" (123), lacking in her discussion is attention to the distinction between emotions (as belonging to the human inclinations) and feeling as an aesthetic capacity that is itself based on an act of judgment; the *Critique*

hope that through one's own efforts one is able to get on the path leading thereto" (*RV* 51).

While one cannot, then, speak of gradual improvement when the question is strictly that of the order of the maxims in choice making, in the complete account that involves also the reform of the sensibilities, as well as the issue of the organization of the community, there is in fact room for the notion of development and progress. The familiar association made in Kant's writings with this latter notion is the concept of virtue, a concept that also names the state of comportment of mind realized upon the establishment of character. "Virtue" is the "*Gesinnung* commensurate with the law out of respect for the law" (*KpV* 128). The inquiry into the connection

---

of Judgment is not accorded a place in her argument that relies heavily on the account of the emotions in order to draw the comparisons with Aristotle. The distinction is an essential one, for Kant never goes back on his fundamental position that "principles must be based on concepts," that "all feelings" (here in sense of emotions) are inadequate as the basis for character and moral *Gesinnung* just because their inherent nature is to be fleeting; they "must produce their effect in the moment when they are at their height and before they subside, else they have no effect at all" (*KpV* 157). The supportive spiritedness (as argued for in chapter 5) has for its basis not emotions, but reflective judgment—the reflection on purposive form.

The current debate on Aristotle versus Kant is in its second decade, with Alasdair MacIntyre's *After Virtue: A Study in Moral Theory* (Notre Dame: University of Notre Dame Press, 1981) setting the stage for it (at least in Anglo-American studies). Among the most interesting studies are those that argue that contemporary ethics needs both Aristotelian and Kantian elements (studies that go back over a decade and include those by Otfried Höffe and Ronald Beiner). George Lucas has so argued in explicit response to MacIntyre, affirming insights arrived at by MacIntyre, but also defending Kant in regard to just those insights: "Moral Order and the Constraints of Agency: Toward a New Metaphysics of Morals," in *New Essays in Metaphysics*, ed. Robert C. Neville (Albany: State University of New York Press, 1987), 117–40; "Agency after Virtue," *International Philosophical Quarterly* 28 (1988): 293–311. Ronald Beiner's argument for both Aristotelian and Kantian elements concerns the "dimensions of judgment" needed for a "comprehensive theory of political judgment": on his view, "from Kant we are to get the transcendental perspective by which to provide an account of the formal constitutive features of politics as such. . . . From Aristotle we get the substantive features of political life by which to fill in the content of this formal delineation" (*Political Judgment* [Chicago: University of Chicago Press, 1983], 102–3). Although he was reading Kant as a deontological ethicist, even Paul Ricoeur has argued for the need for both Kant's and Aristotle's philosophies for a theory of action: "The Teleological and Deontological Structures of Action: Aristotle and/or Kant?" *Archivio di filosofia* (1987): 205–17. For additional references see Jürgen-Eckardt Pleines, *Eudaimonia zwischen Kant und Aristoteles. Glückseligkeit als höchstes Gut menschlichen Handelns* (Würzburg: Königshausen und Neumann, 1984); Otfried Höffe, "Universalistische Ethik und Urteilskraft: Ein aristotelischer Blick auf Kant," *Zeitschrift für philosophische Forschung* 44 (1990): 537–63 (an English version appears as "Universalist Ethics and the Faculty of Judgment: An Aristotelian Look at Kant," *Philosophical Forum* 25 [1993]: 55–71); Maximilian Forschner, "Synthesis und Handlung bei Aristoteles und Kant," in Prauss, *Handlungstheorie und Transzendentalphilosophie*, 82–97; Christine Korsgaard, "Aristotle and Kant on the Source of Value," *Ethics* 96 (1986): 486–505; and Roger J. Sullivan, "The Influence of Kant's Anthropology on His Moral Theory," *Review of Metaphysics* 49 (1995): 77–94, an essay that uses the *Anthropology* as a point of departure for comparing Kant with Aristotle.

of character and moral evil cannot, then, be completed without also examining the counterrelation, that of virtue and character; doing so will further allow us to look at Kant's understanding of virtue in a new light.

VIRTUE: EMBATTLED MORAL COMPORTMENT OF MIND (*GESINNUNG*)

In both *Religion* and *Perpetual Peace,* Kant explicitly addresses the notion of virtue in direct connection with the problem of evil. To mistake the "true adversary of the good" is also to misunderstand the true nature of "virtue's battle" (*RV* 59, 58n). In the 1795 essay we read that the "true valor" of "virtue" consists in "squarely facing and vanquishing the maliciousness of the evil principle in ourselves—that by far more dangerous, deceitful and treacherous, but also sophistical" principle that "would have us believe that the weakness of human nature justifies all transgressions" (*F* 380). While the *Groundwork* simply identifies the "morally good *Gesinnung*" with "virtue" (an identification repeated many times in Kant's writings), in the *Critique of Practical Reason,* the problem of evil is already implicit in Kant's treatment of "virtue" as synonymous with the "embattled moral *Gesinnung*" (*G* 435; *KpV* 84). This interchangeable use of the terms is of particular importance for the articulation of the meaning of virtue as it is directly connected with Kant's conception of character. In the *Metaphysical Principles of Virtue* we find the further relevant distinction spelled out between duties of virtue (of which there are many and which belong to the "material" side of the discussion) and the "formal" sense of virtue, the single commitment to virtue we are obligated to make (*eine Tugendverpflichtung*) (*MST* 410).[33] The identification with comportment of mind here again follows immediately: there is only one such obligation, for there is "only one virtuous *Gesinnung*" that serves "as the subjective ground of determination for fulfilling all one's duties" (*MST* 410; see also 383, 395). The parallel between this passage and another from the *Religion* is striking: "*Gesinnung,* that is, the primary subjective ground of the adop-

---

33. Both the distinctions of the German terms *Verpflichtung* and *Pflicht* and the Latin provided by Kant (*obligatio* and *officium*) are important for fully grasping the differences between virtue considered formally and materially. The term *Verpflichtung* includes the connotation of indebtedness, of owing someone, particularly owing a debt of gratitude. This connotation is similar to that of *obligatio,* which entails the notion of being bound by some form of pledge. *Officium,* on the other hand, means duty in the sense of a service, an office, a function to be fulfilled. Hence, it is used in direct reference to objects, purposes that are duties for us, while the single commitment to virtue we are called to make is a "duty" we owe to the humanity within us.

tion of maxims, can only be one" (literally, "a single one") (*RV* 25), and, of course, where that ground is morally good in form we have (to express it also in the words of the *Groundwork*) "virtue in its true form (*Gestalt*)" (*G* 426).

Thus, as in the case of subjectively practical reason and free power of choice, we once more have distinct terms that are yet identified with one another. In order both to understand wherein the distinction lies and what the import of the identification is, we will examine this notion of virtue in its singular sense by beginning with the two etymologies Kant offers. The "word *virtue* (*Tugend*)," writes Kant in 1797, "comes from to be fit [or suitable, *taugen*] for" something (*MST* 390). This notion of fitness had already (as early as 1763) been introduced as definitive of the concept of an "aptitude" as the inherent "dynamic principle" enabling an organism to "adapt advantageously to many conditions" (*BG* 126). Two decades later, Kant is using the notion of fitness in its moral application. The "morally good *Gesinnung*, or virtue," he notes in the *Groundwork*, makes the rational being "fit to be a member" in a "realm of purposes" (*G* 435). In the *Critique of Practical Reason*, the "practical meaning" of the "concept of perfection" is said to be the "fitness" (*Tauglichkeit*) or "adequacy" (*Zulänglichkeit*) of "something for various purposes" (*KpV* 41). The highest stakes, of course, are in regard to humankind's vocation, its final purpose, named in the idea of the *summum bonum* and whose attainment rests with the perfected practical use that reason makes of the other human capacities. As Kant puts it in the *Anthropology*, human "inner perfection" consists in "having control over the use of all our capacities, in order to subordinate them to our free power of choice" (*ApH* 144). So, the early concerns and intimations of Kant's writings—for example, the 1755 concern as to how rational beings attain the perfection of their natures as thinking beings, or the 1764 discussion of virtue—by 1797 are consummated as a shifting of the classical sense of virtue. Rather than signifying self-control characterizing the human inclinations, virtue is in effect self-control characterizing the human processes of thinking, specifically of choice making or the subjectively practical use of reason in human moral life. It is a self-control that makes us fit as thinking beings to fulfill our human vocation and as such remains definitive of what it means to have good character.

Kant explicitly refers to the Greek and Latin senses of virtue, at least in terms of his understanding of these senses. In both cases, he observes, "virtue designated courageous spirit (*Mut*) and fortitude (*Tapferkeit*)" and hence also "presupposed an enemy" (*RV* 57). Again, in the *Metaphysical*

Principles of Virtue, such "deliberate resolve" in the face of an "unjust adversary" and the capacity to resist is said to be none other than "virtue," for which Kant here provides the Latin cognate *virtus*, as well as *fortitudo moralis* to express its meaning (*MST* 380).[34] *Virtus* of course refers first and foremost to manliness or virility and thus also to the notions of strength, valor, or bravery. As qualities most highly esteemed, the term then derivatively comes to refer to moral perfection. What the essence of the latter consists in for Kant, is a singular notion that he repeats from the beginning to the end of his corpus. "True virtue," he writes in 1764, can only rest on "principles" that are the "more sublime and noble" the "more universal they are" (*B* 217, 218). The discussion in this text is carried out in terms of the medieval humors, but *steadfastness* in the ordering of one's sensations under principles (as manifest in the melancholic soul) is here already praised (*B* 220).[35] "Strength of resolve," we read in Kant's 1797 text, "can alone be truly called virtue" (*MST* 390);[36] such "strength of resolve" is "strength of mind [or soul, *Seelenstärke*]" when "by soul we mean the human principle of life in the free use of one's powers" (*MST* 384; see also *KpV* 147). Several pages later Kant gives the Latin *robur* for this moral strength that is virtue, a term whose various meanings include "vigor of mind" (*MST* 397). Among the relatively few references to virtue in the *Anthropology*, one again finds the same point expressed: "Virtue is moral strength in the observance of one's duty, which must never become a matter of habit" (that is, a merely mechanical employment of power), "but must always emerge from one's *Denkungsart* in a completely new and original" way (*ApH* 147).[37]

34. See also *MST* 390, 405. In the latter citation, Kant further identifies such moral strength as that which constitutes the "greatest and sole military honor (*Kriegsehre*)."

35. Kant goes on to describe the good sense of the melancholic soul as contrasted with the condition in which it has gotten out of hand. Especially in his later writings he emphasizes cheerfulness in the execution of one's duty (in conjunction with retaining steadfastness of resolve). For example, "the cheerful heart in the observance of one's duty" is the "mark of the genuineness of a virtuous *Gesinnung*" (*RV* 24n).

36. For other references to such strength of resolve or strength in the observance of one's maxims, see also *MST* 394, 409, 477. In the *Metaphysics of Morals* Kant is (explicitly at least) silent on the issue of radical evil. In conjunction with this fact, the *Wille/Willkür* distinction is far less attended to; at one point Kant goes so far as to attribute virtue as moral strength to volition as such (*Willens*) (*MST* 405).

37. In *Metaphysical Principles of Virtue* Kant also explicitly rejects the notion that one can think of virtue as a "habit of morally good actions, acquired by practice"; virtue considered as anything but the "effect of deliberate, firm and ever purer principles" would be like "any other mechanism of technically practical reason" and would not be secured against "change and new incitements" (*MST* 383).

In the *Religion* (47) Kant employs the empirical/intelligible distinction in relation to virtue and there allows a kind of "habituation in the observance of the law" whereby a "gradual reform of conduct (*Verhaltens*)" is achieved. This "phenomenal" sense of virtue does still rest on "steadfast maxims," only these are maintained not on the basis of respect for the law, but only in accordance with the law for reasons of self-love (analogous to, for example, turning to a life of moderation for the sake of one's health). "No change of heart, only a change of morals is needed," and for this, the helping hand of nature and the just civil constitution are well suited. Virtue's empirical character here is *not* the same as reason's empirical character precisely because it is not the effect of the synthetic unity of causality in which the empirical receives direction from the *internal* intelligible ground. The sense of virtue of immediate concern for the present discussion, however, is virtue in its "intelligible character" or "virtus noumenon"; for it, the inner "revolution of *Gesinnung*" is necessary.

Virtue in this latter sense, as referring to the acquired mental moral posture characterizing the power of choice such that it is adequate to the task of executing choices serving human final purpose, constitutes the "state of health in moral life" (*MST* 409; see also 384, 405, 419). Not only is it a matter of an inner state of health, but its salutary effects in the world, asserts Kant, are greater than what either nature or art are able to achieve (*RV* 23n). The firmness, the steadfastness of resolve that is its hallmark, represents the opposite of the state of oscillation between incitement and command that is for Kant, from the moral point of view, a condition of a Sisyphean standstill. Just as a lack of health weakens the entire system of corporeal powers (*MST* 384), so the Sisyphean state of mind undermines the entire set of relations belonging to human moral self-preservation. Strength is the "mind at rest" (*Gemüt in Ruhe*, *MST* 409), the state of calm effected by establishing moral character. It is a state of firm commitment to the moral law as one's highest maxim for all one's choice making. As a state of calm or rest, it does not mean something like the poetic version of an original, carefree, idle golden age; for it is just through action that life gains its worth (*M* 114, 122). Indeed, as Kant also says, "Virtue is always progressing and yet also always begins anew" (literally, "from the start") (*MST* 409). This claim, however, raises a further question. How is a comportment of mind characterized by singular commitment, by strength and by calm, to be understood as being also continually in progress?

In Kant or any other thinker, the idea of progress is itself a complex notion involving secular and historical, as well as moral and theological, aspects.[38] Certainly it is a pervasive motif in Kant's thought, one frequently linked with some allusion to moral improvement that is further connected with the question of immortality. For example, in the first *Critique* discussion of the paralogisms of reason, using terminology that we can now recognize as intrinsic to his conception of character, Kant even there reflects that mere "consciousness of the uprightness" of one's *Gesinnung* is enough to give rise to an inner sense of being "called to make oneself, through one's conduct (*Verhalten*) in this world . . . fit for citizenship in a better one" (*KrV* B425–26). In the second *Critique,* in connection with the discussion of the postulate of immortality, Kant is very explicit about the meaning of progress as a change from a "lower to a higher level of moral perfection," proceeding into infinity toward the goal of a "blessed future" (*KpV* 122–23, 123n). The affirmation of a kind of inevitability of this progress is underscored by Kant's further declarations elsewhere that even moral evil ultimately serves its ends: "Moral evil has the intrinsic, ineliminable attribute (especially in relations with others of like mind) that it works against its own intentions and subverts them, thus making room for the moral principle of good, even if progress" thereby is "slow" (*F* 379). These and like passages have occasioned many questions in the scholarship, but our concern here is how to understand such statements about the nature of progress in relation both to virtue and to the conception of moral character as presented thus far: namely, as an account of practical reason's efficacious causality *in this* world, indeed in relation to living nature, and as based on a single moral form of maxim adoption, a form that cannot be conceived as either partially or gradually achieved.

In one sense, the issue seems readily resolvable. Regarded from the point of view of humanity, together with the consideration of the problem of evil, if there is progress tangibly evident, then it must be construed to be on the part of the human race as a whole, as ever more individuals and nations participate in forms of organization and conduct that more nearly realize standards of justice. This of course appears to be Kant's own conclusion in his well-known statement that such progress is precisely something pertaining to the species, but not to the individual (*M* 115, *ApH* 324). Not only is it unsatisfactory to leave matters here from the point of view Kant mentions, namely that the result is that individuals do not

38. For a recent study of this notion in Kant, see Pauline Kleingeld's *Fortschritt und Vernunft: Zur Geschichtsphilosophie Kants* (Würzburg: Königshausen & Neumann, 1995). For a historical analysis of the Western idea of progress from the Greeks to the present, see Robert Nisbet's *History of the Idea of Progress* (New York: Basic Books, 1980).

gather the fruits of their own labors, benefiting instead future generations, but prima facie such a conclusion implies also a limitation on the individual's achievement of moral character. However specific character may be as the moral form of humanity and however universal its fundamental principles, it nonetheless is present in the world only as particular instances of a single character, *einen Charakter,* as Kant himself so frequently refers to it. Even if reason's rule in appearances is more readily seen in the history of the genus than in a given individual life, as Kant observes in the opening lines of his "Universal History" (*IG* 17), the account of moral character is otherwise the account of the work of the individual subject.[39] The question, then, is whether progress can be understood in a way that does pertain to this subject.

A number of second *Critique* passages in fact conjoin the notions of virtue, progress, and firm resolve (which can only be made by the individual qua individual). For example: "With regard to the hope for a share" in the highest good, "all that can lie in store for a created being would be consciousness of one's proven *Gesinnung*"; that is, on the basis both of "one's progress to date from the worse to the morally better state and one's invariable resolve of which one has thereby become aware, one may hope for a further uninterrupted continuance of such progress, however far" into the future "one's existence may stretch, even beyond this life" (*KpV* 123). "The utmost that finite practical reason is able to bring about is virtue"; that is, what reason is able to accomplish is that the "finite rational being" is "certain of constant progress (*Fortschreiten*)," of an "advance (*Progressus*) of its maxims that extends into infinity and of their invariability" (*KpV* 32–33). In relation to both these passages, Kant contrasts this state of virtue as progress or advance possible for the finite being with the ideal of "holiness," a "practical idea that must necessarily serve as an archetype" (*KpV* 32). In the passage cited earlier from the *Metaphysical Principles of Virtue,* Kant refers to such an unattainable ideal as grounds for seeing virtue as always in progress (*MST* 409).

Indeed, where this idea defines the goal, the journey can only be an infinite one, for no revolution of conduct of thought, no state of resolve characterizing the comportment of mind can change the nature of the finite being as finite. Nor is the propensity for evil eradicable (*RV* 51).

---

39. Reinhard Brandt too has concluded that while the individuals may be sacrificed for the sake of the species, as moral persons they are not thus subject: "Everyone can at any point procure a character for himself and, with that, a worth that no history of the race may exploit" ("Kants Anthropologie: Die Idee des Werks und die Bestimmung des Menschen" [paper presented at the Central Division meeting of the American Philosophical Association, Pittsburgh, April 1997]).

Resolve counters but cannot eradicate the permanent possibility, inherent to this being's power of choice, that it adopt as its guiding maxim one derived from an object of the inclinations. The latter order is, in fact, as we have seen Kant himself spelling it out, the natural one. Making the turn to the formal, moral point of departure reorients the natural order, but we cannot transform our human nature such that it would be completely impossible for a maxim contrary to the moral law to be adopted in a given case; we *cannot* make ourselves holy (*KpV* 32, 83–84; see also *RV* 46–47). Human moral status is defined as "respect for the moral law"; the further stage, "love for the law" in fact would "cease to be virtue," for all striving too will have come to an end (*KpV* 84, 83). Moreover, to the extent that "complete commensurability with the moral law" is the condition for "bringing about the highest good in the world," this purpose that defines the human vocation is not completely realizable solely by human effort (*KpV* 122; *RV* 139). While this explanation thus shows Kant limiting possible moral achievement to finite human power, to stop here is to leave matters at the point of the much discussed problematic of moral life directed to an unattainable goal, as well as leaving unclear what it means to speak of progress beyond the requisite revolution in conduct of thought. More can and needs to be said about this notion of progress as characteristic of the infinite journey.

Our previous conclusion had been that it lies within the power and duty of human beings to establish a moral character, a firmness of resolve, a strength of mind, such that we can expect of ourselves and others can expect of us that we actually will choose and act on the basis of the moral law—no matter what the surrounding difficulties of choice might be. This is the hoped-for result as Kant expresses it again in *Toward Perpetual Peace* (355). It is a result that cannot give an absolute guarantee that the expectation will never be disappointed. It is a result that means that "virtue" can be nothing more (but also nothing less) than the "embattled moral *Gesinnung*" (*KpV* 84)—the inner adversary held in check, but not eliminated. What connection is there between this sense of virtue and virtue as progress? What exactly can such "progress" consist in? How is it to be understood? At one end stands the onetime act that is complete in itself, the revolution in the order of maxim adoption, the resolve that guards against the propensity for evil and that must be perpetually, actively maintained. At the other end stands a practical idea between whose object and possible human attainment there will always be an infinite gulf. Certainly, at least part of the answer lies in Kant's distinction between a "subject responsive to the good" and a "good human being" (*RV* 48) and in the attention he gives to the issue of reforming human sensible nature. In regard to the latter, the notion of progress's connoting development and moral improvement is relatively nonproblematic. However, the different terms appearing in the preceding citations from the second *Critique* (*Fortschritt* and *Progressus*), the allusion to humanity's final purpose, as well as our foregoing discussion all offer other possible insights both into the meaning of progress and into another level of significance of the concept of resolve itself.

In the *Critique of Pure Reason* (A510–12/B538–40) Kant explicitly raises the question of the meaning of *progressus* as a term used respectively by mathematicians and philosophers. The context is the discussion of the relation of reason's ideas (which are always ideas of a totality) to a given conditioned series in the world, to a "synthesis of a series" that, as temporally conditioned, can never be brought to completion. The analogy Kant uses is that of drawing a straight line; when the question is what we are able to do in respect to such a line, the answer is that we can indefinitely extend it as long as we wish into infinity (*ins Unendliche*). Just so, says Kant, is the case in all circumstances in which we speak of *Progressus:* that is, when we are speaking of "advance (*Fortgang,* literally going forward) from the condition to the conditioned," which as a "possible advance in the series of appearances continues into infinity" (*KrV* A511/B539). What is striking here is the stated order: "from the condition to the conditioned," *not* from conditioned events toward some unconditioned goal. The order is that of the actor in relation to the line, which is such a line and may continue as such as long as it remains informed by a single condition, idea, or form (a 180-degree angle in the case of the mathematical line). The line could not advance, go forward, progress, if its definitive form were changed or lost; its advance is a function of its form. That the emphasis is on the form, that progress or advance is here not simply meant in its ordinary sense of moving forward from a present point toward a future goal in time, is further underscored by Kant's other example. In consideration of a series as an empirical series in the world, the order of comprehending the synthesis of the series is in fact regressive, not progressive. Thus, for instance, one traces a lineage for a given set of parents by following out the descending line of generation.

In light of this sense of *progressus,* we may come to see an essential connection between the formal meaning of progress and the notion of commitment identified earlier with virtue; that is, these two apparently distinct senses of virtue complement each other. Virtue in its formal sense as synonymous with "constant progress" (*Fortschreiten*), with an "advance

(*Progressus*) of the finite rational being's maxims that extends into infinity" may now be interpreted as follows. It is just on the basis of the singular commitment, of the fundamental act of resolve, that it first becomes possible for the rational human being to take a straight course in life, to cease the oscillation between command and incitement that for Kant is tantamount to standing still, morally speaking. The form of this course remains one and the same, characterized by bringing to bear practical reason's condition on the temporally conditioned and, insofar as what human beings are able to do—what lies in their power, analogous to the mathematician drawing a line—they may thus proceed into infinity along this defined course. Thus to be enabled to strike a course, a steadfast direction in one's life is, in fact, just what the ordinary experience of resolving to do something teaches us. As long as the given resolve informs our choosing and acting, our course of life is shaped thereby, whatever outside circumstances may have to be confronted along the way. Hence too, as Kant puts it in the *Anthropology*, it is the *resolve itself,* the "formal" attribute of "volition per se, to act in accordance with firm principles" that is "estimable and admirable, rare though it is" (*ApH* 292). Thus, further, a being of evil character (such as a Scylla), however horrifying, is *nonetheless* an object of admiration (*ApH* 293, emphasis added); that is, the latter's resolve is awe-inspiring.

It is by such resolve that human moral beings define, fix, shape the employment of their freedom (and it is just this aptitude to do so that Kant sees as having been uncovered among the spectators of the French Revolution). Where it is present, individuals determine their own course from within; therefore each step taken is ipso facto a *Fortschreiten,* a going forth, a taking up of the reins (so to speak), a walking under one's self-given direction. "Progress" in this sense, still considered from a purely formal standpoint, expresses just what is characteristic of the human as actor, whether in a single action or in the conduct of an entire life. It expresses the fact that in and through the particular individual's act that establishes moral character, immanent moral teleology is realized within the conditions of human life. Consonant with the overall structure of Kant's moral philosophy, it is realized not by beginning from an end or goal, but as a consequence of the priority of the formal. Further, progress turns out to express the meaning of moral maturity, as Kant again puts it in the *Anthropology:* "The most important revolution of human inner" life "is 'their emergence from their self-imposed immaturity'"; for "now they dare to progress under their own power (*mit eigenen Füßen fortzuschreiten*)" (*ApH* 229). Each such step exhibits in its form, in its inherent direction, the advance from the worse to the morally better, for it is always informed by the singular revolution in conduct of thought, by the formal order thereby established in the inner moral relation.

Progress thus interpreted is the singular, qualitative difference actualized as the virtuous comportment of mind. Formally regarded, it is not a quantitative measure; for the latter one must turn to the "material" side of its meaning—to the consideration of expected effects in the world, to the duties of virtue. In his *Conflict of the Faculties,* Kant explicitly asks what such progress toward the better yields for the human race. His answer is as follows: The "results of human striving for the better" can only consist in "an increase of products of legality in dutiful actions, . . . in good deeds . . . in the phenomena" that make up "the moral condition of the human race" and "not in an ever growing quantity of morality" in regard to *Gesinnung* (*SF* 91). To repeat our point: the latter, as the formal ground, is qualitative and is either present or absent. No greater share in the morally good comportment of mind than the human moral status defined as "respect for the moral law" is possible for humanity, individually or collectively. Thus to have established moral character in oneself is the limit of what one can make of oneself, but it is also to have completely realized, at the individual level, the formal perfection possible for the human as finite, mortal human (the distance between such and holiness always remaining the same).[40] On the basis of such comportment of mind, each new choice or action is formed in accordance with the morally good order, and so, as Kant says, virtue always begins anew, that is, from the same starting point in each case. The result of proceeding in terms of such resolve, of thus consistently ordering life's choices and actions is, in effect, to draw a straight line, a line that can be seen only by *looking back* (as in the case of the family lineage). In retrospect, its concrete manifestation is now quantifiable as number of deeds. Thereby too one may measure the *duration* of character in the world, but such duration does not increase its merit, which remains a function of the invariable moral quality of the comportment of mind.

If this interpretation of the formal sense of virtue, its identification of

---

40. Thus too, as Kant notes in the *Religion,* it is this quality of comportment of mind at any given point and not the length of time of its existence in the world that is all-important from the standpoint of the Supreme Judge. The gulf between the "good in appearance," what humans are able to effect, and holiness is insurmountable, and no progress can be made from the human side toward closing it. An increased quantity of its effects, of number of good deeds made possible by a longer life, does not increase the merit of comportment of mind and moral character (*RV* 67).

virtue as progress with virtue as commitment, with the resolve that is the essence of character, is correct and if, further, the "character of a living being" is just that whereby we may recognize its vocation or destiny, then how are we now to account for Kant's conclusion that "only the race" (or species, *Gattung*) realizes its purpose, "the development of good from evil" (*ApH* 329)? The gulf between what lies in human power and the ideal of holiness does not address the question, for to speak figuratively, humanity as a species can no more jump beyond its own shadow than can the individual. Indeed, in light of this ideal and the limitation it puts on the attainment of the highest good, Kant's claim about the species realizing its purpose is in fact rather surprising. What is it that humanity per se can accomplish that eludes individual effort?

One might be tempted, on the basis of Kant's remarks as to what moral progress will yield for humanity, to conclude that only by the efforts of all throughout all time can a totality be achieved in appearance that more nearly approximates reason's idea of the highest good. The form of this totality in its concrete manifestation is of course expressed in Kant's moral and political wholes, the ethical and just, civil states. The more complex answer, however, is that it turns out that there is an interconnectedness between the attainment of morally good form as character in the individual citizen and such morally good form of the organization of human society, specifically under the just, republican constitution. Recall that it is in relation to living nature (which for Kant, broadly speaking, includes the social and political realm) that one first properly speaks of character at all. When the discussion of character is further widened from its absolute sense to the subjective employment of freedom as it entails the exercise of the inclinations, when the question is the elevation of nature to the moral order, meaning that all the human aptitudes are to be cultivated as aptitudes for the good, then (as we have seen) Kant conceives of the human individual never in isolation, but always as an intrinsic part of the human community. Only in this context are the human capacities and talents uncovered and developed; only in this context too can humanity's natural purpose (happiness) be sought.[41] And, in just this context, as the foregoing discussion of the inclinations and passions showed, Kant sees the problem of moral evil making its appearance from the very outset.

41. On the basis of a very different line of argumentation, Susan Shell concludes that "the Kantian individual conceives itself neither as a discrete atom nor as the creature of society but as moral substance that sustains itself in and only in reciprocal community" (*The Embodiment of Reason: Kant on Spirit, Generation, and Community* [Chicago: University of Chicago Press, 1996], 311).

The lawless employment of freedom is a problem both within the individual and without. In short, the moral tasks of establishing character and of establishing peace are interconnected, and we turn now to examine their relation.

ESTABLISHING CHARACTER: THE MORAL TASK OF ESTABLISHING INNER AND OUTER PEACE

To speak of a "state of peace" is to speak of conditions "in which laws have force (*Kraft*)" (*F* 366), an account that equally describes the state of the individual in whom good moral character has been established and that of the human community under the just, civil constitution. Reason dictates that bringing about such a "state of peace" is a "duty"; whether as "single individuals" or as "nation states," humanity is "to give up its wild (lawless) freedom" (*F* 356, 357). Indeed, the task is to effect an eternal peace, an idea of reason that, like all such ideas within the critical philosophy, is interpreted for use in human experience as a practical idea.[42] In *Principles of Justice* Kant writes that the "question whether perpetual peace is something real or an absurdity (*Ding oder Unding*), and if we deceive ourselves in our theoretical judgment if we assume the former," is simply not the issue; "we must act as if it were an actual matter (*Ding*)" to be effected. Even if the consummation of this effort were to remain but a "pious wish," to adopt the maxim to work toward it remains a duty (*MSR* 354–55). In his 1795 essay, perpetual peace is said to be "not merely a physical good, but a state of affairs that follows from the recognition of duty," and, as a practical idea of reason, the "reality" of the "concept of duty of perpetual peace" is asserted to be "well founded" (*F* 377, 362).

That this conception of eternal or perpetual peace means (in general) to overcome an *internal source* of conflict within our own nature is already identified by Kant in his *Critique of Pure Reason*. The verbal disputes of reason are here compared with our human relations in terms that are remarkably similar to those of the later essays. "Disingenuousness, misrepre-

---

42. In my article "Reason's Practical Idea of Perpetual Peace, Human Character, and the Pedagogical Function of the Republican Constitution," *Idealistic Studies* 26 (1996): 101–34, I analyze the practical meaning of Kant's idea of eternal peace (or perpetual peace, as it is most often translated). As I show there, the practical meaning of eternal is explicitly connected by Kant with the timelessness of comportment of mind (discussed here in the second chapter). Further, the articulation of the connection between Kant's conception of character and the practical meaning of eternal peace provides the basis for taking up the question of why Kant accords to the republican constitution, which is to secure such peace among peoples, a role in the "good moral cultivation of the people" (an issue taken up in the examination of Kant's pedagogy in the last chapter here).

sentation, and hypocrisy" characterize our human relations while we are in the "state of nature," that state of "war" described by Hobbes as a "state of injustice and violence" from which we have "no option" but to extricate ourselves and to "submit ourselves to the constraint of law that limits our freedom, solely in order that it may be consistent with the freedom of others and with the common good of all" (*KrV* A748/B776, A752/B780). The same "deceit, hypocrisy, and fraud" are found in the "sophistical arguments" brought in defense of claimed hypotheses (*KrV* A749–50/B777–78). In such disputes, writes Kant, the only way to "secure an eternal peace" is to strike at the "*source* of the conflicts"; any other form of "victory" will result in a "merely temporary armistice" (*KrV* A751/B779, emphasis added). A few passages later he repeats the point. "External quiescence (*Ruhe*) is merely specious"; in order to establish an "eternal peace," the "germ (*Keim*) of these disturbances, which lies deep in the nature of human reason, must be extirpated" (*KrV* A777–78/B805–6). In this light, the account of radical evil in *Religion within the Limits of Reason Alone*, in which the "triumph" of the good principle "over evil" is said to "secure eternal peace for the world," is a development of Kant's first *Critique* observations.[43]

As we saw in our foregoing discussion, in the historical order of things, the inherent conflict within produces conflict without, which then hinders the requisite transition from lawless to lawful employment of freedom. One might say that Kant's view here borders on a "tragic sense of life." What the concept of freedom first yields, when brought into relation with the natural inclinations, is the production of conditions that direct human

---

43. Hans Saner interprets Kant's entire corpus (beginning with the piece "Living Forces" from 1747) in terms of the "theme of conflict and unity": "Kant's work is accordingly framed in the polarity of conflict and unity and in the pursuit of whatever unity can be established." The "point is always to eliminate the issue if it is lawless, or to provide the means for its elimination." Noting that Kant's work "as a whole is replete with imagery from the political realm," Saner finds "above all," in the *Religion within the Limits of Reason Alone*, a "thorough-going proximity to the political way of thinking." The "struggle" when it is a question of moving from conflict to peace in the practical philosophy has two forms: (1) the hopeless one whose consequence is war (and in which "the one objective principle of morality has been displaced by contingent, subjective principles")— the "lawless one for a unity without freedom," and (2) its true counterpart—"the lawful one for unity in freedom," "waged on grounds of the absolute," a "fight that is necessarily endless because the idea is transcendent. It is peace, since the principle of peace is at work throughout it; but this peace is also a way throughout, since the unity pursued is only an idea" (*Kant's Political Thought: Its Origins and Development*, trans. E. B. Ashton [Chicago: University of Chicago Press, 1973], 301–5, 279–80; see also 268–69, the discussion of moral order. The original text is *Widerstreit und Einheit: Wege zu Kants politischen Denken* [Munich: Piper, 1967]). All of part 3, "From Conflict to Peace in Critical Metaphysics: Kant as a Metaphysical Peacemaker," provides an insightful reading relevant to the present discussion.

attention outward, to competition with, and a struggle for survival among, the other members of the race. It is a conflict that in principle is different from the struggle for physical self-preservation by the nonrational animal; for, as we concluded previously, it is one essentially informed by the rational concept of freedom, and in it the satisfaction of physical needs fuels, rather than abates, the conflict. Kant's statements about the resulting impediment to the moral cultivation of the human being are very explicit. Whether in the "purposeless conditions" of as yet uncivilized peoples, or the "barbaric freedom" of nation-states, "all the natural aptitudes of our species" are prevented from developing (*IG* 25–26). External conflict, in other words, produces a backlash both at the broader level of the human aptitudes for good and in regard to character in its absolute sense. Nation-states that expend all their resources on "idle and violent aims of expansion" are charged with "unceasingly impeding their citizen's slow efforts at inner formation (*Bildung*) of their *Denkungsart*, even depriving them of all support for this purpose" (*IG* 26). Indeed, "soulless despotism" is held capable of "extirpating the germ of good," after which all will "disintegrate into anarchy" (*F* 367). Thus, citizens in such states are denied attaining their true good, for "all good that is not grafted onto a morally good *Gesinnung* is nothing but illusion and glittering misery" (*IG* 26).

Procuring morally good character, then, continues to be affirmed as the work of the individual, but life in even the so-called civilized state can present (and on Kant's view, thus far has done so) nearly insurmountable obstacles to this endeavor, directing instead the attention, efforts, and energies of its citizens elsewhere, including and especially the war efforts and their attendant miseries. Both in his identification of the problem and the means for its solution, Kant continues to draw explicit parallels and interconnections between the individual and corporately organized peoples. "Peoples [associated] as nation-states may be judged in the same way as are individuals, who in their state of nature (i.e., in their independence from external laws) harm one another just by living together as neighbors" (*F* 354). However, "the mechanism of nature whereby self-seeking (*selbstsüchtige*) inclinations are naturally opposed to one another in their external relations may be used by reason as a means for making room for its own purpose, the rule of law and hereby also, to the extent it lies within the state [to do so], to further and secure both internal and external peace" (*F* 366–67).[44] Under a just republican constitution with its

44. In this regard, Kant makes claims about the beneficial role war plays in the cultivation of humanity in a number of texts, including the *Critique of Judgment* and his 1795 essay. His statement in the *Anthropology* is worth noting, for it also indicates that his references to an "inner"

ability to prevent war, human "progress toward improvement is negatively secured" in that the "hostile inclinations with their aversion for justice are checked" (*SF* 85–86; *F* 357); hence, the "development of the moral aptitudes to an unmediated respect for law is greatly facilitated" (*F* 375–76n). Indeed, the "good moral formation (*Bildung*) of a people is to be expected in the first place" as a product of "a good political constitution" (*F* 366).

Nor is this requirement for civil society organized by a just constitution, if the aptitudes inherently belonging to human nature are to be fully developed, an assertion unique to Kant's 1795 essay. In the *Critique of Judgment*, for example, he identifies it as the "formal condition" necessary for such cultivation (*KU* 432; see also *IG* 22, 27; *ApH* 327). The civil constitution is called upon whenever the discussion concerns the subjective capacities, the conditions under and through which the universal principal is to be concretely realized. Further, in its principles and goals, the just constitution concretely embodies the same moral order that is exhibited in and through good moral character. In the first place, "freedom and law (whereby the former is limited) constitute the two concerns of civil legislation" (literally, "around which it revolves") (*ApH* 330). In his *Perpetual Peace*, Kant quotes the categorical imperative and notes that there can be "no doubt" that this formal principle of reason must be prior to the material principle, the object of our power of choice, in this case the particular purpose, perpetual peace (*F* 376–77). The latter must be derived from "the formal principles of our maxims" (*F* 377). Moreover, the two "branches" of morality, the "duties" of "love for humanity and respect for its rights" (which we can recognize as corresponding to the two dimensions of the magnanimous soul) are to be both honored and importantly, in their morally good order, which, in turn, requires that the political usage "bow before" morality as the "teaching of justice" (*F* 385–86). The doctrine of wisdom for the state, writes Kant, can be summed up in the following statement: "Seek first the kingdom of pure practical reason and its righteousness, and so your purpose (the benefit of perpetual peace) will be yours as well" (*F* 378).

---

as well as "external" war (the latter of which is usually translated as "foreign wars") can in fact also be understood as the inner conflicts of human nature that are, in turn, made manifest in the external (empirically evident) conflicts of human history. Kant writes, "Thus the internal or external war in our species, as great an evil as it is, at the same time serves as a providential mechanism, as the motive spring to leave the brutish state of nature for the civil state, in which the mutually opposing forces, although they impair one another through their friction, are yet maintained for a long time in a regulated course through the repulsion or attraction of other motive springs" (*ApH* 330).

All such parallels and interconnections between the morally good order of human character and the politically just order of civil society may be summed up in the following schema of moves Kant makes in his philosophy. The true enemy of virtue, the propensity for evil inherent to human nature, has for its most obvious and damaging result the external conflict that makes up so many pages of human history. The effect of this conflict in turn is to hinder the individuals' efforts, indeed their task to procure a moral character that is itself the very hallmark of the human race as a species or genus. The solution proceeds by bringing the external conflict under control by an order of governance that both pays homage to and is modeled on precisely the moral order definitive of the righteous, individual character. Within such an external order, within such a state of outward peace (in which reason's laws have force), virtue's empirical character has in effect been realized on the part of its citizens. They are, in other words, "people of good morals (*bene moratus*)" but not yet "morally good people (*moraliter bonus*)" (*RV* 30). Nonetheless, conditions in the state are now conducive for the successful cultivation of inner peace within those individuals, namely, for the revolution in conduct of thought that can only be their own work.

The order of the solution is, of course, the source of the scholarly discussions (which have recently increased their attention hereto) regarding the reconcilability of Kant's formal moral philosophy and his philosophy of history, of his doctrine of freedom and his account of nature's role in relation to it.[45] Cast in terms of the discussion here, the issue involves an

---

45. One does not have to look far to find grounds in Kant's text for these persistent questions. *Toward Perpetual Peace* is no exception: here too the "great artist, nature" is described as the "deep, underlying wisdom" of a "higher providence directed toward the objective, final purpose of the human race," working to bring such about "even against [human] volition" (*F* 360–61). That such statements about nature's designs are ultimately couched within an overarching practical context is generally speaking the avenue taken for reconciling them with the notion of human autonomous, moral action. Recent discussions relevant to the question include those presented by Henry Allison, Reinhard Brandt, Paul Guyer, Pauline Kleingeld, Rudolf A. Makkreel, and Allen Wood in Robinson, *Proceedings of Eighth International Kant Congress,* vol. 1, pt. 1. An earlier article by Georg Römpp explicates the "philosophy of the state" through Kant's moral philosophy, recasting the moral imperative as an imperative of political action (differentiated between national and international relations) ("Moralität und Frieden: Kants Gesetz der Freiheit in der Welt der Staaten," *Kant-Studien* 65 [1990]: 216–33). Or, in another example, Thomas Mertens concludes his analysis of *Toward Perpetual Peace* from the perspective of teleological reflective judgment, with the assessment that Kant's philosophy of history is fundamentally a "moral *Weltanschauung*" ("Zweckmäßigkeit der Natur und politische Philosophie bei Kant," *Zeitschrift für philosophische Forschung* 49 [1995]: 240). An earlier collection of essays dealing with the question of the "relationships between the invisible self and sensible nature (the self as lawgiver

apparent tension between his account of moral character (as the synthetic unity in which the formal order begins with reason) and Kant's pedagogy, his account of the steps in the actual formation of this concrete counterimage of reason's objective moral order. The question is a complex one to which we return in our inquiry focused on the pedagogical issues involved. However, the foregoing examination of evil, conflict, and virtue as these are related to Kant's conception of moral character does allow us to make suggestions and begin drawing some conclusions here.

Reflection on Kant's own metaphor likening the virtuous comportment of mind to a moral state of health leads one to recognize that it is not at all unusual in cases of illness for treatment to begin with the mitigation of the symptoms, for fever and swelling to be reduced (for example), before surgery is undertaken to correct the actual source of these effects or symptoms. By extension, it is no more necessary to assume that the external discipline of the inclinations executed under just, civil governance has become Kant's *basis* for the formation of good moral character, than one would assume that the external application of ice pack and anti-inflammatory medications would correct or even begin to address the underlying cause in a diseased organ. What is evident is that the order familiar to the readers of the critical philosophy also holds in human moral life: a negative task analogous to the relation of the critical philosophy itself to our moral life—"to level the ground beneath the majestic moral edifices and make it capable of supporting them" (*KrV* A319/ B376)—must be completed for the sake of the positive one. Amid the ground as the *plurality* that is humankind, the achievement of a "completely just civil constitution" is humankind's "greatest problem" (*ApH* 333; *IG* 22).[46] It is the duty of each member to work toward this end, but its attainment can only be realized by the human race as a whole.[47] Indeed,

---

of nature and the immediate certainty of self and nature)" was published as *Self and Nature in Kant's Philosophy*, ed. Allen W. Wood (Ithaca: Cornell University Press, 1984).

46. In his *Religion* (1793), Kant is much more attentive than in 1795 to his distinction between the just civil state (under public laws of justice that act as laws of constraint) and the ethical civil state (organized in accordance with laws of virtue that are free of constraint) (*RV* 95). As already noted, such public laws may effect virtue's empirical character and result in a body of citizens exhibiting good morals; that is, their conformity to the law is self-legislated, but legal (not moral) in form. The citizenry of the ethical state would consist of morally mature individuals of good character expressing their own internal, morally well ordered legislation.

47. Reinhard Brandt has made the case that a uniform "argumentative structure" characterizes Kant's writings, namely, that of an *"ascensus* from the individual, determined as a whole . . . or part of the whole, up to the totality itself." Thus, for example, the "categorical imperative is placed in relation to the highest good," which in turn "leads to the postulates" and finally "only at the end is practical reality as a whole visible, in which it is possible for the human being to act morally

it is a "duty" of individuals "toward themselves," a duty "belonging to the worth of humanity in their own person," to be a "member of service to the world" (*MST* 446)—an assertion made by Kant in conclusion to yet another discussion of the cultivation of the natural human aptitudes of which reason may make use. Thus, working on the goal of external, communal peace has intrinsic merit; nature's own "highest intention" is at once also a task (exercised under the voice of command) belonging to reason's means for cultivating the natural order. Thereby the latter is reformed and ultimately made fit for concretely realizing reason's own empirical character as the counterimage of its intelligible one. Where character is thus actualized, the moral individual as synthetic unity of natural and moral truly speaks in the one voice characteristic of the resolute conduct of thought (as we saw Kant describe it in the third *Critique*). And, by implication, in a world composed of citizens in whom such character, such internal peace were once established, the surest foundation too of world peace would be laid.[48] Meanwhile, the outer structure, by keeping the destructive, misanthropic vices (the fever and swelling) subdued, provides a provisional shelter within which the work on the inner moral edifice proper may take place. In Kant's words, once achieved, the "universal cosmopolitan state" would constitute a "womb wherein all the original aptitudes of the human species may be developed" (*IG* 28). Given the ineradicability of the propensity for evil, this outer shelter is not likely to be one that could itself be completely superseded in human history, but under the reading presented here, its systematic connection with the ultimate moral objective of establishing good character, a state of inner peace, has come into view.

In conclusion, two main factors emerge from the examination thus far of Kant's conception of moral character. First, as a concern it has proven to be pervasive from beginning to end in the corpus, intrinsically related to many otherwise familiar distinctions and terms that, in light of this

---

as a sensible and an intelligible being in general." When one turns to the writings concerning the philosophy of history, "here too we have the ascent from the capacities in individual human beings to the totality of the legal order that circumscribes the entire space inhabited by human beings, the earth, and that is the goal of the temporal history of humanity" (*The Table of Judgments: "Critique of Pure Reason" A67–76; B91–101*, vol. 4 of *North American Kant Society Studies in Philosophy*, trans. and ed. Eric Watkins [Atascadero: Ridgeview, 1995], 118–19).

48. Philip Rossi has taken this issue up as an inquiry into virtue as guarantor of perpetual peace: "A Commonwealth of Virtue: Guarantee of Perpetual Peace" (paper presented at the annual meeting of the Midwest Study Group of the North American Kant Society, Loyola University, Chicago, November 1996). Rossi responds to and develops in his paper Howard Williams's claim that "the success of Kant's plan for perpetual peace depends upon the moral progress of man" (in *Kant's Political Philosophy* [Oxford: Basil Blackwell, 1983], 260–68).

connection, can be reconsidered with fresh appreciation. Second, renewed emphasis appears on the comprehension of Kant's moral philosophy as both formal and rigorous, but in a much more interesting sense than either the Hegelian reading of the formalism as abstract and empty, or the deontological reading of it as a rule-driven ethics. To begin with, form has always proven to be a source of difficulty for Kant's readers and critics, for especially in regard to ethics or morality, the most immediate questions that naturally present themselves concern "what is to be done" and "how one is to do it." They involve, in other words, ends to be achieved, the means to achieve them, and the calculative and deliberative processes whereby to ascertain them. We see, however, from such facets of Kant's account of character as the synthetic unity of causality, reason's empirical character as a rule or order manifest in appearances, the problem of the order of maxim adoption that underlies the account of evil, progress and virtue each considered in their formal aspects, that "form is the essence of the thing" [forma dat esse rei].[49] Just this point of departure for his account of character means that it, like the critical philosophy in general (as described in Kant's own words), has "left all the beaten tracks and struck out on a new path" (*Pro* 380).

The significance of Kant's conception of moral character fundamentally in terms of thought (rather than the inclinations), as an issue of the morally good form of thought, might be expressed in terms of a long-standing insight into Kant's life and work. While his readers from his contemporaries to the present have used the question of how his form of life corresponds to Kant's form of thinking as a basis for understanding his work,[50]

49. Kant refers explicitly to this Scholastic dictum a number of times. One such discussion is found in his late essay "On the Recently Adopted Refined Tone in Philosophy" (1796) (*T* 404). His *Reflections on Metaphysics* (*RM* no. 3850, 312) and the Pölitz-transcribed *Lectures on Metaphysics* (*Ak* 28.2.1, 575) are other examples.

50. Ernst Cassirer describes his own task as biographer as consisting in "discovering and illuminating the *Lebensform*, the form of life, corresponding to [Kant's] form of thinking" (the latter being Haden's translation for *Lehrform*, which means that the "thought" Cassirer had in mind was Kant's philosophy itself). Drawing also on Goethe's assessment of the relation of life and thought in Kant, Cassirer notes that "with Kant the relation between form of thought and form of life cannot be understood to mean that the latter came to be only the basis and passive receptacle for the former." Instead, "here that peculiar reciprocal relationship prevails in which each of the two moments that influence each other appears simultaneously as determining and determined." Comparing this relationship also to its forms as found in other thinkers such as Descartes and Augustine, Cassirer goes on to observe that where "thought exhibits itself in its objective structure, as a systematic linkage of concepts and truths," but also such that "in the process the total act of judging and reasoning comes alive," the "ideal and real, world view and process of individual life, have become moments of one and the same indivisible spiritual growth" (*Kant's Life and Thought*, 6, 7).

our investigation into his conception of character proves this notion *itself* to be Kant's *own lifelong attempt* to articulate just such a unity between the forms of thought and life. To put it into our foregoing terminology, in and through his conception of moral character, Kant seeks to give an account of the human actor as thinking being *enacting* morally good form in human life, individually and collectively. Thus far, we have interpreted that account by (1) tracing its historical connections both within Kant's early writings and the larger discourse of the eighteenth century and (2) analyzing its relation to other notions of Kant's philosophy such as cause, maxims, the distinction between intelligible and empirical, human aptitudes, volition, aesthetic feeling, moral evil, virtue, progress, and peace. We have, in other words, located Kant's conception of character in his thought and writings, in relation to his initial concerns, his critical philosophy (of all three *Critiques*), and his biological, anthropological, and aesthetic concepts. Next we turn to the examination of the actual structure of character itself, the maxims formative of its connection with human life—its guiding principles of orientation vis-à-vis reason, nature, community, and the transcendent.

PART TWO

Human Moral Character: Its Structure and Cultivation

Principles of Orientation and the Relational Structure of Character

HUMAN ORIENTATION TO THE GOOD BY THE DAWN OF NATURAL LIGHT

As the *factum der Vernunft*, Kant's construal of moral insight has occasioned much scholarship focusing on its derivation, its possible connection with theoretical reason, and its objective justification. Kant himself often enough treats it simply as a given, characterizing his entire project in the *Groundwork*, for example, as an effort to give philosophical articulation to the "principle" of the "moral cognition of the common human understanding," a principle that this understanding (albeit not expressed in such "abstracted, universal form") "employs as a standard *(Richtmaß)*" or as a "compass" to guide its judgments in any given case as to what is "good or evil, in accordance with, or opposed to duty" (*G* 403, 404). As we have seen, in the *Religion* he holds that "if this law were not given in us, we would not arrive at such through any subtle reasonings," nor would we "foist it on the power of choice" (*RV* 26n). Certainly its objective justification is an important issue, and no doubt Kant's own emphasis in the *Groundwork*—on why morality's fundamental principles cannot be empirically derived, and on developing a metaphysics of morals with no admixture of anthropology, theology, physics, or hyperphysics (*G* 410)—has been in part responsible for the degree of attention given to the objective side of the question.

Equally important, however, is the question of what it means for the human subject concretely to actualize such moral insight. Kant alludes to this dimension both before and after the passage from the *Groundwork* already cited, noting (1) the need for anthropology in regard to the employment of the moral law in relation to human beings (*G* 412) and (2) foreshadowing the second *Critique*'s analysis of making reason subjectively practical: though human beings are capable of the "idea of practical reason, they are not so easily able to make it concretely effective in their conduct of life (*Lebenswandel*)" (*G* 389). We have seen Kant express concern about such "free employment of insight" from his earliest published writings (*NH* 356), and we have argued that in reason's relation to both the understanding and volition, the effect sought is unanimity in the orientation of the various capacities, in accordance with reason's mandate that a possible action be a good action. Among Kant scholars, Dieter Henrich has emphasized the objective line of inquiry, taking up both the epistemology and ontology of moral insight and asking in what kind of knowledge it consists.[1] He does, however, also point to a crucial element of what its concrete effectiveness in conduct of life entails: where human beings follow the good, "the 'natural' morality of personal obligations has lost its *orienting* force" (emphasis added).[2]

To speak of the good, for Kant, is to speak of the "practically necessary"

1. In "Concept of Moral Insight," Dieter Henrich describes a sense of moral insight that received its fullest expression in the Platonic quest for virtue as a kind of knowledge. Moral insight in this sense comprises three essential moments of demand (of the good calling for acceptance), and approval and conviction (on the part of the subject) (63, 56–58); it involves a "conjunction of problems" (ontological, moral, and epistemological) whose "renewal," on Henrich's reading, "emerged unconcealed in Kant's concept of practical reason and its autonomy" (113). It is in this light that Henrich develops his position that "Kant's 'critical business' was undertaken with the goal of justifying the possibility of moral insight and the reality of freedom" (84). Henrich, goes on, however, to follow Kant's Idealist critics in focusing on the issue of an *objective* deduction of Kant's fact of reason; declaring such an effort a failure, he identifies a number of questions he thus sees left unanswered. One such concern is that "theoretical doubt concerning the reality of the moral law" and with that, of the highest good as the fulfillment of the human moral vocation, "is just as possible as the conviction of its reality" (84). Put another way, for Henrich, the lack of a successful objective deduction undermines at the very least the moments of approval and conviction requisite for moral insight. What is surprising is Henrich's lack of development of the relevance of the *Critique of Judgment* in elucidating the full extent of Kant's account of moral insight (and that despite Henrich's passing acknowledgment of the third *Critique*'s relevance). As presented in the course of the discussion in this chapter, one key element that addresses the concern Henrich raises is Kant's notion of rational faith understood as a principle of reflective judgment. Thereby the problem of an objective deduction is not solved, but its failure is proven not to be the obstacle to securing moral insight that Henrich seems to regard it.

2. In connection with this point, Dieter Henrich draws a number of parallels between Kant's account and that of Plato and Aristotle, specifically with regard to moral insight versus evil and the relation of each to character. "Plato's theory of moral education presupposes that anyone who knows the good is also a friend of the good. However, knowledge of the good cannot be obtained, or it is lost again, if it is not grasped by the entire soul. Evil is not the conscious enactment of what is not allowed. It takes place when our view of the good has been obscured. Therefore, it is all-important for moral knowledge that the soul learn to enjoy moral action in the right way, and that the forces that can darken moral insight are overcome. . . . Aristotle [too] means to show . . . that the virtue of moral insight cannot endure without the virtue of a moderate character. The Kantian moral philosophy also sees the concrete phenomenon of evil as a decay

(*G* 412), and (to recast the argument made thus far in our examination of his notion of character) to make such a shift in orientation from natural to practical necessity is to undergo the revolution in conduct of thought (*Denkungsart*) whereby character is first established. Beyond this first and fundamental step in the translation of form of thought into one's form of life, into reason's subjectively practical employment in the world, Kant identifies specific maxims as indispensable for, and belonging to, moral character. It is through these maxims that practical reason ultimately becomes "concretely effective in the conduct of life," that is, not only as understood in relation to the human capacities (as has been our focus thus far), but as these capacities (still in relation to reason, to its moral insight) are actually exercised in human life. Entailed therein is moral judgment, in relation to the good as the final purpose of humanity and in relation to the particulars of human life and community. Such judgment, guided by subjective principles or orienting maxims, is in its form reflective judgment. Rudolf Makkreel has already argued that "by more fully working out his conception of the moral life to include the duties of virtue and the decisions of conscience, Kant makes it possible for us to locate reflective judgment directly in the moral domain, not merely in the cultural and religious applications of morality discussed in the *Critique of Judgment.*"[3]

---

of moral principles. The categorical imperative formulates the demand of the good contrary to all desires that are determined by pleasure. . . . Man subtly refines the moral law until it fits his inclinations and his convenience, whether to free himself from it or to use the good for the justification of his own self-importance. Kant considers his entire philosophy an attempt to refute the sophistry of reason that is in the service of pleasure. In this way he also attempts to give firm support to insight into the good against dialectical artifices. Kant differs in this from Plato and Aristotle only in his conviction that education leading to a good character may not use any means other than the 'representation' of the idea of the good itself. It has enough power by itself to be reason and motive for action. The ontological character of this form of knowledge follows from the fact that the reality of evil is a destruction of moral insight. The self confirms the reality of the good in approving it. Where actions do not correspond to this approval, insight is also exposed to destruction. Approval is thus identical with the affirmation *that* the good exists. . . . The experience of moral life confirms the ontological character of our approval of the good. This is most evident when a human being decides to follow the good, clearly grasping it in a situation in which the 'natural' morality of personal obligations has lost its orienting force" ("Concept of Moral Insight," 65–66).

See also William James Booth, *Interpreting the World: Kant's Philosophy of History and Politics* (Toronto: University of Toronto Press, 1986), which recognizes that "Kant's concept of the practical raises the issue of orientation" (61, 65–66); and Friedrich Kaulbach, "Weltorientierung, Weltkenntnis, und pragmatische Vernunft bei Kant," in *Kritik und Metaphysik Studien*, ed. Friedrich Kaulbach and Joachim Ritter (Berlin: Walter de Gruyter, 1966), 60–75. Kaulbach interprets the concept of orientation, raised by Kant in regard to metaphysical aims, as a "characteristic achievement" of "pragmatic reason" (61).

3. Makkreel, "Differentiating Dogmatic, Regulative, and Reflective Approaches to History," in Robinson, *Proceedings of Eighth International Kant Congress*, vol. 1., pt. 1, 128. In a

The interpretation developed in this chapter goes a step further. With our conception of the "moral domain" incorporating the notion of character in its concrete role in human life, we can come to see Kant's account of reflective judgment as indispensable for completing his account of human morality.[4] For the subjective principles orienting us in relation to the transcendent, to the human community, to nature, and to reason itself complete the formal account of character in action, in relation to the world. Through these principles, the morally good comportment of mind (*Gesinnung*) is further actualized as the "deed (*Tat*) in appearance," or "conduct of life." We begin our interpretation by first examining the notion of orientation.

In its ordinary use (in both German and English) orientation has to do with one's position in relation to the points of the compass, a sense extended to establishing one's position more generally, in relation to given principles, circumstances, and so forth. Further, it can be used in the sense of instructing or informing oneself in relation to something. Prima facie, it is just this ordinary meaning that Kant builds on in "What Is Orientation in Thinking?" (1786, in which all but two occurrences of his use of the term and its cognates are found).[5] Additional interesting dimensions open up, however, when one takes into account the passages in Mendelssohn's *Morgenstunden* to which Kant is specifically responding.[6]

---

more recent paper, Makkreel underscores the point that it "is the transcendental principle of reflective judgment" that "places the subject within the world as an individual who participates in a community. . . . Only through reflective judgment does it become possible to conceive of the subject as a living ego that can respond to its situation. This is because the transcendental principle of reflective judgment is orientational: through the capacity to differentiate between inner and outer, between agreement and opposition, etc., it enables us to orient ourselves in the world" (Rudolf A. Makkreel, "The Various Roles of Judgment in Kant: From Provisional to Reflective Judgment" [paper presented at the twenty-ninth annual meeting of the American Society for Eighteenth-Century Studies, Notre Dame, Indiana, April 1998, 16–17]).

4. As Brandt and Stark have pointed out, Kant already entertains the notion of "reflective pleasure" in moral life in his lectures during the 1770s (introduction, xliv). Specifically, the Pölitz transcriptions provide this detail; Kant is reported to have called the pleasure resulting from the agreement of something with freedom (and hence with the whole of life) the "reflective pleasure" that is the intellectual pleasure enjoyed in the moral realm (*Ak* 28.1, 250).

5. This fact refers to its usage in the works published during Kant's lifetime and is verified by a computerized search of the Academy edition. The other two occurrences are found in the *Critique of Judgment* (193) and the Jäsche *Logic* (57).

6. Moses Mendelssohn, *Morgenstunden oder Vorlesungen über das Dasein Gottes* (Berlin: Christian Friedrich Boß, 1786). Kant cites pages 164–65. The section beginning on page 161 is entitled "Allegorical Dream: Reason and Common Sense."

Kant's general objection to the *Morgenstunden,* stated in both his orientation essay and a second short piece (also from 1786), is that the work remains an attempt to give a demonstrative proof of the existence of God.[7] It is noteworthy, however, that of Mendelssohn's entire book-length study, it is the section entitled "Allegorical Dream: Reason and Common Sense" that impresses Kant enough to respond with an essay of his own. In brief, the *Morgenstunden* recounts the story of travelers in the Alps who are following a pair of guides, a bizarrely attired female persona and a robust, coarse young man. All travel together until a crossroads is reached, at which point the two guides diverge, one taking the left fork, the other the right. The dismayed travelers stop and wait, uncertain whom to follow, when an elder matron comes up from behind to offer them advice. Identifying herself as the one known on earth as Reason (but never saying how she is known by heavenly beings), she recommends that the travelers be of good cheer and wait a short while; their guides, respectively called Contemplation, or Speculative Thought (*Beschaaung, contemplatio*), and Common Sense (*Gemeinsinn, sensus communis*), will return, and Reason will then arbitrate their dispute. In the part referenced by Kant, Mendelssohn translates this dream into a "rule" to serve him as a "guiding principle" or "guideline" (*Richtschnur*); namely, whenever he finds his speculations appearing to have left mainstream common sense (*Heerstraße des Gemeinsinns*) far behind, he will stop, "stand still, and seek to orient himself" by returning to his "point of departure and comparing his two guides (*Wegweiser,* literally signposts)." This rule is to be further applied to the doubts raised by idealists, egoists, and skeptics (with the example given being the question of the existence of the material world). Experience tells him, he notes, that truth usually turns out to rest with common sense, a point

---

7. The second piece referred to is "Some Observations on Ludwig Heinrich Jacob's Examination of Mendelssohn's *Morgenstunden*" (*Ak* 8:151–55). Mendelssohn writes in such a way, notes Kant, that one might think the critical philosophy dealt with unfounded doubts, but he quickly warns of the consequences of the path one takes in the use of reason, with Spinoza as an example of the kind of dogmatism that results from allowing reason in its speculative use to go beyond the sensible limits. Not only has Mendelssohn bypassed the inherent dispute of reason with itself, on Kant's assessment, he has also adopted the maxim of regarding philosophical disputes as mere differences over words. Kant disagrees, concluding instead that in those matters in which philosophical controversy has gone on for a long time, the issue concerns a genuine dispute over the objects involved and cannot be dismissed as a simple difference in the use of terms. Interestingly enough, a letter to Kant (dated May 14, 1787) from one of his former students, Daniel Jenisch, reports the eighty-one-year-old Mendelssohn to have remarked that, while he was now too old to follow up Kant's philosophy with his own response, nonetheless "the essay on orientation in the *Berliner Monatschrift* is the echo of my own profession of faith." Mendelssohn is further reported to have declared his a priori proofs to be "only the playful attempts of a sound human understanding that sees itself corrected by Kant's philosophy" (*Ak* 10, no. 277, 462).

that repeats an observation in the immediately preceding section in which Mendelssohn also concludes that whenever "sound, common human understanding" [gesunde, gemeine Menschenverstand] has been left far behind, it behooves reason to retrace the path leading back to it.

Readers familiar with Kant's original writings will recognize Mendelssohn's terminology and appeal to ordinary human understanding as means Kant himself employs both before and after 1786. "To orient oneself" is new for Kant as a term, but not as a concept. That we orient ourselves in our aptitudes, our inclinations, our choices, our thinking, and that we need do so in accord with proper principles, is a notion that may be traced through Kant's writings as far back as his *Observations* in 1764 (in which he discusses, for example, a "false direction" or orientation being given to the human "sensations" and "natural drives" [*B* 220, 241]). However, Kant expresses this notion and its attendant issues in all his other writings in terms of the variously nuanced verb *richten* and its noun form *Richtung*. Among the examples cited in our study thus far, the passage from Kant's essay of the same year, "Conjectural History," asserts that even a single step, however small a beginning, by giving "a completely new direction [or orientation, *Richtung*] to *Denkungsart*" will initiate an "epoch" (*M* 113). As we have seen, that human volition and the actions it effectuates be directed or oriented toward the ought (*auf das Sollen gerichtet*) is raised as an issue in the first *Critique* (*KrV* A548/B576). In addition to our opening citation referring to the compass used by the common understanding to guide its judgments, in the *Groundwork* we also saw Kant refer to a "particular direction" (*besonderen Richtung*) or orientation that is "peculiar [or proper, *eigen*] to human reason" (*G* 425). The human aptitudes in general, too, were accorded an inherent capacity for "directing" or "orienting" themselves (*sich richten*, GTP 173); or one might in this case use translations such as "adapt to," "act in accordance with," "conform to," or "adjust oneself." In its nonreflexive mode, the verb may simply mean "to straighten out," or it may carry the strong, normative connotation of "to judge"; Kant's uses reflect all of its nuances.[8]

8. Some other examples of Kant's use of this notion and its cognates include the following. *Dreams of a Spirit-Seer* (1766): "Eine geheime Macht nöthigt uns unsere Absicht zugleich auf anderer Wohl oder nach fremder Willkür zu richten" (*TG* 334); "der Betrug der Vernunft . . . der auch großen Theils durch willkürliche Richtung der Gemüthskräfte und etwas mehr Bändigung eines leeren Vorwitzes könnte verhütet werden" (360–61).

Critique of Pure Reason: "Bisher nahm man an, alle unsere Erkenntnis müsse sich nach den Gegenständen richten" (*KrV* Bxvi–xvii) "richtet sich aber der Gegenstand (als Objekt der Sinne) nach der Beschaffenheit unseres Anschauungsvermögen, so kann ich mir diese Möglichkeit ganz wohl vorstellen" (Bxvii); "Regeln oder Kriterien . . . ihren Quellen nach bloß empirisch, . . .

In light of such examples, one may suggest that what Kant finds persuasive in Mendelssohn's work are just those concepts and issues already la-

---

können . . . niemals zu Gesetzen a priori dienen, wonach sich unser Geschmacksurtheil richten müßte" (A21n/B35n); "Alles, was in der Natur unserer Kräfte gegründet ist, muß zweckmäßig und mit dem richtigen Gebrauche derselben einstimmig sein, wenn wir nur einen gewissen Mißverstand verhüten und die eigentliche Richtung derselben ausfindig machen können" (A642–43/B670–71); (discussion of use of transcendental ideas) "haben sie einen vortrefflichen und unentbehrlich notwendigen regulativen Gebrauch, nämlich den Verstand zu einem gewissen Ziele zu richten" (A644/B672); "in Beziehung auf welche [eine gleichsam selbständige, ursprüngliche und schöpferische Vernunft] wir allen empirischen Gebrauch unserer Vernunft in seiner größten Erweiterung so richten, als ob die Gegenstände selbst aus jenem Urbilde aller Vernunft entsprungen wären" (A672–73/B700–701); (in connection with the question of the agreement of the conception of the world with reason's moral employment) "Dadurch bekommt alle Naturforschung eine Richtung nach der Form eines Systems der Zwecke" (A815–16/B843–44); "die menschliche Vernunft, welche schon durch die Richtung ihrer Natur dialektisch ist." Examples of *richten* as judging are found in A551/B579, A755/B783. Examples of *Richtschnur* are found in A782–83/B810–11 and A844/B872; see also *KpV* 163; *RV* 37, 119; *MSR* 302, 313; *LJ* 15.

Prolegomena: "meinen Untersuchungen im Felde der speculativen Philosophie eine ganz andre Richtung gab" (*Pro* 260). *Groundwork* (1785): (about the pitfall of the philosopher) "sein Urtheil aber durch eine Menge fremder, nicht zur Sache gehöriger Erwägungen leicht verwirren und von der geraden Richtung abweichen machen kann" (*G* 404); "Beispiele . . . machen das, was die praktische Regel allgemeiner ausdrückt, anschaulich, können aber niemals berechtigen, ihr wahres Original, das in der Vernunft liegt, bei Seite zu setzen und sich nach Beispielen zu richten" (409).

Critique of Practical Reason (1788): (why principles are not necessarily laws) "weil die Vernunft im Praktischen es mit dem Subjecte zu tun hat, nämlich dem Begehrungsvermögen, nach dessen besonderer Beschaffenheit sich die Regel vielfältig richten kann" (*KpV* 20); "da sie nämlich als reine Vernunft, von den obersten Princip ihres reinen praktischen Gebrauchs ausgehend (indem dieser ohnedem blos auf die Existenz von Etwas, als Folge der Vernunft gerichtet ist), ihr Object bestimmt" (139); "Nachdem aber . . . die Vernunft . . . nicht anders als im Gleise einer vorher wohl überdachten Methode ihren Gang machen zu lassen, so bekam die Beurtheilung des Weltgebäudes eine ganz andere Richtung" (162–63).

Critique of Judgment (1790): "darin besteht eben das Geschmacksurtheil, daß es eine Sache nur nach derjenigen Beschaffenheit schön nennt, in welcher sie sich nach unserer Art sie aufzunehmen richtet" (*KU* 282); (benign intentions of those) "welche alle Beschäftigungen der Menschen . . . gerne auf den letzten Zweck der Menschheit, nämlich das Moralisch-Gute richten wollten" (298); (discussion of appropriate use of principles of reflective and determinant judgment) "welche sich nach den von dem Verstande gegebenen (allgemeinen oder besondern) Gesetzen richten muß" (389); "auf welche letzteren [andern Dingen in der Welt] entweder als Zwecke, oder als Gegenstände, in Ansehung deren wir selbst Endzweck sind, unsere Beurtheilung zu richten, eben dieselben moralischen Gesetze uns zur Vorschrift machen" (447); (discussion of the righteous man) "uneigennützig will er vielmehr nur das Gute stiften, wozu jenes heilige Gesetz allen seinen Kräften die Richtung giebt" (452); "so muß, wenn die theoretische Erkenntniß desselben vorhergehen müßte, die Moral sich nach der Theologie richten" (460).

Religion within the Limits of Reason Alone (1793): "es kann der Vernunft doch unmöglich gleichgültig sein, wie die Beantwortung der Frage ausfallen möge: was dann aus diesem unserm Rechthandeln herauskomme, und worauf wir, gesetzt auch, wir hätten dieses nicht völlig in unserer Gewalt, doch als auf einen Zweck unser Thun und Lassen richten könnten, um damit wenigstens zusammen zu stimmen" (*RV* 5); "Denn so früh wir auch auf unsern sittlichen Zustand unsere Aufmerksamkeit richten mögen, so finden wir: daß mit ihm es nicht mehr res integra ist" (58n); "Wer . . . diesem Geschichtsglauben die Bestrebung zum guten Lebenswandel nachsetzt (anstatt daß die erstere als

tent in his own.[9] In response, Kant takes what he has himself been implicitly assuming and becomes conscious of it as a question that needs to be explicitly addressed: "What *does* it *mean* to orient oneself in thought?" (to translate the title of his 1786 essay more literally). As he notes, "The enlarged and more precisely determined concept of orienting oneself may help us clearly depict the maxim of sound reason" in relation to "cognition of supersensible objects" (*DO* 134).[10] More is at stake than the integrity of the theoretical enterprise found in Mendelssohn's portrayal, as becomes evident when Kant expressly states his concern that the "concept of the highest good be given objective reality" and "not be held simply as a mere ideal" (*DO* 139). It must be remembered that the comportment of mind as identified with virtue is itself the highest term of the *summum bonum*, a fact that lends urgency to this concern. Given further that Kant's conception of character is defined in terms of conduct of thought, the question of orientation so conceived is obviously relevant to explicating this definition itself. In light too of the date of the essay (falling as it does between the *Groundwork* and the second *Critique*), it may be seen as a contributing component to the development of his mature sense of character.

Kant's recasting of the question Mendelssohn is taking up in fact brings to mind his own solution (begun in the *Critique of Pure Reason*, advanced in the *Prolegomena*, and completed and applied in the *Critique of Judgment*) to the problem of cognition of the transcendent: namely, to interpret it practically. Just such "pictorial conceptions," which make rational concepts "fit for use in experience" and allow us to attain to an "enlarged" concept and a "rule for thinking" about the object in question (*DO* 133), are central to Kant's critical sense of analogy whereby the objects of reason's ideas

---

etwas, was nur bedingterweise Gott wohlgefällig sein kann, sich nach dem letzteren, was ihm allein schlechthin wohlgefällt, richten muß), der verwandelt den Dienst Gottes in ein bloßes fetischmachen" (178).

"End of All Things" (1794): "hier mit Ideen zu thun haben . . . die die Vernunft sich selbst schafft, . . . in praktischer Absicht uns von der gesetzgebenden Vernunft selbst an die Hand gegeben werden . . . wie wir sie zum Behuf der moralischen, auf den Endzweck aller Dinge gerichteten Grundsätze zu denken haben (*ED* 332–33).

9. Recall that it was Kant himself who noted in his *Remarks on "Observations"* of 1764–65 that one cannot convince another except by means of the other's own thoughts or ideas (*BB* 30). Construed autobiographically and given, as in the case of Rousseau, latent and implicit articulations of these "thoughts" in Kant's own writings, one may infer that Mendelssohn's writing was virtually another case of "awakening Kant from his own slumber."

10. In his assessment of Kant's early writings, Cassirer has the following to say: "One should not look to this period for fundamental and ultimate philosophical judgments, for everything it contains shows it to belong to the process of intellectual *orientation* which Kant had first to work through for himself. In the later essay, 'What Is Orientation in Thinking?' Kant analyzed the meaning of the expression 'orientation'" (*Kant's Life and Thought*, 43).

are made comprehensible for us.[11] Along the way to this part of his solution, Kant has had to reconcile his own version of Mendelssohn's crossroads. For in his own account (as we will see) he allies moral principles with common sense, yet in one important respect it is *just for the sake of the practical* (which itself must be possible for all humankind) that the road traveled by common sense *must* be quit in favor of the one that speculation chooses for itself. As he had already observed in the *Prolegomena* (362–63): "The actual task of natural pure reason, constituted by the totality of all the transcendental ideas, compels it to leave behind the mere contemplation of nature and transcend all possible experience; this effort gives rise to that thing (be it knowledge or sophistry) called metaphysics." Kant goes on to conclude that "the aim of this natural aptitude, to free our concepts from the fetters of experience and the limits of the mere contemplation of nature, at least to the point of opening a field before us containing only objects for pure understanding, . . . is *not* for the purpose of speculatively occupying ourselves with them" (emphasis added). The aim is "rather that the practical principles" be provided, "for their necessary expectation and hope," with a "domain" in which "they are able to extend to the universality that reason unavoidably requires from a moral point of view." Part of the arbitration in the dispute between speculation and common sense, then, consists in redefining the purpose and scope of the activity undertaken on the former's path.

Moreover, instead of pursuing that path toward the goal of standing in the divine light of the "Platonic sun," in a further parallel to Mendelssohn's allegory and rule based thereon, Kant's account also calls for turning to (as one might put it) the illumination innate to human nature, namely, to common sense, to its principles as a sure and true guide for the concrete realization of moral insight, for the constitution and exercise of character in the world.[12] Indeed, one could go so far as to say that Nietzsche's char-

11. For an analysis of Kant's critical sense of analogy, see my article "'The Beautiful Is the Symbol of the Morally-Good,'" especially 301–9.

12. In short, involved here is a dimension of Kant's conception of immanent teleology, the teleology of reason toward humanity's final purpose. Otfried Höffe has argued for the pervasiveness of teleological elements in Kant's thought and connects these with the notion of orientation. "Ever since Aristotle, teleology, the orientation toward purposes (Greek: *tele*), has strongly influenced Western thought. . . . Kant ascribes an important function to teleology. It is thus wrong to think that Kant belongs to the modern anti-Aristotelian tradition, which disallows all attribution of purpose in philosophy and science. The teleological elements are not pre-Critical residues, which show that Kant cannot, despite his intellectual revolution, completely free himself from traditional philosophy. On the contrary, the attribution of purpose forms an integral part of the transcendental critique of reason. For one thing, Kant emphasizes the subjective nature of teleological judgments. For another, such judgments are found in all of his major works. In the

acterization (which he of course intended be a biting criticism) comes close to the mark in this respect: "Fundamentally the same old sun, but shining through mist and skepticism; the idea grown sublime, pale, northerly, Königsbergian."[13] In conjunction with his initial call for the "free employment of insight to rule over the propensity for passion," Kant had already at this early date (1755) referred to such realization of insight in terms of the "light of the power of judgment" that, "like rays of the sun" piercing through the clouds, could bring elucidation where there is but a state of "confusion" (*NH* 356–57). "To orient oneself," he writes over thirty years later in 1786, in its "actual meaning" refers to locating the remaining quadrants of the horizon by beginning from any given one; "in particular," it means "to find the *Aufgang*" (a word whose range of meaning includes sunrise itself, rising on the part of anything, a way or path up, even a staircase; *DO* 134). For the traditional metaphysician, to call speculation back to the human point of departure, to principles maintained by common sense, is to return to dim illumination indeed, but for Kant it is where and how moral insight dawns in and for the human world, how it makes its appearance in the world.

To express the matter more technically, whereas in the Platonic ascent human cognition is enlightened by a principle taken from the object, the thing in itself, the Form of the Good, here "to orient oneself in thought" is to bring a "subjective principle" or "maxim" to bear on judgment (*DO* 136). The illustrative appeal to our felt difference between our left and right hand, as an analogous "subjective basis" whereby we ascertain dif-

---

Critique of Pure Reason, the theory of regulative ideas relies upon reason's aim of complete knowledge. The teleological idea of the unity of happiness and worthiness thereof underlies the theory of postulates in the *Critique of Practical Reason.* In the philosophy of law and of history, Kant sees eternal peace as the ultimate goal ('meaning') of history. Yet Kant's thought reaches its teleological culmination only in the *Critique of Judgment.* The third *Critique* is connected in many ways with the whole of the critique of reason" (*Immanuel Kant,* trans. Marshall Farrier [Albany: State University of New York Press, 1994], 211–12). The original text is *Immanuel Kant* (Munich: Verlag C. H. Beck, 1983). Ludwig Siep finds that the *Critique of Judgment* provides a substantial portion of Kant's establishment of his philosophy of history, but argues that the teleological contemplation of nature therein follows the "Platonic and not the Aristotelian teleological cosmology" ("Das Recht als Ziel der Geschichte. Überlegungen im Anschluß an Kant und Hegel," in *Das Recht der Vernunft. Kant und Hegel über Denken, Erkennen und Handeln,* ed. Christel Fricke, Peter König, and Thomas Petersen, vol. 37 of Spekulation und Erfahrung. Texte und Untersuchungen zum Deutschen Idealismus (Stuttgart-Bad Cannstatt: Frommann-Holzboog, 1995), 356, 358. See also Jürgen-Eckardt Pleines, ed., *Zum teleologischen Argument in der Philosophie* (Würzburg: Königshausen & Neumann, 1991).

13. Friedrich Nietzsche, *Twilight of the Idols,* trans. R. J. Hollingdale (New York: Penguin Books, 1968), 40. Nietzsche's observation here is part of "How the 'Real World' at Last Became a Myth."

ferentiations in space, had already been made before by Kant in the *Prolegomena* (in the course of his defense of space and time as forms of our sensible intuition, against those unwilling to give them up as things in themselves—unwilling, that is, to give up the traditional and objective standpoint) (*DO* 134; *PRO* 285–86). Now, three years later, this "inner difference" that cannot be "made comprehensible by a concept" (*PRO* 286)—but which is notably (1) common to, and taken for granted by, every human being, (2) indispensable for finding our way in the world, for locating where we are in relation to the points of the compass and without which all objective, astronomic data cannot serve us, (3) relied upon by skeptic and dogmatist alike—this difference is drawn upon by Kant to explain what it means to orient oneself in thought. It is a highly suggestive analogy, then, for fully comprehending Kant's point about human judgment and his understanding of the notion of common sense.[14]

That judgment, indeed moral judgment, is at stake for Kant in this orientation in thinking is immediately and explicitly expressed in his essay.[15] Such a subjective principle of judgment, such a "maxim is necessary" in those cases in which it is not simply a voluntary choice as to whether or not one wishes to reach a certain judgment, but in which doing so constitutes reason's "real need" (*DO* 136). And, a few passages later, reason's twofold need—theoretical and practical—is further distinguished as to their respective urgency. In the former, making such judgments is conditioned (for example, on our simply "wanting" to make judgments about first causes of all in the world), but "far more important is the need of reason in its practical use"; here we "*must* judge," for example judge

14. Much of the scholarly attention given to the analogy considers the technical problem of incongruence. The reading here brings to light another dimension of Kant's reference to the inner sense of left and right.

15. That there is a link indeed between reflective judgment, in particular teleological reflective judgment, and the notion of orientation is argued for by Rudolf A. Makkreel (chap. 8 of *Imagination and Interpretation*). Makkreel's conclusions include the following: "On the level of judgment it is then possible to propose two reflective counterparts to orientation in space and thought; namely, an aesthetic orientation that evaluates the world on the basis of feeling of life and a teleological orientation that interprets culture on the basis of common sense or the *sensus communis*" (155). "Current writings . . . have placed a one-sided emphasis on the fact that every object is oriented *by* its horizon. But it is also important to recognize that the subject orients itself *to* both object and horizon" (159). Makkreel focuses on the hermeneutical role of "reflective interpretation" for orienting both the human and natural sciences: "The inclusion of the interpreting subject in the hermeneutic circle need not lead to a resubjectivization of hermeneutics. This is because direct discriminatory judgments using aesthetic and teleological orientation contribute to the process of finding our place within the overall horizon of the life-world. It is within this horizon that we can then articulate more limited systematic contexts in the way that Kant's teleological ideas can project a variety of purposive systems—organic, social, and cultural" (170–71).

the reality of the highest good (*DO* 139, emphasis added). Hence, the issue of the guiding principles whereby we do so is also all-important.[16] That, furthermore, "common sense" (identified with "sound reason," or the "common human understanding") is essentially involved is more than a matter of carrying over Mendelssohn's notion. Kant in fact challenges Mendelssohn's conception of it, insofar as it is understood to consist in a cognitive or objective insight on the part of reason, or in a kind of inspiration (*DO* 139–40). The allusion to common sense is also more than a matter of its being implicit in the appeal to the human sense of left and right.

Kant's own explicit references for how common sense is to be understood are made within his 1786 essay, as well as a number of other texts, including the third *Critique* and his moral writings. One passage in the Jäsche *Logic* reads as a virtual paraphrase of Mendelssohn's conclusions in the *Morgenstunden:* "The common human understanding (*sensus communis*) is also actually a touchstone for exposing the mistakes of a contrived use of the understanding. That is, to use the common understanding as a test for assessing the correctness of speculation is to orient oneself, in one's thinking or in the speculative use of the understanding, by means of the common understanding" (*LJ* 57). This passage is immediately followed by the "general rules and conditions for avoiding error," namely the three maxims of the common understanding, the third and culminating one being the resolute *Denkungsart* itself. In section 40 of the *Critique of Judgment,* Kant likewise moves from a discussion of the *sensus communis* to these "maxims of the common human understanding," although here he stipulates that "common sense," which is ordinarily simply identified with the latter, should be understood to mean "the idea of a sense shared by all" in the human "community; that is, a power of judging" whereby in our "reflections we take into consideration (a priori)" the way others could and would conceive of the matter at hand, thus avoiding the illusions that result from mistaking subjective and private conditions for objective ones (*KU* 293).[17] Besides continuing the close association of common

16. In the *Critique of Judgment,* Kant also speaks of judgment orienting itself; in this case it is the reflective principle of purposiveness that is the source of guidance, allowing judgment to orient itself amid the immense variety of nature (*KU* 193). In his essay on theory and praxis, in the course of discussing the need for an act of judgment as a middle term between the two, so that one can decide in the practical case whether or not a given particular falls under the rule (in other words, referring here too to reflective judgment), Kant also speaks of judgment orienting itself in accordance with rules; only, here he again resorts to the use of "sich richten" (*TP* 275).

17. Makkreel provides a discussion of the notion of *sensus communis* in Kant as related to "critical hermeneutics," as it allows us to attain to a "better understanding of both the self and

sense with judging, this description parallels that of the second maxim of the common human understanding. A limited discussion of these maxims was given in our first chapter, and we will return to them here to examine the link between them, common sense, character, and the relation of the latter to the human community. At this point, we recall only the additional factor that, in Kant's recounting of these maxims in the *Anthropology*, they are presented as the avenue to attaining wisdom, once in a practical (*ApH* 200) and once in a theoretical (*ApH* 228) context. Both these employments of reason are also discussed in Kant's *Reflections on Anthropology* when he refers to the same set of three as the "maxims of a mature (*reifen*) reason" (*RA* no. 1508, 820–22). Our focus is on the practical employment, in which the necessity of judging is underscored by Kant in his 1786 essay. What we are learning is that the appeal to common sense and to the common human understanding is by no means a singular reference, nor one made simply in response to Mendelssohn.

In fact, Kant makes repeated claims that the main principles and concepts of his moral philosophy are just those known and maintained by common sense.[18] Implicitly and explicitly they are said to share those characteristics previously delineated for the common, human sense of left and right. That is, they are guiding principles that are genuinely universal,

---

the other," as it "provides a mode of orientation to the tradition that allows us to ascertain its relevance to ultimate questions of truth" by "opening up the reflective horizon of communal meaning in terms of which the truth can be determined" (*Imagination and Interpretation,* 156–67). Makkreel emphasizes the distinction between *sensus communis* and the common understanding indicated by Kant in section 40 of the *Critique of Judgment,* noting that it is a "mode of orientation that must be found in each of us," but as a result of its "transcendental status" it "allows us to either assent or dissent from what is commonly held" (163). The latter refers to "beliefs that are actually found to be held in common" (158), but these are in turn distinct from the set of three maxims. For a further discussion of *sensus communis,* see also Rudolf A. Makkreel, "The Role of Reflection in Kant's Transcendental Philosophy," in *Transcendental Philosophy and Everyday Experience,* ed. Tom Rockmore and Vladimir Zeman (Atlantic Highlands, N.J.: Humanities Press, 1997), 92–93. See also Jens Kulenkampff, " 'Vom Geschmacke als einer Art von sensus communis'—Versuch einer Neubestimmung des Geschmacksurteils," in *Autonomie der Kunst? Zur Aktualität von Kants Ästhetik,* ed. Andrea Esser (Berlin: Akademie Verlag, 1995), 25–48.

18. Schiller (for example) accepted them to be such. In the first of his letters in *On the Aesthetic Education of Man,* Schiller makes the following observation about the "main ideas of the practical part of Kant's system": in regard to these, "only the philosophers are at variance; while humankind, as I am confident I will be able to prove, has been in agreement [about them] from time immemorial. One need only free [these ideas] of their technical formulation and they will emerge as the time-honored utterances of common reason and as the data of the moral instinct which nature in her wisdom appointed as humanity's guardian, until [such time as] clear insight would bring [humankind from a state of tutelage] to one of maturity" (*On the Aesthetic Education of Man: In a Series of Letters,* trans. Reginald Snell [New York: Frederick Ungar, 1983], 24; the original is *Über die ästhetische Erziehung des Menschen. In einer Reihe von Briefen* [Stuttgart: Reclam, 1965], 4).

inherent to all humans, not requiring specialized education, and transcending all times and cultures; they are certain, unquestioned in ordinary life, and indispensable. "Only philosophers," writes Kant, "could make debatable the answer to the question" as to what this pure morality as the touchstone of every action is; for "in the common human understanding . . . it has long since been decided, just like the difference between the right and left hand, by customary usage" (*KpV* 155). In the *Groundwork*, in addition to the passages already cited, Kant notes that the concept of "good practical desire, as it is already inherent in the natural, sound understanding," does "not so much need to be taught, but only clarified (*aufgeklärt*)" (*G* 397). One can only "admire," he goes on, "the great advantage the practical power of judgment has over the theoretical one in the ordinary human understanding" (*G* 404). Even in the "Typik" of the second *Critique*, Kant stops to observe that "even so the most common understanding judges"; in this case, in regard to the fact that any maxim of an action must conform to the form of the laws of nature if it is to be also morally possible (*KpV* 69–70). Again, in the *Metaphysical Principles of Virtue*, he asserts that "moral principles" are "nothing but a dimly conceived metaphysics inherent in the rational aptitude (*Vernunftanlage*) of every human being" (*MST* 376).

Likewise, the tenets of rational faith (which, if one is to be consistent, must be regarded as true when and wherever the reality of the highest good is affirmed) are fundamentally tenets held by the sound, common understanding. As one reads in the concluding passages of the *Critique of Pure Reason:* "It will be said, but is this all that pure reason can accomplish in opening up prospects beyond the limits of experience? Nothing more than two articles of faith? As much could very well have been achieved by the common understanding, without seeking the advice of philosophers in this regard!" (*KrV* A830–31/B858–59). As Kant also remarks in the B preface, this is an "insight concerning the universal human condition," and, as such, it is one equally in the reach of everyone in the human community (*KrV* Bxxxiii). These tenets are further identified by Kant with our "practical interest" and represent the case in which our "interest . . . unavoidably determines our judgment" (*KpV* 143; see also *Ak* 28.2.2, 1083). In his grappling with Mendelssohn's allegory and conclusions based thereon, Kant (in his 1786 essay) articulates his own position as we see it expressed in these passages from his *Critiques*. Mendelssohn got it right insofar as he maintained reason as the "ultimate touchstone of truth," and, concedes Kant, it is the case that the "common human understanding always" has reason's "own interest above all in view"

(*DO* 140). Where Mendelssohn got it wrong, at least on Kant's reading, was to credit speculation with insight in the sense of the power of demonstration in regard to reason's interests, especially in relation to the question of the existence of God. Properly understood, the "pronouncement of sound reason" here is a subjective principle, a maxim, more specifically a "source of judgment" that Kant calls "rational faith" (*DO* 140). Such a "pure rational belief (*Vernunftglaube*) is thus the guide (*Wegweiser*) or compass whereby" not only the "speculative thinker orients himself," but whereby "human beings of common, but (morally) sound reason are able to map out their path, both in regard to their theoretical and practical aims, completely commensurate with the *entire purpose of their vocation*" (*DO* 142, emphasis added).

With this statement Kant has explicitly interpreted orientation as a practical or moral matter, namely, as the question of those subjective principles whereby human beings may direct their course of life in a way that befits human moral vocation or destiny (expressed by reason's idea of the highest good). Recapping Kant's conclusions by making rhetorical use of the figures from Mendelssohn's dream, one might put it as follows. In our first chapter, we saw that character involved the question of the unity of thinking and acting as an efficacious moral agent in the world. In the divergence of speculation and common sense, a separation occurs between the two traditional associations made with these respective dimensions of human life. In the arbitration between them, reason (Mendelssohn's elder matron) sides with the "dimly conceived metaphysics" of common sense, denouncing the guidance of Speculation, who would part company with the latter on the road of life by denying, or at the very least undermining, beliefs essentially belonging (on Kant's comprehension of the matter) to the affirmation of the reality of the good—an affirmation identified also by Henrich as an essential moment of moral insight. Theoretically speaking, the task therefore (as Kant understands it) is to "deprive metaphysics of its injurious influence" and provide an alternative "path" (from the directions being taken by, for example, eighteenth-century dogmatists and skeptics) that leads instead back "to the main road (*Heeresstraße*)" (*KrV* Bxxxi, A856/B884); the task is in fact, of course, Kant's self-described task of critique. Moreover, while Kant's explicit challenge to Mendelssohn in the *Critique of Pure Reason* is to his proof for the immortality of the soul (B413ff.), implicitly in this text too, he addresses the position of the *Morgenstunden*. In his consideration of the proofs for the existence of God, Kant from the outset alludes to what is increasingly developed as his own position; namely, that it is just the "practical addition" (consonant with the "commonest understanding") that serves as the solution for "speculation's indecision" (*KrV* A589/B617).

Common Sense, in Mendelssohn's allegory, is an obstinate fellow and not at all drawn to conclusions reached in the intellectual enterprises of elitist byways. However, as Kant notes in the *Groundwork*, "morals are themselves subject to all kinds of corruption," and hence, for their sake, a philosophical articulation of their "guide (*Leitfaden*) and highest norm" is needed (*G* 390). This philosophical articulation (as we have argued all along) turns out to include not only the moral law objectively expressed, but the subjective side of morality's concrete realization in human life. The latter may now be understood to entail subjective principles of orientation, of (quite literally) signposts along the road of life that point the human subject toward ultimate human purpose. It is the natural light inherent to the human subject that provides illumination sufficient for the journey. Conduct of thought in accordance with these maxims or subjective principles realizes the translation of the morally good form of thought into the morally good form of life. Besides the subjective realization of the moral law itself, arguably the other general maxim is just this: adhere to the guidance inherent in the sound, common understanding. Under this rubric, the further maxims for the exercise of judgment on the road leading to the realization of ultimate human purpose may be grouped under three headings. First are those maxims directly related to the fulfillment of the human vocation and the assessment of our efforts in that regard: rational faith and conscience. Second, there is the set of the three maxims of sound understanding that prove, in the final analysis, to be principles for orienting the individual to the other (both to the self as other and to community) in such a way that the unanimity of particular and universal in the resolute conduct of thought is assured. Finally, there are those maxims identified by Kant as specifically "relating to character," principles that bear a remarkable affinity to the initial preliminary articles of the just constitution and themselves turn out to serve the exercise of character in and through human discourse.

REFLECTIVE PRINCIPLES OF ORIENTATION RELATING THE HUMAN SUBJECT AND REASON

Rational Faith

This notion has been received as a component of Kant's views on religion and thus has been examined to reconcile these views with aspects of the critical philosophy.[19] Many passages invite such scrutiny. The postulates or articles of belief falling under its rubric are said by Kant to belong to reason's "need." "No one," he writes, "is completely free of interest in these questions" (*KrV* A830/B858), an interest reason requires from a moral point of view and a claim that accords with the assertion that these are basic beliefs held by the common human understanding. Yet, it is Kant himself who begins the *Religion* with disclaimers to the effect that these articles of belief are in no way required either to "recognize" or "observe" one's duty; that is, either in regard to what concerns morality "objectively" ("volition"), or "subjectively" (the "ability" to do what one ought) (*RV* 3). Prima facie, then, it would appear that the connection of rational faith with character, with reason in its subjectively practical function, is no less problematic than it seems to be in relation to objective morality. However, it is noteworthy that over one-third of Kant's relatively few usages of the term *Vernunftglaube* occur in his 1786 essay, in connection with his explicit inquiry into the question of orientation of thought[20] (although the concept of moral belief appears at least as early as 1766 and references simply to belief are frequent). The following reconsideration of the term *rational faith* in light of the issue of orientation develops what has already been

---

19. Scholarly attention to this notion has focused on the content, the actual postulates or articles of belief. Familiar issues include reconciling Kant's claims with his own objective morality, on the one hand, and with a traditional conception of revealed religion and grace, on the other, as well as examining the relationship of religion so conceived to culture and history. Allen W. Wood pioneered the effort in Anglo-American philosophy to understand Kant's "doctrine of moral faith" as not only "consistent with his best critical thinking," but as "necessary for any genuine appreciation of the critical philosophy as a whole" (*Kant's Moral Religion*, vii); see also Wood's *Kant's Rational Theology* [Ithaca: Cornell University Press, 1978]. The most recent scholarly treatment of these questions continues the argument for situating Kant's account of religion as an integral part of his critical philosophy. See, for example, Rossi and Wreen, *Kant's Philosophy of Religion*. Rossi's other writings on this topic include "Autonomy and Community: The Social Character of Kant's 'Moral Faith,'" *Modern Schoolman* 61 (1984): 169–86; and "Kant's Doctrine of Hope: Reason's Interest and the Things of Faith," *New Scholasticism* 56 (1982): 228–38. For a wider study of the relation of reason and faith that explores "Kant's decisive contribution" consisting in a "practical rational foundation for religious belief," see Franz von Kutschera, *Vernunft und Glaube* (Berlin: Walter de Gruyter, 1990), viii. Based on a comparable reading of Kant and concluding that his "great achievement was to show that a rigorous development of the concepts of practical reason led directly to the main religious ideas of biblical faith, including those that criticized or set limits to reason's pretensions," Ronald M. Green argues for a reinterpretation of Kierkegaard's work as deeply influenced by the philosophical issues raised by Kant (*Kierkegaard and Kant: The Hidden Debt* [Albany: State University of New York Press, 1992], 222).

20. Of the thirty-one total occurrences of the term *Vernunftglaube*, eleven appear in this short essay, while only eight are found in Kant's *Religion*. One instance found near the end of the first *Critique* is also the first occurrence of the term in the works published during Kant's lifetime. Four are found in *Critique of Practical Reason*, four in the *Conflict of the Faculties*, and three in the Jäsche *Logic*.

alluded to, namely, that what is ultimately at stake is maintaining the human orientation to the good in the course of the conduct of life. In the process of inquiry from this perspective, a very specific and technical sense of rational faith emerges.

The explicit association of the two articles of belief (in the existence of God and a future world) is in fact made by Kant, first, with character and, second, with ultimate human purpose, or our human vocation. The "basis therefor lies in the moral *Denkungsart*"; especially in those "moments when the mind (*Gemüt*) is attuned to moral feeling (*Empfindung*)," it is "inclined to expanding its moral *Gesinnung*" (*KU* 445–46). Such "faith"[21] is so "interwoven with the moral *Gesinnung*" that, without forfeiting the one, there is no danger of losing the other (*KrV* A829/B857). These statements of the first and third *Critiques* are foreshadowed already in *Dreams of a Spirit-Seer* (1766). "It is more in keeping with human nature and the purity of morals to base the expectation" of a world beyond this one on a "just soul," on a "noble *Gesinnung*," than to base "good conduct (*Wohlverhalten*) on the hope of another world. The same holds in the case of moral belief" (*TG* 373). Moreover, Kant here describes moral belief (or "moral faith") in terms that correspond to its association with the common human understanding—indeed, in terms sympathetic with Mendelssohn's account twenty years later. Its "simplicity is able to dispense with many of the subtleties of sophistry; it alone and uniquely is suited to human beings under any circumstances, for it leads them straightaway to their true purposes. Let us therefore leave all these clamorous theories about such remote objects to the speculation and care of idle minds. These theories are, indeed, a matter of indifference to us" (*TG* 373).

As indicated by these passages, moral conduct of thought and its attendant comportment of mind are said to be the ground and source of moral, or as Kant comes to call it, rational faith,[22] a point about which he is also

21. *Glaube*, especially in the phrase *Vernunftglaube*, has been most often translated as "faith," although I have here also been rendering it in its basic form as "belief." Standard connotations borne by "belief" and "faith" may both be potentially misleading in conveying the sense in which Kant uses the term: for, "belief" as "opinion" is too little, while "faith" as "religious faith" (especially if the latter is understood in the context of a relationship with a living God) often connotes too much.

22. Some commentators find the use of two notions, moral faith and rational faith, particularly significant. As we see in the examples of the passages cited, both are used by Kant in reference to the postulates and the first introduction of the notion of rational faith in his writings comes in close connection with the reference to moral faith or belief. That first usage of *Vernunftglaube* comes in the first *Critique*'s discussion of opinion, knowledge, and belief. Having just spoken of "moral belief" and the "belief in the existence of God and another world" as being a matter of "moral certitude," without any explanation for changing the terms, Kant goes on in the next

very explicit in his response to Mendelssohn, whose mistake it was to fail to recognize "rational faith" as the "source" of the judgment in regard to the existence of God (*DO* 140). Yet, the role given by Kant to rational faith in relation to the moral conduct of thought and comportment of mind lies in sustaining the latter's steadfastness (for which one of the clearest statements is found in the *Critique of Judgment,* 472).[23] Now if character is resolute conduct of thought and yet first gives rise to rational faith, how are we to understand Kant's point?

In our discussion of the previous chapter, it was the oscillation between incitement and command to which the human agent lacking character (lacking, that is, the singular resolve, the commitment also synonymous with virtue in its formal sense) was subject. In the relevant third *Critique* passages, the poles of opposition are drawn, not between human sensible and moral nature, but within the operations of the rational faculty itself, between the theoretical demand for demonstration (Speculation's chosen path) and the moral insistence on claims that arise in relation to human final purpose and that also accord with the way of Common Sense. Without moral faith, "upon the contravention of theoretical reason's demand for a proof (of the possibility of the objects of morality), the moral *Denkungsart*" enjoys "no firm steadfastness and vacillates instead between practical commands and theoretical doubts" (*KU* 472). A few lines earlier, Kant identifies faith or belief (*Glaube*), considered "not as an act" but as "*habitus*" (the term we saw elsewhere defined as proficiency in choosing), as the "moral *Denkungsart*" on the part of "reason in regarding as true what is inaccessible to theoretical cognition" (*KU* 471). Faith thus identified with *Denkungsart* is the "steadfast principle of the mind to accept as true, *because of our obligation to [our] final purpose,* what we must necessarily presuppose as the condition of its possibility" (*KU* 471; emphasis added to underscore the parallel to the statement of the need for orienting principles in the 1786 essay; see also *KU* 446). A similar statement appears in the *Critique of Practical Reason:* the "principle" that "determines our

---

paragraph to address the potential misgivings that might arise since "this rational faith [or belief] is based on the presupposition of moral *Gesinnungen*" (*KrV* A828–29/B856–57).

23. Among Kant's other passages relating faith or belief with the moral comportment of mind and conduct of thought, the same mutual interdependence is in evidence. For example, in the Jäsche *Logic* one reads that "the greater one's moral *Gesinnung* is, the firmer and livelier will also be one's belief in all that one feels compelled, in [one's] practically necessary aim, to assume and presuppose on the basis of moral interest" (*LJ* 70). On the other hand, as late as 1798 Kant again writes that "only through this belief" (called "rational belief" in a similar context a few pages later) will the *Gesinnung* be characterized by the "courageous spirit" and "firmness" requisite to pursuing a "conduct of life (*Lebenswandel*)" that is well pleasing to God" (*SF* 44).

judgment" to assume the existence of a wise Author of the world is the "basis of a maxim to regard as true in [our] moral aims that which, while subjectively a need, is also however at the same time a means for promoting what is objectively (practically) necessary; that is, it is a pure practical rational faith (*Vernunftglaube*)" that is itself "not commanded," but "has arisen from the moral *Gesinnung*" (*KpV* 146). In the first *Critique*, Kant notes that the "word *belief*[or faith] refers only to the guidance (*Leitung*) that an idea gives me" (A827/B855), and, as we have already seen, in his 1786 inquiry into the notion of orientation in thinking, rational faith is said to be the "guide (*Wegweiser*) or compass whereby . . . human beings of common, but (morally) sound reason are able to map out their path" in life "completely commensurate with the entire purpose of their vocation" (*DO* 142).

In short, Kant understands rational faith or belief exactly in terms of what, by the third *Critique*, is his developed conception of reflective judgment; indeed, at one point in the *Religion* he notes that "one could call" such faith "reflective" (*RV* 52).[24] A problem in general to be solved by the *Critique of Judgment* is just that the realm of reason's ideas "is to have an influence" on the sensible world; namely, "the concept of freedom is to actualize in the sensible world the purpose enjoined by its laws," and that, in turn, requires the possibility of a "transition in *Denkungsart* in accordance with the principles [of freedom] to that in accordance with the principles [of nature]" (*KU* 176). Where this transition is one between reason and understanding, the reflective principle of purposiveness fulfills the need. However, as Kant had noted already in the *Critique of Practical Reason*, when the issue is the "practical task" of actualizing reason's idea of the "highest good" and the sought-for agreement (of this task) is "not only with morals in terms of their form," but with the source of their exercise, with the causality (the moral *Gesinnung*) of rational beings who lack the power over nature to effect the harmony of their happiness and practical principles, then more is needed than the preceding agreement with the form of the laws of freedom (*KpV* 124–25). Essential to the "supreme cause of nature, insofar as it must be presupposed for the highest good," is not only its operation in accordance with the law, but that the "representation of this law" be the "supreme determining ground of its practical desire"; thus it must be conceived as a being of both intelligence and volition—as a God (*KpV* 125). In view of the moral task, practical

24. Adina Davidovich has argued that "in order to begin to read Kant's *Religion*, one must first carefully read his *Critique of Judgment*" ("How to Read *Religion within the Limits of Reason Alone*," *Kant-Studien* 85 [1994]: 1–14).

reason in a reflective mode of judgment avails itself, against the doubts raised through the failure of speculative attempts at demonstration, of the subjective principle of "regarding as true what is inaccessible to theoretical cognition," but necessary from a moral point of view. To do so is just what it means to have rational faith.

Moreover, to do so is also consciously to orient oneself in one's thinking and in one's actions in the world, now in terms not of an inner sense of left and right, but of an individual moral certitude that, on the basis of affirming the conditions of its realizability, allows one unwaveringly to affirm the human vocation, the highest good and human final purpose as one's own (individually and collectively). The one who says "I am morally certain" (*KrV* A829/B857) has achieved the stance of a very deliberately arrived at and articulated moral insight (where the moments of approval and conviction are seen as essential components of such insight). Thus firmly to position oneself in relation to the highest good in thought, supports perseverance in the concrete pursuit of its realization; with this compass in hand, one is always certain of the direction in which one is going.[25] Indeed, such "practical conviction" (as Kant also refers to "moral rational faith") is "often more unshakable than a great store of knowledge," for "in the case of knowledge, one remains attentive to opposing reasons, but not in the case of faith, for here it depends on the moral interest of the subject and not on objective grounds" (*LJ* 72). Knowledge and opinion share a certitude in kind, differing only in its degree; firm belief or faith is accompanied with a "consciousness of its invariability" (*DO* 141, also 141n; see also *KrV* A820–31/B848–59).

Orientation in thinking in this regard really does have to do with the spirit—the degree, consistency, and endurance of effort—with which the moral life is pursued, or, as Kant puts it, with sustaining the steadfastness of the morally good comportment of mind. For where reason has become subjectively practical, where morally good form has been enacted in human thought and life, there is ipso facto (as Kant underscores immediately

25. It lies beyond the scope of the present project to take up the inquiry here, but to the extent that for Kant "rational faith" is the essence of religion, to leave things at this point in the present interpretation would indeed be to see his conception of religion as essentially a moral affair. For instance, one decisive break here with religious orthodoxy is that, unlike an Augustinian or Thomistic position, God is not in himself the final end and good of the human. The journey here is not immediately toward union with the Godhead; the orientation is not to God first and foremost, but to the good that in its perfection requires more than human power is able to effect but remains nonetheless distinct from the Supreme Being. However, this reading does not exhaust all that Kant has to say about religion (and Christianity in particular); for current discussion of these issues see Rossi and Wreen, *Kant's Philosophy of Religion*.

following his opening disclaimer in *Religion*) the question of outcome: "It is impossible for reason to be indifferent as to how the answer to the question, what is to be gained from our just actions, might turn out" (*RV* 5). The issue is not *whether* the good is to be done, at least not within the parameters of Kant's account of morality either objectively or subjectively speaking. The "duty" to work toward the "realization and promotion of the highest good in the world," including our awareness of this as our duty, follows as a subjective effect of the moral law (*KpV* 126); this is the "purpose" toward which we are to "direct" (*richten*) all our "actions" (*Tun und Lassen*) (*RV* 5; see also *LJ* 68n). It is the single-mindedness, the wholeheartedness of the effort on the part of the human rational agent that is now being addressed. Whereas the establishment of character, the realization of reason as subjectively practical entailed, we concluded, enacting morally good form in human thought and life, one might phrase what follows from that as a call to be, not merely responsive as a human subject to practical necessity, but proactive concerning the good in relation to human life in the world (both our own and others).[26] Not just the formal determination of action, but "expanding" our sights "to securing the purpose possible through such action," to effecting (in other words) a successful outcome, is at stake. This means nothing less than (as is well known to Kant's readers) the actualized unity of perfect virtue and of the "possession" of the extent of "happiness proportionate" to our moral worthiness (*LJ* 69n; *KpV* 144).

Wherever this topic is broached by Kant in the various texts, three attendant issues are also raised: the *reality* of the object of reason's idea of the highest good, the *steadfastness* of the moral comportment of mind, and *rational faith*. The 1786 essay on orientation is no exception: the "highest good," unlike the purely formal, moral determination of human volition, choice, and action, "depends" not only on "human freedom," but "also on nature," and it is of the essence that this concept be "given objective reality" if "it, together with the whole of lived morality," is not to be dismissed as a "mere ideal" nowhere to be found in existence (*DO* 138–39). Thus to give reason's transcendental ideas objective reality is, of

---

26. It is important to recognize, as Rudolf Makkreel has pointed out, that "by relating moral belief to reflective judgment, Kant is able to claim that its subjective validity is for us (human beings in general). It is not merely the case that only I in the private sense can be morally certain; rather, we as human beings are entitled to this certainty. It cannot be proved determinantly that God exists objectively; but it can be shown that we are required to judge him to exist in relation to the human community. . . . God is thus transformed from an abstract postulate of private morality into a teleological ideal that can help orient the historical trajectory of the human community" (Makkreel, "Various Roles of Judgment," 14).

course, one of the self-prescribed tasks of the critical philosophy, one that is answered by reinterpreting the problematic, theoretical ideas as practical ones, that is, by recasting them as a moral task, as a maxim that it is the moral agent's duty to adopt. Indeed, Kant writes in the *Critique of Practical Reason* that the task of the "teachings of wisdom" is to "determine this idea" of the highest good "practically, that is, adequately for the maxims of our rational conduct (*Verhaltens*)" (*KpV* 108). Why, in the case of *this* idea, is the critical solution not enough? As already noted, there is no less of a question here in relation to character, to reason's subjectively practical exercise, than there is in regard to the relation of rational faith and Kant's objective morality. Where character is established, the morally good order of maxim adoption characterizes choice, while firm resolve characterizes the comportment of mind. Potential hindrances to morally good choice and conduct arising from inclinations, passions, and the propensity for evil have here all been successfully confronted. Whence could or would wavering in the striving for actualizing the good as human purpose now arise?

Kant is very explicit that it is this "striving," what we have called a "proactive" effort in human life in relation to the good, that is at issue: it must be ensured that this "striving not be seen as utterly futile in its effects" and that "the danger of it thereby flagging" in its efforts be avoided (*KU* 447). The fundamental difference in this aspect of moral life has already been alluded to: unlike the concrete enactment of morally good form in choice and action, the outcome (effects) of such striving depends on more than the individual ground of freedom, its objective determination of choice and subjective actualization as character. And, the "flagging" that Kant is concerned about lies not with physical fatigue, but with maintaining mental strength, conviction, or *fortitudo moralis* in a lifetime of effort, in the face of the perceived human inadequacy to fulfill the task. The threat is again ultimately within; namely in human rationality's becoming a house divided against itself in regard to the "practical employment of reason," to the "feasibility of carrying out" its purpose (*KU* 470–71; also 471n). In a parallel discussion to the one here in the *Critique of Judgment*, in the *Logic* one finds a description of rational faith, of the regarding as true of those conditions under which the highest good is realizable, as the "*casus extraordinarius* without which practical reason cannot maintain [or preserve, *erhalten*] itself in regard to its necessary purpose, and which stands it in good stead *favor necessitatis* in its own judgment." Practical reason "can . . . only oppose whatever hinders it in the use of this idea" (*LJ* 68n).

What can threaten the self-preservation of reason is self-contradiction or per se impossibility. In this case, the antinomy is not simply a theoretical one; reason cannot both author an idea and enjoin the human to actualize it as a purpose and, at the same time, recognize this purpose as "nothing but a chimera [or pipe dream, *Hirngespinst*]" (*KU* 472). The rational, logical consequence of holding the latter view is, as Kant repeats in both the second and third *Critiques,* to call the moral law itself into question (*KpV* 114, *KU* 452–53, 471n). "Dogmatic unbelief" is hence completely incompatible with *Denkungsart* in which the moral maxim prevails, while faith or belief mixed with doubt raises the obstacle (albeit surmountable) of "lack of conviction"; to the latter, "critical insight into the limits of speculative reason" may yet successfully respond on the behalf of practical interest (*KU* 472). Within the parameters of Kant's system, the stakes have been set so high by at least these two factors: (1) his basic assumptions of the nature of reason itself, especially its inherent demand for totality and completeness, entailing that its idea be one of nothing less than a complete good (and this, in terms of human natural and moral purpose is just the idea of complete happiness and perfect virtue);[27] and (2) his account of character, entailing that human agents of morally good character inherently recognize their duty and indeed desire to realize the "good in appearance," the good as a "deed," which is to say, as the whole that is their "conduct of life" (*Lebenswandel*) (*RV* 67).[28] The further recognition on

27. That "reason in its practical employment" seeks totality no less than in its speculative use is explicitly identified as just the difficulty to be dealt with if the idea of the highest good is to be defined in such a way as to make it suitable for the maxims of our rational conduct. For the "practically conditioned (for what rests on inclinations and natural need)," practical reason "seeks the unconditioned totality of the object of pure practical reason under the name of the highest good" (*KpV* 108). The corresponding *Gesinnung* to such an unconditioned totality is that which would be commensurate with the archetype of moral perfection, namely the Son of God (*RV* 61, 74). Reconciling this ideal of holiness with the effect that human beings are able to bring about in conduct of life as the deed that is to correspond to this idea as the "good in appearance" is the topic of "Difficulties Raised against the Reality of this Idea and Resolution Thereof" in the *Religion* (*RV* 66–78).

28. Scholars have debated this notion that the duty to actualize the highest good follows from the moral law. In recent years at least one response has recognized the intrinsic connection with character (albeit the latter is conceived essentially in terms of the notion of will). I am referring to Stephen Engstrom's cogent discussion of how and why the concept of the *summum bonum* "has a legitimate place in [Kant's] conception of morality" ("The Concept of the Highest Good in Kant's Moral Theory," *Philosophy and Phenomenological Research* 4 [1992]: 747–80). Engstrom correctly argues that "the primary focus of attention in Kant's moral theory is not, as is often thought, on isolated instances of choice and action, but rather on a person's disposition or character. . . . Although the moral law does not depend upon or presuppose any material for its *validity,* it does depend upon or presuppose material for its *employment.* . . . An action whose determining

the part of these agents, that neither the whole of conduct of life as the good in appearance in time, nor its basis, the finite, human *Gesinnung* (whose propensity for evil cannot be extirpated), can be brought by human effort into complete commensurability with reason's idea, if and when left solely to the judgment of reason from a practical point of view, entails the rational faith that affirms the conditions of the realizability of its idea by such agents (*RV* 67ff., 139ff., 163). Thereby, steadfastness in their thought and efforts vis-à-vis the good as the human final purpose would be secured.

In regard to this inner obstacle, the assessment of human final purpose as defined by reason as amounting to nothing but a fantasy, Mendelssohn's allegorical dream is again relevant. The two guides on the road of the human journey toward its destination begin in relative concord. For each, the unconditioned transcendent, albeit in a different way and for different reasons, is the shared end. The crossroads is reached when speculation, insisting on the path of demonstration, comes back with theoretical doubts; having failed in its own quest for a definitive, rational proof for the conditions making possible the journey, it points out further that neither human "physical power, nor the cooperation of nature" can be relied upon to complete the journey (*KU* 471). Neither guide (the speculation of the schools, nor the common understanding, which simply relies on the dimly conceived metaphysics inherent in the human soul) wants to

---

ground is the law itself is more than just permissible. It expresses a moral disposition and hence is the virtuous action of a good will. . . . The good is an object desired through reason, and to desire an object through reason is to desire in such a way that the object can agree with the formal features of the concept of the good. . . . For the claim we are concerned with is determined by the disposition of a person's will (that is, by a person's character) and hence can be called the practical attitude that underlies a person's conduct. . . . Whether or not it happens to be expressed in our words or consciously articulated, this attitude, as a practical attitude, is *without fail expressed in our actions*" (748, 752, 756, 758, 760; emphasis added).

Philip Rossi has defended the thesis that the notion of the highest good itself plays a "systematic role" in Kant's critical project, that it "serves as the most complete resolution that Kant gives . . . to the issue of the mutual relation between the exercise of human (moral) freedom and the nexus of causal relationships that constitute nature" ("The Final End of All Things: The Highest Good as the Unity of Nature and Freedom," in Rossi and Wreen, *Kant's Philosophy of Religion*, 132).

For a study that considers the concept of the highest good in the context of a larger analysis of the notion of purpose as such, see Rudolf Langthaler, *Kants Ethik als "System der Zwecke." Perspektiven einer modifizierten Idee der "moralischen Teleologie" und Ethikotheologie,* Kantstudien Ergänzungshefte (Berlin: Walter de Gruyter, 1991), especially 54–79. See also Klaus Düsing, "Das Problem des höchsten Gutes in Kants praktischer Philosophie," *Kant-Studien* 62 (1971): 5–42; Gerhard Kramling, "Das höchste Gut als mögliche Welt," *Kant-Studien* 77 (1986): 273–88; and John Silber, "The Moral Good and the Natural Good in Kant's Ethics," *Review of Metaphysics* 36 (1982): 397–438.

give up these principles, but while the questions raised are hotly debated, human actors wait uncertain at the crossroads, their erstwhile confidence shaken as they listen first to one and then the other. In Kant's parallel and more technically articulated consideration of this scenario in the *Critique of Judgment*, he presents the case of the individual who, "partly due to the weakness of all the so highly praised speculative arguments, and partly due to the many irregularities found in nature and the moral world," has become persuaded that there is no God (*KU* 451). "How," asks Kant, will such individuals "judge their own inner determination to a purpose," following as it does "from the moral law that they actively revere" (*KU* 452). The individual in question is one of good character and *Gesinnung*, one who esteems the good for its own sake and not for personal advantage[29] and "toward which the holy law has" in the first place "directed all his powers" (*die Richtung giebt*), but who quickly confronts the limits to human efforts and the ills endemic to the human situation: one can expect at most nature's contingent cooperation in one's efforts, while vice abounds, on the one hand, and the ills of deprivation, disease, and untimely death visit the righteous with utter disregard for their virtue, on the other (*KU* 452).

The answer to this issue (which as just expressed, amounts of course, to a restatement of the traditional "problem of evil"), the decision to be made at the crossroads, takes for Kant the form of an either/or. Either moral purpose must be given up as impossible, with the unavoidable consequence of impairment to the morally good *Gesinnung*, or human orientation on the road toward this good is maintained by the assumption of rational faith (*KU* 452).[30] The latter, first and foremost, addresses the issue of the "intelligibility" or "comprehensibility" of human final purpose conceived as this ideal of the highest good, as Kant had already indicated in the *Critique of Practical Reason* (*KpV* 126). Just because the pursuit of the good is not a matter either of instinct or inclination, but authored by reason and executed through deliberate choice, the conceptual possibility

29. That the good in question must be desired and esteemed by us for its own sake and that this is just what follows from a morally good *Denkungsart* that rests on formal principles is underscored in *Reflections on Anthropology* (*RA* no. 1518, 871).

30. Kant does not entertain the further question of reconciling the affirmation of the existence of a benevolent Creator with these very ills of the human condition. Not only would such a question broach just the kind of metaphysical speculation that would inevitably fall into interminable debate at the crossroads, but it also has been to a certain extent set aside by the way Kant has cast the human moral task. The latter just is the long road of working ourselves out of an initial brutish, natural state toward a morally perfected one. What must be ensured is that the goal itself is not given up as both a conceptual and actual impossibility.

of grasping it as meaningful in and for the world is crucial. To overcome the vacillation between theoretical doubt and moral command, the voice simply of common sense is not enough. It is itself easily corrupted (as Kant noted at the beginning of the *Groundwork*), and, as also portrayed in Mendelssohn's story, its stance is seen as little more than sheer stubbornness by the opposing party. Nor will the response do that Goethe puts into the mouth of the scholarly Faust: "Call it happiness, heart, love, God, I do not have a name for it! *Feeling* is everything; a name is but sound and smoke" (emphasis added).[31] Difficulties that arise from and within the rational faculty cannot be allayed by resorting to feelings without. Thus too it is Reason, the elder matron who on her own testimony generally finds for common sense, who arbitrates the dispute in Mendelssohn's account. Again restating the point in Kant's terminology, she is wisdom, who defines the moral idea in a way suited for maxims of human practical employment. She exercises that judgment (as Kant describes it in the preface to the third *Critique*) "whose correct use is so necessary and universally required, that nothing else but this power" of judgment can be "meant by the name of the sound understanding" (*KU* 169). For the sake of the human practical vocation, she invokes the reflective principle of regarding as true what is necessary therefor; she invokes the maxim of rational faith, and the human traveler, whose initial orientation toward the final purpose of the highest good had been given by the moral law, may now continue the journey with renewed steadfastness, reconfirmed in the resolve that is the essence of morally good character.

What this renewed steadfastness consists in, what judgment has brought about, is a relationship of inner trust between practical reason and the human agent, a trust that undergirds the proactive working toward the good by the morally good character in the world. To have faith (or belief) purely and simply speaking, writes Kant, is to have "trust (*Vertrauen*) in the attainment of an aim we are duty [bound] to advance, but for which we lack insight in regard to the possibility of carrying it out" (*KU* 472). It is a "free assent" (or "regarding as true") that means also that the individual who maintains it "cannot compel another" thus to assent "on the basis of [given] grounds" (*KU* 472; *LJ* 69n; see also *KrV* A829/B857). Just as the initial establishment of character consists in the revolution in conduct of thought in each subject, likewise this judgment can only be made by the individual. Where it is made, it takes the form of

---

31. Johann Wolfgang von Goethe, *Faust. Eine Tragödie*, in *Goethes Werke*, vol. 3, lines 3454–57.

an inner relationship upon which the external exercise of character in the effort to realize the good concretely in the world depends. More specifically, it is an inner promissory relationship, as Kant characterizes it in *Religion within the Limits of Reason Alone, Critique of Judgment,* and *Logic.* In connection with an explicit discussion of rational faith, he writes, "Faith (*fides*) is actually keeping faith (*Treue*) in an agreement (*pacto*), or a subjective mutual confidence (*Zutrauen*), that the one will keep the promise [made] to the other. . . . According to the analogy, practical reason, so to speak, is the promisor (*Promittent*), the good anticipated from the act, the promised [object] (*Promissum*), and the human being [is] the recipient of and respondent to the promise (*Promissarius*)," the one bound by it who must concretely deliver on it (*LJ* 69n).[32] In the third *Critique,* as a footnote to his identification of faith or belief with reason's moral *Denkungsart* (in regarding as true what is inaccessible to theoretical cognition), Kant's description of what *fides* expresses parallels the statement in the *Logic;* here too reason (through the moral law) is portrayed as making the promise (*Verheißung*) that the final purpose is attainable for the human subject (*KU* 471n). Again, in the *Religion,* Kant observes that human beings are not only "called to a good conduct of life (*Lebenswandel*) by the moral law," but "find within the promise" that they will be able to fulfill this calling (*RV* 144).

In sum, then, on just the human acceptance of the promise of the good, that is, of the latter's reality *for the human,* on this inner relation of trust between human subject and practical reason depends that external positioning or orientation of the self vis-à-vis the good that consists in a lifelong act (conduct of life) that corresponds to the morally good comportment of mind. Accepting the judgment of the elder matron, the human traveler walks on, in and by rational faith. With this essential signpost having been read and heeded, however, further checkpoints must occur

32. The Latin used here by Kant involves the termination "-ario," which has a wide enough semantic variability to generate scholarly examination of its meanings. Hence I have translated *promissarius* by such a lengthy phrase. For a discussion, see Edward W. Nichols, "The Semantics of the Termination -ario," *American Journal of Philology* (1929): 40–63; my thanks to my colleague, Gretchen Reydams-Schils, for this reference. Nichols notes: "-ario- in itself has a tolerably vague possibility of meaning, though it may reasonably be expected to signify instrument, agent, or place, rather than likeness, material, or abundance. The range of its possible meaning is narrowed and its content made more definite when it is appended to a noun stem. When the adjective so formed is attached to a noun the appropriate meaning of the termination usually appears; but the further content is often necessary to make it certain. . . . In each example, the only factors to be considered are the actual meaning of the stems involved and the psychological probabilities or possibilities of the relations between them." Elsewhere he notes three more specific, possible meanings: "working at," "bound" or "obligated by," and "ordinary agent meaning" (62, 60).

along the way to ensure that the traveler has not strayed from the path, inadvertently or otherwise. Here again, an internal relationship obtains within the subject involving a subjective principle of directing or orienting oneself: conscience. To this relation and principle we now turn.

Conscience

Kant's various characterizations of this "marvelous capacity within us" (*KpV* 98) underscore its commonality to all humankind, its connection with character and conduct of life, and its role in providing direction and serving as judge. A "guide" for even the "most questionable moral decisions" (*RV* 185), it is "not acquired," but found "originally in everyone as a moral being" (*MST* 400). "Conscience is practical reason" in its role of "holding before human beings in every case their duty under law, for acquittal or condemnation," and its relation is "solely to the subject" (whose "moral feeling" is thus "affected by" reason's "act") (*MST* 400). So, we see here yet another concept explicitly identified by Kant with practical reason, a fact that by now one must understand to mean that all these concepts so identified represent distinctions in the function and exercise of this one fundamental capacity and are not independent powers found in human nature. As an "authority (*Gewalt*) watching over the laws within," conscience is (as it were) "incorporated into the [very] being" of human nature (*MST* 438). It is thus effectively an "innate judge" of humans over themselves, a "court" before which they stand for sentencing (*MST* 437ff.; *RV* 77, 146n). As such a "presentation of duty," conscience is an "original intellectual moral aptitude," whose "business" is one of "human beings with themselves" (*MST* 438).

Particularly evident in these characterizations is the allusion to an internal relation of the self to itself as an "other." The "distinctions" of the "double self," as the one brought before court and the judge who sentences (as these are expressed in the *Metaphysical Principles of Virtue*) recall the second and third levels of the aptitudes for good delineated in the *Religion:* from a "practical point of view only" (for we remain "one individual"), we regard the "sensible human being endowed with reason" (the rational animal of the *Religion*) as submitting for judgment to the aptitude for "personality" whereby we are morally "accountable"; namely to "morally legislative reason" that, while "distinct," is "intimately present" to us (*MST* 438–40, also 430; see also *RV* 146n). Matters of conscience further involve various stages (for example, before a decision is made to act and after the executed action, *MST* 440) and levels of consideration (justice of a particular action, moral worth of the agent's *Gesinnung*, and accountability for one's entire conduct of life); these stages and levels nonetheless turn out to be intrinsically connected.

That we find ourselves unable to avoid the judicial sentencing of conscience in regard to any given unlawful action, however sufficiently it may have been determined in the realm of appearance by foregoing events and circumstances, accords with the conception of character as a "single phenomenon" that we "have procured for ourselves" and to which the given "action and everything in the past belongs" (*KpV* 98). The unity of character, then, is the presupposition underlying the operation of conscience, but our self-knowledge thereof, as well as of our *Gesinnung*, remains of course necessarily uncertain, based as it is on inferences drawn from the empirical evidence of our conduct of life to date (*RV* 70, 76–77; *ED* 329). In this regard, the least ambiguity obtains in findings against the individual when the evidence indicates that, however often the resolve for the good was attempted, no such resolve was maintained (*RV* 68–69). Where the evidence speaks for the individual, there are grounds for confidence in the steadfastness of one's *Gesinnung* (*RV* 70), but such encouragement can at most be felt as relief (not positively as joy), for as we have seen, human virtue cannot be more than the embattled *Gesinnung* (*MST* 440). Still, it behooves us to "settle the account with ourselves" (so to speak) each and every day, in anticipation of the accounting for the whole that awaits us at life's end (*P* 499).[33]

33. Despite the difficulties that Arendt's noncognitive stance poses (see, for example, Richard J. Bernstein, *Beyond Objectivism and Relativism* [Philadelphia: University of Pennsylvania Press, 1983], 217ff., 221–22) and despite her rejection of any kind of legislative role for reason, basic insights of Arendt's quest for a sense of thinking that accompanies living and inherently gives rise to questions of right and wrong are relevant here. Her discussion of the Socratic sense of thinking that accompanies life, of the inner dialogue that represents for her the model of the kind of thinking that can serve to condition us against evil doing, may be appealed to as a supplement to Kant's discussion of conscience. Arendt puts it that "if there is anything in thinking that can prevent men from doing evil, it must be some property inherent in the activity itself, regardless of its objects" (*Life of the Mind*, 180). In such an exercise of our thinking faculty, we would "do more with this ability than use it as an instrument for knowing and doing" (for science and labor and work) (12). Thinking would be "an activity that is its own end" (197), a *full partner* of the acting human being qua human (whether actions have immediate moral relevance or not, a matter that would first come to light precisely through thinking's engaged questioning) and not a subordinate whose "dignity and relevance" (if realized at all) are bestowed only by the objects of thought (180). For her model, Arendt turns to Socrates, who "first discovered" that sense of thinking which "accompanies life," without which one can in fact carry on life, but only a life that is "meaningless" and "not fully alive" (191). The "property inherent in the activity itself" is the thinking faculty's capacity for the inner dialogue that Socrates put on public display in the market-place (*Lectures on Kant's Political Philosophy*, ed. Ronald Beiner [Chicago: University of Chicago Press, 1982], 37). In this "silent intercourse" in which "we *examine what we say and what we do*"

It is just in regard to this judgment of the whole that Kant's references to the judicial voice within (in terms of a divine judge) shed light on his conception of the nature of this inner relation of the human to conscience and of its full import for human life and character. While these allusions are found both in the *Religion* and *Metaphysical Principles of Virtue,* the most concise statement of what is claimed there is found in *On Pedagogy:* underscoring again the intrinsic connection of the law and conscience, Kant observes that "its reproaches would be ineffective if one did not think" of conscience as the "representative of God, who has [erected] His sublime seat over us, but who has also set up (*aufgeschlagen*)³⁴ a judgment seat within us" (*P* 495). In the *Religion,* in consideration of the question as to what "at [life's] end, human beings may either promise themselves, or have [reason] to fear, based on their conduct of life (*Lebenswandel*)," Kant too explicitly identifies the outer judge with the inner one (*RV* 76). The "verdict of the future judge" is thought of as one's "*own awakening conscience* together with empirical self-knowledge summoned" to one's aid; the basis for passing this judgment must be thought of as "having one's

---

(*Life of the Mind* 191, emphasis added), "living together" is manifest as a fundamental orientation inherent to thought itself. Although as the inner dialogue it is a solitary affair, it is never lonely; in it, thinking is "never altogether without a partner and without company," or as Cato had said, "never am I less alone than when I am by myself" (*Human Condition,* 76, 325; *Life of the Mind,* 74–75, 99–100, 185). It is precisely in this sense that the mind can be said to "have a life," in that "it actualizes this intercourse in which, existentially speaking, [even though] plurality is reduced to the duality, . . . I keep myself company" (*Life of the Mind,* 74). That the essence of thinking is just this inner dialogue, Arendt notes, was agreed upon by Kant, no less than by Plato (*Kant's Political Philosophy,* 40; *Human Condition,* 76; *Life of the Mind,* 186). This inner dialogue entails that one "must be careful to keep the integrity of this partner intact," or destroy the conditions for thought itself (*Life of the Mind,* 187–88, 245). The crucial claim here is that for thought (so understood) it matters in an essential way what the one thinking has said and done; to think about it, to examine it, to reflect on it is to live with it (inescapably under the same roof) (*Life of the Mind,* 188, 191, 245). To avoid living with it, one must cease to think (cease the inner dialogue, *Life of the Mind,* 188). Hence, agreement, consistency with oneself, is the very *conditio sine qua non* of the Socratic inner dialogue; its opposite is literally to be at variance with oneself, to become one's own adversary (*Life of the Mind,* 186, 189; *Kant's Political Philosophy,* 37). "Not even another murderer" would want to "have to live together with a murderer" (*Life of the Mind* 188). In both the Platonic and Aristotelian text, Arendt points out that before it became an axiom of formal logic, noncontradiction expressed *the* guiding principle of inner discourse (*Life of the Mind,* 186; *Between Past and Future,* 220, 244). She further interprets Kant's categorical imperative as essentially appealing to the spirit of this principle (*Life of the Mind,* 187).

34. The term *aufschlagen* connotes a range of meaning that could go so far as to imply that, through conscience, God in effect has taken up residence within the human. It also indicates that this divine voice is revealed to us in our nature. The complete passage reads, "Das Gesetz in uns heißt Gewissen. Das Gewissen ist eigentlich die Application unserer Handlungen auf dieses Gesetz. Die Vorwürfe desselben werden ohne Effect sein, wenn man es sich nicht als den Repräsentanten Gottes denkt, der seinen erhabenen Stuhl über uns, aber auch in uns einen Richterstuhl aufgeschlagen hat."

entire life placed before one's eyes at that time, not merely a segment of it," such as "perhaps the last and for oneself the most advantageous part" (*RV* 77, emphasis added). Later, in his interpretation of the three persons of the Godhead, Kant describes the Holy Spirit as humanity's judge who "speaks to our conscience according to the holy law known by us" and in terms of "our own reckoning" (*RV* 140n; 145, also 145n). In a parallel discussion in the *Metaphysical Principles of Virtue* (*MST* 439–40), conscience is said to "lead inevitably" to the idea of an "ideal person," to that of "an authorized judge" who is an "infallible interpreter of hearts." The idea of the actuality of "such a supreme being outside of oneself" is "given subjectively by practical reason, which obligates itself to act in keeping with this idea." In this light, "conscience" itself is "thought of as a subjective principle of being rendered accountable before God for one's deeds"; it is this "concept" that is "always contained in every moral self-consciousness" whereby human beings receive "direction" (or guidance, *Leitung*). "Conscientiousness (also called *religio*)" is just to conceive of oneself as thus accountable. In sum (as Makkreel has also already pointed out), conscience is a "subjective reflective principle of directing or orienting oneself to an ideal interpreter,"[35] and to do so is just what it means to conduct oneself in a self-consciously, morally responsible way.[36]

However, as the preceding citations indicate, it is important to underscore that thus to adopt the principle of seeing ourselves accountable before a supreme being beyond us does not mean that the judgment to which we are immediately subject now comes from outside us. It remains the case that we are held accountable *by our own conscience*, which is to say by our *own practical reason*. As in the case of rational faith, the adoption of the subjective principle in our moral judgment is for the sake of practical guidance, guidance by the idea of a judge construed as capable of laying the whole of our lives before us and of disclosing the true nature of our *Gesinnung* and character. Kant's claim here, as expressed in *Religion* and supported by passages in both the second and third *Critiques*, has to do with (among other things) the self relating to itself as other and yet remaining "one individual"; the claim is that the verdict is not only pro-

---

35. Makkreel, "Dogmatic, Regulative, and Reflective," 132.

36. It is worth noting, too, that rational faith as a subjective principle for guiding judgment is here also clearly presupposed. Only where immortality is assumed will the prospect of judgment thus rendered on the whole of one's conduct of one's mortal life be an effective guide and motivator in daily decision making. However, as our continued examination will show, Kant ultimately understands the role of this principle in a sense other than such directing of our attention to (literally and figuratively) a future judgment day.

nounced over an individual's life and conduct, but that the individual too acknowledges precisely the same verdict and, thus, as rational, moral human being speaks in one voice (which, as we now know, is just what the resolute conduct of thought as itself a maxim means). At stake too, obviously, is once again human, moral freedom. The consequences that befall us as a result of our conduct of life must be consequences we would impose on ourselves.

Kant's further claim is that it is just so that the strictest possible judgment is pronounced over the character and lives of human beings. Placed before an inner judge (thought of in terms of an all-knowing, righteous being from whom nothing can be hidden), human beings nonetheless find themselves before their own inexorable reason (that is, a reason not subject to being influenced, *RV* 77). Or, as he has put it earlier, "To be concerned that reason through conscience would judge too leniently is to be greatly mistaken. . . . just because reason is free and must pass judgment even over the individual herself, it is inexorable (*unbestechlich*)"; individuals anticipating "soon standing before [such] a judge" may be left to "ponder thereon" and "in all probability will judge themselves with the greatest severity" (*RV* 70n). Kant here implicitly once again relies on the principle of noncontradiction, adherence to which is indispensable for reason's self-preservation. For reason to give the law, to judge character and actions of life by the measure of the law, and as conscience to assess its own act of judging, but yet to issue a verdict that in any way deviated from the law in its rigor would be for reason to contradict itself. So, too, we can speak of reason as inexorable. By contrast, writes Kant, human beings envisioned as coming before a judge other than their own reason would bring with them all manner of excuses based on appeals to human frailty; instead of freely submitting, they would oppose the strictness of the sentence, seeking instead to circumvent it (*RV* 77). It is reason itself, it must be remembered, that avails itself (in its role as judge or conscience) of the idea of the divine judge. For the idea to serve effectively as a guide for moral judging—for conscience to "serve as motivation" for "strengthening" those of good *Gesinnung* and for encouraging those in whom the morally corrupt order of maxims still reigns to "break with evil [just] as far as possible" (*RV* 69)—imagining the possibility of negotiating with one's judge and holding anything less than the totality of one's actions and character as the basis for ultimate judgment must be abrogated from the outset.

Thus one reads in the *Critique of Practical Reason*, for example, that the "respect for ourselves in the consciousness of our freedom" whereby the "law finds easier access" to our *Gesinnung* is "well established" precisely "if human beings dread nothing more than finding themselves, upon their inner self-examination, to be contemptible and reprehensible in their own eyes"; further, upon such respect so established, "every good moral *Gesinnung* may be grafted" (*KpV* 161). In the third *Critique,* such inner self-examination is discussed in terms of humility and the feeling of the sublime. "Even humility (*Demut*), as the strict judging of our defects . . . is a sublime attunement of mind," namely, "voluntarily to subject oneself to the pain of self-censure, in order gradually to eradicate the cause" of these defects; the latter "may otherwise be easily cloaked with the frailty of our human nature," especially when we are also "conscious of our good maxims (*Gesinnungen*)" (maxims that, as we know from previous discussion, may nonetheless not be well ordered) (*KU* 264). Later Kant identifies adherence to the voice of conscience as one of three moments in which the "mind is attuned to moral feeling" (the others being gratitude for one's existence and, in the course of performing one's duty through self-sacrifice, the feeling that one has been obedient to a higher authority) (*KU* 445). Having even "unthinkingly violated their duty," within individuals of such an attunement of mind, including in those instances when their action "did not result in their being accountable to other people," expressions of "strict self-censure will be spoken as if they were the voice of a judge to whom they must account" for their deeds (*KU* 445–46). "Humiliation" (*Demütigung*), the "submission to deserved punishment," Kant goes on, is one of three "attunements of mind to duty" (*KU* 446). Such passages as these thus prove to be earlier expressions of Kant's account of conscience (with its intrinsic links to character) more explicitly developed in the later texts.

One question remaining is this: while conscience so construed in terms of an ideal interpreter, exercised by our own inexorable reason against ourselves, and before whom we stand accountable for the whole of our conduct of life, can readily be seen to have the familiar, negative critical function (in this case, promoting our avoidance of evil), in what sense does it serve, as Kant claims, as a "guide in any and all moral decisions?" The question is what sort of positive guidance (if any) we gain from adopting this subjective principle for judgment. Given the unavoidable uncertainty for the acting human being in regard to the actual motivating maxim in any particular case, or the actual moral worth we have realized in our comportment of mind, how can such a conception of strict judgment serve positively in just these daily, uncertain situations? How is it that conscience in these situations may still be upheld as infallible? In

1791 Kant observes that "moralists speak of an erring conscience," but that such a notion is an "absurdity" (a point he repeats in *Metaphysical Principles of Virtue*). For, if there were truly such a thing, "one could never be certain that one had acted justly [or rightly], since in the final stage of appeal even the judge might be mistaken" (*VT* 268; *MST* 401). In his *Religion* he states that the "demand that one not only judge and opine that any action one proposes to undertake is not unjust, but that one be certain of it, is a postulate of our conscience" that stands in opposition to "the principle of probabilism"; according to the latter, "the mere opinion that an action could very well be just [or right] warrants undertaking it" (*RV* 186). The postulate manifests Kant's negative moral formulation: it prohibits the unjust action without specifying in what the just action would consist. The stipulation of certainty is inherent to it, but what exactly can we be certain of in such a judgment? Or, so conceived, what does the notion of conscience add to that of legislative reason demanding adherence to the moral law?

Kant continues the passage in the *Religion* (*RV* 186) by noting that one "could define conscience as the "power of moral judgment passing judgment on itself." That is to say, "conscience does not judge actions as cases that fall under the law"; this is the work of "reason insofar as it is subjectively practical. Rather, here *reason judges itself*, as to whether it has really undertaken in all diligence such judgment of actions (as to whether they are just or unjust), and it calls upon individuals to be witnesses for or against themselves as to whether or not" such judgment has been exercised (emphasis added). It is just in this "subjective judgment, as to whether or not I have compared" a given case with "my practical (here judging) reason, for the purpose" of making the objective judgment as to whether or not the thing considered is a matter of duty, "that I cannot be mistaken," writes Kant in the *Metaphysical Principles of Virtue* (*MST* 401). To be mistaken in that is "not to have exercised practical judgment at all," and so too, "unscrupulousness is not a lack of conscience, but the propensity to ignore such judgment" (*MST* 401). There are two levels involved here in the process of judgment; we will see shortly how and where error can enter.

In sum, thus far, the conception of such strict judgment serves the positive role of maintaining the traveler's moral self-consciousness on life's road. In its function as conscience, reason is carrying out an ongoing self-assessment to ensure that its guiding activity, the bringing of all contemplated and executed actions before it for moral judgment, is not allowed to lapse. It is a voice as inescapable for human travelers as their "shadows";

"through amusements and distractions they may stupefy themselves or fall asleep, but they cannot avoid now and then coming to themselves or awakening, at which point they will immediately hear the terrible voice. In their greatest depravity, they can at most bring themselves to the point of ignoring it, but they cannot avoid hearing" this voice (*MST* 438). In his *Religion*, Kant does allow for an element of self-deception present in what is there described as the third or greatest degree of moral corruption; namely, to "hold oneself justified before the law" on the grounds that one's "actions did not ensue in any evil consequences" (*RV* 38). We return to this point in our discussion of truthfulness as an indispensable, formal condition of having character, here broaching only the link with conscience. For it is this "deceitfulness of the human heart," notes Kant, that is responsible for the peace of mind enjoyed by the "many" who falsely "deem themselves to be conscientious" (*RV* 38). It is also not surprising then, that the "first command" of our "duties toward ourselves" is "know thyself," a "moral self-knowledge" esteemed by Kant as the "beginning of all human wisdom" (*MST* 441).[37] Or, as he has also put it earlier in the text, "while acting in accordance with conscience is not itself a duty" (for otherwise an infinite regress would be set up, always requiring yet another conscience to become conscious of the acts of the previous one), we do have a "duty to cultivate our conscience"; this entails "sharpening our attentiveness to the voice of the inner judge and employing all means . . . to obtain it a hearing" (*MST* 401).

In regard to our "unconditioned duty" that an "action that we undertake be a just one," it is the "understanding" (here clearly used in its wider sense of rational comprehension) that "judges" (*RV* 185–86), and it is in this "objective judgment, whether something is a duty or not," that we "may indeed occasionally err" (*MST* 401; see also *VT* 268). Therefore, in addition to the postulate that conscience demands we adhere to, we are

---

37. That such self-knowledge entails penetration of depths that for us are extremely obscure and, hence, that this is the most difficult of tasks, is here again immediately acknowledged by Kant. Elsewhere, the familiar references to the uncertainty in regard to our moral comportment of mind repeat the point. In "End of All Things" (1794) Kant lists the good characteristics of our temperament, those we might have the fortune to be born with as natural gifts, which must be identified and from which we must abstract if we are to ascertain our moral worth or the moral state of our character in its absolute sense (*ED* 329–30). This discussion parallels points also made in the *Metaphysical Principles of Virtue* in Kant's identification of the duty thus to assess one's actions in terms of the *Gesinnung* informing them, as one of "broad obligation" (*MST* 392–93). What is of the essence is that the inherent, ineradicable uncertainty cannot, must not become an excuse not to examine the moral state of our character, for that examination is itself bound up with the cultivation of character as morally good conduct of thought.

also "obligated to enlighten our understanding in regard to what is or is not duty" (*RV* 186). To rephrase Kant's point here, while we cannot be mistaken as to whether or not we have followed through on the assessment per se, we may make mistakes in assessing whether or not a given particular falls under the universal law. Enlightenment in this regard may come through a number of sources, including the observance of the second maxim of the sound, common human understanding: to consider the matter from the universal standpoint of humanity. With the internal relations in place orienting human travelers to the good and securing their moral self-consciousness, we turn next to these further subjective principles for guidance in their journey in the world.

Conduct of Thought (*Denkungsart*) and the Maxims of Sound Understanding

The three maxims of the "common human understanding" are repeated by Kant in a number of different contexts in his corpus. In the *Critique of Judgment* (in what has recently become the most familiar of these passages), Kant presents them as three distinct, but intrinsically interconnected principles. The third and final one, the maxim of "reason" or the "resolute *Denkungsart*" (which we now recognize as also definitive of character in its absolute sense) is said to be the one most difficult to achieve and to be attainable only as the union of the first two maxims (of thinking for oneself, or maxim of the understanding, and thinking from a universal standpoint or maxim of judgment); such a union is realized when repeated adherence to the first two has become a matter of an accomplished observance (*Fertigkeit*) of them (*KU* 294–95). While Kant names the three human rational capacities of cognition (understanding, reason, and judgment), his discussion here and elsewhere reveals that what is at stake with these maxims or subjective principles is the right use or employment of reason: more precisely, the practical employment of reason.

The goal is that our traveler exercise judgment in the course of life's journey in a way that at least approaches "wisdom," the "idea of a practical employment of reason that is perfectly in accord with the law" (*ApH* 200). While the categorical imperative serves as the fundamental formative principle of character, comportment of mind, choice, and volition, all of these in their actual exercise in life entail assessing and relating particulars to this normative universal and to reason's ideas. To be perfectly in accord with the law in such exercise of judgment is "no doubt to ask too much of human beings," Kant goes on, "but the prescript to achieve" such wisdom "contains three maxims leading to it," the maxims of *thinking* for oneself, from the standpoint of others, and with unanimity (*ApH* 200, 228). Moreover, as we have just seen, for the demand of conscience to be fulfilled not only in spirit, but in concrete execution in the world, cultivation of right judgment of the particular case is essential.

While theoretical wisdom, the cognitive quest for truth, is also served by adherence to these three maxims (*ApH* 227–28; *LJ* 57), Kant's overriding concern with the practical is evident in each of his discussions of these principles. In the third *Critique,* Kant is explicit that not only is the striving for knowledge not the goal, but such "intellectual curiosity" in fact hinders the attainment of "true enlightenment," which is achieved far more easily by "those who only want to measure up to their essential purpose" (*KU* 294n). The third maxim (the consummation of the first two) is already by definition (as we have learned) the call to employ our reason such that it is "not merely a comprehending, but rather an efficacious and propelling principle" that "acts in the place of a natural cause" in the world. It is the maxim definitive of subjectively practical reason, whose effect in the world (as Kant repeats in his Introduction to the *Critique of Judgment*) is in accordance with the concept of freedom and consists in the concrete realization of final purpose. In the case of the second maxim, too, Kant underscores that it is "not the capacity of cognition" that is at issue, but "rather making a purposive use of *Denkungsart*" (*KU* 295).

The first maxim of thinking for oneself is further identified as that of "a reason that is never passive" (*KU* 294) and, in the *Anthropology,* such passivity is once again spelled out as a moral problem. For, especially in morality, in matters involving acting and refraining from acting (*Tun und Lassen*), people are inclined to forgo the use of their reason and passively and obediently observe given statutes (*ApH* 199, 200). The opposite use of reason in an active or nonpassive mode may be elucidated by its contrast with rote learning. In his *Reflections on Anthropology* Kant presents these three maxims explicitly in contrast to academic learning, which is there said to require "memory and understanding," whereas "going beyond what one has learned" and "applying" one's learning in life is said to take "wit and reason"; that is, it requires "judgment" in accordance with these principles that Kant also calls the "maxims of a mature reason" (*RA* no. 1508, 820, 822). This requirement of something more beyond what can be received through instruction, the call to thinking for oneself, and the account of character, all accord with Kant's point in the *Anthropology* that the wisdom to which these maxims are said to lead "cannot in the least degree be infused by another; rather every individual must produce it from within themselves" (*ApH* 200).[38]

In short, it is just these three maxims that are indispensable for being the enlightened citizen and traveler, en route to achieving wisdom and concretely realizing humanity's final purpose. In his explicit identification of enlightenment with the first maxim of thinking for oneself (*LJ* 57, *DO* 146n), Kant also explicates the different senses of what it is to be thus enlightened.[39] Its negative sense is that of freedom from coercion, or more specifically from prejudice, especially the "greatest of prejudices," superstition (*ApH* 228; *KU* 294). The latter is defined by Kant as consisting "in thinking of nature as not subject to the rules that the understanding, through its own essential law, lays down as the basis of nature" (*KU* 294). To appreciate some of what is at stake here for Kant (in what one might call his critical interpretation of the meaning of superstition), it is worth repeating a point in our previous account of the synthetic unity of causality and of the importance of the relation between reason and understanding for the human being as efficacious agent in the world; namely, that the moral law has "no other mediating cognitive capacity for its application to the objects of nature than the understanding," which, in lieu of a "sensible schema" and for the purpose of moral judgment, provides the "idea of reason" with the "form" of a "law of nature" (*KpV* 69). Or, as we also put it, reason as higher and directing cause avails itself of the form of the causal order of the understanding in order to bring its rule to bear in the world. To eliminate the understanding as lawgiver of nature is thus to eliminate reason's via media to bring its own active rule to bear on nature (for reason determines the understanding in accordance with its ideas and not nature directly, *KrV* A547/B575). Or, as Kant expresses it in the third *Critique,* superstition leaves one in a state of blindness, a claim that may have several implications but, in light of the connection with the second *Critique* passage and with the notion of efficacious cause, may be interpreted to mean that a reason that has succumbed to superstition and re-

38. In the Jäsche *Logic* (22–26) Kant is also very explicit that such thinking for oneself, such concern with the "use of reason" and not the actual "propositions," is just what it means to philosophize (in contrast to learning the factual history of philosophy).

39. Kant's use of the notion of thinking for oneself is in fact very limited in the corpus, occurring only twelve times in the works published in his lifetime (starting with the *Prolegomena* in 1783 and appearing again in the *Groundwork, Critique of Judgment,* "What Is Enlightenment?" "What Is Orientation in Thinking?" *Anthropology,* Jäsche *Logic,* and a 1783 review of Schulz's writings on a "Moral Teaching for All Humankind").

fuses to see the understanding in its role in the determination of nature, also cannot see a way clear to the concrete realization of its own ideas; the very comprehension of these ideas as a practical task is thus jeopardized. In this respect at least, then, the subjective principle of thinking for oneself (as the contrary to superstition) is indispensable for the execution of moral agency in the world.

More generally speaking, the call to freedom from prejudice may also be understood in the original sense of that latter term; that is, quite apart from the issue of their rightness or wrongness, it is a call to move beyond unthinking adherence to ideas and principles, to hold these with rational comprehension and not "blindly" (to give this notion another nuance).[40] While superstition is equated with the state of blindness in which, "above all, the individual's need for guidance from others and thus the condition of a passive reason is revealed" (*KU* 295), prejudice (in general) results in what can be called a mechanical use of mind, in contrast to active judging. Blindly and unthinkingly held and acted upon, any principles would amount to little more than what Kant calls (in his essay on enlightenment) an appeal to "rules and formulas, those mechanical instruments of a rational use, better said, *misuse* of our natural gifts and the shackles of unending immaturity" (*A* 36, emphasis added). From the standpoint of the human subjective capacities, especially of choice, it is not difficult to see how and why principles thus passively held, without understanding, could not meet the requirement of resolve, that is, of conviction and consistent adherence, and would be vulnerable to pressures from without: from the inclinations, circumstances, and dictates of others. And the problem, Kant tells us, is *not* an issue of the *ability* to understand, but rather a matter of "laziness and cowardice" (*A* 34). The child mentality is to take the easier route, the mere following of rules, especially to the extent that doing so also happens to satisfy the demands of the inclinations.

The opposite to such mere rule following, once again, is the exercise of judgment. As Kant explains the point in his *Anthropology:* "Instruction consists in the communication of rules," and by means of such instruction, the human understanding may be furnished with many concepts and rules, but the ability to judge (whether technical, aesthetic, or practical judgment) if a given case is an instance of the rule or not cannot be taught; only years of practice can yield maturity and understanding in this sense

---

40. For a discussion of preliminary judgments versus prejudices, see Rudolf Makkreel, "Role of Reflection," 89ff. See also Makkreel's "Kant, Dilthey, and the Idea of a Critique of Historical Judgment," *Dilthey-Jahrbuch für Philosophie und Geschichte der Geisteswissenschaften* 10 (1996): 68ff.

(*ApH* 199). Thus, as Kant underscores in the *Critique of Judgment* (*KU* 294n), thinking for oneself is attained only slowly and with difficulty, particularly wherever the traveler's guide is pulling another way, drawn by curiosity to the striving for knowledge (which, by the eighteenth century, may very well be satisfied in the form of something like encyclopedic information gathering). The effort Kant calls for, however long and arduous, is on his account not merely well worthwhile; it is of the essence. Nothing less than character depends upon it, for beyond the revolution in conduct of thought whereby it is established, the very life of character (so to speak) consists in the ongoing resolute acts of moral judgment. In this regard, Kant makes the following observation in his *Reflections on Anthropology:* "In order to give the appearance of having character, or in order that they might be satisfied with themselves in their lack of character, people often adhere to rules or make some for themselves that frequently go against what the heart [desires], just because they have no confidence in their power of judgment to make decisions apart from such rules" (*RA* no. 1158, 513).

Another sense of enlightenment already alluded to (and probably the one most familiar) is its association with maturity. In light of the present interpretation of thinking for oneself, both the connection with maturity and Kant's further claim (made in "What Is Enlightenment?" and elsewhere), that nothing less than the call to fulfill the vocation proper to the human being is entailed, may be understood as again referring to requirements for the cultivation of moral character. As the following passages show, these notions are in fact discussed by Kant precisely in those terms central also to his account of character. A "germ" (or rudiment, *Keim*) innate to human nature, "the propensity and calling to free thinking" is one for which "nature . . . cares most tenderly"; once uncovered, this germ "gradually in turn impacts (*wirkt zurück*) the *Sinnesart* (sensibilities) of the people" (whereby they "become more and more capable of acting" in accordance with freedom). And, finally, it even impacts "the principles of government, which itself finds it beneficial to treat human beings, who are now more than machines, commensurate with their dignity" (*A* 41–42). Earlier in the essay, Kant credits those few of the requisite "resolve and courageous spirit" (who have for themselves "thrown off the yoke of immaturity") with "disseminating about themselves the spirit of a rational estimation for both the individual's own worth and the calling of all human beings to think for themselves" (*A* 34, 36). Only where individuals are actively thinking for themselves can one talk at all of the employment of freedom, and only where the latter is exercised can one talk about moral agency and character.[41]

Rule following and imitating, versus thinking (judging) for oneself in other words, may now be seen as particular specifications of the general distinction between mere movement and the activity proper to humanity qua humanity (discussed in our second chapter). The difference is between being and remaining a marionette (to use one of Kant's favorite expressions) and procuring and exercising moral character for oneself. Another parallel to this point is the difference between a lawless and lawful employment of freedom (discussed in our third chapter). As Kant notes too in his essay on orientation in thinking, the "consequence of a lawless employment of reason," that is, one "not subject to reason's own law," is that it must become subordinated to another's law, for "without any form of law whatsoever, nothing, not even the greatest nonsense" can persist for long; in short, "lawlessness in [one's] thinking" is ultimately to "forfeit freedom of thought" (*DO* 145). Again referring to our foregoing examination of Kant's conception of character and, in effect, coming full circle to conclusions reached before, one could say that the most that an individual can accomplish in such submission (be it voluntary or involuntary) to the rule of another is virtue's empirical character (but only when and if such rule is indeed in conformity with the moral law). Virtue in its intelligible character as identified with the moral *Gesinnung* is found only where that "most important revolution within individuals, 'their emergence from their self-imposed immaturity,'" has taken place—as Kant repeats his point in his *Anthropology,* in conjunction with his discussion there of the three maxims of the common understanding (*ApH* 229). Later in the same text, he explicitly identifies the individual who is a mere "imitator" of others in moral life as being "without character, for the latter consists in originality in *Denkungsart*" (*ApH* 293). Taking into account the eighteenth century sense of the original and its intrinsic connection with the notion of authorship, in addition to Kant's continued explanation in the text, one recognizes here yet one more statement expressing the inherent connection of "enlightenment" as humanity's "calling to think for itself" and his conception of what it is to have character (see also *RA* no. 1508, 822).

Finally, "enlightenment" as the "maxim always to think for oneself" is

41. Norbert Hinske notes that the "concept of maturity . . . directs attention to the whole individual. Enlightenment is for the latter not only a matter of thinking for oneself, but equally a [matter of] acting for oneself (*Selbsttuns*)" ("Eklektik, Selbstdenken, Mündigkeit," *Aufklärung* 1 [1986]: 6–7).

further defined by Kant (in his 1786 examination of the notion of orientation) as the maxim of "seeking the highest touchstone of truth in oneself (in one's own reason)" (*DO* 146n). This entails far less, he goes on, than those who identify enlightenment with the acquisition of knowledge imagine, for it requires only ascertaining the reason or ground on the basis of which one accepts a given thing to be true, and then asking oneself the further question, if one could adopt such a basis as "a general rule for the use of one's reason." This "test" is nothing more or less, he goes on, than the "maxim of the self-preservation of reason" (*DO* 146–47n). A general example and a second one related to our opening discussion of the issue of orientation in thinking may illustrate Kant's point. Suppose I find myself willing to attribute a given occurrence (say, symmetrical patterns appearing overnight in wheatfields) to superhuman causes and, pressed for a reason for such an assumption, I confess that my basis is simply a lack of any other explanation. The test required, and lying within everyone's purview, is to ask whether one could make such a basis (in this case, lacking other information, having no evidence to the contrary) a general rule for using one's reason, for regarding something as true. Most students of informal logic, confronted with illustrations of this (and other) fallacies in reasoning, quickly recognize that something is amiss, that one could not in fact generally reach correct conclusions on such a basis, and they do so well before learning "rules" of reasoning that are named and are to be remembered. Just so, on Kant's view, will anyone of sound, common understanding judge.

What *is* required, however, is just that one actually judge, that one *think* for oneself, that one engage in an exercise of self-knowledge, examining one's own processes of thinking and reasoning, that one question oneself. Such activity we also saw to be indispensable if one is to respond to the behest of conscience. It is indispensable, too, if one is to reach that point of conviction (itself a prerequisite for securing human orientation to the good as humanity's final purpose) that expresses itself as "*I* am morally certain that God exists" (with an emphasis on "I"). As presented earlier, this statement is pronounced by the moral human subject attentive to reason's law (which continues to remain fundamental to this entire discussion) who, by an exercise of judgment, adopts the subjective principle of regarding as true what is required from a moral point of view. The answer to the question here, whether one could make such a principle the basis for one's employment of reason in general, is not only answered in the affirmative, it is deemed a matter of necessity precisely for the sake of consistency with reason's practical demands. And such an individual, who has thus on internal, rational grounds (the *factum der Vernunft*) freely adopted the maxim of rational faith by an exercise of her own judgment, will remain unshaken, on Kant's understanding of the matter, by being presented (for example) with Hume's *Dialogues concerning Natural Religion*, or with archeological evidence against claims of the authenticity of the Garden Tomb, or with historical and scientific evidence against a literal reading of Genesis, and so forth.[42] For the critical philosophy stands as surety that the postulates of reason cannot be demonstrated to be false, while rational faith directs or orients the subject's efforts toward fulfillment of reason's ideas interpreted as practical tasks.[43] Considerations such as these also add new meaning to Kant's observation in "What Is Enlightenment?" that immaturity, or lack of thinking for oneself in "religious matters," is above all other instances the "most injurious and degrading" (*A* 41).

Ultimately, this maxim of enlightenment consists in a positive orientation toward human reason itself. In this regard it is worth noting that Kant has raised his concern about "misology," the "hatred of reason," already in the *Groundwork*, where he sees it resulting from reason being directed (or, given his standpoint, better said "misdirected") toward just those kinds of pursuits usually associated with the received, historical notion of enlightenment reason (acquiring knowledge and securing the means for the attainment of human happiness and contentment) (*G* 395–96). Again, in his essay on orientation, one of Kant's explicit objectives is to challenge the would-be "detractors of reason" (*DO* 144). Where, by contrast, the maxim of thinking for oneself in Kant's sense of that term has been adopted as a principle for the use of one's reason, once again, in effect, a trust relationship obtains between the human rational subject and this highest faculty within.

All the emphasis on the primacy of thinking for oneself notwithstanding, further examination proves both the first and second maxims of the

42. For such individuals thus oriented in their thinking, the reality of the good as humanity's true and final purpose also could not be dismissed (as it is in some quarters in the century following Kant) as some psychoanalytical quirk of human nature, as something we merely wish for in vain. For any felt desire for this good follows precisely *consequent to* reason's imperative and inferences based thereon.

43. To those who would further seek to bring empirical evidence against the possibility of success in such efforts, pointing to humanity's dismal record in this regard, Kant's answer remains unequivocal. Resolve in these matters cannot be impacted by such evidence, for "one is not even justified" to bring such evidence of previous failure "against pragmatic or technical intentions (for example, flights with aerostatic balloons), let alone in the case of a moral duty whose results are not demonstratively impossible" (*TP* 309–10).

sound, common human understanding to be in fact principles formative of judgment as the latter is *necessarily* exercised *in interrelation with one another* on the part of the human travelers on life's journey. As such, both principles (the first one negatively and the second one positively) define the orientation of individuals to others, to the human community, in their exercise of judgment. The first maxim specifies the mode of interrelation *from* which the individual traveler must first be freed, namely, that form of subordination to the dictates of another which entails an intellectually passive "following along"—a form of human interaction to which the philosophical objections are at least as old as Socrates' teachings, but for which human history abounds with examples. Within the parameters of Kant's account, as previously detailed, nothing less than moral character is at stake in this first step. Its principle is "negative," as Kant notes in his *Anthropology* (*nullius addictus iurare in verba Magistri*) (*ApH* 228) and may be understood in terms of the negative function so prevalent in Kant's writings: that of clearing away the impediments—in this case, the superstition, prejudice, and passivity that stand in the way of the praxis of judging occurring at all.

If the first maxim is thus necessary for making individual judgment possible, the second, whereby such individuals (now reliant on their own reason) immediately and freely relate to one another, is equally necessary if their exercise of judgment is to be done *well*. The second maxim entails the practice of a "liberal *Denkungsart*," as Kant puts it in his *Anthropology*, of "making the effort to take others' conceptions into account" (*ApH* 228–29). His use elsewhere of this notion of a liberal *Denkungsart* connects it with his understanding of what (for example) the Christian conception of love for humanity involves, namely, freely to incorporate the desire (or will) of another into one's own maxims (*ED* 338–39). As such, this maxim is consonant with the unity of resolve and friendliness that we saw (in our second chapter) constituting the magnanimous soul. What it effectively means to adopt this maxim, and its import for individual judging is brought to light by Kant's other way of characterizing it: as the maxim of enlarged or expanded (*erweiterte*) *Denkungsart*.

In all three *Critiques* this term typically refers to the enlarged employment of reason beyond the critical, theoretical limits, for the sake of its practical purposes. As the second maxim of the common understanding, the widening of one's thinking called for has to do with one's self-perception in relation to others; it effectively shifts the orientation from self to the wider sphere of humanity. An intimation of such a shift, arising naturally from within human nature, appears as early as 1764 in Kant's

Observations: individuals pursuing their inclinations on the stage of the world are said to be "at the same time moved by an inward impulse to adopt a stance beyond themselves in their thinking, to judge the propriety of their conduct (*Betragen*), how it appears to others looking on" (*B* 227). As we have also already seen, earlier in the *Anthropology* Kant speaks of opposing egoism with pluralism, that is, with that *Denkungsart* whereby individuals do not hold themselves as "encompassing the entire world in their own selves, but rather regard and conduct (*verhalten*) themselves as simply world citizens" (*ApH* 130). Such a "cosmopolitan (*weltbürgerliche*) *Gesinnung*" is treated in *On Pedagogy* as a level of cultivation even beyond that of "love for humanity" (*P* 499), and references to such a cosmopolitan *Gesinnung* may be found in other texts too (for example, *Metaphysical Principles of Virtue, MST* 473). The point to be made here is that the general notion of thinking of ourselves as one among many and of that fact's making a difference for how we conduct ourselves in thought and hence in relation to others in the world is expressed by Kant in a number of different ways.[44] It is implicitly connected also with an observation he makes in his discussion of the ideal of the highest good in the *Critique of Pure Reason:* "carrying out the idea" of a moral world, of a system of proportionate happiness conjoined with morality, in which rational beings are the "originators of their own and also of other beings' lasting welfare," rests "on the condition that everyone does what he ought to do" (*KrV* A810/B838). To such a wider vision belongs the enlargement of thought.

By his discussion in section 40 of the *Critique of Judgment* in 1790, the issue of how one's choices and resulting actions appear to others has been refined beyond a concern about how one affects others (which in its own right, we recall, is an element belonging to character considered in terms of the human sensibilities). "How it looks to others" has become a touchstone serving judgment once again for its own self-assessment. Judging in accordance with the maxim of the enlarged *Denkungsart* entails "reflecting on one's own judgment," to ensure that one is not, after all, in actuality judging in accordance with the principle of self-love, but that one has gone beyond the "private conditions of judgment" (*KU* 295). It is just such self-reflection on one's own judgments, too, that we saw was inherent to the operation of conscience. Also as noted previously, this second maxim is most closely connected with Kant's notion of the *sensus communis.* As

---

44. In *Reflections on Anthropology*, Kant discusses this point in terms of the distinction between mere mortals (literally, son of the earth, *Erdensohn*) and world citizens (*Weltbürger*), as well as explicitly in terms of the distinction between a universal and private spirit (*Geist*) characterizing *Denkungsart* (that is, both thinking and volition) (*RA* no. 1170, 517–18; no. 1208, 530).

Makkreel underscores, in regard to this notion, too, Kant explicitly indicates that the comparison to be made is with the "possible rather than actual judgment of others," meaning that the enlargement of thinking called for does not demand that we "transpose ourselves into the actual standpoint of someone else," but rather that we conceive of or "imagine possibilities that are not merely variations of the self."[45] By operating in accordance with the maxim of enlarged thinking, judgment checks itself to ensure that its principles, which on the one hand must arise in "originality of *Denkungsart*" (that is, be authored by the individual, judging subject) if one is to speak of active judging (and hence of character), are yet "valid for everyone" (*ApH* 293); that they truly do express a "universal standpoint" that we know is required from the moral point of view as it is also objectively commanded (*KU* 295).[46]

This conception of universality instantiated in and through particular judgment by the individual, with its inherent need for reference to the other and, indeed, for the use of public reason, had already been explicitly spelled out by Kant in a *Critique of Pure Reason* discussion (quoted in what

45. Makkreel, *Imagination and Interpretation*, 160. For aesthetic reflective judgments to be constitutive for the subject means that they "help to constitute a communal or public world" (Makkreel, "Kant, Dilthey," 71).

46. Thus under the present interpretation, the so-called publicity test is seen as more intrinsically interconnected with the "universalizability test" than it is in Makkreel's interpretation ("Differentiating Approaches to History," 131). The difference arises on the basis of understanding the subject (in the present interpretation) as a concrete instantiation of the objective (of character as the subjective realization of objective morality). For the subject, the self-assessment of judgment by means of checking it against the (morally) possible standpoint of the other is precisely a way of measuring the extent that it indeed realizes the universality required from a moral point of view (objectively speaking). Makkreel's example does in fact point to just this: "If I am willing to be treated the way I treat others, then I may think that my maxim passes the universalizability test. But a public use of reason may disclose that others do not want to be treated this way. The public use of reason makes possible the expanded mode of thought that we linked earlier with reflective judgment and the *sensus communis*."

The closer connection between the "publicity" and "universalizability tests" is compatible, too, with the interpretation of the categorical imperative in terms of its legislatability; i.e., that the "law which maxims must be capable of becoming is a law for the whole community of rational beings" (Ronald M. Green, "The First Formulation of the Categorical Imperative as Literally a 'Legislative' Metaphor," *History of Philosophy Quarterly* 8 [1991]: 164). Andrews Reath, too, interprets and critiques the "legislation thesis" of the moral law ("Legislating the Moral Law," *Nous* 28 [1994]: 435–64).

Philip Rossi defends the Enlightenment ideas that "before we can make moral claims on one another, we must be able 'to stand in one another's shoes,'" and that of the "requirement of 'universality' for our moral judgments," as ideas that "retain significant power even in a post-Enlightenment, 'post-modern' world" ("Moral Imagination and the Media: Whose 'World' Do We See, Whose 'World' Shall It Be?" in *Mass Media and the Moral Imagination*, ed. Philip J. Rossi and Paul A. Soukup [Kansas City: Sheed and Ward, 1994], 264).

follows) of the lawful constraint whereby individual freedom is limited so that it can exist in harmony with the freedom of others. In light of this further connection, one can see judgment in accordance with the second maxim of the common understanding as essential, too, to the realization of virtue consisting (as we concluded in our third chapter) in self-control characterizing the human processes of thinking, whereby we become fit as thinking beings to fulfill our human vocation. Whereas initially external constraint keeps the inclinations in check such that their exercise in accordance with the concept of freedom does not result in infringement upon the freedom of others, where judgment that takes into account the standpoint of the other is consistently exercised, an internal, individual source of self-restraint is effectively in place. So, too, the individual is thereby now subjectively (as well as objectively) truly self-legislating.

For such conduct of thought to be realized, however, Kant, not only in the first *Critique,* but again in the essays on orientation and enlightenment, expressly calls for a free, public interchange of ideas—the point Hannah Arendt first understood as being so important in his philosophy.[47] It is just in and through such exchange that, subjectively speaking, the individual can come to recognize in what universal human reason will concretely consist. "Freedom" entails the right to voice "publicly for assessment our thoughts [and] our doubts that we cannot resolve by ourselves." This right is one of the "original rights of human reason, which recognizes no other judge than, in its turn again, that universal human reason wherein

47. Arendt, "Truth and Politics," in *Between Past and Future* (234–35). It was Arendt who underscored the significance (long before Anglo-American scholarship took the *Critique of Judgment* seriously) of the fact that here (and elsewhere) Kant discusses the necessity not only of being in agreement with one's own self, but of also being able to "think in the place of everybody else," a thinking process Arendt translates as "enlarged mentality" (*erweiterte Denkungsart*) that "finds itself always and primarily, even if I am quite alone in making up my mind, in an anticipated communication with others with whom I know I must finally come to some agreement"; in other words, ultimately for Kant, thinking "depends on others to be possible at all" (*Between Past and Future,* 220–21, 234–35, 241–42; *Kant's Political Philosophy,* 10, 39–43; *Life of the Mind,* 94, 99). What Arendt found here in Kant's works resonates with her observation that the nature of thought is such that "no other human capacity is so vulnerable, and it is in fact easier to act under conditions of tyranny than it is to think" (*Human Condition,* 324).

In "The Fact of Politics: History and Teleology in Kant," Larry Krasnoff takes quite the opposite approach, arguing for the efficacious political agency of the spectators, for the "fact that we are able to confront existing authority with a moral demand, a demand with which we expect that authority to comply" (*European Journal of Philosophy* 2 [1994]: 32). Otfried Höffe is critical of Arendt's and also Saner's political reading of the *Critique of Judgment* but does draw on Kant's maxims of the ordinary understanding and of his notion of common sense to defend Kant against solipsism ("Eine republikanische Vernunft. Zur Kritik des Solipsismus-Vorwurfs," in *Kant in der Diskussion der Moderne,* ed. Gerhard Schönrich and Yasushi Kato [Frankfurt am Main: Suhrkamp, 1996], 396–407).

everyone has a voice. And since all improvement of which our [human] condition is capable must be derived [from this source], such a right is sacred and must not be restricted" (*KrV* A752/B780).[48] Under the present interpretation, at stake is ultimately the moral right to the cultivation of character, the uncovering and development of this aptitude within human nature (to which, as we have seen, Kant explicitly refers in the conclusion to "What Is Enlightenment?"). Again, in "What Is Orientation in Thinking?" Kant asks rhetorically "how much and with what soundness[49] we could hope to think, if we did not think, so to speak, in community with others, to whom we communicate our thoughts and who inform us of theirs!" (*DO* 144). He warns that such "external forces that tear away humanity's freedom publicly to communicate its thoughts, also take away its freedom to think" (*DO* 144). Thus, too, as Kant had put it two years earlier, enlightenment requires the freedom to make public use of one's reason in all matters (*A* 36).

The first two maxims of the common understanding, then, however concisely they are expressed by Kant, as interpreted here encompass a wide range of issues pertaining to the cultivation of the subjectively practical exercise of reason, of the actualization of conduct of thought as the particular, concrete counterimage of objective, universal morality. As noted at the outset of our discussion, Kant in this context defines the resolute conduct of thought as the culmination, the union, of the first two when repeated adherence to them has become a matter of an accomplished observance of them. The traits characteristic of the accomplished thinking on the part of such a subject—literally the accounting of the progress made by our traveler on life's journey—may be summarized from the foregoing as follows. A subjective employment of freedom that comes as close as is humanly possible to wisdom, or the practical employment of reason in perfect accord with the law, it is an active exercise of judgment engaged in an ongoing Socratic exercise of self-examination and self-assessment by comparison with the possible (moral) standpoint of the other travelers on the road, thereby assuring itself that its particular judgments are indeed

---

48. John Christian Laursen has interpreted Kant's use of the terminology of *public* and *publicity* in connection with his systematic analyses of reason and its rights as a political statement, an expression of "opposition to the ruling princes" under the "cover of his philosophy" ("The Subversive Kant: The Vocabulary of 'Public' and 'Publicity,'" in *The Politics of Skepticism in the Ancients, Montaigne, Hume, and Kant* (New York: E. J. Brill, 1992), 213–32.

49. Kant's term here is *Richtigkeit*, which carries a range of connotations that are difficult to capture in a single term. It is connected in its root with the term meaning "to judge" and may itself mean simple correctness or rightness, truth, advisability, appropriateness, regularity, and soundness. The latter translation seems to carry the widest possible nuance.

oriented in terms of the universal that constitutes its own true interest.[50] For the turn within requisite for active, individual exercise of judgment can only be carried out in a way that fulfills human purpose or vocation when the individual also freely submits that judgment to the measure of the universal ascertainable by adopting the standpoint of the other in one's self-reflection. Such enlightened, mature, self-legislating, self-controlled conduct of thought incorporates an interdependent orientation of the self to its own reason and to human reason as such, articulated in and through the human community. Where and when it has been realized, the individual truly "thinks in one voice" (*KU* 294),[51] in agreement with self, for the unanimity of individual judgment and universal moral form has been actualized. Thus to achieve this state of agreement is itself the third and final maxim of the sound human understanding.

CHARACTER AND HUMAN DISCOURSE

To recap: the principles of orientation or general forms of judgment serving as compass and guidepost to direct the human journey toward the good as final purpose, an end that includes the perfected realization of character itself, are now in place as principles relating the individual to reason, to the self as other, and to the human community. Over and above these, Kant provides yet another set of five principles that simply "relate to character" (*ApH* 294). Incorporated into a discussion of "attributes that follow from the mere fact that one does or does not have character" (*ApH*

---

50. For a discussion of Kant's Socratism, see Richard L. Velkley, "On Kant's Socratism," in *The Philosophy of Immanuel Kant,* ed. Richard Kennington (Washington, D.C.: Catholic University of America Press, 1985). As part of his account of Kant's "transformation," not "repetition," of the Socratic way, Velkley underscores Kant's appeal to "common reason" and its need of "the philosopher's metaphysical criticism"; namely, "common moral reason is thereby enlightened as to the limits of speculation, and as to its own sufficiency in the moral-teleological realm. Man is unified on the plane of reason, of a reason forever deprived of speculative ambition" (89, 104, 105). Another early recognition of the connection between Socratic and Kantian thought and of the significance of this connection is articulated by James N. Jordan, "Socrates' Wisdom and Kant's Virtue," *Southwestern Journal of Philosophy* 4 (1973): 7–23. Dieter Henrich, as has been noted in earlier references, is attentive to the Socratic/Platonic dimensions of Kant's thought. See also Gerhard Mollowitz, "Kants Platoauffassung," *Kant-Studien* 40 (1935): 13–67. For an interesting opposite perspective, see Daniel T. Devereux, "Socrates' Kantian Conception of Virtue," *Journal of the History of Philosophy* 33 (1995): 381–408; Devereux suggests that "perhaps the closest parallel to the Socratic conception is Kant's notion of moral character," which Devereux takes to consist fundamentally in the "good will" (407). As he further notes, to support this conclusion would require a full discussion of what good moral character is for Kant.

51. Again, in his *Reflections on Anthropology,* Kant expresses this point explicitly in terms of character: "Individuals without character . . . are not in unanimity (or agreement) with themselves (*mit sich selbst nicht einstimmig*)" (*RA* no. 1220, 534).

293–95), these prove to address a further dimension of the concrete exercise of character, namely its exhibition and self-preservation in and through human discourse, both inner and outer. "To think" is just to "converse with oneself," and "speech is the foremost vehicle of understanding ourselves and others," writes Kant in an earlier section of his *Anthropology* (*ApH* 192). Given our discussion thus far—character defined in terms of conduct of thought, the maxims of thinking for oneself and from the standpoint of others, the reflective principles of conscience and of rational faith adopted on the basis of an act of judgment—the relevance of principles governing the human *means* for carrying out these acts is readily apparent. We begin our examination of these principles formative for human discourse by recounting them as itemized in the *Anthropology*.

These principles are best formulated negatively, observes Kant, and the first one in his list (*ApH* 294) is a very familiar prohibition indeed. Do not lie, or as Kant literally puts it, do not "intentionally speak untruths" (*vorsetzliche Unwahrheit* being also the phrase he identifies in his *Metaphysical Principles of Virtue* as the "ethical definition" for the lie, *MST* 429, 430). Therefore, he goes on, take care in choosing your words, so as not to draw upon yourself the disgrace of having to take them back. Second, do not play the hypocrite, overtly displaying good will and covertly harboring ill will. Third, do not break your promises (those permissible under the law in the first place), a precept that incorporates honoring the trust and confidentiality of friendship, including those relationships that may now be a thing of the past. Not only is the third maxim (of promise keeping) again very familiar to Kant's readers, but in addition, these first three principles bear much affinity with the initial, fundamental articles of the just, cosmopolitan constitution (the significance of which is addressed below). The fourth principle advises against keeping the company (at least socially) of those who are morally deficient in their thinking (*schlechtdenkenden*), while the fifth counsels ignoring libelous gossip whose source is but insipid and malicious opinion; moreover, in general one should guard against fashions and certainly never allow the latter's dictates to take on the status of morals.

On the face of it, these are but commonsense moral principles pertaining generally to human conduct in relation with others. Kant has, however, specified that they "relate to character," and that they may be understood as formal conditions for discourse, whereby character is exercised and maintained in relation to others, becomes evident from his references to these principles in other texts. Character itself, we recall, is a formative activity peculiar to the rational being in relation to living nature

(the latter including human community and history). That we thus procure a character for ourselves in relation to (but not from) nature is just
the leading characteristic of the human genus and entails the cultivation of
all of our natural powers of mind, body, and soul as means for all possible
purposes. Among these, the "communication of thought" is an "inner purpose" (*MST* 430), and the power of "speech" is the "premier way of signifying thought" (or making it manifest, *ApH* 192).[52] Previously we concluded too that character as the moral form of organization or structure
of the human system of powers (as these are employed by reason, practical
desire, and choice), analogous to character of the physical order, indicates
an original, extant, purposive aptitude for self-preservation of one's kind
(in this context, as moral being). On the following interpretation, the
function of these five principles selected by Kant as "related to character,"
insofar as they serve to guide conduct vis-à-vis the other, do so not primarily for the sake of the other, or even our relation to the other, but first
and foremost for the sake of the cultivation and preservation of character
exercised in these relations of human discourse.

It is just in such terms that Kant himself explicitly speaks of the first
of these formal conditions, truthfulness. As the principle most elaborated
by Kant, it is also the main focus of our discussion here. "Having made
truthfulness one's highest maxim both in one's inner admissions to oneself
and in one's bearing (*Betragen*) toward everyone else," he asserts, "is the
only evidence in one's consciousness that one has character" at all (*ApH*
295). The "lie," by contrast, Kant declares to be nothing less than a
"throwing away and, as it were, annihilation of one's human dignity"
(which latter we know consists in the morally good comportment of mind)
(*MST* 429). The lie results in the opposite of the "natural purposiveness
of one's capacity for communicating one's thoughts"; it makes manifest
"not the individual herself, but a mere deceptive appearance of the human
being" (*MST* 429). From the beginning to the end of his corpus, Kant's
emphasis on truthfulness and on its explicit connection with character is

52. Kant's discussion here of *Gedankenbezeichnung* and of *Sprache* as the *Bezeichnung der Gedanken* is part of a larger consideration of the "capacity of signifying" as such, which includes an
examination of symbols, signs, characteristics in relation to concepts. The term *Bezeichnung* means
more than simply giving "expression to" thoughts and is quite well rendered by "signify" or "act
of signifying" when this is understood to mean "to show or make known," that is, to give thoughts
a fixed concrete form whereby they become accessible and available (for example) for attaining
to self-knowledge. Clearly, we are here getting into the domain of the philosophy of language,
and it is beyond the scope of the present project to analyze the merits or deficiencies of Kant's
account in this regard. Our objective is to establish his claims for the purpose of comprehending
the relation and importance of truthfulness and these other precepts to his conception of character.

unwavering. In the *Observations* of 1764 it is described as "sublime," and the melancholic character (Kant's choice among the medieval humors as the one whose characteristics prove to foreshadow his mature account of character) is there presented as "hating the lie or dissemblance" (*B* 221). In the Herder transcriptions of his lectures from this same early period, the "love of truth" is declared to be the "ground of all virtue," while the "lie" is charged with tearing "human society apart at its heart" (*Ak* 27.1, 59–61).[53] His *Reflections on Anthropology* (from the early 1780s) reiterate that the "maxim of a good character is to speak the truth" (*RA* no. 1518, 869). In his essay dealing with the topic of theodicy, one finds Kant asserting that "honesty, an uncomplicated[54] innocence [or simplicity] and straightforwardness in *Denkungsart* . . . is the least one can always demand in regard to a good character" (*VT* 269–70). In his *Metaphysical Principles of Virtue*, Kant explicitly connects the lie with the problem of radical evil (a point discussed separately in the following), and in his last published work, *On Pedagogy*, one finds the unequivocal statement that "truthfulness is of the essence for and the principal attribute of character. Individuals who lie have no character, and should good be found in them, it can only be attributable to their temperament" (*P* 484).

In one respect, from the standpoint of Kant's conception of character as it has been explicated throughout our study, the reasons—one could even say necessity inherent to his account—for his adamant stance in regard to this principle are self-evident. Character as conduct of thought, as the counterimage of objective moral form, concretely conveyed through the activity of free choice-making, whereby the natural order is elevated to the moral one and reason's empirical character is realized as a rule in appearances, is indeed vitiated in its own very core by any inner intentional effort to make outward appearance belie, instead of exhibit the inner. Unanimity, speaking in one voice on the part of all the human capacities, would simply be out of the question, if truthfulness were not the funda-

---

53. Another edition is available as "Immanuel Kant. Aus den Vorlesungen der Jahre 1762 bis 1764. Auf Grund der Nachschriften Johann Gottfried Herders," *Kant-Studien Ergänzungshefte* 88, ed. Hans Dietrich Irmscher (Cologne: Kölner Universitäts-Verlag, 1964); for these passages see 148–49. In Herder's transcription of Kant's lectures on metaphysics (based on Baumgarten), one finds a threefold distinction of logical, metaphysical, and moral truth. The latter is defined as the "agreement of thoughts with words" (*Ak* 28.1, 16).

54. Just as in the title of *Religion within the Limits of Reason Alone*, Kant's use of *bloße* is more difficult to translate than it first seems. Scholars have made a case that in the 1793 work, for example, it should be rendered as "bare" and not as "alone" (as it is in the Greene and Hudson translation). Here too the sense is much closer to "bare," but given the nuances this term can have in English, I have chosen "uncomplicated" for the sake of clarity.

mental principle of the communication of thought. All the human capacities are furthermore, we recall, properly natural aptitudes for good, and reason makes use of these in its subjectively practical employment. The lie, however, as Kant expressly notes, entails not a use, but an explicit misuse of the natural capacity and thus abuses, not cultivates, its inherent aptitude for good: "Individuals as moral beings cannot use themselves insofar as they are physical beings as a mere means (as a talking machine) not bound to the inner purpose (of the communication of thought); rather, they are bound to the condition of being in agreement with the declaration (*Erklärung, declaratio*) of the moral being and are obligated to themselves to be truthful" (*MST* 430).

Conceived in such general terms, one would expect few to argue with this fundamental call for truthfulness, but as an absolute maxim for a given particular action, the objections to it date back to Kant's own lifetime, to his 1797 essay. These objections are seriously made and deserve the hearing they have received in the scholarship. Our focus here, however, will be limited to the attempt to understand the relation of this first principle to character; this relation equally deserves to be articulated, and the general inattentiveness to Kant's conception of character as such has heretofore precluded consideration of the requirement of truthfulness in this light.[55]

55. The criticisms raised range in scope from the demand for the social "white lie" to the demand that there very well could be cases where the lie avoids the greater injury (the familiar murderer at the door example). Kant, as is well known, rejects both kinds of cases as ones permitting the lie (in "On the Supposed Right to Lie for the Sake of the Love of Humanity," from 1797), repeating the point he makes elsewhere that the lie at all times does injury to humanity as such, by "making the source of right [or justice] unserviceable" and rejecting also the notion that the duty of truthfulness makes a distinction between people (those that do or do not have a right to truth), for "truth is not a possession that we have the right to grant as we will" (*RL* 426, 428, 429). In his consideration of the issue in terms of the casuistical questions he raises in the *Metaphysical Principles of Virtue*, Kant casts his conclusion in terms already alluded to in his examples in the *Groundwork*. The one who lies is responsible before her conscience for any and all events that follow directly consequent to the deliberately false statement (*MST* 431; *G* 402–3). "On the Supposed Right to Lie" also raises the issue of maintaining the integrity of contractual relationships and in this sense bears a relation to the first of the preliminary articles of the just constitution. What we first want to understand in our present examination is precisely how and why the intentional untruth is intrinsically inimical to character (hence at all times injurious to humanity as such). It is remarkable, after all, that in the other casuistical questions (for example, in regard to suicide), Kant does entertain the possibility of just such "worst-case scenarios" in which, what is under "normal" life circumstances otherwise clearly a violation of the categorical imperative, might indeed appear justified. In these examples, the consideration of the common good (of Prussia, for whose sake the king is willing to take his life) or more simply of the good of other individuals (in the case of the man whose illness can cause him to be dangerous) is raised as a relevant issue. What is it exactly that stands in the way of a similar contemplation of such a possibility in the case of the lie? Why is it that the lie always does injury to the good of humanity as such, irrespective of such considerations? Does the inherent link with character provide the

We do not want to lose sight of the larger point of our present discussion, namely, that the fundamental connection we are seeking to elucidate is between specific principles of human discourse and moral character, for which the first one, truthfulness, is both exemplary of this relation and fundamental to all five of the principles Kant lists.

The passages already quoted from Kant's various texts point us to what can be seen as the crucial element of Kant's position in this regard. His inclusion of the Latin in *Metaphysical Principles of Virtue* (*declaratio*, *MST* 430) underscores that what is at stake is just the act of disclosing or making evident—speech identified with the "inner purpose of the communication of thought" and construed as the activity that signifies thought (to use the language of the *Anthropology*) in concrete and hence sensibly discernible form in the world. That truthfulness of the declaration is thus of the essence becomes clear precisely in light of Kant's conception of character as the synthetic unity of causality of the human moral being in relation to its natural capacities. In this unity, it is fundamentally the natural capacity of speech whereby reason discloses its empirical character in the world. The truthfulness at issue in this light is *not* in regard to our statements insofar as they make assertions *about* some object, action, or event. To check the accuracy of our judgments in this respect we appeal (among other things) to the standpoint of the other in a public use of reason. The issue now is the integrity of moral judgment itself as expressed: does it articulate what a self-assessment of our thinking would show we actually regard as true? Those who "do not themselves believe what they tell another," even if that other is an "ideal person" (as in the case of the exercise of conscience), "have even less worth," writes Kant, "than if they were a mere thing," for the latter would at least be "something actual and a given fact" of which another could "make some use"; whereas the articulation of words that express the contrary of what one thinks contradicts the "natural purposiveness of one's capacity for communicating one's thoughts" and is tantamount to "renouncing one's personality" (*MST* 429). The latter is, as we know, the third level of the human aptitudes for good whereby we first can be said even to be moral beings, that is, beings to whom one can attribute moral accountability.[56] The act of lying, then, violates "moral

---

answer? It is from this perspective that we approach our inquiry here. What is it that is singularly at stake in the case of truthfulness?

56. It is useful here to recall Kant's definition for "personality," namely as a "rational being" that is "at the same time capable of being held accountable" (*der Zurechnung fähigen Wesens*) (*RV* 26). Accountable or responsible are the usual translations of *Zurechnungsfähig* and, while technically quite correct, may nonetheless obscure (to the extent that they seem to be simply restatements

truth," already defined by the early Kant as the "agreement of thoughts with words" (*Ak* 28.1, 16). Moreover, as we can also glean from the discussion thus far, the act of lying (for Kant) violates the formal condition of truthfulness fundamental for having character at all. The task at hand, then, is to explore further what this means and how and why Kant comes to take this position.

Such "truthfulness in [our] declarations" extends to wider aspects of human discourse as well. As Kant describes it, it may also be called "honesty" (or frankness, candor, openness, *Ehrlichkeit*), and "sincerity" (or fairness, *Redlichkeit*) when such statements "are at the same time promises; in general, [truthfulness is one's declarations] is called uprightness" (*MST* 429). The latter term, we recall, is just how Kant designates the morally good character whereby "the law is given graphic form" (in his first reference to it in the *Critique of Practical Reason, KpV* 77). Moreover, so described in terms of honesty, openness, sincerity, and fairness, the principle of truthfulness underlies also the second and third of Kant's selected "principles related to character" (the prohibition against hypocrisy and the call to keep one's promises), while the last two are in this light clearly an exhortation to avoid those circumstances in human life informed by an opposite state or condition.

Perhaps the most interesting parallel may be made with the order and content of Kant's constitutional articles, the requisite formal conditions if the agreements drawn up between nations in the name of peace are actually to realize this end. Given the parallels and connections we have already seen (in our third chapter) between the just civil constitution and good moral character, this should not surprise us. We saw the civil constitution called upon precisely when the discussion concerned the subjective capacities, the conditions under and through which the moral universal is to be concretely realized. In its principles and goals, the just constitution concretely embodies the same moral order exhibited in and through good moral character. While on the one hand Kant traces all human conflict to an inner source in human nature, a position that receives its full articulation through the concept of radical evil, nonetheless it is the establishment

---

of Kant's conception of duty) the most important nuance of the term. Its basic sense is the possession of that soundness of mind which allows one to be deemed an individual capable of being held thus responsible or accountable in the first place; in short, it is the juridical term for sanity, for *compos mentis*. This meaning underscores the point that what is at issue here is just that moral soundness of our mental state which allows us to make a claim to the status of moral being. Conceiving of the lie, therefore, as an act that fundamentally undermines the soundness of our mental state is consonant with Kant's repeated charge that lying annihilates our human dignity. What we need to understand is how or why the act of lying is inherently such an act.

of the external order whereby conditions conducive to the cultivation of the inner are provided. The achievement of such a "completely just civil constitution"—said to be humankind's "greatest problem"—we saw further, belongs to the "duty" of individuals "toward themselves," a duty "belonging to the worth of humanity in their own person," to be a "member of service to the world." Such service, we might add here, depends essentially upon human discourse or communication.

The express purpose of the constitution is to effect eternal peace; in turn, to speak of such a "state of peace" is to speak of conditions "in which laws have force," and this, we saw, equally describes the state of the individual in whom good moral character has been established and that of the human community under the just, civil constitution. Turning to the articles of the latter, we find the first requirement underlying all the others, without which (so to speak) we cannot so much as get to square one, to be the genuine spirit of honesty, candor, and sincerity with which we enter into the agreement at all, harboring no mental reservations, no hypocritical intentions to resume conflict at the earliest opportunity, instead giving and keeping our promise wholeheartedly to the other (F 343–44). Even during conflict, as the sixth article stipulates, such acts, which would permanently destroy any possibility of some modicum of confidence in the *Denkungsart* on the part of the other, cannot be allowed, for such acts would destroy too the very possibility of entering into a peace agreement (F 346–47). In short, subjectively speaking, truthfulness is the cornerstone that must be in place, if either a just, civil order or character, either world peace or peace within, is to be concretely realized. It is essential for providing just such conditions under which laws may have force.

The central point in this parallel between the constitution of individual character and the constitution of the state (the corporate body of citizens) is once again a question of form; that is, of a fundamental formal requirement, on the basis of which alone stated ends or purposes may be achieved. Objectively speaking, in both cases, this requirement or condition is the moral law; subjectively speaking, in regard to the exercise of, the manner of use that is made of, the natural human capacities (above all, the capacity of speech), the guiding principle is truthfulness. That is to say, the concrete actualization of the moral law itself as a principle formative of the human order on either an individual or corporate, political level (as the principle inherent to that order and not simply as the imperative external to and above it) requires truthfulness as the supreme formal principle for human utterances (in all forms and levels of the latter). Truthfulness is the basis upon which one can confidently expect that human beings will actually carry out any given agreement (in letter and in spirit in accord with its objective principles). For where truthfulness is in fact absent, a given appearance in conformity with the objective universal law (be it as individual action or conduct of life, or as some kind of contractual arrangement) belies the actual intent of the given concrete expression. We are touching here, of course, on the familiar distinction of Kant's moral philosophy between action in mere conformity with and arising from respect for the moral law, with the difference being that in the case of insincerity, not only does the motivation not consist in the moral ground, but giving expression to the latter is being used to serve other ends. Respect is characteristic of the morally good comportment of mind, but it is truthfulness that is the *formal subjective condition* providing *surety against the instrumentation* (actual or potential) of the moral universal itself by the human subject.[57] And it provides that surety both within and without: for the individual before self in conscience and mutually for individuals in their express human relations with one another. Truthfulness, specifically truthfulness in the communication of thought both within and without, fulfills the indispensable need for a subjective ground to serve as the basis for trusting the appearance authored by the human (of the self before itself and in relation to others): for being confident that the appearance truly exhibits what it purports to present.

That human beings have a propensity for "dishonesty in their declarations" (*MST* 430), for deliberately making themselves "appear better than they are," for "giving expression to maxims (*Gesinnungen*) that they do not in fact hold," had already been noted by Kant in his first *Critique's* analysis of the inner source that must be addressed if human conflict (in any of its forms) is to be overcome (*KrV* A748/B776ff.). While he is willing to accord a marginal initial usefulness to such conduct in human

---

57. Reinhard Hiltscher explains the perversity wherein the guilt of the liar consists in just such terms (albeit not in an effort to explain the link with the conception of character, but as an analysis of the inverted relation that obtains in the lie between the moral law and the inclinations). As Hiltscher points out, the decisive factor is that the moral law cannot be eliminated from the human mind; it is the *factum* of reason. The liar must presuppose the validity of the moral law, indeed, of the law as a subjective ground, a motive power of human activity, of the law as an imperative recognized and adhered to by human beings, in order successfully to use, or rather misuse, the law as a means for the satisfaction of purposes arising out of his or her appetitive inclinations. The liar employs the law as an instrument in the service of his or her private ends or, at the very least, in the service of subjective ends belonging to the contingent realm and, hence, by nature subordinate to the law, thereby making the comportment of mind also a matter of mere instrumentation (*Kant und das Problem der Einheit der endlichen Vernunft* [Würzburg: Königshausen & Neumann, 1987], 81–92).

development from the natural to the moral state (familiarizing brutish nature with the "manner of the good"), Kant asserts it to be, in the long run, a state of "falsehood" that must be "vigorously combated," for it "corrupts the heart" and stands in the way of the cultivation of the "morally good *Gesinnungen*" (*KrV* A748/B776). These observations are consonant with his repeated claim that the lie does violence to human dignity.

Considering this claim in light of the foregoing subjective principles of orientation for the exercise of character in the world may help us elucidate it further (first summarized here and followed by a more detailed discussion). As itself the expression of an inherent propensity to present oneself as something one is not, to the point of instrumentalizing the moral, the lie is intrinsically connected with the problem of radical evil. Related to this point is the fact that where inner discourse is deceitful, the possibility and effort of self-knowledge is seriously undermined or thwarted altogether. In turn, the operation of conscience is undermined and with that, so too moral self-consciousness. In addition, such corruption of inner discourse and self-knowledge stands in the way of attaining to the true conviction of rational faith. To the extent this conviction is essential for maintaining human orientation to the good, the attainment of final purpose also is undermined. Finally, "once the supreme principle of truthfulness has been violated, from such a rotten spot (the falsity that seems to be rooted in human nature) the evil of untruthfulness spreads" to external discourse, "in relation to other people" (*MST* 430). In this domain, it serves to undermine the various forms of public agreement, hence once again ultimately undermining the striving for humanity's final purpose (understood in this sphere in terms of the collective effort to realize the just cosmopolitan constitution). So seen, the lie as the perversity of the formal condition of discourse[58]—as the perverse employment of the primary vehicle of the disclosure of character, of its concrete appearance in

---

58. Any one instance of the lie constitutes a violation of the formal condition. Thus as Kant notes in "On the Supposed Right to Lie," the individual intentional expression of untruthfulness is effectually to contribute to that state of affairs in which declarations in general are met with disbelief (426). That a single, or even a few instances, would not bring about such a general state of affairs is of course not the point. Cast in terms of our traveler motif, one could restate Kant's claim as follows: The responsibility of the individual travelers to themselves and to humanity as such is just to establish concretely those conditions under which the purpose of life's journey may be attained. Each violation of these formal conditions is, in effect, to steer the course of humanity as such (to the extent of that individual's role therein) in the opposite direction. The nature of the formal condition fulfilled by truthfulness (understood, it is important to underscore, as the agreement of thought with its sensible expression) is explored further in the continued discussion.

the world to the self and one's companions in the human journey—stands in the way of realizing the vocation or destiny proper to humanity both formally and materially.

Kant (in his *Religion*) expressly links the problem of radical evil with the notion of inner "insincerity" whereby we "mislead ourselves" (*sich selbst blauen Dunst vorzumachen*), with the "deceitfulness of the human heart" that stands in the way of self-knowledge of one's actual moral state and results in peace of mind being enjoyed by those who falsely "deem themselves to be conscientious" (*RV* 38). As he also does in the *Metaphysical Principles of Virtue*, he here holds that this dishonesty before oneself is carried over, "expanded outwardly in falsehood and deception of others" (*RV* 38). If not "wickedness" per se, nonetheless this falsity pertains to the "radical evil of human nature," which, as it were, renders "moral judgment dissonant with [literally, out of tune with] the value one is to attach to human beings and [thus] makes both inner and outer [moral] soundness (*Zurechnung*)[59] completely uncertain" (*RV* 38). Clearly, Kant has more in mind than the failure of lying as such to pass the moral universalizability test. To attempt to clarify all that is at issue here, what the distinction from (and yet connection with) radical evil consists in, it is helpful to turn to his reading of the Genesis story and his treatment of the problem of deception in its terms.

"It is noteworthy," Kant observes, "that the Bible dates the first crime whereby evil was introduced into the world, not from Cain's fratricide (which, after all, arouses natural outrage), but from the first lie" (*MST* 431). Moreover, he goes on, the "human propensity for dissemblance," for which "reason is unable to specify any further basis," must be assumed to "have preceded" this first lie (*MST* 431). This way of casting the Garden of Eden story puts the emphasis on the side of the human (not as it traditionally is, on a willful act of disobedience), on the latter's readiness to accept a false appearance, both on the part of another and as something to adopt for themselves. In the face of this, moral judgment no longer operates in agreement with the true value of humanity.[60] For where the

---

59. See note 56 on the meaning of *Zurechnungsfähig*.

60. Human wickedness, we recall from our third chapter, consists in that *Gesinnung* so oriented that when an "inclination entices one to the commission of a transgression [against the law], one does *not want* to resist" the inclination (*RV* 58n). The "root (*Grund*) of this evil" can lie neither in "human sensibility" (*Sinnlichkeit*) and its "inclinations," nor in "a corruption of morally legislative reason" (*RV* 32–34). To attribute it to the former would be "too little," for the level of sensibility is only that of our aptitudes for animality, while a reason that releases itself from the moral law is too much; it would make of the subject a "diabolical being" (*RV* 34). The diabolical

human is satisfied with the false appearance, or even gives preference to it, this turn to the lie (to put it more bluntly) erects a barrier to the very forging and consummation of the human relation to the moral law, to what we have come to understand as the synthetic unity of causality synonymous with character, whereby the law itself receives "graphic form" (as Kant had put it in the second *Critique*). The law remains unchanged as an imperative for the human, but as we have seen Kant put it in the first *Critique* (and again in the *Religion*), such deception of self and others "thwarts the establishment of a true moral *Gesinnung* in us" (*RV* 38; *KrV* A748/B776). In other words, falsity in human discourse, in communication of self before self and others, indicates for Kant a subjective propensity within human nature that effectually leads human travelers *away from* the true guides, the subjective principles of orientation, indispensable to maintaining their course on their journey toward the realization of human purpose. The cultivation and ongoing preservation of character (wherein humanity's work and value lies) is literally sidetracked by the false appearance whose acceptance stands in the way of adhering, for example (to cite the most obvious one), to the reflective principle of conscience.

Moreover, falsehood is not so readily opposed by *natural* feelings of outrage (such as those aroused by a crime like fratricide), especially when its exercise serves to promote feelings of self-satisfaction (as in the case of those who assume, apart from the rigorous examination before conscience, that their moral state is unobjectionable), or when it is called upon in the name of serving a particular good. Where, to cast the matter metaphorically (and again in terms of the Garden of Eden story), something "appears as good for food, as a delight to the eyes, or as desired to make one wise," where further, unlike the sequence of events of this first occasion, not only no felt injury is experienced, but perhaps such a kind of injury in the particular case is even avoided, it is not difficult to imagine such "insincerity" defined by Kant as "lack of conscientiousness, that is, [a lack] of integrity in the confessions before one's inner judge" (*MST* 430) as the resulting state of affairs. In the Genesis version, "the eyes of

---

being in this story, then, is placed outside of and distinct from the human, but it is significant that Kant does not then focus on the exercise of choice in accordance with self-love, in accordance with a maxim taken from the inclinations (in the face of what appears as good for food, as a delight to the eyes, and as desired to make one wise), despite the clear awareness of both Adam and Eve that their action is contrary to what they have been commanded. Instead he emphasizes the failure to see the false appearance for what it is, from which, in turn, error in moral judgment follows as its consequence—error in recognizing wherein the value of the human lies, what its proper relation to the law must be.

both were opened"; transgression was followed by immediate consequences. While Kant does take such an "awakening of conscience" to be
ultimately inevitable, complete with its appropriate sequel, meanwhile, as
Herder's notes already report him to have warned from the outset, "self-
examination is a very slippery" business; for, it is easy to veil one's vices
with the "pretty side of kindheartedness," and just such a "lack of truthfulness" ends at last in "self-deception" (*Ak* 27.1, 61). Finally, in a parallel
to his observation that immaturity, or lack of thinking for oneself in "religious matters," is above all other instances the "most injurious and degrading" (*A* 41), Kant finds one of the more insidious forms of self-deception
to consist in a profession or declaration of faith where a truthful and conscientious self-examination would reveal no such actual belief, but only a
fear of punishment mistaken as an inner veneration of God's law and a
profession of faith made solely to curry divine favor, on the grounds that
it cannot hurt and may even be useful (*MST* 430; see also *VT* 268–69).
Quite apart from the posture of deception adopted by the human being
toward God (also already noted by Kant in the Herder lecture notes), such
a false declaration cannot bear with it the *conviction* of rational faith, the
trust relation between reason and self described previously as essential for
maintaining that orientation of the self vis-à-vis the good which consists
in a lifelong act (conduct of life) corresponding to the morally good comportment of mind.

Considered, then, in terms of any aspect of Kant's conception of moral
character, truthfulness is the subjective, formal condition upon which all
else depends. In light of this, it is not surprising that Kant, even in his
consideration of casuistical questions (wherein, for example, he is willing
to contemplate seemingly justified cases of suicide), will not, indeed cannot (for the sake of systematic integrity alone) condone any instance of
the act of lying.[61] As an intentional expression of what one does not in

61. Sally Sedgwick, "On Lying and the Role of Content in Kant's Ethics," *Kant-Studien* 82
[1991]: 42–62, argues for indications in Kant's writings that he could recognize permissible exceptions to the prohibition against lying. Similar to John E. Atwell, *Ends and Principles in Kant's
Moral Thought* (Dordrecht: Martinus Nijhoff, 1986), 193–202, she interprets Kant's essay as a
discussion restricted to the "realm of a 'Metaphysic of Right'" in which "Kant can exclude as
impermissible exceptions in the name of prudence or expediency *as a class*, simply by reflecting
on the nature of duty as he has defined it." Sedgwick goes on to say that the questions "whether
duty may on some occasions be excepted to on *other* grounds (on *moral* grounds)," or whether
Kant's thought provides "some objective means of arbitrating among duties when they conflict,"
such as the duty not to lie and the duty to protect the life of my friend, "belong outside that
domain of inquiry." She goes beyond Atwell to argue that "at the applied level Kant's legal theory
does recognize such a right" (i.e. a right to lie) (51, 53). For positive evidence that Kant entertains
cases when lying is permissible, Sedgwick appeals to the Menzer *Lectures on Ethics*, to Kant's

fact hold to be true, it is a way of proceeding that consists not simply in what one might describe as moral failure: the failure to test one's maxim against the moral law, or the failure to effect the revolution in conduct of thought on the basis of which one can first say that moral character has been established. It is not such failure, but a deliberate misuse of human capacities. It is an act of negation of the formal condition and activity whereby character makes its concrete appearance in the world: "Between truthfulness and the lie (as *contradictorie oppositis*), there is no middle" (*MST* 433n). On the basis of this interpretation of the act of lying, Kant's uncompromising statements (such as the following) are its logical consequence. Unlike the juridical requirement of ascertaining the extent, if any, of damages incurred (for example, as a result of a broken contract), this additional consideration of the measure of injury is not needed in the case of the lie, "for it always injures another, if not a particular individual [externally], yet [it does injury] to humanity as such, in that it makes the source of justice [in the world] unserviceable" (*RL* 426).

If we may thus understand what is at stake for Kant in maintaining a prohibition against lying in order to assure the integrity of character, our interpretation nonetheless raises to an acute level the ancient question of whether it is possible to be a just individual in an unjust state. As we have seen, character is further intrinsically connected in its exercise with the

---

reported concession that when force is used against us to extort a statement from us that we are convinced will be improperly used, then we have the "only case in which I can be justified in telling a white lie" (Kant, *Lectures on Ethics*, 228). In these same lectures, however, Kant is reported as repeating a number of times that nonetheless "a lie is a lie, and is in itself intrinsically base whether it be told with good or bad intent. For formally a lie is always evil," and, whatever the particular case may involve (in which, for example, I would not be committing an injustice to the individual who is either first lying to me or using force against me), "yet I act against the right of humankind," a point Kant explicitly repeats in 1797 (*RL* 229, 227). In short, neither the prohibition against "*arbitrary* exception" (Sedgwick, "On Lying," 54), nor the absence of legal injury against a particular individual, can remedy or allow as permissible the violation of humanity in regard to which the lie is always evil. The interpretation of Kant's account of character and the intrinsic connection with human discourse offers a way of illuminating what this violation of humanity entails, namely, more than the violation of "the right to live in a civil society" (as Atwell understands it, 196). To put it another way, the present analysis is compatible with the arguments proffered by Atwell for the "reasonableness" of Kant's stand against a legally established right to lie (202), but insists that Kant further maintains on ontological grounds his stance against the lie as such. For further discussion, see Christine M. Korsgaard's "The Right to Lie: Kant on Dealing with Evil," *Philosophy and Public Affairs* 15 (1986): 325–49. Korsgaard analyses Kant's essay in light of the Formulas of Humanity and of the Kingdom of Ends, as well as the Formula of Universal Law, concluding that under the first two, the prohibition stands, but not in the last case. Also see Georg Geismann and Hariolf Oberer, *Kant und das Recht der Lüge* (Würzburg: Königshausen & Neumann, 1986); J. Ebbinghaus, "Kants Ableitung des Verbotes der Lüge aus dem Rechte der Menschheit," *Revue Internationale de Philosophie* 8 (1954): 409–22.

wider human community; in this community the harsh reality is confrontation with speech that is already deceptive (such as seemingly merely asking for factual information when the actual intent is to secure the means for the commission of some further unjust act).[62] The broadest and long-term solution in Kant's philosophy is that which deals with the just form of the social and political environment, namely the institution of the republican form of governance. To the extent each of us is called upon as a citizen to be of service toward the attainment of that goal, we are also called upon to contribute to the institution of forms of discourse that are truthful. In the interim (until the wider just forms of societal institutions and discourse are firmly established), an interim that can be very long indeed, more immediate guidance for responding under circumstances that are already morally perverse is certainly a desideratum. The route usually taken in such considerations is to seek to qualify the universal in more particular terms and to amend it with "exception" clauses. Kant's conception of character gives us good reason to take seriously the issue of the application of the universal in terms of an alternative solution to such exceptions.[63]

62. Such manipulative means are not simply a matter of a worst-case scenario (the storm trooper demanding to know if Anne Frank is in our attic) that few of us are likely to face in daily life. The more widespread problem of information seeking for ulterior motives and the like is commonly enough found, for example, in daily business contexts. Hence, corporations institute policies that, while their first objective is the corporation's own self-interest, effectively give their employees an avenue for avoiding the potential conflict between the duty of loyalty and the prohibition against lying. The question is whether something like the ready appeal to "I'm sorry, it is against our policy to give out that information, or to discuss that matter," etc., is available within ordinary life. In nonviolent situations, at least, it is not inconceivable that one should be able to express one's preference not to discuss a given subject.

63. While on the one hand Vittorio Hösle regards "Kant's practical philosophy" as a "landmark in the history of philosophy" whose "importance can be compared only with that of Socrates" and urges that in our "time of moral, political, artistic, and intellectual decay" our "interest in Kant's thought must not be only historical," yet in regard to the absolute prohibition against lying, Hösle joins the ranks of Kant's sharper critics, describing Kant's injunction (when the life of an innocent person is at stake) as "absurd and immoral." He goes on to claim that "every moral theory wishing to be taken seriously must explain rationally the necessity of exceptions, and even more, it must recognize that there are norms which are valid only under certain conditions and not valid under others." In order to avoid therefore transforming "ethics into an empirical science of hypothetical imperatives," he proposes a notion of "implicative imperatives," having the structure "under the conditions A you must do B" to serve as the second premise of a syllogism in which the first premise identifies the value which is to be realized. Thus to include exceptions to moral rules requires also obviously a "hierarchy of values and goods" (which Hösle explicitly admits). Such a hierarchy of values raises, of course, its own problems, for there must now be criteria for ranking such values and ways of deciding on these criteria. And, in this regard, it is not simply obvious that life (our modern philosophers such as Nietzsche and Schopenhauer notwithstanding) is a more fundamental value than moral integrity. That the entire issue is a far

* * *

The teachings of the elder matron, of Reason, counseling the traveler at the crossroads, as Kant might have had her articulate his position, may be summarized on the basis of the chapter's discussion as follows. Take your bearings from the following principles for exercising moral judgment in your journey; they will serve to guide you as surely as your inherent sense of left and right allows you to distinguish east from west, north from south. Your own reason has set before you the idea of your destination, but it is not Speculation's desired theoretical account that you need, but only those principles whereby you will perfect the practical employment of your reason. So pursue your course steadfastly by heeding the sign post of rational faith, reason's promise in regard to the reality of the highest good. Check in regularly, daily, with the guide of conscience, to ensure that you have not strayed in your particular judgments from the universal path defined by the law. This necessary self-assessment of judgment requires too that you compare your choices with the collective reason of humanity pursuing this course with you, for you need to guard against the temptation of merely private concerns making their demand to assume the rule of your course. This all entails, of course, that you at all times actively think for yourself and that you do so in complete openness, honesty, truthfulness to yourself and before others. Shun, above all, false appearance in any of its forms, for it can only lead you in the opposite direction of your own true purpose. Abide by these principles shared by humanity's Common Sense and you will both preserve that resolute con-

---

deeper one than being a "self-absorbed egoist" who "refuses to dirty his hands" is clear when it is seen in light of Kant's account of character. Hösle recognizes there is an ontological issue at stake for Kant, but he describes it in the familiar terms of the "phenomenal world" being "ontologically inferior to the noumenal." Hösle's essay has been published in two languages: "The Greatness and Limits of Kant's Practical Philosophy," *Graduate Faculty Philosophy Journal* 13 (1990): 133–57; and "Größe und Grenzen von Kants praktischer Philosophie," in *Wissenschaftsethik unter philosophischen Aspekten,* ed. Klaus Giel and Renate Breuninger (Ulm: Humboldt-Studienzentrum, 1991), 9–39. The passages cited are found on 133, 140, 147–48 and 9, 18, 28 respectively. A further discussion of implicative imperatives is found in Vittorio Hösle, *Hegels System. Der Idealismus der Subjektivität und das Problem der Intersubjektivität,* 2 vols. (Hamburg: Felix Meiner Verlag, 1987) 2: 484ff. Here he differentiates the structure of implicative from hypothetical imperatives; the latter as Kant identifies them consists in the form, "If A is desired, then B must obtain."

Certainly the entire question is a very thorny one, and the present interpretation of what is at stake sheds more light on why Kant would see the lie as the very introduction of evil into the world than it points to an avenue for a happy resolution. Hösle's notion of the implicative imperative is highly suggestive and, at the very least, in the case of the more common, nonviolent scenarios involving deceptive speech and inquiry, may be adaptable into guidelines for handling them that would not require exceptions. For example, one may adopt as one's implicative imperative to respond to all questionable queries with a Socratic examination designed to unveil their true intent.

duct of thought (on the basis of which you first embarked on this journey toward the highest good) and be of service, as you should be, in humanity's effort to give concrete reality to its final purpose. For these principles will direct your relations with reason, yourself, the human community, and the transcendent in a way that realizes the unanimity of particular and universal in your conduct of thought and ensures your progress on the journey.

Kant's conception of the procurement of human *moral* character, of the development of our travelers on life's journey from simply rational human beings to morally competent and accountable ones, is an overall account of how the shift is effected in the orienting force for the human aptitudes from natural to moral necessity. Establishing and maintaining such moral character in relation to nature and exercising it as conduct of life commensurate with the morally good comportment of mind involves what one might call its two moments: causal and reflective. The synthetic unity of causality whereby reason's empirical character is realized as a rule in appearances enacts morally good form in human life. The maxims or subjective principles of moral judgment secure human orientation toward its own proper destiny in the particular judgments of human life. The first concern refers to the notion of the human agent as efficacious cause (examined in our second chapter); the objective must be made subjectively practical. The second concern is to carry out the subjectively practical in relation to human life and nature. Free choice must first be actualized; then the question of the ability to do what one ought is addressed. Reason in relation to the human is both author of the moral order and partner in what amounts to a fiduciary relationship with the human actor called upon to fulfill the practical task, the latter effectually a making immanent *in* the realm of the phenomenal what begins as a relationship of the intelligible *to* the sensible.

In short, morally good character and conduct of life is the exhibition (*Darstellung*) of the good in concrete appearance. To the extent that its production, both as the effect of reason's causal operation and as the ongoing work resulting from the reflective operations of judgment, involves a "production through freedom, that is, through a power of choice that bases its acts on reason" (*KU* 303), character procured as the result of these acts meets Kant's general definition of what may be properly called a work of art.[64] A work, a structure forged out of the relations between reason and

64. Kant does, of course, distinguish in his definition between "effect" and "work" but here "effect" is used to refer to the result of an instinctual operation of nature. Notably, this effect is ascribed as "art" precisely to the "creator" of that nature, and thus, to the extent that human

human powers of agency and these, in turn, in relation to nature, community, and the transcendent, it exhibits the form of purposiveness of the human vocation. The "*Denkungsart* in accordance with moral laws," observes Kant in the *Critique of Practical Reason*, has a "form of beauty" that we "admire" (*KpV* 160). In the *Critique of Judgment*, he notes that the "intellectual" ground, that which is "in itself purposive, the morally good," is "aesthetically judged" to be "sublime" (*KU* 271); as we have seen, the sublime in fact, properly speaking, always has reference to our *Denkungsart*. In his *Anthropology*, Kant further points out that our representation of the sublime must itself be beautiful or we will be put off by it all together (*ApH* 241). Character incorporates all these dimensions. It serves as a systematic link of the moral, aesthetic, and anthropological parts of Kant's philosophy. The exhibition of the law in graphic form, the counterimage of legislative, practical reason realized in and through the human subjective capacities, character is beautiful in its form and sublime in its essential nature.[65]

With the account in place of what Kant's conception of moral character consists in, the remaining question is how he understands the pedagogical function of its cultivation. What are the respective roles of nature, the aesthetic, religion, formal morality, the constitution, the community, and the individual? Addressing this question will conclude our study of this notion in Kant's philosophy.

---

reason's operation parallels that of the creator (giving form to the material, albeit not producing the material itself), the analogy of its efforts with the production of the artwork holds.

65. In an analogous point, Kirk Pillow argues that in the work of art as such, beauty and the sublime are brought together, specifically that the "sublime may only be presented in the work of fine art *by means of* the beautiful" ("Form and Content in Kant's *Kritik der Urteilskraft:* Situating Beauty and the Sublime in the Work of Art," *Journal of the History of Philosophy* 32 [1994]: 444).

❦ 5 ❦

Pedagogy: The Formation (*Bildung*) of Character

AIMS AND NATURE OF PEDAGOGY IN GENERAL

In attending to Kant's philosophy, to Kant as philosopher, it is tempting to treat Kant the educator under a separate heading, as a biographical note. Even taken by itself, his work in education is impressive; for if one includes the early period as private tutor, Kant's years of experience in, and service to, the teaching profession span almost half a century.[1] That pedagogical issues are not far from the mind of the philosopher is evident from allusions to pedagogy in his writings and from his very conception of philosophy. Reexamining both reveals that it is not the case that the critical philosopher simply gives a theoretical account of one more topic, pedagogy; rather, the *critical philosopher is the educator.* Kant's remarks on the components and stages in the development of moral character lead us to insights into how this philosopher-educator understands the relation between philosophy and pedagogy, and their relation (in turn) to the formation of character. Thus the inquiry into Kant's conception of cultivation of character yields, as the account of character itself has done, a much more integrated comprehension of his thought than one might have expected.

1. Commentators rarely fail to point to the wide range of subject matter taught by Kant, or to marvel at the workload he carried in over forty years, uninterrupted even by a sabbatical leave, at the Albertina University of Königsberg. Lewis Beck begins one of the relatively few essays in the Anglo-American scholarship devoted to an examination of Kant's conception of pedagogy with an overview of Kant's professional life ("Kant on Education," in *Education in the 18th Century,* ed. J. D. Browning [New York: Garland, 1979], 10–24). Tabular presentation of all of Kant's lectures during his tenure as professor from 1770 to 1796 (complete with detailed annotation) is to be made available on the Marburg website: <http://www.uni-marburg.de/kant/welcome.htm>. One of the more detailed accounts of Kant's life as tutor, master, and professor is found in Vorländer's biography (*Immanuel Kant,* 1:63–143, 175–212; 3:38–80, 266–70).

That *On Pedagogy* is not the sole, and perhaps not the best, source of Kant's views on education has of course been recognized.[2] Among other relevant texts, of obvious importance are his *Lectures* and *Reflections on Anthropology*. In Kant's own words (which affirm our previous conclusion, that the cultivation of character and human civic relations are intrinsically interdependent), "The sum of pragmatic anthropology in regard to the human vocation and the characteristic of [humanity's] development [or training, *Ausbildung*] is as follows. Human beings are determined by reason to be in society with others and therein [in the same stages as identified in *On Pedagogy*] to cultivate, civilize, and moralize themselves through art and science." They are further determined by reason, "however great their propensity may be for animality (for surrendering passively to the incitements of ease and comfortable living they call happiness), instead to be active, to make themselves worthy of their humanity in battle with the hindrances adhering to them through the crudeness of nature" (*ApH* 324–25).

Important discussion is found too in *Religion within the Limits of Reason Alone*, in particular discussion of the human aptitudes. Given Kant's account here of the aptitudes and their development as central to his conception of character, Cassirer's assessment of the text is a good one: the

2. Beck in "Kant on Education" rejects Traugott Weisskopf's conclusion (in *Immanuel Kant und die Pädagogik* [Basel, 1970]) that *On Pedagogy* "cannot be regarded as an authentic work of Kant's and should be removed from the corpus." "In fact," writes Beck, Weisskopf "has shown very good reason to take *Über die Pädagogik* seriously as a compendium of *echt-kantische* views on education" with the caveat, however, that "one should be warned against using any part of the text of Rink which has no counterpart in authentic Kant works or manuscripts. . . . one should use other authentic works as a guide to and commentary on the Rink compilation" (17–18). Werner Stark's statistics confirm that Kant lectured only four times on pedagogy (1776–77, 1780, 1783–84, 1786–87). As Vorländer has already noted, for the first of these lectures Kant used Basedow's *Methodenbuch* (to which we will return in our discussion) as the basis for the course, changing, at the behest of "königliche Vorschrift," to Bock's *Lehrbuch der Erziehungskunst für christliche Eltern und künftige Jugendlehrer* in the summer of 1780 (*Immanuel Kant*, 227). Samuel Ajzenstat proposes taking the 1803 essay seriously, but as one more source that points us to tensions found in the main body of Kantian philosophy ("Kant on Education and the Impotence of Reason," in Browning, *Education in 18th Century*, 25–43). German scholars (for example, Jürgen-Eckardt Pleines, Gerhard Funke, and Erwin Hufnagel, whose writings are referenced where relevant in the investigation here) tend to be more positive and seek to reconstruct Kant's concept of education from the admittedly aphoristic collection of statements that make up his essay. However, Werner Stark's most recent assessment expresses the caveat that the Rink *On Pedagogy* "should not be seen and used in the full sense of the term as a work by the Königsberg philosopher" ("Kants Lehre von der Erziehung: Anthropologie, Pädagogik und Ethik" [paper presented at the conference "L'Antropologia di Kant e l'attualita dell'illuminismo," Goethe Institute, Rome, October 1997]).

Religion is one of Kant's "pedagogical works" in which "he was speaking as educator of the people and of the government as well."[3] The *Critique of Judgment,* with its attention to the role of the aesthetic in moral cultivation and to the notion of cultivation (*Cultur*) itself, constitutes a substantial part of the complete account of the formation of character.[4] The shorter essays from the period 1784 to 1795 also contain a number of relevant references, while more sustained discussions are found in the "Doctrines on Method" of the *Critique of Practical Reason* and the *Metaphysical Principles of Virtue* (part 2 of the *Metaphysics of Morals*). All of these sources, as well as other parts of his works, will be our basis for inquiring into Kant's understanding of how moral character is to be formed.

Our focus will be the conceptual, not the curricular, elements of pedagogy. As Kant himself states in the *Critique of Practical Reason,* his intention is there "only to indicate the most general maxims of the methodology of moral formation and exercise" (*KpV* 161). He thought he was proposing something unprecedented, stating that such methodology had "never yet been put into operation" and that "experience can therefore tell us nothing about its results" (*KpV* 153). Details of nurture and curriculum, attesting to the century's newfound awareness of the psychological and physiological development of children, appear in Kant's writings, and even more so in the wider eighteenth-century debate on education and its reform. Issues addressed include such wide-ranging topics as the care of the infant, physical exercise, sex education, format and divisions of the curriculum, the value of play, and the role and place of religion. These details make a fascinating read of the historical development of systems of education (such as K. A. Schmid's *Geschichte der Erziehung*).[5] However, our purpose is not to recount these here (which in any event would be a practical im-

---

3. Cassirer, *Kant's Life and Thought,* 381, 387. Cassirer's intention in thus assessing Kant's 1793 work *Religion* was thereby to dismiss it as inferior. In the present context, in light of its importance in regard to Kant's conception of character, we are able to appreciate the systematic contribution the *Religion* makes to his complete account of moral philosophy.

4. This is the only text not included in Erwin Hufnagel's list of writings that serve for him as a check on the text of *On Pedagogy* ("Kants pädagogische Theorie," *Kant-Studien* 79 [1988]: 44).

5. The complete title is *Geschichte der Erziehung vom Anfang an bis auf unsere Zeit,* prepared in six volumes, with Georg Schmid and others contributing to its completion (Stuttgart: J. G. Cotta'schen Buchhandlung, 1898). The discussion of the Age of Enlightenment is found in the fourth volume with over four hundred pages devoted to the conception of education instituted as *Philanthropinismus* (of which in turn pages 27–316 deal with the Philanthropinum in Dessau founded by Johann Bernhard Basedow in 1774).

possibility), but rather to illuminate their guiding principles and concepts that are particularly relevant to moral character.[6]

The call for education reform and its ensuing debate were well in progress by the time of Kant's birth. Emphasis on praxis and not theoretical learning, stress on practical reason and the exercise of judgment together with the disapproval of memorization, perception of education as a maieutic and philanthropic art, attention to providing conditions conducive to the development of human aptitudes, a conception of ordered stages of development all relating to one overarching moral end—these key notions turn out to be elements of a shared vision in the eighteenth century, one that both influences and is influenced by Kant. We will begin by taking a brief look at this wider historical context, identifying its constitutive issues and gaining some sense of the purpose of the educational institute to which Kant gave his enthusiastic support: Basedow's Philanthropin in Dessau.

Not only will the historical backdrop help us better understand how Kant both as practitioner and philosophical thinker conceived of education, but it will help the contemporary reader gain some familiarity with the eighteenth-century conception of pedagogy. Its assumptions are not necessarily shared today. As Jean-François Lyotard has observed, the "technological transformations" of our computerized age impact our conception of knowledge and its relation to the individual; the result is a "thorough exteriorization of knowledge with respect to the 'knower'" and, thus, "the old principle that the acquisition of knowledge is indissociable from the training (*Bildung*) of minds, or even of individuals, is becoming obsolete and will become ever more so."[7] Jürgen-Eckardt Pleines, seeking to articulate a notion of education (*Erziehung*) as the "training (*Ausbildung*) of the capacity of judgment," also discusses what education has come to mean in the face of appeals to nonrational bases of motivation and to empirical experience as an adequate guide for action. Under these circumstances, he notes, we have the task of "bringing praxis and reason once again into a peaceable relation with one another."[8] For Kant's

6. A thesis on Kant's conception of moral education has been published in French: Paul Moreau, *L'Education morale chez Kant* (Latour-Maubourg: Les Éditions du cerf, 1988). Moreau interprets the "final end of education" as "freedom" (200) and discusses character within that context.

7. Jean-François Lyotard, *The Postmodern Condition: A Report on Knowledge,* trans. Geoff Bennington and Brian Massumi (Minneapolis: University of Minnesota Press, 1989), 4.

8. Jürgen-Eckardt Pleines, "Pädagogisches Handeln und dessen Beziehung zur Urteilskraft," in *Kant und die Pädagogik. Pädagogik und praktische Philosophie,* ed. Jürgen-Eckardt Pleines (Würzburg: Königshausen & Neumann, 1985), 66–67, 69, 71–72.

account of moral character, it is axiomatic that they do stand in such agreement.

Mention of the eighteenth century today often brings to mind the Encyclopedists' zeal for amassing and disseminating information and, with that, an instrumental notion of reason. The complete story lies in hearing out the opposing voices within the century and fully appreciating Kant's self-professed practical turn, which accords with a widely held premise of his time that the overall goal of pedagogy is the production of a moral and civic-minded citizenry. Whether systems and institutions of education have a function and responsibility in the moral development of their students, a question that today has no self-evident response,[9] was decided in advance by the leading proponents of education reform in the eighteenth century. Not whether, but *how*, was the question of the age. It follows that ontology, epistemology, and anthropology as connected with the possibility and kind of ethics in question, were also involved in pedagogical theory.[10] Far from being a narrow curricular methodology for imparting information in the arts and sciences, eighteenth-century and Kantian conceptions of pedagogy cannot be disengaged from the questions "What can I know?" "What ought I to do?" "What may I hope?" "What is man?" To realize this is to become aware of how much is at stake when Kant (from the *Groundwork* in 1785 to *Perpetual Peace* in 1795) consistently argues, against empiricist skeptics and political moralists alike, for the actuality of the morally good comportment of mind, for the human capacity for cultivation for the good. Asking "what pedagogy in Kant's sense of the term can be and can accomplish," Gerhard Funke remarks that if

9. Recent discussions of just this question of pedagogy and its wider implications considered in relation to Kant's practical philosophy have been presented by Vittorio Hösle and Thomas Kesselring in their respective essays, "Größe und Grenzen von Kants praktischer Philosophie," and "In welchem Sinne gibt es eine Moralentwicklung?" in *Wissenschaftsethik unter philosophischen Aspekten*. In particular, see Hösle 12–17 and Kesselring 71ff. Kesselring takes into account Kohlberg's work on moral development seen in terms of stages in moral judgment and remarks too on the contrast with Piaget.

Opening remarks in Joel J. Kupperman's recent book *Character* (Oxford: Oxford University Press, 1991) indicate just how basic assumptions today can differ from those in the eighteenth century: "It would be a mistake to link the concept of character too closely to morality. . . . From the point of view of someone who is moralistic. . . . character will appear to lie entirely within the domain of morality. The education of character, then, will seem coextensive with moral education, and to have a good character equivalent to being morally virtuous to a high degree. Most of us in the latter part of the twentieth century are not moralistic and, thus, will have a less simple and reductive view of what good character is" (7, 9).

10. For a discussion of the unavoidability of these questions, see Hösle's "Greatness and Limits."

"Kant is to speak to us today" at all, it presupposes that we must at least "agree with him that what matters is to be a 'moral being.' "[11]

On the basis of the general discussion of the aims and nature of the pedagogy at issue, the investigation turns to the essential question: how, specifically in Kant's conception, these ideas, principles, and stages of education relate to the ultimate task of the formation of moral character. The inquiry proceeds in terms of a threefold division: discipline (of the inclinations), cultivation (of the human aptitudes), and formation (of character). These distinctions encompass both the negative and the positive functions propaedeutic to moral education proper. Under the propaedeutic functions, particular attention is given to the roles of the example and of the development of the human aesthetic capacities. The essence of moral education is the cultivation of moral judgment, indeed of a habit of such judgment, of (one might even say) a philosophical habit of mind.[12] The question of the relation of these distinctions and stages to one another entails the unavoidable issue, not so much of the relation of nature and freedom, but of the reconcilability of Kant's pedagogical and moral orders, the latter of which must *begin* from the establishment of character.[13] More precisely, how and why is the republican constitution, an agency of external constraint, held to be an indispensable vehicle of *moral* cultivation?

The findings presented in the chapter also serve to reply to those among Kant's critics who share the objection that Kant "does not even seem to see that his strict moral philosophy has, and can have, no place for moral

11. Gerhard Funke, "Pädagogik im Sinne Kants heute," in Pleines, *Kant und die Pädagogik,* 99, 102.

12. The notion of a "philosophical habit of mind" cultivated by a good liberal education is, of course, the goal espoused by John Henry Newman in *The Idea of a University* (Notre Dame: University of Notre Dame Press, 1982), 76–77. However tempting it might be to draw parallels to Kant's project, particularly when one reads (for example) Newman's understanding of what "education" means ("But education is a higher word; it implies an action upon our mental nature, and the formation of a character; it is something individual and permanent, and is commonly spoken of in connexion with religion and virtue" [86]), to do so lies beyond the scope of the present investigation. Here we only seek to show that Kant has what amounts to a notion of a philosophical habit of mind and to articulate what that means in terms of Kant's conception of character and its cultivation.

13. Pauline Kleingeld resolves the purported tension between Kant's moral philosophy and his philosophy of history by interpreting history as a learning process, a solution that, she argues, avoids leading to any historization or relativization of the moral principle itself. However, she notes (and I agree with this point) that at the level of the individual (but not at that of the species), there is a tension between Kant's theory of education (or upbringing) and his moral philosophy (*Fortschritt und Vernunft,* 206–10).

education."[14] The conclusion in this chapter is that pedagogy, as a matter of instruction, upbringing, discipline, and cultivation in which nature and community play an essential role, affects the *conditions* under which the individual task of what one is to make of oneself is most readily achieved—if, that is, one is to realize humanity in oneself, the form of one's species as a moral being. The ultimate responsibility does lie with the individual; the essential act of the revolution of conduct of thought (as we will see) is just the virtue that cannot be taught. In connection with the fact that character is a matter of the subjectively practical realization of freedom, this conclusion resolves the apparent contradiction between Kant's pedagogical and moral orders.

Finally, in the epilogue to our entire discussion we draw upon a metaphor employed by Kant himself, the praxis of grafting taken from the gardener's art, to depict character as the achieved unity of the natural and moral, a unity that has been an underlying issue of our entire account and that a successful pedagogy is to effect. Through the metaphor, the role and limits of the pedagogical function may be restated in another form: character as the work of art specific to the human may be seen as a work that, far from opposing nature, requires nature's cooperation and stands in essential relation to it, but cannot be brought about by nature itself. Parallels with conditions that must obtain if a graft is to be successful help us to comprehend how and why the provision and fostering of external

14. Beck, "Kant on Education," 22. Ajzenstat argues that a second look at the "appearance of incompatibility between Kant's views on education and the more or less received account of his thought [on the 'two-tiered' account of self]" is instructive for rethinking the interpretation of Kant's theory of self ("Impotence of Reason," 32–33). P. J. Crittenden essentially agrees with Beck's point, claiming there is a "conflict between [Kant's] commitment to moral education and his strict moral philosophy"; for "since there is no transition from the phenomenal to the noumenal, processes of moral formation must appear ineffectual" ("Kant as Educationist," *Philosophical Studies* 31 [1986–87]: 30). The general problem that Kant's critics see is apparent: if morality is a matter strictly speaking of a noumenal will and if this remains unaffected by education or cultivation of phenomenal capacities, then it is incongruent to speak of moral education. Most recently, Werner Stark has argued that "Kant himself recognized the fundamental moral-pedagogical problem and sought to develop ways of approaching a solution" ("Kants Lehre von Erziehung").

Throughout, the present study has sought to underscore that Kant, through his conception of character, articulates his pervasive concern that morally good form be concretely enacted and exercised in the world, for which purpose the natural (phenomenal) aptitudes of human nature must be cultivated so they are fit for, adequate to, the task of carrying out reason's idea. The central question that must still be addressed is precisely how instruction, discipline, civilization, cultivation relate to the ultimate act of character formation that remains the individual's responsibility. This question is addressed in the course of this chapter's discussion.

For a comparative study, see William K. Frankena, *Three Historical Philosophies of Education: Aristotle, Kant, Dewey* (Chicago: Scott, Foresman and Company, 1965).

conditions and ultimate individual responsibility do not contradict one another.

Returning then to the first step on our way to these conclusions, we begin with a synopsis of the eighteenth-century view of pedagogy. The citations we saw in our first chapter from Arnauld, Pascal, Rousseau, and Goethe provided evidence of the wider concern with the notion of conduct of thought and its causal connection with conduct of life. It is not surprising, therefore, to find among the political, literary, and philosophical figures of the day, the repeated express connection between *bien raisonner* (as Frederick the Great identified the pedagogy he "recommended as the goal for all teachers"),[15] pedagogical purpose and method, and the task of forming a moral and civic-minded citizenry.[16] The king himself affirmed "morality as society's strongest bond and the source of public peace; [hence] the exemplary school would always be the one effecting the best influence on lived morality and making society more secure, benevolent, and virtuous."[17]

Scientific and technological advance, the burgeoning of theoretical learning, was seen as not only *not* synonymous with these moral pedagogical goals, but even detrimental to them, a concern perhaps most familiar

15. Friedrich Paulsen, *Immanuel Kant: His Life and Doctrine* (New York: Frederick Ungar, 1963), 61.

16. For another discussion of "the moral improvement of people" as "one of the main objectives of German enlightenment" see Sabine Roehr, *A Primer on German Enlightenment: With a Translation of Karl Leonhard Reinhold's "The Fundamental Concepts and Principles of Ethics"* (Columbia: University of Missouri Press, 1995), 43ff.

17. Schmid et al., *Geschichte*, 15. For an account (by a prominent Prussian jurist and member of the Wednesday Society) of Frederick the Great's stance on the best way to rule his people, see Ernst Ferdinand Klein, "On Freedom of Thought and of the Press: For Princes, Ministers, and Writers," trans. John Christian Laursen, in *What Is Enlightenment? Eighteenth-Century Answers and Twentieth-Century Questions*, ed. James Schmidt (Berkeley and Los Angeles: University of California Press, 1996), 87–96. Drawing on Frederick's own writings, Klein paraphrases his views, a sampling of which includes the following: "Does not my higher station, my royal office, give me the duty to be gentler, more benevolent, more virtuous, and in a word more humane than they? . . . I want to rule over a noble, brave, freethinking people, a people that has the power and liberty to think and to act, to write and to speak, to win or to die. . . . the resistance of inertia [is that] through which superstition, priestly despotism, and intolerance work against the development of talent and inventiveness and against the natural drive of men to be active. . . . The dawn of philosophy and good taste shall also rise over my subjects. They shall throw off the chains of superstition. Power-hungry priests shall not limit their freedom to think. No religion shall rule. All faiths shall be taught with equal freedom. . . . the beneficial influence of philosophy shall not be limited by any coercive laws. Wolff shall come back to my state, and whatever does not plainly contradict the state, good morals, and the universal religion shall be taught freely and publicly" (88, 89, 90). Frederick's father had dismissed Christian Wolff from the University of Halle; he returned in 1740 (96).

to us today through Rousseau's articulation: "Could knowledge and virtue be incompatible?"[18] Indeed, Jean-Jacques shields Emile—in the various stages of the latter's "apprenticeship" in becoming a man, in learning the "job" of "living" by learning first and foremost "how to think"—from all book learning save for *Robinson Crusoe*.[19] This widely read book of the eighteenth (and even nineteenth) centuries is, by Defoe's own account, an "allegorical history" whose "just and only good end" is "moral and religious improvement."[20] Rousseau was not alone in his misgivings. A striking passage from Goethe's *Wilhelm Meister* has Wilhelm commenting to an astronomer on the purported joys of bringing the universe closer by means of the telescope: "I have found in life as such, that on average these means by which we come to the aid of our senses do not exert any morally favorable effect on human beings. Those looking through spectacles consider themselves wiser than they are, for their external senses are thereby thrown out of balance with their inner competence for judgment. . . . We shall not ban these glasses from the world any more than any machinery, but it is important for the observer of morals to find out and to know whence many things about which people complain have crept into humanity."[21] *Wilhelm Meister*, of course, is the archetype of the entire genre of the bildungsroman whose emergence in this period attests further to the pervasive concern with how the development of young persons is best fostered.

Not only the giants of the age, but many lesser-known figures participated in the debate on pedagogy throughout the course of the century. As described in Schmid's historical account,[22] the debate was carried on in part through contributions to over five hundred weekly publications devoted to moral issues (with the first ones on the Continent appearing

18. Jean-Jacques Rousseau, *Discourse on the Question Has the Restoration of the Sciences and Arts Tended to Purify Morals*, in *First and Second Discourses*, 47.

19. Rousseau, *Emile*, 445, 41, 33, 184ff.

20. Daniel Defoe, *Robinson Crusoe*, ed. Michael Shinagel (New York: W. W. Norton, 1994), 242.

21. Goethe, *Wilhelm Meisters Wanderjahre*, 120–21.

22. Schmid et al., *Geschichte*, 1–26. The summary that follows in the body of the text is taken from these pages. Annette Bridgman, in her introduction to Browning, *Education in 18th Century*, also reports on the "fascination with education that was unprecedented in its intensity" in the eighteenth century. Grimm is said to have observed in 1762 that "writing on education 'is the mania of the year.' " In France too, notes Bridgman, "nearly 200 books and pamphlets on education—written by everyone from prominent lawyers to military men, literary hacks, private tutors, and aristocratic fathers—were published between the death of Louis XIV and the outbreak of the Revolution. Conscious, to varying degrees, of contemporary theories of learning and affected by the century's new sensitivity to the child, these authors criticized the educational status quo and called for sweeping reforms" (1, 5).

between 1721 and 1725 in Zurich, Hamburg, Halle, and Leipzig).[23] Locke's *Some Thoughts concerning Education* served as an early point of departure, with Rousseau gradually gaining prominence in the discussions. Many of the questions addressed have a decidedly modern tone. For example, new conceptions of both the nature of the soul and physiology of children became bases for proposing reforms in established methods of discipline and instruction. Such inquiries led to questioning the value of instruction in the classics and foreign languages and debate as to how other subjects should be treated. It was suggested, for example, that history's practically useful role in the curriculum was as a collection of morally good and evil examples in humanity's past. In accord with this approach, Kant himself quite deliberately chose to make geography a study encompassing "physical, moral, and political" elements, so it would incorporate what could be "preparatory for and serviceable to practical reason" (*N* 312). The criteria of selection for curricular subject matter (moral, perfectibility, usefulness, and so forth) themselves became topics of debate. As the decades passed, the role of reason as fundamental for directing human affairs was opposed by voices decrying the neglect of the imagination. The diminishing role of Scripture at the level of the family (where its status in the Christian world had been seen as a parallel to Homer's role in the ancient world) was a matter of deep concern and entailed the further question of the place of religion in the curriculum. Appeals to external authority were contrasted with the possibility of reliance on the self. Kant's famous shibboleth for enlightenment, *sapere aude,* itself became part of the debate. As Schmid summarizes them, leading principles of the Enlightenment educators included the following: "We will teach (1) established truths that can be made comprehensible to the ordinary understanding through examination, experience and direct judgment; (2) whatever enlightens the mind (*Geist*) concerning the products of nature and their various treatments by the human arts, (3) what will clear away common and harmful prejudices, (4) [what will] make the most appropriate and best

---

23. A more recent study of these so-called moral weeklies (*Moralischen Wochenschriften*) as a literary genre providing a source for an enriched conception of the literature and culture of the period of Enlightenment in Germany has been completed by Wolfgang Martens: *Die Botschaft der Tugend. Die Aufklärung im Spiegel der deutschen Moralischen Wochenschriften* (Stuttgart: J. B. Metzlersche Verlagsbuchhandlung, 1968). Other bibliographies referenced in Martens's research indicate there were 557 such weeklies, but he recommends more conservative estimates and concludes that publications that can be legitimately counted as belonging to this genre number 110 in the German-speaking regions (162). On Martens's assessment, the weeklies of greater scholarly interest (and least deserving of the perception of this literature as a merely trivial and tedious popular one) were published before 1760.

applications of nature and art understandable and hence [result in] prudence in the affairs of human life; (5) finally [what] will ennoble conduct of thought (*Denkungsart*) and improve taste."[24]

In light of the foregoing, Kant's own pedagogical principle (as stated in his 1765–66 "Announcement" of his lectures and elsewhere), that his students were "to learn not thoughts, but how to think," in effect echoes the call of the age (*N* 306).[25] His further express connection of this point with what it means to philosophize is by no means limited to statements made in his lectures on logic (*LJ* 22–26). Already in his 1765–66 announcement, Kant goes on to describe the "method of teaching in philosophy (*Weltweisheit*)": the "philosophical author is to be viewed . . . not as the model of judgment, but rather solely as the occasion" for exercising "judgment in regard to, even against his own" position; for "what the apprentice[26] actually seeks and what can also solely be of service to him is proficiency in the method of thinking for oneself and drawing conclusions" (*N* 307).[27] Both points, in regard to Kant's pedagogy and his understanding of philosophy, are affirmed by the Marburg research.[28] They were also already attested to, for example, in Stuckenberg's 1882 biography: "While in his profounder lectures he gave the students the results of his own investigations, it was his principal aim to teach them to think, and

24. Schmid et al., *Geschichte,* 25. The "educational goal of mutual and societal enlightenment" was borne out by the "rigorously ordered agenda" of the Berlin Wednesday Society (whose internal name was "Society of Friends of Enlightenment"). The society existed in Berlin between 1783 and 1798 and included among its membership the royal physician Johann Karl Wilhelm Möhsen (from essay published as "Die Berliner Mittwochsgesellschaft" by Günter Birtsch, trans. Arthur Hirsh, in Schmidt, *What Is Enlightenment?* 235, 236). Möhsen's lecture of December 1783, "What Is to Be Done toward the Enlightenment of the Citizenry?" is translated by James Schmidt in the same volume (49–52).

25. For a new historical study of Kant's own early schooling see Heiner F. Klemme, *Die Schule Immanuel Kants. Mit dem Text von Christian Schiffert über das Königsberger Collegium Fridericianum,* vol. 6, *Kant-Forschungen,* ed. Reinhard Brandt and Werner Stark (Hamburg: Felix Meiner Verlag, 1994). In their introduction to volume 25 of the Academy edition, Brandt and Stark note the parallel in Kant's program of education as presented in his lectures with that outlined in Friedrich Gabriel Resewitz's *Erziehung des Bürgers* (1773), a more precisely worked-out version of Frederick II's *Über die Erziehung* (1770); with Locke being the underlying influence, the educational program in all these cases seeks to impart learning about conduct in civil society (Brandt and Stark, introduction, xx).

26. It is not insignificant that Kant here uses the term *Lehrling;* recall that Rousseau too saw his Emile as an apprentice.

27. For Brandt and Stark, it is highly noteworthy that Kant did not publish a textbook of his own for use in university instruction, something that was a practice of the day. They attribute this to Kant's basic pedagogical principle that his students were to learn how to think and not to memorize the thoughts of another (Brandt and Stark, introduction, lxvii).

28. See also Dieter Henrich, "Zu Kants Begriff der Philosophie. Eine Edition und eine Fragestellung," in Kaulbach and Ritter, *Kritik und Metaphysik Studien,* 40–59.

he so frequently emphasized this that his hearers could not make the mistake of imagining that he expected to do the thinking for them. According to his *Logic,* a philosopher is one who philosophizes. One man cannot make another a philosopher, however much learning he may impart, though he may help him to become one; for it is only by the exercise of his own reason, by thinking for himself, that one becomes a philosopher."[29] Or, as Friedrich Paulsen reports, it was Kant's self-professed aim "by means of philosophy to form men of independent thought and upright character. . . . The one thing which all" students working toward different professions "required was practical wisdom"; without it, "science" was deemed by Kant to be a "dangerous possession and to have the tendency to make one conceited, rude, and inhuman. Now it is just the task of the academic teacher of philosophy to guard against this," to guard against the student becoming a mere "cyclops," someone equipped with "only one eye" who sees "things only from a single standpoint, that of his specialty. The task of philosophy is to furnish a second eye to the scientifically instructed youth, 'which shall cause him also to see his object from the standpoint of other men. On this depends the humanity of science. . . . The second eye is thus the self-knowledge of human reason, without which we can have no proper estimate of the extent of our knowledge.' "[30]

The self-knowledge and discipline of reason that is the work of the first *Critique;* the affirmation of the "vocation of all human beings to think for themselves" of the essay "What Is Enlightenment?"; the maxim of enlarged thinking (from the standpoint of humanity); the assertions of the *Anthropology* and other texts that the attainment of wisdom consists in developing the "complete use of reason" or its "practical employment

29. Stuckenberg, *Life of Immanuel Kant,* 74.
30. Paulsen, *Immanuel Kant,* 63–64. In our own time, the call for responsibility and wisdom in the face of scientific and technological advances has been forcefully expressed by Hans Jonas: *Das Prinzip Verantwortung. Versuch einer Ethik für die technologische Zivilisation* (Frankfurt am Main: Insel Verlag, 1979), translated as *The Imperative of Responsibility: Foundations of an Ethics for the Technological Age* by Hans Jonas and David Herr (Chicago: University of Chicago Press, 1984). More recently, Vittorio Hösle's work has focused on establishing ethical principles in the face of what he sees as the crisis of contemporary philosophy and the relation to our ecological problems; see *Die Krise der Gegenwart und die Verantwortung der Philosophie. Transzendentalpragmatik, Letztbegründung, Ethik* (Munich: C. H. Beck, 1990). A key thinker for Hösle in this regard is Karl-Otto Apel, who articulated humanity's "obligatory collective responsibility" as corresponding "to the intersubjective validity of norms or at least to the basic principle of an ethics of responsibility" (Karl-Otto Apel, *Towards a Transformation of Philosophy,* trans. Glyn Adey and David Frisby [London: Routledge and Kegan Paul, 1980], 228; the original is *Transformation der Philosophie* [Frankfurt am Main: Suhrkamp Verlag, 1972]).

in perfect accord with the law": all can thus be seen as rooted in and directly connected with these fundamental principles and purposes of Kant's pedagogy. Further statements appearing in close association with Kant's self-professed turn to the primacy of practical reason (in his 1764 *Remarks on "Observations"*) are also relevant here and can be better appreciated in this context. "One of the greatest detriments of science (*Wissenschaft*) is that it takes away so much time that the youth are neglected in regard to morals" (*BB* 37). Humanity's most urgent business is "to know how to fulfill its place in creation properly and to understand rightly what it is to be a human being" (*BB* 36). To this end, the "science genuinely needed by humanity" is precisely the one that "teaches" us how to fulfill "fittingly our place allotted to us in creation" and "from which we may learn what one must be in order to be a human being" (*BB* 39). For the goal is explicitly not "to be a seraph," but rather to take "pride" in being human (*BB* 40). To be such, we must not forget, is just to be a *moral* human being.[31] The pedagogical roles of nature, the aesthetic capacities, and the republican constitution all, as we will see, serve as avenues to this end.

However inspired Kant's early remarks may have been by his reading of Rousseau's *Emile,* he was disappointed by its pedagogical methodology. While he notes at one point that a Rousseauian education is the "only means" of improving society, the twenty years devoted by the tutor to raising a single individual to adulthood was simply impracticable and afforded no clear sense as to how such instruction might be translated into a system of education for the schools (*BB* 129, 27–28). There was, however, an actual institution of education based on both Enlightenment and Rousseauian principles first founded in 1774 by Johann Bernhard Basedow: the Philanthropin. As evidenced by his strong statements printed in the Königsberg newspaper (once in 1776 and again in 1777, *Ph* 447–52), his correspondence, and as reported by Schmid, Vorländer, and others, Kant gave sustained and enthusiastic support to the Philanthropin, not only recommending it to all of Europe's citizenry and urging public support, but personally engaging in fund-raising efforts, praising it in his anthropology seminars, and offering encouragement in turn to each of its two main directors, Joachim Heinrich Campe and Christian Heinrich Wolke.[32] In a letter to Wolke in August 1778, Kant commends

---

31. As Gerhard Funke has also noted, these early statements by Kant are effectively inquiries into "those conditions under which humanity can be human" ("Pädagogik," 100).

32. Vorländer, *Immanuel Kant,* 220–30; Schmid et al., *Geschichte,* 235–38; *RA* no. 1501, 792, 792n. Besides communiqués with Basedow, Wolke, and Campe, the correspondence appearing

him as the one in whom all hope has been placed by the supporters of the school, the "idea" of which gladdens the hearts of all who share in it (*Ak* 10, no. 125, 220). He describes how he won over an erstwhile critic of the school, a Königsberg chaplain, Wilhelm Crichton, not only to support the school in principle, but actively to work on its behalf. In the course of his report, Kant states what is for him the chief role and importance of education. Admitting that he and Crichton remain "worlds apart" on their conception of education, Kant explains that Crichton "sees theoretical learning (*Schulwissenschaft*) as the only thing necessary and I the formation (*Bildung*) of human beings, in regard to both their talents and their character," but that both aims could be well met under Wolke's direction (*Ak* 10, no. 125, 221).

Publicly, Kant hailed the school as an "institution of education" whose founders were "dedicated to the well-being and improvement of humanity," whose pedagogy was genuinely "in keeping with nature as well as all civic purposes" and thus capable of effecting the "development of the natural aptitudes inherent in human nature" (*Ph* 447–48). He called upon "all humanitarians" (literally "friends of humanity," *Menschenfreunde*) to give their support to and inform themselves about this new school and its "true method of education," which not only benefited its students, but served to educate teachers in accordance with its ways (*Ph* 449–50). Upon the school's failure (by 1794, due to administrative and financial difficulties), Kant reaffirmed the verity of its idea of education, noting that experiments in education are necessary and that one ought not give up on such an idea because of initial difficulties in its execution.[33] The very conception of education as *Philanthropinismus* is in itself highly suggestive and implies a connection as well to the wider efforts conducted in the eighteenth century in the name of philanthropy or humanitarianism.[34] A brief review,

---

in volume 10 of the Academy edition includes Kant's July 17, 1778, letter to Wilhelm Crichton (a local chaplain) persuading him not only to adopt more positive views on the Philanthropin, but to take over subscriptions to its journal and other matters that Kant had himself been handling. There is correspondence as well with August Rode, with Friedrich Wilhelm Regge (whom Kant persuades to go to Dessau to be of service to the Philanthropin), and with Johann Ehrmann, a teacher at the school. Also a writer of children's books, in 1779 Campe published a translation of Defoe's *Robinson Crusoe*.

33. Vorländer, *Immanuel Kant*, 2:230.

34. In the eighteenth century, charitable functions formerly carried out under the auspices of religious orders and institutions were beginning to be assumed by both the state and individual citizens; at the same time, the term philanthropy itself came into widespread usage. As Schmid reports, one of the weekly publications dedicated to moral/pedagogical issues was *Der Menschenfreund* (*Geschichte*, 6). Schmid's complete discussion of the entire pedagogical movement of *Philanthropinismus* extends from pages 27 through 445 of his fourth volume and, in addition to

then, of the school's program will help us gain a further sense of the meaning and purpose of pedagogy as understood by Kant and others in his time.

The Philanthropin's complete description was "a school of humanitarianism and proper knowledge for students and young teachers, rich and poor; a *fideicommissum* [entrusted] to the public for the improvement of the educational system everywhere in accordance with the plan of the *Elementarwerk*. Recommended by J. B. Basedow to those among the nobility, humanitarian societies, and private individuals who search for and act [on behalf] of the [common] good."[35] Its "pedagogical purpose," indeed its raison d'être, the "reform of the foundations of the educational system," was to be effected through six steps outlined by Basedow: (1) providing prospective teachers with practical training, not just through lectures, but supervised experience, in the "difficult art of the instruction and education of young people"; (2) basing instruction on a well thought out curriculum; (3) eliminating all memorization and translation of terms (which by such means remain uncomprehended); (4) training governesses and tutors employed by the nobility so that "greater insight and virtue might be attained by the higher classes"; (5) separating civic and ecclesiastical instruction; (6) revising the method of teaching Latin so that this language, so useful to all refined persons, might be acquired without ordeal.[36] Depending on their own level of achievement, its students were intended to become teachers for the aristocracy and in the higher schools, schoolmasters in the country schools, and governors and governesses.[37]

It is worth underscoring that this program of educational reform had

---

Basedow, includes discussions of the efforts and writings of its other central adherents: Christian Heinrich Wolke, D. Karl Friedrich Bahrdt, Christian Gotthilf Salzmann, Joachim Heinrich Campe, Ernst Christian Trapp, and Piere Villaume. The connection as such of a notion of friendship and the promotion of human excellence is in fact, of course, a classical one. Aristotle's books on friendship in *Nicomachean Ethics* affirm friendship itself as a virtue "indispensable for life"; concord in the state is held to be the result of friendship, and living together with good men (the *conditio sine qua non* of true friendship) provides training in virtue or excellence (1155a1–5, 1167a21ff., 1170a11–12).

35. Schmid et al., *Geschichte*, 199n. Schmid presents most of his information about the school, its purpose, principles of learning and instruction, and curriculum in the form of quotes from Basedow's own writings. The brief summary provided here, then, recapitulates the description of the school in large measure in Basedow's own words or a paraphrase thereof.

36. Schmid et al., *Geschichte*, 204.

37. Schmid et al., *Geschichte*, 210. Since the students entered the school as children, they did not all ultimately pursue their intended professions.

the support of authorities and rulers. Basedow's commission to found his school at all was due to the goals and ideals of the local sovereign in Dessau.[38] The Prussian minister in charge of education as of 1771, Karl Abraham von Zedlitz (himself influenced by Locke's treatise and an initiator of reforms at the university level), was sympathetic to the *Philanthropinismus* movement and shared Basedow's conviction that the main deficiency of the current schools consisted in the rote learning of things that the students never came to understand and in the associated fact that the students did not learn how to think[39] (albeit, as Brandt's and Stark's findings have concluded, the reforms in Prussia at the levels prior to the university did not take effect until the middle of the 1790s; too late, that is, for providing Kant with students better prepared for their studies).[40]

It was not finally the Dessau Institute itself, but Basedow's ideas and writings as these were adopted by others, that can be considered to have made an impact. Born in the same year as Kant,[41] Basedow too worked as a private tutor prior to returning to his doctoral studies, which he completed in 1752 at Kiel with a dissertation on the best method for the instruction of youth.[42] In the course of both this early experience and research, his basic ideas began to take shape. In 1753 he received a professorship in Soröe, Denmark,[43] and by 1758 published his *Practical Philosophy for All Walks of Life,* to be used as a textbook at the university level; in 1771 (the year of his arrival in Dessau) he still regarded it as one of his best writings. It began as a commentary on Hutcheson's writings, but by his own account, Basedow's main reliance was on Locke's book on educa-

---

38. Dessau's sovereign, Leopold Friedrich Franz, acted under the resolve "to do something at the expense of his house, for the benefit of homeland and posterity, which the general public was to make use of, carry on, and expand" (Schmid et al., *Geschichte,* 197).

39. Schmid et al., *Geschichte,* 308–9.

40. Brandt and Stark, introduction, lxviii. For a study of the state of the universities in eighteenth-century Europe, see Theodore Ziolkowski's *German Romanticism and Its Institutions* (Princeton: Princeton University Press, 1990).

41. There is apparently some confusion in the historical record on this point. Schmid notes that the correct date of birth according to the baptismal records of the St. Nicolai Church is September 9, 1724. Basedow's grandson (Max Müller, author of the article found in the *Allgemeine Deutsche Biographie*) gives the date of birth as September 11, 1723.

42. Schmid et al., *Geschichte,* 28–39. The biographical information following in the text is found in on pages 56–60.

43. Schmid reports the appointment as being one of professor of morality and the *schönen Wissenschaften.* It is not clear exactly what is covered under the rubric of the latter, but given the attempt in general in the eighteenth century to make connections between morality and aesthetics, presumably "aesthetics" would be a fair way to render the phrase.

tion. A review of *Some Thoughts concerning Education* bears out his claim.[44] It was only in 1768 that Basedow began to take Rousseau's *Emile* and its increasing influence in Germany into consideration; in the same year his *Presentation to Humanitarians* appeared, its full title reading *Vorstellung an Menschenfreunde und vermögende Männer über Schulen, Studien und ihren Einfluß in die öffentliche Wohlfahrt, mit einem Plane eines Elementarbuchs der menschlichen Erkenntniß.*[45]

Basedow's ultimate purpose in this work remained the improvement of the school system; its three parts dealt with "state supervision of education, schools, and studies," with "opinions, doubts, questions, and suggestions

44. In his edition of Locke's treatise, Peter Gay notes that "Locke was both an expression and a cause" of a "shift in sensibility" in regard to children. Previously, children had been very casually treated—among other reasons was their uncertain life expectancy. Little grief was expressed at their death; parents were not always sure just how many they had lost. Most remained illiterate, and even when they were educated there was little conception of the gradual evolution of rationality and self-discipline in the growing child. "To the extent that children were important at all, their importance was economic and legal," as sources of labor and links in the chain of inheritance. "It took books like Locke's and a half century of insistent propaganda," writes Gay, "to diffuse the notion that children are human, with their own rights, their own rhythm of development and their own pedagogical needs. . . . in stressing the crucial significance of education for the total physical and psychic economy of the human being, Locke was the true innovator. . . . Locke developed his pedagogical program, not in isolation, but as part of a total view of the world. It was as a philosopher that Locke the educator appealed to experience, expressed confidence in the flexibility of human nature, regarded human beings as organisms of interacting psychological and physical characteristics, and advocated humane treatment and utilitarian training" (Peter Gay, introduction to *John Locke on Education* [New York: Bureau of Publications, Teachers College, Columbia University, 1964], 2, 3, 4, 5). Gay cites from the last edition of Locke's *Some Thoughts concerning Education*. The latter begins with the statement that "a sound mind in a sound body, is a short but full description of a happy state in this world. . . . He whose mind directs not wisely, will never take the right way; and he whose body is crazy and feeble, will never be able to advance in it" (19). As the text continues, it is evident to a reader that the hallmarks of the whole Enlightenment debate on education may first be found in it: the general purpose of education, the emphasis on praxis and play, the repeated references to virtue. Passages that particularly stand out as ones echoed in Basedow's writings are found (in the Gay edition) on pages 49, 53, 55, 57, 65–66, 72, 99, 111–12, 147–48, 150, and 176.

A critical edition of Locke's work has been prepared by James L. Axtell: *The Educational Writings of John Locke* (London: Cambridge University Press, 1968). For a relatively recent study of *Some Thoughts concerning Education* as "the richest source for Locke's vision of human nature and moral virtue," see Nathan Tarcov, *Locke's Education for Liberty* (Chicago: University of Chicago Press, 1984).

45. Schmid et al., *Geschichte*, 87; *Allgemeine Deutsche Biographie* 117. A literal translation of the title of this work would read: *Presentation [or Conception] of Schools, Studies and Their Influence on the Public Well-Being, with a Plan of a Book about the Elements of Human Knowledge, [Made] to Humanitarians and Men of Means.* It was followed shortly by the publication of an abridged version entitled *The Essentials of the Presentation to Humanitarians.* In the interim, in 1763 Basedow had published his *Philalethie*, a book offering new theological interpretations. In the latter years of his life he returned to his theological writings (Schmid et al., *Geschichte*, 68; see also *Allgemeine Deutsche Biographie* for more details on this dimension of Basedow's work).

for education, schools, and studies," and a description of his work in progress, the *Elements of Human Knowledge*.[46] The conception of public schools
he presented was that of "nurseries" (*Pflanzgärten*) in which "virtue, patriotism, and the public happiness" were to be cultivated.[47] Essential, therefore, in these schools was the "moral education" they provided, for which,
in turn, Basedow saw "*exercise* in virtue" as indispensable (emphasis
added); when combined with "instruction" such a pedagogy was "all that
human beings could do for the well-being of family, state, and posterity."[48]
Recommended modes of schooling to be employed included methods
Basedow had himself already put into practice in his early years as tutor.[49]
Children should, wherever possible, even during times set aside for amuse-
ment, be learning something useful. In fact, play could be so adeptly organized that the young charges will have learned much about a given subject
without their even being aware that instruction had been the intent. In
all cases, whatever is onerous in the learning process was to be alleviated;
children should enjoy learning. The question whether they were ready
both in heart and understanding for some particular knowledge must always be taken into consideration before seeking to impart it. Example,
taste, and exercise must always precede the presentation of theory; the
latter then becomes only the means whereby that which has already been
learned is now repeated, retained, and expanded in an orderly fashion.
For the level of gymnasium studies, Basedow emphasized that "the most
important thing" was that the students "read on their own, thereby thinking and inquiring, and following up their inquiry with their own work."
He also presented a detailed description of the teachers with whom the
schools were to be staffed: five at the public level (the educator who by
example and supervision of the students' communal life taught virtue
through its praxis; the teacher of the elements of human knowledge—
including reading, writing, and arithmetic; the moral instructor responsible for religion, morals, and the laws of the land; the teacher of the civil—
as opposed to ecclesiastical—knowledge of the natural universe; and
finally the one who taught the civil knowledge of history); four at the level
of the *Gymnasium* (the educator and the teachers of rhetoric, of philosophy
and mathematics, and of Greek and antiquities). At this level of education,
"everything was to be geared to the one overarching purpose of making
the youth wise, virtuous, and patriotic."

46. Schmid et al., *Geschichte*, 88, 109.
47. Schmid et al., *Geschichte*, 95.
48. Schmid et al., *Geschichte*, 100.
49. The summary following in the text is taken from Schmid et al., *Geschichte*, 101–5.

As indicated in the complete title of his *Presentation,* Basedow had begun work on his *Elementarbuch* in 1768. In 1770 he initially published two parts, the *Methodology (Methodenbuch,* revised in 1771, again in 1773 and used by Kant in his first lectures on pedagogy) and the *Elementarbuch;* the two together made up his *Elementarwerk,* which underwent further revisions (albeit still heavily indebted to both the *Presentation* and the *Practical Philosophy*).[50] The program of instruction in the Philanthropin itself followed the principles and curriculum laid down in the *Elementarwerk;* the school's stated pedagogical goal (*Bildungsziel*) for each student was to "form a European" (a statement that indicates that the ideal of patriotism was a cosmopolitan and not a narrow one).[51] Its book of protocol identified four points of essence for the new mode of education: "(1) The youth were to be taught no superfluous information; (2) the most natural mode of teaching would be sought, and when it was found and corrected by experience, it would be promulgated for wider use; (3) moral education and preparation for future civic life was the main thing; (4) educators were to be formed through instruction and practice."[52] The *Elementarwerk* outlived the school in Dessau. Over fifty years after Basedow's death and almost eighty years after his initial publication of it, a third edition was published in 1847. The latter's introduction credited Basedow as being the one who provided the original inspiration for efforts everywhere to improve schools and the education of children. As already noted, upon the closing of the Dessau Institute, Kant once again publicly affirmed the merit of its effort to embark on an experiment in new modes of education. The institute and Basedow were further credited with having brought the development of thinking about pedagogy itself to the level of a science. The *Elementarwerk* inspired additional writings, and, finally, the entire project proved to be a motivating impulse for the production of specifically children's literature.[53]

In light of Kant's conception of moral character as the resolute conduct of thought—requiring the cultivation of all the human aptitudes for good in order to effect the shift in orientation from natural to moral necessity and, above all, requiring the attainment of that proficiency and resolve in the exercise of judgment that constitutes speaking in one voice, to have overcome the oscillation of volition between self-love and moral command

---

50. Schmid et al., *Geschichte,* 111–13; for a detailed description including many excerpts from the text of the *Elementarwerk,* see Schmid 130–84.

51. Schmid et al., *Geschichte,* 279, 254.

52. Schmid et al., *Geschichte,* 254.

53. Schmid et al., *Geschichte,* 312–15.

as well as of judgment between skeptical doubts and the moral command directing humanity to its ultimate purpose—it is readily understandable why he was so impressed with the program of the Philanthropin. In its express purpose and its basic principles, it accords well with Kant's concerns. From the preceding synopsis, three points in particular are worth underscoring. First is obviously the primacy placed on moral cultivation and the subordination of theoretical learning to that end. Second is the emphasis on the education of the teacher, a point to which we will return in our discussion of the question already broached of the relation between philosophy and pedagogy for Kant. Third is the intrinsic connection between moral cultivation and the development of proficiency in using reason well, of learning to think for oneself. This fundamental maxim of enlightenment, often received negatively as the hallmark of an undesirable individualism, may here be seen in terms of its classical connection with the quest for wisdom.

We have already discussed Kant's treatment of this maxim as a principle of reflective judgment indispensable for the exercise of moral character in the world. The *sapere aude* of his essay on enlightenment, when understood in the context of Horace's *Epistles* (which is its original source), underscores the connection with wisdom. The intent of the communiqué to the young man studying rhetoric in Rome is to interest him in moral philosophy, to impress him with the importance of right living. *Sapere aude* here constitutes an exhortation to the young man to "dare to be wise," literally to have the courage or spirit to live a morally upright life and no longer to "put off the hour of right living"; reading Homer for examples of life and instruction in manners is essential thereto, for Homer "tells us what is fair, what is foul, what is helpful, what is not."[54] The connection, in turn, of wisdom with exercising one's own reason and judgment, as opposed to rote learning or memorization, is also documented (for example) in Plato's *Phaedrus*. In the story recounted by Socrates of the conversation between the Egyptian king and the proud inventor of writing as a means of improving memory and wisdom, the problem the king sees is that *thinking itself is replaced* by the memorized term; readers will no longer recollect things from within themselves and hence, protests the king, "it's not a recipe for memory, but for reminding, that you have discovered." He goes on: "And, as for wisdom, you're equipping your pupils with only a semblance of it, not with truth. Thanks to you and your invention, your

---

54. Horace, Epistle I.ii, in *Satires, Epistles, and Ars Poetica*, trans. H. Rushton Fairclough, Loeb Classical Library, vol. 194 (Cambridge: Harvard University Press, 1991), 260–67, lines 1–4, 40–43.

pupils will be widely read without benefit of a teacher's instruction; in consequence, they'll entertain the delusion that they have wide knowledge, while they are, in fact, for the most part incapable of real judgment. They will also be difficult to get on with since they will have become wise merely in their own conceit, not genuinely so."[55] For Kant, exercising real judgment has become an issue of even having the "courage to make use of one's own powers of comprehension" (*Verstand* in its broader sense, *A* 35), and, as we have learned, to do so is of the essence for his conception of moral character. We turn now, then, to what Kant himself had to say about the cultivation of judgment, how he understood its connection with his wider discussions of the cultivation of the human aptitudes and its relation both to propaedeutic pedagogical functions and to authorities external to the individual.

PROPAEDEUTIC FUNCTIONS IN RELATION TO CHARACTER DEVELOPMENT

Character as the Guiding Principle for Pedagogical Theory

In his *Reflections on Anthropology*, in the context of reflections about bringing good out of evil as the "plan of universal history" (observations that accord very much with his 1793 *Religion* and other texts), Kant provides a list of twelve items pertaining to the education of the child. Prefaced with the admonitions that "everything befit nature, society, and the polity" and that things "not be done prematurely," the list closes with an explicit reference to Basedow's institute. The items refer to granting children their freedom, a cheerful state of mind, esteem and force of law, the stature of childhood, dissimulation, the role of and stance toward the opinions of others, love of truth, kindness, the rights of humanity, humanity in one's own person, and social relations with others (*RA* no. 1501, 792).[56] While connections both to other texts in Kant's corpus and to Basedow's program of education may be readily recognized for these topics, nonetheless the

55. Plato, *Phaedrus,* trans. W. C. Helmbold and W. G. Rabinowitz (New York: Macmillan/ Library of Liberal Arts, 1956), 275b. Hannah Arendt notes this problem of the "weakness of words" in both earlier and later works (*Human Condition,* 169; *Life of the Mind* 115–16).

56. In the concluding section to the Friedländer lecture notes (appearing in *Ak* 25.2.1, 722– 28), Kant is reported to have said that the "present-day Basedow institutes are the only ones that have come about in accordance with a complete plan" of education. Kant goes on to extol them as "the greatest phenomenon to have appeared in this century in regard to the improvement of the perfection of humanity" (722–23). A number of familiar motifs of Kant's moral philosophy, account of character and of pedagogy, are alluded to in these brief pages. Notably, over a page of discussion is devoted to Kant's remonstrance against the lie.

list illustrates well the prima facie eclectic nature of Kant's notes (including the 1803 essay) on the subject of pedagogy. In seeking to articulate what his concept of education is, commentators have sought to uncover a systematic structure inherent in Kant's remarks. The fourfold division of discipline, cultivation, civilization, and moralization (*P* 449–50) has served as one answer, addressing as it does the initial transition from animality to humanity and the hierarchical realization of individual capacities qua individual, individual in community, and qua humanity in one's person.[57] Moreover, both Kant's stages of human history and his delineation of the human aptitudes correspond to this division.[58] In this regard, then, it serves well for the analysis of his pedagogical theory.

However, the question of systematic structure (if there is one) calls for a principle that connects the divisions themselves to one another and to the ultimate purpose to be achieved by these pedagogical stages, thereby unifying them into a systematic whole. Further, Kant (as his commentators have been quick to point out) does not use his terminology consistently, often crossing over the lines of the division. The term for education (or upbringing, *Erziehung*) is usually treated as the umbrella concept, and, while the term for formation (*Bildung*) is generally held distinct from "education," it is sometimes used as if it were synonymous.[59] The notion of schooling or training (*Ausbildung*) also appears, and, in relation to all of these terms, Kant employs the notion of "cultivation" (*Cultur*). In their essence, to civilize is to cultivate taste and to moralize is to cultivate reason. Even more broadly, the development of any and all of the human aptitudes is a matter of their cultivation. Hence, as we read in the *Metaphysical Principles of Virtue* (*MST* 391, 392), for example, it is a matter of duty to "cultivate the crude aptitudes of our nature," indeed to "cultivate all our capacities in general" (both "physical" and "moral") for the sake of "promoting the purposes set before us by reason"; through such "cultivation we make ourselves worthy of the humanity" that is our vocation and that corresponds to the stage entailed under the rubric of moralization. Whether these purposes are identified as matters of skill,

---

57. See, for example, Hufnagel's "Kants pädagogische Theorie" and Funke's "Pädagogik."

58. Beck goes so far as to claim that "Kant's philosophy of history is a much more important base for his educational theory than his epistemology and *Anthropology*" ("Kant on Education," 18).

59. That is, *Erziehung* incorporates the fourfold division of disciplining, civilizing, cultivating, and moralizing, but is also said to cover the threefold division of nurture, discipline, and instruction (*Unterweisung*) (*P* 449, 441). Nurture refers to early upbringing and includes fulfilling the child's physiological needs. When *Bildung* is used in a sense synonymous with *Erziehung*, it too is said to include discipline and instruction, *P* 443.

prudence, and morality (which in the 1803 essay are also all held to belong to "practical education," *P* 486), or as belonging to our technical, pragmatic, and moral aptitudes (*ApH* 322), the call for their cultivation applies to all levels.

The one distinction that remains clear and consistent throughout the various texts of the corpus is that of the negative and positive dimensions of development and pedagogy, corresponding to the notions of discipline and cultivation. One of the best general definitions of the terms of this distinction is found in the *Critique of Pure Reason* discussion of the discipline of reason, at a point where Kant explicitly distinguishes his use of the notion of discipline from the sense usually given to it in school: "The restraint whereby the continual propensity to deviate from certain rules is curbed and finally eradicated is called discipline. It is distinguished from cultivation (*Cultur*),[60] which is only intended to provide a proficiency, without however annulling another [proficiency] already present. Hence discipline will make a negative contribution, cultivation and doctrine on the other hand, a positive one to the formation (*Bildung*) of a talent that already on its own has a drive to manifest itself" (*KrV* A709–10/B737–38). It is important to underscore here that discipline and cultivation involve a negative and positive operation respectively brought to bear on something *that is already present* and hence are indeed formative (and not creative). One can thus see why Kant uses *Bildung* in this way that also corresponds to the sense of education (*Erziehung*) consisting in these two components. However, *Bildung* is also used in a more restricted sense in the question of the formation of character.[61] In the course of our analysis here, of Kant's understanding of the education required for producing moral character, we will treat its main pedagogical divisions as consisting in discipline, cultivation, and formation.

As indicated by our textual references thus far, the employment of these terms is in most cases directly connected with a discussion of the human natural aptitudes, whose cultivation (as we know from our foregoing account) is a central factor in bringing about "a character" in and by the

---

60. We will return shortly to a discussion of the meaning and translation of this term, which has more often than not been rendered as "culture." Pluhar usually provides both: "culture" in the text with "cultivation" in a footnote concerning the translation of the term. The modern spelling, of course, is *Kultur*.

61. In the reflection referred to earlier, Kant gives a series of four steps that use *Bildung* both in this broader sense of being formative through cultivation and discipline (of what are in effect our natural aptitudes) and then specifically in the sense of the "*Bildung* of reason and character" (*RA* no. 1501, 791).

individual.⁶² It is worth reflecting, then, on Kant's statement in *On Peda-gogy* that "the *idea* of an education that develops all the human natural aptitudes must be admitted to be true" (emphasis added); as an idea it is a "concept of a perfection not yet to be found in experience," a concept of an education that in its own "form befits humanity" (*P* 443–45). Human beings can realize their vocation only through their education (a point Kant had already explicitly asserted in his praise of the Philanthropin in 1776, *Ph* 449; see also *ApH* 324–25, *RA* no. 1523, 895), and it is thus incumbent on every generation to "work on the plan of a more purposive education"; the latter is in fact the "greatest and most difficult problem that can be assigned to man" (*P* 445–46).⁶³ These remarks are made within the context of a discussion of humanity's providential endowment with "all aptitudes for the good," natural aptitudes that entail the mandate that human beings take up the task of developing them so as to produce moral-ity and thus first acquire their humanity (*P* 445ff.). To do so is literally to make human beings out of animal beings and where there is evil, to produce good (*P* 446). From Kant's account of virtue, to history, to the establishment of character, this mandate to effect change to a better state is a familiar one.

Nor is such a mandate original with Kant. From one perspective, we again have here an ancient conception of the essence of education. As Socrates asserts in the *Theaetetus* (precisely in the context of asking on what grounds Protagoras is entitled "to claim for himself that he justly deserves to be the teacher"): "he's the very one who's wise, whoever by inducing a change makes appear and be good things for anyone of us to whom they appear and are bad. . . . this holds as well in education—one has to effect a change from another condition to the better."⁶⁴ The dia-logue's exercise in the Socratic method leaves Theaetetus at its conclusion

---

62. Hufnagel gives a cogent discussion of "aptitudes" as a key concept for Kant's philosophy. To understand Kant's conception of education, specifically of discipline, rightly, concludes Hufnagel, requires referring to his "systematically developed theory of the human aptitudes and the human vocation in *Religion within the Limits of Reason Alone*. Kant seeks to make the 'possibility of human nature' comprehensible on the basis of a theory of original aptitudes. Aptitudes, in Kant's sense are not simply biological, [that is] respectively physiologically based drives or socially induced needs. . . . Kant's concept of aptitudes includes natural and nonnatural aspects (technical, prag-matic, and moral), grounded in the concept of practical reason and its structure" ("Kants pädagog-ische Theorie," 47).

63. As we have seen previously, Kant also identifies the establishment of the republican consti-tution as humanity's most difficult and urgent problem. The two points converge in the further assignment of an essential pedagogical role to this constitution.

64. Plato, *Theaetetus*, 161e, 166d–167a.

in a better condition morally, not only better prepared for future inquiry because of the "present review" (that is, purged of his errors), but more "moderate" and agreeable toward his fellows.[65] Thus, Kant's own turn (as we will see), to the Socratic method as central for human moral cultivation, is in accord with the methodology of these early pedagogical efforts.

Perhaps more importantly for our immediate purposes, not only do Kant's statements (as quoted previously) once again implicitly affirm Basedow's efforts, as well as agree with his repeated call elsewhere for the cultivation of all capacities for carrying out purposes set by reason, but they give a clear indication of his very approach to the subject of education. It is one consistent with his ideal and transcendental approach: to begin with a concept of perfection and to ask about the conditions of its possibility and realizability. The idea is treated not theoretically, but practically; it defines a task, work we are to perform to bring about a concrete manifestation of reason's idea in the world. As such it is consistent with Kant's affirmation that experiments in education are necessary; the experiment lies in finding ways of putting the idea effectively into practice. Thus too, a failed experiment (such as the Dessau Institute) is no grounds for abandoning the idea whose validity remains independent of any particular instantiation past, present, or future; the practical task of realizing our vocation proper to us as humanity remains and we are exhorted to try anew. In his interpretation of Kant's pedagogical theory, Erwin Hufnagel states the point very well. We must realize that "even in the case of discussions of the sphere of animality, for Kant it is a matter of a humanly determined animality, one [that is essentially] related to humanity. Kant does not have a so-called graduated anthropology in mind, but rather a transcendental doctrine of human [nature]; that is, a teaching [consisting in] a science of principles."[66] Or, as Gerhard Funke has also put it, where humanity's task is so defined, to elevate itself as animal species to the level of a moral species, the requisite cultivation entails that we "not simply live, but conduct our lives" (*nicht nur leben, sondern ein Leben führen*); thus to subjugate our conduct (*Verhalten*) to principles, requires knowledge of its presuppositions, the critical investigation of the conditions of the possibility of the human as moral species.[67]

In short, what first defines the structure of pedagogical theory and praxis is the idea that defines what work is to be performed. That work, as expressed by Kant to Wolke, or as stated in his *Anthropology*, is again

65. *Theaetetus*, 210c.
66. Hufnagel, "Kants pädagogische Theorie," 48.
67. Funke, "Pädagogik," 104.

reaffirmed in his 1803 essay: "The primary endeavor of a moral education is to establish a character" (*P* 481). Thus, Kant's critically formulated conception of moral character is *itself* the guiding principle for pedagogical theory. The notions of discipline, cultivation, formation are to be understood, then, in terms of what is required for effecting the relation of the idea of such perfected humanity to the natural conditions in which it is to be concretely realized. What will bring about the requisite shift in orientation from natural to moral necessity? The awareness that this is the question in terms of which Kant considers the various aspects of pedagogy and their relation is also the first step in resolving the apparent contradiction of the moral and pedagogical orders. As Kant puts it even in the *Critique of Practical Reason*, "preparatory training is needed" (*KpV* 152), and discipline and some dimensions of cultivation are, in the empirical, historical course of life, propaedeutic stages to moral education properly speaking. However, the empirical pedagogical process itself is determined and directed in the first place by reason's idea. The role herein that Kant accords to nature must of course be considered, but first we turn to a more detailed examination of the meaning of the terms we have identified as constituting the main distinctions in Kant's conception of pedagogy.

Discipline, Cultivation, Formation

Although Kant gives his general definition for discipline (*Disziplin* or *Zucht, MST* 485, *P* 441) in the context of reason's requisite discipline (as quoted previously from the first *Critique*), it accords perfectly with what he elsewhere describes as necessary in regard to the inclinations and passions. As we have already explained in our third chapter, at issue is the state of barbaric or lawless freedom, a condition of wildness or unruliness (*Wildheit*) that, in degree and kind, is peculiar to just the animal capable of rationality and hence conscious of the concept of freedom, but whose aptitudes still lack the discipline and cultivation whereby it may realize the form of a rational and finally moral being. It is the propensity to deviate from law, specifically justice, or the rights of humanity, that must be eradicated and not, as Kant repeats more than once, the natural inclinations and drives themselves. These must be "tamed," not "uprooted" (*RV* 34–35, 58); the "natural drives are to be opposed only to the extent that one is able to master them when those cases arise in which morality is threatened" (*MST* 485). The ability to control self is to replace the urge to lord it over others, but those forms of asceticism that go to the extreme of leaving no room for the natural inclinations are explicitly rejected by Kant.

His object, rather, is to "make room for the development of humanity" (*KU* 433). It is an objective that is informed by the goal to be achieved, moral character. To view the natural inclinations and drives from that standpoint is to discern that the "condition" for their "fitness for purposes" determined by reason calls for "freeing" human volition from the "despotism of the inclinations" (as Kant spells it out in the *Critique of Judgment* and elsewhere, *KU* 431–33). This is the "negative" work of education as discipline; it "transforms animality into humanity" and, as such, is its indispensable first step whose "omission can never be replaced" (*P* 441, 444). As Kant had warned also in the *Critique of Pure Reason,* merely external forms of politeness, simply a "veneer of decency, integrity, and modesty," constitute a "duplicity" that threatens permanently to suppress the development of the morally good *Gesinnungen* (*KrV* A748/B776). Without the discipline that effects the internal change, one is left with Rousseau's polite society *sans vertu* at best, or a state of unceasing warfare at worst. Either way, the essential characteristic of the state of human nature is an independence from law, instead of the subjective realization of freedom that consists in an adherence to law and is the *conditio sine qua non* for humanity.[68] As Erwin Hufnagel has expressed the point: "Kant's pedagogy demands nothing less than the presence of the educational goal already in disciplinary procedures."[69] What must be realized is that Kant uses the term *animality* not so much in a "biological nor even descriptive-psychological" sense, but rather as a "normative counterconcept for lived morality."[70] The pedagogical means for bringing about this step toward the attainment of humanity (that is, for effecting the transformation from animality by discipline) must be "judged in the light of the highest telos of education (unconditional reasonableness)" and not in accordance with particular criteria of a given educator.[71] This interpretation is consistent with our own earlier conclusion that Kant's conception of pedagogy as such is determined by reason's idea. To restate the point in terms of our discussion of the inclinations in the third chapter: regarded from the standpoint of what it is to have moral character, the lawless exercise of human nature appears feverish and swollen and calls for discipline as the propaedeutic first step in bringing about a state of moral health by alleviat-

---

68. See also Funke's discussion of this point ("Pädagogik," 105).
69. Hufnagel, "Kants pädagogische Theorie," 51.
70. Hufnagel, "Kants pädagogische Theorie," 50.
71. Hufnagel, "Kants pädagogische Theorie," 49. Later he remarks that "moralization takes up its difficult and paradoxical work [from the standpoint] of the idea of humanity as a norm transcending history" (55).

ing the symptoms. Only then are the human capacities fit for, able to undergo, their positive cultivation, which is the next step.[72]

The concept of *Cultur* is another instance of a term for which Kant himself played a contributing role in its adoption and meaning in modern language. Derived from the Latin term for cultivation or tilling of the soil,[73] the concept reportedly entered European usage only toward the end of the seventeenth century and did so initially as a Latin term in scholarly, scientific discourse.[74] Tracing Kant's usage of the term[75] is not only instructive for getting clear on what he intends to convey thereby, but for gaining insight both into specifics of his pedagogical concerns and their connection with his critical philosophy. In the works published in his lifetime, it is not until the *Metaphysical Principles of Virtue* that Kant explicitly notes the Latin form *cultura*, which he then renders as *Anbau*, literally meaning cultivation in its agricultural sense, but used in the passage in its expanded sense of the care of mind and body (a meaning that already adheres to its Latin form): the "cultivation of all its natural powers (of mind, soul and body) as means for all kinds of possible purposes is a duty

72. To the best of my knowledge, Kant never makes reference to Boethius's *The Consolation of Philosophy*. Yet it is precisely in terms of the imagery of medicinal cure beginning with the reduction of fever and swelling that Lady Philosophy restores Boethius to his own true nature: "In your present state of mind, while this great tumult of emotion has fallen upon you and you are torn this way and that by alternating fits of grief, wrath and anguish, it is hardly time for the more powerful remedies. I will use gentler medicines. It is as if you had become swollen and calloused under the influence of these disturbing passions, and by their more gentle action they will temper you ready to receive the strength of a sharper medicament" (trans. V. E. Watts [New York: Penguin Books, 1984], 49).

73. *Cultura* from *cultus*, past participle of *colere*, to till. *Cultura* came to mean care provided for body and mind. Eventually culture came to be paired with nature as its opposite term, i.e. all that humans achieved (acquired habits, skills, art, instruments, sciences, and institutions) as contrasted with what is given by nature.

74. *Brockhaus Enzyklopädie*, 24 vols. (Mannheim: F. A. Brockhaus, 1990), vol. 12. Surprisingly, Grimm gives no discussion of this term. The *Brockhaus* article names Pufendorf, Vico, Voltaire, Rousseau, Kant, Herder, Schiller, and Hegel as key figures in defining the usage of the term up to the nineteenth century. Kant is credited with giving "prominence to the educational function of *Kultur*: the intended function of cultivation is to produce the moral fitness of a rational being for society."

For an analysis of the distinction between culture and civilization in modern thought, see Richard Velkley, "The Tension in the Beautiful: On Culture and Civilization in Rousseau and German Philosophy," in *The Legacy of Rousseau*, ed. Clifford Orwin and Nathan Tarcov (Chicago: University of Chicago Press, 1997), 65–86. Velkley writes: "Civilization . . . conveys the idea of the entire progress of humanity as culminating in the modern liberal state and its way of life, seen as inherently civil, polite, and pleasant. . . . Two primary meanings of culture emerge from this period: culture as the folk spirit having a unique identity, and culture as cultivation of inwardness or free individuality" (67).

75. The data presented here has been verified with a computer search of the CD-ROM version of the first nine volumes of the corpus.

humanity [owes] to itself" *MST* 444). A similar statement, but using *Cultur*, appears in the second half of the *Critique of Judgment:* "Producing the fitness of a rational being for any purposes whatever of its choosing (thus [producing its fitness for] freedom) is culture" (or "cultivation," as it is perhaps better rendered, *KU* 431). Even just these two passages indicate a number of things that a review of Kant's other usages of the term corroborates. His fundamental sense of the notion is the active sense of cultivation (as opposed to culture as referring to the totality of human achievements in language, art, institutions, and so forth in a given time and place). The cultivation at issue in its widest sense refers to all three levels of the human aptitudes and thus concerns developing skill, prudence, and ultimately moral character (with the question of how the first two relate to the final stage still with us). While discipline brings unruliness under control, cultivation gives form to the crude (*rohen*), undeveloped natural aptitudes. The notion of cultivation thus inherently implies the pedagogical question; to recognize this is also to realize the pervasiveness of the latter question in Kant's corpus.

The term first appears in his 1765–66 "Announcement" of his lectures in the context of Kant's claim there that the chosen logic text lends itself to the study of both "the formation (*Bildung*) of the active and sound, albeit common understanding" and "the cultivation (*Cultur*) of the more refined and learned reason" (*N* 311). This use of *Cultur* in regard to the cultivation of reason continues to characterize Kant's next employment of it, which does not come until the *Critique of Pure Reason*.[76] From its passages (which include the definition of culture/cultivation already cited), we begin to get an indication of the further intrinsic connection of the critical philosophy itself to the pedagogical question, the latter being cast by Kant initially in terms of the issue of the cultivation of reason. It is worth quoting some of what, for many, are familiar lines (from A849–51/B877–79), for in the present context their pedagogical import is more readily manifest. "From the entire course" of its discussion, writes Kant, a reader of the "critique will have been sufficiently persuaded" of a number of conclusions. These include the fact that "human reason, which is already dialectical by the direction [or orientation, *Richtung*] of its nature, can never dispense with such a science as one that restrains it [literally, reins it in] and one that prevents, through a scientific and completely evident self-knowledge, the havoc that a lawless, speculative reason

---

76. As a computerized search verifies, not even the verb form of the term is used by Kant until the first *Critique*.

would otherwise unfailingly wreck in morality as well as religion. . . . Thus, what may be called philosophy in the genuine sense is made up of metaphysics, both of nature and of morals, but above all, of the critique of that reason which ventures forth on its own wings, [the critique] that precedes [metaphysics] as a preparatory exercise (propaedeutic). Philosophy relates everything to wisdom, but through the path of science that, when it has once been paved, is never overgrown and permits no straying. . . . Metaphysics [constitutes] also the completion of all cultivation of human reason, which is indispensable. . . . For [metaphysics] examines reason in regard to its elements and highest maxims, which must underlie the very possibility of some sciences and the use of them all."

The conclusion of the *Critique of Practical Reason* (162–63) echoes and expands on points Kant has laid down here in the first *Critique*. Noting the errant ways that have been pursued both in contemplation of the universe and morality, Kant observes that "so it goes with all the still crude attempts in which the main part of the business depends on the use of reason" (*KpV* 162). For the use of reason "does not come of itself like that of the feet, from frequent exercise, especially when it concerns attributes that cannot be so directly exhibited in common experience" (*KpV* 162–63). The remedy for the "error of still crude, unpracticed judgment" is the critical philosophy as the science required for the cultivation of reason, a science to be mastered by those who would take upon themselves a pedagogical role in relation to others: "Science (critically sought and methodically instituted) is the narrow gate leading to the doctrine of wisdom, when by this is understood not merely what one ought to do, but what ought to serve teachers as a guideline in order [that they] may clearly and capably pave the path to wisdom that everyone should follow and keep others from going astray. Philosophy must at all times preserve this science" (*KpV* 163). In short, the critical philosopher has here explicitly cast himself as ipso facto the educator of the teachers who, in turn, are directly responsible for the cultivation of young minds, to direct them rightly onto the path of wisdom. From rendering reason's ideas as practical tasks, in particular the idea of the highest good, to the maxim of thinking for oneself (which, as we saw in the fourth chapter, includes the freedom from prejudice entailed in thinking of nature as subject to the rules of the understanding), to the moral proof for the existence of God: for all the ideas and principles that ultimately bear on moral judgment, the critical philosophy explores their legitimate employment within the bounds of human reason. And this, for Kant, is the guideline needed for pedagogical instruction.[77] Moreover, as Stark has documented, there "was no difference in content between the teachings of the lecturing professor and the views formulated in his writings for a wider audience."[78]

Further references to the cultivation of reason in the first *Critique*[79] are expanded in subsequent writings to explicit allusions to the cultivation of practical reason (in the second *Critique*)[80] and eventually to the use of the term in relation to the human aptitudes generally. In the *Critique of Judgment*, Kant continues to use *Cultur* in relation to the need for the cultivation of the powers of the mind, specifically now as the power of aesthetic

77. To have said this is, of course, by no means to have exhausted the consideration of the critical philosophy as itself a pedagogical enterprise. Further development of this interpretation lies beyond the scope of the present project and will be the focus of my next one.

78. Stark, "Kant's *Lectures on Anthropology*," 3.

79. The other instances not yet discussed of Kant's use of the notion of cultivation in the *Critique of Pure Reason* are as follows. In the preface to the B edition, Kant speaks of the contrast between the "cultivation of reason generally" as effected by pursuing the "secure course of a science," and the "baseless groping and careless roaming-about when there is no critique" (Bxxx-xxxi). This observation ties directly, of course, to the passages just cited from the "Architectonic of Pure Reason." Also in the B preface, in his advice to scholars to limit themselves to what is attainable through the sound, common understanding, Kant exhorts them to "confine themselves solely to the cultivation of these universally comprehensible and for moral aims sufficient proofs" (Bxxxiii). In the "Natural Dialectic of Human Reason," in the course of his discussion of ideas having a "good and purposive vocation in the natural aptitude of our reason," Kant charges their detractors with being in fact "indebted" to the "cultivation" they have enjoyed as a result of "reason's government," a cultivation that in the first place "enables them to rebuke and condemn that government" (A669/B697). In the section on the "Ideal of the Highest Good," Kant observes that without the "purposive unity" laid down by nature itself, we "would not have any reason, since we would have no school for it and no cultivation [of reason] through objects that would offer to it the material for such concepts of purposes" (A817/B845). A few lines later, Kant notes that "in the history of human reason, before moral concepts were sufficiently purified and determined, . . . even a considerable degree of the cultivation of reason in various other sciences could produce in part only crude and erratic concepts of the deity, and in part they left people with an amazing general indifference regarding this question" (A817/B845). In his discussion of the moral proof for the existence of God in his *Critique of Judgment*, Kant again connects the cultivation of reason with a correspondingly better conception of God: the moral proof as he has articulated it is "by no means a newly discovered basis for proving [the existence of God], but at most a new elucidation" of that basis as it has "resided in the human power of reason even before it began to germinate." "As the cultivation of reason progresses," so too the basis of proof is "developed more and more" (*KU* 458).

80. In the *Critique of Practical Reason* Kant speaks of the "cultivation of the intellectual talents (*Geistestalente*)" as something from which we derive satisfaction (24), of the distinction between "innate talent" and the "fruits of cultivation," of personal "diligence" (78), of the "establishment and cultivation of genuine moral *Gesinnungen*" (153), of "exercises" in assessing actions for their objective and subjective moral status and of the "cultivation of our practically judging reason, to which [these exercises] give rise, necessarily gradually producing a certain interest in [reason's] law and thus in morally good actions" (159–60), and of the "development and cultivation" of the "most noble attribute of human nature" (162).

judgment, especially the judgment of the sublime in nature.[81] The aim of the work, as Kant states it in the preface, is transcendental, and not the "formation and cultivation of taste" itself (*KU* 170), but what the text does do is raise the issue of the pedagogical role of the aesthetic, namely, its role in the "cultivation of the powers of mind" (*KU* 306), a role in regard to which Kant goes so far as to deem it a "standard" whereby to "assess the value of the fine arts" (*KU* 329). The connection of this role of the aesthetic and conduct of thought deserves a closer examination, and we will return to it shortly.

In Kant's shorter essays, in particular "Idea for a Universal History," "Conjectural Beginning of Human History," "End of All Things," and *Perpetual Peace,* the chief reference of cultivation is to that of the human aptitudes generally, from an initial state of crudeness to one of adequacy for carrying out reason's purposes. This broader usage of the term corresponds with the one found in both the *Metaphysical Principles of Virtue* and the *Anthropology.* Again, nature's role and, more precisely, the pedagogical function of the republican constitution require a separate discussion (given in the conclusion of this chapter). The 1803 essay on pedagogy both continues the wider sense of cultivation and underscores the fundamental distinction from discipline that Kant spells out in the first *Critique.* Unruliness must be eradicated and hence calls for the negative task of discipline, while the unformed (and thus crude, *roh*) capacities must receive the "instruction" (*Unterweisung*) that may be called "cultivation" (*P* 444). Here, as in other texts, Kant speaks explicitly of "moral cultivation" (*P* 480) and uses the notion of *Bildung* synonymously at times not only with education, but also with cultivation. Nonetheless, since the formation of character strictly speaking is still something more than the cultivation of the human aptitudes (including reason), we now turn to Kant's employment of the notion of *Bildung* to see what additional pedagogical dimension it conveys.

81. In particular, see sec. 29, 264ff. This passage is a good example of where the English cognate "culture" might tempt one to place the primary meaning of the term on the skills and artifacts of human achievements, instead of on the active sense of cultivation that first gives rise to the latter. The explicit inclusion in Kant's discussion of the elements of what *Cultur* means as we saw it defined and used in the previous *Critiques* makes it clear that the same sense of the term continues to be used. Moreover, Kant specifically points out that cultivation is not itself the origin of the power of judgment of the sublime, that we are still concerned with the development of the aptitudes inherent to human nature. In the case of the judgment of the sublime, its "foundation in human nature" is nothing else but the "aptitude for the feeling for (practical) ideas, i.e. for moral [feeling]" (*KU* 265). This reminder that cultivation is a means for developing a given capacity and not the author thereof agrees with its definition given in the first *Critique,* i.e. that it provides a proficiency.

In the first place, even in its ordinary sense, the term as based on the verb *bilden* points to just the function explicitly denied to "cultivation," namely, to generate, produce, bring about, found, establish—concepts all used by Kant when he speaks of moral character in its absolute sense. Cultivation involves developing what is already present in a nascent form; formation introduces something new. *Bildung*'s most enduring, general signification, as reported by Grimm, is that of form, species, or shape, not only in reference to humanity, but also to animals and all natural bodies.[82] This is indeed the initial sense in which Kant employs the notion in his earlier writings (and again in later ones, including the third *Critique*), that is, in regard to the formation, creation, and development of natural bodies and organisms.[83] In the *Critique of Pure Reason* we saw the term used in Kant's distinction of discipline and cultivation (and this is in fact his only employment of the term in that text).[84] It is in "Idea for a Universal History" (1784) that Kant first explicitly relates *Bildung* to conduct of thought, in the context of the state's proper role in the "formation of its citizens": extant nation-states are charged with "unceasingly impeding the inner *Bildung* of the *Denkungsart* of their citizens" (*IG* 26). The role of a good state constitution in the "moral formation of a people" receives a fuller discussion in *Perpetual Peace* (1795) (*F* 366). The first instance of the phrase "moral formation" occurs in the *Critique of Practical*

82. Jacob and Wilhelm Grimm, *Deutsches Wörterbuch*, 33 vols. (Munich: Deutscher Taschenbuch Verlag, 1991), 2:22–23. The original sense of the term, *imago*, was conveyed as well by *Bild* or *Bildnis*. Its use in regard to the specific cultivation of human nature (*cultus animi, humanitas*) appears, for example in Goethe's writings, as well as its reference to education (*formatio, institutio*). What Grimm does not report on is the use of the term in the burgeoning scientific biological discourse, for example by Johann Friedrich Blumenbach, who communicated his work on *Bildungstrieb* (involving the reconcilability of physicomechanical and teleological principles in explanations of nature) to Kant (see Kant's letter to Blumenbach in August 1790, *Ak* 11, no. 411, 176). As Kant testifies in this letter and as is evident not only from his use of the notion in the *Critique of Judgment*, but also in earlier occurrences such as in *The Only Possible Argument in Support of a Demonstration of the Existence of God* (1763), just this issue in connection with *Bildungstrieb* had received his attention for some time. In short, just as with the terms *Anlagen* and *Keime*, Kant is beginning with a term in a biological context and then transferring it to his moral discourse. In the examination here we are searching out the meaning that it retains and/ or receives in the latter.

83. Occurrences of the term appear as early as Kant's essays in 1754 on the earth's rotation on its axis and its aging (*Ak* 1), with numerous instances found in the *Universal Natural History* of the following year. *The Only Possible Argument in Support of a Demonstration of the Existence of God* (1763) and "On the Different Human Races" (1775) also contain a number of references that involve issues reconsidered again by Kant in the third *Critique*.

84. Pluhar translates *Bildung eines Talents* as "molding a talent," which is perhaps more appropriate than "formation," as we rendered it in our earlier citation, since Kant's use of it here is closer to its wide sense, synonymous with "education" (found also in *On Pedagogy*).

Reason (1788), in the identification of acting out of respect for the moral law as being the "true purpose of all moral formation" (*KpV* 117).

It is, however, Kant's discussion of "free formation" in nature in the *Critique of Judgment* that explicitly identifies the crucial mark of differentiation between this notion and cultivation. The "formation" in question "occurs by a sudden solidification, not by a gradual transition from the fluid to the solid state, but as it were by a leap; this transition is also called crystallization" (*KU* 348). Character as conduct of thought, we recall, is held by Kant to be that which defines or sets (*fixirt*) freedom. This act is a matter of a sudden change, a revolution, and it is precisely in this sense that Kant uses *Bildung* in relation to morality in *Religion within the Limits of Reason Alone.*[85] "Thus it follows that human moral formation must begin, not from an improvement in morals, but from the transformation of *Denkungsart* and the establishment of a character" (*RV* 48).[86] This distinction between a gradual change (which human sensible nature undergoes) and an act of crystallization (as it were), of setting or defining a permanent form, also corresponds to the distinction between the propaedeutic functions (of discipline and cultivation) and the formation proper of moral character. The human aptitudes are gradually developed so as to be fit for executing reason's ultimate moral purpose, but the act without which human nature (morally speaking) remains fluid and subject to change is that revolution in conduct of thought which ends the oscillation between moral command on the one side and self-interest and skeptical doubts on the other and secures the human being against such wavering in the future.

As we have already seen in our discussion of character as the guiding principle for pedagogical theory, ultimate human "moral formation" must be kept in view on the part of the teacher in every phase of education; "otherwise errors easily take root," and if these are once present, "thereafter the entire art of education is but a labor in vain" (*P* 455). One way of understanding what this general basic pedagogical principle means in pedagogical praxis might be Kant's discussion in *Metaphysical Principles of Virtue* of our duties to others, specifically the duty of the "love of humankind (philanthropy)" that mandates the exercise of an "active, practical benevolence that makes the prospering and well-being (*Wohl und Heil*)

---

85. This is the primary text too in which Kant relates the critical, causal account of character to his conception of the human aptitudes and the rudiment for good inherent to human nature.

86. In *Reflections on Anthropology*, Kant also reserves *Bildung* for "character," as contrasted with the functions of discipline and positive instruction; see, for example, *RA* no. 1210, 531; no. 1501, 791.

of others one's own purpose" (*MST* 452). Kant's reflections here are prefaced with his observation that the duties of love and respect are, "according to the law, basically at all times joined together in one duty" (*MST* 448). Thus the duty of love can be executed only within the parameters of respect for others, indeed in a way that promotes others' respect for themselves and paves the way for what must ultimately be their own act, the revolution in conduct of thought. As cultivation of human talents, education most directly promotes the prospering and well-being of others. As an example, what it would mean to do so under the call to keep ultimate moral formation in view, clearly and capably to pave the path to wisdom that everyone should follow, can be illustrated by one of Kant's remarks in the course of his discussion of duties to others—remarks that fairly resonate with the autobiographical voice of the professor of logic and metaphysics whose overriding concern is moral: "Upon this is based a duty of respect for human beings even in the logical use of their reason: not to censure their errors under the name of absurdity, inept judgment, and the like, but rather to presume that in such inept judgment, there must yet be something true and to seek it out. In doing so, one should at the same time expose the deceptive semblance (the subjectivity of the grounds determining the judgment, which were held by mistake to be objective) and, thus, by virtue of explaining the possibility of erring, still preserve the others' respect for their own understanding. If in regard to a given judgment, one uses such expressions as to deny one's opponent all understanding, how can one [expect] to instruct him that he has erred? It is just the same in the case of the reproach of vice, which must never lash out in complete contempt and denial of all moral worth of the wrongdoer, because on that hypothesis he could also never be improved. [Such a hypothesis] is incompatible with the idea of human beings, who as such (as moral beings) can never entirely lose their aptitude for good" (*MST* 463–64). As Kant also puts it, the wise one, who by the ancient definition effects the change to a better state, does so both by instruction and the example of his own person (*LJ* 24, *MST* 479). In general, the example plays an important role in moral cultivation, and we now turn our attention to it.

Example, Religion, and Internal Discipline

A brief passage in Kant's *Groundwork* proves to be a good summary of the role of the example and of the main issues in regard to it: "Imitation has no place in moral matters, and examples serve only for encouragement;

that is, they put the feasibility of what the law commands beyond doubt and they present graphically what is more generally expressed by the practical rule. But they can never justify our setting aside their true original inherent to reason and our guiding [or orienting] ourselves by examples" (*G* 409). The full significance of what is said here may be best understood by following out points made in other texts. Thereby, we can understand an assertion about the role of the example made in *On Pedagogy* that stands prima facie in contradiction to what Kant has otherwise claimed in regard to the formation of character: "In order to establish moral character in children, . . . we must teach them the duties they are to fulfill, as far as possible through examples and the arrangement of the instruction whereby they learn" (*P* 488).[87]

That the example as such is indispensable we have already seen Kant affirm in another context in the *Critique of Practical Reason*. There he notes that "without something it can use in actual experience as an example," common sense (*gemeinste Verstand*) "could not make use of the law of pure practical reason in applying it" in the world (*KpV* 70). More, however, than the schema of a law (the issue in this passage) is needed. Nor, as Kant elaborates in his *Metaphysical Principles of Virtue*, is it enough to have an example simply in the sense of an illustration, such as might serve to explicate the meaning of a term (*MST* 479n). What is needed above all is an "exemplary instance" (*Exempel* as distinguished from *Beispiel*), a "particular case of a practical rule," to serve, however, "not as a model, but only as proof of the feasibility of dutiful" conduct (*MST* 480). The provision of such constitutes "the experimental (technical) means for the formation of virtue," namely, "the good example of the teachers themselves (their own conduct and leadership[88] being exemplary) and the admonitory [example] of other people" (*MST* 479). The agreement here

87. The German phrase used by Kant is "Beispiele und Anordnungen." The latter term has dual meanings; it can simply mean "orders, directives, rulings," but it can also mean "making arrangements." Given the background on pedagogical theory and praxis as conceived by Basedow and the other teachers in the Philanthropin, we know that the arrangement of the setting was of central importance in their reforms in instruction. The role of the educator, of play, of learning even classical languages by praxis, not memorized declensions and grammar, and above all, the learning of virtue by praxis and not theory, by the supervised communal life of the students, were all paramount. Thus the translation here seeks to convey this sense.

88. Kant here uses the term *Führung*, which entails a number of applicable connotations. As "leadership" it covers the range from straightforward direction or guidance (as a teacher would, for example, provide in regard to theoretical learning), to management (giving direction in the classroom), to political leadership, to moral leadership (which Kant is likely to have in mind). *Führung* can be used in reference to one's conduct of life, or behavior in particular contexts. Hence the translation is "conduct and leadership."

with Basedow's educator is evident, but what exactly is meant by an example that does not serve as a model? How does the appeal to an example relate to, even fit with, the establishment of character as a revolution in conduct of thought?

The appeal is repeated a number of times in Kant's writings. In the *Groundwork* we find the claim that "no one, . . . when confronted with an example of probity of intentions, of steadfastness in the observance of good maxims, and of sympathy and general benevolence" toward others, "would fail to wish to be likewise *gesinnt*" (*G* 454). Even those unable to follow suit would nonetheless wish "to be free" of the obstructive "inclinations that are burdensome even to themselves" and, hence, "transpose themselves in thought into a completely different order of things" (*G* 454). In the *Critique of Practical Reason,* Kant goes to some length to discuss examples of morally good actions specifically in the pedagogical process. "In this way my youthful listener can be led step by step from mere approval, to admiration, from there to marveling, and finally to the greatest veneration and a lively wish that he himself could be such an individual" (*KpV* 156). Again in *Religion within the Limits of Reason Alone,* we read that "by giving an example of good human beings (of what deals with their lawfulness) and by letting one's moral apprentices judge the purity of various maxims based on the actual motivations of their actions," the "aptitude for good" is "cultivated" in a way that bears "no comparison" with any other (*RV* 48).

The type of example employed and how one makes use of it in moral instruction are essential. As Kant spells it out in the *Critique of Practical Reason,* the young moral apprentices are "to be spared" exposure to "examples of the so-called noble (supermeritorious) actions that fill our sentimental writings" (*KpV* 155). The thrust of Kant's objection here is instructive; it is not simply a matter of his having reservations about such literature as *The Sorrows of Young Werther* (which had appeared in 1774). His problem with "romantic heroes" is that, in their "feeling for exaggerated greatness," they give themselves too much credit, with the result that "common and everyday responsibility seems to them to be but a paltry matter" and thus "they absolve themselves from observing it" (*KpV* 155). "It is entirely advisable," Kant goes on to note, "to extol actions displaying a great, unselfish, sympathetic *Gesinnung* and humanity," but what we must attend to therein is not the "fleeting" feeling "uplifting the soul," but the "subjection of the heart to duty" (*KpV* 155n). If, for instance, we were to cast the sacrifice of someone's life in the course of rescue efforts in a shipwreck as a meritorious and magnanimous action for the sake of one's country, the result of such an example intended for emulation would be to weaken the "force of the model and its inducement for imitation"; so presented, the case abounds with unanswered questions about conflicts with duty to self and other misgivings (*KpV* 158). What genuinely "strengthens and elevates the soul" is the example of "inexorable duty" that convincingly presents the capacity of human nature to rise above all inclinations contrary to the moral law, the example that first "reveals to us a hitherto hardly recognized capacity of inner freedom" *within ourselves,* an ability to "free ourselves from the impetuous importunity of the inclinations" (*KpV* 158, 161).[89] In other words, the morally instructive example makes us attentive to the fact itself that we are moral beings endowed with the essential capacity for freedom. Moreover, it conveys the dignity of the moral action as that which merits our highest estimation.

Underlying Kant's point here, of course, is the distinction between the proper moral, formal criterion of action and the estimation of its worth in terms of ends to be achieved. There is, however, a further dimension at stake, one that relates more directly to the exemplary individual previously alluded to: the distinction between imitation (or emulation, *Nachahmung*) and following after (*Nachfolgen,* following in the same steps, being a successor to). One of the best articulations of the distinction is found in the *Critique of Judgment:* "The proper expression for any influence that the products of an exemplary author (*Urheber*) may have on others is to follow (*Nachfolge*) by reference to a precedent, not imitation (*Nachahmung*); and this means no more than to draw upon the same sources from which one's predecessor himself drew and to learn from him only the way in which one goes about doing so" (*KU* 283). Herein lies the key to understanding how the example has an essential pedagogical function within the complete framework of Kant's morality and his account of character.

In his *Anthropology* he states even more strongly, in a way that incorporates the essence of the distinction given in the third *Critique,* the point we saw in the initial quote from the *Groundwork:* "The imitator (in moral

---

89. As Brandt and Stark have pointed out, Kant's criticism of sentimentality (*Empfindsamkeits-Kritik,* especially in reference to Christian Fürchtegott Gellert's writings) found in the transcriptions of Kant's lectures (e.g. Collins 24, Parow 249, Mrongovius 113), corresponds to the teaching of his pure moral philosophy that we are "not to direct ourselves in accordance with self-satisfied feelings, but rather in accordance with principles of reason that are qualified for public and worldly employment (*öffentlichkeits- und weltfähigen Grundsätzen der Vernunft*)" (Brandt and Stark, introduction, xxii).

affairs) is without character; for the latter consists precisely in the original-ity[90] of *Denkungsart*." Individuals of character "draw upon a source for their conduct (*Verhaltens*) that they have themselves opened up" (*ApH* 293; see also *MST* 479–80, *RA* no. 1111, 496). Neither an account found in literature (be it fictional or historically factual), nor the exemplary indi-vidual (who in the first instance is to be the teacher herself), is to be emulated in *what* in particular they do. They are to serve as a source of instruction for *how* one goes about drawing upon one's own inherent prin-ciple of guidance, one's own inherent practical law for directing those choices and actions that lie within one's own purview. Moreover, they serve as a source of encouragement that so to conduct one's life and to procure such character for oneself does indeed lie within the bounds of human possibility.

Recall that Kant referred to the exemplary instance as a "technical means for the formation of virtue." As such a pedagogical means it is not a mathematical or logical methodology that may be mechanically exer-cised; it is an exhortatory means of awakening the powers lying within its witnesses, of serving as an incitement to make their own attempts at putting these capacities into practice, of calling them likewise to follow the path of practical reason and thus orient or direct their conduct of thought by the supreme moral principle as inherent to their own faculties. Kant's distinction between imitation and following after may be explicated by drawing an analogy with an artistic performance. What is required is not a copying of the motions, a technically correct playing (for example) of a musical instrument, but a *rendering of one's own performance*—as mas-terfully as one can. The difference is qualitative; it is a question of bringing forth a live exhibition from the same sources in one's own being and nature that are also the wellspring in the nature of the master or exemplary in-stance. Every such performance is original, but not individualistic in the pejorative sense of that term. Each is an original work of art, a concrete particular manifestation of the universal expressed by the idea of reason.

In *Metaphysical Principles of Virtue*, Kant specifies how the instructor is to handle the presentation of the example. "The teacher will not say to her badly behaved pupil, 'Let that good (orderly, diligent) boy be an exam-ple for you!' For to do so will only cause the pupil to hate the boy through whom he has been put into an unfavorable light" (*MST* 480). Rather, "the good example," the "exemplary behavior," is to be appealed to as proof

90. Given the close connection in the eighteenth century between the notions of an original and authorship, Kant's point here may be rephrased as follows: character consists in being one's own author of one's *Denkungsart*.

of its feasibility. Properly used, the example focuses the pupils' attention, not on what lies beyond themselves, but inward, directing them to self-knowledge as moral beings. Kant concludes: "Thus, not the comparison with any other human being (how they are), but with the idea of humanity, how one ought to be, and so with the law, must provide the teacher with an infallible standard for education" (*MST* 480).

Kant's conception of the nature and role of the example connects with, on the one hand, his objections to familiar modes of religious instruction and, on the other, his own position on the role of religion in moral cultivation. His explication (in the *Critique of Judgment*) of the distinction between imitating and following makes explicit reference thereto: "Even in religion . . . one will never accomplish as much through general precepts, which one has either received from priests or philosophers, or even found within oneself, as through an example of virtue or holiness" (*KU* 283). And, the exemplary instance par excellence is just the archetype of humanity well pleasing to God, his Son (*RV* 60–78). To follow after (and not imitate)[91] the example here is to strive to actualize the "*Gesinnung* of the archetype" within oneself: "To raise ourselves up to this ideal of moral

91. What Kant means by imitation and what he objects to might be illustrated by some passages from Pascal. In the course of his discussion of the wager, Pascal advises the nonbeliever seeking faith to "learn from those who were once bound like you and who now wager all they have. . . . They behaved just as if they did believe, taking holy water, having masses said, and so on. That will make you believe quite naturally, and will make you more docile. . . . Custom is our nature." Anyone who grows accustomed to faith believes it and can no longer help fearing hell" (Pascal, *Pensées* no. 418, 152; no. 419, 153). Such imitation of the motions of rites, rituals, and devotional exercises is, for Kant (as is well known), the sure route to treating these as ends in themselves, as substitutes for what is needed, the inner change of heart (for example, see *RV* 199ff.). Thus, such external forms are effectively used only where the morally good comportment of mind is already in place, to enliven and support it. In a letter to Wolke in 1776, Kant discusses at some length the order in religious instruction that he explicitly advocates in *Religion within the Limits of Reason Alone* (1793), that is, introducing devotional exercises only when "an active fear of God and conscientiousness in the observance of one's duty" is in place (*Ak* 10, no. 98, 179). The letter refers to the agreement between how the Philanthropin handles religious instruction and the actual upbringing received by a young boy (Robert Motherby's son, George) on whose behalf Kant is writing to urge Wolke to welcome him to the institute. Kant is reported by Mongrovius to have made parallel observations in his lectures on moral philosophy: God's command "be holy" does not mean that "we are to imitate him; but that we should follow [or pursue, *Nachgehen*] the ideal of holiness that we cannot attain. It is impossible to imitate a being different in species, but we can comply and be obedient. We are not to imitate this archetype; rather we must try to be conformable to it" (*Ak* 27.2.2, 1465; Kant's use of the phrase here meaning "comply," i.e. "Folge leisten," also draws attention to this latent connotation in the notion of "following after"). Again in *On Pedagogy*, we read that "praise, prayer, and church attendance are only to give human beings renewed strength and spirit [or courage, *Mut*]" for the work required, their "improvement." These are but "preparations for good works, but not themselves already good works, for one can be pleasing to the Highest Being in no other way than by becoming a better human being" (*P* 494).

perfection, that is, to this archetype of the moral *Gesinnung* in its complete purity, is our universal duty as human beings; indeed for this end the idea itself, which reason puts before us so we may strive [to realize it], can give us strength" (*RV* 61). Five years later, Kant expresses the point thus: having defined grace as the "enlivened hope in the development" of the "original aptitude for good within us," a hope enlivened by belief in this aptitude and by the "example of humanity well-pleasing to God in his Son," he asserts that such grace "can and should become more powerful than sin in us (as free beings), if only we let it act in us, that is, if we let *Gesinnungen* of a conduct of life (*Lebenswandels*) as shown in that holy example become active [in us]" (*SF* 43).

Just as rituals and devotional exercises are thus to be seen not as works in themselves, but as a hortatory means to renew humanity's strength and spirit for the work proper to it, its moral cultivation, so too the "practical use" of Scripture, "especially its public use," affirmed by Kant as "undoubtedly conducive to the improvement of human beings and the quickening of their moral motivations (their edification)," should be a "hortatory" one (*SF* 68). The treatment of Scripture for this pedagogical end is best given in Kant's own words. An explication of the Bible given to the people "must be guided, not by what scholarship draws out of Scripture by philological studies, which are often no more than ill-conceived conjectures, but by what one brings to it through a moral *Denkungsart* (that is, according to the spirit of God) and by teachings that never deceive and also can never fail to have a salutary effect. . . . A sermon directed to edification (*Erbauung*) as its final end (as any sermon should be), if the *Gesinnung* effected thereby is to be pure, must develop its lesson from the hearts of the listeners, namely from the natural moral aptitude [present] even in the most unschooled individual. The testimony of Scripture connected with these teachings should also not be treated as historical arguments confirming their truth (for morally active reason requires none such, and besides, empirical knowledge cannot yield them); rather, [the testimony should be seen as] mere examples in which the truth of reason's practical principles is made more perceptible through their application to facts of sacred history" (*SF* 68–69).

Thus we see Kant consistently adhering to these characteristics and employment of the example, whether it is reported, or whether it is presented in the persona of the teacher (or preacher), or in the archetype of humanity: (1) it exhibits the morally good comportment of mind, good moral character and its corresponding conduct of life; (2) its appeal is directed to the learner's inherent moral aptitude and offers support and

encouragement for what is to be effected within by the learner's own capacities of practical reason and judgment. It can also (as we will see
shortly) therefore be the occasion for practice in exercising moral judgment and thereby play a role in moral education proper; its hortatory function, in awakening and quickening the inherent moral aptitude for good,
is propaedeutic or preparatory to this further role. Its supporting, preparatory function may be seen as belonging to the stage of education that
consists in cultivation. That it can have this role at all is based, of course,
on the underlying assumption of Kant's moral and anthropological account of human nature. The same holds true as it does for the "subjective
exhibition of pure virtue": if "human nature were not so constituted, no
way of presenting the law through recommendations and roundabout
means could ever bring forth morality of *Gesinnung*" (*KpV* 152).

In regard to religion's role in moral cultivation, the matter may also be
put thus. In its hortatory sense, the example provides the encouragement
of spirit that accompanies the work of rational faith as a subjective principle of reflective judgment, reinforcing the latter's conviction about the
reality of human final purpose and the wholehearted effort of the human
agent in its pursuit (as described in chapter 4). There is, however, also a
disciplinary side to religion's role (to religion in its inner, rational sense).
As Kant puts it in his *Anthropology:* it is intrinsic to "the character of our
species" that it "requires discipline through religion, so that whatever cannot be achieved through external constraint," such as provided by a civil
constitution, "may be effected through the inner [constraint] (of conscience)" (*ApH* 332–33n). The larger picture of what is at stake is alluded
to in Kant's plea voiced in 1793: "Oh, uprightness! You, Astraea, who
has fled earth for the heavens, how do we draw you (the foundation of
conscience and, with that, of all inner religion) from there back again
down to us?" (*RV* 190n).[92]

As we saw in our fourth chapter and as Kant notes in *On Pedagogy* and
elsewhere, the voice of conscience is (as it were) the divine voice within
(*P* 495); hence, "conscience" itself is "thought of as a subjective principle
of being rendered accountable before God for one's deeds" (*MST* 439).
Through the act of self-examination on the part of practical reason that
consists in adherence to conscience, in conjunction with the other maxims
of a sound understanding, inner self-control is realized. Pedagogically

---

92. Astraea was the Roman goddess of justice and was identified with the constellation Virgo.
Held to have lived among humankind during the golden age, reportedly she retired to the moun-
tains in the silver age, until finally the wickedness and impiety of humanity during the bronze
and iron ages caused her to leave earth altogether for the heavens.

speaking, what is required is that we "cultivate our conscience," that we "sharpen our attentiveness to the voice of the inner judge and employ all means . . . to obtain it a hearing" (*MST* 401). Such cultivation has the effect of promoting the exercise of the disciplinary role of conscience. As an original aptitude within everyone as a moral being, conscience does have both a positive and negative role. It "serves as motivation" for "strengthening" those of good *Gesinnung* and for encouraging those, in whom the morally corrupt order of maxims still reigns, to "break with evil as far as possible" (*RV* 69). It is also identified by Kant as one of three moments in which the "mind is attuned to moral feeling" (*KU* 445). As the "power of moral judgment passing judgment on itself" (*RV* 186), it has the positive role of maintaining moral self-consciousness. Itself, then, both disciplinarian and instructor, one may see the cultivation of conscience (of attentiveness to it) as propaedeutic to moral formation proper, but its exercise as intrinsically bound up with that of moral judgment. Before turning to moral judgment, however, more needs to be said about the role of the aesthetic in relation to moral cultivation.

Moral Spiritedness and the Relation of Aesthetic and Moral Cultivation

Again there is a direct connection both with conscience and with the role of the example, whose influence is exercised in part through their aesthetic effect. As we have seen, humility as the strict judging of our defects . . . is a sublime attunement of mind (*KU* 264), and, when confronted with "the law given graphic form in the example" of an individual of "upright character," we are affected by a feeling of humility that in its double movement is analogous to the feeling of the sublime (*KpV* 77). Moreover, truly speaking, the "sublime must always have reference to our *Denkungsart*" (*KU* 274), while in the judgment of taste and the feeling of the beautiful, we enjoy the supportive attunement of mind, the consciousness of "a certain ennoblement" and freedom from the compulsion of the senses that characterizes moral action and choice-making as well (*KU* 268, 353).

An extended discussion of these and other aspects of the relation between character and the aesthetic capacities of feeling has already been given in the concluding section of our second chapter. We can now recognize dimensions of the role of aesthetic described earlier, as paralleling what we have just seen in the case of the example or exemplary instance: the role of the sublime in "awakening moral *Gesinnungen*" (*RV* 50) and the turn in aesthetic reflection upon ourselves, whereby we come to feel the dignity of our own essential nature. Given these supportive and hortatory roles of the aesthetic in relation to the moral comportment of mind and moral feeling, the pedagogical questions that naturally present themselves include the following: Does Kant in fact have a conception of aesthetic education? If so, does it agree with Schiller's account? What can the relation of aesthetic cultivation and moral education be for Kant?[93] Could one go so far as to say there is an implicit moral mandate for aesthetic education in his thought, and, if so, do beautiful forms in nature and art equally qualify as its objects?[94] Klaus Düsing answers the first question in the affirmative, concluding that given the formal nature of Kant's aesthetic, its cultivation can only consist in "practice in the contemplation of beautiful forms." Such "cultivation of a personality," however, "remains a stage prior to morality"; for one can "also achieve a moral comportment of mind without it."[95]

In our analysis of Kant's use of the notion of cultivation, we have already seen his references to the cultivation of taste, and it seems fair to say that he indeed has an operative notion of aesthetic education. We even have an indication of what constitutes part of such education, the study of the "humanities (*Humaniora*)"—"oratory, poetry, a wide reading of the classical authors, and so forth," all the things that "serve to cultivate taste in keeping with the model of the ancients" (*LJ* 46; see also *KU* 355). The issue is how we are to understand its connection with moral education, specifically the formation of moral character. A part of the answer lies in

93. Klaus Düsing considers these questions in his article "Der Übergang von der Natur zur Freiheit und die ästhetische Bildung bei Kant," in *Humanität und Bildung*, ed. Johannes Schurr, Karl Heinz Broecken, and Renate Broecken (Hildesheim: Georg Olms Verlag, 1988), 87–100.

94. Jane Kneller has broached this question. Arguing for a "third kind of love, neither practical nor pathological," a feeling of love for nature based on contemplation and, given the reciprocal connection that Kant draws between such an interest in nature and an attunement of mind advantageous for our moral feeling of respect, Kneller concludes that two things may follow from his claims: "that we have a moral obligation to develop a love for nature in ourselves" and "that, if love of nature furthers moral feeling, then we may have an obligation to bring about the conditions in which reflective judgment of beautiful nature is possible for others as well as for ourselves." By extension, she suggests a case can be made for an equal obligation in regard to art and to the ideal beauty of human beings, i.e., that here likewise we are obligated to provide aesthetic reflective conditions conducive for moral cultivation ("The Interests of Disinterest," in Robinson, *Proceedings of Eighth International Kant Congress*, vol. 1, pt. 2, 777–86). For a discussion of why nature (in the sense of our ordinary experience of the external world, of its beautiful particulars) remains ultimately privileged over products of our own agency when the question is that of interest in beautiful forms as an indicator of our moral comportment of mind see G. Felicitas Munzel, "The Privileged Status of Interest in Nature's Beautiful Forms: A Response to Jane Kneller," in Robinson, *Proceedings of Eighth International Kant Congress*, vol. 1, pt. 2, 787–92.

95. Düsing, "Übergang von der Natur," 96.

taste's essential characteristic of being eminently communicable; hence its development most immediately facilitates social communication, including communicating character itself to one another. As noted by most commentators, the cultivation of taste relates to the civilizing of human beings, and, so considered, it does constitute a phase prior to moral formation.[96] However, as such it cannot be the complete answer. In the *Anthropology*'s discussion of the civilizing function of taste, thus to civilize human beings is not yet to form them as moral beings; "ideal taste," Kant says there, "has a tendency to promote morality *externally*" and could even be called "morality in its *external* appearance" (*ApH* 244, emphasis added). Moreover, for all his acknowledgment of the judgment of taste as the vehicle for communicating our feelings to one another and of the traditional role of the symbol in communicating moral principles (*KU* 296, *ApH* 241, *RV* 111, 134–36, 145, 176, 193), Kant never treats the symbol (specifically beauty as the symbol of morality) as a source of moral motivation, nor does he develop a permanent, positive role for it in human moral cultivation.[97] There is the further question of how to understand the asserted reciprocity in moral and aesthetic cultivation: the "propaedeutic for establishing [good] taste consists in the development of moral ideas and the cultivation of moral feeling" (*KU* 356).[98]

96. Not only Düsing, but Hufnagel, "Kants pädagogische Theorie," and Funke, "Pädagogik," discuss this connection between the cultivation of taste and civilizing in their articles cited previously. Düsing, who acknowledges that the "formation of moral character" is "for Kant the premier goal of education," does note that "civilization" or civilizing of the human "through the aesthetic lived experience is preparatory to the formation of moral character" ("Übergang von der Natur," 94).

97. Munzel, " 'The Beautiful Is the Symbol of the Morally-Good,' " 329.

98. For Düsing, this order of cultivation, namely that good taste requires the prior development of moral feeling, is a "culturally moralistic" position that Kant had held early on, but which is "hardly reconcilable with the systematic conception of the transition [from nature to freedom] that is presented in the *Critique of Judgment*" ("Übergang von der Natur," 95). It may be a bit hasty to draw such a conclusion. As we see in the discussion of our main text, the allusion to such reciprocity is not a one-time statement. In the case of the "feeling of the sublime," Kant explicitly rejects that it is either a "product of culture, or a matter of convention"; rather, it "has its foundation in human nature . . . namely in the aptitude for a feeling for (practical ideas), that is, for moral [feeling]" (*KU* 265). What perhaps could be said, then, is this: cultivation is always of present human aptitudes and to this extent—in accordance with the very primacy of practical reason and the unity of all interests in reason's interest—the complete cultivation of all aptitudes is intrinsically connected with the full actualization of the aptitude for good. It is in connection with character effecting the unity of the inner principle of our conduct of life that the reciprocity obtains. While the cultivation of other aptitudes promotes their fitness for realizing reason's interests, their own operation in an "environment" (so to speak) of moral perfection is proportionally enhanced. As Kant puts it (in a passage quoted next in our main text), in its connection with

That Kant sees a connection not just with the level of civilizing, but between the aesthetic feeling of pleasure in beautiful forms and morality, specifically moral character, is clear. In the following passage, we also get an indication of the basis for his stance on a reciprocal relation between the two. In this connection we are now going beyond what pertains to taste purely speaking: "It is true that taste gains in this connection of being aesthetically pleased and being intellectually so, in that taste is thereby fixed [or defined, *fixirt*]"—a function that we have seen Kant attribute to character or conduct of thought in relation to freedom. He goes on here to note that, although taste thus fixed "is not universal, rules can be prescribed for it in regard to certain purposively determined objects. By the same token, however, these rules are not rules of taste, but merely of the agreement of taste with reason, that is, of the beautiful with the good, whereby the former may be used as an instrument [in the service of] our aims in regard to the good," that is, "in order for that attunement of mind which sustains itself and is subjectively universally valid to serve as a basis for the *Denkungsart* that can only be maintained through arduous resolve, but that is objectively valid." Kant immediately qualifies his point; the gain is properly speaking on the part of the whole and not on one side or the other. "Actually it is neither [the case that] perfection gains through beauty, nor beauty by perfection" (and especially given the context, it is implicit that the perfection in question is moral); "rather, because in using a concept in order to compare the presentation whereby an object is given to us with the object [itself] (with regard to what it is meant to be), we inevitably at the same time hold [the presentation] up to the sensation in the subject, the entire power of conception (*Vorstellungskraft*) gains when both states of mind are in agreement" (*KU* 230–31).

Minimally, what we have here is a statement about at least one way in which character effects the unity of the inner principle of our conduct of life. It stands to reason that when taste is so cultivated that it is not only in accord with, but amenable to prescription by, reason's practical rule, the possibility of conflict that might otherwise threaten such unity is eliminated. The further positive dimension of supporting the effort of resolve with a spontaneous feeling of pleasure, in this case in the good as inherent to the choice and action contemplated, is repeated by Kant particularly in reference to beautiful forms in nature. Here again we find an allusion

---

the intellectual, "taste becomes fixed"—*fixirt*, the term we have seen him use in regard to the relation of character and freedom: character as conduct of thought defines or sets (*fixirt*) freedom. The latter is the basis, too, for the exercise of the reflective judgment of taste.

to the reciprocal nature of the relation: "Immediate pleasure in the beauty of nature" both "presupposes and cultivates a certain liberality of [our] *Denkungsart,* that is, independence of being pleased from mere sensual enjoyments" (*KU* 268). The "harmony" in the play of the cognitive powers "contains the basis for the [feeling of] pleasure" and also "promotes the responsiveness of the mind for moral feeling" (*KU* 197), while direct interest in nature's beautiful forms really characterizes only those whose "*Denkungsart* is either already trained to the good, or is exceptionally responsive to this training" (*KU* 301). Then again, from the standpoint of teleological judgment we may go so far as to say that the "display of so many beautiful forms" is a "favor" on the part of "nature," which has thereby in effect taken it upon itself "to promote our cultivation" (*KU* 380n).

Thus, to cultivate our capacity in general for taking pleasure in a purposive form (which is the essence, too, of character), we need not wait for finding such form in moral life; the cultivation in general of this capacity may be seen as a particular aspect of developing the fitness of the human capacities for furthering reason's interest. In our earlier analysis, we said that the aesthetic capacities may be seen as a partner in reason's efforts to bring about the requisite enlargement of sensibility for the sake of producing the concrete counterimage of the moral law, of procuring character in relation to living nature. To repeat our previous conclusion: the feeling of pleasure plays the role of middle term between reason and desire in relation to what is just the fundamental interest of the inclinations, self-preservation and well-being. While reason determines volition through practical desire, the apparent rebuff to the inclinations' interests is translated into a newfound pleasure in serving a higher order of self-preservation. Hence, too, the inner unity for our conduct of life is achieved not in terms of a kind of defeat, or a passive subordination of human nature to reason's causal exercise, but by a genuine, cooperative responsiveness that allows for a single, united effort in realizing moral form in its subjective, concrete actualization.[99] Thus to make a case in these terms for *why* the cultivation of the aesthetic capacities belongs to the complete account of human moral development is not yet, however, to exhaust all that can be said for *how* it fulfills this role.

By its very connotation, to call the aesthetic reason's partner is implicitly to raise the question of Schiller's relation to Kant. It is beyond the scope of this project to give anything approaching a complete analysis thereof,

---

99. As Klaus Düsing has also expressed the point, the "realization" of the concrete moral purposes of freedom "in principle cannot be thwarted by opposition of particular circumstances of the world of sense" ("Übergang von der Natur," 88).

but we must at least clarify the sense of "partner" we are claiming in Kant's case. That we do not ultimately have the same account as Schiller's conception of the harmony of sensibility and reason may be indicated by even a few selected passages from the essay "On Grace and Dignity."[100] On Schiller's estimation, it makes a sad statement about someone if a person "can so little trust the voice of instinct (*Trieb*) that he must in every case bring it before the moral principle" for assessment and approval; "rather, one greatly respects the one who relies on instinct with a certain assurance, without danger of being thereby misled. For that proves that both principles are already present in him" in the state of "harmony that constitutes the seal of perfected humanity"; such a state too is "what one means by a beautiful soul."[101] In this soul it is no longer the case that the "moral spirit" is the authoritative voice exercising "power" over sensible nature; the "instincts" of the latter coexist in complete "harmony with the laws of rational nature," and "virtue is nothing but an inclination to one's duty."[102] Any other way of ordering the relation of sensible and rational nature is unthinkable for Schiller, for otherwise "sensible nature" could "not offer up" the full measure of the "enthusiasm" or "spiritedness" (*ganze Feuer*) "of its feelings" for the exercise of moral life.[103] Telling too, are the examples to which he appeals: Niobe and Apollo.[104] Kant's "upright man . . . preferred in the eyes of the divine judge" is Job (*VT* 267).

Schiller's partnership, then, is one of equals so "intimately connected" with one another that separation could not occur without "violence."[105] The hierarchical order of causality found in Kant is abandoned, and, not surprisingly given Schiller's explicit return to ancient mythology, no conception of moral corruption is taken into account in his essay *Anmut und Würde*.[106] Thus, "The fundamental significance of aesthetic education (*Bil-*

---

100. Friedrich Schiller, "Über Anmut und Würde," in *Schillers Sämtliche Werke*, 16 vols. (Stuttgart: J. G. Cotta'schen Buchhandlung, 1894), 14:1–65.

101. Schiller, "Über Anmut und Würde," 41–42. Calling the "ideology of moral beauty" "not just a central aspect of Enlightened moral philosophy," but a concept that "helped to produce a large part of the discourse that constituted that very tradition," Robert E. Norton interprets "both Schiller and Kant as responding to the same complex field of historical forces, albeit in their own necessarily idiosyncratic ways" ("Kant and Schiller: The Apotheosis of the Beautiful Soul," in *The Beautiful Soul: Aesthetic Morality in the Eighteenth Century* [Ithaca: Cornell University Press, 1995], 224, 225).

102. Schiller, "Über Anmut und Würde," 33–34, 37–38.

103. Schiller, "Über Anmut und Würde," 41.

104. Schiller, "Über Anmut und Würde," 57.

105. Schiller, "Über Anmut und Würde," 41.

106. My thanks are due to Mark Roche for clarification on Schiller's position on moral corruption. As he pointed out, especially Schiller's earlier plays do manifest an interest in evil and a recognition of many complex factors as generating evil. Already in Schiller's first play *Die Räuber*,

dung in its broad sense) for the development of human personality" is quite different for Schiller than it is for Kant.[107] In our next section we look at its role from the standpoint of the aesthetic as a power of reflective judgment, another dimension that does not enter into Schiller's discussion in *On Grace and Dignity*. Most immediately, we continue to regard it

---

one finds two different forms of evil. One brother is absolutely malicious and corrupt, while the other, who is inspired by ideals, turns tragic, using his ideals to commit substantial crimes. Other characters manifesting a variety of problems are Wurm (In *Kabale und Liebe*), Don Carlos, Posa, the Grand Inquisitor, and the king. Roche concludes that "the path back to the good is often motivated in Schiller's plays by some form of inspiration (love or another character who acts as a model or an inspiration)."

107. Düsing, "Übergang von der Natur," 99. The outright inversion of the order of the terms is also evident in Schiller's statement of his project in *On the Aesthetic Education of Man*. "I allow beauty to have precedence over freedom," he writes there, something "I believe I can not only excuse [on the grounds] of my inclination, but justify on principle"; a few lines later he asserts that "it is through beauty that one may arrive at freedom" (*Über die ästhetische Erziehung*, second letter, 7; see also *Aesthetic Education*, 27). Hans Saner gives a very good analysis of Schiller's rejection of "Kant's model of subordination." Retracing Schiller's position as he also stated it in his essay "On Grace and Dignity" (also translated as "Charm and Dignity"), Saner notes: "Two principles which conflict, but of which neither one can be eliminated, are unifiable either by coordination or by subordination. . . . Rather than subjugate either of the two principles, a beautiful soul reconciles them with each other; it does not put a stop to their conflict 'dictatorially' but overcomes it easily, cheerfully, and freely. In perfect harmony it blends the duality of the twofold being into one." Saner goes on: "And, after all, why not? Did Kant himself not give his consent to the draft?" Moreover, "Schiller's essay makes it perfectly clear that he knows how to draw the necessary lines. With Kant, he holds that, 'in the field of pure reason and moral legislation,' subjective principles are rightly 'spurned altogether'; it is only 'in the realm of appearance and in the real exercise of moral duties' that the objective moment must always be reached by way of the subjective one. . . . In other words, [Schiller] is not refuting Kantian principles [but] complementing Kant from a standpoint that opens a vista of the subjective conditions of morality in man. . . . At first glance, this reduction of duality to unity by demonstrating that the contradiction is only apparent reminds us of the formal resolution of the antinomies. One might think that formally Schiller's solution is more Kantian than Kant's. This would be a delusion, however. A closer look proves it to be un-Kantian on several grounds. . . . (*a*) . . . Schiller obviously failed to see something fundamental. The moral law is not an anthropological law; it is precisely not a law of the ever-fragile *ratio humana*, but an absolute law of the *ratio universalis*. Yet man, who ought to live up to it, is always seen anthropologically by Kant, as a creature that keeps foundering and is thus always in need of constraint. . . . The cost of Schiller's conception of unity is either an anthropological relativization of the law or an elevation of man from the anthropological realm into that of the absolute. (*b*) On the formal side of the unity, Schiller does something completely un-Kantian. He 'reduces' the objective duality (acting because one ought to, or because one likes to) to a subjective unity. . . . Kant always proceeds the other way: to him, the subjective contradiction proves to be objectively a mere apparent contradiction. From the subjective split he returns to an objective unity, cutting through the surface divisions in order to point to the unity in the depths. What Schiller does in vaulting the divisions in the depths, so as to have unity on the surface, is the opposite of what Kant wants; Schiller achieves an outward peace instead of the inner one between conflicting principles. Kant views this peace as delusive. . . . (*c*) Schiller's construction is a blow at the universality of the law. Kant would be the last to deny that a coincidence of inclination and duty may occur by chance in the individual human being; we can conceive

in terms of feeling, specifically with respect to the requisite courage or spiritedness for the exercise of the moral life. By exploring whence this "fire" (as Schiller calls it) arises for Kant, we will seek to define more closely what sort of partner the aesthetic is with reason and, on that basis, reevaluate the relation of aesthetic education and moral formation.

That both thought or intellect and spirit are needed for the moral life is, of course, a classical conception.[108] In his *Politics*, Aristotle credits its free life governed by the best constitutions for the fact that the Hellenic race is endowed with both spirit and intelligence; he goes on to claim that "clearly both are needed if men are to be easily guided by a lawgiver towards virtue."[109] In his *Nicomachean Ethics* he concludes that "the kind of courage that comes from a spirited temper seems to be the most natural and becomes true courage when choice and purpose are added to it."[110] Implicit in Schiller's critique of Kant in his essay is just this emphasis on the necessity of a positive role of spiritedness, which not only Schiller has taken to be missing from the critical moral philosophy.[111] It is true that the purely objective account of reason's determination of volition does not address this question, and it is also true that for the procurement of character the inclinations must be disciplined. The familiar conclusion drawn is that one is apparently left with no more than the rigorous, formal demand of duty. Notably, too, to the extent that Schiller understands the "concept of beauty" as "having none other than a sensible cause and being a completely free effect of nature," beauty so defined would thus also be excluded from a rigorously interpreted Kantian moral framework.[112]

---

of men inclining toward the law. But this unity would still be codetermined by something material, by an object of the inclinations. . . . The beautiful soul may be conceivable as a beautiful accident, but its principle of union does not suffice for a general principle of unity. . . . Kant takes the consequences. He rejects the coordination of the principles and achieves their possible unity by subordination. In doing so, he does not negate the contingent principles as such; their claims are legitimate as long as they do not try to qualify as an objective principle in the supreme determining ground of all maxims" (*Kant's Political Thought*, 265–68).

108. I am indebted to Ann Hartle, commentator for my paper delivered at the American Philosophical Association meeting in Atlanta, 1996, for asking for a greater treatment of this issue in light of Aristotle's point.

109. Aristotle, *The Politics*, trans. T. A. Sinclair (New York: Penguin Books, 1981), 1327b28–37.

110. Aristotle, *Nicomachean Ethics*, 1117a3–5.

111. Ajzenstat, for example, writes: "That emphasis on natural feeling which gives the *Emile* so much of its richness is in Kant to a large extent what education must teach us to be able to cut away in order that we may claim our full moral patrimony" ("Impotence of Reason," 27).

112. Schiller, "Über Anmut und Würde," 31. For a discussion of Schiller's conception of beauty and the differences to Kant, see Manfred Frank, *Einführung in die frühromantische Ästhetik* (Frankfurt am Main: Suhrkamp, 1989), 107ff.

Kant, however, in his criticism of ethical asceticism has the following to say about the "exercise of virtue": its "rules proceed from two attunements of mind, a hardy spirit and a cheerful one (*animus strenuus et hilaris*) in the observance of its duties. For virtue must do battle with hindrances whose overthrow require mustering all one's strength, and at the same time one has to forgo many joys of life whose loss can sometimes make the spirit (*Gemüt*) gloomy and sullen. What is not, however, done with pleasure, but only as a compulsory service, has no inner worth for the one who so complies with duty. Such action is not loved; on the contrary [one who is thus disposed] avoids, as much as possible, occasions for practicing virtue" (*MST* 484). The Stoical call for forbearance is deemed by Kant to be a "kind of dietetics" useful for maintaining one's "moral health"; but since health cannot be felt and is "only a negative" sense of "well-being," something "must be added that affords life agreeable enjoyment and is still simply moral. This something is the virtuous Epicurus's ideal of an ever cheerful heart." A "monkish ascetic," by contrast, with its "self-elected and self-inflicted punishment cannot engender the cheer that accompanies virtue and, even more, cannot take place without causing a secret hatred of virtue's commands. . . . The discipline practiced by individuals upon themselves can therefore become meritorious and exemplary only through the cheer accompanying it" (*MST* 485).

Nor is this simply a belated addendum to his thought on Kant's part. We have seen (in our discussion in chapter 3 of Kant's sense of virtue) that he explicitly understands the very notion of virtue to connote just the "courageous spirit (*Mut*) and fortitude (*Tapferkeit*)" designated by the classical sense of the term (*RV* 57) and, that the "deliberate resolve" that is the hallmark of character is none other than this "virtue" (*MST* 380, 384, 390). Orientation in thinking, we concluded, has to do with the issue of the spirit in which the moral life is pursued. In our foregoing discussion of the hortatory function of the example, we have identified another expression of the need for arousing the spirit. We have seen that Kant's *sapere aude* is a call to muster the "spirit" or "courage" (*Mut*) needed "to make use of one's own powers of comprehension." In his note (in *Religion within the Limits of Reason Alone*) responding to Schiller's essay, Kant repeats what he has said before; namely, when it is a matter of the results of the exercise of virtue in the world (virtue here understood in its formal sense as the "self-established *Gesinnung* to fulfill one's duty"), then morally oriented reason calls upon the capacities of sensibility. Without question, the "aesthetic quality" of virtue, or its temperament, is "spirited and cheerful," while a "slavish attunement of mind" is ipso facto one "harboring a hatred for the law"; again, "the cheerful heart in the observance of one's duty . . . is a sign of the genuineness of the virtuous *Gesinnung*" (*RV* 23–24n).

That Kant has a conception of spiritedness, that it constitutes an indispensable and notably *aesthetic quality* of the morally good comportment of mind, is thus evident. The source of this "fire" is for Kant neither an instinctual drive that harmonizes with reason, nor a morally well habituated inclination operative in a conjunction of right reason and right desire. Given both the formal parameters of Kant's morality and the assumption of the innate propensity for evil, his account cannot be anything but hierarchical, with practical reason occupying the position of authority. The subjective human aptitudes, as we have seen, when accordingly cultivated are capacities of responsiveness to moral direction, not simply passively subordinate. A spirited response (as is by now obvious) has to do with our taking pleasure in performing our moral task, and here we must also remember that the procurement of character is itself such a task. The aesthetic capacity of feeling, as the capacity for taking pleasure in purposive form, is reason's partner in this task precisely by being the condition for the possibility of feeling pleasure in the exercise of moral life, in the effort of realizing our proper vocation. Discipline as the negative condition of first making room for the latter (by taming the unruly inclinations) does come first, but as Kant also reminds Schiller, the virtuous *Gesinnung* is literally a benefactor, and, by implication, its works are a blessing and a delight; it *acts* for good (*wohltätig*) and is beneficent in its results "beyond all that nature and art might achieve in the world" (*RV* 23n).

In short, not drives, instincts, or inclinations, but *consciousness of our own inherent moral capacity*, as Kant already insisted in his formal moral account, is the ultimate source of spirited response to the moral life. How this is so may be developed here. First and foremost, in the moral effort of combating opposing natural impulses we become "conscious of our regained freedom," a result that leaves us heartened and cheerful (*MST* 485). The basis for the latter aesthetic possibility was spelled out in the third *Critique*. The moral result parallels the freedom from compulsion by the senses gained in the feeling of the beautiful, and thus the latter's attunement of mind can be called upon to support that conduct of thought otherwise maintained through arduous resolve. What Kant does grant in a discussion of "affects" (that is, "nature within us") in the *Critique of Judgment* is that "every affect of the valiant (*wackeren*) kind (namely, which makes us conscious of our powers to overcome any resistance, *animi strenui*) is aesthetically sublime" (*KU* 272). The first example he gives belonging to this kind of affect is anger, even desperation, provided it is "indignant rather than despondent" (*KU* 272). Further, we may readily love character or "*Denkungsart*" in accordance with moral laws," for the latter has a "form of beauty" (*KpV* 160), and through the aesthetic feeling of the beautiful we are prepared to love something. Again, in the double movement of the sublime, the second moment is a feeling of pleasure, and so we may enjoy the elevation, the ennoblement of soul, when we suffer humility immediately conjoined with reverence for the highest faculty within us—a faculty we may glimpse vicariously in the exemplary instance. Finally, there is an aspect of aesthetic judgment connected with teleological judgment on which we have not yet touched, but is relevant here. As Kant first alluded in 1771, it is an issue for us as practical, rational beings that we find the world so ordered that it is suited for the exercise and realization of our aims.[113] Any indication that it is so again serves to hearten our spirit: "Beautiful things indicate that human beings" find the world to be a place "suited to them (*daß der Mensch in die Welt passe*) and that even their intuition (*Anschauung*) of things agrees with the laws of their intuition" (*Ak* 16, no. 1820a, 127).[114]

---

113. As Reinhard Brandt has put the point: determination [or destination] for a purpose presupposes that the ascertainable determined particularities are adequate to this purpose ("Kants Anthropologie"). Rudolf Makkreel's discussion of the "link between reflective and determinant judgments" as suggested by the conception of the human being as the ultimate purpose of nature is also relevant here. The link "involves the intersection of a reflective teleological judgment about man as a natural purpose with a determinant judgment of practical reason about man as a final purpose" (*Imagination and Interpretation*, 137–38). For John Zammito, the "crucial relation between man's duty and his destiny in the world," the question of whether there is a "place" in the "world of things" for "moral choices," constitutes the "ethical turn" in the *Critique of Judgment*. His conclusion regarding the ultimate meaning of the third *Critique* is stated even more strongly: "The *Third Critique* finds its decisive concerns neither in questions of beauty nor in questions of empirical biology, but rather in the ultimate questions of the place of man in the order of the world—his freedom and his destiny" (*Genesis of Kant's Critique*, 267, 268, 342; see also 306).

114. Birgit Recki has done considerable work in exploring the relation of Kant's aesthetics and moral philosophy. One of the points on which she focuses is the "promise of happiness" that results from the agreement in teleological judgment between the beautiful forms of nature and human purposive action. See Birgit Recki, " 'Was darf ich hoffen?' Ästhetik und Ethik im anthropologischen Verständnis bei Immanuel Kant," *Allgemeine Zeitschrift für Philosophie* (1994): 1–18. Recki's other relevant writings include "Ganz im Glück. Die 'promesse de bonheur' in Kant's Kritik der Urteilskraft," in *Naturzweckmäβigkeit und ästhetische Kultur. Studien zu Kants Kritik der Urteilskraft*, ed. Karl-Heinz Schwabe und Martina Thom (Sankt Augustin: Academia, 1993), 95–115; "Das Gute am Schönen. Über einen Grundgedanken in Kants Ästhetik," *Zeitschrift für Ästhetik und Allgemeine Kunstwissenschaft* 37 (1994): 15–31; and "Ästhetische Einstellung und moralische Handlung: Die Perspektiven der Vernunft im Gefühl des Erhabenen," in *Perspektiven des Perspektivismus. Gedenkschrift für Friedrich Kaulbach*, ed. Volker Gerhardt and Norbert Herold (Würzburg: Königshausen & Neumann, 1992), 161–83.

Paul Guyer's collection of essays exploring the "connection between aesthetics and morality"

When one now reconsiders the relation of aesthetic education and moral formation, it becomes necessary at least to qualify such conclusions as reached, for example, by Klaus Düsing. Granted, the inclusion of the aesthetic quality of the moral comportment of mind in no way changes the moral order that calls upon us to exercise morally good choice without any sort of *dependent* recourse on the enjoyment of aesthetic pleasure therein. However, even an individual action, let alone character and our conduct of life, would be deficient without the accompaniment of a cheerful spirit. Even more, without such spirit (as we have seen Kant admitting), from a subjective point of view we would de facto simply be unlikely to pursue the moral life, however urgent the latter might be de jure. Hence the cultivation of our capacity to take pleasure in purposive form remains distinct from moral education strictly speaking, but ultimately is in fact required from a moral point of view for the complete realization and exercise of moral character in the world.[115] The case becomes even stronger when we consider the question further in terms of the *judgment* of taste,[116] rather than solely in regard to its consequent feeling of pleasure. The role played by an acquired proficiency in the capacity of judging beautiful forms will be explored as part of our next focus, moral judgment.

Moral Education Proper

Moral Discernment: Cultivating a Taste for the Law

Given Kant's strictest sense of character (as discussed in our second chapter)—the law of causality of an efficacious cause that, concretely speaking, we interpreted to mean that the formal moral law is actualized by moral character as its counterimage in the world—moral education in its strict

---

focuses on a "gulf that needs to be bridged" that he identifies as obtaining, not between "noumenal and phenomenal causality, but between feeling and freedom—that is, between the arbitrary realm of sensation and the law-governed autonomy of reason." On Guyer's interpretation, Kant "looked to aesthetics to solve what he had come to recognize as crucial problems *for* morality," namely the need for "sensible *representation*" of the "rational demands of morality" (Paul Guyer, *Kant and the Experience of Freedom: Essays on Aesthetics and Morality* [Cambridge: Cambridge University Press, 1993], 18, 19, 33, 42).

115. Thus we have in effect presented an argument from a different point of view (the requirement of spiritedness) that nonetheless corroborates the claim that Jane Kneller has proposed. John Zammito too addresses this point: "Kant's position is that aesthetics can only be placed properly within a scheme of philosophical anthropology which stresses the primacy of the practical and the groundedness of human meaning in a supersensible order of value. Art can serve, in that context, as a vehicle for moral education" (Zammito, *Genesis*, 292).

116. This is again another dimension absent in Schiller's discussion in *On Grace and Dignity*, that is, the primacy of judgment over feeling in the aesthetic (as Kant conceives of it).

sense must also refer to the relation to this law. The phrase (which has seemed so oxymoronic in a Kantian framework to many of his readers) the "*cultivation* of morality" (*MST* 392, emphasis added) means to "form *Denkungsart*" (*P* 480), a pedagogical process itself "based on maxims, not on discipline"; to "establish morality, one must not" resort to "punishment" (*P* 480–81).[117] Involved is thus the cultivation of the use of reason, which Kant has told us "requires attempts, exercise, and instruction" (*IG* 19). Even more precisely, in the case of character as conduct of thought "freedom in thinking" must be realized; that is to say, thinking, the use of reason, must be practiced in being "subject to" reason's own law (*DO* 145). For if "objectively practical reason is to become subjectively practical," then "entry into the human mind" must have been secured for "the laws of pure practical reason" (*KpV* 151). In his *Critique of Practical Reason*, it is at this point that Kant takes up moral education's role in forming character (under the rubric of "the doctrine of method of pure practical reason"). The "method" is a two-stage process in the cultivation of moral judgment, steps that he explicitly relates to the beautiful and the sublime respectively.

The operative assumption for Kant's account here is that "human nature is so constituted" that "even subjectively, the exhibition of pure virtue can have more power over the human mind (*Gemüt*) and can provide far greater motivation" not only to effectuate the "legality of actions," but "to produce firmer resolve to prefer the law to everything else purely out of respect for it," than could ever be generated by appeals to the "attractions . . . of all that may be counted as happiness or even by all threats of pain and harm" (*KpV* 151–52). In the case of a "still unschooled" or "unruly mind," some "preparatory training" may be needed, "to entice it" with appeals to its "own advantage, or to alarm it" with the threat of "injury," but having had even "some effect," such "mechanical means" (*Maschinenwerk*) must as soon as possible be replaced with "introducing the soul to the pure moral motive"; only thus "can character (practically resolute *Denkungsart* . . .) be established" and "individuals taught to feel their own worth" (*KpV* 152).[118] That the moral law is itself also subjectively speaking

---

117. The very notion of maxims entails the requirement for a process of moral judgment. As Otfried Höffe has put it, "Maxims only provide the general plan (*Grundriß*) of an action. The task of judgment is to undertake, in accordance with the terms of the maxims, the productive process of interpretation and assessment required for the concretization [of the action]" (*Ethik und Politik*, 95–96).

118. A few pages later Kant underscores that the process of moral education he is here outlining is especially needed in his day in which the current practice is to try to influence the mind (*Gemüt*)

the true source of moral motivation is, of course, a familiar Kantian dictum, but less attended to is the aesthetic dimension and its role therein.

Kant's relatively brief discussion (at the end of the *Critique of Practical Reason*) of the two-stage process in the cultivation of moral judgment thus merits being repeated with such commentary as will shed light on the import of the points he is making (*KpV* 159–61). The first step in cultivating moral judgment is to "occupy the power of judgment" with exercises that allow the moral apprentices (to borrow an earlier term) to "feel their own cognitive powers." These exercises entail reflecting on examples of moral actions and "sharpening" the ability to discern what pertains to the "needs of humanity" and what to "justice," or whether the action is objectively commensurate with, and subjectively based on, the moral law. The resulting felt "benefit," indeed the turnabout in one's stance toward what may initially be experienced as "offensive," is illustrated by Kant with an analogy to what occurs in the course of a naturalist's investigation. Where the latter proves to reveal "purposiveness," one "finally finds" one's object of inquiry "dear" (or lovable, *lieb*).[119] Just so, the students come to the point of "gladly entertaining themselves with such judgments"—a factor that reminds us of Basedow's basic pedagogical principle that learning is not to be arduous, but achieved as much as possible by praxis, preferably in play.

Here the students have been "allowed to feel [or be conscious of, *empfinden*, literally "have a sensation of"] the enlarged use of their cognitive powers," and, any "contemplation" that thus affects them, further causes them to find its object "worthy of being loved."[120] As we know from Kant's use elsewhere of the phrase "enlarged use of our cognitive powers," and given the details of his illustrative analogy, what the students have become aware of and have learned to *enjoy* is the expansion of their rational faculty beyond natural instincts; in short, they have begun to be cognizant of and to appreciate their own inherent ground of freedom, here realized in judgments that are themselves purposive. For these allow "reason" to be active in respect to just that sole "order of things" with which, "given its capacity for determining [matters] a priori on the basis

---

with yielding, soft-hearted feelings or high-flying puffed-up pretensions, a description that reminds one of his objections to the romantic hero model (which we described earlier in this chapter) (*KpV* 157).

119. And, yes, this is the case even if that object of inquiry is a roach!

120. *Lieb*, of course, has a relatively wide range of meaning, from dear, sweet, lovable, kind, good, nice, to pleasant, in addition to its use in idiomatic phrases. Given Kant's explicit references in these passages to purposiveness, beauty, etc., the translation "lovable" has been made, rather than "to one's liking" (as it is usually rendered).

of principles," it can come to terms. Kant's point here is reminiscent of the issue already alluded to; namely that we, as rationally thinking beings are concerned with finding the sphere (the world) in which we must exercise our powers as being in fact conducive to such successful exercise. The exercise of moral judgment, making moral discernments in respect to examples of actions in the world, in effect opens up a sphere of operation in relation to the world in which reason may find itself at home. Thus, too, in such an "occupation of our powers of judgment," we find "virtue or *Denkungsart* in accordance with moral laws" having a "form of beauty" that, at this initial stage is admired (for we can appreciate its purposiveness), although it has not yet therefore become something we seek for ourselves (become purposive with a purpose). "Subjectively," however, its "contemplation arouses a consciousness of the harmony of our powers of conception [or presentation, *Vorstellung*], whereby we feel fortified in our entire cognitive capacity"; thus too it "produces in us a sense of being pleased that, in turn, may be communicated to others." So elucidated, Kant's remarks here clearly show that, in his understanding of moral education proper as the cultivation of moral judgment, the development of the aesthetic quality of our comportment of mind (which, we have seen, is intrinsic to moral spiritedness) goes, indeed both must go and naturally goes, *hand in hand* with the cultivation of our cognitive powers of discernment.

The "second exercise" is designed to take the moral apprentices the additional step from disinterested reflection upon character or morally good *Denkungsart,* that is, from a reflection in which there is not yet an interest, a felt urgency, in the issue that such *Denkungsart* be extant in the world, to just such a state of interest, specifically in the realization of such character in themselves. The incomparable manner of cultivation of the "aptitude for good," which Kant again affirms in 1793 is effected by "giving an example of good human beings . . . and by letting one's moral apprentices judge the purity of various maxims based on the actual motivations of their actions," results in the aptitude for good itself "gradually making the transition to [or passing over into, *geht allmählig über*] *Denkungsart*" (*RV* 48). In the second *Critique,* Kant's description of this process of cultivation recalls much of what we saw previously in the hortatory function of the exemplary instance.

By using examples to "draw attention to the purity of practical desire in the spirited [or lively, *lebendigen*] exhibition of the moral *Gesinnung,*" the students' "consciousness of their freedom," now from the compulsion of the inclinations, is "keenly maintained"; indeed, such examples of "pure moral resolutions" reveal to their witnesses their own "previously hardly known capacity of inner freedom." Initially the denial of the "inclinations as grounds of determination" arouses "a sensation of pain," but at the same time the prospect presents itself of "being freed from the manifold discontent" associated with our needs; thus our mind (*Gemüt*) becomes "responsive to satisfaction [arising] from other sources." Here we have the double movement that parallels the feeling of the sublime (which, as we know from the third *Critique,* is held by Kant to pertain primarily to conduct of thought). The "consciousness of independence from inclinations" and the contingencies of our "circumstances and of the possibility of being sufficient to oneself" is "salutary too in all other respects," but especially so in regard to "the observance of the moral law" that allows us to "feel" its "positive worth." Through the resulting "respect for ourselves in the consciousness of our freedom," the law gains "easier entry" into our *Gesinnung.*

The cultivation effected by exercises in moral judgment, metaphorically speaking, prepares the soil in which the concrete counterimage of the law is to take root and flourish, and it involves *both* our felt response and sharpened powers of discernment. Again, as Kant develops the point in the *Critique of Judgment,* we have the capacity for "being pleased intellectually"; its object is the "moral law in its might," and "aesthetically judged," the good that is "intellectual and intrinsically purposive (the moral good)" is "sublime" (*KU* 271). What the teacher must guard against in this entire process, is that the observance of duty does not get established on the basis of perceived "advantages or disadvantages," which would reduce the entire affair to "mere pragmatic prescriptions" (*MST* 482–83), the kind of rule-following that Kant had spoken out against in "What Is Enlightenment?" (*A* 36) and that would effectually bypass the formation of character altogether.[121] Thus, the negative exhibition, that of the "law of duty that

---

121. To state the point in terms of its classical counterpart: "There exists a capacity called 'cleverness,' which is the power to perform those steps which are conducive to a goal we have set for ourselves and to attain that goal. If the goal is noble, the cleverness is laudable, but if the goal is base, the cleverness is mere villainy; hence we call clever both men of practical wisdom and villains. [So] in fact this capacity is not practical wisdom, although practical wisdom does not exist without it. And this eye of the soul acquires its formed state not without excellence or virtue, as has been said and is plain" (Aristotle, *Nicomachean Ethics,* 1144a23–31; reference here has been made both to the Ostwald and W. D. Ross [as revised by J. O. Urmson: *The Complete Works of Aristotle: The Revised Oxford Translation,* ed. Jonathan Barnes, vol. 2 (Princeton: Princeton University Press, 1991)] translations).

Jürgen-Eckardt Pleines, in his articles "Pädagogik und praktische Philosophie" (in *Kant und die Pädagogik*) and "Pädagogisches Handeln und dessen Beziehung zur Urteilskraft," addresses what he takes to be a central, contemporary problem, namely, that in and through modern decision

commands," is the "sole exhibition that cultivates the soul morally" (*KpV* 85; see also *KU* 274–75).

What it achieves in the moral apprentices is that they literally begin to acquire a *taste for the law*, a conclusion implied by Kant already earlier in the *Critique of Practical Reason:* the moral law in its subjectively practical form, as the "true motivation" having its source in pure practical reason, "allows us to perceive" [or more literally, "get a sense, feel, or taste of," *spüren*] the "sublimity of our own supersensible existence" (*KpV* 88). The intrinsic link between moral and aesthetic judgment is rooted in the concept of taste itself, in an etymological connection to which Kant explicitly refers and that gives a deeper sense than otherwise possible to such statements as the following about character formation: "Precise meticulousness in the discrimination [or discernment] of what belongs to the rights of humanity and supreme conscientiousness in its observance forms one['s] character" (*RA* no. 1166, 516). Taste, discernment, and wisdom stem from a single root, on the significance of which Kant makes the following remarks. In his *Anthropology*, he poses the question as to how it has come to be that "the aesthetic capacity of judgment is designated by an expression (*gustus, sapor*), that refers only to a certain tool of sense . . . and to the discrimination [or discernment], as well as choice of things, that may be enjoyed" by means of this same tool (*ApH* 242).[122] "Even more peculiar" is the fact that "skill in testing through sense whether something is an object of enjoyment by one and the same subject (not if the latter's choice is universally valid) (*sapor*) has even been raised" (literally "spiraled upward," *hinaufgeschroben*) to the status of being "the designation for wisdom (*sapientia*); presumably for the reason that an unconditionally necessary purpose requires no deliberation or trial but, rather, is as directly assimilated by the soul [or mind, *Seele*], as it were, as when tasting wholesome"

---

theory, the power of judgment has been reduced to a matter of the mere application of rules. He makes a case for the urgency of recovering the sense of practical reason and submitting both the praxis and science of pedagogy to it (9–11, 66–67).

The observation (quoted in chapter 4) from Kant's 1784 essay reads: "Rules and formulas, those mechanical instruments of a rational use, better said, *misuse* of our natural gifts, are the shackles of unending immaturity" (*A* 36, emphasis added).

122. For a discussion of "taste conceived as a 'faculty of judgment' " as the "precipitate of taste conceived as an activity" in the Spanish, French, and British literature, see Howard Caygill's "Taste and Civil Society," in *Art of Judgment* (Cambridge: Basil Blackwell, 1989), 38ff. For a historical analysis of the development of the concept of taste in the philosophy of the seventeenth and eighteenth centuries, see Fr. Schümmer, "Die Entwicklung des Geschmacksbegriff in der Philosophie des 17. und 18. Jahrhunderts," *Archiv für Begriffsgeschichte* 1 (1955): 120–41. For a book-length study of Kant's theory of the pure judgment of taste, see Christel Fricke, *Kants Theorie des reinen Geschmacksurteils* (Berlin: Walter de Gruyter, 1990).

food (*ApH* 242–43).[123] It is thus assimilated by the soul, that is, of one whose subjective capacities of responsiveness, whose conduct of thought, capacity of choice, and comportment of mind have been schooled through the pedagogical stages previously described. Where "wisdom," the "idea of a practical employment of reason that is perfectly in accord with the law" (*ApH* 200), has been realized, there too the taste for the law has been simultaneously cultivated to its perfection. To say this is to express aesthetically what it is to have adopted the moral law with firm resolve, to have "directly assimilated" it as one's abiding, supreme maxim of choice making. Moreover, taste is fundamentally linked with the human moral vocation, as is evident in the statement that "taste is basically an ability to judge" the way in which "moral ideas are made sensible" (*KU* 356).[124] Having recognized the link, more needs to be said, however, about the details involved in the cultivation of moral discernment and judging.

Socratic Method: Cultivating the Habit of Moral Judging

Students enjoy their exercises in making discernments and discriminations in a learning process that, for Kant, is connected with, indeed draws on, innate characteristics of human discourse manifest even in mundane conversations (*KpV* 153). His account thereof and the consequent, recommended pedagogical approach includes Basedowian elements: for example, the emphasis on praxis, on beginning with what people already do, engaging in a kind of play, and so forth. As Kant describes it in the *Critique of Practical Reason* (153–54), one can easily observe that people sim-

---

123. *Sapio, sapere:* to taste, or to discern, perceive, be wise. *Sapor:* taste of a thing, or elegance in discourse, or good taste in behavior. *Sapientia:* the range of meaning given in the *New Collegiate Latin and English Dictionary* is good taste, common sense, prudence, wisdom, science, philosophy. This connection between taste and knowledge/wisdom is one that etymological accounts show pervades classical and scriptural literature (see, for example, Psalm 34.9: "O taste and see that the Lord is good!").

Aristotle observes that "the function of taste consists in the discrimination of flavors, which is done by wine-tasters and people who season dishes; but they hardly take pleasure in making these discriminations, . . . but in the actual enjoyment" (*Nicomachean Ethics,* 1118a27–29). The point we have seen Kant making is that, in regard to taste and discrimination used in their second meaning, it is precisely the discriminations themselves that are found to be enjoyable. In his paper on Kant's judgment of taste, Manfred Riedel takes up the etymological references to the ancient uses of these terms: "Zum Verhältnis von Geschmacksurteil und Interpretation in Kants Philosophie des Schönen," *Akten des Siebenten Internationalen Kant-Kongresses,* ed. Gerhard Funke (Bonn: Bouvier, 1991): 715–33.

124. For the connection of this notion of making moral ideas sensible with Kant's conception of symbolic presentation adequate for practical cognition, see Munzel, " 'The Beautiful Is the Symbol of the Morally-Good,' " 305.

ply enjoy "arguing" (*Räsonniren*); as a form of pastime it outlasts the telling of stories (which are soon no longer a piece of news and hence lose their interest), or cracking jokes (which soon falls flat). Especially when it is a question of ascertaining the moral substance of an action as a basis for assessing someone's character, even those who normally find the subtleties of theoretical questions dry and tedious, quickly join in and become exacting, meticulous, and subtle in ferreting out anything that might undermine or merely cast suspicion on the purity of the intent and hence the degree of virtue of the action. For Kant, this activity manifests a "propensity of reason"—namely, "to pursue with delight even the most subtle examination of practical questions that have been posed"—of which "educators of youth" ought to avail themselves.[125]

Given our discussion in chapter 4 of the role of human discourse in the concrete exercise of character, Kant's appeal to it in a pedagogical context should not surprise us. The claim, that through their "judgments" expressed in everyday discourse one can catch a glimpse of the "characters of those judging another" (*KpV* 153), is in accord with our earlier findings. In one light, this activity is an avenue whereby we communicate to others who we ourselves are; it is a social activity, even if it is not always sociably carried out. As Kant puts it in his *Anthropology,* "Any exhibition [or presentation, *Darstellung*] of one's own person . . . presupposes a social condition (to impart information about oneself, *sich mitzuteilen*), which is not always sociable (having sympathy for the pleasure of others), but is in the beginning commonly barbaric, unsociable, and merely contentious" (*ApH* 240).

That within this social aspect, the presentation of self is nonetheless inextricably linked with the development of self is an element to which we saw Kant making reference already in the first *Critique.* There, even the effort to make ourselves "appear better than we are," to "give expression to maxims (*Gesinnungen*) we do not in fact hold," was described as a provisional means of bringing ourselves out of a state of crudeness by adopting at least a manner of good (*KrV* A748/B776). In the long run, of course, such a state of "falsehood" stands in the way of the cultivation of morally

---

125. At least in some quarters today, of course, such activity would be frowned upon. The call for tolerance for diversity can bring with it a reluctance to exercise such judgments, or even an outright opposition thereto. For Kant's account it must be remembered that the point of comparison is not with others, but with the supreme moral principle (either in itself or as it is concretely manifest in individual action and character). For reflections on the "possibility of wide-spread moral judgment" in modern democracy, see William M. Sullivan, "The Democratization of Moral Judgment: Moral Leadership and Moral Symbols in Public Culture," in Rossi and Soukup, *Mass Media,* 34–42.

"good *Gesinnungen*" (*KrV* A748/B776) for as we have also seen, truthfulness is an indispensable maxim for having character at all. In the scenario cited from the second *Critique*, the presenting of self, of character, is portrayed at an initial unreflective, even unconscious level; one could call it a simple, natural self-display (such as one would get also for temperament). The cultivation of reason's natural propensity into explicit moral judgment entails the further dimension of making a shift from such a simple self-display to a conscious self-presentation, not now in the sense of imitating good maxims for the sake of show, but in the sense of giving truthful, concrete expression to what it is to be a follower of an exemplary instance of the morally good comportment of mind.[126] With this backdrop in place of the wider social context interconnected with individual development, we now return our attention to the pedagogical process that is to avail itself of the human propensity for arguing about moral questions. Notably, it is one for which Kant suggests biographies (of both ancient and modern times) as source material for the cultivation of moral judgment (*KpV* 154).[127]

126. Although (among other differences) her account is devoid of the primacy of the moral law at the center of Kant's, Hannah Arendt's articulation of this distinction (also made in connection with a discussion of judgment and character) is helpful in elucidating some of the qualitative differences involved. "In addition to the urge toward self-display by which living things fit themselves into a world of appearances, men also *present* themselves in deed and word and thus indicate how they *wish* to appear, what in their opinion is fit to be seen and what is not. This element of deliberate choice in what to show and what to hide seems specifically human. . . . Self-presentation is distinguished from self-display by the active and conscious choice of the image shown; self-display has no choice but to show whatever properties a living being possesses. Self-presentation would not be possible without a degree of self-awareness—a capability inherent in the reflexive character of mental activities and clearly transcending mere consciousness, which we probably share with the higher animals. Only self-presentation is open to hypocrisy and pretense, properly speaking, and the only way to tell pretense and make-believe from reality and truth is the former's failure to endure and remain consistent. [To make the decision in accordance with] the old Socratic 'Be as you wish to appear' [is to make] an act of deliberate choice among the various potentialities of conduct with which the world has presented me. Out of such acts arises finally what we call character" (*Life of the Mind*, 34, 36–37).

127. The context of this discussion also helps us to see the import of a statement in the *Anthropology* that might otherwise be construed as simply an autobiographical expression of preference on Kant's part: his assertion that there is no "situation in which sensibility and understanding united in a single enjoyment may be so often repeated with pleasure or so long carried on as [partaking of] a good meal in good company" (*ApH* 242). In such "breaking of bread together" we have a human activity that, unlike participation in research endeavors, business enterprises, and the like, is not directed to goals external to the individuals involved, but serves as an occasion to practice the communication of self to others. As Kant goes on, in this setting the meal serves as a vehicle for the sake of the companionship.

Otfried Höffe's discussion of the role of maxims in the biography of an individual affords a way of better appreciating Kant's appeal to this medium. According to Höffe, maxims connect the parts of a biography into a unified whole with a coherent meaning, in regard to which the

In general, the pedagogy Kant proposes is explicitly the Socratic maieutic (the classical methodology for effecting a change for the better): from the *Groundwork* (*G* 404), to the *Anthropology* (*ApH* 200), to the *Metaphysical Principles of Virtue* (*MST* 411, 478), to *On Pedagogy* (*P* 477), Kant repeats the point that one need only do "as Socrates did" and "make [reason] attentive to its own principle," its "compass" or "standard" whereby in any given case it is "very well able to distinguish what is good or evil, in accordance with, or opposed to duty" (*G* 403, 404).[128] As he describes it in his 1797 text, an indispensable preparatory step thereto is a "moral catechism," a "fundamental doctrine [or teaching] of the duties of virtue" that, in terms of "its contents, can be developed from ordinary human reason" (*MST* 479).[129] In the use of such a catechism, the mode of instruction is not yet that of the Socratic dialogue in which both teacher and student engage in question and answer; rather, the teacher questions the student (who has yet to learn how to pose the questions). The answers are nonetheless "elicited from the pupil's reason" and then worded in "definite terms that are not easily altered" so they can be "entrusted to the pupil's memory" (*MST* 479, 480). Thus Kant's entire process of moral cultivation to this point (as we have described it) exemplifies one of Basedow's basic dictums; namely, that example, taste, and exercise precede the presentation of theory, which becomes the means whereby that which has already been learned is now repeated, retained, and expanded in an orderly fashion.

Put most succinctly, the pedagogical method is geared to awakening, clarification, and articulation of the pupil's own insight. Its basic assumption, of course, is that such insight, indeed concepts, are inherent to the very nature of reason. As Kant already put it in the *Groundwork,* the concept of good practical desire is "inherent to the natural, sound understanding" and "need not so much be taught, but rather only clarified" (*G* 397). As he reiterates the point in the *Metaphysical Principles of Virtue*, the "dia-

---

categorical imperative serves to test whether the connection is merely subjective or also objective and valid for every rational being (*Ethik und Politik*, 101).

128. Gerhard Funke answers his own question, "What can pedagogy in Kant's sense of the term be and accomplish, and what is it to bring about?" as follows. "In exerting an influence upon another, it can only actually produce something if it helps others [turn] completely to themselves (*wenn sie ihm von Grund auf zu sich selbst verhilft*; literally, help "from the outset" or "from the ground up"). Completely: that means, from themselves, with themselves, for themselves—maieutically!" ("Pädagogik," 100).

129. In *On Pedagogy*, Kant speaks also of a "catechism of justice" or of "right" to serve for the education (*Bildung* in its broad sense) of children in a way that promotes their "uprightness" (*P* 490).

logical, Socratic method" presupposes that "concepts of duty" are "naturally present in reason and need only be developed out of it" (*MST* 411).
Or again, "by questioning" and appealing to case studies, "the teacher
guides the pupil's thought process in that she merely develops the aptitude
for certain concepts" in the student's own mind; she is the "midwife for her
pupil's thoughts" (*MST* 478). There is a reciprocal benefit here: students
become "aware of their own capacity to think for themselves," and the
teacher, in responding to the students' "counterquestions," and in accordance with the motto "learn by teaching" (*docendo discimus*), "learns how
to question well" (*MST* 478).[130] The culminating step in this process of
bringing moral apprentices to an awareness of their own "original [moral]
aptitude"—to a consciousness of their inherent freedom, of which they
cannot be deprived and on the basis of which they enjoy the ability to
master the "ills, tribulations, and sufferings of life"—is that the following
question naturally suggests itself to them: namely, what is this within us
that "dares to do battle with all the forces of nature within and round
about one, and to conquer these if they come into conflict with one's moral
principles?" (*MST* 483). To take this question (which cannot be answered
by speculative reason) to heart, asserts Kant, "uplifts the soul and animates
it" into upholding the "holiness of its duty only the more strongly, the
more it is assailed" (*MST* 483).

This latter point begins to address the first of at least two issues that
remain even if one grants this account of the uncovering of moral insight,
of awareness of one's innate moral aptitude. Simply to have brought the
students to this insight is not yet for them to have achieved what we have
seen Kant call *fortitudo moralis*, the courage and strength actually to execute or carry out morally good choices. As he has put it earlier in the text,
"through mere instruction in how one is to conduct (*verhalten*) oneself in
order to measure up to the concept of virtue," one "does not procure the
strength to carry out its rules" (*MST* 477). It is at this point that the
cultivation of spiritedness previously discussed must be incorporated into
the pedagogical process. As Kant repeats in a number of his texts, nothing
less than the "motivating force of the pure conception of virtue, when it

---

130. Beck remains unconvinced by Kant's account, describing his moral catechism as "not very
realistic" and being equally unimpressed by the particular examples or case studies Kant suggests
(such as the story of Ann Boleyn as an example of innocence being unjustly punished) ("Kant
on Education," 23). It is one thing, of course, to object to particular examples chosen for one's
case studies and another to object to the principles of the methodology per se. Beck neither does
the latter nor explicitly calls into question (as one might perhaps have expected) the fundamental
conception of mind that is entailed here.

is properly recommended to the human heart," is called for (*KpV* 152). Ultimately, what is required is "strength of resolve," a "resolution" that must be "embraced completely and all at once" (*MST* 384, 477), if virtue as self-control characterizing one's conduct of thought is to be realized. As we saw in our fourth chapter and our foregoing discussion here, in this connection rational faith and conscience as principles of reflective judgment are also directly relevant. We will return to this question of realizing resolve in our conclusion. First we will examine the second remaining issue, that of correctly exercising judgment in the particular case.

Conscious moral insight is not yet proficiency in the application of its maxims to circumstances in the world. Ethics "inevitably leads to questions that call upon the power of judgment to ascertain how a maxim is to be applied in particular cases and, in such a way, that [judgment] in turn furnishes a (subordinate) maxim (concerning which one may again ask for a principle for applying [*Anwendung*] this maxim to cases as these arise); thus ethics gets into a casuistics," for which Kant goes on to give examples (*MST* 411, 423–37). Such casuistical questions he further recommends be introduced in catechistic moral instruction in connection with each analysis of duty; the "assembled children are to be allowed to try out their powers of comprehension and [to see] how each of them believes to have solved the proposed tricky assignment" (*MST* 483). Such an approach to the "cultivation of reason," deems Kant, is "best suited to the ability of one still unschooled" in the use of reason (*MST* 484). For "it is far easier to decide questions concerning duty" than speculative issues (meaning, of course, metaphysical questions about first causes). Thus such cultivation is "in general the most apt way to sharpen" the powers of comprehension in youth, and this is especially true because "it is innate to human nature to love what one, through one's own work,[131] has brought" to the level of a "science (with which one is now conversant), and, so, through such exercises, without their being aware of it, the apprentices are drawn to take an interest in lived morality" (*MST* 484). Here again the echo of Basedow's recommendations is unmistakable.[132]

Perhaps even more importantly, Kant is here proposing in effect the cultivation of a *habit of judging*, of a *philosophical habit of mind*. Nor, again, is this a belated addendum to his thought. The description of the sense

131. Kant here uses a term whose original meaning refers to the tilling or cultivation of the soil (*Bearbeitung*). Thus, in effect, this work which the children come to love is precisely the cultivation of their own capacities.

132. That is, I am suggesting congruence with (not influence by) Basedow to be found in evidence in Kant's thought.

of judging involved (as given in the *Metaphysical Principles of Virtue*) is earlier expressed almost verbatim in the *Critique of Practical Reason* (154), while the general account of this judging, one that also underscores the distinction between this activity of mind and first attaining to insight, is found in the *Critique of Pure Reason* (A132–33/B171–72).[133] The power of judgment is the capacity for "distinguishing whether or not something falls under a given rule"; that is, whether "a given concrete case belongs under a universal" that one may know or have insight into only abstractly. One could very well be instructed in, even be a teacher of such universal principles (as, for example, in the respective sciences of medicine, jurisprudence, or politics) and still blunder when trying to apply them. For the power of "judgment is a special talent" that cannot be acquired by instruction, "but can only be practiced." And just this is the "singular and great benefit of examples: that they sharpen one's power of judgment." Kant has here described nothing less than a classic case for the pedagogical art of cultivation, of providing the students with exercises that allow them to acquire proficiency in the use of capacities they already possess. Moreover, it is just the art without which the most learned theory, insight into the most esoteric knowledge, is of little consequence in life (at best), or even outright dangerous if misapplied (at worst). In the background here stands Kant's early articulated dictum that the one thing required first and foremost by *all* is practical wisdom, so that they not conduct themselves in the world as one-eyed Cyclopes.

To conduct themselves instead as individuals of morally good character, that is to say as actively putting into practice their moral insight, is (as we claimed previously) to be exercising a philosophical habit of mind (where philosophy is identified with practical wisdom). The sense of "habit" involved here is not, of course, the mere "mechanism of sensibility" that consists in habituation understood as the "establishment, without any maxims and by means of its frequent gratification, of a steady inclination"

---

133. Hannah Arendt's articulation of these distinctions is instructive here. "The faculty of judging particulars (as brought to light by Kant), the ability to say 'this is wrong' 'this is beautiful,' and so on, is not the same as the faculty of thinking. Thinking deals with invisibles, with representations of things that are absent; judging always concerns particulars and things close at hand. But the two are interrelated, as are consciousness and conscience. If thinking—the two-in-one of the soundless dialogue—actualizes the difference within our identity as given in consciousness and thereby results in conscience as its by-product, then judging, the by-product of the liberating effect of thinking, realizes thinking, makes it manifest in the world of appearances, where I am never alone and always too busy to be able to think. The manifestation of the wind of thought is not knowledge; it is the ability to tell right from wrong, beautiful from ugly. And this, at the rare moments when the stakes are on the table, may indeed prevent catastrophes, at least for the self" (*Life of the Mind*, 193).

(*MST* 479).[134] What is called for is that we get in the habit of exercising moral judgment in connection with life's actions, that we be accustomed to effectuate the mutually referential unity of thinking and acting described by Goethe as the "sum of all wisdom."[135] In Kant's own words (from the second *Critique*), the first step is "*to make judging* in accordance with moral laws a *natural activity* accompanying all our own free actions, as well as our observations of those of others," to make such judging "as it were, *into a habit* (*Gewohnheit*) and to sharpen it" (*KpV* 159, emphasis added). To achieve it, as we saw in the passage cited from the first *Critique*, and as Kant notes in the second *Critique* and elsewhere, "frequent practice" is needed (*KpV* 154). Such exercises, even if "only pursued as a game of judgment in which children may vie with one another, nonetheless leave a lasting impression . . . that, through merely the habit (*Gewohnheit*) of repeatedly regarding such actions as praise or blameworthy, would make a good basis for uprightness in their future conduct of life (*Lebenswandel*)" (*KpV* 154–55). Or again, as Kant spells it out in *On Pedagogy*, for "moral cultivation" that "gives form to *Denkungsart*," one "must see to it that children become accustomed (*sich gewöhnen*) to act in accordance with maxims and not on the basis of certain motive impulses" (*P* 480).

In our fourth chapter we identified the maxims or principles of judgment held by Kant to be indispensable for the exercise of moral character in the world. A review of these maxims within the context of the present analysis of Kant's conception of pedagogy can help us better appreciate the claim we made early on; namely, that the fundamental sense of maxims in his philosophy is that of principles formative of character. For these are maxims formative of the judging activity itself whereby character is *manifest in the world* (which, it must be remembered, is still distinct from its initial establishment); for judgment, only repeated practice can bring about proficiency in the employment of maxims. The moral law remains of course the supreme maxim, but the relevant point here is that the use of reason itself be practiced in being "subject to" reason's own law (*DO* 145). Moreover, for the activity of judging that Kant has in mind to be thus habitually exercised presupposes the adoption of the maxim of thinking for oneself. Since we do not have here a matter of mere rule following or of decision theory (in the sense of a formula identifying sequential steps

---

134. This is, of course, how Kant reads the Aristotelian sense of habituation that he rejects as having a place in morality properly speaking.

135. As Erwin Hufnagel too has concluded, even discipline is not exhausted by procedures that inculcate habits, "although Kant has in all clarity pointed out the indispensability of habituation that consists in the internalization of lawfulness" ("Kants pädagogische Theorie," 51).

to be taken in applying maxims to concrete cases), but are dealing with a sense of judgment as a power of discernment, a "so-called mother wit for whose lack no school can compensate" (*KrV* A133/B172; see also *ApH* 199), the ongoing test of our assessments is precisely the further maxim of adopting the standpoint of humanity. Kant's portrayals of the children's exercises are always of group activity (in which each individual is necessarily confronted with how others think about the matter and hence becomes accustomed to making ultimately the reference to how the other, as rational being, would judge). This requirement of interaction with others, specifically their peers, also underlies one of Basedow's objections to the pedagogy of Rousseau's *Emile* (in which the student is deliberately removed from his peers). Such exercises in assessment and judgment can, however, turn thought to the skeptical doubts occasioned by speculative reason, and, as a bulwark against these, the internal trust relation secured by the maxim of rational faith is further of the essence. Without the maxim of truthfulness one cannot, for Kant, speak of character at all; for it is the formal subjective condition providing surety against the instrumentation (actual or potential) of the moral universal by the human subject before self and others (against, that is, the employment of the law as itself an instrument or means in the service of subjective ends). Of the essence is the habit of the ongoing self-assessment of judgment before conscience, to ensure that the foregoing maxims have indeed been duly carried out. In its strict sense, finally, we cannot properly say of someone that she has "*a* character" until the individual has adopted the penultimate maxim (the resolute conduct of thought). We will return to the question of the relation of the adoption of this resolve to the whole pedagogical process, to the relation (in effect) of formation (*Bildung* in its narrow sense) to cultivation and discipline, after we first examine how and why Kant sees the republican constitution as having an indispensable role in regard to all three of these pedagogical divisions.

Relation of Pedagogical and Communal Roles to Individual Responsibility for Establishing a Character

Pedagogical Function of the Republican Constitution

If discipline and cultivation make the immediate human world of an individual's capacities fit for, or adequate to, the task of executing reason's purposes, we saw in the second and third chapters that the republican constitution is accorded just such a pedagogical role on the behalf of its citizens in the wider sphere of the human community in history. As our examination showed, it is the cultivation of the subjective employment of freedom and hence the exercise of character that constitutes the dimension of Kant's morality essentially connected with communal relations. Repeatedly he makes the point that a "principal feature" of the "character of the human genus" is the "necessity of being a member of a civil society" (*ApH* 330). Such a society under a just constitution is the "formal condition" necessary for the cultivation of the human aptitudes; conversely, in its absence the "depravity of human nature," specifically "unlawfulness in *Denkungsart*," results in the "perpetual threat of hostilities" and ultimately open warfare. By "checking the hostile inclinations with their aversion for justice," the republican constitution "negatively secures human progress." While this goal of external, communal peace is "nature's own highest intention," it is also at once a task (exercised under the voice of command) belonging to reason's means for cultivating the natural order so that it be fit for concretely realizing reason's own empirical character.[136]

In regard to the question of how to understand the relation of the exercise of such external agency (whether by nature's hand or the political order) to moral cultivation, our earlier findings in effect saw it as a propaedeutic function. As a negative task, discipline eliminates the obstacles to cultivation, both in terms of the expenditures of resources and the effectuation of a "state of peace in which laws have force." Moreover, the formal moral order is not only maintained intact, but indeed through this constitution, the formal principle of universal justice is concretely embodied in the historical, human community. Its first principle is the categorical imperative; this universal (and not the local and particular well-being and happiness of the citizens) is the guide for both individual and corporate action. In our earlier analogy drawing on Kant's health metaphor, we noted that it is, however, no more necessary to assume that such external order and discipline is the *basis* for the formation of moral character (and effecting ultimate moral health) than one would regard the external alleviation of the symptoms of an ailment as constituting the overcoming of its cause and the establishment of permanent health. As a continuation of this discussion, now in connection with our preceding inquiry into the

---

136. Kant's rejection of such a civil constitution in the *Critique of Practical Reason* does not necessarily contradict the other texts, for it is made in relation to the question of a universal principal of morality and the objective ground of determination of volition (or the rational faculty of practical desire) (*KpV* 39–41). The civil constitution is called upon whenever the discussion concerns the subjective capacities, the aptitudes we possess by nature, the conditions under and through which the universal principal is to be concretely realized. His affirmations of the need for civil society and constitution are repeated in *Reflections on Anthropology;* see, for example *RA* no. 1501, 789.

principles of a pedagogy whose ultimate purpose is the attainment of moral character, we turn to the question of the role of the republican constitution in regard to the cultivation of moral judgment and the formation of moral character.[137]

Here again, in our discussion of the fourth chapter, we saw the parallels between the articles of the republican constitution and those maxims "relating to character" essential to the latter's exercise in and through human discourse. In both cases, the requirement underlying all the others was truthfulness, a genuine spirit of honesty, candor, and sincerity before self and others. Thus, the governance of this constitution provides both the example of and command for the praxis of reason "subject to" its own law, in conjunction with the subjective principle ensuring such exercise against its mere instrumentation. Moreover, it positively facilitates the cultivation of human capacities of judgment by both providing the freedom for and calling upon its citizens actively to exercise their capacity of thought. By contrast, nation-states that expend all their resources on "idle and violent aims of expansion" are charged by Kant with "unceasingly impeding their citizens' slow efforts [to effect] the inner formation of their *Denkungsart,* even depriving them of all support for this purpose" (*IG* 26;

---

137. A complete analysis examining the truth of the claims Kant makes for the republican constitution would require an account of the nature of the political theory it entails. Here we will limit ourselves to the question of how it may have a pedagogical function in relation to human moral cultivation at all and how such a function is reconcilable with the moral order of Kant's formal moral philosophy. For a book-length study of the political theory Kant presents in *Perpetual Peace,* see Volker Gerhardt's *Immanuel Kants Entwurf "Zum Ewigen Frieden" Eine Theorie der Politik* (Darmstadt: Wissenschaftliche Buchgesellschaft, 1995). As Gerhardt points out, "moral self-conception" constitutes the "irrevocable point of departure for argumentation" in Kant's *Perpetual Peace,* and his "conception of morality . . . incorporates also the conception of justice" (or rights); what Kant ultimately presents is a "doctrine of justice [or rights] for world peace" (9). It is worth underscoring that Kant explicitly distinguishes a republic from a democracy (*ApH* 331). Fundamental thereto is precisely the overriding universal principle of justice, the categorical imperative that unites all other principles beneath it. To the extent that democracy is understood as first and foremost securing the material goals of the pursuit of life, liberty, and happiness without the stipulation of the constraint of worthiness to be happy, the sense of peace and agreement that it seeks to forge is very different from that of the republican constitution. For, the overriding goal of democracy so construed is external; it is not the overcoming of inner conflict within human nature and the attainment of the human moral vocation. Its goal is far more what Kant would describe as the prudential ends of humankind.

For a book-length study of Kant's notion of justice or right see Leslie Arthur Mulholland, *Kant's System of Rights* (New York: Columbia University Press, 1990). Mulholland examines the moral basis of Kant's doctrine of rights, arguing that "Kant cannot construct a system of rights without reference to ethical obligation"; however, the argument treats the moral law as a deontological principle (25–26). George Parkin Grant goes to some length to distinguish the Rawlsian notion of justice from Kant's account thereof in *English-Speaking Justice* (Notre Dame: University of Notre Dame Press, 1985), 23ff.

see also *F* 367). Thus the inner moral edifice is indeed affirmed as being the work of the individual, but life in the so-called civilized state can present (and on Kant's view, thus far has done so) nearly insurmountable obstacles to this endeavor—presumably by forcibly directing the attention, efforts, and energies of its citizens elsewhere, including and especially the war efforts and their attendant miseries. So seen, the function of the republican constitution is once again negative; that is, the removal of impediments present under other forms of political organization.

Identified as chief among these is just the impediment to the free, public interchange of one's thoughts. Its importance lies not only in the fact that the voice of the teacher of justice might otherwise not be heard (a concern Kant explicitly raises in *Conflict of the Faculties*, 89). As summarized also by Hannah Arendt (from Kant's essays "What Is Orientation in Thinking?" and "What Is Enlightenment?"), for Kant, " 'the external power that deprives man of the freedom to communicate his thoughts publicly, *deprives him at the same time of his freedom to think*,' and . . . the only guarantee for 'the correctness' of our thinking lies in that 'we think, as it were, in community with others to whom we communicate our thoughts as they communicate theirs to us.' Man's reason, being fallible, can function only if he can make 'public use' of it, and this is equally true for those who, still in a state of 'tutelage,' are unable to use their minds 'without the guidance of somebody else' and for the 'scholar', who needs 'the entire reading public' to examine and control his results" (*DO* 144, *A* 37).[138] What Arendt (who herself drew an intrinsic connection between "the activity of thinking" and the "problem of good and evil") found here in Kant's works resonates with her observation that the nature of thought is such that "no other human capacity is so vulnerable, and it is in fact easier to act under conditions of tyranny than it is to think."[139] This state-

138. Arendt, "Truth and Politics," in *Between Past and Future*, 234–35.

139. Arendt, *Human Condition*, 324. When one considers (for example) Alexis de Tocqueville's critique of the tyranny of the majority in America, coupled with the effects of the principle of equality that he sees holding sway, the wider relevance of this concern (beyond freeing societies from explicit dictatorial powers) comes into view. Just as we have seen Kant speak of the inclinations as a form of tyranny that must be overcome, so other kinds of tyrannies too may exist. Given also Kant's distinction between what he calls a republican constitution and a democracy (*F* 351–52), passages such as the following from Tocqueville help us see the greater scope of what is at stake: "Thus intellectual authority will be different, but it will not be diminished; and far from thinking that it will disappear, I augur that it may readily acquire too much preponderance, and confine the action of private judgment within narrower limits than are suited either to the greatness or the happiness of the human race. In the principle of equality I very clearly discern two tendencies; the one leading the mind of every man to untried thoughts, the other which would prohibit him from thinking at all. And I perceive how, under the dominion of certain

ment, in turn, is paralleled by Kant's comments in *Perpetual Peace*, in which he accuses "soulless despotism" of "extirpating the germ of good" from humanity and of "exhausting all [its] powers" (*F* 367).

Putting what Arendt's assessment underscores in terms of our previous discussion: the republican constitution best facilitates the exercise of the first two maxims of the ordinary human understanding, thinking for oneself and from the standpoint of others, and hence is of the essence for the cultivation of judgment as it is necessarily conducted in interrelation with one another on the part of the human travelers on life's journey. The provision made by this constitution is not simply a matter of tolerance for such exercise. Included among the objectives of a republican form of governance (even if its constitutional form has not yet been established) is precisely that its citizens become capable of "self-legislation (which is itself originally grounded on justice)" (*F* 372). Concretely speaking, this objective would likely entail (for example) just the sort of support for reforms in education and the establishment of schools that was initiated in Kant's time. In such respects, the republican form of governance makes a positive (and not merely negative) contribution to human cultivation. In regard to the second maxim, to being able to see and move beyond "private conditions of judgment" and "to reflect on one's own judgment" from a "universal point of view" (*KU* 295), one can again readily see how interactive discourse with other members of the community, especially in a setting in which all have before them the principles of a just constitution founded on practical reason's supreme law, provides the requisite practice to become proficient in such a mode of reflective judgment, or the "enlarged *Denkungsart*."[140] Perhaps most importantly for Kant, at least as he expresses it in his essay on enlightenment, is that the people be allowed to think for themselves in matters of religion; immaturity in this regard he deems as the "most injurious and degrading" of all (*A* 41). On the basis of our preceding discussion of both religion's hortatory function and its

---

laws, democracy would extinguish that liberty of the mind to which a democratic social condition is favorable; so that, after having broken all the bondage once imposed on it by ranks or men, the human mind would be closely fettered to the general will of the greatest number." Another remarkably parallel theme occurs as well: the notion of the public realm and its institutions as an educational agency. "Political associations may therefore be considered as large free schools, where all the members of the community go to learn the general theory of association." This is important: "If men are to remain civilized, or to become so, the art of associating together must grow and improve" (*Democracy in America*, ed. Richard D. Heffner [New York: Penguin Books, 1984], 149, 206, 201–2).

140. Kant's notion of *sensus communis* is also relevant here. For an analysis of this concept, see Rudolf Makkreel, *Imagination and Interpretation*, 155–66. Makkreel also notes the role of reflective judgment in practical wisdom ("Dogmatic, Regulative, and Reflective," 135).

role in inner discipline (which is connected with conscience), as well as of rational faith as a reflective principle of judgment, we can appreciate the significance of this point in relation to moral character. Where such immaturity obtains, the inner trust relationship undergirding the human pursuit of the good is wholly undermined and religion's pedagogical functions of cultivation and discipline cannot be properly realized.

To have thus identified the connection Kant sees with each of the principles of judgment essential for character and the political order of the republican constitution does not yet, however, exhaust the scope of the latter's pedagogical role in moral cultivation. Two major dimensions remain: its "sanctioning" the philosophers "their role as *philosopher*" citizens of the state[141] (as specified by Kant in his "secret article for perpetual peace," *F* 368–69) and the issue of its relation to the maxim of the resolute conduct of thought itself. Earlier we identified the pedagogical aspect of the critical philosophy, in particular, as the science required for the cultivation of human reason and thus as necessary in the education of teachers who, in turn, pave the path to wisdom for others by guiding them Socratically to the use of their own reason. In addition, the critical philosophy includes such essential investigations as the critical examination of the very possibility of the human as a moral species. In connection with the latter, in *Perpetual Peace* Kant concludes that the moral politician requires above all the knowledge "of what can be made of human beings," for which the "higher standpoint of anthropological observation" is needed (that is, of pragmatic anthropology as contrasted with a purely empirical account of human behavior in history) (*F* 374). The label *pragmatic* means that it consists in "knowledge of human beings as cosmopolitan citizens (*Weltbürger*)" (*ApH* 120). Such a requirement of the knowledge of "human nature . . . and its peculiar place in creation, so that one could know" ultimately what its "conduct" at the "highest level of physical or moral excellence" would be, is identified by Kant as early as his 1765–66 "Announcement" of his lectures.

More generally, however, it is in regard to their being citizens who are exemplary instances of the "free exercise of judgment" that sanctioning the philosophers' role is so important. As Volker Gerhardt has expressed

---

141. Volker Gerhardt has given a very good analysis of Kant's conception of the relation of philosophy and politics, as it contrasts with the Platonic view of the philosopher-king, in "The Abdication of Philosophy: On the Modernity of the Relation between Philosophy and Politics in Kant," trans. Joel Golb, *Idealistic Studies* 26 (1996): 175–88. The phrase quoted is from the discussion of "A Philosopher's Kingdom?" (179). The original version is found in *Immanuel Kants Entwurf* (126–45).

the point: it is "their ability to contribute to popular enlightenment—
hence to the *general civic formation of judgment*"—that constitutes their
"sufficient," but also indispensable, activity in the state; hence, too, one
need only "grant them their activity as philosophers," for "speaking publicly will come by itself," and thereby "their 'duty according to general
(moral-legislative) human reason'" will be fulfilled.[142] Free of the cor-
rupting possession of, or proximity to, the political power enjoyed even
by jurists, philosophy "carries the torch before its gracious lady" (rather
than "holding her train")—carries it, that is, before all the faculties: theology, jurisprudence, and medicine (*F* 369). For a "true testing of all the
important arguments" can only "be termed philosophical," and "those engaged in the reflecting become philosophers, if only they dig deeply
enough into the issues."[143] It bears repeating here that Kant's express rejection of the notion of the Platonic philosopher-king extends only to his
changed conception of the relation of philosophy and politics. The Socratic model obtains in regard to the persona of the philosopher. The "true
philosopher," the "one who thinks for himself," remains the "practical philosopher, the teacher of wisdom through instruction and example" who
"shows us the ultimate purpose of human reason"; "among all of humanity," it was Socrates who, in his "conduct (*Verhalten*) came closest to the
idea of the wise one" (*LJ* 26, 23, 29). So too, in 1765/66, Kant announced
that the "mode of teaching" to be employed in his course was such that
the youth should "learn how to philosophize" and, in 1784, he remained
confident that there would "always be a few" who were "thinking for themselves" and who "would disseminate about themselves the spirit of a rational appreciation for their own worth and for the calling of each person
to think for himself" (*A* 36).

However, whether the pedagogical source is the philosopher, the constitution, nature, or home and school, and even under the general comprehension of cultivation as "a schooling that makes us responsive to higher
purposes than nature itself can deliver" (*KU* 433) and of discipline as a
taming of unruliness that makes such cultivation possible, the entire account thus far of this natural pedagogical order still leaves open the question of its reconcilability with the moral order that *begins* from the establishment of character. The crucial question is that of the relation of the
pedagogical functions of discipline and cultivation to formation (*Bildung*
here understood in its narrow sense). Or to put it more precisely, is there

---

142. Gerhardt, "Abdication of Philosophy," 179; *Kants Entwurf,* 132.
143. Gerhardt, "Abdication of Philosophy," 180; *Kants Entwurf,* 133–34.

a way of accounting for the necessity of the first two (a necessity that can hardly be refuted in the wake of our investigations) that does not violate the primacy of the individual's act of establishing her own character? It is on the basis of addressing this question that Kant's claim for the republican constitution must ultimately be understood, namely, that the "good moral formation (*Bildung*) of a people is to be expected in the first place" as a product of "a good political constitution" (*F* 366).[144]

The Virtue That Cannot Be Taught

To pose the issue in terms of the relation of discipline and cultivation to formation is, of course, to restate (in hopefully a fruitful way for its resolution) a problem that has currency in the scholarship: the compatibility of Kant's philosophy of history with his moral philosophy. The apparently deeper tension, as has been brought to light here, lies in the reconcilability of both the formal morality and the founding of character in its absolute sense with his pedagogy. Kant's own repeated allusions, indeed his emphasis on the distinction of the natural and moral orders, implies not only his awareness of this apparent tension, but suggests that his statements may very well be referring to just the point to be realized in light of it. Let us begin by recounting some of these passages.

In connection with yet one more affirmation that the "civil constitution" constitutes the "highest degree of raising [or heightening] by means of human efforts (*künstlichen Steigerung*) the good aptitude [present] in the human race to the final purpose of its vocation," Kant explicitly observes that nature's order inevitably leads to modes of instruction that are contrary to that purpose (notably citing religious education, which "ought to consist in moral cultivation" but is carried out as a historical study amounting to no more than "mere cultivation of memory"); for nature's order is to move from culture to morality, instead of making the moral law the point of departure for guiding one's efforts toward purposive culti-

144. Especially given the reference to the whole people (*eines Volks*), it would seem that the better translation here of *Bildung* would be of its wider sense of "education" (in Kant's use of it as synonymous with *Erziehung* and hence simply encompassing discipline and cultivation). However, in both *Perpetual Peace* and "Idea for a Universal History," Kant makes it clear that what is at stake is *Denkungsart*. In the passage quoted earlier from the latter, it is the "inner formation of their *Denkungsart*" on the part of "its citizens" that is said to be obstructed by the state that unceasingly pursues war (*IG* 26). As we also saw in our third chapter, both the ultimate source of all conflict and the ultimate achievement of peace are *within*. Even a quibble (or argument) about the sense of *Bildung* meant in this passage does not in any way affect the basic question to be answered: how do the first two stages of pedagogy relate to the individual act of revolution of conduct of thought that alone can establish character and that is accorded primacy by Kant?

vation (as reason prescribes it be done) (*ApH* 327–28). The constraint imposed by the constitution on the "inclination to mutual acts of violence" is a "step toward morality," but "not yet a moral step" (*F* 375–76n). So too, to be a "good citizen" is "not yet to be a morally good person" (*F* 366). For legality, the conformity of actions with duty independently of the question of their motivation, yields "good deeds" and a phenomenal form of the moral life (even, as we saw previously, a kind of empirical character), but as every student of Kant's ethics knows, it can very well coexist with a perverse order of maxims in one's power of choice (*SF* 91, *KpV* 71, *RV* 36). Indeed, the very fact that the "cultivation of talents, skill, and taste" tends "naturally to rush along in advance of the development of morality" makes for a state of affairs that is most "burdensome and dangerous for lived morality as well as for physical well-being" (*ED* 332). In sum, Kant's own statement could hardly be expressed more directly: "The moral formation (*Bildung*) of human beings must begin, not from an improvement in morals, but from a transformation of *Denkungsart* and the establishment of a character" (*RV* 48). Why this is so and what the implications are will now be interpreted on the basis of the pedagogical divisions described earlier.

In defense of the order under which the republican constitution exercises its pedagogical role, the following can be said. Given that its own first principle is the categorical imperative, it itself represents just such a realization in the conversion of thought (from the prudential order of maxims beginning from the material principle informed by a desire for well-being, to the moral order). The assumption of freedom and of the moral law based thereon is the fundamental assumption of this sense of politics as "practical wisdom" (*F* 372). Thus at the general level, for the relation of the state constitution to its corporate body of citizens and the human species, the point of departure for instituting purposive cultivation in the whole is the law as specified by reason. Moreover, there is no serious objection to the initiation of the reform of the sensibilities in the case of the individual beginning with an external authority itself grounded on practical reason's supreme law. The requirement is only that there be such a "gradual reform of the sensibilities" as "observation of the law" can bring about (*RV* 47).

How does law embodied in such constitutional form relate to law as the principle inherent in individual human reason? As we have seen, wisdom, or the idea of perfection in the practical use of reason, a use in accordance with law, "cannot in the least degree be infused by another; each must give rise to it from within themselves" (*ApH* 200). This point accords with Kant's repeated statements that one "procures character for oneself," that "character in one's *Denkungsart*" is "not from nature" (*KpV* 98, *ApH* 294; see also *IG* 20). Thus, as Kant himself has posed it, "the essential question in regard to the aim of perpetual peace" (whose intrinsic connection with character was revealed in our third chapter) is what nature does on the behalf of human moral purpose, to ensure that "what human beings ought to do according to laws of freedom, but fail to do," is yet done by means of "nature's constraint" but "*without jeopardizing freedom,*" and in all three areas of public law (*F* 365, emphasis added). Recast in the terms of our discussion, the essential question is what discipline and cultivation accomplish on behalf of the formation of character without jeopardizing the individual act of freedom that establishes the latter.

Kant is clearly rejecting a conventional assumption of upbringing and moral pedagogy, one that accords with the notion of attaining moral virtue by habituation of the inclinations and is held by empiricists and behaviorists. He is in effect emphasizing just the point that stands in complete agreement with his formal moral principles, namely that the individual as moral being is never a mere product of circumstance, fortune, and training, and that this is so *irrespective of the need we do have as human beings for discipline and cultivation.* That this latter need does not conflict with ultimate individual responsibility for one's character is, of course, the point of contention for many of his critics. On the basis of our foregoing analysis, we will propose the following interpretation in response.

That all the levels of pedagogy are to be taken into consideration is affirmed again in *Reflections on Anthropology* (*RA* no. 1518, 873), which lists the following four steps under the heading "good character does not come from nature; it must be procured": (1) "through education," which we now know includes discipline and cultivation; (2) "through deliberation and discussion [with respect to] the determination of principles," which we may recognize as referring to the exercises in moral judgment already described; (3) "through the solemn adoption [of such principles] (a kind of rebirth)," which refers to the adoption of the maxim of the resolute conduct of thought itself, marking (as Kant notes elsewhere) a "new epoch" in the life of the individual (*RV* 21, 47–50; *ApH* 294–95); (4) "through the inviolability of these principles . . . and conscientiousness in keeping one's character unsullied"; Kant's allusion to the lie whereby one incurs contempt for oneself makes it clear that this fourth step is the call to the maxim of truthfulness for the lifelong maintenance of one's character. "Finally, one can say one is an upright [or honest, righteous, *rechtschaffener*] person." As Kant notes here and elsewhere, it is only approximately around age forty that "the right *Denkungsart* is formed" (see also *ApH* 294); in another passage in the *Anthropology* lectures, he places only the achievement of prudence at this point in life, leaving wisdom as an accomplishment for one's sixties (*ApH* 201).

It is time, then, to come to terms with Kant's conception of this singular resolve that is the hallmark of good moral character, "this steadfastness and perseverance in principles in general" that can never be "gradually achieved by education, example, or instruction, but rather is effected, as it were, through an explosion that ensues all at once upon a surfeit of the vacillating state of instinctual" life (*ApH* 294). Such resoluteness in conduct of thought, without which one cannot, strictly speaking, say of someone that she has "*a* character," put into the terms of our preceding discussion, entails that moral judgment be consistently exercised, that its form be, as it were, crystallized and, hence, permanently beyond the fluid, potentially or even actually changeable and wavering state that has gone before. Its adoption is not itself a matter of discernment that can be sharpened by repeated efforts of employing it in relation to examples and under the guidance of instruction. It is, rather, a matter of the individual in effect saying "yes" once and for all, of freely committing herself for life to the employment of moral judgment informed by and proficient in bringing the maxims outlined previously to bear on its praxis. It is therefore a step that lies beyond the pedagogical art of cultivation and beyond simply the habitual exercise of judgment in accordance with the specified maxims. It is a step that ensures, in fact, that the latter not be reduced to a trained ability that, once acquired, could be literally unthinkingly exercised. Indeed, without this step that unifies, holds together all one's talents and abilities under the overall orientation directed to the final purpose of humanity in one's own person, these capacities are but an aggregate of more or less well-disciplined and cultivated aptitudes with no absolutely reliable guide or assurance as to what interest they are employed to serve. Hence it is wisdom that is wanted, and neither the humanities nor the sciences (let alone professional skills) in and of themselves can give rise to it.

The relation of the formation of character, of the adoption of resolve in one's conduct of thought, to discipline and cultivation may be understood in terms of an analogy with the relation of preparatory training to taking an oath of office. In this case, of course, the office is that of the vocation of our humanity. No amount of schooling equipping us (in our subjective capacities) to carry out the office well, even if essential for conducting ourselves well in office, can *necessitate* our taking the oath of office, our committing ourselves consciously and freely to assuming personal responsibility for fulfilling it. This choice to make it our own vocation, to make the promise (in effect) to ourselves and others that we will duly perform it can only be our own.[145] It is not a degree ceremoniously conferred upon us that we may passively receive at the conclusion of our studies; we cannot be made or pronounced by another to be a person of good moral character. In principle, consistent with Kant's description of the adoption of this resolve as a conversion or transformation in conduct of thought and with his fundamental premise of freedom, there is in fact nothing to prevent someone from taking this particular oath of office in the absence of preparatory schooling and then acquiring the latter as a kind of on-the-job training. Pragmatically speaking, to do so would be to take the hard road (whether under the duress of circumstance, or one's own prior failures), but it would *not be per se impossible.*

Communal and state pedagogical responsibility nonetheless does turn out to be substantial. Discipline and cultivation prepare the conditions most conducive to the formation of character in its strict sense. In effect, they translate into actuality the promise that reason find the world fit for the execution of its interests—both in regard to the immediate world of an individual's human capacities and the wider world of the human community, in interaction with which character is manifest and exercised. In the first place, nothing less than a cosmopolitan world order of justice and peace is called for by Kant. Under its reign, obstacles, that is, temptations to the transgression of duty, are to be eliminated (or at the very least, mitigated). Inclinations are to be tempered and empirical character cultivated by the use of constraint and the enforced, habitual, legal conformity to law. Example and encouragement are to be supplied. Conditions conducive to the active exercise of human capacities of thought, reflection,

---

145. This act of free choice is something more than acting in accordance with the law in regard to individual action. As Kant notes in *Metaphysical Principles of Virtue*, "to establish and enliven this *Gesinnung* within oneself . . . goes beyond the law of duty of actions and makes the law itself also the motivation" (*MST* 391). As Gerhard Funke has also expressed the matter: "Bei dem Thema: Disziplinieren, Kultivieren, Zivilisieren, Moralisieren wird also erst in der Endstufe der Entwicklung deutlich sichtbar, daß es sich insgesamt überhaupt nicht *um gehabte Erfahrungen* handelt, die an Naturverhältnissen abgelesen werden, sondern vielmehr *um Forderungen,* die gestellt werden müssen, wenn menschliches Handeln sinnvoll und *nicht bis* in den Abschluß hinein *absurd* sein soll. Zur Annahme einer solchen Forderung kann *niemand* gebracht werden, der daran Anstoß nimmt; es sei denn, es erfolgte ein Anstoß zur eigenen *Besinnung* mit anschließendem Einsichts-Erlebnis, in dem der Sinn der Forderung evident wird" ("Pädagogik," 107). Earlier in the essay, Funke also makes these relevant observations: "Selbstverständlich ist alles Handeln besonderes Handeln, allgemein ist nur das von Sonderbedingungen absehende vernünftige Handeln. Die Philosophie wird die Analyse dieser Zusammenhänge vornehmen und vorführen: aha-sagen muß nach solcher Analyse der Einzelne und die Lücke zwischen Einsicht und Verwirklichung der Einsicht schließen, was eine Revolution in seiner Einstellung bedeutet" (101).

and judgment (aesthetic and moral) are to be promoted, including ensuring that the philosophical voice is always free to speak and be heard. For all such efforts, the point of departure must be reason's law, not the end of the well-being and happiness of the citizens. Implicit in all of this is that each citizen is responsible for being of service to the community in these efforts. Individual freedom with its concomitant responsibility thus remains intact in every way. There is a limit to the extent to which it lies within the state to bring about the moral formation of humanity. As Socrates first concluded: the reputed wise of the city can give and teach their children all things, but they cannot ultimately make them good. Virtue in this sense cannot be taught.[146] With the maxim of the resolute conduct of thought, human destiny on behalf of self and the human race is placed in the hands of the individual citizen.

146. Plato, *Meno,* trans. G. M. A. Grube, in *Five Dialogues* (Indianapolis: Hackett, 1981), 93b–94e. Thus too, in a related point, while for the political institution it is very desirable that an ethical civil society in accordance with laws of virtue exist within it, no legislator could or should attempt to bring such about by means of a constitution enforced by constraint (*RV* 95).

Character as a Grafted Entity

It bears underscoring that Kant refers to *character* more often than not as "a character" (*einen Charakter*), which it is "characteristic of human beings in the system of nature to procure for themselves" (*ApH* 321). Thereby he emphasizes that the character in question is a singular entity, a "unity and a concord" (*Eintracht* meaning both) achieved through the use of reason where "nature" first sowed the "seed of disunion and discord (*Zwietracht*)" (*ApH* 322). Out of the separate spheres of the laws of freedom and the laws of nature, of reason and of sensibility, one unified character is to be produced, or literally "brought forth." Thus even the stage of civilizing, the cultivation of the human aptitudes so as to produce a "well-mannered" (*gesittet*) if not yet "moral" (*sittlich*) being, is to make of it a "being determined (or destined, *bestimmtes*) for unity and concord" and thereby to raise it to "a higher level" (*ApH* 323).

The general, inherent philosophical difficulty in conceiving of such a unity effected by contact and/or combination of distinct things was a matter of debate in ancient philosophy. Recognition of this long-standing issue adds another dimension of significance to the wider eighteenth-century concern with it and to Kant's particular efforts to resolve it. As Aristotle describes the problem in *On Generation and Corruption,* for "some thinkers, it is impossible for one thing to be combined with another. They argue that if the combined constituents continue to exist and are unaltered, they are no more combined now than they were before, but are in the same condition; while if *one* has been destroyed, the constituents have not been combined—on the contrary, one constituent *is* and the other *is not,* whereas combination demands uniformity of condition in them both; and on the same principle even if *both* the combining constituents have been destroyed as the result of their coalescence, *they* cannot be combined since *they* have no being at all."[1] Aristotle's own solution is to resort to his metaphysical principle of actuality and potentiality, thereby allowing the constituents to remain potentially what they were before, neither persisting actually, nor destroyed, while "the compound may be actually other than the constituents from which it has resulted."[2]

Kant's solution is his account of character as the concrete counterimage of the moral law, which is to say, of reason in its subjectively practical exercise. Just how complex the account of unity in these terms is, we have had ample opportunity to see. He does, however, also appeal to an image whereby we may think or comprehend this unity of nature and freedom (when conceived in its broadest terms) and, thus ultimately, of the respective sciences of anthropology and morality.[3] His appeal is to that longstanding horticultural art which in fact achieves just such a union of two constituents in a way that neither is destroyed, but both combine to form a new entity. The art is the praxis of grafting, which dates back to Chinese civilizations as early as 1000 B.C. and which enjoyed renewed interest with the Renaissance in Europe.[4] One of Kant's most explicit statements drawing upon the analogy to grafting appears in "Idea for a Universal History" (1784): "All good that is not grafted on to a morally good *Gesinnung* is nothing but illusion and glittering misery" (*IG* 26). In turn, as he notes in his *Critique of Practical Reason*, a "good moral *Gesinnung*" may be "grafted" upon a well-founded "consciousness of freedom" (*KpV* 161). Further, the "aptitude of our nature" consisting in the very "possibility" of steadfastness and resolve characterizing our "free power of choice" is an aptitude upon which "nothing evil can be grafted" (*RV* 27). Or, as

---

1. Aristotle, *On Generation and Corruption*, trans. H. H. Joachim, in *The Complete Works of Aristotle*, ed. Jonathan Barnes, 2 vols. (Princeton: Princeton University Press, 1984), 327b1–6.

2. Aristotle, *On Generation and Corruption*, 327b20ff.

3. Stark has noted that "the difficult mutual relation [between intelligible and empirical character] produces, on the plane of philosophical theory, the tension between anthropology and morality." Yet Kant "leaves no doubt, that it is always one and the same human being whose two characteristics are being contemplated" ("Kant's *Lectures*," 11–12).

4. Hudson T. Hartmann, Dale E. Kester, and Fred T. Davies, *Plant Propagation: Principles and Practices* (Englewood Cliffs, N.J.: Prentice-Hall, 1990), 305. Mara Miller in *The Garden as an Art* describes the changing and developing relation between humanity and nature as follows: "From the fifteenth century Italian gardens on, one improved nature—the wilderness inherited through Adam and Eve's sin—by revealing its inner, obscured rationality, or imposing rational form upon it. From the beginning of the 'natural' movement in the eighteenth century, one remade Nature herself. . . . The next step was the garden as autobiography or self-portraiture, invented by Alexander Pope" (Albany: State University of New York Press, 1993), 112.

Kant observed as early as his *Observations* of 1764, "True virtue can only be grafted onto principles" (B 217).[5]

All analogies have their limits,[6] but the inherent philosophical difficulties in an account of unity in general and the technical complexities of Kant's critical account of unity of character in particular, virtually beg for the use of such imagery. We have also seen a transfer from biological terminology to moral discourse about human aptitudes and rudiments of human nature that makes the analogy of grafting quite apt. An extended interpretation of character as a grafted entity proves well suited to the critical conception of character and illuminates aspects of it otherwise not readily seen. The interpretation further affords a less technical summary of the findings of our investigation.

Based on Kant's appeal to the analogy in 1784 and on the two parts involved in horticultural grafting, we will proceed by paralleling the resolute conduct of thought and its accompanying moral comportment of mind (exhibiting the spirit of the law and grounded on a consciousness of freedom), with the (root)stock, while all other goods (the human aptitudes, actions, choices, and their results ultimately comprising one's whole conduct of life) are seen as the scion, the upper portion of the graft from which the stem and branches of the grafted plant grow. Included in the reasons for grafting in horticulture are the benefits obtained from a certain rootstock, the special forms of plant growth grafting makes possible, and the ability thereby to repair damaged parts.[7] The parallels to be drawn in Kant's account are respectively to conduct of thought and its attendant comportment of mind (whose benefit is summed up by the final purpose of humanity), the elevation of the natural to moral form (made possible by the synthetic unity of intelligible and empirical causality), and the effort to straighten the crooked wood of humanity.

In a successful horticultural graft, the objective achieved is a single entity consisting in the organic union of the strongest possible root system from one plant combined with the limbs of another plant to add the desired qualities of beauty or productivity. Neither original component is,

---

5. Kant makes relatively sparing use of this notion of grafting; there are sixteen references in the works published in his lifetime. It is notable, however, that (save for one in the third *Critique* that explicitly mentions the horticultural process) all deal with characteristics of human nature, for the most part with virtue and vice. Other references are found in *Observations*, 234; the essay on illnesses affecting the mind (*Ak* 2:262); *Religion*, 26, 27; *Conflict of the Faculties*, 86; *Anthropology*, 303, 312; "Orientation," 143; *Perpetual Peace*, 365.

6. Analogy is here being used in its ordinary sense, not in the critical sense of Kant's qualitative analogy.

7. Hartmann, Kester, and Davies, *Plant Propagation*, 307.

strictly speaking, of greater or lesser value; both are indispensable. In Kant's discussion of botanical propagation in the *Critique of Judgment,* he refers to the mutual dependence between the preservation of one part of a tree and another (*KU* 371). For character as the concrete counterimage of the law, both orders of causality, freedom and nature, are likewise interdependent. The natural order is elevated to an interest in preservation of a higher (moral) order, which entails a duty to secure the preservation of the natural without which the moral order cannot be concretely actualized. The interdependence of the parts in a successful graft is such that in both our intuition (*Anschauung*) and our conception thereof, we see and think a single entity (rose tree, weeping cherry, colonnade apple tree), not two conjoined plants. Similarly, the new entity, the moral being incarnate as natural being, lives, flourishes, and dies as one (for even under the assumption of immortality, the demise of the individual removes the appearance of the moral being from the world).

While the vigor, size, and overall shape of the resulting plant are largely a result of the rootstock, a complete explanation of the new plant's characteristics recognizes that "the scion, the interstock, the rootstock, and the graft union itself all interact to influence each other and determine the over-all behavior of the plant."[8] Vigor, moral fortitude, spiritedness are, as we have seen, precisely a function of the moral comportment of mind, and moral form is conveyed to the whole through the form of the operative maxims of conduct of thought. On the other hand, particularly as shown by the account of the second chapter detailing the relation of the strict and wide sense of character (the latter encompassing all the human aptitudes for good), it is clear that only all taken together constitute the complete account of character as concretely exhibited and expressed in the world.

Implicit in the preceding description of the purpose of horticultural grafting and included in its very definition (even used synonymously in the German for *pfropfen,* grafting) is the notion of *Veredelung,* typically translated as two distinct terms, "refinement" being used in reference to plants (and other things), "ennoblement" in reference to humans. In general, *Veredelung* is always a higher development, an institution of a higher order that is brought to bear on, or even substitute for, the basic form of a given thing. Kant's use of the term in connection with humanity's achievement of its moral vocation may now be seen as maintaining the analogy to grafting; the latter, in turn, also entails the meaning of elevation

---

8. Hartmann, Kester, and Davies, *Plant Propagation,* 332, 336.

(*Erhebung*) that is typically used by Kant when he speaks of going beyond sensibility (in ways that remain legitimate within the critical limits; for example see *KpV* 158; *KU* 353; *MST* 436, 483). As we have also seen in the course of our study, to teach what will ennoble conduct of thought was one of the leading principles of Enlightenment educators.

In this light, passages from various texts, from the *Anthropology* to the *Critique of Practical Reason* to the *Critique of Judgment,* may be understood as all pointing to this singular human work depicted in terms of the gardener's art. Individuals "endowed with a moral aptitude," even if they are "only at the stage of subordination to discipline (civil constraint)," through the "consciousness" of these laws as ones they would "give to themselves, feel ennobled (*veredelt*), namely belonging to a species commensurate with the vocation of humanity as reason presents it to them in an ideal" form (*ApH* 329). The graft here has been physically put in place, and the citizen is aware of it and its benefits, even if its consummation has not been realized. Indeed, even those who are still far from allowing the "concept of virtue" to "influence their maxims" "feel themselves to be to a certain degree ennobled even just through the idea" (*RV* 183). In the relation of the beautiful and the morally good, observes Kant, our "mind is conscious of a certain ennoblement and elevation above the mere receptivity for pleasure" derived from "sense impressions" (*KU* 353). Again, when we "contemplate with respect [nature's] immensity, we feel ourselves ennobled in this contemplation" (*KU* 380). In these aesthetic perceptions we, in effect, enjoy a foretaste of the state to which we are raised by the completed graft. In the second *Critique,* Kant spells out how such a union must be brought about: the law shall give the form of supersensible nature to sensible nature, without disrupting the operation of its laws (*KpV* 43). Such a combination that elevates without undermining its constituent parts is just what is achieved in grafting.

The image of character as a grafted entity, in other words, captures how morality, anthropology, and reflective judgment are linked in Kant's critical conception of character. This point may be clarified by following out the parallel in terms of the conditions that must obtain if a graft is to be successful. The first requisite is that the stock and scion be compatible. There "is no definite rule that can predict exactly the ultimate outcome of a particular graft combination except that *the more closely the plants are related botanically, the better the chances are for the graft union to be successful.*"[9] Noteworthy here is the inherent uncertainty in the process; what

---

9. Hartmann, Kester, and Davies, *Plant Propagation,* 349, 324–25.

lies within human control is ascertaining and providing those conditions most conducive to the development of the process to its hoped-for end. What we can claim to know is essentially negatively formulated: we know that in the absence of certain conditions the graft will fail, but in their presence we can at most *hope* for success. In the ancient philosophical account, as reported by Aristotle, a similar first condition is identified: "all things which admit of combination must be capable of reciprocal contact," and according to some (such as Empedocles), "combination takes place only between bodies whose pores are in reciprocal symmetry."[10]

Against this background, the full moral consequence of Kant's inquiry into the possible cooperation of the laws of nature and of freedom, first in the third antinomy and again in terms of the notion of purposiveness, comes to the fore. Without a basis for presuming the world to be essentially suited for realizing reason's interests, the work of procuring a character as a grafted entity would be doomed. It is the necessary (albeit not sufficient) condition for producing character within the "system of living nature." Thus, already in the *Critique of Pure Reason*, Kant writes that "moral purposive unity is necessary and has its basis in the essence of the power of choice itself. Hence natural purposive unity, which contains the condition of the moral unity's application *in concreto*, must likewise be necessary" (*KrV* A817/B845). It is the work of the *Critique of Judgment*, of course, to expound on the subjective principle of reflective (teleological) judgment that allows us to presuppose such "natural purposive unity," to presuppose the condition of the possibility of human final purpose in nature, specifically "in the nature of the subject as a sensible being, namely as a human being" (*KU* 195–96).

The second and third requirements, without which a graft cannot be successful, are related. "Intimate contact" must be made between scion and stock, and it "must be done at a time when the stock and scion are in the proper physiological stage."[11] To a certain extent, "intimate contact" is provided for in the very constitution of human beings as rationally endowed natural beings with such capacities as moral feeling and conscience. To put it in Kant's more general terms, it is provided for in the aptitudes and rudiments (*Anlagen* and *Keime*) intimately present to one another in each individual's human nature. However, as we have also seen, the pedagogical process complete with propaedeutic functions that prepare and develop these aptitudes, even initially awakening them to a state of moral

---

10. Aristotle, *Generation and Corruption*, 322b28, 324b31ff.
11. Hartmann, Kester, and Davies, *Plant Propagation*, 349–50.

responsiveness, is deemed by Kant to be essential. Without, for example, the discipline that tames unruliness, the inclinations are certainly far from a "proper stage" for grafting the natural on the moral.

The fourth step calls for attending to the "environmental requirements" that must be met if the cell tissue constituting the graft is to develop; these include, above all, "protecting" the point of union "from desiccation."[12] It is further "essential that the two original graft components be held together firmly . . . so that the parts will not move about and dislodge the interlocking . . . cells after proliferation has begun."[13] The fifth (and final step) specifies that "proper care must be given the grafts for a period of time after grafting," including providing support for vigorous growth and removing wild shoots that appear from below the graft union.[14] In regard to all of these, the parallel here points (among other things) to the role in particular of the republican constitution in the formation of character. As the reign and legal enforcement of the principle of justice, it provides the requisite environment, especially the stability that is afforded by conditions of peace. It is a powerful check against wild shoots that might emerge and is in itself an antidote to the sorrow inimical to morality, which latter could literally threaten to dry up a budding moral character. For Kant, as we have seen, it is the quintessential source of the support that the citizens of a state need for their efforts to forge the "inner formation of their *Denkungsart.*"

The latter brings us to our final point of parallel, one already alluded to: the lack of a guarantee as to success and, related thereto, the placement of the ultimate agency in the process. "In the healing of a graft union, the parts of the graft that are originally prepared and placed in close contact do not themselves move about or grow together. The union is accomplished by cells that develop *after* the actual grafting operation has been made."[15] In other words, the formation of the actual union is ultimately the work of the plant, of its inherent biological processes, which it may or may not bring to fruition under the conditions provided by the horticulturalist. Something new is generated that goes beyond the skills of cultivation; only the plant can produce the unifying tissue through which will flow the "lifeblood" of the new entity. This imagery helps us better comprehend Kant's point that, however many external agencies are involved (nature, parents, teacher, philosopher, constitution) on the behalf of human moral

---

12. Hartmann, Kester, and Davies, *Plant Propagation,* 320, 350.
13. Hartmann, Kester, and Davies, *Plant Propagation,* 315.
14. Hartmann, Kester, and Davies, *Plant Propagation,* 350.
15. Hartmann, Kester, and Davies, *Plant Propagation,* 312.

purpose, individual freedom is not jeopardized. The others' efforts of discipline and cultivation stop short of the indispensable act of formation; they can only prepare the human capacities to be "responsive to higher purposes than nature herself can deliver" (*KU* 433). "New cells" must be generated, the constitution of the individual's human power of choice as a *free* power of choice and the resolve that is the *conditio sine qua non* for the enduring form and stability of the entity effected by the union. This generation, this unifying act of formation that transforms "intimate contact" into a singular whole, is left to each individual to undertake. Moreover, the result of a graft does not propagate itself; another plant like it can only be produced from a new graft, consciously cultivated and formed in the same way. Likewise, moral character is not hereditary; only the bare aptitudes therefor, which include the "elements necessary" for the very "possibility of human nature" as well as the "forms of their connection" needed for "such a being," are "originally" provided (*RV* 28). Thus endowed, the progeny of the wise may still not prove to be an honor to his family name.

In sum, the pedagogical art (*Erziehungskunst oder Pädagogik, P* 447) in fact shares many aspects of the horticultural art of grafting. It is done in the face of the fact that, "as anyone experienced in grafting or budding knows, the results are often inconsistent, an excellent percentage of 'takes' occurring in some operations, whereas in others the results are disappointing."[16] Even when a graft *seems* initially successful, at a later date the appearance of wild growth, or even an outright break at the point of union, proves otherwise. As Kant so often noted, it is the negative evidence that is most certain; it clearly indicates when and where the revolution in conduct of thought has not been made. The risks notwithstanding, the horticultural art has persisted for millennia, with human gardeners continuing to find their products well worth the effort; the disappointments have, in the praxis of this art, never become an excuse to resort to something like the naysaying of the skeptical empiricist or the political moralist in regard to the human moral endeavor. In the face of such an example of human persistence when only pleasure and usefulness are at issue, it is easy to be sympathetic to Kant's finding naysaying intolerable in a matter in which nothing less than ultimate human worth and dignity is at stake. Precisely by casting humanity's highest endeavor as a moral *task* of producing the concrete counterimage of reason's idea, an exhortation founded on his

16. Hartmann, Kester, and Davies, *Plant Propagation,* 319.

critical, transcendental inquiry into the conditions of the possibility of its attainment and on an articulation in his anthropological and historical writings of what those conditions consist in, Kant has sustained throughout his corpus the effort of "putting an end, for all future time, to all objections against lived morality and religion" (*KrV* Bxxxi). His conception of moral character in its full complexity is his complete argument against the skeptical inference from historical events to the denial of reason's function in giving direction to human life. Subjectively considered, morality conceived in terms of rational principles and ideas and the rationality of concrete, human historical life is indeed not simply a given in the latter's experience, as so many of our nineteenth- and twentieth-century authors have maintained. Kant is the first to admit this, but also at once concerned to show how and why one is not, on such historical grounds at least, forced to cast about for an alternative to rational determination and direction of human life (such as we have seen, for example, proposed in the form of economic, physiological, and neurological accounts).[17]

17. Any number of authors might be referred to as examples of the orientation that thinking did take in the centuries after Kant. Just for the sake of illustration, consider the following statements made by C. G. Jung: "But we *know* that there is no human foresight or wisdom that can prescribe direction to our life, except for small stretches of the way" (emphasis added). "But has it ever been shown, or will it ever be, that life and fate are in accord with reason, that they too are rational? We have on the contrary good grounds for supposing that they are irrational, or rather that in the last resort they are grounded beyond human reason. . . . Hence reason and will that is grounded in reason are valid only up to a point. The further we go in the direction selected by reason, the surer we may be that we are excluding the irrational possibilities of life which have just as much right to be lived. . . . It may justly be maintained that the acquisition of reason is the greatest achievement of humanity; but that is not to say that things must or will always continue in that direction. The frightful catastrophe of the first World War drew a very thick line through the calculations of even the most optimistic rationalizers of culture" ("On the Psychology of the Unconscious," in *Two Essays on Analytical Psychology*, trans. R. F. C. Hull [Princeton: Princeton University Press, 1966], 48–49). The worry that "irrational possibilities" are being denied their "right to live" is, of course, characteristic of much of anti-Enlightenment sentiment, but do these include just those "frightful catastrophes" that are also being appealed to as evidence that reason does not ultimately provide direction for life? The interpretation we are presenting of Kant's account of character agrees in fact with the point that it "is not to say that things must or will always continue in that direction." For, the point is precisely that the rational, moral order of human life depends upon the degree that individuals concretely actualize it in their lives (each separately and collectively as nations in the form of a republican constitution)—that they adopt the very task as a maxim of their thought and action. Kant maintained that the inherent aptitude for moral progress had made itself manifest in the spectators of the French Revolution, but also admitted that it could be covered over (so to speak) for an unspecifiable period of time by a regress of events. It is further noteworthy that in the modern authors (for example a Nietzsche, Marx, or Jung), the denial of reason's function in the direction of human

The gardener's art exemplifies production, generation, formation that results from human ideas giving direction to natural processes. Its products are *not against* nature, but they are also not simply works *of* nature. They remain *human works of art*, works nature of its own accord would not produce and which are thus not possible without the intervention of human rational direction. But equally, they are works not possible without the employment of the natural operations. Thus this art serves so well as an image in terms of which to comprehend the procurement of moral character in relation to living nature, technically articulated in terms of intelligible causality availing itself of empirical causality. As we previously concluded, such procurement of character is the human work of art par excellence. A "production through freedom, that is through a power of choice that bases its acts on reason" (*KU* 303), it is the work specific to human beings, the effect we are obligated to bring forth in relation to nature as a result of our own act, our formative activity that is peculiar to us as rational beings. The realization of moral character is thus the primary instance of the relation of nature and freedom.

In the final analysis, then, the successful formation of character is an ontological achievement. As articulated by Kant, it does bear the hallmarks of an eighteenth-century comprehension of metaphysics and of the human in nature, but without resorting either to naturalism or to skepticism. In his complete development of his conception of character, Kant remains true to his conclusion in 1766 that metaphysics must be brought from the heights back to earth and that it must serve the common good (*Gemeinnützigkeit*). Such a metaphysics is a moral metaphysics, meaning that reason's ideas are given a practical interpretation. Through the account of moral character we can fully appreciate what is entailed, for Kant, by thus construing reason's ideas as a moral task. The form of good is not a given, neither metaphysically nor by nature, but it is a moral form to be achieved, brought about, by the human working on and with nature, specifically the natural human aptitudes. In light of such a conception of moral character as the concrete realization of reason's idea, understood as a kind of grafted entity, the closing lines of *Candide*, paraphrased by Kant

---

life is juxtaposed with the view of the human as the "herd animal." Using Jung again as the example, "morality" is now conceived as "the instinctive regulator of action which also governs the collective life of the herd" (27). Some might argue that giving up the sense of human dignity embraced by Kant is acceptable or even in accord with physiological data. It is hoped that the richer comprehension of Kant's moral thought afforded by the analysis of his conception of character might afford a basis for reconsidering that view.

as his own "practical conclusion" to his *Dreams of a Spirit-Seer*, gain new urgency: "We must cultivate our garden."[18]

18. Kant expresses it as follows: "Let us seek our fortune, go to the garden and work" (*TG* 373). The closing lines of *Candide* read as follows, beginning with the arrival of Candide, Pangloss, and Martin at the Turk's house:

> "I have only twenty acres," replied the Turk; "I cultivate (*cultive*) them with my children; work keeps away from us three great evils: boredom, vice, and need."
>
> As Candide returned to his farm, he reflected deeply on the Turk's observations . . . "I also know," said Candide, "that we must cultivate our garden." — "You are right," said Pangloss; "for when man was put into the Garden of Eden, he was put there *ut operaretur eum*, to work; which proves that man was not born for rest." — "Let us work without arguing (*Travaillons sans raisonner*)," said Martin; "it's the only way to make life endurable."
>
> The whole little society entered into this praiseworthy plan; *each started to exercise his talents* [emphasis added]. The little property produced much. . . . Pangloss sometimes said to Candide: "All events are linked in the best possible worlds; for, after all, if you had not been expelled . . . you would not be here eating candied citrons and pistachios." — "That is well said," replied Candide, "but we must cultivate our garden (*mais il faut cultiver notre jardin*)."

Voltaire, *Candide; or, Optimism*, trans. Peter Gay (New York: St. Martin's Press, 1963), 295–99.

BIBLIOGRAPHY

Kant's texts are cited from the standard German edition, *Kants gesammelte Schriften*. For a list of Kant's works cited, see the list of abbreviations at the beginning of this volume.

TRANSLATIONS OF KANT'S WORKS CONSULTED

The following English translations have been consulted; unless otherwise indicated, translations are my own.

The Cambridge Edition of the Works of Immanuel Kant: Theoretical Philosophy, 1755–1770. Trans. David Walford and Ralf Meerbote. New York: Cambridge University Press, 1992.

The Conflict of the Faculties. Trans. Mary J. Gregor. New York: Abaris Books, 1979.

Critique of Judgment. Trans. Werner S. Pluhar. Indianapolis: Hackett, 1987.

Critique of Practical Reason. Trans. Lewis White Beck. New York: Macmillan, 1993.

Critique of Pure Reason. Trans. Werner S. Pluhar. Indianapolis: Hackett, 1996.

Ethical Philosophy. Trans. James W. Ellington. Indianapolis: Hackett, 1983.

Foundations of the Metaphysics of Morals. Trans. Lewis White Beck. Indianapolis: Bobbs-Merrill Educational Publishing, 1959.

Kant's Latin Writings: Translations, Commentaries, and Notes. Trans. Lewis White Beck et al. New York: Peter Lang, 1986.

Lectures on Ethics. Trans. Louis Infield. 1930. Reprint, Indianapolis: Hackett, 1963.

Prolegomena to Any Future Metaphysics. Trans. Paul Carus. Rev. James W. Ellington. Indianapolis: Hackett, 1985.

WORKS CITED

Ajzenstat, Samuel. "Kant on Education and the Impotence of Reason." In *Education in the 18th Century,* ed. J. D. Browning, 25–43. New York: Garland, 1979.

Albrecht, Michael. "Kants Maximenethik und ihre Begründung." *Kant-Studien* 85 (1994): 129–46.

Allison, Henry E. *Idealism and Freedom: Essays on Kant's Theoretical and Practical Philosophy.* New York: Cambridge University Press, 1996.

———. "Kant on Freedom: A Reply to My Critics." In *Idealism and Freedom: Essays on Kant's Theoretical and Practical Philosophy.* New York: Cambridge University Press, 1996.

————. *Kant's Theory of Freedom.* New York: Cambridge University Press, 1990.

————. *Kant's Transcendental Idealism: An Interpretation and Defense.* New Haven: Yale University Press, 1983.

Ameriks, Karl. "Kant on the Good Will." In *Grundlegung zur Metaphysik der Sitten. Ein kooperativer Kommentar,* ed. Otfried Höffe, 45–65. Frankfurt am Main: Vittorio Klostermann, 1989.

Ameriks, Karl, and Dieter Sturma, eds. *The Modern Subject: Conceptions of the Self in Classical German Philosophy.* Albany: State University of New York Press, 1995.

Anderson-Gold, Sharon. "God and Community: An Inquiry into the Religious Implications of the Highest Good." In *Kant's Philosophy of Religion Reconsidered,* ed. Philip J. Rossi and Michael Wren, 112–31. Bloomington: Indiana University Press, 1991.

Apel, Karl-Otto. *Towards a Transformation of Philosophy.* Trans. Glyn Adey and David Frisby. London: Routledge and Kegan Paul, 1980. Originally published as *Transformation der Philosophie.* Frankfurt am Main: Suhrkamp, 1972.

Arendt, Hannah. *Between Past and Future.* New York: Penguin Books, 1977.

————. *Eichmann in Jerusalem: A Report on the Banality of Evil.* New York: Penguin Books, 1964.

————. *The Human Condition.* Chicago: University of Chicago Press, 1958.

————. *Lectures on Kant's Political Philosophy.* Ed. Ronald Beiner. Chicago: University of Chicago Press, 1982.

————. *The Life of the Mind.* New York: Harcourt Brace Jovanovich, 1978.

————. "Thinking and Moral Considerations: A Lecture." *Social Research* 38 (1971): 417–46.

Aristotle. *Nicomachean Ethics.* Trans. Martin Ostwald. New York: Macmillan, 1962.

————. *On Generation and Corruption.* Trans. H. H. Joachim. In *The Complete Works of Aristotle,* ed. Jonathan Barnes. 2 vols. Princeton: Princeton University Press, 1984.

————. *The Politics.* Trans. T. A. Sinclair. New York: Penguin Books, 1981.

Arnauld, Antoine. *The Art of Thinking: Port-Royal Logic.* Trans. James Dickoff and Patricia James. Indianapolis: Library of Liberal Arts, 1964.

Atwell, John E. *Ends and Principles in Kant's Moral Thought.* Dordrecht: Martinus Nijhoff, 1986.

Axtell, James L. *The Educational Writings of John Locke.* London: Cambridge University Press, 1968.

Baron, Marcia W. *Kantian Ethics Almost without Apology.* Ithaca: Cornell University Press, 1995.

Beck, Hamilton. "Kant and the Novel: A Study of the Examination Scene in Hippel's 'Lebensläufe nach aufsteigender Linie.'" *Kant-Studien* 74 (1983): 271–301.

Beck, Lewis White. *The Actor and the Spectator.* New Haven: Yale University Press, 1975.

————. *A Commentary on Kant's "Critique of Practical Reason."* Chicago: University of Chicago Press, 1960.

————. *Early German Philosophy: Kant and His Predecessors.* Cambridge: Harvard University Press, 1969.

————. "The Fact of Reason: An Essay on Justification in Ethics. Internal and External Questions." In *Studies in the Philosophy of Kant,* ed. Lewis White Beck, 200–214. Indianapolis: Bobbs-Merrill, 1965.

———. "Kant and His Predecessors." In *Critique of Practical Reason and Other Writings in Moral Philosophy.* Chicago: University of Chicago Press, 1949.

———. "Kant on Education." In *Education in the 18th Century,* ed. J. D. Browning, 10–24. New York: Garland, 1979.

———. "Kant's Theoretical and Practical Philosophy." In *Studies in the Philosophy of Kant,* ed. Lewis White Beck, 3–53. Indianapolis: Bobbs-Merrill, 1965.

———., ed. *Studies in the Philosophy of Kant.* Indianapolis: Bobbs-Merrill, 1965.

Beiner, Ronald. "Kant, the Sublime, and Nature." In *Kant and Political Philosophy: The Contemporary Legacy,* ed. Ronald Beiner and William James Booth, 276–88. New Haven: Yale University Press, 1993.

———. *Political Judgment.* Chicago: University of Chicago Press, 1983.

Beiner, Ronald, and William James Booth, eds. *Kant and Political Philosophy: The Contemporary Legacy.* New Haven: Yale University Press, 1993.

Beiser, Frederick C. "Kant's Intellectual Development." In *The Cambridge Companion to Kant,* ed. Paul Guyer, 26–61. New York: Cambridge University Press, 1992.

Benhabib, Seyla. "Judgment and the Moral Foundations of Politics in Arendt's Thought." *Political Theory* 16 (1988): 29–51.

Bernstein, Richard J. *Beyond Objectivism and Relativism.* Philadelphia: University of Pennsylvania Press, 1983.

Birtsch, Günter. "Die Berliner Mittwochgesellschaft." Trans. Arthur Hirsch. In *What Is Enlightenment? Eighteenth-Century Answers and Twentieth-Century Questions,* ed. James Schmidt, 235–52. Berkeley and Los Angeles: University of California Press, 1996.

Boethius, Anicius Manlius Severinus. *The Consolation of Philosophy.* Trans. V. E. Watts. New York: Penguin Books, 1984.

Booth, William James. *Interpreting the World: Kant's Philosophy of History and Politics.* Toronto: University of Toronto Press, 1986.

Bradshaw, Leah. *The Political Thought of Hannah Arendt.* Toronto: University of Toronto Press, 1989.

Brandt, Reinhard. "Kants Anthropologie: Die Idee des Werks und die Bestimmung des Menschen." Paper presented at the Central Division meeting of the American Philosophical Association, Pittsburgh, April 1997.

———. *The Table of Judgments: "Critique of Pure Reason" A67–76; B91–101.* Vol. 4 of *North American Kant Society Studies in Philosophy.* Trans. and ed. Eric Watkins. Atascadero: Ridgeview, 1995.

Brandt, Reinhard, and Werner Stark. Introduction to *Kant's Vorlesungen über Anthropologie.* Vol. 25, bk. 2.1 of *Kant's gesammelte Schriften.* Berlin: Walter de Gruyter, 1997.

Bridgman, Annette. Introduction to *Education in the 18th Century.* Ed. J. D. Browning. New York: Garland, 1979.

Browning, J. D., ed. *Education in the 18th Century.* New York: Garland, 1979.

Buchdahl, Gerd. "The Relation between 'Understanding' and 'Reason' in the Architectonic of Kant's Philosophy." In *Kant's Critique of Judgment.* Vol. 4, *Immanuel Kant: Critical Assessments,* ed. Ruth F. Chadwick and Clive Cazeaux, 39–53. New York: Routledge, 1992.

Callahan, Daniel, ed. *The Roots of Ethics.* New York: Plenum Press, 1976.

Canovan, Margaret. *Hannah Arendt: A Reinterpretation of Her Political Thought.* New York: Cambridge University Press, 1991.

Carnois, Bernard. *The Coherence of Kant's Doctrine of Freedom.* Trans. David Booth. Chicago: University of Chicago Press, 1987.

Cassirer, Ernst. *Kant's Life and Thought.* Trans. James Haden. New Haven: Yale University Press, 1981. Originally published as *Kants Leben und Lehre.* 1918. Reprint, Darmstadt: Wissenschaftliche Buchgesellschaft, 1977.

Cavell, Stanley. *The Claim of Reason.* Oxford: Clarendon Press, 1979.

Caygill, Howard. *Art of Judgment.* Cambridge: Basil Blackwell, 1989.

Chadwick, Ruth F., and Clive Cazeaux, eds. *Kant's "Critique of Judgment."* Vol. 4, *Immanuel Kant: Critical Assessments.* New York: Routledge, 1992.

Crittenden, P. J. "Kant as Educationist." *Philosophical Studies* 31 (1986–87): 11–32.

Davidovich, Adina. "How to Read 'Religion within the Limits of Reason Alone.'" *Kant-Studien* 85 (1994): 1–14.

Defoe, Daniel. *Robinson Crusoe.* Ed. Michael Shinagel. New York: W. W. Norton, 1994.

Denneny, Michael. "The Privilege of Ourselves: Hannah Arendt on Judgment." In *Hannah Arendt: The Recovery of the Public World,* ed. Melvyn A. Hill, 245–74. New York: St. Martin's Press, 1979.

Devereux, Daniel T. "Socrates' Kantian Conception of Virtue." *Journal of the History of Philosophy* 33 (1995): 381–408.

Dostal, Robert J. "Judging Human Action: Arendt's Appropriation of Kant." *Review of Metaphysics* 148 (1984): 725–55.

Düsing, Klaus. "Das Problem des höchsten Gutes in Kants praktischer Philosophie." *Kant-Studien* 62 (1971): 5–42.

———. "Der Übergang von der Natur zur Freiheit und die ästhetische Bildung bei Kant." In *Humanität und Bildung,* ed. Johannes Schurr, Karl Heinz Broecken, and Renate Broecken, 87–100. Hildesheim: Georg Olms Verlag, 1988.

Ebbinghaus, J. "Kants Ableitung des Verbotes der Lüge aus dem Rechte der Menschheit." *Revue Internationale de Philosophie* 8 (1954): 409–22.

Engelhardt, Paulus, ed. *Sein und Ethos. Untersuchungen zur Grundlegung der Ethik.* Mainz: Matthias-Grünewald Verlag, 1963.

Engstrom, Stephen. "The Concept of the Highest Good in Kant's Moral Theory." *Philosophy and Phenomenological Research* 4 (1992): 747–80.

———. "Kant's Conception of Practical Wisdom." *Kant-Studien* 88 (1997): 16–43.

Engstrom, Stephen, and Jennifer Whiting, eds. *Aristotle, Kant, and the Stoics: Rethinking Happiness and Duty.* New York: Cambridge University Press, 1996.

Esser, Andrea, ed. *Autonomie der Kunst? Zur Aktualität von Kants Ästhetik.* Berlin: Akademie Verlag, 1995.

Fenves, Peter D. *A Peculiar Fate: Metaphysics and World History in Kant.* Ithaca: Cornell University Press, 1991.

Flanagan, Owen, and Amélie Oksenberg Rorty, eds. *Identity, Character, and Morality: Essays in Moral Psychology.* Cambridge: MIT Press, 1990.

Flynn, Bernard. "Arendt's Appropriation of Kant's Theory of Judgment." *Journal of the British Society for Phenomenology* 19 (1988): 128–40.

Forschner, Maximilian. "Synthesis und Handlung bei Aristoteles und Kant." In *Hand-*

lungstheorie und Transzendentalphilosophie, ed. Gerold Prauss, 82–97. Frankfurt am Main: Vittorio Klostermann, 1986.

Foucault, Michel. *The Foucault Reader*. Ed. Paul Rabinow. New York: Pantheon Books, 1984.

Frank, Manfred. *Einführung in die frühromantische Ästhetik*. Frankfurt am Main: Suhrkamp, 1989.

Frankena, William K. *Three Historical Philosophies of Education: Aristotle, Kant, Dewey*. Chicago: Scott, Foresman, 1965.

Fricke, Christel. *Kants Theorie des reinen Geschmacksurteils*. Berlin: Walter de Gruyter, 1990.

Fricke, Christel, Peter König, and Thomas Petersen, eds. *Das Recht der Vernunft. Kant und Hegel über Denken, Erkennen und Handeln*. Vol. 37 of Spekulation und Erfahrung. Texte und Untersuchungen zum Deutschen Idealismus. Stuttgart-Bad Cannstatt: Frommann-Holzboog, 1995.

Friedman, Michael. *Kant and the Exact Sciences*. Cambridge: Harvard University Press, 1992.

Funke, Gerhard. "Pädagogik im Sinne Kants heute." In *Kant und die Pädagogik. Pädagogik und praktische Philosophie*, ed. Jürgen-Eckardt Pleines, 99–109. Würzburg: Königshausen und Neumann, 1985.

———, ed. *Akten des Siebenten Internationalen Kant-Kongresses*. Bonn: Bouvier, 1991.

Gay, Peter, ed. *The Enlightenment: A Comprehensive Anthology*. New York: Simon and Schuster, 1973.

———. Introduction to *John Locke on Education*. New York: Bureau of Publications, Teachers College, Columbia University, 1964.

Geismann, Georg, and Hariolf Oberer. *Kant und das Recht der Lüge*. Würzburg: Königshausen und Neumann, 1986.

Gerhardt, Volker. "The Abdication of Philosophy: On the Modernity of the Relation between Philosophy and Politics in Kant." Trans. Joel Golb. *Idealistic Studies* 26 (1990): 175–88.

———. "Handlung als Verhältnis von Ursache und Wirkung. Zur Entwicklung des Handlungsbegriff bei Kant." In *Handlungstheorie und Transzendentalphilosophie*, ed. Gerold Prauss, 98–131. Frankfurt am Main: Vittorio Klostermann, 1986.

———. *Immanuel Kants Entwurf "Zum Ewigen Frieden" Eine Theorie der Politik*. Darmstadt: Wissenschaftliche Buchgesellschaft, 1995.

———. "Kants Kopernikanische Wende," *Kant-Studien* 78 (1987): 133–52.

———. "Vernunft und Urteilskraft: Politische Philosophie und Anthropologie im Anschluss an Immanuel Kant und Hannah Arendt." In *John Locke und Immanuel Kant. Historische Rezeption und gegenwärtige Relevanz*, ed. Martyn P. Thompson, 316–33. Berlin: Duncker und Humblot, 1991.

Gibbard, Allan. *Wise Choices, Apt Feelings: A Theory of Normative Judgment*. Cambridge: Harvard University Press, 1990.

Giel, Klaus, and Renate Breuninger, eds. *Wissenschaftsethik unter philosophischen Aspekten*. Ulm: Humboldt-Studienzentrum, 1991.

Gilligan, Carol. *In a Different Voice: Psychological Theory and Women's Development*. Cambridge: Harvard University Press, 1982.

Goethe, Johann Wolfgang von. *Faust. Eine Tragödie*. Vol. 3 of *Goethes Werke*. Ed. Erich Trunz. 14 vols. Munich: C. H. Beck, 1981.

————. *Wilhelm Meisters Wanderjahre*. Vol. 8 of *Goethes Werke*. Ed. Erich Trunz. 14 vols. Munich: C. H. Beck, 1982.

Goicoechea, David, and John Luik, eds. *The Question of Humanism*. New York: Prometheus Books, 1991.

Gram, Moltke S., ed. *Interpreting Kant*. Iowa City: University of Iowa Press, 1982.

Grant, George Parkin. *English-Speaking Justice*. Notre Dame: University of Notre Dame Press, 1985.

Green, Ronald M. "The First Formulation of the Categorical Imperative as Literally a 'Legislative' Metaphor." *History of Philosophy Quarterly* 8 (1991): 163–79.

————. *Kierkegaard and Kant: The Hidden Debt*. Albany: State University of New York Press, 1992.

Grimm, Wilhelm, and Jacob Grimm, eds. *Deutsches Wörterbuch*. 16 vols. Leipzig: S. Hirzel, 1860. Reprint, 33 vols., Munich: Deutscher Taschenbuch Verlag, 1991.

Guyer, Paul. *Kant and the Experience of Freedom: Essays on Aesthetics and Morality*. Cambridge: Cambridge University Press, 1993.

————, ed. *The Cambridge Companion to Kant*. New York: Cambridge University Press, 1992.

Hare, John E. *The Moral Gap: Kantian Ethics, Human Limits, and God's Assistance*. Oxford: Clarendon Press, 1996.

Hartmann, Hudson T., Dale E. Kester, and Fred T. Davies. *Plant Propagation: Principles and Practices*. Englewood Cliffs, N.J.: Prentice-Hall, 1990.

Heimsoeth, Heinz. "Freiheit und Charakter. Nach den Kant-Reflexionen Nr. 5611 bis 5620." In *Kant. Zur Deutung seiner Theorie von Erkennen und Handeln*, ed. Gerold Prauss, 292–309. Cologne: Kiepenheuer und Witsch, 1973.

Hendel, Charles W. Foreword to *The Art of Thinking: Port-Royal Logic*. Trans. James Dickoff and Patricia James. Indianapolis: Library of Liberal Arts, 1964.

Henrich, Dieter. *Aesthetic Judgment and the Moral Image of the World*. Stanford Series in Philosophy. Studies in Kant and German Idealism. Stanford: Stanford University Press, 1992.

————. "Der Begriff der sittlichen Einsicht und Kants Lehre vom Faktum der Vernunft." In *Die Gegenwart der Griechen im neueren Denken*, ed. Dieter Henrich et al. Tübingen: J. C. B. Mohr, 1960. Trans. Manfred Kuehn as "The Concept of Moral Insight and Kant's Doctrine of the Fact of Reason." In *The Unity of Reason: Essays on Kant's Philosophy*, ed. Richard L. Velkley, 55–87. Cambridge: Harvard University Press, 1994.

————. "Ethics of Autonomy." Trans. Louis Hunt. In *The Unity of Reason: Essays on Kant's Philosophy*, ed. Richard L. Velkley, 89–121. Cambridge: Harvard University Press, 1994.

————. "On the Unity of Subjectivity." Trans. Guenter Zoeller. In *The Unity of Reason: Essays on Kant's Philosophy*, ed. Richard L. Velkley, 17–54. Cambridge: Harvard University Press, 1994.

————. "Das Problem der Grundlegung der Ethik bei Kant und im spekulativen Idealismus." In *Sein und Ethos. Untersuchungen zur Grundlegung der Ethik*, ed. Paulus Engelhardt, 350–86. Mainz: Matthias-Grünewald Verlag, 1963.

————. "Über Kants Entwicklungsgeschichte." *Philosophische Rundschau* (1966): 252–63.

————. "Über Kants früheste Ethik. Versuch einer Rekonstruktion." *Kant-Studien* (1963): 404–31.

————. *The Unity of Reason: Essays on Kant's Philosophy*. Ed. Richard L. Velkley. Cambridge: Harvard University Press, 1994.

————. "Zu Kants Begriff der Philosophie. Eine Edition und eine Fragestellung." In *Kritik und Metaphysik Studien*, ed. Friedrich Kaulbach and Joachim Ritter, 40–59. Berlin: Walter de Gruyter, 1966.

Henrich, Dieter, et al., eds. *Die Gegenwart der Griechen im neueren Denken*. Tübingen: J. C. B. Mohr, 1960.

Herman, Barbara. "Making Room for Character." In *Aristotle, Kant, and the Stoics: Rethinking Happiness and Duty*, ed. Stephen Engstrom and Jennifer Whiting, 36–60. New York: Cambridge University Press, 1996.

————. *The Practice of Moral Judgment*. Cambridge: Harvard University Press, 1993.

Hill, Melvyn A., ed. *Hannah Arendt: The Recovery of the Public World*. New York: St. Martin's Press, 1979.

Hiltscher, Reinhard. *Kant und das Problem der Einheit der endlichen Vernunft*. Würzburg: Königshausen und Neumann, 1987.

Hinske, Norbert. "Eklektik, Selbstdenken, Mündigkeit." *Aufklärung* 1 (1986): 5–7.

Höffe, Otfried. *Ethik und Politik. Grundmodelle und Probleme der praktischen Philosophie*. Frankfurt am Main: Suhrkamp, 1979.

————. "Grundbegriff Sittlichkeit." In *Ethik und Politik. Grundmodelle und Probleme der praktischen Philosophie*, 281–310. Frankfurt am Main: Suhrkamp, 1979.

————. *Grundlegung zur Metaphysik der Sitten. Ein kooperativer Kommentar*. Frankfurt am Main: Vittorio Klostermann, 1989.

————. *Immanuel Kant*. Trans. Marshall Farrier. Albany: State University of New York Press, 1994. Originally published as *Immanuel Kant*. Munich: C. H. Beck, 1983.

————. "Kants kategorischer Imperativ als Kriterium des Sittlichen." In *Ethik und Politik. Grundmodelle und Probleme der praktischen Philosophie*, 84–120. Frankfurt am Main: Suhrkamp, 1979.

————. "Eine republikanische Vernunft. Zur Kritik des Solipsismus-Vorwurfs." In *Kant in der Diskussion der Moderne*, ed. Gerhard Schönrich and Yasushi Kato, 396–497. Frankfurt am Main: Suhrkamp, 1996.

————. "Universalistische Ethik und Urteilskraft: Ein aristotelischer Blick auf Kant." *Zeitschrift für philosophische Forschung* 44 (1990): 537–63. Translated as "Univeralist Ethics and the Faculty of Judgment: An Aristotelian Look at Kant." *Philosophical Forum* 25 (1993): 55–71.

Horace. *Satires, Epistles, and Ars Poetica*. Trans. H. Rushton Fairclough. Loeb Classical Library, vol. 194. Cambridge: Harvard University Press, 1991.

Hösle, Vittorio. "The Greatness and Limits of Kant's Practical Philosophy." *Graduate Faculty Philosophy Journal* 13 (1990): 133–57. Also published as "Größe und Grenzen von Kants praktischer Philosophie." In *Wissenschaftsethik unter philosophischen Aspekten*, ed. Klaus Giel and Renate Breuninger, 9–39. Ulm: Humboldt-Studienzentrum, 1991.

————. *Hegels System. Der Idealismus der Subjektivität und das Problem der Intersubjektivität*. 2 vols. Hamburg: Felix Meiner Verlag, 1987.

————. *Die Krise der Gegenwart und die Verantwortung der Philosophie. Transzendentalpragmatik, Letztbegründung, Ethik*. Munich: C. H. Beck, 1990.

————. "Moralische Reflexion und Institutionenzerfall. Zur Dialektik von Aufklärung und Gegenaufklärung." In *Praktische Philosophie in der modernen Welt*, 46–58. Munich: C. H. Beck, 1992.

———. *Praktische Philosophie in der modernen Welt*. Munich: C. H. Beck, 1992.

Hufnagel, Erwin. "Kants pädagogische Theorie." *Kant-Studien* 79 (1988): 43–56.

Jackson, Michael W. "The Responsibility of Judgement and the Judgement of Responsibility." In *Hannah Arendt: Thinking, Judging, Freedom*, ed. Gisela T. Kaplan and Clive S. Kessler, 42–55. Sydney: Allen and Unwin, 1989.

Jaumann, Herbert, ed. *Rousseau in Deutschland. Neue Beiträge zur Erforschung seiner Rezeption*. Berlin: Walter de Gruyter, 1995.

Jonas, Hans. "Acting, Knowing, Thinking: Gleanings from Hannah Arendt's Philosophical Work." *Social Research* 44 (1977): 25–43.

———. *Das Prinzip Verantwortung. Versuch einer Ethik für die technologische Zivilisation*. Frankfurt am Main: Insel Verlag, 1979. Trans. Hans Jonas and David Herr as *The Imperative of Responsibility: Foundations of an Ethics for the Technological Age*. Chicago: University of Chicago Press, 1984.

Jordan, James N. "Socrates' Wisdom and Kant's Virtue." *Southwestern Journal of Philosophy* 4 (1973): 7–23.

Jung, C. G. *Two Essays on Analytical Psychology*. Trans. R. F. C. Hull. Princeton: Princeton University Press, 1966.

Kaplan, Gisela T., and Clive S. Kessler, eds. *Hannah Arendt: Thinking, Judging, Freedom*. Sydney: Allen and Unwin, 1989.

Kaulbach, Friedrich. *Immanuel Kants "Grundlegung zur Metaphysik der Sitten."* Darmstadt: Wissenschaftliche Buchgesellschaft, 1988.

———. "Weltorientierung, Weltkenntnis, und pragmatische Vernunft bei Kant." In *Kritik und Metaphysik Studien*, ed. Friedrich Kaulbach and Joachim Ritter, 60–75. Berlin: Walter de Gruyter, 1966.

Kaulbach, Friedrich, and Joachim Ritter, eds. *Kritik und Metaphysik Studien*. Berlin: Walter de Gruyter, 1966.

Kennington, Richard, ed. *The Philosophy of Immanuel Kant*. Washington, D.C.: Catholic University of America Press, 1985.

Kesselring, Thomas. "In welchem Sinne gibt es eine Moralentwicklung?" In *Wissenschaftsethik unter philosophischen Aspekten*, ed. Klaus Giel and Renate Breuninger, 41–84. Ulm: Humboldt-Studienzentrum, 1991.

Klein, Ernst Ferdinand. "On Freedom of Thought and of the Press: For Princes, Ministers, and Writers." Trans. John Christian Laursen. In *What Is Enlightenment? Eighteenth-Century Answers and Twentieth-Century Questions*, ed. James Schmidt, 87–96. Berkeley and Los Angeles: University of California Press, 1996.

Kleingeld, Pauline. *Fortschritt und Vernunft: Zur Geschichtsphilosophie Kants*. Würzburg: Königshausen und Neumann, 1995.

Klemme, Heiner F. *Die Schule Immanuel Kants. Mit dem Text von Christian Schiffert über das Königsberger Collegium Fridericianum*. Vol. 6, *Kant-Forschungen*. Ed. Reinhard Brandt and Werner Stark. Hamburg: Felix Meiner Verlag, 1994.

Knauer, James T. "Hannah Arendt on Judgment, Philosophy, and Praxis." *International Studies in Philosophy* 21 (1989): 71–83.

Kneller, Jane. "The Interests of Disinterest." In *Proceedings of the Eighth International Kant Congress*, ed. Hoke Robinson, vol. 1, pt. 2, 777–86. Milwaukee: Marquette University Press, 1995.

Köhl, Harald. *Kants Gesinnungsethik.* Berlin: Walter de Gruyter, 1990.

Kohlberg, Lawrence. *The Philosophy of Moral Development: Moral Stages and the Idea of Justice.* San Francisco: Harper and Row, 1981.

Kohn, Jerome. "Thinking/Acting." *Social Research* 57 (1990): 105–34.

Kohnen, Joseph. *Theodor Gottlieb von Hippel. Eine zentrale Persönlichkeit der Königsberger Geistesgeschichte. Biographie und Bibliographie.* Lüneburg: Nordostdeutsches Kulturwerk, 1987.

Konhardt, Klaus. "Faktum der Vernunft? Zu Kants Frage nach dem 'eigentlichen Selbst' des Menschen." In *Handlungstheorie und Transzendentalphilosophie,* ed. Gerold Prauss, 160–84. Frankfurt am Main: Vittorio Klostermann, 1986.

Koppers, Rita. *Zum Begriff des Bösens bei Kant.* Pfaffenweiler: Centaurs Verlagsgesellschaft, 1986.

Korsgaard, Christine. "Aristotle and Kant on the Source of Value." *Ethics* 96 (1986): 486–505.

———. "The Right to Lie: Kant on Dealing with Evil." *Philosophy and Public Affairs* 15 (1986): 325–49.

Kramling, Gerhard. "Das höchste Gut als mögliche Welt." *Kant-Studien* 77 (1986): 273–88.

Krasnoff, Larry. "The Fact of Politics: History and Teleology in Kant." *European Journal of Philosophy* 2 (1994): 22–40.

Kuehn, Manfred. "The Moral Dimension of Kant's *Inaugural Dissertation:* A New Perspective on the 'Great Light of 1769'?" In *Proceedings of the Eighth International Kant Congress,* ed. Hoke Robinson, vol. 1, pt. 2, 373–92. Milwaukee: Marquette University Press, 1995.

Kulenkampff, Jens. "'Vom Geschmacke als einer Art von sensus communis'—Versuch einer Neubestimmung des Geschmacksurteils." In *Autonomie der Kunst? Zur Aktualität von Kants Ästhetik,* ed. Andrea Esser, 25–48. Berlin: Akademie Verlag, 1995.

Kupperman, Joel J. *Character.* Oxford: Oxford University Press, 1991.

Kutschera, Franz von. *Vernunft und Glaube.* Berlin: Walter de Gruyter, 1990.

Langthaler, Rudolf. *Kants Ethik als "System der Zwecke." Perspektiven einer modifizierten Idee der "moralischen Teleologie" und Ethikotheologie.* Kant-Studien Ergänzungshefte. Berlin: Walter de Gruyter, 1991.

Laursen, John Christian. *The Politics of Skepticism in the Ancients, Montaigne, Hume, and Kant.* New York: E. J. Brill, 1992.

———. "The Subversive Kant: The Vocabulary of 'Public' and 'Publicity.'" In *The Politics of Skepticism in the Ancients, Montaigne, Hume, and Kant.* New York: E. J. Brill, 1992.

Locke, John. *John Locke on Education.* Ed. Peter Gay. New York: Bureau of Publications, Teachers College, Columbia University, 1964.

Lucas, George. "Agency after Virtue." *International Philosophical Quarterly* 28 (1988): 293–311.

———. "Moral Order and the Constraints of Agency: Toward a New Metaphysics of Morals." In *New Essays in Metaphysics,* ed. Robert C. Neville, 117–40. Albany: State University of New York Press, 1987.

Luik, John. "An Old Question Raised Yet Again: Is Kant an Enlightenment Humanist?" In *The Question of Humanism,* ed. David Goicoechea and John Luik, 117–37. New York: Prometheus Books, 1991.

Lyotard, Jean-François. *The Postmodern Condition: A Report on Knowledge.* Trans. Geoff Bennington and Brian Massumi. Minneapolis: University of Minnesota Press, 1989.

MacIntyre, Alasdair. *After Virtue: A Study in Moral Theory.* Notre Dame: University of Notre Dame Press, 1981.

———. "Can Ethics Dispense with a Theological Perspective on Human Nature?" In *The Roots of Ethics,* ed. Daniel Callahan, 122–28. New York: Plenum Press, 1976.

Makkreel, Rudolf A. "Differentiating Dogmatic, Regulative, and Reflective Approaches to History." In *Proceedings of the Eighth International Kant Congress,* ed. Hoke Robinson, vol. 1, pt. 1, 123–37. Milwaukee: Marquette University Press, 1995.

———. *Imagination and Interpretation in Kant: The Hermeneutical Import of the "Critique of Judgment."* Chicago: University of Chicago Press, 1990.

———. "Kant, Dilthey, and the Idea of a Critique of Historical Judgment." *Dilthey-Jahrbuch für Philosophie und Geschichte der Geisteswissenschaften* 10 (1996): 61–79.

———. "The Role of Reflection in Kant's Transcendental Philosophy." In *Transcendental Philosophy and Everyday Experience,* ed. Tom Rockmore and Vladimir Zeman, 84–95. Atlantic Highlands, N.J.: Humanities Press, 1997.

———. "The Various Roles of Judgment in Kant: From Provisional to Reflective Judgment." Paper presented at the twenty-ninth annual meeting of the American Society for Eighteenth-Century Studies, Notre Dame, Indiana, April 1998.

Martens, Wolfgang. *Die Botschaft der Tugend. Die Aufklärung im Spiegel der deutschen Moralischen Wochenschriften.* Stuttgart: J. B. Metzlersche Verlagsbuchhandlung, 1968.

McCann, Hugh J. "Practical Rationality: Some Kantian Reflections." *Journal of Philosophical Research* 15 (1990): 57–77.

Meerbote, Ralf. "*Wille* and *Willkür* in Kant's Theory of Action." In *Interpreting Kant,* ed. Moltke S. Gram, 69–84. Iowa City: University of Iowa Press, 1982.

Mendelssohn, Moses. *Morgenstunden oder Vorlesungen über das Dasein Gottes.* Berlin: Christian Friedrich Boß, 1786.

Mertens, Thomas. "Zweckmäßigkeit der Natur und politische Philosophie bei Kant." *Zeitschrift für philosophische Forschung* 49 (1995): 220–40.

Michalson, Gordon E. *Fallen Freedom: Kant on Radical Evil and Moral Regeneration.* Cambridge: Cambridge University Press, 1990.

Miller, Mara. *The Garden as an Art.* Albany: State University of New York Press, 1993.

Minnich, Elizabeth K. "To Judge in Freedom: Hannah Arendt on the Relation of Thinking and Morality." In *Hannah Arendt: Thinking, Judging, Freedom,* ed. Gisela T. Kaplan and Clive S. Kessler, 133–43. Sydney: Allen and Unwin, 1989.

Möhsen, Karl Wilhelm. "What Is to Be Done toward the Enlightenment of the Citizenry." Trans. James Schmidt. In *What Is Enlightenment? Eighteenth-Century Answers and Twentieth-Century Questions,* ed. James Schmidt, 49–52. Berkeley and Los Angeles: University of California Press, 1996.

Mollowitz, Gerhard. "Kants Platoauffassung." *Kant-Studien* 40 (1935): 13–67.

Mönch, W. *Voltaire und Friedrich der Große. Das Drama einer denkwürdigen Freundschaft. Eine Studie zur Literatur, Politik und Philosophie des XVIII Jahrhunderts.* Stuttgart and Berlin: W. Kohlhammer, 1943.

Moreau, Paul. *L'éducation morale chez Kant.* Latour-Maubourg: Les Éditions du cerf, 1988.

Mulholland, Leslie Arthur. *Kant's System of Rights*. New York: Columbia University Press, 1990.

Müller, Max. "Basedow: Johann Bernhard B." In *Allgemeine Deutsche Biographie*. Leipzig: Duncker und Humblot, 1875.

Munzel, G. Felicitas. "'The Beautiful Is the Symbol of the Morally-Good': Kant's Philosophical Basis of Proof for the Idea of the Morally-Good." *Journal of the History of Philosophy* 33 (1995): 301–30.

———. "The Privileged Status of Interest in Nature's Beautiful Forms: A Response to Jane Kneller." In *Proceedings of the Eighth International Kant Congress*, ed. Hoke Robinson, vol. 1, pt. 2, 787–92. Milwaukee: Marquette University Press, 1995.

———. "Reason's Practical Idea of Perpetual Peace, Human Character, and the Pedagogical Function of the Republican Constitution." *Idealistic Studies* 26 (1996): 101–34.

Nenon, Thomas. "Freedom, Responsibility, Character: Some Reflections on Kant's Notion of the Person." *Jahrbuch für Recht und Ethik/Annual Review of Law and Ethics* 1 (1993): 157–68.

Neville, Robert C., ed. *New Essays in Metaphysics*. Albany: State University of New York Press, 1987.

Newman, John Henry. *The Idea of a University*. Notre Dame: University of Notre Dame Press, 1982.

Nichols, Edward W. "The Semantics of the Termination -ario." *American Journal of Philology* (1929): 40–63.

Nietzsche, Friedrich. *Twilight of the Idols*. Trans. R. J. Hollingdale. New York: Penguin Books, 1968.

Nisbet, Robert. *History of the Idea of Progress*. New York: Basic Books, 1980.

Noddings, Nel. *Caring, a Feminine Approach to Ethics and Moral Education*. Berkeley and Los Angeles: University of California Press, 1984.

Norton, Robert E. *The Beautiful Soul: Aesthetic Morality in the Eighteenth Century*. Ithaca: Cornell University Press, 1995.

Nussbaum, Martha C. *The Fragility of Goodness: Luck and Ethics in Greek Tragedy and Philosophy*. New York: Cambridge University Press, 1986.

O'Neill, Onora. *Constructions of Reason: Explorations of Kant's Practical Philosophy*. New York: Cambridge University Press, 1989.

———. *Towards Justice and Virtue: A Constructive Account of Practical Reasoning*. New York: Cambridge University Press, 1996.

Orwin, Clifford, and Nathan Tarcov, eds. *The Legacy of Rousseau*. Chicago: University of Chicago Press, 1997.

Pascal, Blaise. *Pensées*. Trans. A. J. Krailsheimer. New York: Penguin Books, 1966.

Patzig, Günter. "Principium diiudicationis und Principium executionis: Über transzendentalpragmatische Begründungssätze für Verhaltensnormen." In *Handlungstheorie und Transzendentalphilosophie*, ed. Gerold Prauss, 204–18. Frankfurt am Main: Vittorio Klostermann, 1986.

Paulsen, Friedrich. *Immanuel Kant: His Life and Doctrine*. New York: Frederick Ungar, 1963.

Pico della Mirandola, Giovanni. *Oration on the Dignity of Man*. Trans. A. Robert Caponigri. Chicago: Regnery Gateway, 1956.

Pillow, Kirk. "Form and Content in Kant's *Kritik der Urteilskraft*: Situating Beauty and the Sublime in the Work of Art." *Journal of the History of Philosophy* 32 (1994): 443–59.

Pippin, Robert. "Hegel, Ethical Reasons, Kantian Rejoinders." *Philosophical Topics* 19 (1991): 99–132.

Plato. *Meno.* Trans. G. M. A. Grube. In *Five Dialogues.* Indianapolis: Hackett, 1981.

———. *Phaedrus.* Trans. W. C. Helmbold and W. G. Rabinowitz. New York: Macmillan/Library of Liberal Arts, 1956.

———. *Plato's Theaetetus.* Trans. Seth Benardete. Chicago: University of Chicago Press, 1986.

Pleines, Jürgen-Eckardt. *Eudaimonia zwischen Kant und Aristoteles. Glückseligkeit als höchstes Gut menschlichen Handelns.* Würzburg: Königshausen und Neumann, 1984.

———. "Pädagogik und Praktische Philosophie." In *Kant und die Pädagogik. Pädagogik und praktische Philosophie,* ed. Jürgen-Eckardt Pleines, 9–15. Würzburg: Königshausen und Neumann, 1985.

———. "Pädagogisches Handeln und dessen Beziehung zur Urteilskraft." In *Kant und die Pädagogik. Pädagogik und praktische Philosophie,* ed. Jürgen-Eckardt Pleines, 65–74. Würzburg: Königshausen und Neumann, 1985.

———, ed. *Kant und die Pädagogik. Pädagogik und praktische Philosophie.* Würzburg: Königshausen und Neumann, 1985.

———, ed. *Zum teleologischen Argument in der Philosophie.* Würzburg: Königshausen und Neumann, 1991.

Potter, Nelson. "Maxims in Kant's Moral Philosophy." *Philosophia* 23 (1994): 59–90.

Power, F. Clark, Ann Higgins, and Lawrence Kohlberg. *Lawrence Kohlberg's Approach to Moral Education.* New York: Columbia University Press, 1989.

Prauss, Gerold, ed. *Handlungstheorie und Transzendentalphilosophie.* Frankfurt am Main: Vittorio Klosterman, 1986.

———. *Kant. Zur Deutung seiner Theorie von Erkennen und Handeln.* Cologne: Kiepenheuer und Witsch, 1973.

Reath, Andrews. "Legislating the Moral Law." *Nous* 28 (1994): 435–64.

Recki, Birgit. "Ästhetische Einstellung und moralische Handlung: Die Perspektiven der Vernunft im Gefühl des Erhabenen." In *Perspektiven des Perspektivismus. Gedenkschrift für Friedrich Kaulbach,* ed. Volker Gerhardt and Norbert Herold, 161–83. Würzburg: Königshausen und Neumann, 1992.

———. "Ganz im Glück. Die 'promesse de bonheur' in Kant's *Kritik der Urteilskraft.*" In *Naturzweckmäßigkeit und ästhetische Kultur. Studien zu Kants Kritik der Urteilskraft,* ed. Karl-Heinz Schwabe und Martina Thom, 95–115. Sankt Augustin: Academia, 1993.

———. "Das Gute am Schönen. Über einen Grundgedanken in Kants Ästhetik." *Zeitschrift für Ästhetik und Allgemeine Kunstwissenschaft* 37 (1994): 15–31.

———. "'Was darf ich hoffen'? Ästhetik und Ethik im anthropologischen Verständnis bei Immanuel Kant." *Allgemeine Zeitschrift für Philosophie* (1994): 1–18.

Richardson, William J. "Contemplation in Action." In *The Public Realm: Essays on Discursive Types in Political Philosophy,* ed. Reiner Schürmann, 206–24. Albany: State University of New York Press, 1989.

Ricoeur, Paul. "The Teleological and Deontological Structures of Action: Aristotle and/or Kant?" *Archivio di filosofia* (1987): 205–17.

Riedel, Manfred. "Imputation der Handlung und Applikation des Sittengesetzes. Über den Zusammenhang von Hermeneutik und praktischer Urteilskraft in Kants Lehre vom 'Faktum der Vernunft'." In *Urteilskraft und Vernunft*, 98–124. Frankfurt am Main: Suhrkamp, 1989.

———. *Urteilskraft und Vernunft*. Frankfurt am Main: Suhrkamp, 1989.

———. "Zum Verhältnis von Geschmacksurteil und Interpretation in Kants Philosophie des Schönen." In *Akten des Siebenten Internationalen Kant-Kongresses*, ed. Gerhard Funke, 715–33. Bonn: Bouvier, 1991.

Robinson, Hoke, ed. *Proceedings of the Eighth International Kant Congress*. 2 vols. Milwaukee: Marquette University Press, 1995.

Rockmore, Tom, and Vladimir Zeman, eds. *Transcendental Philosophy and Everyday Experience*. Atlantic Highlands, N.J.: Humanities Press, 1997.

Roehr, Sabine. *A Primer on German Enlightenment: With a Translation of Karl Leonhard Reinhold's "The Fundamental Concepts and Principles of Ethics."* Columbia: University of Missouri Press, 1995.

Römpp, Georg. "Moralität und Frieden: Kants Gesetz der Freiheit in der Welt der Staaten." *Kant-Studien* 65 (1990): 216–33.

Rossi, Philip J. "Autonomy and Community: The Social Character of Kant's 'Moral Faith.'" *Modern Schoolman* 61 (1984): 169–86.

———. "A Commonwealth of Virtue: Guarantee of Perpetual Peace." Paper presented at the annual meeting of the Midwest Study Group of the North American Kant Society, Loyola University, Chicago, November 1996.

———. "The Final End of All Things: The Highest Good as the Unity of Nature and Freedom." In *Kant's Philosophy of Religion Reconsidered*, ed. Philip J. Rossi and Michael Wren, 132–64. Bloomington: Indiana University Press, 1991.

———. "Kant's Doctrine of Hope: Reason's Interest and the Things of Faith." *New Scholasticism* 56 (1982): 228–38.

———. *Kant's Doctrine of the "Fact of Pure Reason": The Foundation for Moral Rationality*. Ann Arbor: UMI, 1975.

———. "Moral Imagination and the Media: Whose 'World' Do We See, Whose 'World' Shall It Be?" In *Mass Media and the Moral Imagination*, ed. Philip J. Rossi and Paul A. Soukup, 264–72. Kansas City: Sheed and Ward, 1994.

Rossi, Philip J., and Paul A. Soukup, eds. *Mass Media and the Moral Imagination*. Kansas City: Sheed and Ward, 1994.

Rossi, Philip J., and Michael Wren, eds. *Kant's Philosophy of Religion Reconsidered*. Bloomington: Indiana University Press, 1991.

Rousseau, Jean-Jacques. *Emile; or, On Education*. Trans. Allan Bloom. New York: Basic Books, 1979.

———. *Discourse on the Origin of Inequality*. Trans. Donald A. Cress. In *Basic Political Writings*. Indianapolis: Hackett, 1987.

———. *The First and Second Discourses*. Ed. Roger D. Masters. Trans. Roger D. and Judith Masters. New York: St. Martin's Press, 1964.

Sabini, John, and Maury Silver. "Emotions, Responsibility, and Character." In *Responsibility, Character, and the Emotions: New Essays in Moral Psychology*, ed. Ferdinand Schoeman, 165–75. New York: Cambridge University Press, 1987.

Sala, Giovanni B. "Das Gesetz oder das Gute?" *Gregorianum* 71 (1990): 67–95, 315–52.

Saner, Hans. *Kant's Political Thought: Its Origins and Development*. Trans. E. B. Ashton. Chicago: University of Chicago Press, 1973. Originally published as *Widerstreit und Einheit: Wege zu Kants politischen Denken*. Munich: Piper, 1967.

Schiller, Friedrich. *Über Anmut und Würde*. In *Schillers Sämtliche Werke*, vol. 14. Stuttgart: J. G. Cotta'schen Buchhandlung, 1894.

———. *Über die ästhetische Erziehung des Menschen. In einer Reihe von Briefen*. Stuttgart: Reclam, 1965. Trans. Reginald Snell as *On the Aesthetic Education of Man: In a Series of Letters*. New York: Frederick Ungar, 1983.

Schilpp, Paul A. *Kant's Pre-Critical Ethics*. 1938. Reprint, Evanston: Northwestern University Press, 1960.

Schmid, K. A., et al. *Geschichte der Erziehung vom Anfang an bis auf unsere Zeit*. 6 vols. Stuttgart: J. G. Cotta'schen Buchhandlung, 1898.

Schmidt, James, ed. *What Is Enlightenment? Eighteenth-Century Answers and Twentieth-Century Questions*. Berkeley and Los Angeles: University of California Press, 1996.

Schmucker, Josef. *Die Ursprünge der Ethik Kants in seinen vorkritischen Schriften und Reflektionen*. Meisenheim am Glan: Anton Hain, 1961.

Schoeman, Ferdinand, ed. *Responsibility, Character, and the Emotions: New Essays in Moral Psychology*. New York: Cambridge University Press, 1987.

Schönrich, Gerhard, and Yasushi Kato, eds. *Kant in der Diskussion der Moderne*. Frankfurt am Main: Suhrkamp, 1996.

Schott, Robin May, ed. *Feminist Interpretations of Immanuel Kant*. University Park: Pennsylvania State University Press, 1997.

Schümmer, Fr. "Die Entwicklung des Geschmacksbegriff in der Philosophie des 17. und 18. Jahrhunderts." *Archiv für Begriffsgeschichte* 1 (1955): 120–41.

Schürmann, Reiner, ed. *The Public Realm: Essays on Discursive Types in Political Philosophy*. Albany: State University of New York Press, 1989.

Schurr, Johannes, Karl Heinz Broecken, and Renate Broecken, eds. *Humanität und Bildung*. Hildesheim: Georg Olms Verlag, 1988.

Schwemmer, Oswald. "Das 'Faktum der Vernunft' und die Realität des Handelns. Kritische Bemerkungen zur transzendentalphilosophischen Normbegründung und ihrer handlungstheoretischen Begriffsgrundlage im Blick auf Kant." In *Handlungstheorie und Transzendentalphilosophie*, ed. Gerold Prauss, 271–302. Frankfurt am Main: Vittorio Klostermann, 1986.

———. *Philosophie der Praxis. Versuch zur Grundlegung einer Lehre vom moralischen Argumentieren*. Frankfurt am Main: Suhrkamp, 1971.

———. "Vernunft und Moral. Versuch einer kritischen Rekonstruction des kategorischen Imperativs bei Kant." In *Kant. Zur Deutung seiner Theorie von Erkennen und Handeln*, ed. Gerold Prauss, 255–73. Cologne: Kiepenheuer und Witsch, 1973.

Sedgwick, Sally. "On Lying and the Role of Content in Kant's Ethics." *Kant-Studien* 82 (1991): 42–62.

Seigfried, Hans. "Kant's 'Spanish Bank Account': *Realität* and *Wirklichkeit*." In *Interpreting Kant*, ed. Moltke S. Gram, 115–32. Iowa City: University of Iowa Press, 1982.

Shell, Susan. *The Embodiment of Reason: Kant on Spirit, Generation, and Community*. Chicago: University of Chicago Press, 1996.

Sherman, Nancy. *Making a Necessity of Virtue: Aristotle and Kant on Virtue*. New York: Cambridge University Press, 1997.

———. "Wise Maxims/Wise Judging." *Monist* 76 (1993): 41–65.

Siep, Ludwig. "Das Recht als Ziel der Geschichte. Überlegungen im Anschluß an Kant und Hegel." In *Das Recht der Vernunft. Kant und Hegel über Denken, Erkennen und Handeln*, ed. Christel Fricke, Peter König, and Thomas Petersen, 355–79. Vol. 37 of Spekulation und Erfahrung. Texte und Untersuchungen zum Deutschen Idealismus. Stuttgart-Bad Cannstatt: Frommann-Holzboog, 1995.

Silber, John. "The Moral Good and the Natural Good in Kant's Ethics." *Review of Metaphysics* 36 (1982): 397–438.

Sloan, Phillip R. "Preforming the Categories: Kant and 18th C. Generation Theory." University of Notre Dame, Notre Dame, Indiana. Typescript.

Sommer, Manfred. *Identität im Übergang. Kant.* Frankfurt am Main: Suhrkamp, 1988.

Stark, Werner. "Anthropologie und Charakter. Beobachtungen und Überlegungen zur Entstehung von Kants Lehre vom intelligiblen Charakter." Paper presented at the conference "L'Antropologia di Kant," Institute for Philosophy, University of Padua, Italy, March 1998.

———. "Kant's *Lectures on Anthropology*." Paper presented at the Central Division meeting of the American Philosophical Association, Pittsburgh, April 1997.

———. "Kants Lehre von der Erziehung: Anthropologie, Pädagogik und Ethik." Paper presented at the conference "L'Antropologia di Kant e l'attualita dell'illuminismo," Goethe Institute, Rome, October 1997.

Stuckenberg, J. H. W. *The Life of Immanuel Kant.* 1882. Reprint, Bristol: Thoemmes Antiquarian Books, 1990.

Sturma, Dieter. "Self and Reason: A Nonreductionist Approach to the Reflective and Practical Transitions of Self-Consciousness." In *The Modern Subject: Conceptions of the Self in Classical German Philosophy*, ed. Karl Ameriks and Dieter Sturma, 199–215. Albany: State University of New York Press, 1995.

Sullivan, Roger J. "The Influence of Kant's Anthropology on His Moral Theory." *Review of Metaphysics* 49 (1995): 77–94.

Sullivan, William M. "The Democratization of Moral Judgment: Moral Leadership and Moral Symbols in Public Culture." In *Mass Media and the Moral Imagination*, ed. Philip J. Rossi and Paul Soukup, 34–42. Kansas City: Sheed and Ward, 1994.

Tarcov, Nathan. *Locke's Education for Liberty.* Chicago: University of Chicago Press, 1984.

Teichner, Wilhelm. *Die Intelligible Welt. Ein Problem der theoretischen und praktischen Philosophie I. Kants.* Meisenheim am Glan: Anton Hain, 1967.

Thomas, Lawrence. "Trust, Affirmation, and Moral Character: A Critique of Kantian Morality." In *Identity, Character, and Morality: Essays in Moral Psychology*, ed. Owen Flanagan and Amélie Oksenberg Rorty, 235–57. Cambridge: MIT Press, 1990.

Thompson, Martyn P., ed. *John Locke und Immanuel Kant. Historische Rezeption und gegenwärtige Relevanz.* Berlin: Duncker und Humblot, 1991.

Timm, Hermann. *Gott und die Freiheit. Studien zur Religionsphilosophie der Goethezeit.* Vol. 1, *Die Spinozarenaissance.* Frankfurt am Main: Vittorio Klostermann, 1974.

Tocqueville, Alexis de. *Democracy in America.* Ed. Richard D. Heffner. New York: Penguin Books, 1984.

Todorov, Tzvetan. "Rousseau and Humanism." Paper presented at the twenty-ninth annual meeting of the American Society for Eighteenth-Century Studies, Notre Dame, Indiana, April 1998.

Van de Pitte, Frederick P. *Kant as Philosophical Anthropologist.* The Hague: Martinus Nijhoff, 1971.

Velkley, Richard L. "The Crisis of the End of Reason in Kant's Philosophy and the Remarks of 1764–1765." In *Kant and Political Philosophy: The Contemporary Legacy,* ed. Ronald Beiner and William James Booth, 76–94. New Haven: Yale University Press, 1993.

———. *Freedom and the End of Reason: On the Moral Foundation of Kant's Critical Philosophy.* Chicago: University of Chicago Press, 1989.

———. "Freedom, Teleology, and Justification of Reason: On the Philosophical Importance of Kant's Rousseauian Turn." In *Rousseau in Deutschland. Neue Beiträge zur Erforschung seiner Rezeption,* ed. Herbert Jaumann, 181–95. Berlin: Walter de Gruyter, 1995.

———. *Kant as Philosopher of Theodicy.* Ann Arbor: UMI, 1978.

———. "On Kant's Socratism." In *The Philosophy of Immanuel Kant,* ed. Richard Kennington, 87–105. Washington, D.C.: Catholic University of America Press, 1985.

———. "The Tension in the Beautiful: On Culture and Civilization in Rousseau and German Philosophy." In *The Legacy of Rousseau,* ed. Clifford Orwin and Nathan Tarcov, 65–86. Chicago: University of Chicago Press, 1997.

Voltaire. *Candide; or, Optimism.* Trans. Peter Gay. New York: St. Martin's Press, 1963.

Vorländer, Karl. *Immanuel Kant. Der Mann und das Werk.* Hamburg: Felix Meiner, 1977.

Ward, Keith. *The Development of Kant's View of Ethics.* Oxford: Basil Blackwell, 1972.

White, David A. "Kant on Plato and the Metaphysics of Purpose." *History of Philosophy Quarterly* 10 (1993): 67–82.

Williams, Howard. *Kant's Political Philosophy.* Oxford: Basil Blackwell, 1983.

Wood, Allen W. "The Emptiness of the Moral Will." *Monist* 72 (1989): 454–83.

———. *Kant's Moral Religion.* Ithaca: Cornell University Press, 1970.

———. *Kant's Rational Theology.* Ithaca: Cornell University Press, 1978.

———. "Unsociable Sociability: The Anthropological Basis of Kantian Ethics." *Philosophical Topics* 19 (1991): 325–51.

———, ed. *Self and Nature in Kant's Philosophy.* Ithaca: Cornell University Press, 1984.

Wundt, Max. *Kant als Metaphysiker. Ein Beitrag zur Geschichte der deutschen Philosophie im 18. Jahrhundert.* 1924. Reprint, Hildesheim: G. Olms, 1984.

Zahn, Manfred. "Contemporary Trends in the Interpretation of Kant's Critical Philosophy." *South African Journal of Philosophy* 8 (1989): 129–47.

Zammito, John H. *The Genesis of Kant's "Critique of Judgment."* Chicago: University of Chicago Press, 1992.

Ziolkowski, Theodore. *German Romanticism and Its Institutions.* Princeton: Princeton University Press, 1990.

Zoeller, Guenter. "Main Developments in Recent Scholarship on the *Critique of Pure Reason.*" *Philosophy and Phenomenological Research* 53 (1993): 445–66.

Index of References to Kant's Writings

INDEX OF MODERN AUTHORS

General Index